CW01500352

SWISSAIR

JASON BURKE

The Revolutionists

The Story of the Extremists Who Hijacked the 1970s

THE BODLEY HEAD
LONDON

3 5 7 9 10 8 6 4 2

The Bodley Head, an imprint of Vintage, is part of the
Penguin Random House group of companies

Vintage, Penguin Random House UK, One Embassy Gardens,
8 Viaduct Gardens, London SW11 7BW

penguin.co.uk/vintage
global.penguinrandomhouse.com

First published by The Bodley Head in 2025

Maps by Bill Donohoe

Typeset in 10.2/13.87pt Sabon LT Std by Six Red Marbles UK, Thetford, Norfolk
Printed and bound in Great Britain by Clays Ltd, Elcograf S.p.A.

The authorised representative in the EEA is Penguin Random House Ireland,
Morrison Chambers, 32 Nassau Street, Dublin D02 YH68

A CIP catalogue record for this book is available from the British Library

HB ISBN 9781847926067
TPB ISBN 9781847926074

Penguin Random House is committed to a sustainable future
for our business, our readers and our planet. This book is made
from Forest Stewardship Council® certified paper.

For Tessa Rachel Burke, in memoriam

Contents

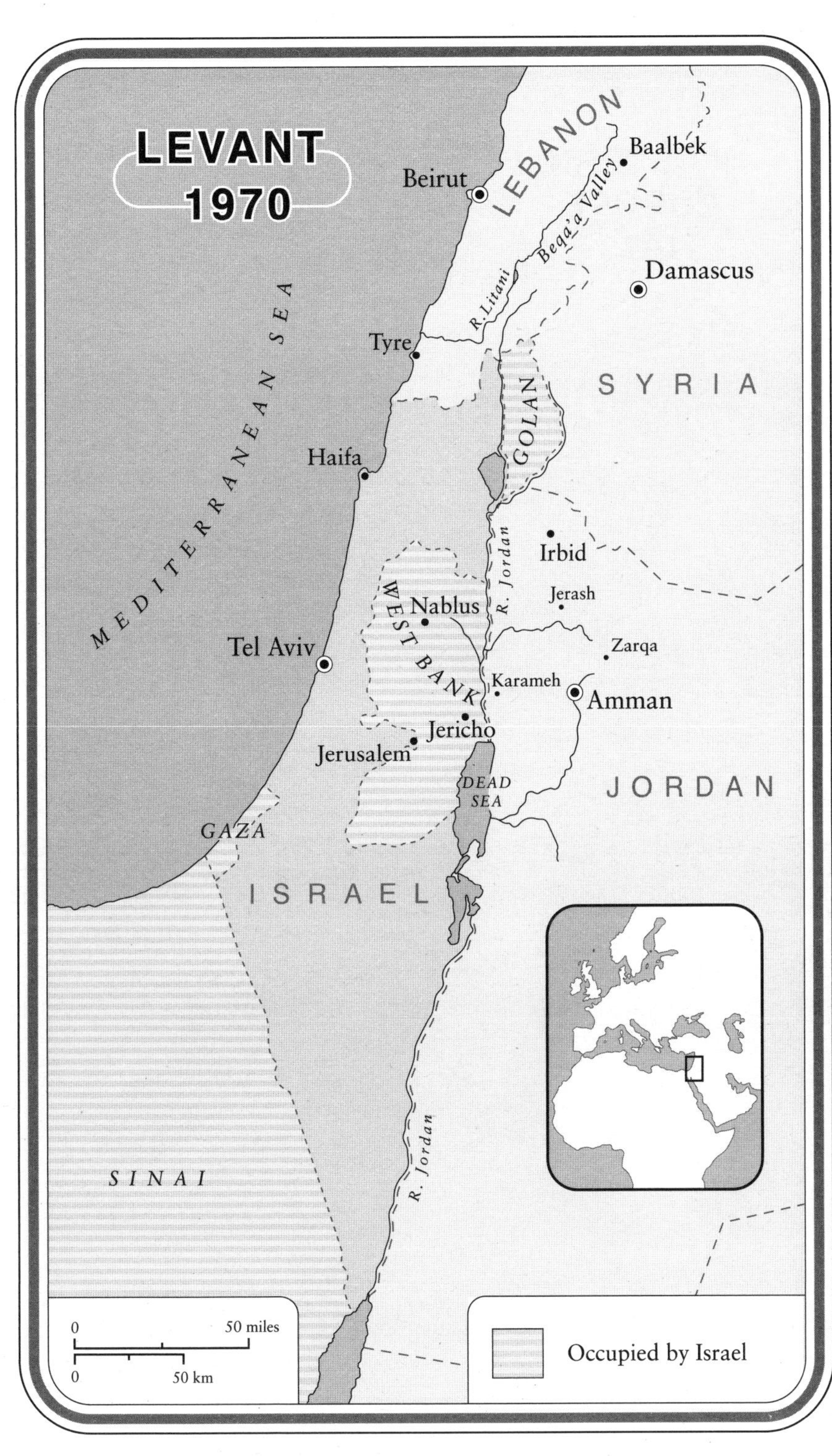

LEVANT
1970
MEDITERRANEAN SEA
LEBANON
Beirut
Baalbek
Beqa'a Valley
R. Litani
Damascus
Tyre
SYRIA
GOLAN
Haifa
R. Jordan
Irbid
Jerash
WEST BANK
Nablus
Tel Aviv
Zarqa
Karameh
Amman
Jericho
Jerusalem
DEAD SEA
JORDAN
GAZA
ISRAEL
SINAI
R. Jordan
0
50 miles
0
50 km
Occupied by Israel

WESTERN EUROPE 1973
SWEDEN
Lillehammer
NORWAY
Stockholm
NORTH SEA
DENMARK
Malmö
BALTIC SEA
NETHERLANDS
Hamburg
UNITED KINGDOM
The Hague
WEST GERMANY
Berlin
EAST GERMANY
Rotterdam
London
Cologne
BELGIUM
Frankfurt
Stuttgart
Paris
Munich
Vienna
FRANCE
Zurich
SWITZ.
AUSTRIA
Geneva
Trieste
ITALY
Rome
SPAIN
MEDITERRANEAN SEA
0
300 miles
0
300 km

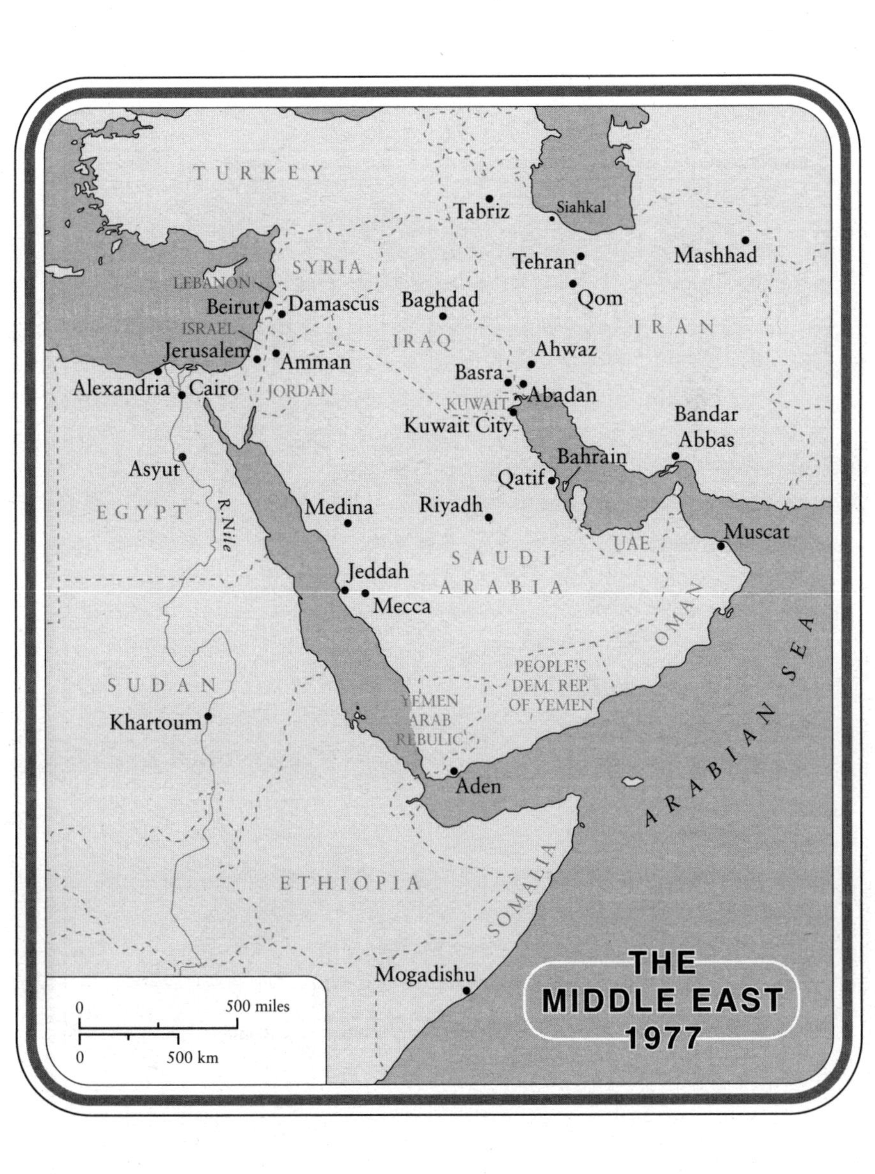

TURKEY
Tabriz
Siahkal
Mashhad
Tehran
SYRIA
LEBANON
Beirut
Damascus
Baghdad
Qom
ISRAEL
IRAN
IRAQ
Jerusalem
Ahwaz
Amman
Basra
Alexandria
Cairo
JORDAN
Abadan
KUWAIT
Kuwait City
Bandar Abbas
Asyut
Bahrain
Qatif
EGYPT
R. Nile
Medina
Riyadh
Muscat
UAE
SAUDI ARABIA
Jeddah
Mecca
OMAN
PEOPLE'S DEM. REP. OF YEMEN
SUDAN
YEMEN ARAB REBULIC
Khartoum
ARABIAN SEA
Aden
ETHIOPIA
SOMALIA
Mogadishu
0
500 miles
0
500 km
THE MIDDLE EAST 1977

CENTRAL EUROPE 1980
Berlin
EAST GERMANY
POLAND
Cologne
WEST GERMANY
Prague
CZECHOSLOVAKIA
Karlsruhe
Stammheim
Munich
Vienna
Budapest
FRANCE
SWITZ.
AUSTRIA
HUNGARY
ITALY
YUGOSLAVIA
Belgrade
0
200 miles
0
200 km

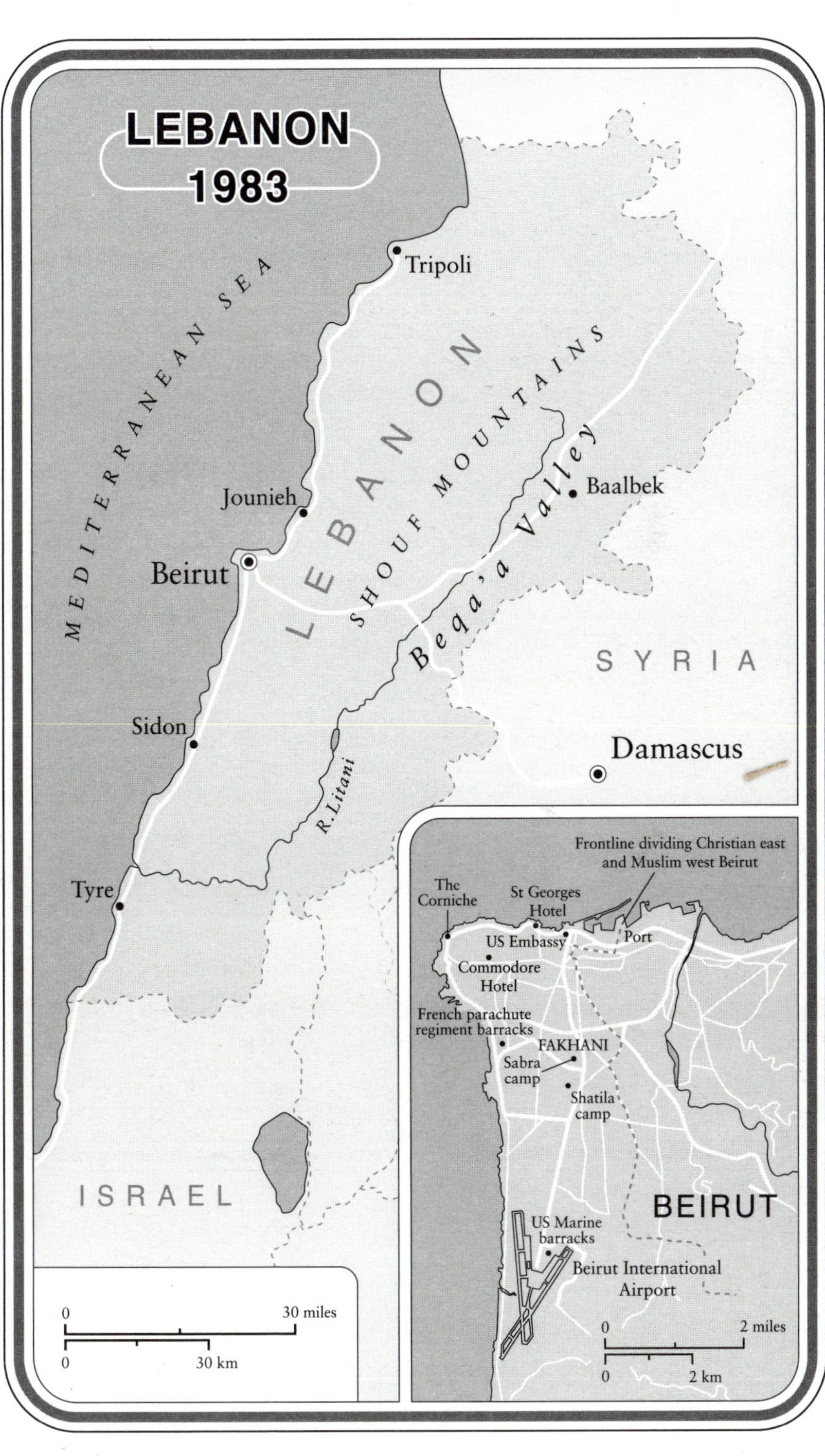
LEBANON
1983
MEDITERRANEAN SEA
Tripoli
LEBANON
SHOUF MOUNTAINS
Beqa'a Valley
Baalbek
Jounieh
Beirut
SYRIA
Sidon
Damascus
R.Litani
Tyre
ISRAEL
0
30 miles
0
30 km
Frontline dividing Christian east and Muslim west Beirut
The Corniche
St Georges Hotel
US Embassy
Port
Commodore Hotel
French parachute regiment barracks
FAKHANI
Sabra camp
Shatila camp
BEIRUT
US Marine barracks
Beirut International Airport
0
2 miles
0
2 km

Preface

This is a book about violence, and people who use it in an effort to bring about radical change. Specifically, it deals with the violent expression of political and religious extremism between the late 1960s and the early 1980s that we have come to call terrorism. The pages that follow describe attacks in two dozen countries, on four continents, committed by a hundred or so citizens of around thirty different nations. They include young women and old men, literature students and high-school dropouts, penniless refugees and scions of wealthy families, sociopaths and idealists, social care assistants and hardened assassins, puritans and hedonists, idealists and cynics, sadists and aspirant saints. They came from all over the Middle East, from Europe, Latin America, Japan and the US. Some took other people's lives as they sought to bring about revolution. Some were killed themselves. Those who tried to counter their activities used violence too, sometimes with forensic precision, sometimes with deliberate lack of discrimination. This book describes the lives, ideas, acts and occasional deaths of those involved in this extraordinary and important conflict, which did so much to shape the world we live in today.

The Revolutionists focuses on Europe and the Middle East in the years between 1967 and 1983 because it was here, during this period, that two important and interrelated events took place. The first, in the early years, was the emergence of a new kind of transnational terrorism. Enabled by mass media and air travel, an unprecedented wave of spectacular violence spread around the world. Its epicentre was the Middle East, and the conflict between Palestinians and Israelis, but its extent was much greater. For the most part, it was informed by a secular, often left-leaning revolutionary view of the world. The second, in the later years, was the rise of violence associated with a very different set of revolutionary ideas: Islamic extremism.

Previous accounts have focused on one or other of these phenomena, and have almost always presented them in isolation from one another, not to mention from their broader political, social and cultural context. This book seeks to do something different. Through the stories of the individuals involved, it tells the story of both movements – the leftist and the Islamist – showing how the former influenced the latter, and indeed how the failure of the first contributed to the emergence of the second, as well as how both were part of a broader revolutionary moment. Terrorism in this period has often been considered with only passing reference to some of the most significant events to occur in the Middle East, indeed the world, at this time. Its role in the Iranian revolution has been obscured, for example. The importance of events beyond the Middle East, meanwhile – such as the war in Vietnam, other conflicts in Africa or Latin America, the changing dynamics of the Cold War and the global economic crises of the 1970s – has generally been ignored altogether.

Through exploring the whole world of the Revolutionists, we can understand how they reflected as well as formed their environment. Above all, we can see how extremist violence was not simply the unthinking product of a particular ideology but a tool that its users chose, often because they believed it to be an essential means of bringing about the radical and necessary transformation of society. These are insights that resonate eerily today, and which are all too often forgotten. We may strongly disagree with the change that violent men and women seek, but we fail to understand their motivations at our peril.

The first pages of this book describe the events that led to one of the most spectacular acts of political violence ever witnessed: a multiple hijacking of passenger planes in September 1970. As the attackers made their final preparations, President Richard Nixon was in the White House; Led Zeppelin were about to finish a US tour with a sell-out concert at Madison Square Garden; and American troops in Vietnam had just launched their last major operation. In Britain, the release of the Mark III Ford Cortina was delayed by industrial action; a vast, chaotic, ecstatic music festival on the Isle of Wight had just ended; and Prime Minister Edward Heath was settling into Number 10 Downing Street after a surprise election victory. At Semipalatinsk, in what is now Kazakhstan, the Union of Soviet Socialist Republics, led by Leonid Brezhnev, had just completed a new series of nuclear explosions.

In its details, the differences between this world and our own are striking. This was a time when plane travel was still glamorous and expensive, when spies met contacts in bars in Beirut or Rome or Paris, when international phone calls were luxuries and credit cards almost unknown; when terrorists casually dropped hand grenades into French bistros, planned spectacular attacks while reading newspapers on a terrace in a Roman piazza, and made demands that powerful elected officials not only debated, but frequently granted.

But looked at on a wider scale, the similarities between then and now are striking, too. These years were a time of rapid and destabilising change. Much of this sense of dislocation was caused by technological innovation, particularly in the media, which exposed hundreds of millions to shocking images, radical ideas and extreme opinions. Suddenly billions of people could watch what was happening on the other side of the world in real time. This had an immense impact. Some fell victim to a proliferation of paranoiac conspiracy theories. Others realised they had the power to hold their rulers to account or challenge them in violent ways. Repeated and sudden economic shocks led to the realisation that an improvement in quality of life from generation to generation was not inevitable and that the planet's resources were finite, which exacerbated a profound loss of confidence in the integrity of political leaders and their ability to solve the problems of the day. Both the West and the Middle East saw a surge in identity politics and culture wars. Ideologies that had been accepted or imposed for decades were being interrogated and renewed or discarded. Histories were being contested in ways that were disturbing for some, empowering for others. This was a time when 'liberation' and 'revolution' meant something very real and urgent. We use a different vocabulary now, but there are many today who dream of the radical transformation of our world – and some who are prepared to use violence to achieve it.

Just a decade or so later however, the zeal for 'revolution' had faded in the West, while in the Middle East it evolved into something dramatically different. The attacks of the early 1970s were undoubtedly traumatising for their victims but rarely caused many deaths. Hijackers handed out sweets and pamphlets to former hostages. Gunmen carefully emptied planes of passengers before blowing them up. The aim of much of the violence was to have 'a lot of people watching and not a lot of people dead', in the words of one perceptive contemporary commentator. Though they may have considered the US to be their enemy, few among this new wave of violent extremists saw it as a target for violence. By the early 1980s, all this had changed. Smiling young men were driving trucks packed with explosives into their targets, convinced that they were on their way to heaven. Others were planning attacks designed to cripple the entire infrastructure of major cities, potentially leading to the deaths of tens of thousands. Instead of secular slogans promising a socialist utopia, many attackers now chanted the words of faith. To explain how we went from one to the other is one aim of the pages that follow.

This is a book concerned to understand if not the individual psychology then at least the worldview that motivated these attackers. It will take us deep into their lives and minds; at one level, all politics is personal. But for all the diversity of their personalities and backgrounds, there was one overarching conflict that defined everyone's worldview, no matter who they were. The Cold War that pitted the USSR and its immediate satellites against the US and its allies also caused a much broader cleavage across the Middle East, Africa and beyond. Though its frontlines appeared to Western observers to run across the plains and cities of central Europe, much more actual fighting and dying took place in these other theatres as individual rulers and leaders aligned themselves with one superpower or another to gain advantage in their own battles for power and resources. These local conflicts belied frequent attempts by observers to misrepresent this complex reality as a simple binary battle between good and evil. Some actors were manipulated and exploited by great powers – but others did much manipulating and exploiting of their own. The same is true today.

Writing this book took me not only on a chronological journey from the late 1960s to the early 1980s but on a geographical one too. My research spanned four continents and drew on sources in twelve languages (English, French, Arabic, Italian, German, Swedish, Danish, Norwegian, Dutch, Spanish, Serbo-Croat and Hebrew). I conducted dozens of interviews, read hundreds of books and logged thousands of air miles. I watched wars flare and fade, and saw vast change sweep through the lives of hundreds of millions of people. I spent weeks in the company of long-dead men and women with long-dead ideas, and days in the company of people who were very much alive and as committed and enthusiastic about transforming the world as they had ever been. Some were sympathetic and likeable; others were the opposite. I spoke to hijackers, soldiers, activists and ideologues, retired and active security officials, single and double agents, smooth former diplomats, regretful ex-ministers, protagonists who had been famous, others whose acts had never been known, and victims on all sides who still grieve lost husbands, wives and children. It was an extraordinary and powerful experience, as history should be, full of noise and emotion, shouted exclamation and moments of reflection, violence and its opposite, hope and pain, despair and reconciliation, courage and anger, cowardice and compromise.

There are one or two explanations about style, sourcing and much else that are due here. I have preferred familiarity to absolute accuracy with the transliteration of names and places. This will displease purists. On the other hand, I see no reason why the man known to most simply as Carlos should not be known by his real name, which is Ilich Ramírez Sánchez. I have taken the liberty of shortening this to Ramírez to save space.

Any author writing about the Middle East, Israel, Palestine, extremism and terrorism knows they have entered a terminological minefield. This is amply demonstrated by the fact that the definition and use of at least six of the words in the previous twenty-word sentence could provoke bitter argument. I have stuck broadly to the rules that have informed my more than three decades of work on the region and extremist violence. I use 'terrorism' to describe a tactic – the use of violence or the threat of violence against civilians to advance a political, religious, economic or similar agenda – and 'terrorist' as an adjective. I do not use 'terrorist' as a noun, not because I sympathise with anyone who uses terrorism or seek to belittle the suffering of their victims, but because I do not think reducing complex individuals to single-word descriptors is helpful. Some will say that seeking to understand 'terrorists' is wrong. I disagree. No one should base important decisions, moral or strategic, on ignorance. Know your enemy.

Equally, the use of terms such as 'armed struggle' or 'counter terror', all part of language used at the time of the events described, does not indicate any personal judgement on the justification or otherwise of the use of violence. Arguments about what could or should be described as state terrorism are legitimate, but not for this book. A 'revolutionary' project, at least in these pages, is one that seeks to achieve radical and irrevocable social, political and economic transformation of a society or societies. A 'revolutionist' is therefore someone who works towards this goal.

I encourage readers to turn to the expanded notes at the back of this book as they read through. This has been included in the place of more conventional references, and should provide adequate details of sources, as well as some additional information, and suggestions for further reading.

Finally, I should say this book is not a comprehensive account of any one of the various conflicts it describes. Some readers will be angered by the omission of something that appears to them of vital importance. Others by the inclusion of something they see as inaccurate or misleading or even dangerous, particularly in any moment of heightened sensitivity and conflict, which is most of the time. This is their right, of course. Inevitably, new evidence will emerge. For the moment, though, I have done my best to tell this history as it was.

Prologue

They met at Stuttgart airport in the late morning of 5 September 1970. She knew only that 'an American comrade' would be waiting outside the terminal. He had been told just that 'Shadia' would find him there.

Handsome, with his dark hair combed back in a wave, a tailored blue-grey plaid suit matched with a blue shirt and tie, he was posing as one half of a wealthy, newly married Latin American couple on honeymoon in Europe. Sunglasses, false travel documents with stamps from countries favoured by tourists and his flawless Spanish completed the disguise.

She was the other half, pretty and petite in a navy-blue miniskirt, fitted jacket and matching shoes. A series of painful operations recently conducted by a surgeon in Beirut had altered her features, broadening her sharp nose and rounding her oval eyes. This, along with her Honduran passport in the name of Luna Maria Chavez Britto and striking companion, would convince even the most suspicious security staff that she was an innocent traveller.

Together, they flew from Stuttgart to Frankfurt, arriving in the early afternoon. There they checked into separate hotels before meeting for dinner in a recently opened restaurant on the top floor of the tower of a giant grain silo run by a local brewery. Looking out over the lights of western Europe's financial centre, they discussed global revolution, the civil rights movement in the US and the armed struggle against Zionism, imperialism and capitalism. He spoke of the revolutionary Sandinista movement against the repressive right-wing regime in Nicaragua, where he was from. She described the recent history of the Palestinians, which was hers. Then they paid the bill, left the restaurant and went back to their hotels.

She fell asleep almost instantly and did not wake until the next morning, when the two of them returned to the airport and took another flight, this one delivering them to Amsterdam's Schiphol airport around midday. The El Al flight from Tel Aviv was due to arrive within three hours, making a short stop before flying on to New York. That's when they would board.

Their luggage was checked and re-checked. They had rehearsed their answers but in the event a few words of Spanish and a smile were all it took to satisfy the first El Al security agent. 'Do you have a weapon? Anything sharp or dangerous?' a second asked. 'Why would a girl like me have a dangerous weapon?' she laughed. He apologised and waved her through.

Her partner was not overly troubled either, despite the converted Italian-made starting pistol jammed into the tight waistband of swim shorts he wore under his suit trousers. The gun had had all its metal parts removed and replaced with plastic substitutes to avoid detection by any scanners, but was still lethal. She was carrying two carefully concealed grenades, each about the size of a soft-drink can and made entirely of non-ferrous materials. These too went unnoticed. So far, everything had gone very smoothly.

The only setback was the absence of the two Palestinian men they were supposed to have met in the departure lounge. Both were big and would have intimidated anyone thinking of resisting, and their first-class seats were to have positioned them perfectly to secure the cabin. There had been no sign of either, but the young couple had decided to go ahead with the plan anyway.

It was both very complex and very simple. Three planes would be hijacked as they left European airports bound for the US. Two would be making stopovers, having departed originally from Israel. The third would be flying from Switzerland. Each plane would be commandeered by at least two hijackers, and no more than four. Once under their control, all three aircraft would be diverted to a makeshift runway in Jordan, referred to as 'Revolution Airport'. The Popular Front for the Liberation of Palestine (PFLP) would then have possession of hundreds of passengers and three planes worth tens of millions of dollars, to be traded as ransom for prisoners in Israeli and western European jails. The attackers were instructed to be polite but firm. They were not to hurt anyone but could use their weapons to defend themselves if necessary. The only plane on which they expected to meet resistance was the single El Al flight, as the Israeli airline now flew with armed air marshals among the passengers. The other flights were run by airlines that did not consider such precautions necessary.

Quite how the deal for the hostages and aircraft might be done was unclear, but the plan's architects were confident such challenges would be met. Whatever happened, one thing was certain: a message would have been sent in the most forceful possible way that the Palestinians' cause could not be ignored – not by leaders in the West, nor by rulers in the Arab world, nor by anyone trying to negotiate peace between Israel and its neighbours, nor by ordinary people anywhere on the planet.

Great care had been taken over the selection of the ten hijackers. The inclusion of the woman and her Nicaraguan-American companion was to demonstrate the international support that existed for the Palestinian cause as well as the PFLP's own progressive politics and its commitment to 'revolutionary struggles' around the world. The young couple had been paired for practical reasons too: her frontline experience would complement his untested enthusiasm. Despite his involvement with the Sandinistas, he had never used a deadly weapon to threaten, let alone harm.

The couple took their seats in the first row in economy, just behind the first-class section. In his pocket, the young man carried his own US passport and a scrap of paper containing notes of their instructions written in Spanish. These included the order to attack within the first twenty minutes of the flight to avoid the risk of catastrophic depressurisation if the fuselage was punctured by a bullet or grenade shrapnel. She carried a prepared statement to read over the plane's intercom once it was under their control.

As they sat waiting for take-off she observed that no one on board seemed to have recognised her.

'Who are you?' he asked.

When she told him, he nodded and touched his fingers to his forehead in mock salute.

The minutes passed. They waited, as they had been instructed to do. Then the plane with its 138 passengers and ten crew taxied, took off, and climbed over the Dutch coast before setting a course due west, across Britain, Ireland and the Atlantic. Drinks were served, and then, after twenty-one minutes, with the plane now at 29,000 feet and just crossing the British coast over Clacton in Essex, it was time.

I

1

'Where are we going?'

Leila Khaled was born in the port city of Haifa in what was then British-run Palestine. Her father had arrived there as a boy, travelling with his father from southern Lebanon in the 1910s or 20s. He had opened a grocer's shop and brought Khaled's mother from Lebanon a few years later to start a family. The Khaleds lived on Stanton Street, a narrow, busy thoroughfare that linked the crowded Arab neighbourhoods of Wadi Salib and Wadi Nisnas. Theirs was a traditional three- or four-storey house faced in local limestone with high, round windows and steep stone steps on one side. To the north was the port complex that the British had built, with its soaring cranes and busy jetties. Inland were the regular, spacious streets of the new suburbs that had been built before the First World War to accommodate Jewish immigrants and which had much expanded since, as successive waves arrived seeking refuge from persecution in eastern Europe. Beyond lay a belt of shanty towns, home to the poorest, most recent arrivals: Arabs from outlying villages seeking escape from hunger and hardship.

In early 1948, as the British prepared to withdraw from Palestine and war broke out between Jewish militia and Arab forces, this much coveted commercial centre, with its population split more or less equally between the two communities, was claimed by both. For months it had been the site of skirmishes, bombings and many deaths. In the initial phase of the war, however, fighting was concentrated around Jerusalem or in remote rural areas, and Haifa remained relatively calm, if very tense. Then, as Jewish forces went on the offensive and made advances throughout the territory of the Mandate, the city's Arab residents began to flee. Reports of atrocities, some entirely accurate but others often deliberately exaggerated by both sides, accelerated the departures. In early April Khaled was placed in a hired car with her mother and siblings and driven north across the Lebanese border to the small, picturesque port of Tyre, twelve miles from the frontier. Just over a week later, the British withdrew to Haifa's port area and Jewish fighters took over the city, prompting mass flight of almost all its remaining Arab residents. Within a month, Haifa was part of the newly declared independent state of Israel. This new status did not look likely to change in the immediate future. In intermittent rounds of fighting through the rest of 1948, the new Israel Defence Forces beat back the badly co-ordinated and poorly equipped forces of neighbouring Arab powers and seized much new territory, with further mass displacement of previous inhabitants.

To begin with, the Khaleds moved into the crowded home of a maternal aunt on the outskirts of Tyre. The contrast with their previous life was sharp. The family lived on rations distributed by the United Nations and when Khaled went to school, it was in a tent with a dirt floor. Her parents were among the more affluent of the 120,000 who had fled to Lebanon from what had been Palestine by the time the fighting had come to an end. Most had few skills, scarce funds and few or no local contacts. They lived in insalubrious camps in packed rows of tents, very cold in winter and unbearably hot for much of the rest of the year. But despite the defeat of the Arab armies in 1948 they, like most of the approximately 750,000 Palestinian refugees scattered across the region, still believed they would one day regain their villages, land, businesses and property.

The *nakba*, meaning simply 'catastrophe', as it became known, prompted feverish debate among the refugees and throughout the Middle East. One result was the massive reinforcement of a newly emerging identity. Instead of seeing themselves primarily as members of a family, or a village clan, or as Muslims, or simply as former residents of a province of Ottoman-ruled Syria, some began to think of themselves as Palestinians.

There had been the Peleshet or Philistines of biblical reference, a Greek Philistia and a Roman province named Syria Palaestina. The first Arab invaders of the seventh century CE had named one of their military districts Falestin, and by the mid-nineteenth century the description of the territory roughly between the Litani river in the north, the Jordan river in the east and the Sinai Desert to the south as 'Palestine' was common. But it was only from the turn of the century that Arab intellectuals in any numbers started talking about being 'Palestinian' in the sense of belonging to a clearly-defined community with a shared history, identity and territory. The resistance to Zionism and British rule after the First World War had reinforced this new thinking, but the principle rallying cries during the 1920s and 30s were often the centuries-old ones: defence of Islam, tradition and community and the resolution of local grievances. In the aftermath of the 1948 wars, however, the idea that the Palestinians were a nation with a homeland – one that had just been robbed from them – held powerful appeal among its former residents.

This appeal was further heightened by two apparently contradictory forces. On the one hand, the host populations in their places of exile were often deeply unsympathetic to their plight. On the other, the idea that the Arabs as a whole were a nation, with a common civilisation, language, history and destiny, was also on the rise. With its roots in the intellectual debates of the late nineteenth century about how best to respond to an increasingly fragile Ottoman Empire and the technological, military and financial superiority of the West, the idea of a strong, independent, unified Arab nation had gathered momentum among the hundreds of millions of Arabs who found themselves ruled by colonial powers in the 1920s and 30s. The new thinking took many different forms: some were influenced by fascism, others by revolutionary socialism; some were rooted in faith, but many were secular.

Khaled's older brothers were rapidly drawn into the wave of argument and activism catalysed by the conflict of 1948 and the creation of Israel. Two had won scholarships to the American University of Beirut (AUB), one of the most prestigious educational institutions in the Middle East. There they joined an organisation called the Arab Nationalist Movement (ANM) that had been started a decade earlier by a group of students from across the region. Heavily influenced by earlier Arab nationalist and Islamist groups, the organisation they created was secretive, hierarchical and confrontational. Its motto was 'Unity, Liberation and Revenge' and discipline was strict, if slightly sophomoric: cigarettes and alcohol were banned, orders were supposed to be obeyed without question and members were admitted only after a lengthy trial period.

When they returned home to Tyre during holidays, Khaled's brothers tried to convince their conservative father that the instrument of 'The Return' to Palestine was a single man: Gamal Abdel Nasser, the former army officer who had taken power in Egypt in 1954, two years after participating in the Free Officers coup that had overthrown the Egyptian monarch. Nasser's electrifying speeches, broadcast from Cairo by the Sawt al-Arab, the Voice of the Arabs radio station, commanded a vast audience across the Middle East. In Tyre and the surrounding refugee camps, Palestinians like the Khaled family and many Lebanese listened rapt to the young Egyptian leader's promise to create a new Arab nation that would be united, technologically powerful, prosperous and more than capable of defeating and destroying Israel. Khaled's parents were among many to name a new-born son after the Egyptian leader. By then the family had moved into their own six-roomed top-floor apartment in Tyre. By her early teens Khaled was climbing down drainpipes from her bedroom to attend nocturnal meetings of the ANM in flagrant breach of a ban imposed by her parents. When in 1961 she followed her brothers to the American University of Beirut, she sought out the organisation immediately.

By the time she joined, the ANM had expanded considerably since its foundation but was now riven by internal argument. Should the battle against Israel be prioritised over that against reactionary Arab rulers? How could the class struggle be reconciled with Palestinian nationalism? Should the ANM accept the support offered by Nasser or other sympathetic leaders? If so, which ones? Soon Khaled was passing most of her time either plunged into these debates, organising meetings, or at the forefront of demonstrations. When in 1963 she failed to win a scholarship to continue her pharmacy studies, her father told her she would need to earn her own living as he could no longer support her. The obvious option was to follow the large number of Palestinians who had been heading east over the previous decade, seeking employment in the booming monarchies of the Persian Gulf. Khaled had no great desire to travel, but when she was offered a post teaching young children English in Kuwait, she felt she had little choice but to accept.

Khaled had been working in Kuwait for four years when she heard that war had broken out between Israel and the combined forces of Egypt, Syria and Jordan. She was so certain of victory she began stitching an embroidered picture to hang on the wall of the family home in Haifa to celebrate their return. When Khaled learned of the total defeat of the Arab armies in just six days, she was stunned. 'I felt catatonic for a month,' she remembered. 'All hope was gone.' She gave the embroidery to a friend who had family in the West Bank with instructions to somehow get it to her native city.

She was not alone. All across the Arab and Islamic worlds, Israel's crushing victory in the war of 1967 prompted grief equivalent to a bereavement. Disguising the immensity of the disaster was impossible: the Sinai, Gaza, almost all of the Golan Heights, the West Bank and above all the holy city of al-Quds, or Jerusalem, had all been lost. A second major war between combined forces of multiple Arab powers and Israel had ended in a second crushing defeat. For many, the disappointment was all the more bitter for the euphoria with which they had greeted the outbreak of hostilities. Tawfiq al-Hakim, a leading Egyptian dramatist whose writing had influenced Nasser's vision of Arab nationalism, described sitting 'open-mouthed like a moron'. King Hussein of Jordan, who had reluctantly joined the offensive against Israel and lost the West Bank as a consequence, spoke of 'a dream, or more a nightmare'. Umm Kulthum, the Egyptian singer whose monthly concerts were broadcast across the region to tens of millions of radio listeners, refused to leave her home for two weeks after the war's end, emerging finally to sing of loss, disillusionment and betrayal, leaving her audience sobbing. That September, the Arab powers pledged 'No peace with Israel, no negotiation with Israel, no recognition of Israel'.

Through the rest of the summer, Khaled and other Palestinian colleagues discussed the new situation. Like many others, she recognised that the failures of the Arab armies and the expansion of Israel had fundamentally and irrevocably altered the politics of the Middle East. Those who had spent time in the territories newly occupied by Israel tended to believe that the communities there could rise up and somehow overcome the victorious Israelis. Anyone who had spent the summer elsewhere in the region, such as Khaled, was sceptical of such hopes and remained 'frustrated, confused, dismayed'. There she was, in Kuwait, in a place of 'eternal boredom', doing nothing except running fundraising drives at her school in the small town of al-Jarrah, reading out Palestinian poems over its public address system, and trying to organise protests against rules that prohibited female staff from wearing short sleeves.

Khaled had already been asked by colleagues to join Fatah, one of the various Palestinian factions that had formed over the previous decade, committed to a violent campaign against Israel. Founded by Yasser Arafat and half a dozen other activists in the late 1950s, Fatah was by far the largest of them. But Khaled was not impressed when she attended Fatah's meetings in Kuwait. The culture of the organisation struck her as hierarchical and overly deferential to authority. There was none of the cut-and-thrust that she had enjoyed at ANM meetings in

Beirut, and she considered the oath of loyalty that Fatah required all its members to swear to be an insult. You acted for the revolution out of conviction, not because you had made a promise to someone, she complained to a friend. When Khaled asked about joining Fatah's military wing she was told that, as a woman, she would be better employed in the effort to raise money for the fledgling social welfare system they were building.

In late 1967, Khaled returned to Lebanon to see her parents and seek out the leaders of the ANM. Most remembered her from her activism in Beirut half a decade before. Many were still frequent visitors to her family home. Once again, she asked to play a frontline role in the 'armed struggle' against Israel. To her intense disappointment, her request was denied.

One reason that the ANM could not accept Khaled as a frontline fighter was that the organisation, weakened by its internal divisions, had effectively collapsed following Israel's military triumph that summer. A second was that the successor organisation that had just been set up was still uncertain about its objectives or strategy. This was not the time to be recruiting untested if enthusiastic schoolteachers, even if their ideological pedigree was impeccable.

The leader of the new group was George Habash, a charismatic, chain-smoking former doctor from a prominent Christian family in the town of Lydda, in what was now Israel. Habash had been studying medicine at AUB before the 1948 war but was radicalised by atrocities that he witnessed when he returned home during the conflict and was among the founders of the ANM in 1951. Sixteen years later, he remained fully committed to the Palestinian and Arab causes, but Marxist ideology had become a primary influence too. Habash had drawn a crucial lesson from the war in 1967: the Palestinians could not rely on the support of unwilling or incapable Arab states if they wanted to defeat Israel. Through the autumn of 1967, he worked to fuse the Palestinian branch of the ANM with three smaller factions to form a new group. In December, a statement addressed to 'the Masses of our Arab nation and the Masses of our Palestinian people' proudly announced the establishment of the Popular Front for the Liberation of Palestine. The 'only weapon left in the hands of the people with which to redirect history into its proper course, with which to bleed the resources of the enemy and eventually to overcome him, is revolutionary violence', it read. And not only would the PFLP fight for the 'liberation of Palestine', it would be part of a broader struggle too: 'a counter-alliance grouping all anti-imperialist forces throughout the world'.

What this meant in practice was unclear. Habash spoke of launching a 'popular war of liberation' inspired by the anti-colonial uprisings of the previous two decades. These included the bloody eight-year struggle that led to France's withdrawal from Algeria in 1962, Mao Zedong's campaigns in China and the ongoing war in Vietnam, then reaching a new intensity. If the Viet Cong could successfully fight a bush war against the heavily armed forces of a superpower, surely the Palestinians could too. Yet Habash could offer little concrete detail when it came to how such a campaign might actually be organised on the ground.

The de facto deputy leader of the new group had a more precise strategic vision. Wadie Haddad was another Palestinian whose family had been forced to flee their home in 1948, when he was twenty-one. Haddad had also studied medicine at AUB and had worked very closely with his friend Habash in the early years of the ANM, even breaking him out of a Syrian prison. He was also Christian, though from a more modest background. Haddad lacked the good looks, eloquence and charisma of Habash but by late 1967 he had spent more than twenty years organising, recruiting and evading a variety of potentially lethal enemies, and he had proved himself an original, creative and formidably practical thinker.

Haddad was sceptical of Habash's strategy of popular uprisings and wars of resistance. On a practical level, with its networks in the West Bank and Gaza wiped out following Israeli occupation, the ANM lacked the basic infrastructure necessary to launch an insurrection. On a strategic one, Haddad believed that nobody, let alone one small group like the Popular Front for the Liberation of Palestine, could fight Israel's formidable military 'plane for plane, tank for tank, soldier for soldier'. Earlier in the year, he had pushed a series of resolutions through the ANM executive committee describing the need to 'strike the enemy everywhere' and find 'isolated, sensitive targets that are susceptible to shock'. These could include embassies, diplomats, companies, individuals, anything or anyone that was vulnerable, the planes and offices of El Al, Israel's national airline, being one obvious example. This version of the 'armed struggle' would allow the weaker force to keep the initiative, but still spur a wider mobilisation among Palestinians. Eventually, the chance would come to 'move to a higher stage of conflict' and 'cleanse the occupied homeland' of all 'traces of the Israeli presence', Haddad believed.

There was nothing intrinsically original about waging unconventional guerrilla warfare against a massively superior conventional military force, but Haddad envisaged a campaign that was radically different from anything that had gone before. First, he wanted to 'expand the circle of the battle with Israel' geographically. This meant attacks across the Mediterranean, into western Europe, wherever Israeli interests or citizens could be reached. This expansion would take the PFLP's offensive into places that had never witnessed this kind of conflict. In the words of the group's newsletter, *al-Hadaf* ('The Target'), the struggle would move from the forests to the skies.

Second, the group would use tactics that were also unprecedented. There had been scores of hijackings over the previous decade, but most had taken place in the US and been undertaken either for money or to reach Cuba. At one point, so many hijackers sought to reach Havana that neutral diplomats there had pre-printed forms ready to expedite the return of planes to the US, and American comedians joked about stewardesses aboard US domestic flights offering passengers 'coffee, tea or rum daiquiris'. Almost none had been carried out for political reasons. If the PFLP started to seize aircraft, they would surprise and shock their enemies. Finally, Haddad planned to deploy attackers the like of which had never been seen before, and this was where someone like Khaled might be very useful.

When Khaled had asked to join the armed struggle as a frontline fighter, Haddad had given her a task: to find ten new members for the PFLP in Kuwait within a year. If she managed that, he promised to reconsider his decision. On her return to al-Jarrah, Khaled convened a meeting of friends at the school where she was teaching, and spent the night discussing whom among their colleagues might be recruited. Local former ANM contacts supplied Khaled with leads. A bookshop in the centre of Kuwait City served as a meeting place or 'dead drop', where messages could be left or retrieved. Well before a year had passed, Khaled had recruited more than twenty new members of the PFLP.

By then Haddad's campaign was well underway. In July 1968 an El Al flight returning to Israel was hijacked twenty minutes after taking off from Rome. The three attackers threatened to detonate grenades, beat the navigator into unconsciousness and fired shots in the cabin. They then told the pilot to divert to Algiers, the Algerian capital where authorities were sympathetic to the Palestinian cause. Israel was forced to negotiate for the safe return of the plane, crew and twelve Israeli passengers and eventually agreed to release sixteen Arabs convicted of violent offences as a 'humanitarian gesture'. It was the first time the state had entered into any kind of talks with a representative of the Palestinians, let alone a 'resistance' group explicitly committed to violence. The Algerians then allowed the hijackers to leave unhindered. In almost every aspect, the operation was a spectacular success, and Haddad set to organising more.

Seven months later, Khaled was in al-Jarrah, listening to the BBC World Service in her hostel, when she heard reports of a new attack. A team of four PFLP attackers had opened fire on an El Al plane as it taxied at Zurich's airport, fatally wounding the co-pilot and injuring six passengers. The aim had been to force the aircraft to a halt so that they might destroy it with explosives – after passengers had been disembarked – in a spectacular propaganda stunt. But the plan had gone badly wrong. An Israeli security guard on board shot dead one attacker and the others were arrested by Swiss police. Newspapers ran pictures showing the corpse of a young man sprawled in the snow and, among the surviving attackers, a young woman, twenty-three-year-old Amina Dahbour, surrounded by her captors, wrapped in a warm coat, smiling and nonchalantly lighting a cigarette.

That a woman had participated in such an operation prompted amazement across the region. Khaled was tremendously impressed. 'The news struck me like lightning. A woman, a revolutionary . . . I ran out in my pyjamas screaming throughout the dormitory. Everyone thought that I had gone mad,' she wrote later. Within days, Khaled had got a message to Haddad that she wanted to participate in a similar operation. Two months after that, in April 1969, she was on her way to Jordan, a new recruit to a very new war.

Patrick Arguello was the 'very restless child' of an Irish American mother from Wisconsin and a Nicaraguan cook who met in San Francisco. He had grown up in Nicaragua on a farm a short distance outside the capital Managua, below the volcano of Momotombo. In 1956, he and his family had been forced to flee when a relative was implicated in the assassination of President Anastasio Somoza García, the founder of the Somoza dynasty's corrupt and authoritarian rule. The family moved to the US, and Arguello, aged thirteen, was sent to a high school in Los Angeles where he felt very out of place. On graduation he won a place at the University of California in LA, where he majored in Latin American Studies.

Though not quite as febrile as some other US campuses at the time, UCLA had its fair share of activists campaigning in support of the civil rights movement and against the war in Vietnam. Like them, Arguello saw the various battles against colonial rule in Africa, against US-backed repressive regimes in the Asia-Pacific region and South America, and against racial discrimination in the US itself as part of the same struggle. 'A child dies of hunger while others enjoy Cadillacs and furs – and I ask myself: WHERE ARE WE GOING?' he wrote to a friend. 'The crises facing the peoples of all continents affect each one of us and we have obligations to respond to the aggression that the capitalist systems have unleashed on the defenceless, bleeding populations.'

Arguello was clever, graduating magna cum laude and winning a Fulbright scholarship to study for a master's in political science in Chile. There a moderate Christian Democrat government was being challenged by a radical left-wing movement led by a former physician and Marxist activist, Salvador Allende. The country was restive and unstable, with many strikes and protests. Arguello's academic schedule at the University of Santiago was demanding, but left plenty of time to enjoy the company of its bright and idealistic students in a 'politically lively, socially aware atmosphere'. Arguello saw little of his fellow Fulbright scholars. When one twenty-two-year old scholar met him for the first time she was unimpressed. 'His family is from Nicaragua, and he's lived there for many years. As a result he is more Latino than American and is constantly trying to prove himself a "macho" by having an array of females at his "disposal" – and that would seem a good summary of his real feeling about women', she noted in her diary. Arguello enjoyed, and to some extent cultivated, an air of mystery. When he disappeared for weeks on end, other students wondered among themselves if he had set out to find one of the many revolutionary groups across the region.

In fact, [illegible] of his absences were the result of lengthy road trips with a local sculptress, but Arguello was at least emotionally invested in Latin America's struggle against repressive right-wing regimes. In August 1967, shortly after arriving in Santiago, Arguello received news that a friend whom he had 'loved as a brother' had been killed in a new wave of repression in Nicaragua, following a disastrous attempted insurrection by the Frente Sandinista de Liberación Nacional (FSLN), the radical underground opposition group known as the Sandinistas. Six weeks later, Che Guevara, the Argentinian insurgent who had played a leading role in Fidel Castro's takeover of Cuba, was caught and shot in Bolivia by CIA-trained special forces as he attempted to raise rural masses against their right-wing government. The two deaths powerfully affected Arguello. He consoled a Nicaraguan friend with the hope that neither signalled 'the end of the struggle'. Though 'the price may be high, [the] spirit does not weaken, [but] grows back stronger'.

At the end of that academic year, Arguello spent some months travelling, in conscious emulation of Guevara, before making his way to Nicaragua, where he arrived in June 1968. There he began working with radical students and eventually, having overcome considerable suspicion that he was a CIA spy, began running clandestine errands for the Sandinistas. By the spring of 1969, he was trusted sufficiently by them to act as a guide for their training expeditions in the forests near Momotombo, where he had grown up.

A year later, he was invited by student activists to address them at the Central American University in Managua. The main inspiration for the speech he gave was the work of a young Frenchman called Régis Debray, who had spent time with Guevara in Cuba and Bolivia. His book *Revolution in the Revolution?* had been promoted by Fidel Castro, reprinted by left-wing publishing houses in the US and Europe, and was then being read by aspirant revolutionaries everywhere. In it, Debray had presented Guevara's theory that a small number of committed individuals could use a mixture of coercion, spectacular violence and ideological persuasion to lead a successful popular uprising. This so-called 'Foco' or 'Focus' strategy went against decades of traditional Marxist orthodoxy, which maintained that successful revolution depended on the right 'objective conditions' and the importance of patient work by activists over decades to raise the consciousness of the masses. Instead, 'Foco-ists' argued, revolutionary violence created its own conditions for success and anyone could overturn the established order with little more than authentic revolutionary commitment, courage and modern automatic weapons.

In the crowded auditorium in Managua, following a poetry reading and a lecture on the US civil rights movement, Arguello spoke to hundreds of students about insurgency and revolutionary warfare. It did not matter that he had little direct experience of either. The audience was shocked by his daring. Merely to mention the Sandinistas in public was extremely risky, but Arguello appeared entirely fearless as he explained how to set about overthrowing their government.

The Nicaraguan security services had been watching Arguello ever since he made a brief visit to the country eight years previously. Unsurprisingly, his rousing rhetoric attracted their attention. Had he not been a US citizen, he would have been detained and then tortured or killed. Instead he was expelled, and so launched on the journey that would ultimately allow him to fulfil at least one of Debray's injunctions: 'Victory means to accept the principle that life is not the most precious thing for a revolutionary.'

By the time Arguello had left Nicaragua, Khaled had been training for several weeks at a camp among ancient pine forests spread across limestone hills in Jerash, thirty miles north of Jordan's capital Amman. Villages studded the slopes around, each surrounded by fields of wheat, groves of olives and orchards. At dawn cocks crowed and donkeys brayed. At night the sky was very clear, and full of stars. The facility was rudimentary: little more than rows of tents pegged into the stony earth beneath the trees, a clearing for parades and physical exercises, a shelter for meals, some trenches. Khaled had joined nineteen other female volunteers on a basic course of military instruction, and she was very pleased to be there.

That so many women were being trained by the PFLP was something of a sensation. Khaled had faced resistance to her activism from male members of the ANM, and her own family, since she was a teenager. Most Palestinian men believed that the role of women was to raise a new generation of fighters, not take up arms themselves, and mocked the female volunteers who marched through the refugee camps. The domestic arrangements of the senior PFLP leaders were entirely traditional and if there were women among the group's pantheon of martyrs, there were none among its decision-makers. Nonetheless, the PFLP's policy was, in theory, to encourage discussion of such issues and within twenty-four hours of arriving at the camp in Jerash, Khaled found herself drawn into an intense debate about the kinds of relationship that revolutionary women should have with 'parents, boyfriends or husbands'. When one volunteer said she would have to obtain formal permission from her parents to stay in the training camp, Khaled and another female fighter rounded on her for her antiquated attitude.

But before the debates came the drill. Khaled and the other trainees completed long marches through the hills, sleeping out in caves, under makeshift shelters or simply below the pines. There were moments of hilarity and of intense anxiety. One night the volunteers opened fire wildly at a supposed intruder after a jumpy sentry raised the alarm. At dawn, the cause was found to be an errant donkey, now riddled with bullets. On several occasions, Israeli jets flew low overhead, looking for targets. Once, while the volunteers were hosting 'a group of Iraqi artists who wanted to live the revolution and witness the work of revolutionaries', the camp and the surrounding hills were strafed. There were few luxuries and training was intensive, though the routine was broken by 'consciousness-raising sessions' in nearby villages. Breakfast consisted of hard biscuits, green olives and scalding tea. Camp rations were beans, lentils, potatoes, pasta, eggs, tomatoes and tinned sardines or corned beef. Meals were eaten standing up to discourage idle conversation. But Khaled enjoyed the freedom, the open air and the camaraderie, and, despite the strict segregation of the camp, began to form a close (though entirely chaste) friendship with the older, male commander of her training unit.

Then, three months after she had arrived, Khaled was summoned back to the PFLP's headquarters in Amman and told to travel to Beirut. There she met Haddad. When he asked if she was ready to die, Khaled told him that she was. When he said that the more realistic question was whether she was prepared to spend many years in prison, Khaled gave the same answer. Only then did Haddad explain that he wanted her to travel to Rome to hijack an American passenger jet.

Tanned, slim, with short brown hair, wearing casually elegant summer clothes and sunglasses, Leila Khaled did not look out of place when she flew into Rome from Lebanon in August 1969. The summer had been very hot, and though temperatures were now dropping, the city remained humid and enervated. The high temperatures had temporarily calmed the restless workers who had been protesting at the factories on the outskirts, and even the paparazzi following Hollywood stars to fashion shows and photoshoots lacked their usual energy. But Khaled was full of nervous excitement. The further training she had received in Beirut had gone well. She had asked if she could arrive earlier in Rome than the thirty-six hours she'd been allocated to allow some sightseeing. 'You are going for a mission, not on holiday,' Haddad replied.

The shuttle provided by Pan American airlines delivered her from Fiumicino, Rome's international airport, to the bus stop on Via Giovanni Giolitti near the city's main train terminal. From there she walked the short distance to the Grand Continental Hotel on the Via Cavour. At more than $50 a night, it was not a cheap place to stay but the PFLP was not short of funds.

Mindful of Haddad's instructions to maintain maximum security, Khaled left the Grand Continental only once: to book the plane tickets she needed for her onward journey. At the newspaper stands, the front pages carried stories of the most recent bombings in northern Italy by leftist extremists, Moscow's warning to Beijing to avoid 'military adventures', and the discovery by scientists in the US that plants grew 'greener and stronger' in the lunar dust brought back to Earth just six weeks earlier by the first men to walk on the Moon. Khaled rebuffed numerous offers of personal tours of the city from single men and made sure none of the staff saw her when she returned to the Grand Continental, slipping swiftly through its grand pillared entrance and lobby. Once back in her room, she found the bag containing a handgun and ammunition that had been left in a cupboard while she was out.

The following morning Khaled woke early and dressed in leather sandals, a soft wide-brimmed white hat, her large dark sunglasses and a loose white trouser suit, her favourite, bought a year earlier while on holiday in Damascus. She was pleased with the outfit, and especially fond of the hat, which she secured to her hair with a ribbon. The journey through the morning traffic back to the airport was short and uneventful.

Khaled's accomplice was an older PFLP veteran called Salem Issawi who had overseen some of her training in Jordan. According to the instructions she had received before leaving Beirut, Issawi would be waiting for her in the departures hall. And so he was: tall, broad-shouldered and, despite his pressed, grey trousers and smart blue blazer, looking exactly like the amateur boxer he had once been. He had spent the previous forty-eight hours in a more expensive hotel a short walk from hers and had not left his room at all, ordering sandwiches from room service. Though they had met before, they did not acknowledge one another, checking in separately for Trans World Airlines' Flight 840 from New York bound for Israel's principal international airport just outside Tel

Aviv. It was a similar routine to the one she would follow just over a year later – with Arguello – but this was her first time.

Soon Khaled was in the airport's lounge, looking out onto the planes, surrounded by her fellow passengers. There was a delay of half an hour. A middle-aged man travelling alone attempted to engage her in conversation. She brushed him off, politely. On the bus to the aircraft yet another single man tried to talk to her, so she opened a book – a biography of Che Guevara that had been an international bestseller that spring – and ignored him.

Arriving at the plane, Khaled mounted the steps and found her seat in first class. A few moments later, her accomplice sat down beside her. There were few other passengers and the three cabin staff, in the new TWA uniform of yellow, red and gold, with their jaunty scarves and short skirts, were very solicitous. Khaled and her accomplice continued to ignore one another as a stewardess offered drinks: she chose a coffee, he a beer.

The Italian coastline was still visible through the portholes on the right of the plane when Khaled and her accomplice stood up, retrieved their hand luggage from the racks, and moved swiftly up the aisle holding handguns and grenades high above their heads. Within a minute, they were in the cockpit.

Khaled took the pin out of a grenade and showed it to the pilot. 'Do you know what this is?' she asked. 'I am your new captain.' The pilot nodded. Khaled then read a prepared statement to the passengers, explaining that the Che Guevara Commando of the Popular Front for the Liberation of Palestine had taken over the flight.

As they approached Israeli airspace, she contacted local controllers and told them with some satisfaction that the plane's new call sign was 'Flight PFLP Free Palestine'. As they neared the airport outside Tel Aviv, three Israeli jet fighters flew alongside them. At this point, Khaled ordered a new route that would take the aircraft over Haifa, explaining to the crew that she wanted to see her home town. Finally, she ordered a new destination: Damascus.

By the time the airport of the Syrian capital was in sight, the hijacked plane was almost out of fuel. Any landing was going to be at the limit of the Boeing 707's range and the crew warned the 120 passengers to prepare for a crash. The stewardesses collected watches, pens, shoes and 'anything that keeps going at impact, because when you hit, everything that's not tied down keeps going with the speed that the aircraft had'.

In the event, TWA Flight 840 landed without incident and taxied to the runway furthest from the terminal. Khaled had already told the crew and passengers to evacuate the plane 'within sixty seconds' because the plane was wired with explosives. This was not true, but it meant terrified passengers slid down the emergency slides and onto the rocky, briar-strewn ground very quickly. Only then, with the aircraft empty, were explosives placed and detonated, neatly destroying much of the nose of the craft and causing $10 million in damage.

It was now late afternoon. Khaled joined the exhausted and traumatised passengers as they were collected by the airport staff and ferried in buses to the terminal. To her surprise, her cheerful attempts to distribute sweets and cigarettes met with a frosty response. She gave a brief speech to the assembled passengers and crew, now very clearly prisoners of the Syrians who had surrounded the airport and plane with troops. The hijacking had aimed to 'tell the world about the crimes the Israelis inflict upon our people' and TWA had been targeted because the US was an 'imperialist country' which supported Israel financially, diplomatically and through weapons sales. 'We are a part of the Third World and the world revolution,' Khaled said, and offered 'Greetings to all lovers of the oppressed!'

The crisis prompted by the hijacking would last many weeks. Syrian authorities were far from overjoyed at being chosen as the theatre for this particular Palestinian drama. The attitude of the regime in Damascus to both the PFLP and its tactics was hostile, with one soldier telling Khaled sternly that the seizure of a plane was the action of a 'terrorist'. Authorities allowed the TWA crew and all but six of the passengers to go free almost immediately, and held four Israeli women for just twenty-four hours. But negotiations for the release of two Israeli male passengers dragged. Eventually, after six weeks of complex diplomacy by the US, the International Committees of the Red Cross and other intermediaries, a deal was done. Once Israel had reluctantly released dozens of Syrian and Egyptian soldiers captured during and since the 1967 war, the final Israeli hostages were repatriated and the affair, long taken out of the hands of the PFLP, was over.

Khaled and Issawi remained in detention in Damascus throughout – to their intense annoyance. A series of hunger strikes did little to change their situation, but an interview with the Syrian minister of defence, an ambitious thirty-nine-year-old Ba'ath party official called Hafez al-Assad, did. Soon after this encounter, Khaled and Issawi were also released, and travelled straight to Jordan where they were feted as heroes.

But for the failure to destroy the entire plane – it was refitted and was flying again within months – Haddad and the PFLP considered the operation to have been a major success. In the weeks following the attack, Khaled gave dozens of press conferences and interviews. Reporters from major international newspapers fought to see her and a series of photoshoots with news agencies was arranged. One set of pictures showed Khaled outside a tent in a forest drinking from a tin cup with her accomplice and other fighters. Another showed her in combat fatigues standing next to a plane like the one she had hijacked.

In some images, Khaled wore a soft cap similar to those popularised by Mao, but in most she wore the *keffiyeh*, the traditional chequered Arab headdress that offered cheap and practical protection against the heat and dust of the region but which had become a symbol of nationalist resistance in the late 1930s during the Arab Revolt, a major uprising against British rule in Palestine. The scarf, along with a ring made from ammunition that Khaled wore to symbolise her 'engagement to the revolution', instantly became an integral part of her public persona. The keffiyeh evoked the culture, identity and traditions of the Palestinian people, and resonated with a more conservative constituency than might usually have supported the Popular Front. But that a woman could wear the keffiyeh was itself an important and radical statement. In the best-known set of pictures, Khaled smiled and carried an AK-47 or Kalashnikov assault rifle, the emblematic weapon of revolutionaries around the world. It had been handed to her by a journalist during the shoot.

Popular Front publicists did all they could to encourage this attention. They commissioned an 'autobiography' from a ghostwriter, to be published in English and Arabic, and sent Khaled on a three-month publicity tour of the Middle East, with bodyguards and an entourage. She was paraded at embassy parties, gave talks on campuses and drew hundreds to public meetings. When, tired of interviews and photoshoots, Khaled tried to avoid a meeting with an Italian TV team in Beirut, she received a 'very angry' call from George Habash, the leader of the PFLP, who told her in no uncertain terms to co-operate with the journalists.

Khaled's new celebrity was a gift to the movement but an obvious problem when it came to future deployments. Her jet-black hair, oval eyes, sharp chin and high cheekbones made her instantly recognisable.

Some breathless observers compared her to a young Audrey Hepburn. There was now little chance that she could slip through even the rudimentary security at most European airports without detection. So when, nine months after the Rome attack, Wadie Haddad cast Khaled in the starring role of his new spectacular, planned for the late summer of 1970, he came up with a radical, if extremely painful solution.

A Lebanese surgeon in Beirut was engaged to conduct a series of operations on Khaled to alter her appearance. After five months of work on almost every part of her face, there would be no further comparisons to Audrey Hepburn. Khaled and Haddad agreed that only her close relatives or friends would recognise her. She was now ready to be the public face of Operation Revolution Airport, the most ambitious hijacking operation ever launched by the PFLP, or indeed anyone else.

2
Spies Across the Jordan

In April 1970, Khaled had appeared as a 'hero of the resistance' at a mass meeting organised by the PFLP in a refugee camp in Amman to commemorate the anniversary of the birth of Lenin. Among the excited crowd was a foreign guest of the PFLP who had recently arrived from Sweden: a slim young man of medium height, with floppy dark hair and a narrow handsome face, featuring a neat moustache and goatee beard.

Gunnar Ekberg had grown up in the Swedish city of Malmö, the son of a typographer who had been conscripted in the Second World War and a nurse who had treated concentration camp victims. An uncle had married a Jewish woman in Germany and been forced to flee, while other family members and neighbours had been involved in the Danish resistance or helped Jewish families escape Nazi persecution. All talked frequently about the recent struggle against the Nazis and the immediate threat from the USSR. In his words, these were people who understood 'the difference between democracy and its opposite'.

In 1964, aged nineteen, Ekberg and a friend, both keen divers, had swum down to the wreck of a Soviet signalling vessel that had sunk off the coast of Malmö that April. Together they collected a handful of trophies. News of the exploit reached the local coastguard, who passed it on to Sweden's Intelligence Bureau, a secret and arguably illegal organisation that operated under the loose authority of the Ministry of Defence but was unknown to many parliamentarians and all but a handful of elected officials. The IB, known by those familiar with its operations as 'The Firm', asked Ekberg to repeat the feat, but this time to systematically empty the vessel of everything useful. A similar expedition to a second sunk vessel followed, and the IB then arranged for Ekberg to complete his compulsory military service as a diver in the Swedish navy.

When The Firm asked Ekberg to do some more work for them as

a civilian, he agreed readily and was given his first overseas mission: a covert information-gathering operation in Cuba. In 1966 Havana had hosted the Tricontinental Conference, a gathering of socialist governments and radical revolutionary organisations from across Asia, Africa and the Americas. The event had profoundly worried Western security services, who saw it as the centrepiece of a global effort to sow subversion and dissidence. The plan was for Ekberg to gain access to Cuba, which was virtually closed to western Europeans, by competing in the World Spearfishing Championship, scheduled to be held there in September 1967. He duly won a place, and was soon on his way to Havana via East Berlin. When not spearing barracuda in the Caribbean, the debutant spy toured the Cuban capital, noting the huge street portraits of Fidel Castro and Che Guevara, then serving as a sort of roving ambassador of revolution, as well as the Soviet-supplied jets at the airport. When one night a young female guide sent by the government invited him to her hotel room before dinner and then removed most of her clothes, he suspected a trap, made his excuses and left.

On Ekberg's return from Cuba, The Firm proposed a new mission. Sweden, despite its social democratic government and progressive values, had not been spared the wave of discontent and protest that had been building among students and young people in the West for much of the decade. Some had already labelled this surge of activism, different in so many ways from traditional schools of Marxist thought, as the 'New Left'. Swedish security services feared that their Soviet, Polish and eastern European counterparts, as well as the Chinese, were recruiting agents and informants among these new groups' members. The service asked Ekberg to infiltrate some of these rapidly proliferating left-wing organisations at home.

Ekberg was also asked to learn about anyone who might be in touch with Palestinian activists and organisations. The assessment by both the Intelligence Bureau and SAPO, the Swedish security police, was that the refuge and support Sweden had offered to many Palestinians over previous decades would insure against any actual hostile action against them. Prime Minister Olof Palme was a vocal critic of US foreign policy and a supporter of liberation movements around the world, and certainly those who had been granted asylum, housing and social assistance in Sweden were considered very unlikely to commit acts of violence themselves. The concern of both SAPO and IB was that the presence of activists among the Palestinian community in Sweden who raised money for Palestinian organisations and provided logistical support to those involved in violence might encourage such actors to use Scandinavia as a secure rear base for operations in Europe, and they did not want to see the conflicts of the Middle East imported onto the streets of Stockholm.

It was not hard for the novice spy to find and infiltrate the groups that interested his handlers. His first step was to get involved with a group in Gothenburg dedicated to protesting against the war in Vietnam. Using the credibility he gained here, he then joined the Communist League (Marxist-Leninist), which his IB handlers believed had the closest connections to Moscow of all Swedish groups. Many hours spent digesting texts by Communist thinkers allowed him to intervene convincingly in their many theoretical debates. His engaging manner helped too. When his new comrades learned that he had completed his military service – as students, most of them had avoided the twelve-month stint in the armed forces – and served as a specialist diver, his stock rose further. Soon he was travelling deeper into the world of radical revolutionary activism.

At the Swedish-Cuban Association, he got involved in discussions about the development of a 'scientific Marxist model of resistance to capitalist states'. At the Swedish-Chinese Association, Ekberg listened to lectures on the Soviet-Chinese border conflict, and at the Chinese Embassy he applauded a film about China's first nuclear bomb test in the Gobi Desert in 1964. Many of the activists Ekberg was spending time with were fervent admirers of Mao Zedong, then in his nineteenth year in power in China, and were inspired by the Cultural Revolution, then entering one of its bloodiest and most radical phases, about which they knew virtually nothing. While at the offices of one Marxist organisation, Ekberg took a key and pressed it into clay he had concealed in a matchbox. Some days later he used a duplicate made by his handlers from the imprint to break in, then photographed hundreds of documents.

Ekberg's frequent reports were long and full of the minutiae of meetings, debates, ideological arguments and factional disputes. His handlers at The Firm complained to each other that much of it was of little real interest, and some officials at SAPO were dismissive of the Intelligence Bureau's hyperactive agent. Ekberg signed up for a university degree in political science, went diving, planned his marriage to his long-term girlfriend and read much of the work of August Strindberg. Then came a breakthrough: an invitation from activists who had links to armed

Palestinian factions to 'join the comrades' in Egypt and Jordan for a few weeks.

Before he left Sweden, his handlers told Ekberg that his primary objective should be to gather information on the various armed Palestinian groups, about which the IB, like most Western services, was profoundly ignorant. Ekberg's instructions were to 'observe and memorise' without drawing attention to himself. There was no real discussion of the risk the young spy was running. It went without saying that there was almost nothing his Swedish employers could do if he ran into trouble. He would be entirely on his own.

On his first morning in the Middle East, Ekberg was woken by the call to prayer crackling through the speakers of Cairo's mosques, and he walked out of his run-down pension on an island in the Nile to find a city apparently at war. Blast walls shielded the entrances to government buildings and machine gun barrels glinted behind sandbagged positions on street corners. Windows, streetlights and headlights were coated with blue paint to dim their glare at night and so, in theory, avoid attracting the attention of Israeli bombers. Garish painted billboards advertised the latest productions of the Egyptian film industry, while down at street level the walls were covered with posters featuring stylised images of Palestinian fighters waving weapons, maps of the Middle East and explosions.

Ekberg watched and listened and remembered. Though still the cultural and political centre of the Arab world, Cairo was clearly much diminished. The ongoing low-intensity 'War of Attrition' between Israel and Egypt that had followed the 1967 war had made life difficult for the city's six million inhabitants. Hawkers offered the young Swede everything from perfume and black-market exchange to brothels. Shelves in the groceries were often empty. The streets were battered and potholed. President Gamal Abdel Nasser, who had offered to resign immediately after the war, was still in power but clearly weakened. It was obvious that the trauma of the defeat had yet to heal.

Some Egyptians argued that their leader's populist blend of authoritarian nationalism and 'Arab socialism' remained the only viable answer to the region's problems, insisting that 'el Rais' had not gone far or fast enough with his reforms. Others believed that Egypt needed to ditch socialism and its increasingly close relationship with Moscow as well. For good reason, any such views were expressed very discreetly, if at all. During a long afternoon drinking cold beers at the exclusive Gezira sports club, Ekberg asked some local students how he could meet Egyptian Marxists. His enquiries were met with embarrassed silence and a denial that any such people existed. In reality, years of brutal repression had reduced local Communists to a shadowy existence. Most were either underground or had been forcibly subsumed into the ruling Arab Socialist Union. The Muslim Brotherhood, a mass Islamist movement founded sixty-one years earlier, had also been decimated by a wave of arrests, mass incarceration and torture. To mention either would have been to risk disappearing into one of the grim cells of Cairo's Tora prison complex or one of the detention camps built out in the desert.

After several days of sightseeing and meetings with 'revolutionary' factions from across the region whose presence in Cairo was tolerated by the security services, Ekberg and his half-dozen fellow activists flew to Beirut. There their Palestinian-Swedish guide loaded them into taxis for the seventy-mile journey east over the mountains to Damascus, and from there they embarked on the longer journey south to Amman.

In the Jordanian capital, Ekberg had the perfect opportunity to build up his 'map' of the various Palestinian factions. The retreat of Jordanian forces from the eastern half of Jerusalem and the hilly West Bank in 1967 had turned the River Jordan into a new frontline between Israel and its Arab neighbours. Militant groups vied for control of the crowded refugee camps while sending their fighters on often ill-fated raids into the now occupied West Bank or to plant bombs in Israeli cities. Some were also turning their attention to targets further afield, he learned. There was even talk of a takeover of Jordan itself. On his first night in the city, Ekberg was woken repeatedly by gunfire in the streets outside his cheap hotel, confirming that tensions between the armed Palestinian factions and the forces of King Hussein, the young monarch who had been on the throne since 1952, were sharpening.

Of the many armed groups, only three appeared genuinely significant. Fatah, led by the physically unprepossessing but energetic former engineer Yasser Arafat, had the most fighters and the most political influence. Then there was the Democratic Front for the Liberation of Palestine, the DFLP, a relatively small faction which had been founded just a few months earlier and had since raised its profile through loud advocacy of the most doctrinaire Marxist-Leninism. The DFLP took Ekberg to a makeshift training camp just outside the city where he spent the next two days firing weapons and performing drills. But the group that most interested Ekberg's employers was the Popular Front for the Liberation of Palestine, the PFLP, and especially its key strategist, Wadie Haddad, about whom they knew very little. Once more, Ekberg impressed his hosts. The PFLP officials he met were not only convinced of his commitment to the Palestinian cause, they seemed keen to develop their relationship with him. Once again, a major attraction was his military diving skills. Another was the possibility that he could obtain Swedish passports for them. The PFLP asked him to come back as soon as he could.

In April 1970, nine months after his first trip, Ekberg set out again for the Middle East, this time as a personal guest of the PFLP. He carried the half-dozen genuine Swedish passports that the PFLP had requested, obtained by the simple expedient of relaying the Palestinians' demands to the leaders of the Communist League, who in turn promptly instructed some of their members to 'lose' their travel documents. He also carried some carefully concealed pornographic films. These were easily obtainable and relatively cheap in Sweden, but were rare and costly in the Middle East. Ekberg planned to sell them to raise funds that would allow him to explain how he, a penurious activist, was able to afford such a journey. The idea had been his own.

This second trip exceeded everybody's expectations. Amman was chaotic and violent as before. A day after Ekberg arrived in the city, hundreds of students, led by members of the PFLP and other uniformed factions and carrying placards announcing 'The Commandos will never surrender', stormed the United States Embassy compound, smashing windows, burning cars, tearing down the embassy shield, and replacing the Stars and Stripes with the black, green, white and red flag of Palestine. The protest had been prompted by a new plan to bring peace between Egypt and Israel that was being pushed by Washington but that did not involve the Palestinians in any significant way. Tensions between the armed Palestinian groups and King Hussein were sharper than ever and every night the streets rang with gunfire.

But the PFLP was happy to see him, and very pleased by the passports he had brought. Over the following days, Ekberg visited a school for 'ideological training', where students read Mao, Lenin and Marx before lengthy sessions of self-criticism. He met a 'colonel' in a villa on the slopes of one of Amman's many hills who requested a dossier on how to train military divers to use explosives. The PFLP's apparent confidence in their new recruit was confirmed when they told Ekberg that any Swedish compatriots who wanted to follow in his footsteps would only be accepted following his personal endorsement. Some of his hosts' questions were especially interesting to the IB back in Stockholm: What might happen if the PFLP tried to land a hijacked plane in Sweden? one senior member asked.

After a week, one of the PFLP's more senior officials drove Ekberg back to his hotel and stayed for a beer at the bar. He had a message. Ekberg should go to Beirut as soon as possible, and get in touch with the editor of *al-Hadaf*, the newsletter run by the Popular Front, when he arrived there. Haddad had heard about him, the official said, and wanted to meet.

Ekberg had little difficulty finding *al-Hadaf*'s offices, which turned out to be housed on the third floor of a modern building on the Boulevard de Mazraa, set back from the seafront in Beirut's commercial district, not far from the Popular Front's headquarters. 'The Target' had been launched two years earlier, and had become an influential publication, though the logistics of distribution limited its reach. Its offices were plastered with portraits of revolutionary icons such as Guevara, Ho Chi Minh and Mao, as well as dramatic, graphic posters of fighters waving weapons, flags and fists. Ekberg was greeted by Ghassan Kanafani, a celebrated Palestinian novelist who was *al-Hadaf*'s editor, a key spokesman for the Popular Front and one of its most influential strategic thinkers. The young Swede sat, drank tea, noted the gun that his host had just taken from a holster and placed in a drawer of his desk, the fins from spent mortar shells used as paperweights and the spent artillery ammunition piled in corners. Kanafani told him that he had an appointment with Haddad the very next day.

Very pleased, Ekberg took a taxi back to his hotel, then walked along Beirut's seafront boulevard, the Corniche, under the palm trees and past the luxury hotels. On the ridge of the promontory to the east was the superb campus of the American University of Beirut. Below the paved walkway, the waves of the Mediterranean crashed over a breakwater. The sun was warm on the back of his neck. The following morning, Ekberg returned to the seafront shortly after dawn and dived through the clear water to the limestone bottom, then showered, ate, and walked through the waking city to *Al-Hadaf*'s offices.

The meeting lasted an hour. Around five feet six inches tall, balding, with a small well-groomed moustache, there was nothing in Haddad's appearance to indicate the role he played, or the ruthless talents that had earned him the nickname 'the Master', apart from perhaps a sharp scar between his mouth and chin. With his spreading waistline, white shirt, dark trousers and homburg hat, Haddad looked very much like the paediatrician he once had been, or a moderately successful local shopkeeper. He was polite, serious, focused and very well informed. Not only did Haddad know of Ekberg's delivery of Swedish passports to Amman and his expertise in military diving, which interested him greatly, he also knew that Ekberg had sold the Swedish pornography in a brothel near Beirut's Martyrs' Square on his arrival from Damascus a day earlier. This led to some muted ribaldry, but also made clear how effective Haddad's intelligence network could be.

For the next hour, the two men drank tea, ate chocolate pralines and talked about how Ekberg could best help the PFLP. First Haddad asked if his visitor could detail what might be needed to train and equip a team capable of underwater attacks. As the conversation moved to broader issues in the Middle East and then western Europe, Haddad requested details of the political situation in Scandinavia, which he made clear he saw as a potential base for the PFLP's overseas operations, which were being expanded. The group needed around ten more Swedish or other western European identity documents, 'preferably unused', and was also looking for suitable recruits in Scandinavia, he said, hinting that Ekberg could help here too. 'There are always young people who are frustrated and hate someone or something around them,' Haddad observed. 'They often end up far to the left in politics, where they can vent their anger. We must keep our eyes open for such people, for young people who want to do something that makes a difference.'

The key thing was recruitment, he explained. If that was properly managed, the practicalities of any attack would not be challenging. 'It is easy to get them to perform the operation itself,' Haddad told his visitor. 'Take a target such as a popular restaurant. It takes two kilos of ordinary explosives, a simple clock, an electric lighter, and a small battery. That's all. . . . They then conceal the bomb in a small bag hidden under a table, in a bin, in the toilet, or you can have the bomb in the pockets of your overcoat that you hang in the closet. Then just pay and walk out to the street in plenty of time before it blows up. It's that simple.' Haddad did not volunteer any further detail of what he might be planning, though Ekberg was sceptical that the PFLP would want to recruit foreigners and obtain identity documents merely to bomb eateries. But he could ask no further questions without raising suspicions and soon the conversation was over and 'the Master' was gone.

Elated, Ekberg returned to his hotel, where he enjoyed a bottle of wine and a hearty dinner. In the morning, he returned to the *al-Hadaf* office where one of Haddad's aides had briefed him on future arrangements: all communications would be sent to a mailbox address in Beirut and written in a simple code: passports were 'pictures', passport stamps were 'pencils', explosives and underwater mines were 'books' and potential candidates for future missions would be known as 'friends'. In due course, Ekberg would be notified of an address where he could collect money and airline tickets. He would be provided with two passports: one to travel to Beirut or Amman in order to receive instructions, a second to travel 'on assignment' to Israel or to another country. Then he was given a thousand dollars in cash and a task: to track down another Swedish activist whom the Popular Front now suspected of being a double agent. Ekberg was given photos, a recent telephone number and a postal address. 'We trusted him but he tricked us,' the aide said. 'We will set an example for others . . . But do not worry. You're not going to kill him. We have other people to do that, and we have other assignments for you.'

Ekberg would spend the summer of 1970 in Stockholm, working to fulfil the list of requests given him by the PFLP that April. Reviewing what he had heard in Beirut and Amman, the questions about hijacking in Europe, the requests for multiple sets of European identification documents, and other potential clues to the extraordinary attack that later unfolded on 6 September, he would curse himself for failing to join the dots.

3
The Fedayeen

In the spring of 1970, Wadie Haddad faced a problem. The Palestinian nationalist movement was beset by ruthless internal rivalries, its many factions continuously vying for position. Haddad's new tactic of directing violence against 'isolated, sensitive targets that are susceptible to shock', wherever they might be, had in part been a response to this. Such violence not only damaged and demoralised Israel, it also raised the PFLP's profile, attracting new recruits with its growing reputation for audacity and technical competence and in turn winning political leverage that was vastly disproportionate to the group's size. This gave Habash and its leadership access to powerful rulers such as Nasser and forced those in Moscow, Washington and throughout the Middle East at least to acknowledge their agenda. But it all depended on being seen and heard by the widest possible audience.

In the Middle East that was made difficult by state control of media, which filtered any news of an attack to its own ends. Further afield and across the West, meanwhile, Haddad was having to compete for attention with an astonishing series of events. The summer of 1968 had been witness to the aftermath of the protests that had rocked Paris and other European capitals in May; the killing of hundreds in a brutal crackdown at the Olympics in Mexico, where African American athletes on the US team had raised their fists in a Black power salute from the podium; the bloody invasion of Czechoslovakia by Soviet and eastern European troops who sought to oust the reforming premier, Alexander Dubček; and running street battles at the US Democratic party's National Convention in Chicago. Amid such turmoil, the Middle East was largely forgotten. Things did not much improve the following year. Khaled's hijacking in the summer of 1969 had won massive attention, but soon similar attacks that lacked such a striking participant were being ignored again. In 1970, the *New York Times*' coverage for one of them extended to a single column on page 120 under the headline 'Another Ransom Hijacking'.

This led Haddad to a further radical innovation. Henceforth, the group would prioritise not Israeli citizens or planes as legitimate targets, but those of other nations implicated in the conflict as well. Given the number of planes now flying around the world, the chances that any passenger might actually be a victim of a hijacking was infinitesimally small, but this was irrelevant. The point was that those who had once had the luxury of being onlookers would find themselves on the frontline of what had hitherto been a very distant conflict. As a consequence their elected leaders would be, too.

That the PFLP's young men and women would be described as terrorists in the West was inevitable, if unfortunate and unjust, men like Habash and Haddad reasoned. But then the same was true of the participants in almost all the struggles that had inspired them: the Viet Cong, the Algerians, Latin American groups like the Uruguayan Tupamaros, the African National Congress in its battle against apartheid in South Africa. The Israelis, of course, used the noun 'terrorist' to refer to more or less any Palestinian attacker. This was the nature of their enemy, the PFLP's leaders believed, and of the conflict they were engaged in.

Such was the thinking that lay behind the attack planned for September of that year. And the man given responsibility for attracting the 'global attention' that was one of the principal aims of the attack, and then explaining this new strategy to its bewildered victims, was the twenty-four-year-old deputy editor of *al-Hadaf*, Bassam Abu Sharif.

Sharif had been born into a well-known and once wealthy family which had lost properties and a hotel business in Jerusalem after the war of 1948. His father was a banker, and Abu Sharif had grown up in Amman among other wealthy Palestinian exiles speaking Arabic, French – which was still used by the Lebanese and Syrian elite – and English he had learned at expensive schools. Animated and articulate, he too was a graduate of the American University of Beirut, a great admirer of Gamal Abdel Nasser, and on his first day at university had joined the Arab National Movement. After an interview with George Habash in the ANM co-founder's apartment in Beirut, Abu Sharif had been given a series of mildly risky clandestine missions in the West Bank, then still under Jordanian rule.

In 1967, like Khaled, he had welcomed the outbreak of war and made an abortive attempt to join the fighting, despite a total lack of military experience, travelling in a bus with dozens of other students as far as the Lebanese border with Syria before the extent of the Israeli victory became clear. Bitterly disappointed at his and his companions' failure, he then spent several weeks in Jordan working with the United Nations among newly arrived Palestinian refugees, but found himself ill-suited to physical labour in a chaotic and uncomfortable environment. So instead he got involved in the formation of the PFLP and had then been appointed to work on its newsletter. When Haddad outlined his new strategy a year later, Abu Sharif had been hugely excited – 'the world had tilted slightly on its axis', he said later – and with his various languages he saw a role for himself helping to publicise and explain the planned wave of attacks.

While Gunnar Ekberg was talking to Wadie Haddad over tea and chocolate pralines in the offices of *al-Hadaf*, the key players in Operation Revolution Airport were gathering. Some were right nearby: Bassam Abu Sharif had been in one of the other rooms of the office as they spoke, while Leila Khaled was working on logistics in Haddad's home a short walk away. Others were making their way to Amman for their final preparations, among them a tall, muscular twenty-six-year-old who had recently been freed from a Greek jail, where he had been serving a lengthy sentence for murder and arson, and who had been picked by Haddad to lead the detachment on the ground at Revolution Airport itself. The story of his career as an armed militant to that point involved some of the most important events for the Palestinian nationalist movement since the war of 1967, and a frontline role in the bloody new form of unconventional warfare that Haddad had pioneered.

Like Leila Khaled, Mahmoud Issa had fled his home in what had been the British Mandate of Palestine in 1948. His large family had travelled north from Acre, across hills and fields into Lebanon, where Issa had grown up in a refugee camp. He enrolled to train as a teacher but abandoned his studies, having been forced to leave Lebanon by its security services who were concerned by his activism and outspoken support for the Palestinian cause. He then spent two years in Egypt, before eventually travelling to Jordan in the aftermath of the 1967 war, where he joined Fatah.

Fatah not only had four or five times as many fighters as the Popular Front, but the PFLP's recruits tended to be more educated and relatively affluent. Christians were over-represented in its ranks and the group made much of its commitment to socially progressive politics. By contrast Fatah, as Khaled had found out in Kuwait, was much more conservative, appealing to those like Issa from a poorer, more traditional background. Contemporary reporters described the organisation as 'very square' compared to the PFLP. The fighters in Fatah's propaganda videos held copies of Mao's Little Red Book and portraits of Che Guevara were prominently displayed in Fatah's offices and camps, but the organisation was careful to cleave closely to the values of its key constituency. Some of its posters featured a deep-rooted tree or a proud horse, evoking the rural village life that many displaced Palestinians mourned. It encouraged the publication of homespun proverbs, songs and stories, and the revival of skills such as embroidery, and its network of social services took over and expanded the activities of religious bodies and community associations. Folk dances reinforced its image as the authentic heir to and protector of the down-to-earth traditions and identity of the Palestinian *fellahin*, farmers or agricultural labourers. Fatah's members called each other 'Revolutionary Brother', not 'Revolutionary Comrade'.

Many of the organisation's leaders, including Arafat, came from relatively devout backgrounds, prayed five times a day and neither smoked nor drank. A significant number had been involved with the region's leading Islamist movement, the Muslim Brotherhood. They recognised that to reject religion or Islamic culture entirely would be to alienate many potential supporters. The name Fatah was a reverse acronym of Harakat al-Taḥrir al-Watani al-Filasṭini, or the 'Palestinian National Liberation Movement', but it also meant 'conquest', a word used as shorthand for the spectacular early expansion of the Muslim Empire and the name of one of the most famous verses of the Koran. When a photographer and a journalist from *Life* magazine were invited to view Fatah's bases in Jordan in late 1968 the carefully choreographed scenes that they were allowed to photograph included rows of fighters at prayer. This was in sharp contrast to the culture of the PFLP and even more so that of the radical Marxist-Leninist faction, the Democratic Front for the Liberation of Palestine (DFLP).

Issa knew little about Arafat. Few people did. The Fatah leader's real name was Mohammed Abdel Rahman Abdel Raouf Arafat al-Qudua al-Husseini, but since childhood he had been known as Yasser, and he deliberately kept much of his biography obscure. One key fact that Arafat was especially keen to keep quiet was that he had been born not in Palestine but in Cairo, though he spent much of his childhood in Jerusalem. He also allowed it to be understood that he was in some way linked to the prestigious al-Husseini family of Jerusalem, though in fact he was the son of a fairly unsuccessful businessman from Gaza and there was no such connection. Nor had he been an aide to one of the most famous Arab commanders in the war of 1948, as he liked to claim, though he had helped supply arms to Palestinian irregulars in or around Gaza during the fighting. This tendency to lie, systematically and sometimes outrageously, would anger and frustrate those who dealt with him throughout his career, but it was a strategy learned in a hard school.

Arafat had been a student from 1949 at Cairo University, where he had just about found time between his political activities to complete a civil engineering degree. He won election to the head of the Palestinian Students' Union, despite such posts being reserved for the scions of notable families. The victory was a testament to both his unlikely charm and capacity for hard work. He also showed considerable political talent. While his opponents campaigned on single ideological causes – pan-Arab nationalism, Communism, Islamism – he presented himself as a unity candidate. This inclusive approach to politics would remain central to Arafat's strategy over the decades to come.

Though a fervent admirer of Nasser, Arafat was deeply frustrated by the practical restrictions the Egyptian leader placed on Palestinian activists. After several unpleasant brushes with Egypt's increasingly intrusive security agencies, Arafat left Cairo in 1956, heading, like so many other Palestinians, to the Gulf, where he found employment as a government engineer in Kuwait. There he set about transforming a group of like-minded allies, committed to forming yet another Palestinian nationalist faction, into something much more structured and effective.

From the outset, Fatah was different. Like the leadership of other groups, Arafat and his associates were convinced that the Palestinians could not wait for Arab armies to defeat Israel but needed to act themselves. But unlike their contemporaries, Fatah's leaders explicitly eschewed any interference in the internal affairs of any Arab country. Fatah's slogan 'Revolution or death' was a call for radical upheaval and sacrifice in the cause of Palestinian nationalism, not for transformative social or political change across the Middle East. To its new recruits, the cry revolution meant hope, pride and resistance, not Arab rulers swinging from makeshift scaffolds. Naturally this eased fundraising among powerful and wealthy donors. In the early 1960s, Arafat won substantial sums of money from King Faisal of Saudi Arabia and King Idriss of Libya, from Kuwait's ruling elite and from newly independent Algeria.

Much of these funds was spent on an expensive effort to convince other Palestinian nationalist groups to join Fatah, and the rest disappeared fast as offices and functionaries proliferated around the Middle East. Arafat's appeals were reinforced by the grandiose promises made in its newsletter *Filistinuna*, 'Our Palestine', which gave the impression that his organisation was a major force with significant combat capabilities. Only a few people close to Arafat knew that in reality Fatah had only a few hundred members and its entire armoury consisted of a handful of rusty rifles, a single malfunctioning machine gun and a few stolen commercial detonators.

In January 1965, Fatah launched its first strike: against Israel's new irrigation infrastructure, which had caused anger and concern among neighbouring Arab states. Militarily, the operation was an almost total failure. Lebanese security forces prevented one Fatah team crossing the frontier into Israel, while the explosives attached to a pumping station by a second group of fighters failed to explode. Other attacks that were supposed to be part of Fatah's great opening salvo were either abortive or went unnoticed, but this mattered little to Arafat. Even before the results of the attacks were known, Fatah had issued a communiqué claiming that its 'revolutionary strike forces had gone into action to show to the colonialists and their henchmen, and to world Zionism and its financiers that [the] Palestinian people ... ha[ve] not died and will not die'.

Through 1965, the raids continued and became marginally more effective. In 1966, Fatah launched dozens of operations attacking Israel. By May of the following year, the total had risen to well over a hundred. Thirteen Israelis had been killed, including four soldiers. This tempo was hard to sustain but had begun to show results. In early 1967, Israel warned Damascus to curtail raids from Syrian territory by Palestinian groups or face military attack. The threat fuelled the crisis that would eventually lead to war some months later, vindicating Arafat's judgement that the Palestinians could win political influence and leverage through violence.

Like George Habash of the PFLP, Arafat had studied the experiences of other nationalist insurgents in the developing world and believed their lessons could be applied. Alongside the ideas of Guevara, who had met Fatah officials in Algiers in 1965, and Mao Zedong's victory over initially vastly superior forces in China, by far his greatest influence was the bloody but successful effort waged against the French colonial regime in Algeria. But Arafat's confidence in the late summer of 1967 that he could recreate such successes in the territories captured by Israel that June proved wildly misplaced, and his efforts to galvanise a revolt among the Arab population of the West Bank failed utterly. The Fatah leader himself narrowly escaped capture and the organisation's networks were as comprehensively dismantled as the PFLP's had been.

This was a blow to Arafat's prestige and authority, and it threatened the dominance Fatah had established within the Palestinian movement. The competition for recruits between the various factions based in Amman fuelled a fierce propaganda war. 'Commando broadcasts resound from radios everywhere. . . . Commando leaflets are legion and commando handbills shout silently from hundreds of walls,' wrote one visitor. Multiple groups often claimed responsibility for the same attack and all systematically exaggerated even the smallest success. Operations were given grandiose names – The Che Guevara Offensive, Scythes of the North, Ho Chi Minh – or sometimes simply invented. A committee was set up to try to co-ordinate policy between Fatah, the PFLP and the smaller factions. 'We nearly all smoke like chimneys and there is talk, much talk,' one of its members admitted, but an attempt to run a cost-benefit analysis of offensive operations failed when its members either refused to take part or provided grossly distorted data. Still, in the first nine months following the 1967 war, the raids, mortar strikes, bombings and other attacks on Israel and the occupied West Bank killed sixty-five Israeli soldiers and fifty civilians.

One of Israel's various reactions to this onslaught was to dispatch sizeable detachments of troops across the border into Jordan on missions to destroy the infrastructure of the armed Palestinian factions and pressure King Hussein to shut them down. When in March 1968, a school bus in the far south of Israel struck a mine and a doctor and a student were killed, the Israeli cabinet agreed to launch the largest such incursion to date. Its target was Karameh, a small town just over the River Jordan that had become the de facto headquarters of Fatah.

Yasser Arafat was made aware of the impending attack by the Jordanians, who had themselves been warned by the CIA, but he decided to ignore the advice of his close associates, who urged a tactical withdrawal, and the joint strategy agreed with other groups to avoid any major confrontations. Instead, as the Israelis massed their powerful forces on the other side of the river, the Fatah leader told his fighters to prepare to resist. This proved an astute choice. Though Israeli troops eventually penetrated deep into the town, they failed to deliver a decisive blow and in the late afternoon Palestinian fighters launched a counter-attack.

Issa had been among those who had launched this final assault. 'The [Israelis] began to pull back, following their tanks . . . Since their stunning victory of 1967, these men were invincible,' he remembered several years later. 'We had been waiting since the morning. We were waiting for this moment. At the instant when the tanks drew level, a signal gave us the order to attack . . . It was . . . an indescribable relief. As if we had held our breath too long . . . Only late at night did calm return,' he wrote. 'We stood among ruins lit by the light of flaming [Israeli] tanks. We repeated to ourselves again and again: we had won.'

Militarily speaking, this was not quite accurate. Though twenty-eight Israelis were dead, so too were at least ninety-two Fatah fighters, and hundreds more were injured. But the raw statistics were not important. Images of burned-out Israeli tanks and trucks allowed the inconclusive encounter to be portrayed as the first major victory ever won by the *fedayeen*, meaning 'those prepared to sacrifice their lives', the romantic name now used by millions to refer to Palestinian fighters. Arab rulers across the region recognised that any win over the Israelis could help restore their own battered reputations, however minimal their actual involvement, and so directed their state media to spread the glad tidings of this glorious Arab victory and the emergence of a new Arab military force. King Hussein of Jordan, whose artillery had actually inflicted most of the losses on the Israelis at Karameh, was moved to declare that 'all of us are fedayeen'. That Karameh meant 'dignity' in Arabic also helped. Within weeks Arafat's portrait was tacked next to that of Nasser on the wall of cafés from Marrakesh to Aden.

One immediate consequence was a huge surge in funds for Fatah, as Arab states and individual donors sought to outdo one another in their displays of support and enthusiasm for the struggle against Israel. Money flowed in from almost everywhere, though the Saudis were especially generous. Recruitment went up too. Fatah officials claimed that 20,000 students and former soldiers in Egypt had sought to join, while its office in Baghdad was receiving 1,500 applications each week. One PFLP member remembered that, following Karameh, 'a Palestinian fedayi could travel right across the Arab world with nothing more than his organisation card and be welcome everywhere. Nobody . . . dared to raise a voice against a fedayi.' The battle even attracted the attention of the Western media. Six months after Karameh, Arafat made the first of many appearances on the cover of *Time* magazine.

It was not just Israel and the West that Arafat was now able to defy. The 'victory' at Karameh allowed him to consolidate his control over the Palestine Liberation Organisation, the umbrella organisation founded four years earlier by the various Arab states in order to corral and control the many armed Palestinian factions. Though by now the organisation officially included a dozen or so different groups, including the PFLP and the DFLP, all with a say in its overall strategy and most with a particular state sponsor, it had come to be reviled for its lack of action and for embodying the many shortcomings of the region's rulers. At a meeting in February 1969 in Cairo, 'Fatah settled into the empty shell' of the PLO, Eric Rouleau, the Middle East correspondent of *Le Monde*, wrote.

This was a considerable achievement, as whoever ran the PLO gained significant authority over the entire Palestinian nationalist movement, control of a nascent state structure bankrolled by donations or levies from Arab states that amounted to many millions of dollars a year, and a legitimate claim to be able to represent all Palestinians politically. The pan-Arabist language and sentiment that had been included in the PLO's charter four years earlier was now stripped out and replaced with more revolutionary rhetoric. The 'armed struggle' led by the fedayeen was now described as 'the only way'. One of Arafat's first acts as chairman of the PLO was to call able-bodied Palestinian nationalist supporters around the Middle East to concentrate in Jordan. 'Our new generation is tired of waiting for something to happen,' he told them. 'Isn't it better to die bringing down your enemy than to await a slow, miserable death rotting in a tent in the desert?' Some, like Mahmoud Issa, had little need for the choice to be spelled out for them and had already sought out Fatah.

The battle at Karameh had reinforced Arafat's belief that a guerrilla campaign fought along more or less classic lines could bring victory, but most of those who answered Arafat's call rapidly discovered that the disparity between the resources of the Israeli military and those of the Palestinian fighters was as wide as it had ever been. Fedayeen sent across the River Jordan now faced minefields, electronic detection devices, arc lights and mobile patrols. The Israelis claimed to have captured or killed more than thirty-five of the fifty attackers who made the crossing during a single ten-day period in the spring of 1968. Veterans of the raids, such as Issa, suggested an even higher rate of attrition.

All armed factions sought to steal each other's best fighters, and at some point in the summer of 1968 the PFLP convinced Issa to join them. Quite how they did this is unclear. At the time the smaller group's leaders were still engaged in mutual recriminations over their decision not to join Fatah's fight at Karameh. Perhaps the better salaries paid to their fighters by the PFLP was a factor in Issa's decision. Perhaps he was attracted by their politics. Perhaps it was that they offered a clear alternative to being shot by border guards in a gully, spending years in an Israeli prison, or the humiliating death in a tent derided by Arafat. Or it may simply be that he was flattered to be asked to join an organisation that had established an elite reputation. Whatever the reason, by the late summer of 1968, two years prior to Operation Revolution Airport, Haddad had picked Issa to lead one of the new high-profile overseas attacks that the PFLP were then planning.

Even on an overcast day with the waves of the Saronic Gulf whipped by a fierce wind and rain spattering against its vast windows, the view from the main transit lounge of the new terminal at Athens' Ellinikon airport would have been impressive. At around 11 a.m. on Boxing Day 1968, Mahmoud Issa, aged twenty-five, and a nineteen-year-old whom he knew as 'Moussa' would have been found sitting on its grey-upholstered minimalist chairs. The two young men had spent the previous week together in Beirut and had got on well. Issa had spent his last evening with friends at a restaurant, eating well and drinking slightly too much wine. When his father asked how he would hear news of his son's first overseas trip, Issa had told him to listen to the radio.

The two young men were posing as wealthy Arab tourists on their way to Milan and Rome for a short break, and wore fedoras, sharp leather shoes, open-necked shirts and jackets. No one had checked their bags at Beirut airport and, as they were transit passengers in Athens, no one had bothered them on their arrival in the Greek capital either. They'd sat silently, lighting one cigarette from another. On the marble floor at Issa's feet was a sports bag containing grenades, an automatic rifle and clips of ammunition.

To avoid the suspicion of the security guards, they pretended to be drunk, staggering across the hall towards the glass doors that led onto the apron. Most planes served unlimited free alcohol to passengers, so airport staff were used to such sights. As the Boeing 707 of El Al Flight 253 from Lod airport came to a halt outside, Issa and Moussa pushed through the doors and began to run towards the plane, pulling the assault rifle and grenades from the bag. A few dozen yards from the plane, Issa opened fire, sending dozens of 7.62mm rounds through the fuselage of the aircraft and fatally wounding a fifty-year-old maritime engineer called Leon Shirdan. Moussa had circled the plane, throwing grenades into its engines. As the airport's emergency services converged, he had tried to hand out leaflets to the terrified passengers who were now evacuating the plane at their instruction. These carried a lengthy justification of their actions in English and French. At this point, Issa began trading shots with police and security men. After a lengthy standoff, the two young men eventually surrendered.

They were beaten, handcuffed and stripped, held for several hours in an airport cell, then put in a police van and driven to a high-security prison in the city. Issa had watched the crowds on the streets of Athens through the bars of the vehicle. 'The city was beautiful with its Christmas decorations,' he remembered later. 'It was the first time I had ever been in Europe.' The attack was the first lethal operation carried out by a Palestinian organisation outside the Middle East.

Issa and Moussa were tried, convicted and received lengthy prison sentences, but no one thought they would spend very long in jail. When in April 1970 the PFLP hijacked an Olympic Airlines plane with fifty-five passengers on board and demanded Issa and Moussa's release, the Greek authorities swiftly acquiesced. Five members of a PFLP team that had thrown a hand grenade into an El Al office in the Greek capital, killing a small child, were also freed. All were put on a plane and flown to Cairo, where they were driven to the luxurious Semiramis Hotel in the centre of the city. On a table in Issa's room lay flowers and chocolates. These were the personal gift of Gamal Abdel Nasser, the Egyptian president, an accompanying card informed him.

Despite the offer of a week's holiday in the city paid for by the government, Issa did not linger in Cairo and was on a flight to Amman within thirty-six hours of his arrival from Greece. He was welcomed at the airport outside the Jordanian capital by a guard of honour of policemen, and was then driven in a convoy of fifteen Land Rovers to Wahdat refugee camp, on the southern outskirts of the Jordanian capital, one of the biggest of the dozens of camps that had initially housed Palestinians displaced by the 1948 war and then been forced to accommodate a new wave of refugees in 1967. There a huge crowd of relatives, fedayeen well-wishers and supporters had gathered to greet him.

Wahdat was a stronghold of the PFLP. Here the group provided hand-outs of fuel and food, ran some rudimentary public services and had set up summary courts handing out rough justice to spies, traitors and other offenders against the revolution. Elsewhere, other factions did the same. This angered and worried King Hussein and his advisers. The support the kingdom's armed forces had offered at the battle of Karameh now seemed a strategic error. Since, the fedayeen in his kingdom had grown stronger and more confident, with louder calls by their more radical elements to take control of the state altogether and turn Amman into a 'Palestinian Hanoi'. For months, the fedayeen had been setting up checkpoints on roads in Amman, ignoring repeated demands not to flaunt their weapons, and detaining even prominent Jordanian citizens. Clashes between local security forces and fedayeen were increasingly frequent, with the Jordanians often forced into ignominious retreat. Only months before, police and soldiers had been able to prevent Leila Khaled speaking to a mass meeting in Wahdat. Now, they stood aside reluctantly as another hijacking hero was brought in.

Among those waiting for Issa in Wahdat was George Habash, the leader of the PFLP, who congratulated the young fighter on his successful return, accepted an invitation to stay for dinner in the modest family home, and posed for photographs. Issa was then given leave to travel to Tripoli, the northern Lebanese port where he had grown up, where his marriage to an eighteen-year-old distant relative had been arranged by his family. Once again, he was welcomed by huge crowds. But after two weeks, the celebrations were cut short.

Shortly before Ekberg's visit in April 1970, Habash had tried to impose a ban on overseas operations such as hijackings, on the basis that they were unpredictable and often counter-productive. This had angered Haddad, who had continued his planning for the massive attack in the autumn anyway. Three months later, however, the prohibition was lifted, prompted by an agreement between Egypt and Israel to end their 'War of Attrition', raising the possibility of a deal, based on the ambiguous United Nations Security Council resolution 242, by which the Arab states would formally recognise Israel's right to exist in return for its withdrawal from either some or all of the territories it had conquered in 1967. From the PFLP's point of view, any such deal would crush Palestinian hopes of their own state on the land they believed rightfully theirs. Haddad argued that a spectacular terrorist attack would disrupt the diplomatic effort and underline the need to include the Palestinians in the negotiations or even put an end to them. Habash had been convinced, and a new date for the Revolution Airport operation was set: the end of August 1970. Issa's nuptial festivities were curtailed because he had been issued with orders to return to Beirut and then travel on to Amman to prepare.

By now, the day of the attack was only a few weeks away. Leila Khaled, with her new face, was ready. Abu Sharif had prepared his media strategy and trained some of the participants in how to talk to hostages or journalists. Most of the hijackers had been drawn from the ranks of the PFLP, others from the training camps in Jordan. Once again, Haddad had added a new element: foreigners, whose presence among the attackers was designed to reinforce the impression that the Palestinian cause was part of a greater revolutionary struggle around the globe. One was the young, idealistic former Fulbright scholar turned aspirant Sandinista, Patrick Arguello.

Much later, when the immediate shock of the events had passed and there was time to think about how such things could happen, his mother would wonder if it was merely a letter mislaid by a teenage sister that led to his involvement. The reality was that, following his expulsion from Nicaragua, the twenty-seven-year-old had been swept, or had jumped, into a revolutionary movement in full spate, and it was this current that bore him thousands of miles from Central America to Europe and eventually the Middle East.

Having been expelled from Nicaragua in the wake of his fiery speech to the students of Managua, Arguello flew first to New York to visit friends and then, after a couple of weeks, on to London where he hoped to take up a scholarship to study political science at the London School of Economics. The course was starting in September, so the timing of his arrival would have been perfect but for one problem: he had missed the deadline to formally register as a student. When his paperwork had arrived in the mail in Nicaragua that spring, Arguello had been away on the country's Atlantic coast. By the time it was found by his sister, the registration deadline had passed, and when the prospective scholar arrived several months later in London the LSE's staff were unwilling to bend the rules.

Rather than dwell on his disappointment, Arguello sought out some friends he had met during his year in Chile who were now living in Geneva. The Swiss-French lakeside city had become the effective headquarters of the Sandinistas in Europe, home to a handful of representatives who spent much time in cafés and student meetings 'discussing Vietnam, Africa and so on' with local activists and other exiles. Unsure of exactly what to do with their new arrival, the Sandinistas set Arguello to work on a report on 'Capitalist Development in Nicaragua', which took him most of the autumn.

Arguello had arrived in Geneva at a crucial time. Under pressure from the Soviet Union, Cuba had recently reduced its support for and military training of armed groups across Latin America, including the Sandinistas. In search of alternative sources of instruction, they consulted a Guatemalan insurgent in Havana who introduced them to an Argentine revolutionary who connected them with the Trotskyist Fourth International, a global network of radical socialists based primarily in Europe. This final connection proved to be the key link. When a senior figure in the Fourth International secured them an introduction to a representative of the Democratic Front for the Liberation of Palestine in January 1970, Arguello, as the only English-speaker among the Sandinistas in Europe, was the natural choice as an interpreter. The discussions went well, and when the DFLP offered to host two Nicaraguans in their camps as an advance party for the larger number who would later be sent for training, Arguello was put forward once again. He flew via Rome to Amman in the first week of April, telling his family he was going 'on vacation'. A month later, four more Nicaraguans flew to Jordan from Cuba.

Excited to be in the Middle East, especially as guests of the fedayeen, the Nicaraguans spent only a short time in Amman before moving on to the DFLP's rudimentary training facility in the squalid and overcrowded Baqa'a refugee camp, about twelve miles north of the Jordanian capital. The camp too had been set up to cope with the influx of Palestinian refugees from the West Bank following the 1967 war, and when Arguello arrived the United Nations administrators had yet to replace all of its original canvas tents with prefabricated huts. He was now among the fighters he had read and heard so much about.

The training offered by the DFLP was a disappointment. The routine was 'very simple', with much emphasis on physical fitness. Though

Arguello remained enthusiastic, his more experienced comrades were not convinced that karate sessions, six-mile marches under the hot sun, or learning how to butcher a camel were likely to be of much use back in Nicaragua. By early June, the Sandinista trainees had given up, and were on their way back to Geneva with a disappointed Arguello, now sporting a full beard, in tow. They still wanted instruction, but something more suited to the environment they were likely to be fighting in back home.

Once more they turned to the Fourth International, which this time offered introductions to the Popular Front. The PFLP proved happy to help, but in return for hosting and training the Sandinistas they requested their participation in the attacks they had planned for later in the year. The senior leaders of the Nicaraguan group had no objection and agreed to supply a number of volunteers. Haddad wanted an English-speaker among the hijackers themselves, so once more Arguello was the only choice. It was now the third week of August, and the operation was to be launched at the end of the month.

If Arguello, then twenty-seven years old, was dismayed at being placed so precipitately in the line of fire, he did not show it. From Geneva, he flew to Paris, probably for briefings on his role in the plot and to meet the two big Palestinian men who would be part of his team during the attack. Then, with just five days to go, came disturbing news. There were not yet enough weapons for all the hijackers and the operation would have to be postponed until more were obtained.

By now Khaled had arrived in Stuttgart from Beirut on her false Honduran passport and so urgently had to find somewhere to hide. Within hours, she had been directed to the home of a Popular Front supporter who lived on the outskirts of the city. There she spent several nervous days keeping a low profile and reading English-language newspapers filled with news of the continuing tensions in Jordan. Many speculated that Palestinian armed factions might seek to show their displeasure at the proposed deal between Egypt and Israel with new hijackings, possibly in Europe. Khaled was concerned to see that the city considered most likely to be the site of an attack was Zurich, where one of the three [illegible] as currently waiting to strike. Nobody mentioned her own target, Amsterdam, which offered some reassurance.

Eventually word came from Haddad. The courier – a young French woman with deep radical sympathies whose passport and striking beauty could be counted on to divert the suspicion of airline or security staff – had returned from Beirut to Paris with two grenades in her bra, three revolvers strapped to her body and ammunition hidden in a foil-wrapped cigarette packet. The PFLP's network in France had ensured these had reached the hijack team that had been without its weapons, so the operation could now go ahead. Arguello wrote a letter to his family, less than twenty-four hours before the attack took place, telling them not to worry about him. 'Instead, be happy for each day that we continue to live and advance a little more the struggle necessary for . . . all the countries where a child lives with hunger, abandoned before an unjust society,' he told them. 'It may not be our own eyes that will see [the final] goal, but others' eyes will. To get there . . . means preventing the death and anguish of a child or thousands of children.'

4
Revolution Airport

The first plane to arrive at Revolution Airport was a Swissair DC-8 hijacked less than an hour after its take-off from Zurich. The second was a Trans World Airlines Boeing 707 flying from Tel Aviv to New York. 'This is your new captain speaking. We are taking you to a friendly country with friendly people,' one of the hijackers had told the passengers fifteen minutes after it had left its stopover in Frankfurt. By nightfall, both aircraft had made a precarious but ultimately successful landing at the makeshift airstrip prepared by the PFLP on deserted salt pans twenty miles north-west of Amman. But unlike the first two planes, the third that was successfully hijacked had not been part of Haddad's original plan; nor would it reach Revolution Airport, nor did it have Leila Khaled and Patrick Arguello on board.

The two PFLP men who were supposed to have joined Khaled and Arguello had reached Amsterdam but had not made it to the departure gate. They had planned to buy tickets for the transatlantic flight in the airport – a relatively common and straightforward practice – but their sequentially numbered Senegalese passports, insistence on sitting 'close to the cabin' and last-minute demand for a one-way ticket paid for in cash aroused suspicions. Denied seats on the El Al flight, they complained vociferously and were offered an alternative: a Pan American Airways flight to New York, which they promptly hijacked. Lacking any clear instructions from their PFLP commanders, they improvised, redirecting the almost brand-new Boeing 747 towards Beirut. When Lebanese air traffic controllers informed them that they could not land there because the airport could not accommodate the huge plane, their choice of destination appeared to have been a poor one. But when the authorities were informed that the aircraft would run out of fuel in ten minutes and suddenly decided that they could accommodate the 747 after all, it seemed a masterstroke. PFLP leaders in Beirut hurried to the airport where they were able to ensure that the plane was refuelled and its first-class cabin wired with explosives.

The 747 then took off again and flew to Cairo, where air traffic controllers also attempted to refuse landing. After circling for two hours, one of the hijackers asked cabin staff for some matches, only to be told that smoking was not permitted during the approach to an airport. He laughed, found what he needed and lit the fuses on the explosives, informing the cabin staff that they would explode in eight minutes. Immediately the Egyptian authorities gave permission to land, which was lucky as the hijackers had miscalculated and set the explosives to detonate three minutes earlier than intended. 'Don't wait for me. Don't wait for the captain. Don't wait for Jesus Christ. Just get off this plane,' the flight director told the passengers as they scrambled down the emergency chutes and onto the concrete of Cairo's international airport. According to journalists, the last crew member had 'just run clear of the wing' when the plane disappeared in a 'searing orange fireball of flame and smoke'.

By that evening, Haddad's ambitious operation had in many ways been successful. The spectacular destruction of very valuable, state-of-the-art plane in Egypt was leading news bulletins all over the world. It had demonstrated the attackers' resolve and sent a salutary warning to President Nasser of the risks of ending the conflict with Israel without due consideration of the grievances of the Palestinians. In addition, the PFLP now held almost 300 hostages in Jordan and two valuable aircraft. But in one crucial respect, the operation had gone badly wrong. Khaled and Arguello's attempt to hijack El Al Flight 219 as it left Amsterdam's Schiphol airport had not gone according to plan.

They had followed Haddad's instructions to the letter. Twenty minutes into the flight, as the Boeing 707 reached an altitude of 29,000 feet above the British coastline, they stood up and rushed towards the front of the plane. Just beyond the first-class cabin, before arriving at the cockpit, they reached a small lounge with couches and a well-stocked bar where a steward attempted to block their path. Arguello knocked him to the floor with the butt of his gun. When the man stood up and advanced swinging a bottle of spirits, Arguello shot him five times at very close range.

Two Israeli security officers were on board, both armed but neither close enough to intervene immediately. One was in the cockpit. The other, stationed at the back end of the plane, had pursued the hijackers as they ran shouting up the aisle and now reached them in the lounge. Khaled was banging on the door to the cockpit, holding up her two grenades, both apparently armed to explode if she released their sprung handles, shouting for the crew to let her in.

In the cockpit, there was little doubt what was happening. 'We are being hijacked,' the pilot, an Israeli air force veteran, told his colleagues. Through the spyhole in the cockpit door, the plane's navigator could make out Khaled and her grenades. El Al had advised pilots that in the event of a hijacking they could put the aircraft into a very steep dive, effectively reducing gravity in the plane to almost zero. If the attack occurred relatively soon after take-off, most of the crew and passengers would be strapped to their seats, whereas any hijackers would presumably not be. The pilot now sent the plane into a plunging downward arc. The floor tilted, then tipped steeply as the dive accelerated. Amid tumbling bags, bottles, glasses and cushions, Khaled lost her balance, fell, tried to get up and fell again, holding her grenades tightly in both hands.

Then the plane suddenly levelled, leaving Khaled and her accomplice sprawling. Both tried to stand. The sky marshal now fired seven shots from extremely close range, hitting Arguello three times, shattering his thigh, perforating both lungs and causing massive damage to his lower abdomen. Passengers and cabin crew rushed at Khaled, bringing her to the floor, kicking and punching her, prising the grenades from her hands. The arms and ankles of both hijackers were secured with neck ties and cables. It was four minutes since Arguello and Khaled had left their seats. The attempt to hijack the plane was effectively over.

Though the pilot was under strict instructions to return to Israel in the event of an abortive hijacking, it was clear that the badly wounded steward would die if he did not receive urgent medical attention. So Flight 219 diverted to Heathrow, where it landed and the injured man was removed. To avoid legal problems with the British authorities, the security officer who had shot Arguello dropped out of a hatch under the cabin, ran across the apron to another El Al flight that was about to take off, climbed aboard and disappeared before anyone could stop him.

The British authorities at the airport were more successful in taking custody of the hijackers. Arguello, whose injuries had been of less interest to the El Al crew than those of the steward, remained trussed on the floor of the plane. There was a brief struggle between the Israeli crew members, who wanted to keep Khaled on board in order that they might fly her to Israel, and the policemen who insisted that she was now their prisoner. Eventually she and Arguello were carried out of the plane and placed in an ambulance under armed guard. It then sped off, sirens blaring, towards the nearest hospital in the London suburb of Hillingdon. Khaled's grenades had been rolling about on the floor of the plane and were gingerly gathered and removed.

In the ambulance, medics fought to save Arguello, who had lost a lot of blood and was unconscious. A policeman cut a tie binding his wrists and removed some of the aircraft cabling knotted around his legs. Khaled had not been aware of his wounds until she was placed with him in the ambulance. Now she was shouting in English and Arabic, pleading for her hands to be untied, telling Arguello not to die, crying that as a Palestinian she should have been the one to have been hurt. The ambulance careered through the streets of west London as Arguello's pulse faded. Three minutes before it reached Hillingdon hospital, the medics said he was dead, and the oxygen mask was removed from his face.

Sobbing, blood all over her hands and clothes, mechanically repeating 'Popular Front for the Liberation of Palestine', Khaled was led inside and examined by a doctor who found many cuts and bruises but no serious injury. A journalist, one of several who had followed the ambulance from Heathrow, now approached and asked if she was Leila Khaled. She did not answer. But when the police assigned to guard her asked her again if she was 'really Leila Khaled', she said yes.

Still sobbing, Khaled was then driven to the nearest police station where she spent the night in a cell. Arguello's body was taken to the morgue. He had yet to be identified. Even Khaled did not know his real name.

Out on the barren salt pans north-east of the Jordanian capital the two hijacked planes shimmered in the sun. Within twenty-four hours of the arrival of the first plane, the PFLP had issued its demands in a 'quiet and unemotional manner' to an official at the US Embassy in Amman. Any British citizens among the passengers would be freed in return for the release of Khaled and the restitution of the remains of Arguello, whose fates had been broadcast worldwide within hours of their arrival at Heathrow. Swiss hostages would be exchanged for three militants responsible for the Zurich attack of the year before – all currently serving lengthy jail sentences in Switzerland. German passengers would be swapped for several Palestinians from a smaller, little-known armed faction who had been held in Germany since killing an Israeli passenger while trying to hijack a plane in Munich seven months before. With the failure of Khaled and Arguello's attack on the El Al plane, there were far fewer Israelis among the hostages than the PFLP had hoped. Those, including any who were also US citizens, would be released if Israel agreed to a 'prisoner exchange' involving some, possibly all, of the thousands of fedayeen held in its prisons. If Khaled was not freed, there would be no deal. The PFLP set a seventy-two-hour deadline. If by then their demands had not been met, the planes would be destroyed with the passengers on board.

There now followed a moment of relative calm. After several days of backbreaking labour, Mahmoud Issa was finally able to rest. Having cut short his wedding celebrations in August to receive Haddad's operational briefing in Beirut, he had then led the team responsible for the preparation of Revolution Airport. The site had been used as a landing ground during the Second World War by the Royal Air Force, who referred to it as Dawson's Field. Temperatures had reached thirty-five degrees Celsius as the men lifted rocks, filled ditches and smoothed away tracks worn by the camels that grazed the dry grass around the salt flats. They had put up two large tents to offer shelter from the sun and a Palestinian flag now flew from a pole. Nearby, a military water tank was parked bearing a sign in Arabic that read, 'The Popular Front is at your service'. On the night before the attack, Issa and his men had rolled oil drums across the sand and pebbles, setting them up in long lines and filling them with petrol-soaked rags which, when lit, would act as makeshift landing lights for the incoming aircraft. Once the planes arrived, Issa would be responsible for security, and the several dozen young men under his command would be redeployed from construction to defence. In preparation, Issa had ordered a series of trenches and foxholes to be dug around the perimeter of the airstrip. These faced outwards, to defend against Israeli special forces, the Jordanian military or anyone else who might attempt to free the hostages by force.

Bassam Abu Sharif, the PFLP's public relations co-ordinator during the operation, had been standing alongside Issa when the planes landed. He had spent much of the previous month or two in Amman, organising press conferences and dealing with the Western journalists who had arrived there to report on the growing tensions between the fedayeen and the king. Much of the rest of his time had been spent arguing with other factions and negotiating with his comrades, while smoking and drinking copious quantities of sweet tea in the PFLP's office beneath posters of Lenin and Che Guevara and slogans reading 'Zionism Equals Nazism . . . We Are Not Terrorists, We Are Freedom Fighters'. Now he sought to reassure the hostages. Addressing them through a loudhailer, he apologised for bringing them to the Jordanian desert and set about explaining the PFLP's motivations for doing so. 'We are fighting a just war, for the liberation of our country from Israeli occupation . . . The reason you are in the middle of it is that we want to exchange you for prisoners who were taken in Israel and other countries,' he said, before advising them to 'relax'.

This was easier said than done. No provision had been made for the hostages to receive food or water. Armed fighters had moved through the planes, rifling baggage and examining identity documents. Few of the hostages knew where they were, nor anything much about Jordan, the Palestinians or the PFLP. As the aircraft had begun their descent, the hijackers handed out landing cards for Revolution Airport marked with the group's insignia, which had only increased their confusion. The night was very dark and hot, and when the sun came up they found the airstrip flanked by dozens of armoured personnel carriers, tanks and flat-bed trucks bearing anti-aircraft guns, all plainly visible a couple of hundred yards away, all pointing their weapons at the aircraft. Few would have known their insignia and been able to identify them as Jordanian.

Tensions remained high through the morning. The PFLP fighters ordered the hostages to hand over their passports. Some were made to kneel while their documents were examined. Questioning was sometimes aggressive, though some of the hostages got into conversations with their captors. When the young children among them were allowed down from the planes to play and run on the sand, some parents were reassured. After all, almost all of the many hijackings of the previous decade had lasted no more than a few hours. In the afternoon, their hopes were raised when buses arrived to take all of the Arabs and citizens of 'allied' states to three hotels in Amman, including one luxury establishment seized by the PFLP earlier in the summer. Shortly afterwards, a second fleet of vehicles arrived to take 127 women and young children whom Issa and others at the airstrip had decided were 'not in a condition to endure another night in the desert' to the Jordanian capital too. This was a relief, though of course it left many families divided.

Among those who remained on the planes were American, German and Swiss citizens. There were also a number of Israelis, though all held US citizenship too. One major problem for the PFLP was that none of the hostages appeared to be British, which significantly weakened their demand for Khaled's release. The solution to this was simple but dramatic. The next day, the third of the crisis, a team of two hijackers seized control of a DC-10 belonging to the British Overseas Airways Corporation, the UK's national carrier at the time, as it left Bahrain on its way to London with 105 passengers and ten crew on board. The flight was then diverted to the PFLP's makeshift airstrip in Jordan, where it joined the two already there. To prove the aircraft was under the control of the PFLP and not full of Israeli or US troops mounting a rescue mission, a code word was radioed to the waiting fighters during its approach: *warak diwali*, the name of Haddad's favourite home-cooked dish of vine leaves, rice and minced meat.

The seventy-two-hour deadline came and went. No planes were destroyed and no hostages killed. Across Jordan and throughout the region, in European capitals, in Washington and Moscow, phones rang, diplomats hurried, officials met, presidents and prime ministers made urgent and often angry calls. None had ever dealt with a crisis of such a scale caused by a terrorist attack of such complexity. A Red Cross negotiator was appointed to mediate between the PFLP and the various nations whose citizens were among the hostages – a difficult task made harder by the fact that they held such wildly divergent positions.

The Swiss had agreed to all the PFLP's demands within hours, and then been forced to hastily backtrack after vociferous complaints from Washington and London. The Germans also favoured making swift concessions. The British wanted a deal but were concerned to avoid the appearance of having capitulated too easily. As its officials privately admitted, giving away too much too soon would 'throw overboard' their previously declared policy of not negotiating in such circumstances, while British airlines' and pilots' associations worried that any compromise with the hijackers would set a dangerous precedent. In conversation with their more hardline counterparts in the US, British diplomats claimed that they were under significant pressure from the public to make big concessions, but this was not entirely true. According to opinion polls conducted by newspapers, the public showed no clear preference either way.

For its part, Israel refused point-blank to give in to what Prime Minister Golda Meir angrily called 'blackmail'. To signal their resolve, the Israeli government detained 450 Palestinians in the West Bank and Gaza on suspicion of 'being active in the PFLP'. This prompted the British to complain about Meir's 'obduracy' which, they said, was made easier by the fact that there appeared to be no 'pure Israelis' among the hostages, just a handful of US-Israeli dual nationals.

The PFLP's demands and deadlines evolved too. Its leader, George Habash, was making his way back to the region from North Korea where he had been seeking funds and arms, so was effectively incommunicado. This meant that Haddad continued to be the group's key decision-maker. On the Thursday, the fourth day of the crisis, a new deadline for the destruction of the planes and the killing of the hostages was set, though it was unclear exactly when it would expire, and a shambolic press conference took place, stage-managed by Abu Sharif. A half-dozen passengers and crew from the three planes were ordered to sit on the sand while some of the hundreds of reporters who had flown into Jordan to cover the crisis shouted questions to them. Many passengers, speaking in front of their captors, made light of the situation. One joked that the conditions were bearable but that the repeated lectures on the plight of the Palestinians and the coming revolution were not. Others described the 'guerrillas' or 'commandos' as 'humane' and that they seemed fond of children. Another merely commented that it was 'bloody hot', and there were increasing problems with sanitation. This was evident to everyone. Reporters could smell the overflowing blocked toilets on the planes, and, though a doctor had been brought from Amman, several passengers had already fallen sick. Blurred photographs taken on board one of the planes and published in the British press showed a smiling stewardess, barefoot in a summer dress, distributing water. Hostages later described singing songs and organising a talent competition to amuse the children. The Red Cross, which could speak more freely than the passengers at the airstrip, described the 'mental and physical torture' of being imprisoned for days on end in a superheated tube of metal, wired with explosives. One young woman, a US citizen, managed to get a message to her embassy, possibly carried by a journalist, pleading with them not 'to gamble with our lives'.

Some passengers had greater reason to fear than others. Abu Sharif made repeated protestations that the Popular Front saw Israelis and Zionists as their enemy, not Jews. This echoed what Khaled had said in the many interviews she had given over the previous year and was the official stance of the Popular Front. It was also that of the PLO and Fatah: both had repeatedly claimed to want merely to replace the state of Israel with a multi-denominational, secular democracy, though few Western observers (and almost no Israeli citizens) considered such claims credible. A rabbi among the hostages told reporters that the Jewish passengers were not being treated any differently from the rest, but others disagreed vehemently. Many noted that the PFLP did not ask the passengers about their political views, but about their faith. 'They asked each of us, "Are you Jewish?" I thought it was going to be the firing squad,' remembered one (non-Jewish) hostage afterwards. Others spoke of being forced off the planes and walked some distance away before being questioned at gunpoint. It was also clear to everyone that among the successive batches of hostages who were selected for transfer to Amman, better conditions and the possibility of early release, none were known by their captors to be Jewish.

By day six of the crisis, there had still been no progress in the hugely complex negotiations being brokered by the Red Cross. Meanwhile, in Amman and elsewhere, new and increasingly intense clashes were taking place between the various fedayeen factions and Jordanian forces. There was also increasing disagreement between the factions as to how to proceed. A furious Yasser Arafat ordered the Popular Front to move most of the hostages to the Jordanian capital to allow for their orderly release. The PFLP refused. Further batches of hostages had been moved off the planes, and dozens of those in the hotels in Amman had been allowed to fly home on the few commercial flights still running from the international airport, but 200 remained in the planes.

Sudden sandstorms lashed the planes for three to four hours at a stretch. Food became scarcer as supplies were interrupted by the fighting. The stench from the blocked toilets grew worse. The guards grew rougher. Issa and his men were convinced that an intervention by Israeli or US forces was imminent. So too was Abu Sharif. Twenty-four hours before the extended deadline expired it was still very unclear what would happen. Explosives, or what appeared to be explosives, were still rigged around the planes. Many feared the worst.

In fact, the US had decided against a direct rescue attempt. One of President Nixon's first reactions to the hostage crisis had been to order a series of air strikes against PFLP facilities, though which ones and where they might be was not entirely clear, but the notion had been dropped when Melvin Laird, his secretary of defence, had told the president, not entirely truthfully, that weather conditions over Jordan made such a measure unfeasible. A lively discussion had followed about alternatives, including the use of some kind of nerve gas to incapacitate the fedayeen at Revolution Airport to allow a rescue attempt, possibly by local forces. 'The lack of knowledge of whether suitable gas existed in our arsenal impeded the discussion no more than the absence of a concept of how it was to be delivered,' Henry Kissinger, Nixon's national security adviser, caustically recalled.

Instead the decision was made to rely on diplomacy, both of the conventional and more muscular varieties. One significant concern of the US president and his advisers was that the crisis caused by the hijacking might lead the fedayeen to launch an uprising against King Hussein, which they had been threatening to do for some time. The Jordanian monarch had long been one of the few rulers to steadfastly support Western interests in the region, and this had earned him generous funding and a steady flow of weapons for his cherished military, first from London and then from Washington. Nonetheless, it was far from certain that such supplies would be sufficient for Hussein's fragile rule to survive a concerted attempt to oust him, particularly if the large Palestinian population of his kingdom sided with the fedayeen or regional powers such as Iraq or Syria became involved.

For several days Nixon wavered before deciding to send a significant force to the Middle East to guard against any escalation, assist if an evacuation of US citizens from Jordan became necessary, and to show resolve. The USS *Independence*, an aircraft carrier that was part of the Sixth Fleet which patrolled the Mediterranean, was directed towards the Lebanese coast while six transport planes were sent to the Turkish airbase of Incirlik, just over an hour's flight from Amman, where US fighter bombers had been put on alert. Staff at the US strike command at MacDill air force base in Florida were told to stand by and thousands of troops in Europe readied for a possible deployment. At the same time, US officials intensified efforts with Israel and the three European countries to maintain a united front in their negotiations with the PFLP.

What seemed evident to everyone, whether in Washington, London, Berne or Bonn, was that the threat to the lives of the hostages was genuine. Abu Sharif spoke frequently of the PFLP's desire to avoid deaths, and the group had no history of inflicting the mass casualties that would occur if they followed through on their threat to blow up the planes with the hostages on board. And yet the PFLP's attitude to the survival of hostages was reckless, to say the very least. The hijackers aboard the 747 flown to Cairo a week before had been polite and considerate but had nearly killed everyone on board with their failure to set the fuses correctly. The steward shot by Arguello was in intensive care in a London hospital and was very lucky to be alive, while the second plane to land at Revolution Airport had come to a stop only thirty yards from the first aircraft to put down. A collision could well have caused the deaths of 300 people.

There was also the unavoidable fact that dozens of civilians had been killed by Palestinian armed groups in recent years. There had been attacks on aircraft such as the Athens operation led by Issa, grenades lobbed into El Al offices in Europe, and the bombing of a supermarket in Israel, which killed two and wounded more than twenty others. One of the smaller armed Palestinian factions had recently ambushed a school bus in northern Israel, killing three adults and nine children. Seven months before, another group had blown up a Swissair flight shortly after it departed Switzerland by placing a parcel bomb in its hold. Forty-seven people had been killed. In June 1970, Habash had told an interviewer that his followers had been instructed to spare European lives but also that all those who supported the Zionist project, including any individual anywhere who supported Israel 'economically, militarily, politically, ideologically', needed to be targeted if Israel was to be weakened. This meant the capitalist and imperialist states that had 'conceived Israel', he had explained, as well as those currently 'using it as a bulwark to protect their interests in [the Arab world]'. In addition, it was his firm conviction that many states in western Europe were controlled by the Zionist movement and provided 'bases for Jews to wage war on Arabs'. Given such statements, it was difficult not to conclude that the people holding the hostages in Jordan were prepared to kill at least some of them. And with every day that the negotiations remained stalled, the chances rose that the PFLP might commit some desperate act in a bid to regain the initiative, deter a rescue bid or somehow break the deadlock.

On the morning of Saturday, 12 September, Haddad told Abu Sharif to pick out a cameraman and a photographer from among the horde of journalists in Amman and to send both to Revolution Airport. The two men were duly selected and conveyed to the airstrip, where they were instructed to set up their gear a safe distance from the planes. At around 10 a.m., the pair watched as most of the remaining passengers on the planes were ordered onto a convoy of buses. The fedayeen were agitated, 'rushing around, screaming, arguing amongst themselves'. The buses departed in the direction of Amman, and the fifty or sixty hostages left standing on the sand were told to board the Swissair DC-8. Before anything else could happen, a violent sandstorm brought all activity to a temporary end.

When the choking dust cleared several hours later, the two journalists saw PFLP fighters now moving deliberately and carefully under the fuselage and wings of the three aircraft shimmering in the mid-afternoon sun. Other fedayeen manned jeeps and trucks equipped with anti-aircraft guns and heavy weapons, some aimed at the Jordanian forces who still watched warily from dunes and rocks around the perimeter of the airstrip, beyond the lines of burned-out oil drums.

Suddenly there were shouts, and the men around the planes came sprinting across the gravel and sand. The cameraman turned to his equipment. The photographer focused his lens. At 2.59 p.m. the explosives wired around the three planes exploded, sending huge, roiling gouts of flame and debris spinning through the air, and a vast column of black smoke erupting upwards. When the air cleared and the onlookers raised themselves, they saw that all three aircraft had been almost entirely destroyed. Only the three tail fins remained intact, vertical and stark against the yellow dirt of the airstrip and clear blue sky.

There was a pause, a moment's silence, and then the shooting started. The Jordanian soldiers, thinking the hostages had all been killed, had opened fire. The PFLP fighters attempted to fight back from their trenches. For some minutes, Revolution Airport was a battlefield. Issa knew his lightly armed fighters had limited ammunition and faced a trained, regular military force supported by tanks and artillery. But the fedayeen had one significant asset.

Just before the explosives wired to the aircraft had been detonated, the hostages who remained on board had been hurriedly told to disembark. They had hastily climbed down the rough wooden ladders that had served as steps for the past week and, harried by anxious fighters, made their way to buses lined up a short distance away. These were close enough to the planes that they rocked on their axles when the blasts came. As the Jordanian troops' fire intensified, Issa ordered his men to point their weapons at the men and women huddled inside the vehicles and told the army to stop shooting if they wanted the passengers to remain alive. There were shouted commands among the Jordanians, sudden silence, and a tense pause.

A message asking for instructions was sent by the soldiers to King Hussein in his palace in Amman. A response came back. The buses full of hostages were driven away by the Popular Front. Around an hour later, having crossed numerous checkpoints, their exhausted, frightened passengers were deposited at the Intercontinental Hotel in the Jordanian capital. The crisis now entered a complex new phase.

Over the previous days, Abu Sharif had set about hiding a total of fifty hostages in a series of safehouses that were located in parts of Jordan controlled by the fedayeen. Around half had been taken to homes and offices in or around Amman, including ten who were sent to a hiding place in the heart of the Wahdat refugee camp within the city. Eighteen others were hidden in a house in the industrial town of Zarqa, about twenty miles to the north-west of the Jordanian capital. They were confined to two small rooms where they were brought Pepsi, playing cards, beer, toothpaste, soap and English-language newspapers. Immediately after the destruction of the planes and the ensuing stand-off, Issa had taken a group of six male hostages who were thought to be 'working for the Pentagon' to a deserted school in the northern city of Irbid. This part of Jordan was considered a 'liberated zone', controlled entirely by the fedayeen and outside the jurisdiction of the government, and so beyond the reach of any rescue operation.

When asked what they had done with the fifty missing hostages, Abu Sharif told reporters they had been taken to 'a more cozy place' and reiterated their demands: the release of Khaled and the other prisoners in Europe and Israel and the restitution of Arguello's remains. Though the hostages would be treated 'very kindly' they would be kept 'as prisoners of war until we get what we want', Abu Sharif said, and restated his earlier threats. If the 'western governments had not learned' from the events of the previous days, then the group would be 'forced to take further action', he told the journalists.

The film of the destruction of the planes had been rushed to Amman's airport and onto an otherwise empty eighty-seater passenger jet chartered by the cameraman's press agency. A second plane was standing by in Cyprus to take the film on to Rome. Processed and edited in the small hours of the morning, it was then flown to London, reaching the studios of Independent Television News in time to be broadcast on lunchtime bulletins in the UK. Viewers of the BBC saw it six hours later. Over the next twenty-four hours, images of the spectacular blasts in the desert would lead bulletins everywhere, watched by hundreds of millions of people.

The destruction of planes had injected new urgency into the stalled negotiations but ultimately resolved very little. The crisis was now in its second week. Officials in London were increasingly angry at what they saw as Israel's stubborn refusal to make concessions to the PFLP and worried that the Germans or the Swiss would make a separate deal that would undermine their own efforts. The US Secretary of State, Joseph Sisco, told Israel's ambassador in Washington that the British had 'shown themselves to be terrible', while the Europeans were 'not prepared to stand up . . . at all'. In Jerusalem, Meir was bitterly critical of all the other governments involved, fearing that they would cave to the hijackers' demands and leave Israel isolated.

Haddad may have been aware of how close the PFLP had come to splitting the united front hitherto presented by the hostages' governments but was more worried than ever that US or Israeli special forces would launch a raid to rescue the remaining captives and so deprive the PFLP of their sole means of winning the release of Khaled. In reality, the chances of this were extremely slim. Even if the US military had the capabilities to successfully execute such a difficult operation at such short notice, American intelligence services had been forced to admit to the president himself that they had absolutely no idea where the hostages had been taken. For their part, the Israelis only knew that the missing men were being held in several groups at different sites, possibly including former training facilities or refugee camps, but even this fragmentary information, from a 'secret confidential source', was considered out of date. The British were relying on the Jordanians, who could only tell them that the hostages were repeatedly moved, which was of little help.

Within less than a week of the destruction of the planes, circumstances changed dramatically once again, threatening not only chaos in Jordan but a regional conflagration and ultimately a confrontation between superpowers. Haddad had meticulously planned the hijackings of 6 September 1970 but he had hopelessly misjudged their broader impact. What seemed a spectacular success was about to become a debacle.

5
Black September

Leila Khaled learned about the events at Revolution Airport in the newspapers brought to the small, first-floor 'women's detention room' in Ealing police station where she had been detained since her arrest at Heathrow airport.

She had not been a particularly troublesome guest. For the first five days she had smoked, drunk black coffee, cried occasionally and slept fitfully on a bunk bed. A police surgeon attended to her severe bruising but she was otherwise in perfect physical health. She was guarded by seven armed officers, though no charges had been brought against her and, so far, her detention was justified by a technicality of immigration law. Arguably the most famous activist-terrorist in the world, who had just undertaken the most dangerous task of the most spectacular terrorist attack for many decades, was perfectly, tediously safe.

When news emerged that Khaled was being held in the local police station in Ealing, an entirely unremarkable suburb of west London, a crowd of commuters, local shop assistants, housewives, school children and students had packed the pavement outside. Among them were reporters not only from local newspapers but from international TV networks and news agencies. The BBC had a camera mounted on the top of a van parked among the rows of Mini Coopers and Vauxhall Vivas in the police station car park. Everyone hoped for a glimpse of 'Grenade Girl', as she had been dubbed by the more sensationalist newspapers. But little emerged from the police station's modern glass facade apart from busy, uncommunicative officers who shouldered their way through the throng of reporters without comment.

Eventually, a few details from inside were leaked to the media, and so the journalists learned that once the initial shock of the death of her 'comrade in arms' and the beating she had taken had faded, Khaled had been moody but not disagreeable. By day six of her incarceration, they reported, some of her previous spirit seemed to have returned: the detainee had refused to answer questions, demanded to be treated as a prisoner of war and made lengthy speeches about the sacrifices of her comrades, especially Arguello. She had also shown a less intractable side. In response to her threat of a hunger strike, the officers in charge of her detention and interrogation had told her that they genuinely cared about her health and she had begun eating again.

Khaled also 'made friends' with some of the female police officers who watched her round the clock. One had told her that they had all been worried about guarding 'a terrorist' and were surprised to find someone 'so small and nice'. Khaled even confided that she missed the commander of her unit at her training camp in Jordan, to whom she was now engaged and hoped one day to marry. She was given slippers for her cold feet, taken upstairs to a senior officer's light-filled office to enjoy the sunshine and lent a stub of a pencil with which to write to her mother. 'Do not be anxious at my disaster . . . I am well. Life here is like a dream . . . We must endure . . . I shall return soon. I don't know when but I shall return,' she wrote in Arabic, well aware that the letter would be read by her jailers and by many of her 'comrades' throughout the Middle East. She refused a lawyer and rejected the women's magazines brought to her as reading material. She requested newspapers instead. From these Khaled learned that in Jordan the long-gathering storm had broken.

There had been many clashes between Palestinian fedayeen and King Hussein's troops and police in the previous six months. During Gunnar Ekberg's visit to Amman in April he had returned to his hotel room one evening to find the ceiling damaged by bullets that had ricocheted through an open window during yet another firefight. Ekberg had been surprised at the way the Palestinian fighters brazenly carried weapons in public, flouted traffic regulations, forced businesses to pay entirely illegal 'contributions' to their organisations and blocked roads with checkpoints. Since then, the situation in Jordan had worsened. There had been at least two attempts by Palestinian factions to assassinate the king and several protracted bouts of fighting in which hundreds had died. The PFLP and the DFLP were among the most outspoken critics of the king and his regime, and though Yasser Arafat and other more moderate Palestinian leaders sought to reduce the chances of outright confrontation with the kingdom's security forces, they appeared unable to prevent multiple abductions, shootings and serious assaults on Jordanian citizens. Posters covered the walls of Amman calling for the overthrow of the monarchy. 'All power to the resistance fighters!', read one, echoing Lenin's slogan calling for an uprising in Russia.

The triple hijacking had demonstrated in very public fashion just how far King Hussein's hold on the country had slipped. The PFLP was not only based there, it controlled key pockets of the kingdom, allowing it to recruit and train its attackers there and even build an airstrip entirely under its own control only a short drive from the capital. It now seemed obvious to the king and his advisers that the PFLP were intent on creating a state within a state. The faction had stamped passports in the name of the PFLP, issued landing cards for Revolution Airport, refused royal troops access to the site and had not even thought to involve the kingdom in their negotiations with Western states once the planes were on the sand.

In interviews earlier that year, the young king's distaste for the concessions he had been forced to make to the fedayeen was quite apparent. Hussein was thirty-five years old, enjoyed flying his own plane and driving fast cars, and adored his military and their arms. During the 1967 war, he had been the only ruler actually to expose himself to danger and he was confident that his soldiers, predominantly recruited from the Bedouins of the Jordan's East Bank, remained loyal, whatever the calumnies spread by his enemies. The triple hijacking was a provocation too far, Hussein decided, and he had no choice but to fight again, though this time against a rather different enemy.

He was convinced that any offensive could not be directed solely against the PFLP but would have to target the entire Palestinian militant movement. He knew also that if he was defeated, he would lose his crown, and quite possibly his life. Having sent his English-born wife and young children out of the country, he then set about replacing his civilian government with a military one and solicited a pledge from the Israelis that they would not seek to exploit his momentary vulnerability should he deploy his armed forces against the fedayeen. But they were not the only neighbouring threat. Iraq's Ba'athist regime made no secret of its contempt for the king and the Hashemite dynasty. Since the 1967 war, it had maintained a force of 12,000 troops in Jordan, which could theoretically be ordered into action against him. Then there was the very worrying possibility that Syria, another Ba'athist power and also no friend, might somehow send troops to support the fedayeen or, worse, launch its own full-scale invasion.

The Jordanian army went into action on the morning of 17 September, eleven days after the first hijackings and five days after the destruction of the planes. The king's 40,000 or so soldiers outnumbered the 10–15,000 lightly-armed fighters that the various Palestinian factions could muster, but resistance was much stronger than Hussein and his generals expected. As the days passed and their casualties mounted, the Jordanian military was forced to deploy more and more firepower, making little attempt to spare civilians as tanks demolished buildings at close range and artillery bombarded entire neighbourhoods of Amman, sometimes using incendiary shells. Huge clouds of smoke drifted over the city during the day and fires could be seen burning brightly at night. Power and water supplies were cut off. 'Thousands of houses ... are destroyed, thousands of others are severely damaged ... To cross the street is to risk almost certain death. Broken glass and burnt-out vehicles are strewn in all directions,' reported one foreign correspondent. Western officials spoke of as many as 5,000 casualties among the Palestinians in and around the city, including very significant numbers of children, women and the elderly. The scenes in Wahdat camp, which was located close to a strategically critical crossroads, were particularly distressing, observers said. In the north of Jordan, where Hussein's troops were trying to re-establish control over the 'liberated zone', progress was also slow and civilian casualties high.

Six days after Hussein launched his offensive, Syrian tanks began to move into northern Jordan, realising the king's worst fears and dramatically increasing the regional and global implications of the conflict. The Syrian forces had been equipped, trained and furnished with munitions by the Soviets, and Damascus was key to Moscow's strategy in the region. A regime seen as a Soviet client by the US had now sent its forces against one seen as a Western stooge by Moscow, turning the hijacking crisis into what Kissinger called 'a critical test' of US influence in the Middle East. This meant that the ongoing regional contest between the so-called revolutionary powers of Iraq and Syria on the one hand and the pro-Western Jordan and Israel on the other had now taken on a global dimension.

And yet, with almost half a million troops still mired in a brutal conflict in Vietnam, the US could ill afford any new overseas military commitments. Nor did they want to jeopardise the progress being made in their much broader effort to improve relations between the superpowers. A treaty between the US and the USSR that aimed to prevent the spread of nuclear weapons had come into force just six months earlier. And fundamentally, Kissinger did not see the Middle East as important enough to warrant risking global conflict. 'The axis of history starts in Moscow, goes to Bonn, crosses over to Washington, and then goes to Tokyo,' he had said a year earlier. 'Nothing of importance can come from the South.' The president had his eye on less epic considerations. 'The American people do not have the heart to go into another war,' Nixon told Congress.

Happily, the Soviets too were looking to avoid confrontation. Leonid Brezhnev, the Communist party general secretary, had worked with Lyndon Johnson, Nixon's predecessor in the White House, to avoid escalation during the war in 1967, and Moscow had backed the controversial United Nations Security Council resolution 242 passed in its aftermath. Three years later, the Soviets were heartened by the progress of their efforts to project power in the Middle East and Brezhnev had no desire to risk these hard-won successes – in Cairo, Baghdad and Damascus – and potentially much more besides, by being drawn into a conflict he neither wanted nor expected, in a place and at a time that was very much not of his choosing, and in support of a cause about which he was distinctly ambivalent.

The day the Syrians sent their tanks into Jordan, Nixon's intelligence briefing that morning told him there was no evidence of Soviet hostile intent. Less than twelve hours later, US officials were briefing journalists that Moscow was working to convince Damascus to withdraw its forces, and that this was 'good news'. And so when King Hussein made frantic calls for US air strikes against the Syrian tanks advancing into the north of his kingdom, the US decided against any direct intervention. If anyone was going to get involved in fighting in Jordan, Kissinger and Nixon both felt it would have to be a local ally. This meant the Israelis, and so Hussein's request for instant and decisive support was passed on to them.

But by the time Meir and her ministers finally agreed to act against the Syrians, the military balance in Jordan had already begun to shift in the king's favour. The initial Syrian advance had slowed, then been stopped. Then, having taken heavy losses from Jordanian warplanes and better-armed Jordanian tanks, the Syrians began pulling back. Their own air force had not been deployed to protect them – a politic decision made by Hafez al-Assad, who was still the defence minister – while the Iraqi division outside Zarqa remained immobile. When the news of the Syrian retreat reached Washington, there was some satisfaction. Nixon went to play golf. Kissinger spoke of the 'warm glow of success'.

Hussein's victory was not conclusive, however. After more than a week of fighting, both he and the fedayeen needed respite. The king might have been winning militarily but he was losing diplomatically. He was now reviled throughout the Arab world, portrayed by state-run media as a Western or Israeli proxy who was killing Arabs, and Kuwait's defence minister had accused him of genocide. For the fedayeen, the situation was the exact inverse. They had lost thousands of fighters and been forced out of most of the enclaves they had once controlled in Jordan but had gained massive popular support throughout the Middle East. Though the PFLP had triggered the crisis, Yasser Arafat remained the undisputed overall leader of the various factions now fighting for their lives and had been gifted an opportunity to reassert his authority: as chairman of the PLO, it was Arafat who would have to speak on the PFLP's behalf at any negotiations with the king. Reluctantly, both the king and Arafat agreed to negotiations in Cairo, to be brokered by Gamal Abdel Nasser, the Egyptian president, in person.

The talks were difficult and ill-tempered. Arafat postured in front of the assembled Arab leaders, angry and insulting. Hussein made little effort to hide his loathing for the PLO leader. Both men wore holstered handguns at the negotiating table. Nonetheless, they did eventually reach an agreement: the fedayeen agreed to leave the main Jordanian cities and abide by a ceasefire on the condition that they be allowed to keep their weapons and military infrastructure and continue their raids on Israel. This deal resolved none of the deeper tensions between the Hashemite monarchy and the militant Palestinian groups in Jordan, but it did halt the fighting. The participants posed for a photograph as the summit drew to a more or less successful conclusion: an astonishingly relaxed Arafat smiled broadly in what had become his trademark Ray-Ban sunglasses and keffiyeh; a grim-looking Hussein scowled in military uniform; an intense, handsome Muammar Gaddafi, who had taken power in Libya only a year before aged twenty-seven, stared impassively at the camera. Nasser looked exhausted. Overweight, diabetic, irascible and increasingly paranoid, the Egyptian president died of a massive heart attack within hours of the conference's end, aged fifty-two.

Arafat also agreed to the release of all hostages held by the various factions of the PLO, which included the PFLP. This was clever diplomacy, or at least must have appeared so to those in the know, for he had told Wadie Haddad to free the remaining hostages from the three hijacked planes some days before the Cairo talks had even begun. And in reality, even that request had been rendered obsolete by rapidly unfolding events. While the negotiations were taking place, a dozen of those hidden in Amman were discovered by advancing Jordanian forces, while almost all the rest were simply allowed to go free as the fedayeen's resistance crumbled. The last six hostages were driven from the school in Irbid where they had been held to a hotel in Amman where they were met by TWA representatives, reporters and diplomats. The US ambassador cabled a description of the group to Washington: 'In excellent spirits. Some lost weight but other than that in good shape, rapturous at being back with Americans. Neat suits, clean shirts, shined shoes.' The ambassador and his State Department superiors were unaware what a near-run thing their release had been. As the fighting with the Jordanian military had intensified, Mahmoud Issa had been ordered to move the group to a new hiding place where they could be held until Israel agreed to release a large number of detainees that the PFLP wanted freed. The deal in Cairo had been done while Issa was en route to their hiding place. By the time he had arrived there, they were gone.

Just three weeks after the hijackings of 6 September 1970, Issa, Abu Sharif and their fellow PFLP fighters found their situation dramatically changed. Despite the popular support they had gained throughout the region, public sentiment within Jordan was now turning against them, and the agreement negotiated by Arafat gave their enemies the chance to rest, rearm and reinforce. Days before, they had set the world alight with spectacular violence. Now, even if the fedayeen had wanted to fight on, they no longer had the means to do so.

In the early evening of 30 September, Khaled dressed herself in a long black skirt and jacket lent by a policewoman, climbed into the back of a police van and was driven out of Ealing police station. 'I like this hotel, it is awarded ten stars; the service is very good, and I will ask my comrades to come here,' she joked with her guards before she left. Preceded and flanked by police motorbikes, the van was rushed through west London's traffic to the Royal Air Force base at Northolt. Khaled was then flown by helicopter across the woods and hills of the Chilterns to another military airbase where she was transferred to an RAF Comet passenger jet, which took off minutes later for Munich. The police escort and aircraft crew were instructed not to pose for photographs with 'Grenade Girl', however excited their friends and family might be to see such images.

There was no need to have released Khaled. Even before the Comet had taken off, it was clear that any of the hostages who had not already been liberated by King Hussein's soldiers were about to be freed by the PFLP. Nonetheless, Edward Heath, the British prime minister, decided they had a 'moral obligation' to honour the terms of a bargain they had been discussing with Egyptian officials in the days before the fedayeen collapse, which involved releasing their famous captive. In reality, this was an elegant if cynical solution to the diplomatic problem posed by Khaled's presence, allowing them to avoid the offence they would cause the Egyptians if they complied with Israel's request for her extradition or put her on trial themselves. The lengthy prison sentence that would follow would only lead to further attempts by the PFLP to force her release.

Security at Munich airport was tight. As the plane waited to pick up the three militants whom Bonn had agreed to release in a similar spirit to the British, Khaled peered through the small windows to count the armoured vehicles all around it. The next stop was Zurich where they were joined by Amina Dahbour, freed by Swiss authorities, whose attack on a plane there the year before had so enthused Khaled. She was accompanied by two other PFLP prisoners and several guards. 'I wanted at least to hug Amina, but it was not permitted. We just greeted each other from afar. The night was a long one,' Khaled later recalled.

The plane now carrying seven PFLP militants arrived in Cairo at 8 a.m. on 1 October. The city was in mourning for Nasser. Confined to an Egyptian government guesthouse, Khaled was unable to join the millions of Egyptians who marched in a vast procession behind the remains of the late president. A day later she was provided with clothes – a black suit and dark shades – and was driven with Dahbour to Nasser's tomb where the two women laid a large wreath. 'Do you feel in any way responsible for all that has happened – that you started in train the whole great crisis throughout the Middle East?' a British reporter asked her afterwards. 'Not at all,' she replied.

Then Khaled was flown to Damascus and on to Beirut, where she held a press conference at the offices of *al-Hadaf*, the PFLP's newsletter. This was followed by an evening appearance in a packed auditorium at her alma mater, the American University of Beirut, where she received a five-minute ovation from students chanting 'We want Leila'. She spent much of the event praising Patrick Arguello, who she said had travelled from 'so far' to give his life for the Palestinians and the revolution. The next month was spent giving press interviews, doing photoshoots with international journalists and preparing to marry.

Her fiancé was from Iraq, where he had spent a decade in prison, convicted of being a member of the Communist party, before joining the PFLP. As fellow members of the PFLP the couple were obliged to get its permission to be married. He had proposed in February. They were eventually wed in November. There was no celebration, and after a week's honeymoon in which they visited his family in Baghdad, both husband and wife 'returned to [their] tasks', he to a combat unit in southern Lebanon and she to Beirut. There Khaled contacted the plastic surgeon who had operated on her earlier in the year and asked him to restore her former features. 'This is the last time you come to my clinic,' he told her.

Days before her wedding, Khaled gave an interview to the *New York Times*, wearing a blue roll-neck sweater, pinstripe dungarees of blue, black and lilac, and matching blue high heels. According to her interviewer, she lit Kent cigarettes with a gold lighter as she explained that her celebrity meant an end to 'missions outside' but not of her commitment to the battles against Israel and against patriarchy, 'man and the ideas he practises on women'. For now, she had been deployed as a spokesperson by the PFLP but she told the newspaper that she had been promised 'a harder mission' in a different role. The article prompted an angry letter from a reader in Cambridge, Massachusetts, who noted that it had been published in the 'food, fashion, family, furnishings' section and expressed the ironic hope that the newspaper would 'continue to inform readers of the romantic involvements, sexual attitudes and fashion preferences of other noted criminals and would-be murderers'.

In Britain, newspapers focused on the ordeal of the hostages in Jordan and broadly approved of their government's handling of the hijacking. None of the hostages had been killed, and the only apparent losses were material. In the US, the view that the British were insufficiently resistant to the demands of terrorists had been revised, and Heath's 'delicate exercise in brinkmanship' received praise.

Some were less congratulatory. Enoch Powell, a Conservative member of parliament, told reporters that the government had struck a blow against a principle of justice by freeing Khaled, whom he felt should have faced trial. Woodrow Wyatt, an outspoken journalist, said that Britain should have held on to Khaled to 'break the blackmail chain', telling readers of the *Daily Mirror* that 'too few considered the impact their victory might have on the terrorists themselves, or on others tempted to follow a similar strategy'. 'What's to stop [demands] for parachute drops with £500m in gold or nuclear artillery?' Wyatt argued, somewhat melodramatically. Golda Meir, the Israeli prime minister, angrily told reporters that the decision to release Khaled meant this notorious terrorist 'will do it again . . . Kill men, women and children. That is what her organisation is for.'

But most observers recognised that the British, the US and the other governments involved in the crisis had faced difficult choices. For all their tough talk, even the Israelis had struggled to find effective ways to counter terrorist attacks over previous years. When the PFLP had conducted its first hijacking in 1968, diverting an El Al plane from Rome to Algiers, Israel had planned an operation to free the hostages and destroy the fleet of Air Algérie on the tarmac in retribution against Algeria for being the PFLP's willing hosts. In the event, they had been forced to abandon the idea – possibly because the hostages were moved, possibly because they feared a bloodbath – but the Israelis continued to pursue a strategy of retaliation against states they deemed responsible for hosting and enabling the terrorists who attacked them. Issa's attack in Athens, for example, though planned in Jordan by a Jordanian-based group, had led to an Israeli attack on Lebanon in which twelve passenger planes leased by the Lebanese national carrier and another local airline were destroyed on the tarmac at Beirut airport by Israeli special forces, landed by helicopters. This played well with domestic public opinion in Israel and prompted the Lebanese military to launch operations against the Palestinian armed groups based on their border with Israel in the south, but did little if anything to deter future attacks and had negative consequences for Israel in the long run. Soon after, Lebanese leaders concluded a deal that allowed Fatah, the PFLP and other Palestinian groups authority over the 300,000 Palestinians living in refugee camps in the country – and free rein to attack Israel.

The reality was that, more than two years after the first PFLP hijacking, no coherent policy had yet been formulated anywhere to guide a response to such attacks. When a young Vietnam veteran had hijacked a plane in the US and forced its diversion all the way to Rome in October 1969, he was feted by the Italian media, charged only with possession of an unlicensed firearm and found himself cast in a film about his own exploits. In response to the epidemic of hijackings through the mid- and late 1960s in the US, when dozens of planes each year were being diverted by criminals and cranks to Cuba, airlines there had adopted a strict policy of total compliance with any demands, largely because they had no alternative. Almost everywhere, the laws about such attacks remained vague and difficult to enforce. Khaled had clearly committed many serious offences but commandeering a passenger aircraft did not appear to be a crime in the UK. International legislation was equally inadequate, based on treaties drafted well before the problem of hijacking had become acute. A convention signed by some countries in 1963 which bound them not to negotiate with those who attacked planes was rarely respected. There was not even an agreed vocabulary to describe such people. Were they 'air bandits' or 'air pirates'? Did they hijack or skyjack? No one knew.

The simultaneous multiple hijacking executed by the PFLP in September 1970 posed questions that had never been asked before, partly because they were a response to circumstances that had never been seen before. The Boeing 747 destroyed at Cairo, the iconic double-decked 'jumbo', had been introduced into commercial service only eight months before. It was insured for $25 million, a vast sum. Like the new terminals at Schiphol and Athens, it was a symbol of a new era of science, comfort and consumerism. Until very recently, air travel had been hugely expensive and well beyond the means of ordinary people even in wealthy Western countries. Now a whole network of terminals, flights, sales offices and hotels existed and was becoming a normal part of the lives of hundreds of millions of people. 'With astonishing impunity, the pirates of the skies are able to take over the swift vehicles that represent the most advanced developments of modern technological civilisation,' commented *Time* magazine, shortly after the hostage crisis in Jordan ended. 'The skyjackers are the greatest threat to travel since bandits roamed the Old West.'

Nor had anyone ever dealt with mass media of such reach and velocity. The big surge in television ownership in the developed world had come in the 1950s, but it had continued through the following decade. By 1970, only one in twenty US households were without a television, and one in ten in the UK. The new air transport infrastructure had delivered the images of the destruction at Revolution Airport to the studios of ITN within a matter of hours; the new media infrastructure was able to beam those images into millions of homes within a matter of minutes. *Time* adapted a newly famous phrase, first coined by a media theorist called Marshall McLuhan seven years earlier, to conjure this new connectivity and how it might affect global politics. 'If the world has become a global village . . . the Palestinians have become its most troubled ghetto minority,' the magazine told its four million readers.

The astonishingly international nature of the attack itself had added to its confounding complexity. The operation had involved participants living in at least four countries and had been planned by a group with a substantial presence in at least two, as well as networks that stretched into many more. The targeted planes belonged to American, British and Swiss airlines with crews and passengers who were citizens of two dozen states. This was a direct consequence of Haddad's original insight that a war for territory did not necessarily have to be fought on that territory. Instead, it could be fought on a new battlefield, one without geographic limits, indeed without terrestrial limits at all. Key sites in the crisis – the cockpit of a jet as it hurtled through the air at 29,000 feet; Revolution Airport, constructed and controlled by a stateless people in a lawless zone – were outside a strategic geography that for decades had been defined by nations and borders. In the skies and on the ground, they constituted a new sort of anarchic zone beyond the reach of soldiers, policemen or spies. *Time* magazine's reference to the Wild West captured the nature, or at least the impression, of this new lawless and unexplored frontier.

The contours and features of this new battlefield were different from anything known to Heath and his cabinet, or to Nixon and his advisers. Indeed, governments and security agencies were not just absent from this new terrain, they were in many ways unaware that it existed until September 1970. They now scrambled to catch up. Some suggested banning airlines from flying to states in which the PFLP had a presence, others suggested air marshals on every plane. Some were in favour of the outlandish idea that in order to board their aircraft passengers should be required to put any potentially dangerous objects in a separate bag, which would then be shown to security staff before passing through the new detector systems that were being introduced at airports. Many commentators dismissed this proposal as impractical, on the basis that travellers would refuse to submit to such onerous procedures.

The result was that the fedayeen had the strategic initiative, even if they occasionally lost the tactical one. The destruction of the planes at Revolution Airport had been a gesture of extraordinary power. The 'Palestinian question' had received limited attention in the West since 1948 and had been generally framed as a humanitarian, not a political problem. In the Middle East, Palestinian grievances had been subordinated to the interests of rival powers and individual rulers, and Palestinians themselves had remained politically marginalised everywhere they lived, even under more generous regimes such as that of Jordan where they were offered citizenship. One goal of the hijacking strategy had been to change this. By the end of 1970, they had gone some considerable way towards achieving it. 'For decades world public opinion has been neither for nor against the Palestinians. It simply ignored us. At least the world is talking about us now,' said Habash.

There were costs, though, and these became increasingly evident as autumn turned to winter that year. The ceasefire agreed by Arafat and King Hussein of Jordan did not last. Within weeks of the deal, the king's forces had begun a series of new offensives, bombing and shelling refugee camps as before and inflicting further heavy casualties. By the early summer of 1971 it was clear to everyone that Hussein and his prime minister, Wasfi Tal, sought a decisive and definitive victory. Once again, the Palestinians found themselves outgunned and outfought by trained, well-armed troops who offered them little quarter. The body of one well-known Fatah commander was dragged behind a tank in the northern town of Irbid. Others were tipped into mass graves. Thousands more fighters and sympathisers were rounded up by the Jordanian intelligence agencies.

Among them was Issa. After watching the destruction of the planes and making his abortive bid to retrieve the six hostages hidden in the school in Irbid, he had been ordered to open a secure route into Syria for fedayeen fleeing Jordan. This too had been a disaster. Before they had led even one of their fugitive comrades along the paths and tracks to the relative safety of the neighbouring country, Issa's small group of fighters was ambushed by a much larger force of the king's soldiers. There was little point in resisting and Issa ordered his men to surrender.

He was beaten, detained in a barracks with hundreds of others, blindfolded, loaded into a truck and driven to a desert prison where he was starved, assaulted with batons and bars and subjected to a series of mock executions. Only after several weeks was he handed over to the International Red Cross. Half-starved, in pain, weak and sick, Issa eventually reached Lebanon, where he found that his wife had borne him a son. Issa called the child Khaled, after Khaled bin Walid, a legendary early Muslim general who had fought with the Prophet Mohammed and been one of the most successful military leaders of early Islam.

Later, the PFLP would commemorate the spectacular attack that had led to the war in Jordan by issuing fake airline tickets, so cleverly made as to seem entirely real, were it not for what they said: valid on 'PFLP AIRLINES ONLY', they displayed a flight leaving Gaza and travelling via Tel Aviv and a variety of European destinations to reach 'REVOLUTION AIRPORT in PALESTINE'. They were stamped with the PFLP's distinctive insignia and on the obverse were covered with hundreds of lines of tiny type, stating: 'OUR CODE OF REVOLUTION IS OUR MORALS'.

But even the cleverest propaganda could not disguise the extent of the trauma and loss sustained by groups like Fatah and the PFLP in the aftermath of the triple hijacking of September 1970. The fedayeen's enemies – Israel and Jordan – emerged from the war stronger than ever. Some of the Palestinians' most important supporters in the region, such as Saudi Arabia, were appalled by the violence; others, such as Syria, were destabilised by it. Official Soviet media had implicitly criticised the hijackings for sparking the crisis, while state-controlled press in their eastern European satellites described them as an act of terrorism that would do nothing to improve the condition of the Palestinians. Senior Fatah officials recalled later that the debacle threatened the PLO with 'total collapse' just six years after its foundation and less than two years since Arafat had taken control. Bassam Abu Sharif, the self-confident spokesperson of the PFLP who had once boasted of imminent victory to hundreds of journalists in Amman, was forced to make a rapid and uncomfortable dash for the relative safety of Beirut. He later admitted that the hijacking had 'triggered a disaster for the Palestinian people'. Abu Sharif was not alone in recognising the damage done. Palestinians were soon referring to the month of the hijackings and the war that followed as 'Black September'.

*

The British authorities took several days to establish that the US passport found on the body of Khaled's accomplice was genuine. After liaising with counterparts across the Atlantic, officials in London decided to prevent Arguello's family from retrieving his remains until the crisis was well over. It was not until mid-October that the prime minister received a terse hand-written note informing him that Arguello's body had been 'removed in the early hours ... by his mother and taken to Managua, Nicaragua for burial'. Though they were eventually able to establish most of the details of his childhood and youth, neither British nor US investigators had much idea of the series of events and choices that explained his circuitous journey from California to the Middle East, nor why he was to be buried in Central America. Some officials and journalists suggested Arguello had been a mercenary, paid $5,000 to take part in the September attack. The fact that anyone found this credible reveals how hard people found it to understand why this bright young college student, with his clean-cut all-American looks, had done what he had done.

In fact, Arguello was far from unique. By the summer of 1971, there were hundreds of similar young men and women like him. They saw Khaled, Issa, Abu Sharif and others like them as standard bearers in a global battle not merely against Zionism but against the forces of reaction, imperialism and capitalism. Many wanted to support this struggle, some wanted to participate in it, a few were prepared to risk their lives for it. They came to the Middle East seeking adventure, excitement, political engagement, justice, or sometimes just a safe haven. They came from the USA, from western and eastern Europe, even from Japan, but all travelled under the banner of 'Revolution'.

II

6
The German Connection

Three months before the triple hijacking of September 1970, a group of aspirant revolutionaries arrived in Jordan from West Germany. They sought military training though had barely handled weapons. They sought a guerrilla war in the streets and squares of Europe but had never done anything more than light a fire in a deserted department store. They sought the spurious glamour that training with the fedayeen could confer but were unsure what they would do with any skills they might acquire. Above all, they sought a safe place where they could hide and plan.

Some of the group had flown to Beirut on a direct flight from Communist-run East Berlin with Interflug, the East German national carrier. The better known members – Ulrike Meinhof, a prominent left-wing journalist, and two convicted arsonists called Gudrun Ensslin and Andreas Baader – had faced a more complicated journey. First, they'd had to cross into East Germany, or the German Democratic Republic (GDR) as it was officially known, at the vast checkpoint at Berlin's Friedrichstrasse railway station. They then took a train to Prague and only there did they board a plane to Lebanon. Once in Beirut, things were not straightforward either. Their travel and fake passports had been arranged by the representative of Yasser Arafat's Fatah in West Germany. Fatah's officials had to intervene to get them through Lebanese immigration control and then hold off the suspicious local authorities for long enough to allow their guests to be driven out of the city. Once clear of the capital, they followed the same route taken by Gunnar Ekberg, the Swedish spy, a month or so earlier: a taxi took them east across the mountains and the Beqa'a valley into Syria and from there they went south to Amman.

At the founding of Israel in 1948 and for many years thereafter, most progressive or liberal activists and thinkers in Europe and the US had been largely supportive of the Jewish state. In West Germany, this was bound up with a sense that the country had never acknowledged, let alone atoned for, the crimes of the Nazi era. Meinhof had written favourably about Israel and the kibbutz movement, and was especially interested in encouraging the study of the history of the Jews in Germany. But by the late 1960s such sympathy had been waning for some time. Israel's victory in the 1967 war, its evident military superiority, its sudden and massive territorial expansion, its imposition of military rule in the territories it now occupied and its increasingly close relations with the US resulted in a dramatic reversal of these attitudes. Among the broad coalition of activists and protest groups known as the 'New Left', commitment to the cause of the Palestinians not the Israelis became a test of one's progressive credentials. Israel was no longer seen as a beleaguered outpost of moderate socialism and progressive values surrounded by reactionary, despotic regimes dedicated to its destruction, but was now frequently described by leftists as a bellicose outpost of imperialism, capitalism and 'settler colonialism'.

This shift in attitudes was accelerated by a concerted campaign of Soviet propaganda, as well as the independent efforts of networks of activists across western Europe and in the US, such as the ones infiltrated by the Swedish spy Gunnar Ekberg. Many intellectuals on the left had come to believe that the radical transformation they longed for would never begin in Europe, where the proletariat were more interested in foreign holidays and saving up for fridges or cars than manning the barricades. Instead, they believed, the coming revolution would originate far away, in Asia or Africa or Latin America, where the masses were ready to rise up and fight. It was therefore the duty of aspirant revolutionaries in Hamburg, London or Stockholm to support those fighting the good fight in the global South. Attacks such as those by Leila Khaled and Mahmoud Issa brought the Palestinians much attention in these circles. In 1970 the CIA complained that 'the fedayeen have succeeded in making the New Left in [western Europe] anti-Zionist'.

The agency had concerns about US activists too. The Palestinian issue attracted particular attention among the younger, more extreme militants who had become prominent within the civil rights movement towards the end of the 1960s and who drew a parallel between the plight of the Palestinians and that of Black people in the US. Malcolm X had visited Gaza and spoken at the American University of Beirut less than a year before his assassination in 1965. In July 1967, the Black Panther party, founded a year before as an armed self-defence organisation in California, had reprinted Fatah's first communiqué, and in 1970 described 'the Zionist fascist state of Israel' as a 'puppet of imperialism that must be smashed'. Huey Newton, the group's founder and leader, listed 'Palestinian guerrillas' alongside Castro, Guevara, Ho Chi Minh, Mao and 'liberation' fighters in Angola and Mozambique as inspirations.

For those on the New Left, the US remained international enemy number one and the war in Vietnam their greatest cause. But while the plight of the North Vietnamese undoubtedly roused their sympathies and fired their imaginations – one group of activists in the US tried to live on rice and fermented fish sauce in emulation of Hanoi's fighters – there were almost insuperable obstacles to supporting them on the ground in Vietnam itself, and almost none of the numerous sympathisers who visited Vietnam made any attempt to stay in the north, let alone fight with the Communists. Most encounters occurred instead at the many international conferences organised by activists in Europe, or in the Soviet satellite states or by 'revolutionary' regimes in North Africa and elsewhere. These were often attended by delegations of North Vietnamese fighters who 'dazzled' or 'captivated' those they met. The revolutionary campaigns in Latin America were slightly more accessible but the consequences of getting directly involved could still be very serious if things went awry. By contrast, the Palestinian cause was one of very few where direct involvement was both feasible and relatively risk-free. The Middle East was only a short flight or a cheap bus and boat trip away, and until the autumn of 1970, the worst that could be expected when one returned home would be some slightly difficult questions at border control.

So they came, and in increasing numbers. Fatah's camp in Ajloun, close to where Leila Khaled had trained in Jordan, welcomed between 150 and 200 young volunteers in 1969 and 1970. The biggest contingent was British, though most western European countries were represented too, along with some eastern Europeans and several Indians. They were an ideologically eclectic bunch. When in February 1970 the DFLP offered training and instruction to any 'revolutionary and progressive forces' who wanted to build a 'World Front Against Imperialism, Zionism, and Reaction', about fifty 'militant Maoists, Trotskyites, and members of . . . an extreme left-wing group in France' responded, according to the FBI. During one of his visits to Jordan, Ekberg had come across a group of young men who had deserted from US Army bases in Germany rather than serve in Vietnam. In all several thousand volunteers made the journey to the Middle East. Some even combined the trip with wider travel in the region or used it as the first stage of a longer journey along the hippy trail that crossed Iran and Afghanistan en route to India. Most merely toured refugee camps, workshops and military bases, worked on farms, helped dig trenches and assisted at clinics. Some fired a few rounds from a Kalashnikov. Then 'they picked up their [keffiyeh] headdress, several volumes of Palestinian poetry and went home souvenir-ed and sun-tanned', in the cynical if not entirely unfair words of one foreign correspondent.

A minority had greater ambitions. But though the PFLP was keen to recruit foreigners, other factions were more reluctant. 'It is ridiculous to talk of forming . . . an international brigade or foreign legion. We have more Arab volunteers than we can use,' a Fatah spokesman told journalists in Beirut. Many fedayeen groups also had a justified fear of infiltration by hostile intelligence services. Ekberg was not the only agent to successfully infiltrate the fedayeen's camps. The Israelis had exploited the rush of recruitment that followed the battle of Karameh in 1968 to place hundreds of low-level spies in the ranks of the Palestinian armed groups, and as early as 1969 the FBI were reporting that they had successfully recruited a US citizen whom Fatah had trained and then tasked with sabotage assignments in Israel. A young Frenchman who turned up in a Fatah camp in Jordan around the same time fell under suspicion and was shot dead in a 'training accident'.

Those whose motivations were entirely authentic could be a liability too. A nineteen-year-old Swiss student trained by the Popular Front was arrested in Haifa in 1970 when he stepped off an Italian passenger ship on his first mission. Even before he disembarked, Bruno Bréguet had been betrayed to Israeli intelligence services by a source within the PFLP. Worse, he left an obvious trail of evidence and disobeyed a strict injunction from the PFLP to destroy his written instructions for an attack, simultaneously offering his captors a valuable haul of intelligence and sufficient evidence to convict him. Two British subjects who had 'met fedayeen members' in the Middle East were detained shortly after their return to the UK on suspicion of planning to attack an El Al plane at Heathrow airport. When, after weeks of training in Jordan and discussions in Beirut, it was suggested to a Danish Maoist that he participate in a forthcoming 'external operation', he refused, returned home in some haste and had no further contact with the Palestinians or the radical network in Denmark that had dispatched him. A pair of Swedish sympathisers were sent by the PFLP to reconnoitre Lod airport but attracted the close attention of security staff and were forced to beat a hasty retreat.

A final problem was that even when the trainees were both committed and competent, their former instructors had little influence over how they might deploy their new skills. In 1969, volunteers led by Dieter Kunzelmann, a self-declared agitational artist who cashed cheques from his wealthy financier father while living in communes, returned to West Germany from a Fatah camp in Jordan and promptly attempted to bomb a crowded Jewish community centre on the anniversary of Kristallnacht, the Nazis' first major antisemitic pogrom. Had it been successful, the attack might have killed scores. 'This was not what we had expected,' commented one senior Fatah intelligence official drily, if possibly disingenuously. Kunzelmann may also have planned an attack on a Jewish kindergarten and to daub pro-Palestinian slogans on a concentration camp memorial.

The group that arrived from West Berlin in June 1970 was an odd assortment of violent activists, polemicists, self-publicists, adventurers and intellectuals. Their leader, though not the loudest or best-known among them, was Gudrun Ensslin, the thirty-year-old daughter of a Protestant pastor. Tall, fair and serious, she had been brought up in a small village on the edge of the Swabian mountains in an environment of strict moralism, spiritualism and nostalgia for a Germany unpolluted by either commercialism or war. When she spent a year with a Methodist family in Pennsylvania as a teenager, Ensslin was distressed by the materialism of her hosts. There was no sign of any rebellion in her youthful years, only of a fierce intelligence. Ensslin studied English and German at the University of Tübingen, then won a scholarship to Berlin's Free University to study for a doctorate in literature. She campaigned for the moderately left-wing Social Democrat party (SPD) in elections in 1965, and then, like many others, felt deeply betrayed when the party entered government in coalition with centrist conservatives the following year.

A turning point for Ensslin came in June 1967, when Mohammed Reza Pahlavi, the Shah of Iran and a staunch US ally, visited West Germany, sparking major protests. Tensions were high even before the

Shah's security men attacked the noisy but peaceful demonstrators in West Berlin with wooden staves and a local policeman shot dead a twenty-six-year-old student. Immediately afterwards Ensslin told fellow activists that it was impossible to reason with 'the generation that made Auschwitz' and that only violence could halt a government set on establishing a new authoritarian regime like that of the Nazis.

This was a commonly-held view among young West Germans on the left, many of whom had only discovered the extent of the Nazi-led atrocities during the war crimes trials of the early 1960s and with the publication of books such as the diary of Anne Frank. This widened the gulf that had already opened up between the generations as younger people realised how many of their elders, including teachers and parents, had pasts that were deeply compromised and yet enjoyed complete impunity.

Here Ensslin was particularly exposed and conflicted. Her own parents had been broadly opposed to the Nazis, though they had not actively resisted them, and, unusually for the time, had spoken to their children about the mass murder of the European Jews and the questions of conscience and responsibility they and their compatriots had faced during the war. But Ensslin's partner, a fellow literary student, was the son of a mediocre 'blood and soil' poet who had been a committed member of the National Socialist party and an enthusiastic antisemite. Worse, the couple had edited and published a volume of his poetry to fund Ensslin's own postgraduate studies. In the summer of 1967, as protests intensified across West Germany, Ensslin reached a moment of personal and political crisis. She left her infant son and his father and dived deep into the world of radical activism in West Berlin. There, among the drifters, pranksters, amateur orators, runaways, petty criminals, draft dodgers, deserters, potheads, avant-garde artists and the occasional genuine ideologue who made the city such an exciting, anarchic place, she met Andreas Baader, with whom she fell in love.

Baader was twenty-four years old. His father had been captured on the Russian front during the Second World War and not been heard of since. Baader had grown up surrounded by bereaved women. A first brush with the police aged nine was followed by expulsion from a series of educational establishments and a short time at art school in his home city of Munich. Formal study of any kind bored Baader and he preferred the less demanding pastimes of a local bohemian scene where he was briefly involved in experimental 'action-theatre'. He was, a friend said, 'a Marlon Brando type'.

Spoiled, arrogant and lazy but with a brooding, scruffy charm, Baader often appealed to women, and some men too. He was dark-haired, brown-eyed, gap-toothed and at five feet ten inches slightly taller than Ensslin. He dressed fashionably and expensively, posed for erotic pictures for a gay men's magazine, and occasionally wore make-up. Fast cars held a powerful appeal, though obtaining either insurance or a driving licence did not, resulting in a string of convictions for traffic offences. Baader was uninterested in politics and unmoved by progressive causes. He was attracted to Berlin because it offered its residents looser licensing laws than the rest of the Federal Republic of Germany (FDR), less oppressive policing and, most importantly for Baader, an exemption from military service.

Many Berlin activists found Baader profoundly irritating. One described him as 'impossible to talk to', prone to sulking and foul-mouthed rants. Others saw him as a bully and a braggart who sought to convince people of his revolutionary credentials by belittling others' efforts. In April 1968, an accidental fire in a department store in Brussels killed over 250 people. Baader boasted of his intention to bring about a similar conflagration, but it was Ensslin who organised a car, obtained the necessary materiel and selected a multi-storey department store in Frankfurt as their target. After the attack, which caused substantial material damage but no loss of life, she and Baader headed to a well-known leftist bar to celebrate loudly. This was an error. So too was leaving bomb components in the car and a list of ingredients in a coat pocket.

In the combustible atmosphere of the summer of 1968, even minor incidents could provoke significant unrest. Nine days after the arson attack in Frankfurt, the charismatic German student leader Rudi Dutschke was shot by a right-wing extremist. This botched assassination led to riots and demonstrations of a severity not seen anywhere in Germany since the 1920s. Similar protests broke out in Britain and France. In London, there were bloody clashes with police as hundreds of protesters broke away from a demonstration against the Vietnam war some 30,000 strong and attempted to reach the US Embassy in Grosvenor Square. Most famously, a demonstration against restrictions on male students' access to female accommodation on a campus on the outskirts of Paris set off a chain of events that led to the occupation of the Sorbonne, days of running battles with riot police in the centre of the capital and a strike by nearly ten million workers.

But this 'revolutionary moment' was transient. Despite all the possibilities it conjured and the iconic photographs, posters and slogans it produced, the reality was that the protests of the summer of 1968 never commanded the breadth of popular support needed to destabilise a government. The war in Vietnam remained hugely emotive and polarising, posters of Mao and Guevara continued to adorn bedsit walls, a book by German philosopher Herbert Marcuse which blamed capitalism and consumerism for reducing the masses to a state of stupefied apathy sold briskly, but by the end of the summer the crowds had disappeared from the streets of western Europe's cities. Activists might have rolled up their sleeves or worn jeans, industrial overalls, military cast-offs and steel-capped boots in imitation of manual workers, but their vision of radical, violent change was alien to the vast majority of those they sought to emulate. Even the most obtuse Marxist-Leninist could see that the revolutionary vanguard had failed to mobilise the masses. When, in August, the Beatles sang about 'Revolution', it was to make very clear to their millions of fans that they would not be getting involved.

Many of the activists who had led the summer's protests believed that radical transformation was still possible, but only if the revolutionary cause was pursued with greater vigour. A smaller number believed that this meant adopting a strategy of armed struggle, not mere agitation, though only a minority of these were actually prepared to commit violent acts. Through late 1968 and into 1969, a number of groups emerged from this 'unholy stew' of 'angels, militants, New Left totalists . . . fanatics, far-outs and fucked up', as leftist writer Norman Mailer would describe them. Most remained anonymous but some became known to the wider public: in the UK, there was the Angry Brigade; in the US, the Weather Underground, who took their name from the lyrics of a Bob Dylan song; in Italy, the Red Brigades. In West Germany, despite their grandiose names, most of these various cells and networks involved fewer people than the average amateur sports team.

The errors made by Ensslin and Baader in Frankfurt led to their arrest within thirty-six hours. In October 1968, after six months in custody, they faced trial. In court, Ensslin, wearing a fashionable red leather jacket and dark sweater, waved a copy of Mao's Little Red Book and claimed that the arson had been a protest against the failure of the German people to react to the horrors of the Vietnam war. Baader, wearing dark glasses, a T-shirt and 'Mao jacket', smoked a Cuban cigar in the dock and described students in Germany as the country's equivalent of oppressed Black Americans. They each received three-year prison sentences but were released eight months later pending appeal.

A condition of their provisional liberty was that they devote it to worthy social causes, so the following months were spent working with teenagers in institutions in Frankfurt. Ensslin organised sessions to discuss Mao. Baader appropriated the youths' minuscule financial allowance, took them to bars, drank and lectured them about the coming revolution. When they heard that their appeal had been rejected, Baader and Ensslin fled rather than return to prison to serve the rest of their sentence. They drove west to Paris where they stayed in the spectacular apartment of the author Régis Debray, who was still in jail in Bolivia for his involvement with Guevara's abortive bid to foment revolution there. Hansel and Gretel, as they now called themselves, enjoyed financial support from political sympathisers. They spent large sums of the money they received on expensive restaurant meals and photographed each other in cafés. Tiring of Paris after several weeks, the couple then drove to Italy where they enjoyed the generous hospitality of wealthy leftist activists for some months. In Milan, Giangiacomo Feltrinelli, the very radical and very rich publisher, welcomed them to his home and laid out his collection of guns for their admiration. Another new friend offered the use of his villa outside Rome. There were more long conversations about the forthcoming armed struggle. Somewhat surprisingly, these began to crystallise into an authentic if nebulous plan of action which they resolved to pursue back in Germany. When their car was stolen they took it as their cue: Baader broke into an Alfa Romeo which they drove back to Berlin. In need of somewhere to stay, they sought out Meinhof, whom they had met when the journalist had reported on their trial.

Meinhof was almost a decade older than both. She had grown up in Oldenburg, a small, conservative town in north-west Germany. Her father was a government art historian who was killed by cancer shortly after the outbreak of the Second World War. Her mother died shortly after the conflict, leaving Meinhof and her siblings in the care of a close female friend who was energetic, supportive and deeply committed to a range of moderate left-wing pacifist causes. Meinhof was a conscientious, mature, religious and idealistic young woman who won a scholarship from the Studienstiftung des deutschen Volkes, a German foundation for the promotion of exceptionally gifted students. She studied pedagogy and psychology at university and was active in Protestant groups who helped campaign against the stationing of nuclear weapons in West Germany. She also joined the youth organisation of the Social Democratic party, listened to jazz and smoked a pipe.

At this time she began to publish articles in student magazines. Her opinions were radical but not extreme; her arguments structured and well-researched; her writing fluid and articulate. This got her hired as a columnist for *Konkret*, a left-wing magazine of culture and politics based in Hamburg, where she moved shortly after graduating in 1959. Two years later, she married *Konkret*'s publisher and gave birth to twin girls. Over the following nine years, Meinhof's journalism earned her respect, lawsuits, a good income and a new status as an unofficial spokesperson for the emerging protest movement in West Germany. Her eloquence, grasp of detail and controlled fury led to frequent appearances on television and radio, and she was soon reaching a broader audience. A slightly smitten British correspondent interviewed her at home in Hamburg, and described 'a nervous, pretty woman with two blonde little girls rolling round her feet' who sadly confessed that other more militant activists contemptuously dismissed her as a 'peace-loving pancake'.

But Meinhof was not happy. For many years, she and her publisher husband had been part of the local liberal social elite, invited to dances and dinner parties and spending their weekends at the fashionable coastal resort of Kampen on the island of Sylt in the North Sea. This lifestyle filled her with unease – though not sufficiently to stop her enjoying a holiday at the north Italian castle of Feltrinelli and flying home in his private jet, or buying a big house in Blankenese, one of the most elegant and expensive suburbs of Hamburg. 'Our house, the parties, Kampen, all of that is only partly enjoyable . . . TV appearances, contacts, the attention I get . . . I find it pleasant, but it doesn't satisfy my need for warmth, solidarity, belonging to a group. The part I play . . . corresponds only very partially to my real nature and needs, because it involves me adopting the attitude of a puppet, forcing me to say things with a smile when to me, to all of us, they are deadly serious,' she wrote in her diary.

Luckily for Ensslin and Baader, Meinhof eventually resolved the tension between her deepening ideological commitment and her wealthy lifestyle. In late 1967 she had divorced her unapologetically unfaithful husband and moved with her twin daughters to Berlin, where her apartment became a meeting place for activists, writers, students and young people on the run. When the two fugitive arsonists knocked on her door on their return from Italy she agreed to let them stay.

By 1969, Meinhof's relatively moderate views had become more extreme, the language harsher, the arguments more direct. She was very busy, lecturing while also working hard on an investigation into young female runaways in state institutions, writing prolifically late into the night and early morning, fuelled by cigarettes and coffee. Interviewers found her tense and angry, her already deep voice made harsh by chain-smoking. 'Protest is when I say I don't like this. Resistance is when I put an end to what I don't like. Protest is when I say I refuse to go along with this any more. Resistance is when I make sure everybody else stops going along too,' she wrote in what would be one of her last columns in *Konkret* in April 1969. Her previously sympathetic views on Israel had hardened too.

Ensslin and Baader lived with Meinhof for several weeks, an intense experience for everyone concerned, especially when they all tried LSD. Meinhof's daughters liked Ensslin, who played with them, but disliked Baader, who laughed when they hurt themselves. After a couple of months Hansel and Gretel moved on, though this did little to improve the atmosphere in the apartment. When Meinhof's new partner proposed a Christmas tree, she accused him of bourgeois sentimentality and banned presents or any celebrations. Her daughters frequently missed school. Meinhof told collaborators she couldn't see the point of journalism any more, but also railed against the restrictions imposed on her professional activities by motherhood.

When Baader was re-arrested, driving a stolen car with false papers, and returned to prison to serve out the rest of his sentence, Ensslin asked Meinhof to help her lover escape. The journalist agreed to write letters to the governor of the prison describing a book project that she was to undertake with Baader and so obtained reluctant permission for him to join her for research in a Berlin library. At around 10 a.m. on 14 May 1970, shortly after Meinhof and the prisoner had settled down with cigarettes and instant coffee in the reading room of the Institute of Social Issues, two women gained entry through a ruse, then let in a man armed with a Beretta pistol, then Ensslin. Together, they overpowered the two armed prison guards with tear gas and shot an elderly member of staff, wounding him in the side. Baader promptly jumped from a first-floor window onto the institute's well-tended lawn and ran. Meinhof faced a split-second decision: stay where she was, pretend to have been duped by Ensslin and so return to her writing, activism and children. Or follow Baader and the others and exchange all this for an uncertain and dangerous life as a wanted criminal on the run.

A stolen Alfa Romeo sports car had been prepared for their getaway – later found by police with a tear gas gun and an introduction to Marx's *Das Kapital* inside – but the bloodshed during the raid required a change of plan: now they would need to get further away than a single tank of petrol would take them. To complicate matters further, Meinhof had chosen to follow Baader through the window and they now had a well-known public figure among them. Meinhof had made some arrangements to go underground, taking out a mortgage on her apartment for 40,000 Deutschmarks, but had no support network or false papers, and was encumbered by commitments that would be hard to reconcile with a life of clandestine political activism. One of the first things she did as a fugitive was to call a friend to arrange for her daughters to be picked up from school.

The obvious solution was to leave West Germany, and ideally Europe too. Ensslin was in touch with the representative of Fatah in West Berlin. The organisation had been recruiting in West Germany among Palestinian students with some success for several years and had arrangements in place to facilitate travel to the Middle East for the growing number of young West Germans who wanted to learn about the Palestinian cause first-hand. They had all the necessary knowledge and contacts to organise Ensslin and her comrades' hurried departure. The fugitives were supplied with forged passports issued some time before in the name of the United Arab Republic, a union between Egypt and Syria which had only existed as a political reality from 1958 to 1961 but was theoretically still in force. Amateurishly disguised to match the images in their new travel documents, they assembled at Berlin's Friedrichstrasse station just over three weeks after Baader's escape and set out for the Middle East.

After the chaos and excitement of the journey from West Berlin, Amman initially proved something of a disappointment. Their Fatah hosts had set up the standard itinerary offered to such visitors, but Baader,

Ensslin, Meinhof and the half-dozen others who had accompanied them were not particularly interested in viewing clinics, villages and refugee camps. They had not come as tourists, they told their hosts, they wanted instruction in guerrilla warfare. Despite some misgivings, a Fatah official called Abu Hassan agreed to their request and sent the group to a camp recently set up by the organisation's internal security department in the hills outside the Jordanian capital. Its two stone buildings, shooting range, dirt exercise yard and threadbare tents were guarded by fedayeen and ringed by barbed wire fences. The trainees were issued Kalashnikovs, to be kept at hand at all times. This was considered a rare honour.

The following weeks could not be described as an unqualified success. Fatah instructors taught the Germans how to build incendiary bombs and other explosive devices, as well as how to rob a bank. But none of the volunteers was physically fit or knew anything about guns or explosives. When they had launched the operation to free their leader a month earlier, they had been obliged to hire an experienced criminal to carry the one lethal weapon and at least one of their number had vomited from nerves beforehand. Baader now refused to give up his tight velvet trousers even on an assault course, and Meinhof struggled badly with the physically demanding aspects of their training. When she froze after pulling the pin from a grenade, Baader called her a 'bourgeois sow'.

Almost immediately there was a series of fierce disagreements between the Germans and the middle-aged Algerian, a veteran of the independence struggle against the French, who ran the camp. The first of these was about Ensslin and Baader's insistence that they be allowed to sleep together, which was unheard of in the conservative environment of Fatah's training camps. The row was calmed by the intervention of the suave Abu Hassan, who spoke good German, but there were further disputes. Food was rudimentary – rice mixed with tinned meat distributed by the UN to the refugee camps, flatbread, water and black tea – and the visitors complained about the diet. Then the women insisted on sunbathing either nude or topless, which provoked further outrage as well as possibly other sentiments among the young male fedayeen guards. Baader frequently refused to follow orders and led the trainees in a protest after they had fired off hundreds of rounds with apparent abandon and a limit was placed on the precious ammunition they could expend. Abu Hassan returned to calm tempers once again, but just when peace had been restored and a chicken slaughtered and cooked in his honour, Baader loudly complained that it was unfair and 'unrevolutionary' that a leader might receive better food than ordinary foot soldiers, prompting a new row.

Such tensions and mutual incomprehension were to be expected. The visitors and their hosts had read many of the same texts, venerated many of the same heroes, were familiar with the same slogans of revolution, even wore some of the same clothes, but the international solidarity that this suggested was something of a mirage. Almost none of the visitors spoke Arabic and very few had travelled in the Middle East, or even overseas, before. For all their sympathy for the Palestinians' grievances and undoubted enthusiasm for their cause, the European volunteers were profoundly ignorant of the society, history and culture of their hosts. A senior Fatah official later remembered that their guests' interest in the Palestinian cause appeared 'very recent indeed'. One of the Germans with Baader, Meinhof and Ensslin sent a photograph of himself in combat fatigues, wearing a keffiyeh and carrying a Kalashnikov, to a radical German newspaper with the message: 'Best wishes to your readers from the land of *A Thousand and One Nights*!' For some of the foreign visitors, Jordan and the Palestinian cause were simply a stage on which a new identity could be forged. 'I was given another name, and after a few days I couldn't remember anything my former name had meant . . . In these revolutionary struggles . . . a new person is born,' a German volunteer wrote later. Their pursuit of personal reinvention was not always appreciated, particularly if it was pharmaceutically assisted: when Timothy Leary, the counterculture icon who advocated the use of hallucinogenic drugs, wanted to travel to Jordan he was rudely rebuffed.

The behaviour of some of the foreign volunteers did little to bridge the divide. A group of British International Socialists smuggled alcohol into one camp, got drunk, held an impromptu sing-song and then got into a fight, first with a group of British Maoists then with the guards who tried to confiscate their remaining bottles. Another group of volunteers failed to understand that laundry left to dry on trees might reveal the position of their camp and so attract Israeli air strikes. Others refused to join in with the trainees digging trenches, complaining that they hadn't come all the way to Palestine to make holes in the ground, only to leap into those very holes when an Israeli jet flew low over the camp. At her Popular Front base in Jordan, Leila Khaled had been amused by a group of 'graduates of the 1968 university upheavals in the West' who 'honestly believed they were making a "revolution" if they undressed in public, seized a university building, or shouted an obscenity at bureaucrats'. Their interest in discussing 'sexual problems and issues' seemed to her utterly misplaced.

The group that Baader, Ensslin and Meinhof had led to Jordan was particularly vexatious. In early August, after seven weeks in the camp, Baader provoked another argument by demanding to be treated as a militant commander equal in status to Abu Hassan. Shortly afterwards, Ensslin demanded that the Palestinians execute a member of her own group whom she suspected of being an Israeli spy, largely on the basis that he had listened to a Hebrew-language broadcast on a transistor radio. Abu Hassan's polite refusal led to a new confrontation and a raft of fresh complaints from the Germans. His patience now wearing thin, Abu Hassan terminated the training and told Baader, Ensslin and the others that they had come as friends so would therefore be 'conducted out as friends' and he would arrange for their swift return home. The Germans did not see their host again. None of them had made the slightest effort to learn his true identity, nor even why he spoke such good German, and only much later did the significance and secrets of the man they had been dealing with become clear.

Three days before they had left Berlin, the half-dozen young men and women who had been involved in Baader's escape issued a communiqué, printed in a leftist magazine. It promised a campaign of violence to bring the latent conflict in Germany into the open and, echoing Guevara's call for 'one, two, a thousand Vietnams', promised to 'start [in Germany] what has already started in Vietnam, Palestine, Guatemala, in Oakland and Watts, in Cuba and China, in Angola and New York'. The statement did not attempt to explain the group's actions 'to the intellectual windbags, the know-it-alls and the shitting-in-their-pants brigade', nor to the 'petit bourgeois intellectuals' or 'Lefty ass-kissers'. Instead, its message was meant for the 'potentially revolutionary segment of the population': the underpaid workers, the teenage girls in institutions, the boys in care homes, the factory workers, the families on the housing projects, the labourers and apprentices, all those who were 'exploited but receive no compensation in the form of good living standards, consumption, loans, automobiles'.

The statement, probably written by Meinhof though signed by Ensslin, appeared under an image of a leaping black panther that was clearly inspired by the US activists they most admired. It ended with a series of lapidary exhortations: 'Don't go meekly off to slaughter . . . The end of the rule of the pigs is in sight! . . . Develop the class struggle. Organise the proletariat. Start the armed resistance'. The statement was entitled: 'It is time to build up the Red Army Faction.'

7
Armed Struggle is the Reality

Our view is from the passenger seat. We are in a large car, travelling at moderate speed along a street lined with apartment blocks and palm trees. The sky is blue and empty of clouds. The ride is smooth. The camera pans, tracking objects and individuals with a tourist's avid, superficial interest. We see other vehicles, a line of buses, pedestrians, soft drink stalls, a Ferris wheel. We hear a voiceover: 'Propaganda is information. Information is the truth. And the supreme form of truth is the armed struggle. So armed struggle is the best form of propaganda.'

There is a pause. Now we see a beach, waves, the sea; planes taxiing at an airport, then taking off; television aerials and washing lines above poor housing, all breeze blocks and bleached white sunlight. Dirt roads. Ragged children. An office of the Popular Front for the Liberation of Palestine, posters on walls. A slogan in Japanese flickers over the screen. 'Armed Struggle is the Reality', it says.

The screen clears, and there follows a brief interview with a woman sitting on a bed in a spartan room, an assault rifle carefully positioned beside her and a volume of Lenin on a table. 'I do everything necessary for the armed struggle . . . sometimes it's hijacking, sometimes it's giving interviews, and everything in between,' Leila Khaled tells us. 'I do not think of myself as a hero . . . but to hear someone speak of me that way makes me very happy.'

Now we are in among dry, rocky hills. We are in a bunker, then on some kind of patrol. Fedayeen in jeans and sandals scrabble through scrubby bush carrying an assortment of weapons. 'This is an attack on the Zionist imperialists. The PFLP fights with the people, for the people,' the voiceover continues. The faces of the fighters are serious, determined. A group sits and reads very clean copies of Mao's Little Red Book, their pages fresh and as yet unturned.

The film – entitled *The Call to World Revolution* – was made over two weeks in May 1971 in Beirut and southern Lebanon by a pair of radical Japanese filmmakers who had stopped on their way back to Japan from the Cannes film festival. When they had turned up at the office of *al-Hadaf* in Beirut to see what access might be arranged to Lebanon's Palestinian refugee camps and the fedayeen, they had found a young Japanese activist called Fusako Shigenobu who was helping out with the group's media operations. Shigenobu had also travelled to Lebanon with the aim of doing something to publicise the Palestinian cause, particularly in her homeland, as well as to forge an alliance between Japanese and Palestinian extremist groups. The first goal was relatively easily achieved; the second would prove far more costly.

Shigenobu was the daughter of a temple teacher with extreme right-wing nationalist views who had served during the Second World War as an officer in Japan's infamous military police. The family was too poor to afford her college fees so she worked in a soy sauce factory while attending evening classes at the prestigious Meiji University from 1963. She later claimed to have earned money as a nude dancer in a local bar as well. Like so many students in the mid-1960s, Shigenobu was drawn into the burgeoning local protest movement.

Radicalism in Japan shared much with its counterparts in the West, and particularly with West Germany. As a former Axis power in the Second World War, Japan had its own dark past marked by extremist nationalism, atrocity and catastrophic defeat. Crucially, it too had been occupied by the US whose influence could be felt everywhere from its nascent democratic institutions, capitalist economy and foreign policy to its citizens' emerging taste for milkshakes and rock 'n' roll. Like western Europe, post-war Japan experienced rapid economic growth that produced massive social and political change, including a huge expansion of higher education, even while the universities themselves remained under hierarchical administration and offered old-fashioned teaching and inadequate facilities. In the 1950s, a broad, left-leaning coalition arose in reaction against the foreign policy imposed upon Japan through its common defence treaties with the US, and the following decade was marked by protests against the war in Vietnam and wider unrest: street battles with police, sporadic makeshift bomb attacks on symbolic targets and the occupation of university buildings. Japanese activists paid close attention to the campaigns of their counterparts in other developed countries, reaching out to US-based groups and adopting many of their slogans about the fight against global imperialism, consumerism and capitalism. To Shigenobu the 'barricades', as she called them, were a place of unprecedented social equality, where young people from various backgrounds – whether university graduates or local high-school students or 'girls who'd run away from home' – were able 'to come together and discuss their lives'.

While the unrest in Japan had much in common with that of the West, and was to some extent modelled on it, it continued slightly longer and was marked by an even greater factionalism. In the autumn of 1969, the most violent and marginal fringe of the protest movement made a declaration of 'open war' on the state and tried to trigger an insurrection. Police swiftly rounded up many of the most prominent leaders at a training camp close to Tokyo. The remaining hardliners concluded that finding locations where they could train and plan in Japan, a heavily populated and well-policed island, was impossible. Hence the need for an alliance with an extant revolutionary movement somewhere. In March 1970, a group of seven extremists hijacked a Japanese domestic flight and got themselves flown to North Korea, which was in theory still aligned with Maoist China and thus the broader global 'revolutionary movement'. They quickly disappeared into a re-education camp, from which they did not emerge for many years. Even so, many of Japan's militants saw the hijacking, which severely embarrassed the unprepared Japanese authorities, as a great success.

Shigenobu did not. Capable, intelligent, strikingly beautiful with her fine features and long dark hair, and adept at gathering information and raising funds, she had risen swiftly through the ranks of the student movement to become a leader of its most radical faction. This was named the Red Army, which evoked radical leftism and violent struggle as well as making historical reference to Leon Trotsky's revolutionary force. Shigenobu fervently believed in the creation of an international revolutionary coalition – even a common global leadership – and so had been researching potential partners for the Japanese. She had decided the PFLP was the most obvious candidate and found another activist who had independently arrived at the same conclusion. They married, allowing Shigenobu, who was known to police, to obtain a new passport in the name of her spouse.

When Shigenobu and her husband arrived in Beirut, the PFLP was plunged in recrimination and disagreement. George Habash, its leader, had been incensed by Haddad's handling of the triple hijacking operation, and his authority now suffered the additional blow of his being held responsible for the losses sustained in its aftermath. Habash now sought to ban any further attacks on targets either outside or not directly linked to Israel. Wadie Haddad, meanwhile, made little secret of his contempt for his friend and collaborator's relative moderation.

Shigenobu knew none of this when she presented herself at the *al-Hadaf* offices. Like so many preceding visitors, she was sent to see Bassam Abu Sharif, who had now returned from Jordan to Beirut along with the rest of the PFLP's remaining fighters, and become the first point of contact for foreign volunteers. Shigenobu was soon very busy, sending breathless articles back to Japanese publications, meeting Japanese consular staff, building a network of contacts among journalists in Beirut and, when the filmmakers turned up on their stopover from Cannes, organising their itinerary. This proved a worthwhile use of her time. Attracting activists from Japan had been slow and difficult – Shigenobu later compared it to 'fishing with one line' – but after *The Call to Global Revolution* was screened in Japanese universities in the autumn of 1971, several were inspired to join her in Lebanon.

In the first months of 1972, extremely worrying news began to arrive from Japan. Over the course of the previous year, extremists there had intensified a campaign of bank robberies and sought to obtain firearms. It now emerged that two of the more radical factions had joined forces and then retreated to a remote mountain refuge in the Japanese Alps where they had tortured and killed twelve of their own members, beating some, stabbing others and leaving several to die of exposure in the snow. The survivors were arrested by police, some after a siege that was watched on television by almost ninety per cent of the country's viewers.

The sheer brutality of these 'snow murders' in Japan was incomprehensible to most, but it pointed to a dark aspect of the radical underground at this time. Communes had become common in the US in the 1960s, hosting some three million people by the end of the decade, and there were of course many throughout Europe too: squatted houses or apartments in Berlin's Kreuzberg, Copenhagen's Christiania neighbourhood and London's Notting Hill. For the most part these were relatively benign enterprises, providing adventurous and sometimes supportive homes for a range of misfits, believers, dropouts or simply those unable to find alternative accommodation. Many were also outposts of activism, propaganda and, sometimes, extremist recruitment. In these, the boundaries between hippy haven, shared living space, ideological bootcamp and guerrilla collective easily became blurred. Strict rules imposed either by the group or a charismatic leader were common. Inevitably, levels of coercion were high and some members were vulnerable to abuse. Restrictions were designed to enforce a sense of shared identity, sometimes via humiliation. Some of the 'K-Gruppen' that emerged in Germany in the late 1960s not only banned make-up but any clothes that were not made of a specific uncomfortable fabric, took the doors off all the toilets and ordered that children be educated by the group. The Red Brigades which emerged in Italy slightly later imposed a 'no contact with outsiders' rule on all their members, and leaders would split up couples if thought necessary. A more extreme Italian group ordered that orgasms be simultaneous, but forbade masturbation and oral sex as 'petit bourgeois' practices. In Sweden, 'deviants' and 'revisionists' were locked up in toilets or ordered to stand on apartment balconies for protracted periods in the freezing cold. It became apparent that a marathon 'self-criticism session', supposedly modelled on Maoist practice in China, had led ultimately to the horrors of the snow murders.

After spending time with members of such collectives, Gunnar Ekberg, the young Swedish spy, had wondered at how many 'sinners gladly submitted to their punishments' in this way. In fact, a key aspect of the more extreme groups was an overriding and fiercely held belief that the well-being of an individual was of no importance when weighed against the needs of the collective and the contribution one could make to 'the revolution'. Extended to the world at large, it was a logic that radically devalued the life of anyone outside the group. Shortly after Andreas Baader was freed, Ulrike Meinhof had described a police officer as 'a pig, not a human being', a view that was subsequently repeated in a thousand conversations in the group's safehouses across Germany. The use of violence, even to murder, thus became an unavoidable duty. At the same time, these violent impulses often lacked a clear focus. How does one attack an entire economic, political and cultural system, as historian and Communist party member Eric Hobsbawm asked in 1971? Where do you even begin? The potential targets were almost limitless. Many of the more inexperienced extremists turned their violence against targets that made little strategic or political sense, including against suspected internal enemies.

The snow murders and the subsequent arrest of almost all the main radical leaders in Japan effectively ended the threat from domestic extremism there. Shigenobu's faction in Lebanon became the only active Japanese group remaining. When Haddad suggested that this handful of Japanese volunteers be deployed in a spectacular but high-risk operation targeting Israel, their leader agreed.

In May 1972, following two months of physical conditioning and weapons training, three Japanese men travelled from the Popular Front camps in Lebanon to Frankfurt, where they picked up false passports, and then on to Rome. They stayed first in the plush Anglo-American Hotel on Via delle Quattro Fontane. On the second day of their stay, they returned from a walk to the Trevi fountain to find Czech-made machine pistols, ammunition and Chinese grenades waiting for them in their rooms – just as Khaled had three years earlier. They then moved to the nearby Pensione Scaligera where the manager remembered them as guests who 'came and went very often and behaved very well, like gentlemen', though on one night they asked where they could go for drinks and came back at 4 a.m.

Three days later, the three men packed the weapons in their hold baggage, dressed in freshly ironed light trousers, white shirts and ties, and travelled to Fiumicino airport where they checked in for a flight to Lod airport in Israel, posing as businessmen. One of them, a twenty-four-year-old former agricultural student called Kozo Okamoto, wrote a last diary entry: 'I love cherry blossoms . . . Humans have been contaminating the world with DDT [pesticides] for twenty years . . . I'm setting out on an important business.' Bewildered Israeli investigators later decided that this was not a code but a faithful expression of his thoughts.

Nor was the attack at Lod airport a 'suicide operation' as many later claimed. Haddad's attitude to casualties among the men and women he deployed was certainly unsentimental – in Beirut, he had told Ekberg that all those who were killed on his operations 'would have died eventually anyway' – but no suicide attacks had taken place by the time the PFLP deployed Shigenobu's group to attack at Lod airport. In fact, the idea of making the death of attackers an integral part of the plan was still seen as outlandish. 'Arabs don't blow themselves up, only the Japanese,' one senior British official told Colin Smith, a British journalist, no doubt on the mistaken assumption that the Japanese participants were continuing the 'Kamikaze' tradition of an earlier generation. Members of the Japanese Red Army (JRA), the PFLP, Fatah and all other armed factions described themselves as fedayeen, or fedayi in the singular, but though this could be translated as those who redeem themselves through the sacrifice of their life for a righteous cause, it did not by any means imply the intention to die in a given attack, merely a willingness to take the risk, sometimes very significant, of such an outcome. Fedayeen would become martyrs – *shaheed* – if they were killed, and celebrated as such, but this was not supposed to be their objective. Her comrades set off anticipating 'a festival' not a 'funeral', Shigenobu later said.

The target of the three men was an obvious, if daring one. Three weeks earlier, four Palestinians had flown a hijacked Sabena plane into Israel's main international airport and demanded the release of just over a hundred prisoners from Israeli jails, mainly Palestinians but also a handful of Western sympathisers who were incarcerated. Golda Meir's government had stalled, allowing negotiations with the International Red Cross to continue for several hours. This had allowed an assault team of elite army soldiers to formulate a plan, move into position disguised as technicians in white overalls and then storm the plane, killing two of the hijackers and disarming those who remained, both women. (Among the troops was a young veteran of the battle of Karameh and the 1968 special forces raid on Beirut called Benjamin Netanyahu.) Haddad may have wanted to prove that his organisation could succeed where others had failed, or he may have sought revenge for the Israelis' successful assault. Whatever his motivation, his plan called for the attackers to storm the control tower, or possibly take charge of a plane, and then negotiate with Israeli authorities. They may also have been ordered to engage police, soldiers or airport security staff in the arrivals hall. Either way, Haddad certainly intended this attack on Israel's main international airport to be spectacular and bloody.

On their arrival at Lod airport from Italy, the three Japanese men retrieved their baggage at the carousels. They immediately pulled their weapons from their bags and began firing indiscriminately at the passengers around them. Within seconds, the many security personnel in the airport began shooting back. Two of the three attackers died at the carousels, one fatally injured by the explosion of his own grenade, the other possibly by fire from a fellow attacker's weapon. The third was detained after he ran out onto the tarmac where he began hurling grenades at aircraft. In all, twenty-six people died in less than two minutes, including seventeen Christian pilgrims from Puerto Rico, a prominent Israeli scientist, tourists and airport personnel. The surviving attacker was Okamoto, who had written about cherry blossoms and DDT.

In Beirut, Shigenobu was devastated by the loss of her close comrades – who included her nominal husband – and initially saw the attack as a tragic failure. By contrast, the Popular Front announced that the attack had shown the 'solidarity of revolutionary groups around the world', and its jubilant reaction eventually persuaded her that the heavy losses had not been in vain. At a brief press conference Shigenobu claimed responsibility for the operation in the name of the Japanese Red Army and then disappeared from view. Now dubbed 'the Mistress of Mayhem' by Western newspapers, Shigenobu would not be heard from for several months. When she did finally break cover, it would be with a new wave of violence perpetrated by Japanese volunteers who had been recruited on the back of the publicity and attention generated for her group by the attack on Lod.

Any hopes that it would attract sustained attention from Western populations or policy-makers to the Palestinian cause went unfulfilled. Front pages around the world were dominated by Richard Nixon's summit with Leonid Brezhnev in Moscow, the first visit of a US president to the USSR. In West Germany, meanwhile, the attack competed with the news that on 30 May, after months of increasingly bloody bombings, Andreas Baader and two other leaders of the Red Army Faction had been arrested.

Launching an armed struggle in Germany had proved more difficult than Ensslin, Baader and Meinhof anticipated when they issued their call to arms in the summer of 1970, shortly after their return from the problematic sojourn in a PLO training camp in Jordan. The name they had chosen for their group – the Red Army Faction (RAF) – reflected their belief that theirs was merely one of many efforts worldwide that would collectively bring about the downfall of capitalist, imperialist states such as the US and West Germany. But the reality was that some parts of the world were significantly more receptive to revolution than others. By the late spring of 1971, the group had been back in Germany for some eight months and yet had little to show for its efforts beyond a dozen or so bank robberies.

It was at this time that Ulrike Meinhof sat down to write a text that would focus and explain their campaign of violence to the world, as well as to provide answers to a great number of unanswered questions, among them: How would the great uprising of the oppressed German masses actually come about? And when and against whom could the group use lethal force? For several days and nights, the former journalist sat at a typewriter in a sympathiser's apartment in the city of Heidelberg, surrounded by books, documents and cigarette smoke.

The pamphlet Meinhof eventually produced, entitled *The Urban Guerrilla Concept*, began with no fewer than three quotes from Mao. One laid down a rude credo for the group: 'It is good if we are attacked by the enemy, since it proves that we have drawn a clear dividing line between [them] and ourselves.' Another major influence, apparent from the title, was the Brazilian Communist dissident Carlos Marighella whose eighty-page *Minimanual of the Urban Guerrilla* had reached Germany in the spring of 1970. Marighella had updated Guevara's 'Foco' strategy to argue that any revolutionary struggle should be centred in cities not in rural areas, and offered a multitude of practical tips on logistics, disguise, surveillance, bomb-making, recruitment, propaganda and much else. These had not served Marighella himself particularly well – he was killed by security forces of Brazil's military dictatorship shortly after finishing his book, and his rebellion fizzled – but they were welcomed by activists throughout Europe who were sorely in need of guidance. One West German group sought to replicate the Maoist strategy of 'encircling the city from the countryside' by recruiting in rural Bavarian discos. The effort met with a predictable lack of success.

Meinhof argued that the powerful forces of 'imperialism and colonialism' could only be defeated if forced to fight on many different fronts across the world. The student protest movement of the late 1960s had been useful because it had broken through the 'provincial isolationism' of the 'old Left' and shown those involved that they were facing the same enemy as the Vietnamese, the Palestinians and all the 'exploited peoples of Latin America, Africa and Asia'. She stated that armed struggle was a 'pre-requisite for progress and an eventual victory of revolutionary forces', even while she insisted that the RAF had been forced to take up arms reluctantly. 'The urban guerrilla war is based on the analysis that by the time the conditions are right for armed struggle it will be too late to prepare for it,' Meinhof wrote, a line which echoed Guevara, Debray and others. 'Whether it is right to organise armed resistance at this moment is dependent on whether it is possible – and it can only be made possible by actually doing it.'

The tract was at times perplexing and incoherent but it was effective. Mimeographed and distributed as a booklet at the annual May Day demonstrations, its cover featured the new logo of the RAF: a red star and an assault rifle. It was read avidly in activist circles – as well as by the police – and then reached a far wider audience of ordinary West Germans when it was reprinted by a major newspaper.

Meinhof's text ended with a quotation from Eldridge Cleaver, a prominent leader of the Black Panthers in the US and a vocal advocate of armed struggle: 'Either you're part of the problem or you're part of the solution. There is nothing in between.' The response to her pamphlet suggested that most people in West Germany were very much in between, and a poll was conducted in the summer of 1971 to try to establish their views. Forty per cent of the respondents agreed that the RAF's violence was 'political', eighteen per cent approved of their motives, and six per cent said they would shelter a member of the group for a night. Meinhof, Baader and Ensslin were hugely encouraged by the results, not least because they relied on precisely such popular support to stay ahead of the police.

Life for RAF members was mainly dull, stressful and frustrating, punctuated by infrequent moments of fear or great excitement. 'You join the urban guerrillas and then you find yourself spending a month fixing up an apartment, and there's always shopping to be done, things that are needed. That's ninety-nine per cent of what goes on,' one remembered later. Another described tedious hours spent encoding and decoding addresses and messages. Errors could have serious consequences, though. Meinhof miswrote an address after she and three other RAF members broke into a town hall to steal blank identity cards and all the precious documents were sent to the wrong location and lost. Funds often ran low. Meinhof's wealthy left-wing friends donated money and offered their luxurious weekend homes as temporary hideouts, but food was sometimes scarce and safehouses could be uncomfortable. One, a central Berlin apartment, was almost unfurnished and 'the comrades' sat and slept on the floor. Another, an unused care home, was remote and extremely cold.

Their camaraderie helped ease the discomfort. 'They debated, laughed, and joked with one another . . . They all loved Donald Duck comic books and read them together, laughing like children. Andreas and Gudrun often fooled around, giggling like teenagers. If four or five of them were there, and they had time, they cooked together,' wrote Margrit Schiller, a young recruit. 'I had never met people like [Baader, Meinhof and Ensslin] before . . . Their political discussions, the way they handled weapons, their jokes, how they spoke to and treated one another. They seemed to be connected, to be on the same wavelength, almost as if they shared one mind.'

Music and film provided diversion, too. Meinhof was ashamed of her fondness for the music of Rod Stewart. Baader had no such qualms about his taste in film, modelling himself on the anti-heroes of contemporary gangster films and wearing a trench coat and hat in imitation of the leading men of the *nouvelle vague*. In Jordan, when their Fatah hosts had refused to execute the comrade Ensslin suspected was a spy, Baader proposed that he, she and Meinhof shoot the suspect from different directions so no one would know who had fired the fatal shot. He drew the idea from a spaghetti western. A triple bank robbery was inspired by Gillo Pontecorvo's 1967 film, *The Battle of Algiers*.

Then there were the cars and the guns. The RAF stole many vehicles, but the small, fast BMW 2002 was such a favourite that owners across Germany placed stickers on their windscreens saying 'I am not a member of the RAF' and joked that BMW actually stood for Baader Meinhof Wagen. Such vehicles sufficed for low-ranking members of the group but Baader preferred top-of-the-range sports cars. In the autumn of 1971, he crashed a stolen Porsche 911 at over 100 mph on an autobahn, emerging from the wrecked vehicle without a scratch. Other members of the group later remembered being terrified when he was behind the wheel. 'There were lots of accidents with group members. Andreas always said "that would never have happened to me" and then three days later it did,' remembered one.

Firearms were just as attractive but harder to master. Six weeks training in Jordan proved insufficient, and the first time Meinhof, Ensslin and the others wielded weapons in anger was in order to intimidate bank staff during one of the many robberies they committed while underground. The group's logo showed their ignorance, featuring a German-made Heckler & Koch submachine gun used by local security forces rather than the Soviet-made Kalashnikov that was the instantly recognisable icon of almost every 'liberation struggle' in the developing world. Baader's view was that 'fucking and shooting are the same thing', which perhaps explains his incompetence.

It also helps explain his relationships with women. Ensslin tolerated her lover's abusive outbursts but was deeply irritated by her male comrades' tendency to be more interested in sex than overthrowing capitalism. During a visit to the famous Kommune 2 in Berlin in the summer of 1971, she upbraided Bommi Baumann, one of the leaders of the Hash Rebels, for 'chasing round apartments, fucking little girls, smoking hashish', angrily telling him that such activities were a distraction from the serious work of the armed struggle. Meinhof was not a fan of revolutionary promiscuity either, tartly telling one aspirant recruit from a group with a reputation for sharing sexual partners that 'we don't go in for group sex here [in the RAF]'.

The wanted posters that went up all over Germany from May 1970 made obvious the high proportion of young women among the ranks of the RAF. In one sense, this was a breakthrough. And yet, during the unrest of 1968 women participated – if at all – as 'coffee makers and sleeping partners (and as shoulder-borne visual accessories for the benefit of press photographers)', according to one observer. And in reality the 'free sex' encouraged in many of Berlin's communes was often the opposite of liberating for women. 'It's like training a horse; one guy has to break her in, then she's available for everyone,' said one male inhabitant. Some claimed that for a woman to refuse sex was 'counter-revolutionary'. Baader systematically referred to women, even Ensslin, as '*Fotzen* (cunts)', justifying it as a deliberate repudiation of bourgeois conventions. Beate Sturm, a twenty-year-old who quit the RAF after two months in January 1971, remembered one occasion when female members criticised Baader at a meeting and he shouted them down, screaming: 'You cunts, your emancipation consists of yelling at your men.'

The first casualty in the struggle between the West German authorities and the RAF had been a woman. The twenty-year-old part-time hairdresser first came into contact with the group through her boyfriend and was shot dead as she tried to evade arrest in July 1971. The first murder committed by the RAF came some months later in Hamburg when two members of the gang shot a police officer who was attempting to arrest a third. The killing was barely discussed within the group but it marked the start of a new and more violent phase of activity. A second policeman was killed during yet another bank robbery, then a third. Authorities responded with a series of vast dragnets which met with little success but did hinder the group's ability to move freely.

In April 1972, the RAF's leaders decided that the moment had come to launch the blow that would, by provoking massive repression that would reveal the 'Fascist' nature of the German state, definitively rupture the false consciousness of the working classes and so create the conditions for revolution. As ever, quite how to do this was unclear, and neither Mao nor Marighella offered much guidance. First the group armed themselves with dozens of pipe bombs, using coffee mills and egg whisks to mix fertiliser and household chemicals into explosives. More bombs were made by a sculptor skilled in metalwork who was persuaded that his creations were to be used as props for an avant-garde film project. Only then did the group discuss potential targets. When it was reported in the news that the US Air Force, engaged for several weeks in a massive bombing campaign in North Vietnam, had dropped mines to block the country's principal port, Ensslin suggested bombing the numerous US military installations in West Germany in response. Baader's response was typically unconsidered: 'Let's go then.'

The first target of this new campaign was the sprawling US base outside Frankfurt. The bomb they planted demolished part of the officers' mess, killing an officer. They then released a communiqué written by Meinhof in the name of the Petra Schelm Commando, named after the hairdresser who had been shot by police, which ended with Guevara's call for revolutionaries worldwide to create 'two, three, many Vietnams'. The RAF's next effort wounded five at a police headquarters in Augsburg and was swiftly followed by an abortive attempt to kill a federal judge who had signed many of the warrants for their arrest.

After a brief pause, a bomb was planted at the head office of the conservative newspaper group Springer, long loathed by the German left. Their warning was ignored and when the bomb exploded it injured dozens. Surprised by the public disgust this prompted, Baader telephoned Meinhof, who had overseen the attack, to berate her for her 'stupidity' and ordered the group to revert to military targets. On 24 May the group stole two cars, fitted them both with stolen plates, placed a bomb in each with a timing device and drove them into the Supreme Headquarters of the US Army in Europe at Heidelberg. This attack killed three soldiers. Meinhof once more sent a statement to the press, equating the US air offensive in Vietnam with the Allied bombing of Germany during the Second World War, and saying that any further intensification of the bombing would be 'genocide, the Final Solution, Auschwitz'. Then, with its stock of pipe bombs and its appetite for violence momentarily exhausted, the RAF rested.

Some days after the attack in Heidelberg, police in Frankfurt were told by a resident about a garage under an apartment block in a nondescript neighbourhood on the outskirts of the city where men arrived at odd times of the day and night to work with some kind of powder stored in large sacks. The garage was put under surveillance. Very early on the morning of 1 June, police officers hiding nearby watched a brown Porsche Targa drive the wrong way up a one-way street and come to a stop. Baader and Holger Meins, a former art student and filmmaker who was close to the principal leaders, got out and went to the garage. Police moved in. The resultant standoff lasted several hours. Meins eventually gave himself up when an armoured car was deployed, but Baader continued to shout abuse and shoot until he was hit in the thigh by a police sniper. TV footage showed him being carried on a stretcher to a police van, grimacing in pain, his dark hair dyed a lurid shade of orange. In the garage, police found explosives and a silver-grey ISO Rivolta, one of the most expensive and rare sports cars in Europe, stolen by Baader some weeks before.

Authorities now set about rounding up the rest of the group. The next RAF leader to be caught was Ensslin, who was arrested in a high street store in Hamburg after leaving a coat with a revolver in its pocket outside a fitting room as she tried on some sweaters. A shop assistant noted its weight, checked the pockets, found the gun, and called the police. After a brief struggle, Ensslin was overpowered, arrested and driven away in a police van. 'I am glad that the hunt is now over,' her father told journalists.

That left Meinhof still at liberty. But the violence of the previous weeks had alienated – or at least scared – many who had once been sympathetic to the RAF. Twelve days after the arrest of Baader, when a young teacher in Hanover was asked by an intermediary if he would allow two unidentified people to stay the night, he hesitated, spoke to his girlfriend, and made a phone call. When the police arrived they found a poster of Guevara on the sitting room wall, bags containing guns and a bomb, and Meinhof, underweight and exhausted.

This success could not have been better timed for West German authorities. In a little over two months, more than 10,000 athletes, hundreds of journalists and many thousands of spectators would be arriving for the 1972 Olympic Games, hosted by the southern city of Munich. Bavarian officials had spent a long time discussing potential threats. The two most likely potential scenarios were an aeroplane hijacking at a German airport or an attempt to assassinate a VIP. What they did not consider – simply because no one could imagine it – was an armed invasion of the Olympic village and a deliberate attempt to hold or harm athletes. This was a fateful mistake.

III

8
Munich

On a morning in July 1972 three men met at a café terrace in the Piazza della Rotonda in Rome. One had recently flown in from Beirut, another from Libya and the third from Sofia, where he had just spent several frustrating and ultimately fruitless weeks trying to buy silenced pistols from unco-operative Bulgarian arms manufacturers. All three were members of Fatah, the armed Palestinian organisation led by Yasser Arafat, and had spent much of the previous nine months organising a series of bombings and assassinations across the Middle East and in Europe.

On the table in front of them lay several Arabic- and English-language newspapers. All were full of articles about the forthcoming Olympic Games in West Germany. The choice of Munich as host city had been hotly disputed. The Soviets and the East Germans had grudgingly decided to attend, but disputes over arrangements for their delegations and supporters continued to generate tension. There had also been a venomous row over the possibility that the white supremacist regime in Rhodesia might send a team. The three men were less concerned by either issue than they were at the absence of any Palestinian team at the games, as IOC rules prohibited delegations that did not represent a recognised state. They discussed what might be done. Maybe there was a way to highlight this exclusion or at least underline its injustice? Could they attack the games in some way? Perhaps even take hostages?

It was a bold suggestion. No Palestinian fedayeen group had ever attacked a remotely similar target before and no armed group had ever attacked the Olympic Games. To do so would shatter a number of taboos, not least the traditional truce that was supposed to protect the event, and would mark a very significant escalation of the campaign of international violence. The political consequences were almost impossible to predict, and Arafat's support was by no means guaranteed. Such an operation was sure to be deeply controversial among even the more extreme Palestinian factions. On the other hand, the most successful attacks of the previous three years had been those that had provided striking images: the 747 exploding at Egypt's international airport or the three planes destroyed on the dirt airstrip in Jordan, for example. In Cairo and at Revolution Airport there had been only one or two photographers present but this had been enough to prompt global coverage of the PFLP's actions and cause. At the Olympics, there would be hundreds, possibly thousands of journalists. As a platform for highlighting the grievances, or simply the existence of the Palestinians, the Munich games appeared difficult to surpass.

After ten minutes of discussion, the most senior of the three made a decision. Salah Khalaf, better known as Abu Iyad, was head of Fatah's intelligence and security services. He had been among the founder members of the organisation and was widely considered its de facto deputy leader. Khalaf told the others that he would fly back to Libya, where a batch of Fatah militants were being trained for urban warfare and 'external operations' in one of the half-dozen camps that Muammar Gaddafi's intelligence services had set up to offer instruction to a multitude of different groups from the Middle East and elsewhere. The second man at the table, a more junior Fatah official called Fakhri al-Umari, would accompany him and help with the logistics for a potential attack. The third would travel immediately to Munich to see if any kind of attack might actually be feasible. They would meet again in Athens, eight days before the Olympics were scheduled to begin. If it looked like there was a good chance of success, the operation would go ahead.

In 1971 and 1972, the unprecedented wave of terrorist violence that had washed across the Mediterranean in previous years went global. Activist networks were mobilised in places where few had suspected their existence and extremist groups formed ad hoc alliances to launch attacks across five continents, leaving a trail of destruction from Bangkok to Washington, DC. The multiple hijackings of September 1970 were soon forgotten as policy-makers, security officials and ordinary citizens scrambled to understand this new threat.

As they sought ways to improve their counter-terrorist capabilities, many Western governments also took the pragmatic decision to open channels of communication with Palestinian factions they had previously shunned. Some politicians even looked to strike deals of brutal cynicism with them in order to ensure the security of their own citizens and so avoid the inevitable electoral blowback of having an attack occur on their watch.

In fact this global wave of attacks would eventually ebb of its own accord, as its instigators realised it was becoming counter-productive and risked running entirely out of control. But by then it would be too late. The dozens of attacks from 1968 through the early years of the 1970s undoubtedly made clear that the Palestinians could simply not be ignored, but this came at the considerable cost of undermining much of the relatively new support in the West and elsewhere for the resolution of their grievances. Long after the movement shifted away from using spectacular international violence as a strategic weapon, the Palestinian cause would remain irredeemably tarnished by it. And of the hundreds of attacks associated with Fatah, the PFLP and others in this period, one above all was responsible for this hardening of attitudes.

The opening ceremony of the XXth Olympiad took place on 26 August 1972. First came speeches, the German national anthem and an alpenhorn fanfare played by a dozen men in lederhosen. Then the 121 participating teams paraded around the athletics track of the new Olympic arena. Each entry was accompanied by lively folk music commissioned for the occasion: bouzouki for the Greeks, a bossa nova for the Brazilians, lots of drumming for African nations and barely distinguishable 'traditional' melodies for the Egyptians, Ethiopians, Algerians and Afghans. The serried ranks of the near 600 US athletes marched to a medley of jazz, swing and gospel. Later, school children sang, there was a display of Hispanic dancing, thousands of doves were released and the Olympic flame was lit by an eighteen-year-old policeman. The display surprised everyone, including the Germans themselves. 'As we know we don't do light-heartedness well . . . If it wasn't [happy] enough for some people, we'd have to say: we don't get any more cheerful,' commented one local newspaper editorialist.

The last Olympic competition in Germany had been in Berlin in 1936 and had been a showcase for the Nazi regime. From the outset, the 1972 edition was designed to be an explicit contrast with its predecessor. The games would demonstrate a different Germany to the world: pacifist, polite, prosperous, content and welcoming. Security personnel would be mostly unarmed and wear 'leisure suits' in azure blue, supposedly the same colour as the skies of Bavaria. A 980-foot television tower soared above the six-square-mile Olympic Park so that television networks could beam live images of a record 195 events across the planet via recently developed satellite technology, reaching an anticipated audience of more than a billion people.

The significance of the Israelis' presence in Munich, the historical home of Nazism, was lost on no one. The delegation numbered twenty-seven in all. Only a minority had been born in Israel. Yossef Romano, an immensely powerful weightlifter with a big grin and razor-sharp sideburns, had come as a child from Libya, where there had once been a flourishing Jewish community. Shaul Ladany, a long-distance walker, had been born in Belgrade. Several were originally from Romania, such as Andre Spitzer, the fencing team's coach. The youngest member of the delegation was the most recent immigrant: eighteen-year-old Mark Slavin had grown up in a deeply orthodox family in Minsk, capital of the then Soviet Socialist Republic of Byelorussia, and had taken up wrestling to fight off antisemitic bullies. Though offered a place in the Soviet national team, he had emigrated to Israel four months before travelling to Munich and was considered Israel's best chance of a medal.

None of the team was particularly wealthy or particularly poor, but together were representative of Israel's new working and middle class, a product of massive immigration, the welfarist policies of successive left-wing governments and decades of economic growth. The delegation included a watchmaker, a young lawyer and a businessman. Romano was a painter and decorator, Ladany a scientist. Most had served in the Israeli armed forces and several in at least one war. Shmuel Lalkin, the punctilious but respected delegation leader, had been a member of the Palmach, the then elite of Jewish forces, in 1948 and fought in 1967 too.

The delegation's members were also representative of many Israelis' religious identity. Though most were looking forward to returning to Israel for the festival of Rosh Hashanah, the Jewish new year, few were religiously observant. The team visited a synagogue in Munich shortly after the beginning of the games, where they met members of the city's small Jewish community, but only a handful placed their faith at the centre of their lives. The delegation did not include any of Israel's Arab Palestinian citizens, who constituted roughly a tenth of the 3.5 million population at the time.

Being in Germany provoked profoundly mixed emotions for both the young athletes and their older coaches. The trial of Adolf Eichmann that took place in Jerusalem in 1961 had been televised internationally in order to raise awareness of the Holocaust, but in the decades before and to a lesser extent afterwards the subject remained virtually taboo in Israel, too painful for survivors and the bereaved, and almost incomprehensible to younger Israelis raised in a society that prioritised action, initiative and frequently force. Many members of the delegation had themselves suffered appalling ordeals or loss during the Second World War. The entire family of Yakov Springer, a fifty-one-year-old internationally recognised weightlifting coach, had been killed in Poland. So had all the relatives of the mother of his fellow wrestler Ze'ev Friedman, twenty-eight. 'I saw in every adult German the faces of the murderers of my parents,' Tuvia Sokolovsky, a weightlifter, remembered later. Some of the athletes told dark jokes attributing the warmth of their welcome to the Germans' inability to disobey orders. Dan Alon, a fencer, spoke of his fierce joy at 'marching into this stadium in Germany thirty years after Hitler tried to annihilate my people', writing that 'we proud Olympians ... are proof to the world that we Jews have survived our Holocaust, and we are stronger than ever.'

Others were less conscious of the past and less worried about present dangers. Only three members of the delegation attended an official memorial service in Dachau on the eve of the games, prompting anger in Israel. Romano told his anxious wife not to worry for his safety because 'the Germans think of everything'. Coming from a country where life remained relatively austere, many were astonished and excited by the vast, newly built Olympic village, with its ping-pong tables, fruit stands, news counters, sports equipment stores, souvenir shops, overhead walkways and artificial river. Esther Shahamorov, a twenty-year-old sprinter, remembered the opening ceremony as 'very beautiful ... not only for the sportsmen, but for everyone ... an amazing experience, better than a dream'. Spitzer, who was twenty-eight and had a newborn daughter, told his wife about the joy he felt at being able to mix with other athletes, even those from hostile Arab countries.

The team did creditably in their events, and no one outside Israel took any notice of them. Attention during the first ten days of the Olympics was focused elsewhere. The USSR defeated the USA in a hotly contested and hugely controversial basketball final. Mark Spitz, the mercurial swimmer, won the first of seven golds, the tiny Russian gymnast Olga Korbut wept and smiled. The only problems were a protest by left-wing activists in the centre of Munich, rows over the high number of East Germans who defected, and complaints about the poor value for money offered by local hostelries. Athletes, including some Israelis, began leaving the Olympic village to enjoy Munich's bars, pool halls and pubs in the evening, often returning late at night. On the evening of 4 September, the entire Israeli delegation attended a production of the musical *Fiddler on the Roof*. They returned at midnight to their apartments in a block on Connollystrasse in the Olympic village.

Just over four hours later, eight young men wearing tracksuits walked up to the fence surrounding the village, located a particular gate on its eastern side that they knew to be closed but unguarded, climbed over, took assault rifles and grenades from the sports holdalls they were carrying and headed along a paved ramp to where the Israeli delegation was sleeping, less than a hundred yards away.

While the Israelis had been at the theatre, the third man who had sat around the table in the Piazza della Rotonda was in his hotel near Munich's main station, making final preparations. Mohammed Daoud Odeh had grown up in the Palestinian village of Silwan, a few hundred yards south of Jerusalem's Old City, before training as a teacher. He had joined Arafat's organisation in Kuwait well before the 1967 war. In 1970, he had led Fatah fedayeen during the fighting in Jordan following the triple hijacking of that year, where he had earned the nickname 'the palm tree of Amman'. Since then he had been working on both sides of the Iron Curtain, building up networks of support in West Germany but also spending weeks in Bucharest to negotiate with Romanian manufacturers for specialised weapons that Khalaf felt would give Fatah the edge against the Israeli security services.

Odeh was an odd choice for such complex and delicate tasks. A six-month stint in Fatah's embryonic intelligence service in Amman in 1969 had not been a success, and the arboreal soubriquet he had acquired in Jordan evoked not just his great height and burly frame but a signal lack of subtlety. But Khalaf trusted him, and when he had reported to the older man that an attack on the Olympics in Munich was not just practicable but relatively straightforward, he had been appointed as the tactical commander of the operation.

The plan Odeh had formulated was not particularly sophisticated: a team of eight armed men would break into the Olympic village, seize as many Israeli athletes and coaches as possible and then demand the liberation of hundreds of Palestinian prisoners held in Israeli jails. They would be given two communiqués. The first, in English, laid out their initial demands and was to be handed to German authorities immediately after the hostages were seized. The second was in German and only for use if the crisis lasted more than twenty-four hours, which was deemed the likely limit of the attackers' physical and psychological endurance. It would offer a way for the authorities to resolve what would by then have become a major crisis, asking for planes that would fly the attackers and their hostages out of West Germany to a friendly – or at least not unfriendly – Arab state. There, the hostage-takers would be in a virtually unassailable position and so able to negotiate with the Israeli government from a position of considerable strength. This was the theory. A weakness of the plan was that Israel had not capitulated to such demands in any similar situation for several years and its leaders had made repeated public pledges not to do so.

Odeh arrived in Munich some days before the date chosen for the attack and took delivery of eight AK-47s, ammunition and ten grenades. He would later say that these were brought through Munich airport in a single large suitcase, which stretches credulity as it would have weighed around 50 kg. It is equally unlikely that so many weapons were concealed by a layer of women's lingerie, as he also claimed. In reality, the armoury was either provided by Libya and imported in the diplomatic bag of Libya's embassy in Bonn or supplied by local neo-Nazis, or possibly a mixture of both. Odeh's next task was to make sure the young men who were on their way to Munich to participate in the operation reached their rooms in several cheap hotels around the city.

Their leader was to be a twenty-seven-year-old named Mohammed Massalha, who had been born in a village five miles from Nazareth in northern Israel and grown up in a refugee camp in Syria. He had studied psychology and chemistry at the University of Damascus. Massalha then travelled to West Germany to complete a master's degree, where, like many others, he had become involved with Fatah's local branch. Since then he had lived in West Berlin, and was engaged to a local woman, so he spoke excellent German as well as English, which would allow him to negotiate with the authorities and if need be speak to journalists. His lack of military experience had been partly remedied by a short training course in Libya, provided by Gaddafi's security services.

Massalha's deputy was a Fatah combat veteran who called himself 'Tony', but whose real name was probably Yusuf Nazzal. Tony had grown up as a refugee in Jordan and Lebanon before joining Arafat's organisation in 1965. He had taken part in raids into the West Bank before and after the 1967 war and then fought against Jordanian forces in the autumn of 1970 and spring of 1971. Tony's military experience may well have trumped Massalha's language skills in the eyes of Odeh, and it is likely that he was the designated leader of the forthcoming operation, even if he was to play a less publicly prominent role.

The other six members of the attack had grown up in refugee camps in Lebanon, Syria and Jordan. Several knew each other, some very well. There were two brothers and a cousin. Others had played together in a football team in their sprawling camp on the southern outskirts of Beirut. The youngest was eighteen, the oldest in his mid-twenties. All were former or existing members of Fatah's internal security service and all had spent much of the previous month undergoing intensive training in Libya, an exercise designed to reinforce an *esprit de corps* as much as provide instruction in how to handle weapons or climb obstacles.

Tony had been in Munich for a month to scout the location for the attack, Massalha had arrived a week or so earlier. The six others arrived by train, after long journeys from Syria and Lebanon by circuitous routes via Yugoslavia and Italy. Late that evening, Odeh summoned them to dinner at a cheap restaurant near the city's central train station where he explained what was planned. After the meal they handed over their passports, signed a collective will and retrieved large bags from storage lockers at the train station. These contained identical Adidas tracksuits, tinned food and snacks, lengths of rope, masks made from long socks and nylon stockings, weapons and ammunition. Odeh told the men they should try to avoid bloodshed but could use their assault rifles and grenades if they met any resistance. Then they waited.

As dawn approached the following morning, two cars – one driven by Odeh, the other by a local sympathiser – took them close to the Olympic village. Though they were seen when they climbed over the perimeter fence, they were not challenged by security guards who thought they were sportsmen returning from a late night in Munich's town centre.

The first person to die was Moshe Weinberg, a massively powerful wrestling coach from Haifa. At around 4.40 a.m. one of the gunmen forced the door on the first floor of the Israelis' two apartments. Weinberg grabbed a fruit knife from the table, lunged and was shot in the face. Bleeding heavily, Weinberg was ordered to lead the attackers to a second room, where the delegation's weightlifters were sleeping. There he may have made a second attempt to resist. This time he was hit by a volley of shots to the chest which killed him almost instantly.

The second to die was Romano, the wrestler, shot several times, sustaining grievous wounds to his abdomen, possibly after trying to overpower one of the attackers. Had he received prompt medical attention it is possible he would have lived. Instead the nine surviving athletes would spend the rest of the day corralled into a single room with Romano's corpse on the floor, covered by a sheet.

The sound of the shooting was reported by a cleaner on her way to work. At 5.10 a.m. a policeman arrived at the blue doors of the apartments on Connollystrasse. As he looked at number 31, two pieces of paper were dropped from a first-floor window: the statement of demands given to Massalha along with a separate list of prisoners the hostage-takers wanted released. These comprised more than 200 Palestinians held in Israeli jails, as well as the lone survivor of the Japanese Red Army attack on Lod four months earlier and Andreas Baader and Ulrike Meinhof, a late addition, included out of 'revolutionary solidarity'.

Fifteen minutes later, Massalha opened the blue door. He was wearing a light brown safari suit, a wide-brimmed white hat and dark sunglasses, and had boot polish smeared over his face, an apparent bid to disguise his identity. He gave a signal to those inside and the body of Weinberg was carried out and left on the ground. Tony, in sunglasses, a black cowboy hat, boots with stacked heels and a short-sleeved red shirt open to the chest to show a medallion, watched warily. A gunman briefly appeared on a balcony wearing a makeshift balaclava cut from a sock and was photographed in what would become an iconic image.

The news of events in Munich reached Jerusalem at around 6 a.m. local time. The initial details of what was happening in the Olympic village were unclear but the first reaction of Golda Meir, the Israeli prime minister, was unequivocal: there had been no concessions in May when the Sabena flight had been hijacked and flown to Lod airport, and there would be none now. She met with her closest advisers and cabinet, then issued a statement saying that Israel did not bargain with terrorists and confidently expected the West German authority to 'do all in its power to secure the release of the hostages'. Meir spoke to a reporter in her office. 'If we should give in . . . then no Israeli anywhere in the world will feel that his life is safe. This is blackmail of the worst kind,' she said.

There had been some discussion about sending to Munich the same

Israeli military unit that had successfully stormed the hijacked Sabena plane, but the Germans did not seem to want this and the general consensus among the Israelis was that the authorities in Bonn were both fully conscious of the weight of their responsibility and capable of meeting it.

Massalha's first communiqué had set a deadline. It had explained that if their captors' demands were not met by 9 a.m. West German time, the hostages would be shot one by one. Any attempt by the Germans to 'interfere' would lead to their immediate 'liquidation'. Hundreds of police were now at the village and senior German officials had gathered too. These included the head of Munich's police, state as well as federal ministers and members of the organising committee of the games. They had no prepared strategy and no one had any clear idea of what to do. Germany's chancellor Willy Brandt had been informed of the attack but was not directly involved in planning the response.

This meant the immediate priority for the Germans was to win time. They gained three extra hours by convincing Massalha that they were waiting for a response from the Israeli government, then a further hour by promising that the Israelis were going to agree to the hostage-takers' demands. The scornful rejection of an offer to Massalha of a substantial amount of money in exchange for the hostages prompted some bewilderment. All this took them to around 1 p.m., and was followed by a lengthy pause, punctuated by intermittent attempts at negotiations. By mid-afternoon, with a fourth deadline now approaching, Massalha was becoming increasingly angry and suspicious.

The reality was that the West German officials remained without any workable strategy for resolving the crisis. The German foreign ministry had contacted half a dozen Arab governments, hoping they could act as intermediaries or offer some kind of solution, but none seemed willing to help. A suggestion that some kind of 'knock-out gas' might be used to facilitate a rescue was discussed at length then rejected, wasting valuable time. A plan to somehow seize the gunmen when food was delivered to 31 Connollystrasse was shown to be utterly impractical when a feeble attempt was made to put it into action. Massalha and Tony were obviously the leaders but had not yet been identified and nothing was known about them that might help negotiations. No one even had any idea exactly what group they represented. Nor was there any military or police unit trained for the complex and risky job of an armed assault to free the hostages, should they want to attempt one. No such force existed either in Germany or anywhere in the world outside Israel.

Shortly before yet another deadline was due to expire at 5 p.m., Massalha followed the instructions he had been given by Odeh and told the German officials he wanted two planes to fly the attackers and their hostages to Cairo. There were more talks, and the Germans agreed to provide a single aircraft which they said would be ready in two hours. In the meantime, they would try to contact the Egyptian government, they said. Officials had a brief shouted conversation with Andre Spitzer, the Israeli fencing coach, who had been brought to a first-floor window in order to talk. Calm but evidently very frightened, Spitzer had only time to say that the hostages were 'OK . . . except for one' and that he was prepared to be flown to a third country, before he was hit with a rifle butt and pulled back into the building. 'We are doing everything we can to get you released,' Hans-Dietrich Genscher, the German interior minister shouted to him as he disappeared from view.

The events at 31 Connollystrasse were by now being broadcast live by ABC, the US network that had paid $13.5 million for the rights to lead coverage of the games. This streaming of events to viewers around the globe was a recent innovation, made possible by a series of rapid advances in audiovisual technology over the previous decade. By the middle of the afternoon, an estimated 500 million were watching. The nature of the breaking story, with its single location, led to another significant innovation: ABC's cameras were trained on the scene of the hostage-taking without break, allowing producers to offer viewers a single unbroken live shot of the outside of 31 Connollystrasse hour after hour.

Some chose to watch in person. Tens of thousands had abandoned the boxing, dressage or gymnastics and gathered on the sunny, grassy slopes overlooking the Olympic village. In front of them were hundreds of photographers. More spectators arrived after 4 p.m. when scheduled sporting events were reluctantly suspended by the games' organisers. Less than an hour later, the excitement of the crowd palpably mounted when a team of a dozen armed police officers began moving into position on the roof of the apartment.

These armed men were indeed a makeshift assault team. With no specialist unit available, the German officials had asked for volunteers from a Munich police squad that dealt with organised crime and so had some experience of handling firearms. The policemen had no experience of close-quarter urban combat, though, let alone the kind of highly specialised operation they were about to attempt. Nor was there any reliable information on the number of attackers they would face, let alone where they were posted within the building or what weapons they possessed, nor of the location or condition of their prisoners. Wearing brightly coloured tracksuits and basic body armour, equipped only with antiquated automatic weapons or their service revolvers, the police team planned to gain access to the apartment through ventilation shafts and then somehow overpower the hostage-takers. One later described the effort as 'a suicide mission'. Certainly, their chances of success were low, and the probability of casualties very high.

The skills of the amateur assault team were never put to the test. As the armed policemen climbed gingerly across balconies to take up positions adjacent to or above the rooms where the hostages were thought to be held, they were visible not only to the crowds gathered a few hundred yards away, who shouted encouragement and advice, but to millions of TV viewers too. Later, it would be frequently reported that Massalha was among them, watching on a television in the house at 31 Connollystrasse, and that he had immediately and furiously demanded that the police pull back. In fact, 'Operation Sunshine', as the rescue attempt had optimistically been named, was called off by authorities because they believed Massalha's request for an aircraft to fly the attackers and the hostages to an Arab capital offered new opportunities to intervene in more favourable circumstances. A further round of fruitless efforts to win the co-operation of Arab governments reinforced the apparent need to act decisively, and rapidly.

An hour or so later, as the shadows began to lengthen over Connollystrasse, the Germans conceived a new plan to free the hostages. It was ambitious and risky but Genscher and the local police believed it could work. First, Massalha needed to be convinced that the Germans would actually provide the plane he had requested. Then, when the attackers and hostages walked through the underground car park below Connollystrasse to the helicopters that were to fly them to the aircraft, armed police could strike. If this failed, the Palestinians and all the hostages would be flown to Fürstenfeldbruck airfield, a military airbase twenty miles outside Munich, where a trap had been laid. A Lufthansa plane would be waiting, apparently ready to fly everyone to Cairo. When Massalha and Tony came to inspect the plane, as they would surely do, they would both be shot dead by a dozen armed policemen disguised as its cabin crew. The death of the two leaders would deal such a terrible psychological blow to the rest of the gunmen that they would surrender, the German officials believed, but even if they did not, a team of marksmen was to be positioned around the airfield to kill or incapacitate them all. The hostages would be freed. German honour would be saved. The games could go on.

The very first element of the plan went relatively smoothly: Massalha, though suspicious, agreed to the arrangements proposed by the Germans. After that, things began to go wrong. In the dark car park, Massalha very quickly became aware of the police sharpshooters moving behind the concrete pillars either side of him and refused to go any further. The Germans were forced to resort to their back-up plan. At 10 p.m. a bus pulled up at 31 Connollystrasse's basement door, allowing the gunmen and their prisoners to board without walking through the underground car park. They were then driven the short distance to the waiting helicopters. For some moments, the gunmen stood smiling and posing with their weapons as Massalha hurried the hostages, bound at the wrists and to one another, onto the aircraft. The helicopters then took off for Fürstenfeldbruck amid camera flashes and shouts from thousands of onlookers.

At 10.40 the two helicopters landed at the airfield, and the gunmen stepped to the ground. The journey had taken much longer than Massalha and Tony had anticipated – the pilots had deliberately flown slowly to allow a third helicopter to ferry senior officials from the Olympic village to Fürstenfeldbruck ahead of them – and they now suspected that they were being set up. Nonetheless, just as hoped, the two men began to walk towards the Lufthansa Boeing 707 passenger jet parked 150 yards away. From the airport's administration block, the German authorities watched as the gunmen reached the plane and moved to mount the steps leading to its open cabin door. Then, seconds later, they came running back towards the helicopters, shouting in alarm.

Much later, the multiple failures at Fürstenfeldbruck would become brutally clear. Less than a minute before the gunmen and hostages arrived at the airfield, the police officers hidden in the plane had decided that any attempt to ambush Massalha and Tony could well result in their own deaths and so decided to abandon their mission. They were not convinced that their thin disguise as cabin crew would fool anyone. And so far as they knew the plane's fuel tanks were brim-full, so a stray grenade or even a round from an AK-47 could cause a massive explosion. Either way, their decision meant the entire responsibility of freeing the hostages now fell on the marksmen.

The import of this was lost on no one. When the Bavarian official who commanded the operation from the airfield's administration block was informed that the men in the plane had pulled out, he shouted: 'What am I supposed to do now?' The marksmen lying in the dark around the airfield could well have posed the same question. They were not trained snipers, had been on duty for fourteen hours and were badly positioned. They had telescopic sights but no helmets, body armour or any means of communication. Crucially, their ability to actually make out any target was limited because the three lighting masts that had been hastily rigged around the helicopters' landing zone were too weak to illuminate the whole of the concrete apron. Worst of all, there were only five of them. The idea had been for them to shoot one hostage-taker each. It was only when Massalha led his men out of the Olympic village that it had become clear to the German officials that there were in fact eight attackers, three more than they had counted on.

The police marksmen had a go anyway. But their immediate priority had changed. Instead of shooting first at Massalha and Tony, they were ordered to shoot at the Palestinians standing around the helicopters that had landed in front of Fürstenfeldbruck's administration block. This was because the helicopters' pilots had not been allowed to walk away from their aircraft as agreed, but appeared to be being held at gunpoint. These initial shots killed one of the Palestinians and wounded a second. But by then the element of surprise had been lost and a second round of firing merely succeeded in wounding Tony in the lower leg as he ran back across the apron from the Lufthansa plane. Within seconds, the five other unwounded Palestinians, including Massalha himself, had scattered into the deep shadows around the helicopters and a firefight ensued. The officials in the administration block were forced to throw themselves to the floor as bullets shattered glass and furnishings around them. A thirty-five-year-old policeman beside the control tower was hit by a bullet in the head. 'We all felt paralysed,' Manfred Schreiber, the Bavarian police official in charge of the operation, said later.

Massalha and his men were sufficiently well-trained to know that their ammunition – not more than sixty rounds each – would not last long if they fired indiscriminately, and the initial chaos and noise of the firefight soon subsided into sporadic exchanges between the marksmen, who could barely make out their targets, and the gunmen now almost invisible in the darkness. At least two of the attackers did not fire at all – their Kalashnikov rifles were eventually retrieved with full magazines – and one fired only twice. Through it all, the nine Israeli hostages, some still blindfolded and bound, remained immobile in the helicopters.

The end came shortly before midnight amid more chaos and incompetence. Where there should have been speed, there had been delay: a squad of armoured cars sent earlier to the Olympic village was summoned to Fürstenfeldbruck some ninety minutes after the shooting had started and had then run into traffic jams: no one had thought to close the roads to the hordes of onlookers as they tried to follow the drama. Then, where there should have been delay, there was haste: having finally arrived at Fürstenfeldbruck the armoured cars drove straight onto the airfield and fast towards the helicopters.

Exactly what happened in the next few seconds is unclear. Massalha and the gunmen had no way of taking on several armoured vehicles equipped with spotlights and machine guns and, though their orders had been to avoid harming the hostages if possible, they had been told to kill them all if the operation 'became a hopeless military situation'. As the armoured cars closed in, one of Massalha's men fired off his remaining ammunition, possibly into the cabin of one helicopter. A vast sheet of flame suddenly consumed the entire front half of the aircraft, perhaps caused by a grenade set off by one of the attackers or a flare fired by the police, igniting fuel. The four hostages inside were incinerated. Some witnesses described a second gunman firing into the cabin of the other helicopter, where four other Israelis were sitting. A marksman then killed Massalha, who had stood up and was shooting at the airfield buildings. There was further confusion as the surviving gunmen scattered. Finally, the police deployed dogs to hunt them down. Two were shot, including Tony who was killed after a prolonged exchange of fire by the perimeter fence, and three were captured.

Dawn was still several hours away. At the airport, fourteen people lay dead: in the charred helicopters, on the scorched concrete, and spreadeagled in the grass. A fifteenth, the critically injured policeman, had died in an ambulance on the way to a nearby hospital. At 3.17 a.m., Reuters news agency released an urgent update, telling thousands of editors around the world: 'All Israeli hostages seized by Arab guerrillas killed.' The West German authorities had still not even worked out which group the attackers were from.

9
The Black September Organisation

Just days after the last shots had been fired at Fürstenfeldbruck, German authorities received a request from Libya, where some wealthy businessmen were ready to pay for the transfer of the attackers' remains and their funerals. This was a fiction to hide the identity of the real donor: Muammar Gaddafi, the former military officer now in the third year of his rule, who may well have funded the whole operation in Munich and conceivably even commissioned it. Anxious to assuage anger in the Arab world, where many had been incensed by the deception practised on the fedayeen at Fürstenfeldbruck, the West German foreign ministry broke with customary practice and told Bavarian authorities it had no objection to the attackers' bodies being sent to Tripoli.

Less than a week later, millions across the Middle East and beyond watched footage of the vast crowd accompanying the coffins from the centre of the Libyan capital to the Sidi Munaidess cemetery, where prayers were said over the remains of the 'martyrs'. King Hussein of Jordan had condemned the violence in Munich as 'a horrible crime' that was the work of 'sick minds who are opposed to humanity' but was the only Arab ruler to do so. The semi-official *El Mojahed* newspaper in Algeria blamed Israel's intransigence for the attack but stopped short of expressing explicit approval. Egypt's official news agency described the funeral as a 'majestic spectacle'. A broadcast from Damascus offered 'congratulations on the revolution and on the new man who is bearing the banner of Arabism on the path to victory'. British diplomats in Tripoli informed London that the event had been a 'typical, Arab, shambolic occasion'.

Mohammed Odeh, the Fatah veteran who had been running the operation from his hotel in Munich, had watched the helicopters containing the hostages and their captors take off from the Olympic village on a television in the hotel lounge, surrounded by horrified tourists and travellers. Exhausted, he then fell asleep listening to the running commentary of events on a radio in his room and woke suddenly in the very early morning to learn what he later described as the 'appalling news' of the deaths of the hostages and all but three of the attackers. Within an hour, he was at Munich airport, with a seat booked on a flight to Rome and an attaché case containing the passports of all the men he had sent to the Olympic village less than thirty-six hours earlier. A few days later, he too reached Tripoli.

In Israel, there had been initial joy and relief when early media reports erroneously suggested that all the hostages taken to the airfield were safe. Only hours later did it become clear that the celebrations had been tragically premature. Ankie Spitzer, the wife of fencing coach Andre Spitzer, managed to get a call through to an Israeli journalist in the Olympic press centre in Munich and asked for news. There was a long pause, then the journalist simply said 'Ankie, I am with you.' Jim McKay, the ABC anchor, had been on air for fourteen hours when, with a voice close to breaking, he delivered the news to tens of millions of viewers, saying: 'When I was a kid my father used to say our greatest hopes and our worst fears are seldom realised. Well, tonight our worst fears have been realised . . . They're all gone.'

At an early morning press conference, West German authorities blamed the attackers for failing to make any mistakes, the Egyptians for failing to co-operate and the Israelis for refusing to negotiate. 'The decision of the Israeli state not to give in to the demands of the terrorists was the death sentence for the hostages,' read a statement from the police. Shmuel Lalkin, the Israeli delegation chief, flew to Fürstenfeldbruck to identify the remains of the victims. In Munich, surviving team members gathered the dead men's effects: sports gear, books, team scarves and caps given to them by other nations' athletes, presents for wives and children. In Herzliya, Ilan, Romano's widow, gathered her three daughters, the oldest aged six, and told them that their father was dead.

At 10 a.m. the next day there was a memorial service in the main arena in Munich. The Olympic flag flew at half-mast and the Munich Philharmonic Orchestra played the funereal second movement from Beethoven's Third Symphony. A plane was arranged to fly the body of David Berger, a twenty-eight-year-old weightlifter, to Ohio and his family, while the remains of the other ten Israeli casualties were flown to Lod airport where a vast and silent crowd waited. Dan Alon, the fencer, remembered expecting to hear 'a great keening' when he stepped out of the aircraft into the bright sunlight. Instead, he was greeted by a 'stark, white soundlessness'.

Many Israelis later described the trauma of Munich in terms more usually reserved for major conflicts. Recent years had seen a significant decline in cross-border incursions and raids by armed Palestinian groups, and though Israelis were still being killed in sporadic attacks there was a general sense that the battle against Palestinian militants had been won. As early as 1969, Shimon Peres, an urbane Israeli bureaucrat and politician, had described the fedayeen as a 'temporary myth kept alive abroad'. Moshe Dayan, the maverick soldier turned politician then serving as defence minister, was dismissive of the threat posed by terrorist attacks, claiming that road accidents caused more deaths in Israel. The successful end to the hijacking of the Sabena plane at Lod in May 1972 reinforced the impression that the worst of such violence was over, even if that incident had been swiftly followed by the bloody shooting at the same airport by Fusako Shigenobu's Japanese Red Army.

Such triumphalism was not universal in Israel, nor was the general lack of interest in the past or future of the million or so Arabs who lived either in Israel or, since 1967, in the territories under Israeli military occupation. The Israeli novelist Amos Oz said that Palestinians had a right to live in Palestine equivalent to that of Iraqis to live in Iraq or the Dutch to live in Holland, and a new peace movement took baby steps. Just a year before the Munich attack, Israeli journalist Amos Elon wrote in a bestselling book that the persecution in Europe that had culminated in the Holocaust had 'imbued the Zionist settlers with the relentless drive of drowning men who force their way on to a life raft large enough to hold both them and those who were already on it'. Yet, the raft was smaller than it looked and 'the Arabs bore no responsibility for the centuries-long suffering of Jews in Europe . . . [But] were punished because of it.' Even some senior soldiers and spies argued that force alone would not suffice and that only a durable political settlement would resolve the problem posed to Israel by the Palestinians.

But most Israelis were feeling more secure than they had for many years, and were proud of their expanded borders. The economy had benefited from the cheap labour offered by the poor Arabs of the West Bank and Gaza as well as an influx of tourists after the 1967 war. Many Israelis had themselves travelled into the West Bank to view biblical sites, float in the Dead Sea and bargain in exotic markets for souvenirs.

More began to travel to Europe or the US. The numbers of private cars on Israel's roads had doubled in a decade, most households had fridges and almost all had radios. When it came so unexpectedly in the autumn of 1972, the Munich attack badly shook the nation's new-found but brittle confidence, evoking memories of recent and less recent violence that many hoped to forget. Shops remained closed, people gathered on corners talking quietly, families came together. As significantly, the failures of the West Germans reinforced the profound sense of many Israelis that when it came to their security, abroad or at home, they could rely only on themselves.

Golda Meir, the seventy-two-year-old prime minister, had taken power in 1969 at the head of a fragile alliance of left-wing parties after her predecessor had a heart attack. A committed Zionist from her teens, she had been born in Ukraine, grown up in the US and emigrated to Palestine in 1921, first working on a kibbutz, then rising rapidly through the ranks of the labour movement and finally through a series of senior government posts in the left-wing Mapai, the 'Party of the Workers of the Land of Israel' that had been in power since 1948. Meir's deep, rasping smoker's voice, laconic wit and matronly advice charmed world leaders from Richard Nixon to Charles de Gaulle but even supporters admitted she was stubborn and unsubtle in her thinking. Many Israeli critics went much further, describing her as abrasive, inarticulate and insecure. In the Middle East, Meir's reflexive hostility to Arabs and outright denial of the existence of anything resembling a 'Palestinian nation' made her reviled.

The Israeli government's immediate response to the Munich attacks was entirely predictable. Within days, F-4 Phantom jets recently supplied by the US had bombed a series of targets in Lebanon and Syria described by Israeli government spokesmen as 'training bases'. Any fighters had long deserted the facilities and several of the sites were close to, or even within, refugee camps. This led to claims that the raids killed as many as 200 civilians, which Israeli officials denied. Just over a week later, armoured and infantry columns moved into southern Lebanon where they destroyed around a hundred houses in Palestinian villages which the Israelis said sheltered or at least supported fedayeen groups. What evidence they had for these assertions was unclear, and despite the Israelis' insistence that their targets were purely military, American diplomats worried that faulty intelligence seemed to cause significant civilian casualties 'on every occasion'. Such 'errors' in the information supplied to bomber pilots and artillery men seemed to be oddly systematic, the Beirut embassy cabled to Washington.

Few within Israel's security establishment were under any illusions that air strikes or shelling would significantly weaken those responsible for the massacre in Munich. Indeed, the real problem was definitively deciding who that might actually be. Israel's principal civilian overseas intelligence service, the Institute for Intelligence and Special Tasks – HaMossad leModi'in U'leTafkidim Meyuchadim in Hebrew, more commonly known as the Mossad – had been caught unprepared by the Munich attack. Its focus was the threat posed by hostile neighbouring states and their allies, not the supposedly defeated fedayeen. The safety of Israelis overseas had not been a priority and the country's Olympic team had never been seen as vulnerable. Nor had the Mossad or the Shin Bet, the agency responsible for internal security, thoroughly pursued the few leads that might have given advance warning of the attack. Responsibility for the safety of the delegation to Munich had been given to a minor functionary in the ministry of education.

But for officials, investigators and analysts scrambling to establish what had gone wrong and prevent further attacks, one name stood out as a potential starting point. The statements given by the Munich attackers to the authorities at the Olympic village had been initialled BSO. To those in the know, these were the initials of a group who called themselves the Black September Organisation.

The first clue had come in November of 1971 when the hardline Jordanian prime minister Wasfi Tal had been shot dead by a group of young Palestinians in a hotel lobby in Cairo. While one of the killers knelt to touch his fingers in the dead man's pooling blood and raise them to his lips, another had shouted 'Black September' at the appalled onlookers. This was understood at the time to be an explanation for the attack: a reference to the assault launched by the Jordanian military against the fedayeen just over a year earlier, known widely as 'Black September', in which Tal had played a prominent role. In fact, it was a claim of responsibility.

Over the following months, further evidence emerged that a new armed Palestinian faction was at large. Weeks after the attack in Cairo, a gunman emptied a submachine gun's entire magazine at the Jordanian ambassador as he was driven through the middle of Knightsbridge. A combination of poor aim and the quick reflexes of the embassy driver meant no one was hurt, but there was more to come. The bombing of major oil facilities in the Netherlands, which was seen as pursuing pro-Israeli policies, was followed swiftly by an attack on a West German factory making machine parts for export to Israel. All of these appeared to investigators to be connected to something called the Black September Organisation. In May 1972, meanwhile, the two surviving hijackers of the Sabena plane diverted to Lod told their Israeli interrogators that they had been recruited by Fatah and that, just hours before the attack, they had been informed by those running the operation that they were now members of something called 'Black September'. Finally, in August, responsibility for the bombing of a major oil refinery and storage facility in Trieste was claimed in a statement issued in the name of the group. Then came the attack on the Olympics, and the issuance of demands using the acronym BSO.

A month after the debacle at the Olympics, the CIA circulated a background report on the various armed Palestinian groups they suspected of involvement in the attack. It explained that in the wake of the Jordanian offensive against the Palestinian armed groups in 1970, the fedayeen had lost not only their main base but much public support and credibility. Since then, the governments of Lebanon and Syria had both tightened restrictions on fedayeen activities, leaving 'terrorist operations outside Israel' as their only remaining weapon. The report argued that the increasingly spectacular operations in Europe were seen as great victories by the fedayeen, giving the 'flagging' armed struggle a much-needed 'shot in the arm', and that extremism and violence were likely to intensify in their wake.

The report went on to explain what had already become clear to many intelligence services and some informed journalists: 'Black September' was not really an independent organisation at all but a 'label' designed to distance the leadership of groups like Fatah from the violence. The reasons for this clumsy attempt at plausible deniability were not hard to see. The Soviets had repeatedly made clear their opposition to such 'adventurist' operations by the fedayeen. Nor were the Saudis or the Kuwaitis, major financial supporters of the Palestine Liberation Organisation, likely to be impressed by them. But the fiction was fooling hardly anyone. The CIA reported bluntly that the leadership of Fatah, which it described as 'the largest and heretofore the most moderate guerrilla organisation', and that of the Black September Organisation were 'closely entwined'. All the BSO's members were drawn from Fatah and there could be no doubt that Fatah's leaders knew of the planned attacks, the agency said.

What the CIA either failed or chose not to mention was that, despite its name, the Black September Organisation was not actually very organised. Rather than being a single group, it was more a flag of convenience being adopted by a number of different individuals and factions. Sometimes they co-operated with each other, but on the whole they were better understood as rivals, denigrating each other's attacks, poaching each other's best operatives and competing for resources. A second intelligence report, compiled by the US Embassy staff in Beirut, spoke of 'ad hoc' cells that formed for specific operations. According to *Time* magazine's correspondent in Beirut, fedayeen leaders insisted that Black September was 'less an organisation than a state of mind', with 'no flag, no symbol, no offices', leaders who were 'shadowy, constantly shifting and unknown' and members 'drawn from all guerrilla factions . . . known only when they are killed or captured'. The three men who had sat at the table in the Piazza della Rotonda had comprised one such faction within Fatah, but there were several others.

This chaos, confusion and competition had some advantages. It allowed Fatah's leader Yasser Arafat to play his various lieutenants off against one another, channel the energies of the more radical among them, and satisfy those who felt that his preference for a classic guerrilla war against Israel was misguided. It also reinforced his increasingly tattered revolutionary credentials inside Fatah while just about keeping the violence they perpetrated at a deniable distance. But such subtleties were largely beyond the grasp of many Western security agencies.

Though the CIA had analysts in the Middle East and ran a very small number of very mediocre agents there, much of its understanding of what was happening within the Palestinian movement was derived from other security services. Its western European allies occasionally came up with good material – such as the Swedes who shared the information provided by Gunnar Ekberg with the US – and many governments and actors in the Middle East had their own ad hoc and self-serving reasons for offering knowledge (or sometimes falsehood) to the US. Relations with the Mossad were prickly, but those with the Jordanian intelligence services were excellent, so it was from Amman rather than Tel Aviv that the CIA sourced much of its best information. Both Israeli and Jordanian services ran their own agents within Fatah, the PFLP and other groups, and both also received information from third parties.

The Mossad sometimes learned of developments among Palestinian factions from Turkish agencies which had successfully infiltrated elites in Damascus, for example, or from Iran's increasingly capable intelligence services.

Inevitably, what the spies passed to each other was partial and highly selective. No one sharing intelligence did so without some kind of agenda. Though allies of the US knew better than to attempt to mislead Washington with outright disinformation, they were well aware that, with care, they could selectively deploy the intelligence they gathered to influence its decisions. Many of the dossiers sent by the Jordanians in 1972, for example, focused heavily on the complicity of other states, such as Algeria and Libya, in the attacks of the previous year. The CIA saw such claims as highly plausible, even if definitive proof remained hard to come by, and strongly suspected that Gaddafi's officials had at least provided the weapons used at Munich. In contrast, fairly far-fetched Israeli claims that the Egyptians sponsored fedayeen violence in western Europe were dismissed as unfounded.

The man responsible for such calls was the head of the CIA's Middle East desk, a tall, square-jawed steelworker's son from Philadelphia called Robert Ames who habitually wore cowboy boots and aviator shades but had a genuine affection for the Middle East. He also spoke excellent Arabic, had travelled widely, and was considerably more sympathetic to the Palestinian cause than many of his colleagues. One reason for this was his friendship with a senior member of Fatah who was very close to Arafat. This source had been given a cryptonym or codename: MJTRUST/2. Ames had seen MJTRUST/2 many times after an initial encounter in 1969 when Ames had been based in Beirut. The two men repeatedly dined together, visited each other's homes and remained in contact after the American moved back to the US.

In late 1970, another senior official in the CIA had tried to recruit MJTRUST/2 as a fully-fledged agent, offering very large sums of money at meetings in luxury hotels in Rome. This move had been resisted by Ames and backfired badly. Despite a flamboyant lifestyle, Ames' contact had no need of additional funds and was absolutely committed to the Palestinian cause. His dealings with Ames had been motivated not by greed, nor even by any special affection for the US, but by their personal friendship, the potential protection the relationship offered him, and the advantage it brought over rivals within Fatah. MJTRUST/2 was also well aware that having a confidential channel of communication to the most powerful clandestine intelligence service in the world and so, through it, to the most senior ranks of the US government, was very useful. As Ames had predicted, MJTRUST/2 had been grossly insulted by the clumsy offer of financial reward made in Rome and had broken off the relationship with the CIA immediately.

In the aftermath of the attack at the Olympics, Ames asked an intermediary to reach out again to his old friend. The identity of the contact was known to only a very few people within the CIA and only one person in Fatah – Arafat himself. Ames strongly suspected that his friend had played some role in the wave of Black September attacks over the previous ten months. A key and very obvious question was whether MJTRUST/2 had been involved in the Munich attack itself.

Shortly after the first attack linked to the Black September Organisation, a suave and handsome Palestinian began travelling extensively around western Europe and the Middle East. He remained discreet about his identity, even while he was flamboyant in many other respects. His presence alone prompted questions: who was this man, six feet tall, with his wallet full of local currency and US dollars, with his bodyguards and good humour despite the apparent seriousness of his business? He was clearly young, maybe twenty-eight, twenty-nine years old, with broad forehead, thick dark hair and sideburns, and almost certainly an Arab, but probably not an Algerian as his passport, no doubt false, suggested. A businessman or a wealthy tourist perhaps? Whoever he was, he was obviously at ease as he drove from city to city and across frontiers in Europe, speaking passable English, excellent German, even a little French, frequently changing hotels and cars.

Physically fit, his broad chest revealed by unbuttoned shirts, and casually elegant, seen usually in a black leather jacket and tight trousers or tailored suits, he wore a Swiss platinum watch and had a packet of American cigarettes never far from hand. Some of his pleasures were sophisticated and expensive – French wine, Scotch whisky, rented sports cars – while others, such as his taste for Elvis and Sinatra, were less so. Women were attracted to him, and he to them. This was a weakness he was happy to indulge; others he preferred to hide.

In 1971, he was seen in Paris, where he had contacts among Palestinian political and cultural circles, as well as in Frankfurt and Stuttgart, where he met various members of the growing Palestinian student community, as well as some well-known activists. He had lots of friends in Rome too, where his contacts included not just Arabs but activists from a whole range of extremist organisations: Maoists, Marxists, Trotskyists, Third Worldists, revolutionaries of all kinds, even some from the other end of the political spectrum too. His trail was picked up in the Netherlands, and in Geneva, where he met some well-known right-wing extremists and François Genoud, an extremely wealthy neo-Nazi banker who was supportive of the Palestinian cause and familiar to local intelligence services. He was often seen in the company of middle-ranking officials at Middle Eastern embassies – a deputy trade attaché, the head of the visa section – and wherever he went and whatever he did, money was never a problem. Though his entourage swelled occasionally to double figures, everyone, whether bodyguard, assistant or humble bag carrier, enjoyed their own room in whichever luxury hotel he had chosen to patronise. He preferred a suite, of course.

Some of his friends knew he did something important for Fatah. The better informed among them referred to him as Abu Hassan, the name he had used when running training camps in Jordan for European volunteers between 1968 and late 1970. This had been a tedious job with its share of frustrations – a group of fractious and opinionated Germans led by a bumptious young man called Andreas Baader had been particularly trying. Others knew his real name, and how close he was to Arafat, 'Abu Ammar' himself. They knew too that following the disastrous fighting with the king's forces in Jordan in the final months of 1970, he had joined the other PLO fugitives in Beirut, which is where he was to be found whenever he was not travelling. A few perhaps knew something of his family – the young children, the long-suffering wife. Fewer were aware of the most exceptional aspect of his distinctly unordinary life, which was hardly surprising, as to share that particular piece of information would probably get you killed.

Those who knew his real name – Ali Hassan Salameh – would have known that nothing about him could be understood without knowing something of his father. Born the son of an illiterate day labourer who worked the fields of Jewish settlers near the town of Lod (or Lydda, as the Palestinians knew it), Salameh *père* had made a name for himself during the unrest that became known as the Arab Revolt, which had broken out in 1936. Through the astute manipulation of alliances and via targeted violence, Salameh's father gathered first a small band of followers around his village, and then expanded his operations, earning more recruits, wealth and vital weapons. Among his various exploits was a famous raid to destroy the railway line to Haifa. When eventually the British crushed the rebellion, deploying the full range of brutal tactics they had developed policing their empire over the previous century, Salameh's father, a price of £10,000 on his head, fled to Syria and thence to Iraq where, in 1942, he received training from the recently installed pro-Palestinian, anti-British, pro-Nazi government.

From Iraq, he travelled to Berlin in the entourage of Haj el Amin al-Husseini, the former Mufti of Jerusalem and a pre-eminent, if controversial, Palestinian political leader. Al-Husseini saw the Nazis as an ally in the bitter struggle with the Zionists and in 1944 dispatched his protégé as part of an effort to destabilise British rule in Palestine. Salameh senior parachuted into the West Bank with two German officers to launch an ambitious project of sabotage, which may have involved introducing lethal poisons into the water supply of Tel Aviv. The Germans were swiftly caught but Salameh, though badly wounded, escaped once more to Syria. Three years later he returned, and in June 1948, just over two weeks after the foundation of Israel, he died of shrapnel wounds during fierce fighting for a strategic promontory overlooking the Jerusalem road. His only son – Ali Hassan Salameh – was six years old.

From Damascus the bereaved family now moved to Beirut, where they had more connections. As the widow of a notable war hero, Ali Hassan's mother received donations that allowed her son to be sent to the famous Makassed College and then to a private boarding school at Bir Zeit in the West Bank. In 1958 President Gamal Abdel Nasser himself invited the famous Salameh family to Cairo, where the now teenaged Ali Hassan joined Cairo University to study engineering. When he turned twenty in 1962, he was married to the daughter of a well-known, wealthy Palestinian family. Within a year, his wife gave birth to a son, called Hassan too, allowing Salameh to be known henceforth as Abu, or father of, Hassan. A year after the wedding, Salameh graduated and travelled first to Switzerland to work on his languages and then to Düsseldorf, where he learned fluent German, partied, lifted weights, applied himself occasionally to his postgraduate studies in engineering and showed no interest whatsoever in politics.

And yet he had ambitions – or rather, obligations – that went well beyond earning a decent living to support his young family. 'The influence of my father posed a personal problem to me,' he said in the one interview he ever gave, much later. 'I grew up in a family which considered struggle a matter of heritage which should be carried on by generation after generation . . . When my father fell . . . Palestine was passed to me, so to speak . . . I was made constantly conscious of the fact that I was the son of Hassan Salameh and had to live up to that, even without being told how the son of Hassan Salameh should live.'

Others would decide this for him. On his return from Germany in 1965, Salameh was found a job in the office of the recently created Palestine Liberation Organisation (PLO) in Kuwait, where he was swiftly drawn into the vibrant new Palestinian nationalist scene. Here he was also sought out by Salah Khalaf, the Fatah founder member who would mastermind the Munich attack seven years later, who now invited this young man with a famous name to join his group. In the aftermath of the 1967 war, with Fatah's leader Arafat now chairman of the PLO and Fatah expanding rapidly, Salameh was redeployed. The unexpected flood of recruits prompted by the battle at Karameh brought a new risk of infiltration by its enemies, particularly Israel, and when Egyptian intelligence offered to train a select group from the organisation, Salameh was among those selected for the course. In August 1968, he travelled with a dozen others to a villa in Giza, within sight of the pyramids, for six weeks of instruction in combat, weapons, explosives, surveillance, counter-espionage and related dark arts. Despite his illustrious pedigree, Salameh proved a poor student, preferring the recreational opportunities offered by Cairo's nightclubs. He failed to read most of the texts set by instructors, came last in many of the written tests and faked sickness to avoid a route march across the desert.

Back in Amman, Salameh was tasked with vetting the new volunteers who were now overwhelming Fatah's recruitment centres. This was tedious, detailed work, and he soon tired of it, preferring to ride through the Jordanian capital in a convoy of Land Rovers packed with fighters kitted out in elaborately camouflaged uniforms and wielding powerful firearms. Charged with establishing so-called 'revolutionary bases' on the hills around Amman, the gunmen he recruited to these miniature strongholds distinguished themselves primarily by their 'anarchy, parasitic nature and ostentatious displays'. Salameh also returned frequently to Beirut, where he delivered rousing lectures to potential volunteers and performed best as a guide to foreign visitors. One was Jean-Luc Godard who had been invited by Fatah to make a film about their armed struggle. The suave, polyglot 'Abu Hassan', as Godard knew him, organised the French film director's visits to refugee and training camps and supplied him with a series of pithy quotes about the nature of revolutionary struggle.

Despite Salameh's obvious shortcomings and relative inexperience, Arafat liked the brash young Fatah functionary and, as tensions rose between the Jordanian authorities and the fedayeen, appointed him to lead his own team of bodyguards. During the fighting of late 1970, Salameh shared Arafat's hiding places and managed the complex logistics of his movements. When Arafat needed to get to Cairo for the talks organised by Nasser, it was Salameh who came up with a plan to disguise the most wanted man in Jordan as a Kuwaiti sheik. He then drove with Arafat through Jordanian military checkpoints and was at his side in the plane to Egypt.

But even Arafat could not shield his young protégé from criticism in the wake of the debacle of 1970. Those who had been the most hawkish beforehand were suddenly vulnerable in its aftermath, and Salameh had been vocal in advocating confrontation with King Hussein and his army, despite the misgivings of Khalaf and other more senior men. Salameh was stripped of his formal responsibilities, and found himself in Beirut without a formal role in an organisation in total disarray. Showing something of the unscrupulous verve and competitive instinct of his father, he now set about exploiting the chaos within Fatah and the opportunity offered by the creation of the Black September Organisation to overcome his recent setbacks and re-establish his leadership credentials.

By October 1972, many of the questions that had been asked about the mysterious man who criss-crossed Europe in hired cars with his platinum watch, expensive suits and habit of listening to 'Love Me Tender' had been answered. It was increasingly obvious that Salameh had been involved in a significant proportion of the attacks of the previous nine months. With several groups using the Black September Organisation name simultaneously, the exact lines of responsibility for any given attack remained blurred but Western intelligence services – and the Mossad – believed Salameh had organised both the attempted assassination of the Jordanian ambassador in London and the refinery bombings in the Netherlands. In fact, not only had Salameh organised both attacks, he had also been personally responsible for the bombing of the West German factory which took place shortly afterwards. As Italian and French investigators continued to probe the August attack on the fuel facilities in Trieste, evidence emerged that strongly suggested his involvement in that operation too.

But was Salameh involved in Munich? This was far less certain. Israeli intelligence services said they had telephone intercepts that placed him in East Berlin while the attack was taking place but did not release them, and when the Mossad had given a supposedly comprehensive list of those they deemed guilty to journalists in Germany in early October 1972, Salameh had not been included. A memo on Black September compiled by West German intelligence which reached their British counterparts around the same time listed Salameh but only as the organisation's 'chief of intelligence'. No one else appeared to have any information that suggested he had any connection to the attack on the Olympics either. In a classified briefing four months after Munich, US State Department officials in Washington referred to Salameh as a senior figure in Black September but pointed to Mohammed Odeh as the tactical commander and Khalaf as the mastermind. This was also the conclusion the Israelis reached, the American officials reported.

What was clear was that the Israelis were determined to end the activity of those they saw as responsible for the traumatic – and humiliating – violence at Munich, and would make strenuous efforts to do so. Against whom these efforts would be directed and what form they might take was unclear. Much depended on which group of people the Israelis deemed to pose the greatest threat, and which they had the opportunity to act against.

Even if he had not been responsible for the Munich attack, Ali Hassan Salameh was clearly to blame for a series of others that had caused tens of millions of dollars of damage. He had also shown himself to be a highly effective operator who was entirely prepared to use violence and, quite probably, lethal force. To observers in Washington, this was surely sufficient to make him a target for the Israelis. But the CIA knew one thing that the Mossad did not. Salameh was not just the leader of one of the most effective factions of Black September. He was also MJTRUST/2, the CIA's key source within Fatah. From now on, they would be keeping a very close eye on this hugely valuable asset. As for the precise nature of Israel's strategy, that would soon become apparent to everyone as the bodies began to pile up.

10
The Shadow War

In late November 1972, around ten weeks after the Munich Olympics attack, Golda Meir spent five hours with Oriana Fallaci, an Italian magazine journalist. The Israeli prime minister was at her most maternal and domestic, receiving Fallaci alone at her very modest home in Jerusalem and talking about how she did the cleaning late at night so as not to overburden her maid the next morning.

As she often did, Meir recounted her earliest memories of persecution in Russia, the family's poverty during her upbringing in Chicago and her excitement when she first learned about socialism. Unusually, she also spoke about her unhappy marriage, her disappointment at the failure to build a 'more just, more equal society' in Israel, and her lack of religious faith. She spoke too about Israel's response to terrorist attacks, admitting that the air strikes she had ordered on Lebanon and Syria were effective only 'to a certain extent'. Such raids would not bring peace, she said, but then men like Arafat or George Habash could not be considered human beings so what could you expect? War in the Middle East would undoubtedly continue for many, many years, she told Fallaci, fuelled by the indifference with which the Arab leaders sent their people off to die, but to allow the return of Palestinian refugees to what was now Israel was impossible, as 'for twenty years they have been fed on hatred for us'.

But the Palestinians, the Arabs and their leaders were not the immediate target of her fierce contempt and anger, which was reserved instead for the European governments that had consistently failed to take a tougher line against the 'terrorists' operating from their territory. Meir was well aware that of the dozens of men and women detained by European governments following terrorist acts, many of them directed at Israelis or Jewish communities, only a tiny proportion had spent longer than eighteen months in prison and many had been freed within weeks.

A month before she spoke to Fallaci, either the PFLP or Black September had hijacked a Lufthansa jet flying from Damascus to Frankfurt and the German authorities had bowed to their demand that they release the three Munich Olympics attackers captured at Fürstenfeldbruck. Arriving in Libya, the attackers had been feted as heroes and spoken at a well-attended press conference. This had 'physically sickened her', Meir said, and reinforced her conviction that Europeans cared neither about the deaths at the Olympics nor about fighting terrorism nor about Jews.

'The fact [is] that terrorism has its headquarters in Europe. In every European capital there are offices of so-called liberation movements, and you know very well it's not a matter of harmless offices. But you do nothing against them. You'll be sorry. Thanks to your inertia and your indulgence, terror will be multiplied and you'll pay the price of it too,' Meir told Fallaci.

The subject of Fallaci's last two questions was death. Did Meir fear her own? And had she ever killed anyone?

The answer to the first was straightforward: the prime minister's only worry was to die 'too late'. She was not well, and wanted to go with her faculties intact, her mind 'clear'. As for the second, Meir's response was more nuanced. 'There's no difference between killing and making decisions by which you send others to kill,' she told Fallaci. 'It's exactly the same thing. And maybe it's worse.'

Meir was talking from personal experience. Around two weeks after the last funerals of the victims of Munich, the prime minister had accepted a recommendation from her newly appointed counter-terrorism advisers and the heads of her intelligence services to dramatically expand their efforts against the fedayeen's networks in Europe. The clandestine war that would follow would last almost a year and be fought all over the continent and beyond. It would be waged in hotels, student hostels and safehouses, in airports, car hire offices and railway stations, in embassies, police cells and, on one occasion, a municipal swimming pool. Its victims would die on street corners or in cafés, beneath bombs or bisected by exploding telephones; one would be torn apart by an exploding mattress, another was gunned down by a future Israeli prime minister wearing women's clothes and a wig. Nothing about the conflict was predictable. If its climax took place in Beirut, its end came in an out-of-season Norwegian ski resort.

The principal tool that the Israelis deployed was a highly visible campaign of assassinations. One aim was to eliminate actors who might otherwise go on to harm Israelis. But its broader objective was to intimidate, disrupt and deter the country's enemies. The CIA had predicted that the Israelis would launch a campaign of 'counter terror' in the aftermath of Munich. British diplomats in Tel Aviv thought something similar, suggesting to London that Meir would seek to 'terrorise the terrorists', with teams of 'faceless men' whose existence could be officially denied 'turning the terrorists' [own] techniques and methods against them'. 'The Israelis can be just as, if not more, ruthless than the Arabs, certainly more efficient,' one diplomat wrote, pointing to Israel's efforts to trace and capture Nazi war criminals as proof. The Foreign Office later opened a file on the Israeli response to the attack in Munich which it labelled 'Israeli terrorist activities'.

The Israeli secret services had extensive experience of assassination. In the mid-1950s Israel's military intelligence had killed Egyptian officers in Gaza thought to be behind the recent wave of cross-border raids. A decade later the Mossad had sent lethal letter bombs to German scientists who were helping Egypt develop advanced rockets, prompting outrage in Europe. More recently, there had been several attempts to kill Arafat since Israeli officials belatedly recognised his importance, and in 1970 they had fired explosives into the Beirut home of Wadie Haddad of the PFLP, narrowly missing him and Leila Khaled, who was there at the time. They had also tried to assassinate George Habash but the bomb dropped by an Israeli jet over his villa outside Beirut missed its target. A year later, Ali Hassan Salameh had received a letter bomb at his apartment in the Lebanese capital. In July 1972, the Mossad had killed Ghassan Kanafani, the PFLP's chief spokesperson and editor of *al-Hadaf*, with a massive bomb which reduced the car he and his seventeen-year-old niece had been travelling in to twisted wreckage.

Kanafani was replaced by Bassam Abu Sharif, the self-assured young Popular Front official who had marshalled the international media during the 1970 hijackings in Jordan. Two weeks into the job he received a parcel at the PFLP offices in Beirut. Sharif was reassured by stamps indi[illegible]ing that the package had been put through a scanner at the city's central pos[illegible] and was excited to find it contained a thick biography of Che Guevara. When he opened the volume, Abu Sharif saw a bomb concealed in a hollowed cavity. Moments later there was an explosion. He survived but suffered very serious injuries to his eyes, face and hands from which he never fully recovered.

But the Israeli effort after Munich would be on a much larger scale. Meir had reservations, but to the prime minister and her advisers there appeared to be little alternative. There was significant domestic political pressure to show a firm response to the attack at the Olympics and a need to reassure millions of fearful and angry Israelis. Meanwhile, Black September's offensive had continued through the autumn of 1972. As well as the hijacking that led to the Germans' release of the Munich attackers, a Mossad *katsa*, or collections officer, had been shot and badly wounded by an informant in Brussels, and dozens of letter bombs had been arriving at Israeli embassies and businesses and at the homes of prominent Jewish figures all over the world. As the Mossad traced the devices, it became clear they had been dispatched from locations many thousands of miles apart. The first wave of bombs had been sent from within Europe, the second from East Asia and the third from India. Only one person was killed – an agricultural attaché at the embassy in London – but their provenance suggested that whole areas of the world harboured sympathisers who would assist the fedayeen and who were almost wholly unknown to Israeli intelligence services.

For at least the past three decades, the central doctrine of Israel's security and defence strategy had been the concept of an 'Iron Wall' of 'Jewish bayonets' – derived from a famous 1923 essay by the uncompromising Odessa-born Zionist ideologue Ze'ev Jabotinsky – as the only means of convincing their hostile Arab neighbours that resistance to the establishment and ongoing existence of a Jewish state was futile. Its more hawkish policy-makers and military leaders now argued that the Iron Wall needed not only to be reinforced but its perimeter pushed much further outwards. The challenges of sending operatives into busy Arab capitals and then exfiltrating them safely after an assassination or sabotage attempt were almost insuperable, and so the new Israeli effort would take place, initially at least, in a less hostile environment: the cities of western Europe.

Its first victim was Wael Zwaiter, a poet, writer and part-time translator working at the Libyan Embassy in Rome. Zwaiter was shot dead in the foyer of his modest apartment block as he returned late one evening after seeing an artist friend. The thirty-eight-year-old was unarmed, carrying his half-finished translation into Italian of *The Thousand and One Nights* and some home-baked bread. The Mossad was convinced Zwaiter had played an important role in an abortive attempt to bomb an El Al plane flying from Rome to Israel the previous summer and had also helped with logistics for the Munich attack. But if he was an international terrorist, he was a very poor and impractical one. Some days before he was killed his phone had been disconnected for non-payment, and associates spoke of him as a chaotically disorganised intellectual whose greatest passion was literature. Zwaiter had undoubtedly been a vocal supporter of the Palestinian cause and the de facto ambassador of the PLO in Rome, but there was limited hard evidence that he had ever been directly involved in any violence. When detained in an indiscriminate sweep by Italian police after the attack in Trieste three months earlier, he had been swiftly released. An Italian police report compiled after his death described him merely as Fatah's representative in Italy.

Meir insisted on political and legal oversight of the process by which individuals were selected as targets for assassination, and senior officials from outside of the military and intelligence services were involved in weighing every case. Mossad officials needed to present a dossier of evidence to justify any lethal operation, and here a key resource was reports from Western intelligence services, at least when they suggested a potential target's guilt. A network had been set up in 1971 which allowed eighteen nations, including Israel, to share raw intelligence on Palestinian armed groups active in western Europe. Codenamed Kilowatt, the system meant the Mossad and Shin Bet received a steady stream of timely and detailed information from counterparts in France, West Germany, Italy, Britain and others. It also allowed the Israelis to make sure a carefully curated selection of their own intelligence reached a very select group of western European security officials and sometimes, but not always, their political masters. After the Munich attack, thousands of reports about Palestinian suspects in western Europe and elsewhere circulated by encrypted telex through the system. Much was speculative or inaccurate but this did not always matter back in Israel, as the interrogation by Meir and others of evidence presented by the Mossad was often fairly cursory.

Nor was it simply the identity of victims that mattered. The Mossad's teams, which included forgers, communications experts and inventive bomb-makers, had been instructed not only to kill but to do so in spectacular and innovative ways that would 'evoke fear and trembling'. In mid-December 1972, operatives from one such team broke into the Paris apartment of Mahmoud Hamshari, the PLO's representative in the French capital, and inserted plastic explosives into the base of his telephone. They then called the line, intending to detonate the bomb when he answered. A first effort failed because the remote control within the device was too weak. The Mossad sent a more powerful version, disguised as an ordinary radio to evade detection at border control, which worked. Hamshari was badly injured and died in hospital some weeks later. Again, there was little solid evidence to connect him with any actual violence, let alone Munich. Hamshari was close to Arafat and worked hard to promote the Palestinian cause. Reports reaching Israel through the Kilowatt network suggested he had provided some logistical assistance for one or two attacks, but most of his work was political and diplomatic. Senior French police officers and diplomats certainly had no reservations about meeting Hamshari on a regular basis.

Nor was there much effort to disguise responsibility for the death in Paris of a forty-year-old professor of law at the American University of Beirut called Basil al-Kubaisi. Approached on a street corner by two men as he returned from a meal to his modest pension on the rue de l'Arcade, al-Kubaisi had time to say 'No, No' before shots rang out and he collapsed with nine bullets in his body. Al-Kubaisi's sympathy for the Popular Front's activities were plain – he was one of its leading intellectuals and was in Paris as part of a tour to reinvigorate flagging support for the organisation among European leftists. His direct links to any recent attacks were more equivocal, however. Shortly afterwards, another representative of the PLO – this time in Cyprus – was killed by a powerful bomb placed in his bed in a hotel in Nicosia. There was little evidence this new victim was linked either to Black September or directly to any violent acts.

The fact that many of their targets were connected only tenuously, if at all, to Munich did not concern the Mossad's senior officials or its agents in the field. In their view, the use of 'counter terror' was entirely justified. Nonetheless, as the campaign continued, the Mossad's methods became marginally more subtle. Sometimes it was not deemed necessary to kill in order to get their message across. Relatives of suspected members of Black September were sent flowers with anonymous condolence notes even while they were still alive; others woke to read obituaries of their brothers and sons in local Arabic newspapers; anonymous threats were telephoned to minor functionaries or their wives.

The Mossad's campaign, sometimes referred to as Operation Wrath of God, has been portrayed as a methodical and forensic application of lethal force. In reality, it was often none of these things. The service was given no vast infusion of funds to carry out the campaign, nor did it have the time to recruit and train large numbers of new operatives. Instead, it improvised, drawing heavily on informal support networks among Jewish communities across western Europe and beyond. The actual assassins were seconded by the military, as no one with such aptitudes existed within the Mossad itself. The result was chaotic and subject to the same inefficiencies and frustrations that characterise many government initiatives.

Meanwhile, the threat from the Palestinian factions was only one among many, and far from the most serious, and there was much else for the Israeli intelligence services to be doing: monitoring the intent of hostile states such as Egypt or Syria and the capabilities of their militaries, liaising with allies, obtaining crucial technology through clandestine means, monitoring the movement of the few Jews allowed to leave the Soviet Union, counter-espionage and more. As the Mossad was not a big agency, the new initiative ordered by Meir put immense strain on its resources. The pressure was perhaps greatest on those tasked with getting the intelligence that might be fed to the assassination teams or might prevent a forthcoming attack.

One such individual was a thirty-seven-year-old katsa called Baruch Cohen, whose task was to travel around the continent from his base in Brussels recruiting and interviewing agents. A careful man, aware of his responsibilities both to his young family and the service, Cohen nonetheless fell into a trap laid by Salah Khalaf, the head of Fatah's intelligence service. The Mossad, working with the Shin Bet, found they could often recruit young Palestinians overseas who had family in Gaza or the West Bank. In the time-honoured way, if inducements such as money or medical treatment for relatives did not work, threats were usually effective. In this instance, a young student in Madrid was convinced by a mixture of both to work for Cohen. Discovered or betrayed to Fatah's own spies, he was offered a choice by Khalaf: execution or the chance to clear his name by luring his Mossad handler to a final meeting. Understandably, the student took the latter option. Incapable of handling weapons himself, he was followed to the rendezvous in a bar in the centre of the Spanish capital by a Fatah veteran who shot the Israeli several times, fatally wounding him. This was a significant setback for the Mossad and restored increasingly battered morale within the various factions that comprised the Black September Organisation. Their battle now seemed less one-sided. As one participant recalled many decades later, the Mossad's campaign launched in the wake of Munich 'did not deter us, but made us fight more'. There was 'an exchange of assassinations between us and the Israelis'.

Morale mattered to the Mossad too, and officials knew it was important that teams working in Europe felt they were supported by the Israeli public. News of the successive killings perpetrated by the Mossad's teams was repeatedly leaked by the service or government officials to sympathetic domestic newspapers and politicians. It was not made clear who was responsible for these sudden deaths in distant cities, but no one needed to be told. After the shock of Munich such reports reassured the public and relieved some of the political pressure on Meir.

But not everyone in Israel rejoiced at the murders. After each of them, the Mossad discreetly informed Ankie Spitzer, the widow of Andrei, the fencing coach who had died in Munich. An anonymous phone call would tell her that the murder had been committed to avenge her husband. 'It did not fill me with joy ... I never looked for that revenge,' Spitzer said later. When Nurit, Baruch Cohen's widow, also received word of the killings in Europe she simply thought of 'another family that has been hurt, another woman who has been left alone, a few more children who lost their father'.

Gunnar Ekberg had started working for the Mossad shortly before the Munich attacks. The young Swedish spy had been passed to the Israelis by his handlers in Sweden's Intelligence Bureau in the summer of 1972. Amid the wood panelling, designer 'egg' chairs, colourful carpets and spiral staircases of Copenhagen's SAS hotel, he had met 'Danny', a bright-eyed, besuited, smiling man in his mid-thirties who had enthusiastically set about explaining how his new employers preferred to work.

For the Mossad, Ekberg was a very valuable asset. Its own covert agents and informants provided only fragmentary and often inadequate intelligence. Ekberg, with his contacts in both Beirut and Scandinavia, was perfectly placed to learn not only what key fedayeen leaders in the Lebanese capital might be planning but how activists in Europe might be involved. A recent series of incidents had shown quite how dangerous this intercontinental connection could be, the best example being an attempt in early 1971 by the PFLP to send three young women into Israel with components for a series of incendiary bombs that would be used to attack hotels full of Easter tourists. All three had been recruited in Paris. Two were the daughters of Middle Eastern diplomats but the third was entirely French. At her trial, reporters noted her resemblance to Brigitte Bardot. The plot had been betrayed in advance by one of the Mossad's agents within the PFLP and the unlikely attackers detained on arrival in Israel. It was also widely suspected that German leftists had somehow helped the Black September attackers at Munich. This belief was not justified – if any assistance was given, it was from extremists at the opposite end of the political spectrum – but it led to a keen interest in monitoring these relationships.

The risks of such work were obvious. Ekberg, who was increasingly worried that he would not live to see his thirtieth birthday, admitted that he was indeed scared when asked if the prospect of a return to Lebanon frightened him. This was good, Danny said, as a spy who was not scared would be dangerous.

Ekberg's first trip to Beirut for the Mossad started as his previous visits had done. In late October of 1972, he flew into the Lebanese capital's international airport, took a taxi to a hotel, rested and then made his way to the PFLP's headquarters. On all his previous visits, Ekberg had been received by *al-Hadaf*'s editor, but with Ghassan Kanafani now dead he was met this time by his replacement, Bassam Abu Sharif, himself still recovering from the injuries caused by the Mossad's letter bomb. In a side room, Ekberg found Sharif's old desk with a football-sized hole torn through the metal on one side and blackened matter and burn marks scorched in the ceiling above.

As Wadie Haddad would be unavailable to meet for some time, Ekberg accepted an invitation to visit a training camp where he could 'have a real experience of the struggle' while he waited. An old Mercedes took Ekberg out of Beirut, east across the Shouf mountains and then via the famously ancient city of Baalbek to his destination: a handful of military tents in a grove of pine trees behind a rocky crag close to the border with Syria. The camp was considerably more impressive than the training facilities Ekberg remembered from his time in Jordan almost three years earlier. The dozen or so recruits were all Palestinians, fitter and clearly more competent in the use of weapons than any he had seen before. The instructors appeared to be Iraqi, probably serving soldiers sent from Baghdad in a gesture of revolutionary solidarity. Ekberg drew on his experience as an assault diver during his military service in Sweden to give an impromptu lecture in the use of explosives underwater, enjoyed a dinner of lamb roasted on a campfire with rice, then slept outside wrapped in a blanket. At dawn, he walked a short distance to a stream to wash. He had just knelt to splash water on his face when a tremendous blast of hot air flattened him among the rocks. When he recovered his senses, staring upwards, he saw the afterburners of two Israeli F-4 Phantom jets disappearing into the sky and, very close to him, a small green lizard that he would remember for the rest of his life.

Apart from cuts and bruises, a bloodied forehead and singed hair, Ekberg was unhurt. As he staggered back, unable to hear anything other than the ringing in his ears, he saw men running and gesticulating, a severed leg on the ground, what looked like entrails caught on tree branches. Fires were burning among the trees and the air smelt of roast meat, cordite and faeces. The camp commandant shoved him into the Mercedes that had brought him the day before, now dented and scarred by shrapnel, shouted for the driver, and told him to go before the jets returned. When he reached Beirut some hours later, his Popular Front hosts appeared unimpressed. Such raids were bad for morale and should never be mentioned unless they caused civilian casualties, one warned. Still very shaken, Ekberg walked for a long time through Beirut, went back to his hotel, drank a bottle of wine, slept fitfully and had just changed his flight to travel home early when word came that Haddad was now available.

This was Ekberg's third meeting with the PFLP's head of external operations. Very few other foreigners had spent as much time with this most wanted man. Though the Black September Organisation's various attacks had focused attention on Arafat's Fatah, the PFLP's operations were still the more numerous and effective. Ekberg found Haddad haggard with fatigue. The bitter internal disputes within the PFLP were far from resolved. One of many points of contention was the firm ban George Habash had finally imposed on hijackings or other violence targeting anyone other than Israelis. This had prompted Haddad to consider setting up his own breakaway group – if he could find funds and fighters.

Haddad and Ekberg met in an apartment in a newly constructed block on the outskirts of Beirut and spoke for an hour or more, discussing how to use the Swede's expertise as a military diver and what he should do on his return to Stockholm. Haddad was still very interested in using Scandinavia as a launchpad for operations in western Europe and wanted to attract more recruits in Sweden. 'Our revolution is not like others . . . The struggle is entirely international,' he told Ekberg. But amid the advice and encouragement was a warning. 'This is a job that will not end,' Haddad said. 'Once inside always inside.'

Throughout his years as an agent, Ekberg had been able to provide the Swedish Intelligence Bureau and then the Mossad with detailed information about personalities, ideologies, relationships, strategies and more, but at no stage had he been able to identify concrete evidence of a specific, imminent attack. He often worried about missing something significant. This was much more than a vague anxiety, but a fear felt in the pit of his stomach. On his first trips to Beirut, he had discussed hijackings in Europe and learned of the PFLP's efforts to obtain identity papers, but he had not learned of the plans for Revolution Airport. In Beirut in February 1972, he had glimpsed a letter from Japan and the floor plans of a large building on the desk of Kanafani, and he had seen Fusako Shigenobu, the leader of the Japanese Red Army, in the *al-Hadaf* offices, but it was not until a month later, when twenty-six people were killed by three of Shigenobu's group at Lod airport, that he grasped the significance of what he had seen. On a third trip, he had sat with Khalaf, the man who would mastermind the Munich attack, in a hotel bar and discussed how to recruit people in Scandinavia who might provide logistics for operations in Europe. Ekberg had reported everything to his handlers but had been unable to link the information in a way that would allow him to understand what was being planned. He knew that this was not his role, that to make that leap of imagination was almost impossible and that asking questions that revealed his interest in an impending operation would have been extremely dangerous. But the failure to do so was deeply upsetting nonetheless. On the night of the Munich attack, Ekberg had sat with his wife Elizabeth, the dinner he had cooked cooling on their plates, as they watched images broadcast from the Olympic village. That night he did not sleep.

In February 1973, six months after his last trip, Ekberg returned to Beirut for a fifth visit. Both Haddad and the Mossad wanted him in the city, though for very different reasons. This time, Ekberg was sitting with 'the Master' in the offices of *al-Hadaf* within twenty-four hours of his arrival. In three weeks, the *Sounion*, a moderately luxurious cruise ship, would dock at Beirut to allow its 200 or so predominantly US passengers a day's sightseeing, Haddad said. Its next stop would be Haifa, where they would be dropped off for a tour of Israel. This made the ship a 'perfect target' for someone with experience in the use of underwater explosives, Haddad told Ekberg.

For a sickening moment, the young Swede thought that Haddad was proposing that he attack the *Sounion* himself, but then realised with some relief that his role would be to direct a pair of Popular Front fighters who had already been trained in basic diving. They would plant magnetic mines on the hull of the ship that would later detonate out at sea. In theory those on board would probably have time to reach the lifeboats. Ekberg was driven that night into Beirut's port, where he undertook a thorough reconnaissance of the jetty where the *Sounion* would moor and plotted an underwater route for the divers that would allow them to evade detection. Over the next two days, Ekberg worked with the two PFLP divers out at sea before pronouncing them ready and briefing Haddad on how the attack would be conducted.

For the first time, Ekberg was now in possession of authentic and very detailed information about a forthcoming attack that would endanger the lives of hundreds of people. He waited a day, spending a tense afternoon shopping and reading, then sent a telegram to his wife which used a series of code words to alert her, and so his multiple handlers, of the imminent threat to the cruise ship. Next, he wrote a long letter that would, to the casual reader, appear to be little more than a lengthy and somewhat pedantic discussion of the relative attributes of different types of diving equipment. In between the lines of text, he set down exactly what was being planned by Haddad, writing with a pen pre-filled with ink that would only be legible once the pages had been treated by the Mossad. He sent the letter to one of the addresses Danny had given him.

This still left Ekberg in a very uncomfortable position. If he tried suddenly to leave Beirut, as every instinct told him to do, he risked attracting suspicion. Just mentioning a possible departure before the date of the attack could lead to some very difficult questions. But to be in Beirut if the *Sounion* miraculously escaped unscathed from the planned operation could be more perilous still. After several nervous days, to Ekberg's immense relief, Haddad told him not to wait for the attack on the *Sounion* but to return to Europe so he could start work on his new tasks for them there. Within hours, Ekberg was gone. His first stop was Copenhagen where Danny told him that both he and his wife were to be flown to Israel for meetings.

Ekberg and his wife flew first to Vienna, where they were taken through border control checks but then immediately back through the airport to an El Al passenger plane. Though legally still in Austria, the couple were flown to Tel Aviv where they were welcomed by the Mossad and introduced to two minders, a woman and a man their own age. For the next two weeks, Ekberg mixed business with pleasure. He toured Israel, dived with Israel's specialist military dive unit, got fitted out with a disguise and was given a false Israeli passport. He also spent days in intense sessions with a series of Mossad specialists in offices in Tel Aviv, answering questions about the habits and thinking of the men in the PFLP and Fatah that he had met, indicating the locations of their workplaces and homes on maps, discussing their way of thinking and planning and much more. Ekberg declined an invitation to help assassinate 'the Master' – not with his own hands, of course, his interlocutor assured him, but perhaps by placing an explosive charge in his toilet or poisoning him with an irresistible comestible gift, such as the chocolates Haddad liked so much. One evening Ekberg and his wife were able to slip away from their minders after dinner in picturesque Jaffa, just to the south of Tel Aviv. The young couple found a small bar by the beach. It was cold, raining, and the bar was empty. 'How does this end?' Ekberg's wife asked. He told her that he did not know but could not quit just yet.

After two weeks, word came from Beirut. The *Sounion* had indeed been attacked shortly after it moored in the city's port, but an unexpected delay to its departure had meant that the magnetic mines placed on its hull had detonated while the vessel was still at the quayside. Instead of sinking to the bottom of the Mediterranean, the *Sounion* had simply settled in the shallow water, allowing every one of its crew and passengers to walk to safety. Ekberg heard the news in an apartment surrounded by his new Israeli acquaintances. He sat on a sofa, limp with nervous exhaustion, as the Mossad men and women opened a bottle of champagne.

There were other reasons the Israeli intelligence services were feeling more optimistic by late March of 1973. Almost everywhere, the Mossad's efforts had begun to challenge the freedom of action that Palestinian groups had enjoyed in western Europe and further afield over previous years. Letter bombs continued to arrive at Israeli embassies – but only because they had been mailed from India and delayed many months in the post, and there had been no repeat of Munich. The Iron Wall appeared to have been reconstructed and its perimeter extended deep into new territory.

But there was still much to do: the Mossad had yet to locate the most senior commanders of Black September's various factions, let alone render them *hors de combat*. Some had gone to ground but others continued to move around Europe with relative impunity. The decisive breakthrough came a month after the operation to save the *Sounion*. It drew on information Ekberg had delivered from his recent trip to Beirut and was the result of one of the most complex and audacious missions the Israeli intelligence services had ever undertaken.

The planning for Operation Springtime of Youth had started in October 1972, when agents in Beirut gave the Mossad the locations of the homes of several senior PLO officials in the city. There was little hard evidence that any were involved in specific attacks but this did not particularly matter. It would be how and where the Israelis struck, not whom, that would be most important. Three officials were of particular interest, and apparently poorly-protected. The Israelis set out to kill them all.

For several months, senior officers had considered the many challenges of mounting a mission in a chaotic and hostile Arab city seventy miles from Israeli soil. For a long time such operations had been dismissed as impossible. Special forces had landed at Beirut's airport in 1968 to destroy planes on the runway, but that was very different from sending assassins through the streets of the neighbourhood known to be a stronghold of the PLO. Lebanon was not as viscerally hostile to Israel as Syria or Egypt and its security forces were not particularly sympathetic to the Palestinian militias that were an increasingly powerful and disruptive presence in their country, but it was certain that they wouldn't take kindly to the incursion in their capital of a large force of heavily armed Israeli soldiers either. The solution would have to be a combination of speed and subterfuge.

By the end of 1972, it was decided that a small unit of highly trained soldiers from the Sayeret Matkal, the elite army reconnaissance unit, could be landed into the Lebanese capital, reach the apartment blocks, kill the three Fatah officials in their homes and be gone before any resistance could be organised. In charge of the team would be a tough, intelligent, almost absurdly self-confident thirty-one-year-old soldier called Ehud Barak who had led the successful operation against the hijacked Sabena plane at Lod earlier in the year. Every single resource the Israeli military possessed would be mobilised to ensure success.

In late February, several experienced operatives from the Mossad arrived in Beirut. One posed as an eccentric Englishman who enjoyed nocturnal fishing and so spent a lot of time on beaches at odd hours. Another pretended to be a female TV producer scouting for locations, and so was able to secretly photograph the apartment blocks where the targets of the operation lived. The images sent back to Tel Aviv revealed entirely ordinary, eight-storey modern buildings with neat, railed balconies and entries at street level set back from the pavement. A similar block was found in Israel to allow Barak and his men to practise the attack. The information provided by Ekberg in Tel Aviv was also fed through to the operation's planners.

By late March, an assault team was ready and the plan had been further refined. It now called for Barak and fifteen of his men to be landed at a beach on Beirut's northern seafront, then driven by Mossad operatives across the city to a location a few hundred yards from their targets' homes. The soldiers would finish their approach on foot, nonchalantly disguised as tourists. Any large group of young men would inevitably attract attention, so some of the commandos would be dressed as women. Meanwhile, further detachments of special forces would land on different beaches and cross the city to other targets: offices of the Democratic Front for the Liberation of Palestine, and some workshops where weapons were made by the PLO. There would be further attacks elsewhere along the coast. These secondary operations would act as diversions, amplify the psychological effect of the main operation and provide a well-armed reserve force in case anything went wrong. Offshore a small naval flotilla would be positioned to provide extra support and the air force would be ready to send helicopters or launch air strikes if required. The operation would be one of the biggest by the Israeli armed forces outside of wartime.

In the late afternoon of 9 April, Barak and his men boarded fast navy boats and headed north. Close to Beirut, they transferred to motorised dinghies which took them to a secluded beach. They reached the sand without getting wet, crammed themselves into the waiting hire cars and were driven south through the evening traffic. This was the most nerve-wracking part of the entire operation. Within half an hour, they had been dropped off on the famous seafront Corniche and were climbing a sloping street away from the Mediterranean towards two apartment blocks on the rue Verdun. Their disguises successfully diverted any suspicion. Barak, wearing a brown wig, wide-cut trousers that concealed several weapons and a bra filled with grenades, walked arm-in-arm with a much taller officer wearing men's clothes. Nearby, a commando in a dress with false blonde hair curling to his shoulders led another towards the second apartment block. There was a pause as a third pair made their way to their target and the team who would stay below to guard the street moved into position.

Mohammed Yusuf al-Najjar, a member of the PLO's executive committee who had been linked by the Israelis to the Sabena hijacking a year earlier, died first, killed with his wife by bullets fired through a door he shut in the face of his assailants. Kamal Adwan, an intellectual and founder member of Fatah who ran clandestine operations in the occupied West Bank, was shot dead moments later. The last to die was Kamal Nasser, a poet who was known to never carry a weapon and whose primary responsibility was to manage the PLO's media relations. In the street below, Sayeret Matkal soldiers exchanged fire with local police, but anonymous phone calls made by the Mossad reporting yet another clash between rival Palestinian groups convinced the commanders of the local security forces not to order any substantial deployment.

As the sound of combat below intensified, Barak and his men scooped up as much paperwork as they could and ran down the stairs of the apartment block. An approaching Lebanese police car was stopped with grenades and automatic fire by a soldier wearing women's clothes and a wig standing in the middle of the road. Then the Israelis got in their vehicles, drove back across the city and were soon being ferried by inflatables to the boats that would return them to Israel. The Mossad team that had been in place to guide them was evacuated with the soldiers. Barak and his men had been in Lebanon for less than thirty minutes.

The larger Israeli force that had headed for the DFLP headquarters, located to the south-west of the city in the Sabra refugee camp, had encountered stiffer resistance than expected. A third of its strength was wounded or killed. Nonetheless, it too reached and destroyed its objectives. In addition to the three Fatah officials shot by Barak and his detachment, the Israelis killed several dozen fedayeen fighters, two Lebanese policemen and a number of other civilians including an elderly neighbour who opened her door during the raid on rue Verdun. Most of the Israeli force were back at their bases within hours. Barak's wife woke up in the morning to find her husband, still in women's clothes and lipstick, deep in exhausted sleep on the bed beside her.

More than 100,000 people gathered in Beirut to attend the funerals of the three dead Fatah leaders. The Lebanese government complained to the United Nations of 'repeated criminal operations undertaken by units of the Israeli armed forces in pursuance of a policy of intimidation and state terrorism ... against Lebanese civilian areas, centres and population'. The then West German ambassador to Lebanon was incensed, cabling Bonn that the dead Palestinians were among the most 'rational and responsible' members of the PLO and accusing the Israelis of aiming to scuttle any nascent negotiations that might lead to peace. *Al-Ahram*, the leading daily newspaper in Egypt, said that the operation's aim had been to 'drive into Arabs' hearts the sense that Israel was in control of the region'. This was entirely true. David Elazar, the chief of staff of the Israel Defence Forces, summed up the aim of the entire campaign of violence since the Munich attacks when he told reporters that 'if the terrorists can come to ... Cyprus, to Paris and to Rome, there is no reason to believe that we are not able to come to any place in the world.'

The toll exacted by Operation Springtime of Youth among senior Fatah and Popular Front leaders could have been much higher. Salah Khalaf, who the Israelis knew had a major role in the attack on the Olympics, happened to have refused an invitation to dine at one of the targeted apartments in favour of spending the evening with the recently returned Munich gunmen, and so he survived. Bodyguards managed to rush Yasser Arafat to safety from his home nearby the moment they heard the shooting start. Ali Hassan Salameh, whose apartment was only a hundred or so yards from those attacked, was also unharmed. He later claimed that this was because the Israelis knew he was guarded by fourteen hand-picked gunmen. It is more likely either that the Israelis did not know where he lived or that he was absent on the night of the raid, possibly overseas.

By now, though, the Israelis were more determined than ever to eliminate the man they considered the mastermind of the Munich attacks and one of their most potent enemies within the PLO. For in previous months, they had learned that this flamboyant but increasingly capable and respected man was in touch with the CIA, and this they did not like at all.

11
The Red Prince

When Ali Hassan Salameh moved into his apartment on Beirut's rue Verdun in late 1970, he had found the city dramatically changed since his teenage years. The highlife Beirut offered its most wealthy inhabitants was increasingly decadent; the financial speculation increasingly outrageous; the streets increasingly dangerous. But for all its flaws, or perhaps because of them, Beirut was an agreeable place for a man of Salameh's tastes and talents.

After his early rapid rise, Salameh's career within Fatah had foundered. His violent exploits in Europe – the bombings of oil refineries and German factories, the attempt on the life of the Jordanian ambassador in London – had earned suspicion not praise within Fatah, and when Salameh had five alleged double agents in Cologne shot dead in early 1972, he had been suspended from active duties for three months pending investigation. Though eventually cleared of being either trigger-happy or a double agent, the episode had damaged the thirty-one-year-old's already battered reputation. Salameh had subsequently worked hard to restore his standing. In early May of 1972 he had travelled to Paris, Holland and then Rome to brief the hijackers of the Sabena plane, and in August he returned to Italy at the same time as the Trieste bombings, which it is likely he masterminded.

Despite his many enemies within Fatah, Salameh retained the patronage of Yasser Arafat, who referred to his young protégé as 'my son' and trusted him with very large amounts of Fatah's money for investment in western European businesses. This meant Salameh could ignore older and more senior Fatah officials supposedly in charge of clandestine operations. One of his former colleagues and rivals described a 'strong personality' who 'carried out operations alone', sourcing funds from wherever he could while recruiting followers from among 'a group of young men, most with criminal records'.

By the autumn of 1972, Salameh was acquiring something of a profile in the international media. After the Munich attack, he was repeatedly named in Western newspapers as a key figure in Black September. Many of these articles clearly owed much to briefings by Jordanian and Israeli intelligence or diplomats and portrayed him, largely accurately, as an ostentatious, energetic, hard-living and extremely effective 'playboy terrorist'. Secret Western briefings circulated through the Kilowatt network repeated much the same. But though these reports made clear his repeated involvement in acts of violence, none provided any real evidence that Salameh had been personally responsible for the operation targeting the Olympics, and many did not even suggest this had been the case.

Even so, the 'Red Prince', as those tracking his movements from Israel had dubbed him, remained a suspect by default, and by early 1973, the list of charges against him had grown even longer. The Mossad blamed Salameh for a spectacular attack on the Israeli Embassy in Bangkok, for example, perhaps the most distant operation from the Middle East attempted by the fedayeen, as well as both an attempt to shoot down an El Al plane carrying Golda Meir to Rome and an abortive plot to set off car bombs during the Israeli prime minister's visit to New York. The Israelis also suspected that Salameh was behind the assassination of their defence attaché in Washington.

But the two spectacularly ill-judged operations that took place in 1973, which would ultimately put paid to Black September's campaign of terrorism, were the work of someone else entirely: Salah Khalaf, the real architect of the Munich attack, who remained convinced that striking at high-profile international targets was the best means to advance the Palestinian cause. In March 1973, the month before Operation Springtime of Youth, Khalaf mounted an ambitious attempt to storm the US Embassy in Amman and hold its staff as hostages. No one was to be hurt, at least in theory, but Khalaf believed that if a large enough number of US diplomats were at risk in his capital, King Hussein would be unable to resist the pressure from Washington to release hundreds of Fatah fighters and supporters held in Jordanian jails. The operation was a fiasco, and ended up with Mohammed Daoud Odeh, the former militia commander who had been the organiser on the ground in Munich, joining them behind bars.

There was worse to come. To free Odeh, Khalaf hastily dispatched a team of gunmen from Beirut to Khartoum, the capital of Sudan, with orders to take hostages at the Saudi Arabian Embassy there. Arriving during a cocktail reception, the Fatah gunmen seized the new US ambassador, the outgoing US chargé d'affaires and his Belgian counterpart. They then demanded the release, among others, of Odeh, all Arab women in Israeli jails, Andreas Baader and Ulrike Meinhof.

The standoff lasted nearly three days. Both Sudan's president, Gaafar Nimeiri, and King Hussein made it very clear they were not minded to negotiate the release of the hostages. In an off-the-cuff comment to a reporter, President Richard Nixon, who had won re-election the year before, ruled out 'pay[ing] blackmail', an unexpected reversal of US policy in such situations. Some hours later the three captive men were given Saudi Arabian diplomatic stationery on which to write their final words, then taken to the embassy's basement and shot dead. When they returned from the basement, the Black September gunmen, supposedly hardened fighters, 'did not look like men who had killed before', witnesses remembered.

To attack US diplomats in the embassy of an Arab state that was very supportive of the Palestinian cause and one of its biggest financial backers was an extraordinary misjudgement. There was no doubt over who was responsible. Telephone calls intercepted by US intelligence services revealed the whole operation was masterminded by senior Fatah officials in Beirut. Though the remaining hostages were released unharmed, and the attackers surrendered to Sudanese authorities, the attack still provoked almost universal outrage. A poster on the wall of Khartoum University asked: 'Can any sane mind justify this? Does Israel's inhumanity justify the abandonment of all human values?'

One obvious question was whether Yasser Arafat had known in advance. This had been asked after every such attack without ever receiving a definitive answer, exactly as intended by those who had set up Black September. Now, however, the US was absolutely convinced that the operation 'was planned and carried out with the full knowledge and personal approval' of the Fatah leader, and believed it was designed to punish the 'United States because of its efforts to achieve a Middle East peace settlement which many Arabs believe would be inimical to Palestinian interests'. On the basis of the radio intercepts, the US believed Arafat himself had given the orders to kill their diplomats, giving the code word 'Nahr el Bared', the name of a training base and refugee camp in northern Lebanon raided by Israeli special forces a month before. Seventeen civilians had died in that attack, Lebanese authorities claimed.

No one implicated Salameh in what had happened in either Amman or Sudan, and he himself had a range of motives for distancing himself from international violence at that exact moment. One in particular meant that any personal involvement in the murder of two US diplomats would not have been well timed: he had a meeting with the CIA arranged for the end of the month.

Within a week or so of the bombing of the cruise ship moored in Beirut, Salameh and Robert Ames, his CIA contact, met in a safehouse in the city. The American had recently moved to take up a new post in Tehran but continued to work on wider issues across the Middle East. Since the Munich attacks, Ames had been trying to contact Salameh, whom he had not seen for two years, through a mutual friend. His messages had been ignored, until now.

For some years, there had been a growing sense among some US analysts and policy-makers that the superpower needed to engage more with the Palestinians. A National Intelligence Estimate in February 1971, based on CIA analysis and agreed by all major agencies, stated that 'no lasting mid-East peace settlement is possible unless it addresses Palestinian interests.' Eighteen months later, Joseph Sisco, the US assistant secretary of state for Near Eastern affairs, had told an audience of Jewish war veterans that if the US could talk to China and the Viet Cong then there was no reason why the Middle East should be a 'unique exception'.

There was a more straightforward and practical reason for talking to someone like Salameh too. The Lebanese capital was still described as the 'Paris of the East', but it was increasingly riven by deep sectarian, political and social tensions. The Palestinians who had been living in its crammed refugee camps since 1948 were resentful of their marginal position in the country, while the many Shia Muslims who had swapped the thin fields and poor villages of the south of Lebanon for the wretched shanty towns on Beirut's outskirts were disillusioned at the false promise of a better life. The city's Christians, who still dominated politics, the security forces and the economy, felt ever more threatened. As a consequence, Beirut had become a very unsafe place for US diplomats and other citizens. Preserving good relations with the increasingly powerful and combative Palestinian organisations in the city was a sensible precaution.

At their meeting in March of 1973, Salameh told Ames that the

Khartoum attack had 'made its point of causing the US government to take fedayeen activity seriously' but that there would be no further plans to target Americans or American interests as long as both sides maintained a dialogue. This was not a threat but a recognition that talking was necessary, Salameh said.

Ames sent a memo describing the conversation to the director of the CIA, Richard Helms, and arranged a further meeting with Salameh. This took place at the beginning of the second week of July, again in a safehouse in Beirut. Salameh had been busy in the meantime. One trip took him to Khartoum where Arafat hoped he might smooth relations with Nimeiri, who remained incensed at the attack on the Saudi Embassy. When told that any further such violence would lead to serious reprisals, Salameh had given the blunt guarantee that 'if any man threatens the Sudanese government, I will cut his tongue out.'

Such rough-edged diplomacy was rooted in more than a desire to placate the Arab regimes on whose support the PLO and Fatah depended. When he saw Ames in July, Salameh told the American that there had been an important evolution in Fatah's strategic goals since their earlier talk. In the wake of their recent disasters – the Munich attack, Khalaf's two spectacular misadventures and the subsequent assassinations by Israel's special forces in Beirut – the group's leadership had finally accepted 'a change', he said, and now acknowledged that Israel was 'here to stay'. This meant that the formal goal adopted in 1968 by the PLO – the liberation of the entire territory of the former British Mandate in Palestine through armed struggle – was no longer considered realistic. In return for a pledge not to attack the US or its interests, Arafat wanted US support for a plan to create a Palestinian state in the place of Jordan. Ames, an experienced and prudent operator, made no promises other than to relay the proposal to his superiors.

In fact, the 'change' Salameh had described was authentic, and the culmination of a long process of thought and debate within the PLO and Fatah. Arafat had been considering a shift to a more pragmatic position for some time. As early as 1969 he had raised the possibility in private conversations of a Palestinian state restricted only to Gaza and the West Bank, and he had always been ambivalent about the violence of the Black September Organisation. Arafat was not as viscerally anti-American as others within the PLO either. He had been disappointed at the US's increasingly close relation with Israel since the war of 1967 six years earlier but had come to believe that only the Americans could pressure Israeli leaders into making concessions. The PLO's relations with Moscow were warmer than they had been, but the Soviets had repeatedly made their distaste for attacks like Munich or Khartoum very clear. Further progress in Moscow therefore depended on less violence. The PLO also had financial problems, so could not risk losing the support of Saudi Arabia and others with more rash attacks. Meanwhile, Israel's Operation Springtime of Youth had triggered the collapse of the fragile Lebanese government and led to bloody clashes between Palestinian fighters and national armed forces. Arafat was concerned that these might lead to a showdown which he could ill afford, Salameh told Ames. If the PLO was to avoid another debacle like that in Jordan, it needed all the friends it could get, or at least fewer enemies.

Nor was it possible for Arafat to continue to deny Fatah's involvement in terrorism, or at least cast useful doubt over the exact relationship between the organisation and the attacks across Europe over the previous two and a half years. Odeh, the commander of the abortive attack in Amman, had made a lengthy confession to Jordanian interrogators after being tortured, revealing that 'there was no such thing as Black September' and that 'Fatah announces operations under this name so [as not to] appear as [their] direct executor'. Taped excerpts of his statement were broadcast on national radio in Jordan and printed in local newspapers. This was all familiar to Western intelligence services but still embarrassing to Arafat.

The PLO leader's new thinking did not mean an end to all violence. Any such commitment would have shattered an already fractious organisation. Salameh told Ames that attacks on Israel would continue in order 'to sustain the movement's credibility' and insisted that the 'armed struggle' remained at the heart of their movement. But for the moment at least the pre-eminent leader of the Palestinian nationalist movement believed that diplomatic efforts would bring greater rewards than military ones had done hitherto.

Indeed, even as Salameh was talking to Ames, Arafat was already moving to shut down all the various factions operating under the label of Black September Organisation. Some were led by influential, committed and capable men, so their diversion to other tasks called for a degree of subtlety. Salah Khalaf, who was still in charge of the PLO intelligence and security services, was given the task of 'turning off Black September'. A novel scheme was set up to demobilise a hundred or so of the most committed fighters by introducing them to young, eligible and attractive Palestinian women. They were then told that any who married would be given $3,000, an apartment in Beirut with a gas stove, a refrigerator and a television, and salaried employment that did not involve violence. Any who had children within a year would be rewarded with an additional $5,000.

The continuing rivalries within the PLO made for poor security, and Fatah in particular 'leaked like a sieve', according to one spy. Soon enough the Mossad was able to obtain its internal reports of the meetings that Salameh had held with the CIA. Their content reinforced all of the Israelis' concerns. That the US, supposedly their most important and closest ally, was secretly communicating with Arafat, especially via an intermediary like Salameh, was bad enough. But the possibility that Washington might be ready to consider the possibility of a bilateral understanding with the PLO was appalling.

Salameh was already a marked man, and by May 1973 the Mossad appeared to be closing in. After months of targeting low-level operatives of Fatah or the PFLP, or individuals who had limited involvement with either group, the service finally had in its sights a man who was close to Salameh himself. This was Mohammed Boudia, a colourful and capable forty-one-year-old Algerian who would later be systematically portrayed in Israel and the West as little more than a terrorist accomplice and cynical womaniser – a portrayal that was very incomplete.

Boudia had grown up penniless in Algiers' famous Casbah, dropped out of school and been sent to prison for a series of petty crimes. Behind bars, he enrolled in acting classes run for detainees by the French colonial regime and discovered a talent for drama. On his release, Boudia travelled to France, where he sought to use theatre to mobilise Algerian migrant workers in the cause of independence and ran clandestine networks which conducted bombing campaigns against symbols of French authority. Injured and arrested when an attack went wrong, Boudia spent eighteen months in a prison in Marseille, translating Molière into Arabic and writing a series of political plays, then escaped. When the French left his homeland in 1962, he was appointed the first director of its national theatre. Forced out by poisonous local factional politics, Boudia then returned to Paris, where he took over the management of a small avant-garde theatre in the western suburbs. In addition to organising opposition to the new regime in Algiers, he also spent much time with Palestinian activists in literary circles, and soon became an enthusiastic supporter of their cause.

By late 1970, Boudia had turned himself into a one-man logistics hub for Palestinian armed groups in western Europe. Charming, committed and competent, he had a vast range of contacts on both the extreme left and right, while his highly-regarded work at the Paris theatre provided perfect cover for moving around western Europe. He also had long experience of clandestine work, bomb-making and using his thespian skills to deceive, convince or indeed seduce. Boudia's compulsive womanising was risky but also useful. In Geneva, which he visited frequently, he had two girlfriends living close to each other. This made nocturnal changes of accommodation – vital to evade surveillance – much more convenient. He seduced an assistant, then the daughter of a Middle Eastern diplomat, then dispatched both to Israel to deliver explosives to the PFLP. When he travelled to London to oversee the Black September attempt to kill the Jordanian ambassador, he took a girlfriend with him to divert suspicion.

For Salameh, Boudia was both a kindred spirit and an indispensable collaborator. When Salameh needed explosives for the Black September attack in Rotterdam, Boudia provided them. He also organised an ambitious but abortive effort to attack a transit camp in Austria for Jewish migrants on their way from the USSR to Israel, and the logistics for Salameh's attack on the oil terminal in Trieste. The somewhat motley crew Boudia recruited for the latter operation included a middle-aged French physiotherapist and another assistant at his theatre. Boudia had taken both to bed, then persuaded them to participate in the attack, sending them to Italy from Paris in a hired car packed with a massive quantity of stolen explosives.

The Mossad watched Boudia for many weeks through the late spring of 1973, looking for the best way to kill him without causing a furore in France. Their break came when the Swiss federal police discovered an alias Boudia was using, then identified his car through a parking ticket. Both details were circulated via the Kilowatt encrypted telex network to other security agencies in western Europe and, crucially, to the Israelis who were able to track Boudia down in Paris. Eventually, a specialist Mossad team placed an adapted land mine under the seat of Boudia's grey Renault 16 while it was parked overnight on a street in central Paris outside the home of a girlfriend. The device killed Boudia instantly but harmed no one else.

The bomb had been designed by the Mossad to look like Boudia had died in an explosion of 'terrorist materiel' that he had been transporting. This initially fooled some reporters, and French security services, but not everybody. The PLO issued a statement accusing 'Zionist assassins' of systematically liquidating revolutionary Arab intellectuals. Jacques Poulet, a theatre critic, wrote in *Le Monde* that if Boudia, a close friend, had been 'un terroriste', it was out of necessity and moral obligation. 'You are not born a terrorist, you become one,' Poulet said.

At a further meeting with Ames in Beirut in the summer of 1973, Salameh boasted of having 'recruited' Boudia for Fatah. This was a misrepresentation of their relationship. The two men had been partners. But having brought their collaboration to an end with the bomb in Paris, the Mossad knew they had also taken a big step nearer to killing Salameh himself. For when it killed someone important, other potential targets invariably sought remote or unlikely locations where they could lie low, and because such fugitives still needed to stay in touch with their subordinates, the Mossad could locate them by monitoring potential couriers closely.

In mid-July 1973, a month after Boudia's death, the Israelis learned that an Algerian Fatah official based in Geneva needed to pass a message by hand to Salameh and was about to travel to find him. It seemed too good an opportunity to miss.

From Switzerland, the Algerian official flew to Stockholm then, tracked much of the way by Mossad operatives, took a train to Lillehammer, a picturesque ski resort a hundred miles due north of the Norwegian capital, where he checked in to a small hotel close to the railway station. Almost deserted in the summer, the town seemed an odd place for such a rendezvous but the Israelis knew from Ekberg and others that both Fatah and the PFLP saw Scandinavia as a potential launchpad for operations in northern Europe and a useful haven. Over the previous year, senior officials from both organisations had repeatedly visited Stockholm and regional cities, and both had very recently launched drives to find 'people who could help with secret operations' there or gather intelligence about prominent figures in the local Jewish community. The PFLP also maintained close links with a group of former Communists in Denmark who had trained in their camps in Jordan before returning home to steal money and automatic weapons. The Mossad saw the quiet Swedish port city of Malmö as a particular hotbed of extremism.

Convinced that they had their best opportunity yet to kill Salameh, the Mossad rushed to assemble a team. The twelve men and women who eventually gathered in Lillehammer included several hardened operatives, but the service had been so stretched by recent efforts that others had almost no field experience. They had only one picture of their target – a photograph supplied by the British domestic service MI5 in the immediate aftermath of the Munich attacks.

There are several conflicting accounts of what happened in Lillehammer but none obscure the fact that the operation went horribly wrong. According to one version, the team lost contact with the Algerian official and then combed the resort until they found a man who fitted, very roughly, the description of Salameh. According to a marginally more generous account, the courier from Geneva was tracked to a hotel and then to a meeting in a café with 'another Arab' whom the Mossad team decided was Salameh. When this second man was heard speaking French, the team's leaders took this as confirmation of his identity. Several of the operatives disagreed, pointing out that their famously sybaritic and stylish target was not only unfashionably dressed and rode a bicycle but appeared to have suddenly grown a beard and taken up residence in a modest apartment block on the outskirts of Lillehammer with a heavily pregnant local woman. 'If that's Salameh, then I'm Mother Theresa,' one said. Their concerns were ignored by the senior men leading the mission.

No one disputes what happened next. Early in the evening of 21 July 1973, members of the Mossad team watched their putative target leave his home with the pregnant woman, who seemed to be his wife. The couple took a bus into Lillehammer and then walked to a cinema where they spent the next hour and a half watching Richard Burton and Clint Eastwood kill Nazis in the Second World War action film *Where Eagles Dare*, before setting off back to their apartment. The bus dropped them a short walk from their destination at around 10.40 p.m. It was still perfectly light at such a northern latitude. A moment later, a grey Volvo drew to a halt next to them. Two people got out carrying silenced Beretta pistols and fired thirteen times, killing the man almost instantly.

The murder was as clinical as any carried out by the Mossad over the previous ten months. The problem was that the person they had murdered was not Salameh but a twenty-nine-year-old Algerian-born waiter called Ahmed Bouchiki who had no connection to any form of political activism, let alone violence. He had been in Norway for almost a decade, had lived in Lillehammer for a year and married his local wife in February. It was true that Bouchiki had met the courier from Geneva – an encounter seen by the Mossad team – but they had come across each other by chance and, as people do when they meet a compatriot in a distant land, struck up a conversation, mainly about sports and Arabic music.

The mistake was grave but could have been covered up had the Mossad team not made a series of further errors. Having informed headquarters in Tel Aviv that Salameh was dead, they split up as planned, heading for Amsterdam, Copenhagen, Oslo and London, unaware that two teenagers had not only seen them shoot Bouchiki but had noted the registration number of their Volvo. When one of the team drove the same car to the airport, he was arrested. The operative was chronically claustrophobic – a fact he had disclosed to the Mossad but which had been ignored – and lasted less than twenty-four hours in a police cell before 'revealing everything about his role in the operation'. Within hours the police had rounded up another five members of the team. All the detained Israelis were put on trial in a public court, convicted and sentenced to several years in jail.

The fiasco prompted outrage around the world, and the trial revealed much highly sensitive information: the location of safehouses and dead letter drops, the identities of agents, codenames and code words, secret phone numbers in Tel Aviv. But though this was embarrassing, strict compartmentalisation limited the damage done to the Mossad's operations. Despite the public anger of their political masters, senior officials of intelligence services in western Europe appeared unbothered by events in Norway and continued to share details of potential future targets with the Israelis through the Kilowatt system. Golda Meir decided nonetheless that the diplomatic cost of further killings was too high, and ordered an end to the assassination campaign on the continent.

By mid-summer of 1973, both Black September's campaign of violence and that of the Mossad, one of terrorism and the other of 'counter terror' in the formulation of the CIA, were effectively over. That same summer, Gunnar Ekberg's involvement in 'the war of the spooks' also ended.

After the *Sounion* episode in March, he had flown back to Sweden with his wife entirely unaware that members of the Marxist group which he had infiltrated (and still reported on) had written a long letter to the DFLP denouncing him as a spy. This had actually reached Beirut in advance of his last visit, but its contents had not been passed on to Haddad or his aides by the rival faction. Had the PFLP learned that Ekberg was working for the Swedish Intelligence Bureau, and possibly the Israelis too, he would have been interrogated, tortured and almost certainly shot. Instead, the partial success of the attack on the ship in Beirut had further reinforced his credentials with Haddad and the Popular Front, who had tasked him with setting up a series of mailboxes and finding an apartment in Vienna to use as a base of operations in Europe.

Shortly after arriving in the Austrian capital, Ekberg received instructions from the Mossad to meet a contact at the foot of the Ferris wheel in the city's Prater park. In one of its cabins, rotating above the trees and buildings, he was briefed by a man calling himself Martin. The service had already learned much from the correspondence that was passing through the mailbox system Ekberg had arranged, and it was looking forward to the next stage of the operation. They had picked out an apartment for him to rent in Vienna, fully equipped with listening devices and cameras. Before they went their separate ways, the Israeli pointed back up to the Ferris wheel, made famous by the film version of Graham Greene's spy novel *The Third Man*, and whistled its famous theme tune. Ekberg recognised the melody at once. They would not see each other again, the Mossad man told him, but the service was always watching. 'If someone in your vicinity whistles the ... [film] theme, follow the person in question without attracting attention or making contact yourself. It's a way to get in touch quickly and easily without being noticed,' he said.

Ekberg never got to hear the tune, nor to travel back to Beirut, nor to do any further clandestine work for the Swedes or the Israelis. A month later, a radical Swedish magazine published the details of his collaboration with the Swedish Intelligence Bureau and Ekberg's days as an agent were over.

In the last week of July 1973, Arafat flew from Beirut to East Berlin. It was his third visit to the German Democratic Republic but his first as a guest of the state. The PLO chairman had been invited to attend the Tenth World Festival of Youth and Students in the East German capital. Dubbed 'the red Woodstock', the event attracted tens, possibly hundreds of thousands of visitors from more than a hundred countries for over a week of concerts, parades, debates and sporting events.

The festival was designed to rival the Munich Olympics eleven months earlier and showcase the vitality and vibrancy of the other Germany. Instead of apolitical sport, the festival would be a 'vivid demonstration of the solidarity of young people in the fight against imperialism', according to Soviet official newspapers. Arafat joined guests who included leaders of the Viet Cong, a survivor of the My Lai massacre, British peace campaigners and Angela Davis, the African American intellectual and civil rights activist who had become something of an icon in parts of eastern Europe. There were marches pledging determination in the battle against 'the world's policeman' – which everyone knew meant the USA – and mass meetings where the evils of capitalism were denounced at great length. Soviet soldiers who had died 'liberating Europe from Fascism' were commemorated. At the 'Solidarity Centre', Namibian revolutionaries admired the keffiyehs of the Arab delegates who in turn looked longingly at the Guevara-style berets worn by the Cubans.

Yet, among all the songs about resistance, the banners in support of struggles, the slogans about liberation, there was very little mention of violence. Even Arafat struck an uncharacteristically moderate tone at a press conference, eschewing his usual radical rhetoric and saying that the 'Palestinian people will fight with political, military, ideological and other methods . . . [and not] engage in such senseless actions as hijacking of aircraft' even if Israel persisted in dropping 'bombs . . . on peaceful villages and shells which rake the bodies of innocent children'.

This new language was not simply a matter of mouthing the sentiments that would please his hosts, or signalling for the benefit of other governments his commitment to his recent decision to close down the Black September Organisation. Arafat may have understood that a defence of shootings and bombings on European streets would not have been received at all well by his audience. As far as the delegates were concerned, fundraising for the Viet Cong was one thing, but bombs going off or grenades being hurled in European capitals was quite another. Very few of the vast crowds that massed for the fireworks that closed the festival saw themselves as potential urban guerrillas or even supported those who did. No one was calling for insurrection any more.

At a geopolitical level, meanwhile, the recent detente between the superpowers had lowered tension everywhere outside the developing world. China's tentative move towards normalisation of relations with the United States in 1972 had undermined its status as the leading revolutionary power and the popularity of Mao's brand of revolutionary thinking. The peace accords signed by Kissinger and the governments of North and South Vietnam in January of that year not only signalled the definitive withdrawal of US forces from the conflict but also removed one of the most important rallying flags for the otherwise diverse constituencies who had shouted, marched and sung for global revolution.

Even in West Germany, where chancellor Willy Brandt was making new efforts to engage with rather than demonise the GDR, the revolution was struggling. Gudrun Ensslin, Andreas Baader and Ulrike Meinhof were on trial, and so able to make frequent statements excoriating the 'Fascist police regime' that had imprisoned them. This won them some support, as did the conditions of the hundreds of other young men and women jailed for their involvement with the Red Army Faction. But the group had also described Black September's attack on the Munich Olympics as a revolutionary act of internationalist solidarity that had carried the struggle from 'the periphery to the centre', and accused Israel of 'burning its athletes like the Nazis burned the Jews, as fuel for an imperialist policy of extermination'. Such statements alienated many of their more mainstream sympathisers.

By 1973, it was increasingly clear that any activist hoping for a global uprising against capitalism and imperialism was likely to be disappointed. The slogans and revolutionary invocations of the radical New Left were still widely spoken and popular, but the reality was that the acts they had inspired in the developed world had been neither cathartic nor effective, as Guevara and Marighella had promised, but sordid, bloody and mainly counter-productive.

In the Middle East, there was no sign of the great revolt of the oppressed either. Instead there were indications of something else. In the early autumn of 1973, Richard Helms, the former director of the CIA who had recently taken up a new job as US ambassador in Tehran, sent a memo to Henry Kissinger in Washington containing a sweeping analytic overview of the Persian Gulf. Six months earlier he had considered the prospect of serious instability in the region to be limited, at least in the near future. Now Helms confessed that he had been struck by 'something very interesting that was happening in the Arab world'. There had been 'a swing toward conservative Islamic principles', so pronounced in some regions that even leftists were now 'giving lip-service' to religion. This clearly surprised the former CIA director, who stressed that the change was not restricted to the street but was visible among the sort of people that the US government needed to be most concerned about.

'The leaders of the three most powerful factions in the Arab world: progressive/radical, moderate and conservative/reactionary are all very strong on Islam,' Helms noted. 'This trend is well worth watching.'

Another idea newly influential in analytic circles at this time originated with Brian Jenkins, an expert at the Rand Corporation in California, who had studied art history and was steeped in the radical artistic production of the 1960s. He argued that the use of violence in terrorism was not 'mindless' but carefully designed to communicate a message to specific audiences: terrorism as theatre. In the last days of 1973, an assassination attempt in London would launch the career of the man who would become the best and certainly the most famous exemplar of Jenkins' ideas.

IV

12

Carlos!

The twenty-four-year-old gripping the Beretta 9mm pistol in his gloved hand had enjoyed many names in his short life. To teasing classmates, he had been el Gordo or 'the chubby one'. To fashionable friends in London's nightclubs, he was Illy. To his girlfriends in France, he was Johnny. In the Middle East, he was Saleem Mohammed. To the customs officials who checked his documents at various international airports, he was usually José Adolfo Muller Bernal, a Chilean academic. To British authorities, meanwhile, he was Carlos Martínez Torres, a Peruvian businessman whose passport photograph – clearly in need of updating – showed a nineteen-year-old with a round face, full lips, a prominent nose, sharp chin and eyes obscured by large oval sunglasses.

José, Johnny, Saleem, Adolfo or Carlos had spent the penultimate day of 1973 preparing to shoot dead Joseph Edward Sieff, the Jewish president of Marks & Spencer, a major retail chain whose upmarket shops were to be found on high streets across Britain, and a prominent supporter of Israel. To this end, the young man had travelled to a mock-Georgian mansion on a quiet, elegant street in north London, not far from Regent's Park.

It was a cold evening and the street was unusually dark. In response to Syria and Egypt's surprise attack on Israel that October, aided by massive military support from the USSR, in which tens of thousands of infantry and hundreds of tanks had invaded simultaneously across the Suez Canal in the south and the Golan Heights in the north, the US had leapt to Israel's defence, allowing its forces eventually to repulse the attack after a series of desperate engagements resulting in heavy casualties. In the immediate aftermath of the short war, to protest at US support for Israel, Arab producers did what they had threatened to do for several months and deployed the 'oil weapon', announcing a series of price hikes and production cuts. Coming at the same time as industrial action by British coal miners and railway workers, the consequent energy crisis had led the Chancellor of the Exchequer to announce the country's 'gravest situation since the end of the [Second World] War'. Police were told to replace vehicle patrols with bobbies on foot, a speed limit of fifty mph was imposed, and the nation's three TV channels were ordered to stop broadcasting at 10.30 p.m. On Queen's Grove, where the young man now stood, the streetlights were dimmed, as they had been across much of London, to save electricity.

At around 7 p.m., as Sieff was preparing for dinner, his doorbell rang. His butler opened the door and, seeing the Beretta in the young man's gloved hand, led the visitor to the bathroom where Sieff was dressing. The intruder pushed the door half open, raised the weapon and squeezed the trigger. There was a single deafening report. The weapon then jammed and the attacker fled, running down the stairs, out onto the street, and disappearing into the dark.

To his significant surprise, Sieff survived. Metal dental work in his upper jaw deflected the bullet, and within a month he was convalescing on an extended holiday in Bermuda.

The real name of the man who had tried to kill him, the name written on his birth certificate, issued in the Venezuelan capital Caracas twenty-four years previously, was Ilich Ramírez Sánchez. But it was as Carlos, the name on his favoured passport, that he would become infamous. It was not until excitable tabloid journalists found a copy of Frederick Forsyth's bestselling novel *The Day of the Jackal* in his former girlfriend's apartment that he acquired the second part of his memorable sobriquet. The fact that the book was not his did not bother the headline writers. Ramírez would be known as 'Carlos the Jackal' for the rest of his life.

Before the attack that night in north London, Ramírez had never before fired a round in anger, let alone attempted to shoot someone dead at close range. Within six years, he would be credited with scores of killings perpetrated on almost every continent, as well as almost supernatural powers of infiltration and evasion, a fanatical devotion to revolutionary ideology, and a principal role in orchestrating a network of terrorist operatives who were supposedly some of the Cold War's most effective fighters and influential actors. The many myths and inaccuracies that surrounded him not only disguised the bloody, chaotic and cynical reality of Ramírez's activities, but greatly assisted them. This indeed was the theatre of terrorism suggested by Brian Jenkins of the Rand Corporation.

The reality was that the career of 'Carlos the Jackal', which stretched from the final moments of 1973 to the mid-1980s, did not reveal the strength and success of the international revolutionary 'armed struggle' so much as its incipient decline. For Ramírez, as for many others involved in international extremist violence at the time, the middle years of the 1970s undoubtedly brought opportunities to further their cause and violent careers. Yet, like those who had launched the international armed struggle over the previous decade, they attained very few of their more ambitious objectives, and only a handful of their less inspiring ones. Many failed to reach the relatively modest goal of staying alive.

Newspapers in Britain carried the story of the attack on Sieff on their front pages. Detectives told reporters they were hunting a man who was around five feet eleven inches tall with a foreign accent and dark complexion, wearing a green parka-type anorak with a fur-trimmed hood. The police had overestimated Ramírez's height by an inch or two but most of the other details were correct. Detectives checked hotels and boarding houses in London, asking landlords and -ladies if the suspect had been a guest, and interrogated taxi drivers. Their enquiries bore little fruit, not least because the object of their search lived with his mother and two younger brothers in a two-bed flat in the west of the city and had driven to the scene of the attempted assassination in the family estate car.

Two months later, Ramírez attempted another attack, this time on an Israeli bank in the City of London. Again, his efforts were only partly successful. He failed to throw the shoebox containing his bomb cleanly through the establishment's doors, and so caused only superficial damage to the building and slight injury to a cashier. Once more, police made desultory enquiries and soon lost interest, their investigative resources stretched thin by a recent string of bombings in London by Irish republican extremists. It would be more than two and a half years, after the deaths of five people, including two French policemen, and a series of near misses that could have killed hundreds, before British security services finally identified the perpetrator of the attack.

At the time he tried to kill Sieff, Ramírez had been in Britain for seven years. His childhood was unusual but considerably less eventful than either he or his detractors later claimed. Though he had been given the surnames of both his parents – Ramírez and Sánchez – as was customary in Venezuela, his first name had been chosen by his father, a successful lawyer with strong left-wing views for whom Lenin was a hero. The Russian revolutionary's real name had been Vladimir Ilich Ulyanov, so Ramírez, the second of three brothers, got Ilich. The family were wealthy, and Ramírez enjoyed a comfortable if somewhat unstable upbringing. There were sufficient funds to hire private tutors and for a lengthy tour of Central America and the Caribbean during a period of extreme political instability in Venezuela at the end of the 1950s. While in Jamaica, the Ramírez boys were sent to a very conservative private school to learn English and were punished for refusing to sing the British national anthem in morning assembly.

Back in Caracas, the family rented an apartment in the slightly run-down neighbourhood of El Silencio. Ramírez attended the Liceo Fermín Toro, a public school with a reputation for revolutionary politics and catering to high-society families of slightly bohemian inclinations. Timid and overweight, he was neither very interested in the former nor popular among the confident, stylish offspring of the latter, though like many pupils he did join the local Communist party's youth branch. Party officials and friends who knew him at the time do not remember the teenager doing anything to suggest the violent direction his life would soon take.

When his parents' rocky marriage broke down definitively, Ramírez left Venezuela with his mother and brother for London. He did not particularly impress the teachers at the small, expensive and undemanding school where he was enrolled. 'He is not yet as clever as he thinks or imagines. He talks far too loudly and too long,' wrote one. Slimmer and more self-assured now, dressed in suits and a tie, always charming and polite, Ramírez made more of an impression when accompanying his mother to diplomatic functions on the Latin American cocktail circuit.

Two years later, his son having attained A levels in English, maths and sciences, Ramírez's father flew to Europe to arrange for his further education. One possibility was the Sorbonne in Paris but soaring property prices and recent political unrest made the French capital unattractive. Instead, strings were pulled in the Venezuelan Communist party and Ilich and his brother were found places at the Patrice Lumumba Peoples' Friendship University in Moscow. Here the two brothers found themselves among around 3,000 overseas students from eighty or more countries. Their new home had been set up 'as part of [the USSR's] drive to lessen the traditional ties of newly emerging states with the Free World', the CIA explained in a secret intelligence assessment in 1968, which was only part of the story. The institution was named after the first democratically elected prime minister of the Republic of Congo, who had been ousted and assassinated in 1961 by its Belgian former colonial rulers and their proxies to forestall any possibility that he might swing the newly-independent state into the Soviet camp.

The university was one of an array in the USSR and eastern Europe that offered free education to thousands of students from the developing world. Most courses lasted four to six years, with compulsory Russian language instruction for the first two, and a significant amount of Marxist dialectics throughout. Not only was tuition free, students also received a generous stipend and an allowance to buy warm clothing. The spacious lecture halls and hostels of the Friendship University were significantly superior to its overcrowded counterparts in western Europe at the time, but discipline was strict and students were strongly discouraged from travelling even around Moscow.

Ramírez, who was supposed to be studying chemistry and physics, ignored such strictures. Funded by a sizeable allowance from his father, he ate frequently in local restaurants, drank in bars and repeatedly brought women back to his room, many of them sex workers. Nor did his habit of challenging teachers during lectures win him many friends among the academic staff. When university authorities nonetheless suggested to the Komitet Gosudarstvennoy Bezopasnosti, the USSR's main intelligence service, that Ramírez might be a candidate for recruitment, the KGB demurred, deciding that 'his appalling record as a student' and dissipated lifestyle made him entirely unsuitable as an agent.

The immediate cause of Ramírez's expulsion from the university in July 1970 was not his ostentatious womanising, poor grades or contrarian attitude, but the sudden decision of the fractious Venezuelan Communist party to withdraw its vital sponsorship of dozens of students at the end of his second year. This was not a rare occurrence at the university, where the presence of many students depended on the outcome of factional battles in their countries of origin. Ramírez was not overly vexed by the premature end of his studies in the USSR, but instead of returning to Britain he flew to Beirut where he set about finding the Popular Front for the Liberation of Palestine.

Ramírez had no particular interest in the Middle East, still less the Palestinians, but it was a long-held ambition of his to train as a guerrilla fighter. His father had spoken to him of the exploits of relatives who had fought for radical causes in Latin America, and he had spent his adolescence hearing about men like Castro and Guevara. His immediate aim was to learn the military skills that would allow him to join a breakaway Communist faction in Venezuela that had launched an armed insurgency there. A small number of Nicaraguans at Lumumba University, all members of the Sandinistas, held similar hopes of being trained by the Palestinian fedayeen in order to better fight at home. They may have inspired Ramírez or simply instructed him on how best to fulfil his ambition.

Before departing Moscow, the young Venezuelan had obtained a letter of introduction to the PFLP from Arab fellow students who were involved with the group. With this in hand, he now set out along the well-worn path to the offices of the *al-Hadaf* newsletter in Beirut. On arrival, like so many others before him, he was directed to Bassam Abu Sharif. At first sceptical of the young, smartly-dressed visitor, Abu Sharif soon found himself impressed by his knowledge of current affairs and charmed by the beautifully engineered camera he had brought from Moscow as a gift. The young Venezuelan was dispatched to spend the afternoon in the Shatila refugee camp on what was then the southern outskirts of the city before being dropped at a nearby hotel, as was routine. Usually, the foreign visitors would wait days before the Popular Front got back in touch. This time, however, Abu Sharif decided to take this latest new arrival to dinner at a local Italian restaurant to continue their earlier, enjoyable conversation.

At this point, three years before the Israeli special forces raid into the heart of Beirut put an end to such things, life in the city was much easier for the fedayeen. Soon other members of the Popular Front joined the pair and the increasingly lively group went on to a nightclub. After hours of dancing and drinking, Ramírez was dropped off back at his lodgings. A night or so later, he bumped into Gunnar Ekberg, the Swedish spy, at a small restaurant. The two had seen each other earlier in the day at the *al-Hadaf* office, where Ekberg was waiting to meet Wadie Haddad. Recognising each other, they shared a convivial bottle of Chateau Musar. Shortly afterwards, Ramírez was in a taxi on his way to one of the training camps in Jordan where international volunteers were still being hosted.

Ramírez arrived in Amman at the moment when the fedayeen groups were at the height of their power and belligerence, and the kingdom was teetering on the brink of all-out conflict. Fatah were hosting Andreas

Baader and his comrades at one camp; other foreign volunteers were at the camps where Leila Khaled had trained in the hills further north. Due to the growing tension, Ramírez was among a contingent of newly arrived volunteers who were hosted in cheap hotels in the back alleys of the Jordanian capital rather than being dispatched to the more distant training facilities where foreigners usually stayed. The trainees nonetheless followed much of the usual syllabus, being ferried daily to one or other of the big Palestinian refugee camps under PFLP control for lectures and drills in unarmed combat and very basic weapons handling. Unused to the diet, heat and poor hygiene, Ramírez fell ill, though neither diarrhoea nor stomach cramps prevented him from complaining vociferously about his accommodation, arguing with his instructors about tactics and questioning his hosts' more grandiose claims of military prowess.

In early September, with the multiple hijackings organised by Haddad and a final confrontation with King Hussein's forces both looming, the Popular Front leaders in Amman decided that the foreign volunteers were a liability and arranged for them to be bussed back to Lebanon out of harm's way. This may have been completed before the bitter fighting of the autumn, or it may have occurred after a delay of days or even weeks. Ramírez may have helped guard a Popular Front base in the north of Jordan during the first round of fighting, as some accounts suggest, and he may have been close to targets hit by Israeli jets, as is often reported, but it is unlikely he participated, as he occasionally later claimed, in actual combat.

Once back in Beirut, Ramírez quickly made himself at home. He found the American University a more congenial environment than the battered shacks and open sewers of the Palestinian refugee camp where he was supposed to be staying, and spent much of his time on its campus. Eventually, after more than three months of debate, lectures, occasional physical drills and wine-fuelled evenings, he flew from Beirut to Amsterdam where he pretended to have lost his passport with its tell-tale stamps from Jordan and Lebanon. Once he had obtained clean documents from the Venezuelan consulate there, he travelled on to London in late January of 1971, where he moved into the spare bedroom of the apartment that his mother and brother were now renting in a 1930s mansion block on Kensington High Street. A month later, he was reprimanded by a family friend for not telling his parents where he had been through the autumn and winter. 'I've been in the Middle East, learning how to kill Jews,' Ramírez replied.

One of the first things Ramírez did on returning from Lebanon was to sign up for a course of lectures in economics at the University of London. He also taught Spanish two afternoons a week at a secretarial college near Hyde Park where he tried without success to seduce his students, took some Russian lessons to maintain the moderate proficiency he had acquired in Moscow and continued to accompany his mother to soirées organised by the Latin American community. At a Christopher Columbus Day celebration, he met Nydia Tobón, a tall, intelligent left-wing lawyer fifteen years his senior who had come to London from Colombia after separating from her husband. The two became lovers. They talked a lot about politics – the Middle East, the struggle for revolution around the world, the breaking Watergate scandal in the US – in pubs on the Fulham Road or cafés in Soho and went to the Royal Festival Hall to listen to Tchaikovsky.

London offered various activities for a person interested in revolutionary ideology or political and social transformation. *Time Out* magazine listed 'demos and meetings' alongside 'prog rock' gigs, 'health food' restaurants and experimental 'fringe' theatre. Every weekend protesters somewhere in the city shouted, marched and occasionally clashed with police, whether to highlight the injustices faced by distant populations battling 'imperialist-backed' regimes or those fighting discrimination in Britain itself. Ramírez, who boasted that Napoleon brandy was his favourite drink and enjoyed Cuban cigars with a game of poker, ignored all of this, preferring to spend his free evenings at The Playboy and Churchill's, two expensive West End members' clubs known for their 'hostesses' and occasional patronage by minor celebrities.

Beyond his obvious fondness for the life of a well-heeled young expat in the still slightly swinging British capital, there was another reason for Ramírez to avoid the haunts of London's radical left: he had his heart set on activism of a more disruptive nature. Eventually, more than two years after his return from the Middle East, the call came.

In the autumn of 1973, Tobón detected a change in her lover. He had become preoccupied, tense and uncharacteristically incommunicative. After several bottles of wine in a steak restaurant on the King's Road one evening, Ramírez suddenly revealed the cause of his changed demeanour, blurting out that he had now committed himself entirely to the revolutionary cause, had 'formed a group', and needed her help.

'Nydia, I am not Ilich. I have stopped being him. From now on you must call me Carlos,' he told her. In the immediate aftermath of this declaration, the couple decided to celebrate their new pact of clandestine collaboration with a holiday in France, stopping in Le Havre, Marseille, Saint-Tropez and Paris.

In fact, Ramírez had told Tobón only an approximate version of the truth. Some months earlier, he had briefly returned to Beirut to seek out Haddad, who was then at the beginning of the chaotic and acrimonious process of breaking away from the PFLP, following its decision to eschew further long-range attacks against 'third party' targets in Europe or even further afield. Haddad wanted to keep some ties with the organisation he had helped found five years before – not least because of the resources and legitimacy that membership conferred – but he also wanted his independence. In consequence, Haddad called his own faction the Popular Revolutionary Front for the Liberation of Palestine, though it became more widely known as the Popular Front – External Operations Section, often shortened to Popular Front–XO. The exact relationship between his new breakaway and the original organisation would confound outsiders for many years, though the split was in fact genuine and conclusive.

As the leader of a new group that lacked both cash and personnel, Haddad had welcomed the arrival of Ramírez, and began briefing him on what he could do for the new Popular Front–XO in the UK, a country in which his new group had almost no presence. Ramírez was told that he might also be called on to operate across the Channel, in countries where the Mossad assassination campaign over previous months had thinned the ranks of Haddad's networks. The murder of Boudia just weeks before Ramírez's return to Beirut had been particularly painful and there was now a big gap in France.

The young Venezuelan was enthusiastic about his new tasks, though unhappy not to have been given the leadership role he felt he deserved. Instead he would answer to an experienced Lebanese man called Michel Moukharbal who was being sent to Paris to rebuild Haddad's networks on the continent. For the moment, Ramírez was told, all that was required of him was to return to London and wait. Whether through frustration or trepidation, the waiting had rendered him unusually taciturn.

By October, the wait was over. Ramírez received instructions to travel to Paris to meet Moukharbal and took Tobón with him. The couple found Haddad's new head of European operations at a café called the Parrot's Tavern on the rue de L'Ancienne-Comédie in the heart of the touristy Latin Quarter on the Seine's Left Bank. Despite the martinis they ordered on arrival, the meeting was far from convivial. Ramírez made little effort to hide his resentment at being placed under the authority of the older man. This annoyed Moukharbal, as did, it is probably safe to assume, the presence of his utterly inexperienced subordinate's lover at their first meeting. Their evident mutual dislike did not prevent them meeting on several further occasions over the following days. At one, Moukharbal gave Ramírez an old Beretta pistol and five rounds, explaining that the Popular Front–XO tested all new members with a mission. His would be to shoot Sieff dead.

If Moukharbal or Haddad were disappointed at Ramírez's failure in this endeavour and in his subsequent attack on the Israeli bank, they did not show it. In the late spring of 1974 Ramírez was entrusted with a much more powerful Czech-made automatic handgun, ammunition, grenades and explosives which he hid in Tobón's London apartment. In July, Ramírez was ordered once more to Paris to take part in bombings aimed at three newspapers in the French capital that had been supportive of Israel, as well as the offices of public national broadcasters. Haddad's faction of the Popular Front was still short of funds, and Ramírez was disgusted by the dirty top-floor attic that had been rented for him. He and another operative built the bombs there using instructions that had been provided during his trip to Beirut the previous year, but with so little money he was restricted in his choice of materials, which he also found profoundly irritating. Nonetheless, four out of the five devices he constructed detonated successfully. Warnings had been telephoned to avoid casualties, and the attack was claimed in the name of the 'Mohammed Boudia commando'.

Ramírez had now taken part in three operations for Haddad but was yet to kill. That was about to change.

A short walk from the grubby *grenier* where Ramírez had built his bombs was the Mitsukoshi department store. Opened by the Japanese luxury chain in 1971, the Mitsukoshi was staffed by female Japanese-speaking assistants to cater to the increasing number of wealthy Japanese tourists visiting the city. One was a young woman called Mariko Yamamoto, who was known as hard-working, conscientious, quiet and very good at parting tourists from their money. Codenamed 'Little Miss Full Moon', Yamamoto was also a key member in a network of radical activists working on behalf of what remained of Fusako Shigenobu's Japanese Red Army.

Shigenobu's small group had slowly made good its losses in the bloody attack on Lod airport two years earlier. Though the operation had cost almost half its members, it had won the group notoriety and attracted dozens of fresh recruits from Japan to its bases in Lebanon. This influx had allowed the JRA to launch a series of fresh attacks. In July 1973, a team of new recruits had hijacked a Japanese 747 leaving Amsterdam. Another had launched an attack on oil refineries in Singapore six months later. The first of these operations had gone badly wrong: the leader had blown herself up with a grenade and the hijacked plane had eventually been destroyed on the tarmac in Tripoli. The second had been more successful, causing mayhem and attracting worldwide publicity, after which the attackers had successfully escaped.

Shigenobu had remained personally and organisationally entwined with Haddad's faction of the Popular Front since its schism from the main organisation. Both attacks had been claimed jointly, and the latter had been supported by a simultaneous attack by Haddad's group on the Japanese Embassy in Kuwait designed to put pressure on decision-makers in Tokyo. Shigenobu had also married one of Haddad's deputies in the new Popular Front–XO. But there were tensions too. Shigenobu saw her group as a vanguard of the international battle against imperialism, whose purpose was to shatter the false consciousness of the world's oppressed masses and prompt revolution. Haddad had long since decided that Palestinian liberation took precedence over such sweeping objectives and was under no illusions about the likelihood of there being any kind of revolution, if only a regional upheaval, in the near future. Though eventually these differences would drive the two groups apart, in the summer of 1974 the relationship still worked well.

Shigenobu's recent attacks had prompted a wave of excitement, recruits and offers of support among radical leftists in Europe, especially among Japanese expatriates living in France. One who visited Shigenobu in Beirut in the spring of 1974 suggested a quick way to raise significant funds would be to kidnap senior executives of major Japanese firms overseas and demand ransoms from their employers. To Shigenobu the idea was ideologically attractive and seemed eminently practicable. She decided to send a courier to her sympathisers in France with a sheaf of coded instructions on how to execute planned abductions. And so in early July 1974, as Ramírez and others were preparing to bomb the Paris offices of pro-Israeli newspapers, a member of Shigenobu's group flew in from Beirut carrying $10,000 in counterfeit cash, a stack of documents and three counterfeit passports. Acting on information probably supplied by the Mossad, police stopped the courier at Orly airport, seized the money and then painstakingly decoded the documents. The investigators were particularly intrigued by a love letter. Signed 'Your slave Suzuki', its author said he was 'ill with desire' and wanted to 'embrace your beautiful body again'. It was addressed to 'Little Miss Full Moon' who was eventually located at Mitsukoshi department store.

The arrest of the sales assistant – who turned out to be a master forger – led police to dozens of other members of the conspiracy. Very swiftly, Shigenobu's entire network in Paris had been uncovered and dismantled. Faced with this disaster, she turned to Haddad, who agreed to help organise an operation to force the French to release those detained in the roundup. The obvious thing to do was to take some high-profile French hostages and demand the detainees' freedom as a ransom.

Now it was the turn of the French to commit a significant error. Rather than charge all the Japanese activists arrested over the summer, they decided to expel eight of the most troublesome to Switzerland, allowing them to meet up with Ramírez and Moukharbal in Zurich where they set about planning the hostage-taking. The target would be the French Embassy in The Hague, they decided. It did not take long for Swiss authorities to track them down and arrest them, though they missed the two Popular Front–XO organisers who had already returned to Paris. The Swiss then made the same short-sighted mistake as the French had: they deported their Japanese detainees to West Germany, from where the Germans sent them to the Netherlands, which was exactly where Ramírez and Moukharbal wanted them to be.

This spectacular lucky break was nearly squandered. Ramírez travelled to The Hague to lead the planned attack on the French Embassy but he missed his rendezvous with the assault team, who had been delayed, possibly by the Dutch capital's complex one-way traffic system, and retreated to Paris. Lacking their leader the Japanese went ahead anyway, took control of the embassy without difficulty and announced that they would kill the ambassador and eleven other hostages unless their demands were met: the release of their detained compatriots, a substantial amount of cash and a Boeing 707 with crew to fly them to safety in the Middle East.

Having missed his chance to participate in the assault, Ramírez had been forced to watch from a distance as the crisis played out. After three days, with negotiations dragging, he decided to launch his own freelance operation to pressurise the French into submission. This would be *à l'algérienne*, he decided, inspired by the tactics employed during the final years of Algeria's war of independence from the French, when cafés mainly full of white civilians had been targeted in a series of bloody attacks that proved supremely effective at spreading panic and suspicion.

Late on the afternoon of 15 September, a warm and sunny Sunday, Ramírez took two US-made fragmentation hand grenades and a handgun from one of the Popular Front–XO's secret caches in northern Paris and set off for the Latin Quarter on the other side of the Seine. He was headed for Le Drugstore, a new establishment on the boulevard Saint-Germain decorated in modern American style – all pale wood, windows and chrome – which was fashionable among wealthy young professionals. At 5 p.m., when Ramírez strolled in, the complex was busy with local diners, tourists and many children. He climbed the stairs, entered the toilets and then emerged some moments later and stood among the diners in the café on the mezzanine floor, looking down over the railings to the crowd browsing newspapers, souvenirs, luxury spirits, records and cigarettes in the shops below.

Witnesses later remembered a sudden gesture made by a man of medium height, solidly built, wearing a light grey suit and square tortoiseshell glasses. One spoke of arms suddenly spread; another of one abruptly raised, the other lowered. A moment later, a heavy object 'the size of a pot of jam or mustard' bounced off the marble floor next to the tobacconist on the lower level. Seconds later it exploded. Shards of hot metal shattered glass and splintered wood. The first reporters on the scene described debris and blood mixed together, a bisected body, counters smashed, the acrid smell of the grenade's explosive charge. Waiters from the nearby Brasserie Lipp tried to staunch wounds with white linen napkins. A small boy stared in horror at where his hand had been. Two died and 34 people were injured, several very seriously. Within days, Ramírez was back in London, where he laid low for four months.

In mid-January he returned to Paris – and to the scene of his crime. By now Le Drugstore had been refurbished and reopened. Ramírez browsed the shops and bought some non-essential luxuries, convinced that his attack there had been a success. After all, only two days after the attack, the French had provided the hostage-takers in The Hague with $300,000 and an Air France 707 with a volunteer crew. But as ever, Ramírez's idea of his own talents and achievements was dramatically at odds with reality. In fact, the French officials directing negotiations had been unaware of the bombing in Paris, and the truth was that his record as a clandestine operative for the Popular Front–XO over the previous year and a half was patchy at best. Apart from the bombs he had built, nothing much had worked out as planned.

And yet there was one role in which he had excelled. In the short time Ramírez had been active in western Europe, he had shown an uncanny ability to build relationships. Through the first half of 1975, this would allow him to make a much more significant contribution to the Popular Front's cause than by lobbing grenades, as he used his charm to consolidate an effective operational collaboration between the most extreme elements of the Palestinian nationalist movement and their counterparts amid the fractured, diverse German left. It was an alliance that would lead to an intensification of terrorist violence through the middle of the decade, even if ultimately it would also precipitate its final, catastrophic failure.

13
The Revolutionary Cells

Three months after the attack on Le Drugstore, a young German activist picked up an elderly Frenchman wearing dark glasses and a heavy sheepskin-lined coat from Stuttgart's Echterdingen airport and drove him to the prison on the city's outskirts. There he got out and pushed his way through the small crowd of journalists that had immediately gathered around their battered Peugeot 104 to open the rear door for his diminutive passenger. The reporters fell back, allowing the old man to shuffle past a line of police towards the high, blank concrete walls of the jail.

Jean-Paul Sartre, then sixty-nine, had been an inspiration to many activists of the New Left over the previous decade. An outspoken supporter of the cause of Algerian independence, Sartre had written a preface to Frantz Fanon's *The Wretched of the Earth* in 1961, unequivocally endorsing the book's influential argument that violence would play an essential part in restoring colonised people's dignity and agency. The philosopher had also launched a scathing attack on European liberals who failed to recognise their complicity in the brutal exploitation of the developing world by the West, writing that they were 'living at the moment when the match is put to the fuse'. Though he had mellowed since, Sartre remained a vocal supporter of many of the major New Left causes, and it was his description of the Red Army Faction as 'an interesting force' with a 'sense of the revolution' that had prompted Ulrike Meinhof to invite him to visit the group's leader, Andreas Baader, in prison. Writing from prison herself, where she had been incarcerated since her arrest in June 1972, Meinhof expressed the polite hope that Sartre would accept the opportunity to grant 'the protection of your name and your gifts as a Marxist, philosopher, journalist and moralist'. More pragmatically, she added that such a gesture would make it 'a bit more difficult for the cops' to murder Baader.

Meinhof's fears were comprehensible, if not entirely justified. She had suffered more than 200 days of solitary confinement during which she was kept in a whitewashed, 'acoustically-isolated' cell in the women's psychiatric wing of Cologne-Ossendorf prison, and described its consequences in 'A Letter From the Dead Zone', widely circulated among the other RAF prisoners within the German penal system: 'The feeling that your head is exploding, that your spinal cord is being pressed into your brain, that your brain is gradually shrivelling . . . of falling silent, of pissing your soul away as if unable to hold it in . . . Raw aggression, for which there is no outlet . . . Clear awareness that your chances of survival are none.' Conditions had improved since but the scars remained.

Six months before Sartre's visit, Meinhof, Baader and Ensslin had been transferred to a specially constructed wing of Stammheim prison, the most secure facility anywhere in West Germany, and probably anywhere in western Europe. A steel mesh canopy prevented access from the air and dozens of spotlights lit the entire complex, which was patrolled by hundreds of policemen. A courthouse was built alongside it so that the three could be brought to face trial through an underground tunnel.

Compared to Cologne-Ossendorf though, conditions on the inside were very different. Confident that no escape was possible, authorities felt they could be generous. Prisoners could meet for several hours every day in a corridor full of cushions and blankets, and were allowed radios, televisions and typewriters in their cells. They were also permitted subscriptions to more or less as many periodicals and newspapers as they wanted. Hundreds of books accumulated in a library that soon equalled that of many contemporary social science faculties, featuring works by all of the key thinkers of the New Left, from Carlos Marighella and Régis Debray to Antonio Gramsci, Theodor Adorno, Herbert Marcuse and Noam Chomsky. Increasingly influential French theorists such as Pierre Bourdieu, Michel Foucault and Raymond Barthes filled a whole shelf. Fiction also played an important part. Two of the RAF's favourite authors were Bertholt Brecht and Herman Melville. Ensslin, the former literature student, gave all the members of the RAF codenames based on *Moby-Dick*. Inevitably, Baader was Captain Ahab, while Ensslin decided she was the ship's cook, who 'keeps the pans well scoured and preaches to the sharks'. It did not take a literary critic to spot the parallels between their current situation and Melville's description of a doomed, violent quest by an isolated community surrounded by a hostile sea.

The leaders of the RAF were able to communicate with other prisoners and supporters on the outside thanks to sympathetic lawyers who smuggled messages out of Stammheim and circulated them through what was known as the 'Info System'. The aim of this 'resistance postal service' was to 'prevent solitary confinement from separating and crushing us', remembered junior member Margrit Schiller who had been jailed in 1974, but in reality mutual support was the last thing it offered. 'A harsh tone did predominate,' admitted Schiller. 'Criticism was often used as a cudgel, and it could become a form of self-flagellation. The language used was often unbearable, and relations between us were not comradely.'

It was Meinhof who was most often the target of the abuse. Relations between the former journalist and the other leaders had deteriorated since their arrests, with Ensslin and Baader writing long messages full of vicious insults to the older woman. She was a 'victim, crazy, cracked', a 'liberal cunt' and a 'disorientated pig'. 'You are the knife in the back of the RAF because you never learn,' Ensslin told her. 'You have become a burden . . . you're [one of] the ones destroying us,' Baader added. Meinhof had been the only member of the group not to receive a codename drawn from Melville's novel, and had been dubbed Therese, a long-suffering Catholic saint, instead.

Early in her detention Meinhof had seen her two small daughters several times, but by now she had cut off all contact with them. The growing alienation from the other imprisoned leaders compounded her isolation. She wrote a lengthy work of self-criticism, describing herself as a 'hypocritical bitch from the ruling class' whose 'social development towards fascism through sadism and religion' had been conditioned by the unresolved contradictions of her class background. This savage mea culpa was also circulated among the hundred or so prisoners connected by the Info System. When Meinhof appeared, expressionless and withdrawn, in court in August 1974 to deliver a forty-minute speech in a monotone, watching journalists felt only pity. 'Ulrike Meinhof speaks, turning her sharp mind mercilessly against herself,' one wrote. 'A self-made martyr, a self-elected Joan of Arc of proletarian internationalism, with no army behind her but the people who call themselves the RAF, a spectral image in her poor clever head.'

Over the year, the RAF leadership had ordered a series of hunger strikes in protest at the prison conditions, which attracted massive publicity. A second, then a third round of such protests followed. Some took the logic of the hunger strike to its ultimate conclusion. In November 1974, Holger Meins died in Stammheim after refusing food for two months. The German minister of the interior had given strict instructions that the thirty-three-year-old should be moved into an intensive care ward if his life was in danger but the prison governor and doctor had failed to issue the requisite orders. Shortly before his death, Meins had written to another prisoner that 'everybody dies anyway . . . Only question is how, and how one lived.' For him, the answer was clear, he said. To die 'fighting the pigs as a man for the liberation of mankind . . . That's the way for me: serving the people – RAF.' More than 5,000 people attended Meins' funeral where they dramatically pledged to continue his struggle. In Frankfurt, mourners carried large placards displaying two pictures: the emaciated corpse of Meins and a photo of a naked concentration camp inmate.

Sartre's meeting with Baader took place less than a month later. It was not a success. The philosopher had made clear in an interview two days before that although he was sympathetic to some of the RAF's aims, he did not agree with their methods. Baader greeted his famous guest with a handshake, three minutes of silence and then the words: 'I thought I was dealing with a friend, but they sent me a judge.'

The two men discussed the RAF prisoners' life behind bars and recent hunger strike, before Baader read an incoherent and lengthy prepared statement. Sartre had difficulty following its argument, and asked Baader repeatedly to explain what was meant by references to 'the counter-revolutionary revolution' or a strategy of 'City, city, city, village'. When he told the younger man that any 'revolutionary actions' unpopular with 'the masses' should be avoided, Baader retorted with the results of the well-known poll from 1971 which had shown 'that 20% of the [country's] population are sympathisers'. This statistic was out of date, and Sartre reiterated that conditions in West Germany could not justify violence. The pauses in the exchanges between the two men became longer. Soon Sartre was on his way back to a hotel in Stuttgart for a press conference at which he was critical of the conditions under which Baader was being held but offered little other support. 'Baader was dejected and disappointed . . . that Sartre does not wholeheartedly endorse the actions of [his] group,' an official report of the encounter noted laconically.

Sartre was not alone in his concerns about the RAF's strategy. Many on the left in western Europe were worried that the violence of people like Baader was not only morally misguided but counter-productive and risked undermining the efforts of more moderate activists to bring about change through peaceful means. The spread of such disillusion had accelerated as accounts of the Soviet Union's repression of dissidents circulated more freely and in the wake of incidents such as the indiscriminate murder of dozens of passengers at Rome airport in December 1973 by a minor Palestinian faction. Sartre had been an enthusiastic supporter of Castro's revolution in Cuba but had since turned away from the regime as the extent of its repression became evident, too. Like others, he had revised his previously positive view of China's Communist regime in light of the recently revealed reality of the Cultural Revolution. Those who remained committed to radical change increasingly channelled their energy into other causes: environmentalism, for example, and the battles against racism, homophobia and sexism.

By the early middle years of the 1970s, several countries had lowered the voting age to eighteen; others had promised to do so. There had been reform of higher education and new funds invested in universities. The 'generation gap' had narrowed as businesses and politicians appropriated or assimilated 'youth culture'. Younger people were more prominent in public life, whether as politicised pop singers or celebrity sportspeople. Even for those who had been throwing bricks and bottles in 1968, the revolution was no longer quite so urgent. And the revolutionary was increasingly out of fashion. When John Lennon recorded a double album of protest songs, it was a commercial and critical disaster, whereas when The Who told their millions of fans they 'Won't Get Fooled Again' by those promising radical change they enjoyed massive success. The album which broke all the records in 1973 was Pink Floyd's almost entirely apolitical *The Dark Side of the Moon*. The new search for personal fulfilment often entailed extreme behaviour – the consumption of psychotropic drugs, membership of bizarre and sometimes deeply disturbing cults or sects, sexual experimentation – but not extremism. 'Don't Dream It, Be It', sang the cast of the transgressive but politically inoffensive *Rocky Horror Picture Show*. This was not exactly a call to the barricades.

Many of those who had turned to violence at the end of the previous decade now decided this had been a mistake. In 1970 the Weather Underground recognised their 'military error' and announced they no longer considered 'the armed struggle the only revolutionary struggle'. As effective as guns or bombings were 'grass and consciousness-expanding drugs', the group said in a statement. The Black Panther party split following founder Huey Newton's decision to favour social activism and participate in local government. In the UK, several members of the Angry Brigade were now in prison for their short-lived and amateurish bombing campaign, which had brought the group's activities more or less to an end. In Japan, there had been no resurgence of extremism since the horrific snow murders. The Tupamaros, the Uruguayan 'urban guerrilla' group that had inspired many aspirant revolutionaries across the developed world, had succeeded in their bid to provoke a brutal crackdown but miscalculated the level of their likely support among the masses and were wiped out amid general indifference. In Italy, the Red Brigades were increasingly active but so far could muster only around a thousand or so adherents and just a hundred 'regulars'. By contrast, the violent organisations that appeared to have momentum in western Europe – the Irish Republican Army, nationalist groups in Corsica, separatists in the Basque region – may have seen themselves as revolutionary socialists fighting imperialism, and were steeped in the wider culture of political revolt, but their projects were certainly not internationalist nor even particularly progressive.

Baader had told Sartre that he and his followers were seeking closer ties with revolutionary groups in the developing world, particularly those based in Arab states and South America. In practice, however, the RAF were focused almost exclusively on more proximate battles: primarily the improvement of the conditions of their members in prison. In the late spring of 1973, RAF members had worked with Fatah's Black September to hijack an El Al plane flying out of Amsterdam, but the operation had been aborted at the last minute by Ali Hassan Salameh in order to comply with Arafat's new ban on such targets. Since then, the RAF had had almost no contact with any groups outside Germany, let alone in the Middle East. This meant that when Wadie Haddad's Popular Front–XO reached out in late 1974 to propose its own collaborative projects, the RAF had neither the desire nor the ability to respond positively.

But there were others in Germany who did.

*

The man who drove Sartre from Stuttgart airport to Stammheim prison was a twenty-seven-year-old former thief named Hans-Joachim Klein. Klein's mother had been a concentration camp survivor who killed herself shortly after the end of the war. He had grown up first in a care home, then with foster parents and finally with his own father, a violent, drunken policeman with fascist sympathies. Klein was convinced that his mother had been Jewish and his father an SS officer. This was not true but contributed to his acute sense of the failings of previous generations in Germany and the duty this imposed on their children. Teenage years marked by exclusion from a number of schools, delinquency, car theft and assaults on immigrants and homosexuals led eventually to eight months in jail. In 1967, having finished his compulsory year of military service, Klein attended one of the protests breaking out all over West Germany. This was something of an epiphany. 'I saw three cops beating up a woman. Two images collided, my image of women and my image of cops. I went to help her. I hit out and got hit back. From that moment on I began to think,' he wrote later.

Shortly afterwards, Klein went to a 'teach in' run by left-wing students. Surprised and pleased to find that the largely middle-class activists were attracted rather than repelled by his criminal record and lack of formal education, he was soon a regular at such events. Then came enthusiastic participation in protests against the war in Vietnam, an introduction to the texts of Mao and a serious relationship with another activist. Home became a series of communes in Frankfurt's run-down West End district. Here he noticed that everyone was smoking Gauloises, so he began to smoke them too.

Frankfurt was a centre for the Spontaneous or 'Sponti' movement, which advocated for anarchic acts of revolt rather than the mass mobilisation favoured by the Marxists. From a series of squatted buildings in the centre of the city, leaders organised kindergartens, cultural events and workshops as well as demonstrations, particularly against the gentrification of poor neighbourhoods. Klein spent much time at 'Revolutionary House', a squat where the group 'Revolutionary Struggle' was based. Residents aimed to follow Adorno's call 'to lead the right life in the wrong society' and so, perhaps, prompt radical change through their own example. Others were having similar ideas around this time in Egypt, Saudi Arabia and elsewhere in the Islamic world.

Frankfurt's Spontis had gathered an international reputation, producing a rich network of links with French and other foreign movements. A frequent visitor was Danny Cohn-Bendit, the high-profile German-born activist who had led the protests in Paris in 1968 and whose car Klein occasionally repaired. Protest leaders from the US were admiring – and their appreciation was fully reciprocated in Frankfurt. In 1971, Klein had helped organise a series of rallies in support of the Black Panthers and was among the young men recruited to act as bodyguards for Kathleen Cleaver, the famous activist, when she came to speak at Frankfurt University. Like many other Spontis, Klein had already enthusiastically read *Soul on Ice*, the incendiary book by Cleaver's husband, the Black Panthers' information minister, Eldridge Cleaver.

A year later, Klein travelled to Paris with activist friends for a weekend. He ended up staying several months, earning a living as a mechanic, fighting right-wing thugs, dodging the feared French riot police, reading Fanon's *The Wretched of the Earth* (or at least Sartre's introduction) and enjoying a screening of *The Battle of Algiers*. On his return to Frankfurt, he became more deeply involved in the support groups set up to campaign on behalf of the RAF members in jail, working part-time for a lawyer who represented Meinhof.

Some of Klein's new comrades were close to key members of the 'Revolutionary Cells', a loose coalition of the various small groups, often made up of no more than half a dozen or so friends, lovers or even relatives, that had emerged in West German cities over the previous four years. The cells were committed to violence in the cause of revolutionary change but, influenced by the Sponti scene and reaction against the 'dogmatism and elitism' of the RAF, sought to create 'small nuclei of resistance' that remained free to organise their own actions, without reference to a wider hierarchy, and eschewed criminal activities like bank robberies that would force them underground. Predictably, the RAF dismissed them as 'only playing with the idea of revolution', but while it was true that the Revolutionary Cells preferred blocking train ticket machines with glue to wielding firearms, and that few of the hundreds of bombs they planted caused much damage or any casualties, their members were undoubtedly committed and their actions arguably more effective.

The death of Meins in November 1974 triggered a shift in Klein's attitude. 'We had marched about Vietnam and got smashed in the face. We marched about the racism against Blacks in the USA and the conditions of migrant workers in West Germany and got smashed in the face. We marched to protest the demolition of a neighbourhood, and conditions [in prison], and got smashed in the face . . . And Holger was dead, and I had had enough of the street [where] the only thing we had ever obtained was proof of our own impotence.' From now on, Klein felt that peaceful protest was doomed to failure. For some time, he kept a photograph of Meins' emaciated corpse in his wallet so as not to dull the edge of his 'hatred'.

Tall, thin, clumsy and introverted, with unsightly teeth and a mournful expression, Klein did not initially impress the RAF membership who nicknamed him 'Klein Klein' ('Little Little') and 'Schnitzel', after the only dish he was ever seen to consume in Hamburg's cafés. But the steady nerves he had shown when driving Sartre around Stuttgart demonstrated potential, and he spent the subsequent weeks covering thousands of miles around Germany on errands for his new comrades in arms. Then he was given another, more important mission, one that would prove very significant in connecting the Revolutionary Cells with Wadie Haddad's faction of the PFLP, and so uniting two of the most extreme actors in Europe and the Middle East.

The boast of the Revolutionary Cells that they had no leaders was only partly true. Some individuals had greater authority and influence than others. One was Wilfried Boese, a twenty-five-year-old activist and former publisher of left-wing and feminist literature who had been a founder of the organisation. Klein looked up to Boese and so was glad to be asked to drive him to Paris for what he was told was an important meeting.

This took place in an elegant apartment block in the centre of the city – 'the sort of place where the concierge coughs very discreetly, if at all', Klein remembered. The man waiting for the two Germans in a beautifully furnished room was like no one Klein had previously encountered either in the world of revolutionary activism or beyond. He wore aftershave and a tailored suit and had the appearance of some kind of 'Italian mafioso'. Boese had told Klein that the man they were meeting represented a Palestinian group but as the conversation, conducted in English, was incomprehensible to him, Klein did not linger, instead spending the rest of the day walking through Paris and eating crepes.

The 'mafioso' was Ilich Ramírez who, since the attack on Le Drugstore seven months earlier, had been very busy. In January, he and Michel Moukharbal, the head of the Popular Front–XO's operations in western Europe, had organised two attacks on Israeli passenger planes at Orly, France's international airport south of Paris. Typically, neither had gone according to plan. For the first, they had been promised some of the new shoulder-fired surface-to-air 'Strela' missiles developed by the Soviets, but in the event were given a much inferior rocket-propelled grenade launcher, which had an effective range of only around 300 yards. A specially trained Palestinian had been flown in to fire the weapon but was very nervous at the vital moment and struggled to release the launcher's safety catch. When he did fire from his position at the airport's perimeter fence, the shot missed the El Al plane taxiing for take-off by a significant margin, flew across the apron and struck a Croat plane. Meanwhile, the weapon's recoil upended the firer while its infamous back-blast blew out the windscreen of the Peugeot 504 they had hired for their getaway. The chastened attackers picked themselves up and drove rapidly away, clearing the shattered windscreen as they drove. Given the condition of the vehicle, which was bound to attract attention, they dumped it a few miles from the airport where it was found an hour or so later, with some grenades and a handgun on the back seat, by a policeman on a bicycle.

A second effort fared little better, though its outcome was more advantageous to the Popular Front–XO. The same team had returned to Orly and hidden another rocket-propelled grenade in a toilet close to the viewing terrace overlooking the runways, ahead of an attack planned for the following Sunday. But Ramírez and Moukharbal had overlooked the fact that weekends on the terrace were considerably busier than mid-week, and when the three Palestinians sent by Haddad for the operation tried to retrieve the weapon at the appointed hour they found themselves stuck in a lengthy queue for the facilities. By the time the trio had found, loaded and set up the launcher amid astonished sightseers and plane-spotters on the now very crowded viewing terrace, the El Al plane they had hoped to hit was well out of range. After a chaotic firefight with armed police, the men fled, ending up in another lavatory with a dozen tourists, a priest, a four-year-old child and a pregnant woman as hostages. After lengthy negotiations, French authorities provided a plane and flew them to the Middle East. The PLO issued a statement stressing that it 'had stopped all [such] operations quite some time ago', called the attack a 'criminal act' which constituted 'conspiracy against the Palestinian cause and people' and denied that any fedayeen group was involved in it.

Even so, Haddad's group claimed the attack as a significant victory, and neither of these failures appeared to dismay the ebullient Ramírez, who now had a proposition for Boese. The two men had been in touch for several months, and the Revolutionary Cells had already helped the RAF on a number of occasions by providing weapons, documents and minor logistical assistance. This time however Ramírez had a more ambitious suggestion. He and Moukharbal hoped to raise tens of millions of dollars to pay for a series of major operations in West Germany by kidnapping and ransoming the ambassador of the United Arab Emirates in London, a man of very considerable personal wealth. They had already put together a team but were short of a competent mechanic-cum-driver. Boese said he would send Klein.

Preparations for the kidnap attempt in London lasted much of the late spring, and though it was eventually called off when it became clear that the target was too well protected, it gave Klein the chance to get to know the stylish young man he had met briefly in Paris. 'Johnny', as he knew Ramírez, impressed him greatly. He was 'a real James Bond', a 'very cool guy [who] didn't waste time on details, knew an enormous amount about politics and the Palestinian question, read newspapers by the ton' and showed off his collection of weapons in his hotel room 'as calmly as if he were showing a stamp collection'. Even if Ramírez stayed in a five-star hotel for reasons of 'safety' while the others in the team made do with a modest boarding house or rented basement apartments, this flamboyant and fastidious man still took his turn sitting in parks in the rain watching embassies. Ramírez's explanation for his refusal to eat in 'chip shops and canteens' and his taste for expensive suits was that he had been unable to shed the refinement he had learned as a 'bourgeois child'. The German thought this reasoning showed his comrade had class, in every sense.

When Haddad cancelled the operation in May, Klein returned to Frankfurt's left-wing bookshops and squats. Six months later, Ramírez would call on his services again. In the meantime, a series of attacks by a new West German group dashed any hopes that the incarceration of the leaders of the RAF would put an end to such violence.

On 5 February 1975, a month before Boese and Ramírez met in Paris, the leadership of the RAF ordered their followers in prison to end the third hunger strike. In a letter circulated through the Info System, Meinhof explained that to continue to use this 'ultimate weapon' would not further the 'propagation, mobilisation and organisation of anti-imperialist politics' and so meant sacrificing their lives for no useful purpose. Many had already started eating, others had only been kept alive by forced feeding.

The hunger strike, the death of Meins and the loud campaign to end their 'torture' in jail may not have broadened support for the RAF but it had injected a new energy into radical left-wing politics in Germany, and local authorities were 'now having second thoughts about their earlier conclusion that hard core Baader-Meinhof support had been crushed'. One problem, US diplomats in Germany cabled to Washington, was that both sides in Germany's polarised debate over political violence were exploiting the media very effectively. The 'carefully staged media event' of Sartre's visit to Stammheim was an example of 'the extreme left's strategy for building sympathy for the Baader-Meinhof gang', they said. But 'on the other side of the fence', there was the 'drum fire of headlines about the terrorists and terrorist activities' in conservative newspapers that was 'designed to feed public insecurity' and so discredit a coalition government led by the centre-left Social Democratic party. This tactic appeared successful, the diplomats said: polls showed that people were frightened. Hard days may be ahead, they concluded.

A month after the end of the RAF hunger strike, a well-known conservative mayoral candidate in West Berlin called Peter Lorenz was abducted only days before elections in the city. The response to the kidnapping, the first by extremists for political ends in the post-war history of Germany, was confused, and the identity of those responsible was not immediately clear. Many suspected the RAF, and at least one member of the group was among the ten prisoners whose release was demanded in return for sparing Lorenz's life. But in statements and communications with the police, the abductors identified themselves only as the June 2 Movement.

More a chaotic collective than an organised group, the J2M, as they became known, took their name from the date of the demonstration eight years before when the murder of a student by a policeman catalysed West Germany's protest movement. Like the RAF, the group had emerged from West Berlin's lively scene of communes, cannabis, petty crime, conscription dodging and situationist stunts. Many of those involved saw political activism and even violence as an extension of the rejection of all that was 'square', and continued to wear leather coats, boots and flares even as they swapped joints for homemade explosives.

Like the Revolutionary Cells, the J2M saw the RAF as authoritarians obsessed with esoteric Marxist theory and promoted themselves as an earthier, more proletarian alternative. As slightly fewer of their members came from middle-class backgrounds, this claim had some credibility.

The abduction of Lorenz was a tactical victory for the group. German authorities had paid ransoms before and released prisoners too. But these had been foreigners, not local extremists convicted of serious crimes. Very reluctantly, Helmut Schmidt, who had taken power as chancellor after Willy Brandt's private secretary was revealed to have been an East German spy, forcing Brandt to resign, decided he had little option but to agree to the J2M's demands, though he first checked that none of those being released had been convicted for murder. The prisoners were then collected from various prisons, transported to Tegel airport and flown to the Middle East. Lorenz, who had been relatively well treated, was then freed. 'This is not to be considered a precedent . . . but it will unavoidably have a certain effect,' warned Werner Maihofer, the minister of the interior.

This gloomy assessment was soon shown to be entirely justified. Just over a month after the abduction of Lorenz, six attackers stormed the West German Embassy in Stockholm. Swedish security services had been tapping the telephones of the leaders of the group that Gunnar Ekberg had infiltrated for many years, and so had picked up rumours that some kind of attack in their country by a German group was imminent, but they did not act fast enough. Calling themselves the 'Holger Meins commando', the six men barricaded themselves on the embassy's upper levels with fifteen kilos of explosives, weapons and several hostages. One – the defence attaché – was shot when Swedish police refused to withdraw from the lower floors and a second was executed after the attackers heard that Bonn had refused outright to release Baader, Ensslin, Meinhof or any of the twenty-three other members of the RAF whose liberty they had demanded. There followed a standoff of several hours which ended when the explosives wired around the embassy detonated prematurely, engulfing the top floors of the building in a vast ball of fire.

The attackers had always believed the operation would end either in death or success. The blast and blaze killed one of them. A second died shortly afterwards in a German prison hospital. 'We were only a few comrades, without experience in illegal armed struggle . . . we saw [death] as a victory of sorts too, because if we died we would never be absorbed by the system we hated,' one of the surviving hostage-takers later said.

In prison, the jailed RAF leaders celebrated this evidence of continuing support for them on the outside. Meinhof described the attack as the 'Dien Bien Phu of social democracy', a reference to the catastrophic defeat of French colonial forces in Vietnam in 1954, which served only to underline how utterly out of touch with what was happening outside Stammheim she had become.

On 21 May 1975, amid unprecedented security, the trial of Meinhof, Baader, Ensslin and Jan-Carl Raspe, another RAF second-rank leader, began in the specially constructed courtroom at the prison in Stammheim. They were charged with four actual and fifty-four attempted murders. According to US diplomats, this violence of the previous six years showed how 'a small group of fanatic terrorists can play havoc with highly developed, industrial/technological societies', something that 'has become an accepted fact of life in the 1970's'.

14
Winter in New York, Summer in Paris

An evening in late June 1975 on the rue Toullier, a side street dropping steeply down to the grand, pillared southern facade of the Sorbonne university. At one end, The Shanghai, a Chinese restaurant; at the other, a brasserie called Le Soufflot. The hottest night for almost two decades, and all the shutters and windows of the tall, terraced Parisian townhouses are open. This is not an expensive neighbourhood, despite its proximity to the centre of 'the city of light', so is popular with students and young couples who enjoy what the guidebooks call its 'hippy ambience'. There is laughter, music, occasional shouting and the sound of a four-stringed guitar from an apartment on the second floor of an annexe at the back of number nine.

It is shortly before nine o'clock, and two formally dressed men are knocking at the apartment's door. They are police officers from the Direction de la Surveillance du Territoire (DST), a service charged since 1944 with countering 'activities of espionage and of alien powers on territories under French sovereignty' and, more recently, of terrorism too.

In a car parked around the corner, a two-minute walk along the crowded pavements, is another policeman and a thirty-five-year-old Lebanese man with a narrow face, mop of straight brown hair and moustache. He is Michel Moukharbal, the head of operations in Europe for Wadie Haddad's breakaway faction of the Popular Front, and he is under arrest.

Moukharbal was picked up by the DST a few days after landing at Orly airport from Beirut. It is no mystery how the French security services knew of his arrival. Their Lebanese counterparts, the Sûreté Nationale, had arrested Moukharbal at the airport in Beirut as he sought to board the plane to Paris, interrogated him for three days and then let him go. They then warned the French of his imminent arrival and said he was likely to meet people involved in planning attacks in Paris. So the DST had then followed Moukharbal for several days to see who his contacts might be, before finally taking him off the streets and putting him in a cell where he had been answering questions until a few hours ago, when he reluctantly gave his interrogators an address: the apartment on rue Toullier. He is now waiting with one police officer while the two others set off to find it. But Moukharbal is experienced and clever, and he has a plan.

The first part of his strategy is complete. He has almost convinced his interrogators that he has not been involved in any of the violence perpetrated by Arab groups in France over the previous year, or at least not in any significant way. He is just a travelling salesman, making a poor but more or less honest living buying and selling carpets and electrical goods in Paris and Beirut. Yes, he has admitted, he knows a young Latin American businessman going by the name of Carlos Andres Martínez Torres but their relationship is entirely innocent. Yes, he met Martínez Torres for a coffee the day after his arrival in Paris, while he was under their surveillance, and yes, he and Martínez Torres had enjoyed a lengthy and animated conversation. But no, he can't remember exactly what they discussed nor what was in the bag he handed over to his friend. He can say, however, that Martínez Torres is certainly not a terrorist. What he could also say, but does not, is that the real name of Martínez Torres is Ilich Ramírez Sánchez, soon to be known to the world as Carlos the Jackal.

And so to part two of the plan: Why don't they talk to Martínez Torres themselves, Moukharbal suggests, and then all this unpleasantness can be cleared up. He knows where they can probably find the man they are worried about.

Now Moukharbal is taking a chance. He tells the DST to look for Martínez Torres at the apartment of a Venezuelan anthropology student, an occasional lover, close to the Sorbonne. Moukharbal is confident that the risk of the police actually finding his subordinate and accomplice there is minimal. He knows that Ramírez rarely spends two successive nights in the same place, has several girlfriends and tends to eat in restaurants in the evening. If the DST question the anthropology student, she will probably confirm that her close friend sometimes drops by but is unlikely to know his actual whereabouts. Either way, Moukharbal will have demonstrated his willingness to help, and perhaps then the authorities will proceed with his expulsion from France without any further difficult questions while Ramírez is left free to continue the work of the Popular Front–XO alone. The plan could backfire badly of course, but it is a good one. Or so it must have seemed.

But Moukharbal is unlucky. The anthropology student is not at home, having departed for the airport and her flight home to Venezuela hours before – but her apartment is not empty, as the guests at her leaving party have continued the festivities and are still there when Commissioner Jean Herranz, who has been in charge of the interrogation of Moukharbal, knocks on the door.

After twenty-five years in the police, this is just another investigation and another evening spent checking a detainee's stories in the back streets of Paris. According to the regulations he and his colleagues should be armed, but as they were on their way home they checked in their service revolvers before leaving headquarters. Herranz knocks again, identifies himself when the door is opened, is allowed to enter, and asks to see everyone's papers.

The apartment is small: one room, a kitchenette and a bathroom. Herranz sees a double bed, a desk, a sofa, a cheap rug on the floor and posters on the walls – the inevitable portrait of Che Guevara and one of Fidel Castro. A low table is crowded with dirty glasses, a box of cigarillos, bottles of wine, pastis and J&B whisky. The curtains are drawn and some of the paint is peeling off the walls. The apartment feels crowded, though there are only four people there. All are young, in their mid-twenties. Three wear typical student dress: jeans, scarves, long shirts, denim jackets, bangles and bead necklaces. But one is wearing tinted glasses, a blue blazer and brown trousers, and looks very like the missing associate of Moukharbal. When asked to present his papers, he hands over a Peruvian passport.

Herranz opens the document and reads the name Carlos Martínez Torres. Flicking through its pages, he sees stamps indicating recent trips to Lebanon.

'Do you know any Arabs?', he asks.

'No, I hate Arabs . . . [and] anyone can go to Beirut as a tourist,' its owner answers brusquely.

There is a pause. Herranz says something to the officer who accompanied him into the apartment. Inspector Raymond Dous, a decorated veteran of the Algerian war just weeks from retirement, rummages in a briefcase and then holds out some surveillance photographs. One shows Moukharbal, who is still in the car parked around the corner, alone on a street in Paris two weeks earlier. Another appears to show him with the man whose passport Herranz is holding. The photographs are blurred and indistinct but it is difficult to deny the resemblance. There is tension now. The young man becomes angry, denies any connection to the individual in the photographs, blusters, threatens to call his ambassador or his father who 'is very important' or both, but then abruptly apologises, says he was rude because he was 'nervous', and offers whiskies all round. Herranz searches him for a weapon, finds none, and accepts the drink. One of the other guests strums the guitar and sings for a moment. The tension ebbs. The young man excuses himself, walks the few steps to the bathroom, enters and locks the door behind him. Beside the toilet is a brown washbag containing shaving brushes, razors and a Czech-made pistol loaded with eight rounds.

Later, there would be much criticism of Herranz and his colleagues. Many commentators expressed astonishment that they were unarmed and without radios. Had they no idea of how dangerous 'Carlos' was? they asked.

The short answer to this justified question was no. Herranz was playing to different rules, ones that the man he met on rue Toullier had rejected long before, if he had ever known them.

Herranz had been working on Middle Eastern extremism for two years. In that time, he had dealt with scores of individuals from tens of different groups from a dozen countries and none had tried to kill him. Instead, a series of quiet understandings were negotiated, based on the simple premise that if foreign extremists did nothing to endanger the lives of French citizens or seriously harm the country's broader interests, their activities would be tolerated. The DST was well aware that a particular Arabic-language bookshop in Paris was a meeting place for active members of the Black September Organisation, for example, but preferred to watch the store rather than shut it down. Herranz regularly had lunch with the official representatives of the PLO in Paris, who claimed the organisation was not involved in violence, and knew ma[illegible]ther Palestinian activists in the city, some of whom clearly were. Basil al-K[illegible]he PFLP propagandist and thinker shot dead by the Mossad near L'Opéra in 1972, had been a source of much information, if not a fully paid-up agent.

Such pragmatism made the French capital a congenial and practical base for extremists from places as diverse as Armenia and Argentina.

The city, like London, was still busy with protests, marches and meetings despite the disappointing outcome of the seemingly revolutionary moment of 1968, and there was still plenty of energy and *engagement* in the universities and among critical theorists and historians. Eldridge Cleaver, the former 'Information Minister' of the Black Panthers who was wanted for murder in the US and had recently been granted political asylum in France, lived openly with his family in a house near the Latin Quarter and was feted as a minor celebrity at society parties.

Few French government officials, politicians or police officers were particularly appreciative of the presence of so many foreign extremists on their territory, but most saw the policy adopted by successive governments as sensible, if unsavoury. Such deals were not unlike the unspoken understanding between Western espionage services and their counterparts in Moscow: when spies were caught, they were sometimes imprisoned, to be exchanged in a few years, or just discreetly asked to leave. Certainly, no one started shooting.

As importantly, the French attitude towards extremists in Paris aligned with the country's foreign policy. Though Paris had been a close supporter of Israel from the middle 1950s, a partner during the Suez debacle, its main arms supplier and the provider of the technology for its incipient nuclear programme, the relationship had soured from 1967. At a press conference, President Charles de Gaulle spoke of Jews as a 'domineering, elite people', military sales were curtailed, the Mossad was forced to leave its Paris headquarters, French contacts with Arab leaders multiplied and criticism of Israel became more strident. The French were also profoundly angered by the killings carried out by the Mossad on the streets of their capital city, sending condolences to the family of at least one victim, as well as by Israel's leaders' attitude to attempts to negotiate an end to their conflict with their neighbours. Paris laid the blame for the war in 1973 squarely on Israeli intransigence and responded relatively positively to the PLO's requests for senior-level meetings in its aftermath.

Many other European governments pursued similar strategies, some with the express intention of reducing the chances of being targeted by the Palestinian armed factions. By the time Ramírez was fully active for Wadie Haddad in Paris, both the Swiss and the Italians had come to a tacit understanding with a range of Palestinian groups that they would be allowed to operate without significant hindrance if they targeted their attacks elsewhere. Many political leaders shared the French view that any serious domestic problem with international extremists could be resolved by exporting it to another country, even just over the nearest frontier. When the Revolutionary Cells leader Wilfried Boese was detained in France a month or two later after meeting Ramírez in Paris, he convinced a judge that he was travelling across the Pyrenees to support violent Basque separatists and was released.

In simple practical terms, logistical, legal and cultural obstacles to effective counter-terrorist efforts remained very significant. Ramírez had been briefly put under surveillance by MI5 in London following a tip-off from French security services in 1971. Agents from the British domestic intelligence service followed their target to a laundrette and reported that he appeared 'agitated and nervous'. This was unsurprising as Ramírez was aware that he was being watched. But the investigation was dropped very rapidly, probably because its target differed so dramatically from MI5's understanding of what an 'Arab extremist' looked like. Even after Munich, only a tiny minority of British or French investigators were knowledgeable about or even interested in Middle Eastern terrorism, and most domestic security officials saw the threat posed by such groups as essentially minor.

By mid-1975, however, it was becoming clear to the French security services at least that their approach was inadequate. The assault on the French Embassy in The Hague and the two attacks on Orly airport had come close to killing large numbers of people. In the case of the latter, the most pressing task was to identify those responsible, and yet the French police struggled to make any progress in the investigation. But as men like Herranz reasoned, if they could not find out *who* was responsible, they might at least try to find out *why* some Palestinian groups had decided to escalate their operations at that exact moment, as this could eventually help them find the perpetrators and stop them before they attacked again.

The answer to this question was to be found not in France but in New York.

For Yasser Arafat, the summer and autumn of 1974 had passed in a frenzy of travel. He had been on the move almost incessantly for a decade or more, but his decision in the late spring of 1973 to pivot at least temporarily from an armed to a diplomatic strategy had prompted an almost absurd acceleration of his movements. In the weeks after his appearance at the East German youth festival in July of that year, the PLO chairman and Fatah leader had attended summits or bilateral meetings in Morocco, Algiers and Tripoli. In November, Arafat flew to Riyadh, Baghdad, Cairo, and then, via a stop in eastern Europe, to Moscow for a successful week-long stay. In addition he made dozens of less significant trips, often flying thousands of miles to appear at a parade, sit through a speech, or attend a meeting for a few hours.

The man in charge of Arafat's personal security on these journeys was Ali Hassan Salameh. Now thirty-three years old, Salameh had not just survived the factional battles that had wracked Fatah and the PLO since 1970 but had improved his position within both organisations. He was under no illusions that this achievement was due to anything other than Arafat's continuing patronage, and had amply demonstrated his loyalty to 'the Old Man' by accepting without demur his controversial decision to abandon the campaign of violence outside Israel. This obedience had earned Salameh overall command of Arafat's moderately ramshackle force of bodyguards, and he now enjoyed considerable responsibilities for intelligence-gathering within both Fatah and the PLO. The new post was an important one but dangerous too. The Mossad had made multiple efforts to kill Arafat over previous years and was still convinced that Salameh had been mastermind of the Munich attack. Not only that, they remained profoundly concerned by his contact with the CIA.

In fact, the relationship between Salameh and the American intelligence community had been instrumental in a shift of attitudes in Washington that in the autumn of 1974 saw Arafat making preparations for a landmark visit to the US.

The previous spring, when Salameh had met Bob Ames in Beirut and explained the change in PLO strategy away from international attacks, it had been understood for what it really was: a proposal for an entirely new relationship with the US. The offer had been conveyed to Kissinger in late July of that year by Richard Helms, the former director of the CIA who was ambassador in Tehran. At the end of a long conversation that had ranged over US policy towards Pakistan and Iran's increasingly cantankerous shah, Helms had told Henry Kissinger, the recently appointed Secretary of State, about the meetings between 'a fellow on my staff' and someone highly placed within the PLO. 'I do not even know who the contact is; I do not want to know,' Helms said. 'But I can guarantee you that he is one of Arafat's right hand men . . . The issue is whether you want to have policy talks with the fedayeen or not.'

Kissinger had decided that any serious conversation with the PLO was out of the question but told his staff to draft and send to Arafat what he called a 'nothing message'. Typed on a sheet of plain paper, and left both undated and unsigned, the message stressed that 'a peaceful settlement of the Arab-Israeli problem must take into account the reasonable interests of *all* the people in the area, including both the people in existing states and the Palestinians', but if the PLO was genuinely interested in negotiations, then the US government would be pleased to hear its ideas. Though deliberately anodyne and entirely non-committal, this missive had greatly encouraged Arafat.

Since the war of 1973, Arafat had been attempting to build bridges with Washington. While the conflict had cost Israel almost 3,000 dead, more than a hundred combat aeroplanes and 800 tanks, it had ended with Israeli forces within artillery range of Damascus and sixty miles from Cairo. The huge US resupply effort dramatically underlined the kind of support Israel could now rely on from Washington. The conflict also underlined that the Egyptian president Anwar Sadat had no appetite for an all-out war against Israel. Not only had Sadat lauded the war as a major victory despite failing to 'liberate' any territory of real significance, but all available evidence suggested that he had no intention whatsoever of launching any renewed effort. It was crystal-clear to Arafat that the PLO needed to accept the new reality if it was going to survive. The content of Kissinger's message may have been banal and disappointing, but the fact of it, and its implicit acknowledgement of Palestinian grievances, were highly significant.

Spurred on by its receipt, Arafat had launched a major diplomatic offensive. PLO officials requested meetings with senior British and French diplomats in Cairo and made approaches via a host of unconventional intermediaries: businessmen acting as fixers for US envoys in Beirut, well-connected journalists, junior politicians from Western nations who were visiting the Middle East, friendly Arab monarchs. Even Nicolai Ceauşescu, the Romanian dictator, spoke to Kissinger on Arafat's behalf at a reception in Washington. Though conducted with customary frantic energy, Arafat was attempting a highly delicate manoeuvre: not only to convince Western governments of his abandonment of violent attacks but also to persuade his followers that it was the right time to do so.

The seismic shift in the PLO had come in June 1974 with the decision of its national council to approve a new goal: the establishment of a 'national, independent and fighting authority' on 'any liberated parts of

Palestine'. This was described as an interim objective but it was widely understood to mean accepting a state alongside Israel, not in place of it, and possibly on no more than around twenty-two per cent of the historic territory of the old British Mandate. One senior Fatah official explained to Eric Rouleau of *Le Monde* that, however difficult it might be to surrender their dream of a definitive defeat of Zionism and Israel, he and his comrades had concluded that it was in the overriding interest of the Palestinian people to accept a compromise and the 'often cruel verdict of history'.

Once agreed by the PLO, albeit amid emotional scenes and in the face of much fiery opposition, the next step had been to win the support of those who funded the movement and who might, if not treated right, conclude their own agreements with Israel at the expense of the Palestinians. This was achieved at a summit in Morocco in October 1974 attended by dozens of Arab heads of state where the new objectives and strategy were endorsed. The assembled monarchs and presidents also agreed to recognise the PLO officially as the sole legitimate representative of the Palestinians, much to the chagrin of King Hussein of Jordan who had long claimed the role. These were very significant personal victories for Arafat, consolidating his authority within the nationalist movement and regionally, but the following month they were overshadowed by a spectacular achievement at a global level.

In November 1974, a special session of the UN General Assembly in New York would be devoted to 'the Question of Palestine', with Arafat as headline speaker. The 'guerrilla chieftain', as he was described by the Associated Press news agency, would be the first leader of a national liberation movement and the first person not representing a member government to address the body since Pope Paul VI. The significance of Arafat being given such a platform, with such honours, just a decade after Fatah had launched the armed struggle, six years after Karameh, only four after the bloody debacle in Jordan, two after the Munich attack, and less since the group's gunmen had shot dead two US diplomats in Khartoum, was not lost on his critics, but there appeared very little that they could do about it.

Ever since the foundation of Fatah, Arafat had framed the group and Palestinian nationalism more broadly as part of a global revolutionary effort. This was largely rhetorical and in some sense superfluous: the Palestinian cause had swiftly been adopted by the New Left in the West and by the post-colonial states of the developing world as a continuation of their own struggles, important in its own right, but also a symbol of wider iniquities. Arafat had understood that, hard as it was to unite these diverse actors around a specific course of action, they could form a powerful coalition when in pursuit of a common objective – and the UN provided precisely the forum in which such a coalition could be formed and express itself.

The power of that coalition had been made very obvious when the Arab members of OPEC imposed their oil embargo and production cuts during the 1973 war. The impact on the US economy had been as brutal as it had been in Europe, plunging it into a deep recession and exacerbating the sense among many Americans, already reeling from failure in Vietnam and the Watergate scandal, that their nation was a declining power. A succession of votes lost in the United Nations had seemed to confirm such pessimism. In reality, the defeats owed more to raw arithmetic than sudden US weakness: the wave of post-colonial liberations of the 1950s and 60s meant there were now 138 member states of the institution, not fifty-one as when it was founded at the end of the Second World War. But the defeats stung nonetheless.

One particularly harsh reversal had come in 1972 when the UN tried to find a consensus on practical steps to counter 'terrorism' in the aftermath of the Munich attacks. Even the idea of such a debate was contentious. The Cubans said any discussion of 'terrorism' was 'imperialist', the Mauritanians told the assembly that 'all liberation movements are described as terrorists by those who have reduced them to slavery', and the Chinese said it was 'perfectly just for the oppressed nations and peoples to use revolutionary violence against the violence of imperialism, colonialism, neo-colonialism, racism and Israeli Zionism'. The French pointedly insisted that terrorism was born from injustice. The draft resolution that was eventually presented to the UN's General Assembly horrified the US and Israel. It acknowledged the problem of terrorism but called on member states 'to investigate the underlying causes which give rise to such acts of violence' such as the 'misery, frustration and despair ... which cause some people to sacrifice human lives, including their own, in an attempt to effect radical changes'. It also reaffirmed 'the inalienable right to self-determination of all peoples', explicitly upheld 'the legitimacy of their struggle, in particular [that] of national liberation movements' and condemned 'repressive and terrorist acts by colonial, racist and alien regimes'. The resolution had passed by seventy-six to thirty-seven, with seventeen abstentions.

Now, less than two years later, Arafat was on his way to address the assembly. And it fell to Salameh to work with US authorities on the security arrangements for the visit.

The Americans made little effort to hide their distaste for the whole affair and said they would issue visas for just six people to travel with the PLO leader. The Palestinians demanded sixteen, with permission for some members of the delegation to carry their own firearms. On 11 November, two days before the session in New York was due to begin and Arafat was due to speak, Salameh had a four-hour meeting with US diplomats in Beirut. He warned them that Arafat believed Washington was set on 'demeaning his pride and self-image' and told the diplomats that if they could not help Arafat overcome his 'psychological' problems, he would refuse to travel. Salameh was drily informed that the US government had its own 'psychological hang-ups' too, and these included allowing people like Arafat to bear arms in full view of the American public.

In fact, despite their moaning at 'this latest example of PLO uppitiness, paranoia and silliness', the diplomats were disposed to help and eventually a compromise was found. The delegation that took off for New York numbered sixteen, but none were armed. Salameh travelled on an Algerian passport bearing a false name so as to provide the State Department with an excuse if anyone thought to ask why they had permitted a known terrorist, or indeed freedom fighter, to enter the US.

The words of Arafat's ninety-minute address to the UN had been through scores of revisions. The entire speech had been polished by the celebrated Palestinian poet, Mahmoud Darwish, and an English translation provided by Edward Said, the Palestinian-American literary critic and Columbia professor. To avoid noisy protests the PLO delegation was brought by military helicopter from New York's John F. Kennedy airport to the UN headquarters and dropped in a garden beside the towering building on the East River. Arafat was taken to a fifth-floor sickroom where he rested for a few hours, then he strode out before the assembly in keffiyeh and Ray-Bans, clasping his hands in the air to reveal a holster at his hip that was, after much further argument, empty. The assembly's president, Abdelaziz Bouteflika, the foreign minister of Algeria, introduced him as 'commander in chief of the Palestinian revolution'.

The speech was by turns strident, angry, plaintive and grandiose. Though careful to draw a distinction between Zionism and the Jewish faith, Arafat assailed the former as an ideology of colonialism and terrorism. Repeated references to 'armed struggles provoked by imperialism and racial discrimination' and 'the plundering . . . of the wealth of impoverished peoples' by 'an outmoded but still dominant world economic system' won sustained applause in the crowded chamber. There was little of the more pragmatic thinking that had dominated debates within the PLO over the previous year, and Western reporters and diplomats focused on its blunt, threatening finale as well as its implication that the PLO chairman might actually have been carrying a weapon after all: 'Today I have come bearing an olive branch and a freedom-fighter's gun. Do not let the olive branch fall from my hand,' Arafat told the assembly. 'I repeat: Do not let the olive branch fall from my hand. Wars flare up in Palestine, but it is in Palestine that peace will be born.' Arafat then spent the afternoon and evening after the speech at a lunch, followed by a meeting with Arab diplomats in a corner lobby of the UN assembly, and finally at a sumptuous reception hosted by Egypt.

Salameh had watched the address from the wings and remained at Arafat's side throughout most of the day before breaking away late in the evening for an important appointment. Each member of the PLO delegation had been given a suite at the Waldorf Astoria Hotel on Park Avenue. Salameh was not entirely unfamiliar with such establishments – when the CIA had tried to buy his loyalty almost exactly three years earlier they had done so at the Hilton Cavalieri in Rome, and when in Geneva he stayed at the sumptuous Hotel de la Paix – but this moment was different and impressed him. At one point during the twenty-four hours he spent in New York, he picked up a postcard showing the hotel, drew an arrow pointing at its upper floors, wrote 'The PLO at the Waldorf Astoria!' on its back and posted it to his wife and children back home in Beirut.

At around 10 p.m., a senior CIA officer arrived at Salameh's suite. The two men spent four hours talking. Salameh assured his visitor, the incoming station chief in Beirut, that Fatah's decision to refrain from attacking US interests or citizens and from 'international terrorism' more generally was serious and definitive. Quite what the American offered in return is less clear but, at the very least, Salameh had reinforced his relationship with the most powerful intelligence agency in the world. Merely to have been in New York, to have sat with senior American intelligence officers, to have been driven between the hotel and the UN in armoured limousines was an achievement. That a permanent channel between the PLO and Washington appeared to have been opened was an astonishing step forward. Very early the next morning, Salameh flew with Arafat in an Algerian Airlines plane to Cuba for a meeting with Fidel Castro. The Mossad had tracked his movements and meetings in New York and were not happy.

But they were by no means the only players who were dismayed at what they saw that day, and it was here that the answer to Commissioner Herranz's question was to be found. For many Palestinian nationalist activists, Arafat's talk of olive branches was a betrayal of both their cause and the revolutionary international. George Habash spoke of treachery, telling interviewers that the duty of Palestinian leaders was to mobilise and arm the masses so they could reclaim their homeland piece by piece. And the simplest and most direct way to undermine Arafat's initiative was through violence.

This was the motive that Herranz and his colleagues among French police were searching for as they sought to explain the recent spate of attacks in France. In the aftermath of the PLO chairman's speech, several of the most active fedayeen groups had launched dozens of increasingly indiscriminate attacks in Israel but also in Europe and beyond, with the single aim of derailing Arafat's new strategy. Haddad enthusiastically joined this effort. If his two main European operatives had not been distracted throughout the spring and early summer of 1975 by the abortive plan to kidnap Arab ambassadors in London, there would have been others. By June, when Moukharbal was picked up in Paris by the DST on his way in from Beirut, several new schemes were close to fruition.

But no one, not even Haddad, anticipated what would happen to his European chief of operations and his Venezuelan subordinate on rue Toullier that evening, events that would reverberate around the world, revealing the lines of a new and lethal phase of the conflict between armed Palestinian groups and Western governments.

Shortly after Ramírez returned from the bathroom, Commissioner Herranz had sent his colleague Dous to fetch Moukharbal. There followed a five-minute wait, filled with nervous conversation. The students said they were 'leftists' but did not believe in violence. Ramírez was surly, asking aggressively what kind of *flic* Herranz might be. 'I work for peace and the security of citizens,' the older man answered. 'DST', said Ramírez with contempt, pointing a finger. By the time Dous returned with the detainee and the third officer, a burly thirty-five-year-old called Jean Donatini who had been waiting with Moukharbal in the car, about half an hour had passed since the police first knocked on the apartment door.

Moukharbal was brought into the now crowded room. Ramírez was standing in front of the bathroom, nervously running his left hand through his hair while concealing his right hand behind his back. Though no doubt surprised and alarmed to see him there, Moukharbal showed no emotion. One of the policemen asked him if he knew anyone in the room. The Lebanese 'carpet salesman' told the students to stop talking. Herranz was sitting on the sofa with a whisky in his hand. Moukharbal pointed at Ramírez and said: 'It's him.'

There was a sudden series of blinding flashes and deafening detonations. Ramírez had moved very quickly, raising the pistol and firing from very close range. His first shots were aimed at the two more junior policemen, who he believed to be armed. A bullet hit Donatini under the jaw, knocking the solidly built sportsman to the floor. Another struck Dous in the hand, possibly as he raised his arms to protect himself, and two others pierced his neck. Ramírez then turned on Herranz, pointing the gun almost directly into the older policeman's face. Herranz turned away. Ramírez's aim wavered momentarily: fired from less than two feet away, the bullet struck Herranz above the collarbone. Finally, Ramírez turned to Moukharbal, whom he shot carefully and deliberately in the head. Donatini and Dous died more or less instantly, Moukharbal moments later, lying across their legs. Herranz, badly injured and barely conscious, would survive.

The fusillade had lasted seconds. Ramírez then ran, bolting out of the studio, down a flight of stairs and out along rue Toullier until he turned left, slowing his pace, and crossed the boulevard Saint-Michel. There had been a power cut, and many of the streets were plunged into darkness. Exactly what Ramírez did for the next hours is unclear, but he ended up at the apartment of another former lover on the rue Amélie, a mile or so away across the Latin Quarter.

Arriving shortly after midnight, Ramírez barely addressed the woman as she let him in, going immediately to the bed and reaching underneath it for a bag from which he pulled a handful of documents. Then he sat at a table and made several phone calls. For some years, it had been possible to call numbers in London from Paris without going through an exchange. Ramírez now called a friend of his mother's there, who was out, and then Nydia Tobón. 'Hello my love, it's me,' he said. 'I had to do it. Moukharbal was a coward, the police took him, and he sold us [out] . . . It was him or me.'

When French investigators eventually found the rue Amélie apartment, they discovered huge quantities of handguns, ammunition, detonators, plastic explosives and twenty-eight grenades similar to those used in the Drugstore attack, all hidden in bags under the bed. Had there been an accident, the cache would have demolished not just the building but much of the neighbourhood. In a cupboard was a Savile Row suit, many Nina Ricci ties, several pairs of Italian leather shoes and four passports. They also found two notebooks. One revealed every expense of Haddad's European network over the previous eighteen months, down to the two francs spent on entry tickets for the viewing platform at Orly airport. The other listed hundreds of potential targets in France, including the health minister Simone Weil, a survivor of Auschwitz who had recently overcome determined resistance and abuse from conservative members of the National Assembly to force through laws decriminalising abortion.

News of the shootings in Paris quickly reached London. The reports there prompted a young scientist living with a Basque waitress in London's Bayswater to investigate a mysterious sports bag that belonged to her former boyfriend and which he had found by accident some months earlier in a fireplace behind a sofa. The ex-boyfriend had told the woman that he was a Latin American businessman and travelled frequently to Europe for work. This, along with the man's professed skills as a marksman and protestations of revolutionary fervour, had seemed suspicious at the time and all the more so in retrospect. The bag contained cash, handguns, silencers and what looked like explosives. The scientist, a man of moderate left-wing convictions who was distrustful of the police, phoned the *Guardian*, explained what he had found, and spoke at length to a reporter. The newspaper splashed his story on the front page.

Further investigations by the police and security services established that the bag's owner was indeed responsible for the recent shootings in Paris. More digging revealed him to be the same man who had tried to kill Joseph Sieff in December 1973, thrown a bomb at a bank a month later and drawn up a list of potential targets for assassination in London, including several prominent Jewish public figures such as Yehudi Menuhin, the violinist, and Keith Joseph, a conservative politician. It would be decades before journalists and the public learned the embarrassing fact that this mysterious individual had been briefly put under surveillance by MI5 as early as 1971.

Of the four passports found by French police amid the cache at rue Amélie, only one turned out to be genuine. Investigators in Paris now had the name of their man to accompany his description: Ilich Ramírez, referred to initially as Carlos by French police, dubbed 'the Jackal' by journalists in London following the discovery of a copy of Forsyth's thriller, *The Day of the Jackal*, in the Basque waitress' flat, and now one of the most wanted men in the world.

But where would a twenty-six-year-old Venezuelan member of a Palestinian extremist faction go after killing two policemen and his immediate superior in the centre of a busy European capital? And how would he flee? Neither the French nor the British, nor any other police or intelligence service had any idea. Nor, it appeared, did the fugitive himself.

15
Sand, Sea and Kalashnikovs

At eight o'clock on the morning of 28 June 1975, a twenty-nine-year-old South African secretary called Angela Armstrong was buying a ticket at the Air France terminal near the Eiffel Tower when she saw a familiar figure pushing his way into the crowded office. Armstrong waved and shouted across the queueing customers, and a moment later was introducing her five-year-old daughter to a man she knew as Carlos. They had seen each other occasionally at parties at the small flat of one of the Latin American students with whom she practised her language skills. But Carlos was not his usual bombastic self, and drew her to a corner, putting his arm around her shoulder and asking conspiratorially in English: 'Have you been listening to the news bulletins?'

'No, why?', Armstrong answered.

'I've got problems . . . I've just shot three policemen and a dirty Arab,' he said, the words spilling out this time in rapid Spanish. 'I am not in the habit of killing [but] I kill all those who betray me [and] he had sold me out . . . I'm going to have to get new papers. It's annoying.'

It was not until Armstrong saw the headlines scrawled on newspaper billboards on the street outside that she understood quite what she had just been told. But by then, Ramírez had disappeared. Armstrong would tell police and journalists that his parting words had been: 'I'm leaving for the Middle East. You won't see me again.'

European authorities had never shown much tenacity in pursuing fugitives beyond their borders. If Ramírez could evade their first frantic efforts, there was every likelihood he would escape their clutches indefinitely. The first challenge was to get out of France, but there were several reasons to believe this could be done without major difficulty. Of the three policemen who had ever seen him up close, two were dead. Surveillance photographs taken by the police were too blurred for easy identification and it would take time for investigators to interview the other witnesses to the shooting. Finally, even once the police had created a likeness using one of the recently introduced 'photofit' kits, it would take many hours if not days to distribute it to frontier posts. And as Ramírez knew from his many journeys over the previous five years, most border guards would barely glance at a white male carrying a valid passport if its name or number had not yet been identified as suspect, especially if it had been issued by a friendly state. The document Ramírez had pulled from the bag in his former lover's apartment was a US passport into which his photograph had been pasted and stamped several months earlier. He had never used the document before, and if he avoided obvious itineraries, reached border control before his name and appearance had been circulated and did nothing to attract suspicion, there was no reason why he should not be able to get clean away. But to where?

One possible destination was Libya. Tripoli, the capital, was only a three-hour flight away, and its leader, Muammar Gaddafi, had made great efforts to position his country among the vanguard of 'revolutionary states' in recent years. Having forced the Western oil companies that dominated Libya's oil industry to hand over a majority of their profits to the state, the mercurial thirty-three-year-old was now one of the richest men in the world, and a significant portion of that wealth was channelled into support for the Palestinians, alongside others engaged in armed struggles from Ireland to the Philippines. But Ramírez knew no one in Libya, his Arabic was poor, and Gaddafi had shown profound hostility towards the PFLP, whose secularism he, as an idiosyncratic but devout Muslim, disliked.

A more attractive alternative was to return to Beirut, the de facto headquarters of most major Palestinian armed factions and a city Ramírez knew well. Here at least he could use his passable French and had plenty of friends. But it was entirely possible that Lebanese intelligence services might be looking for him, given that Moukharbal's detention at Beirut airport had started this whole chain of events, and very likely that the PFLP would not be pleased to see him, given the rift between George Habash and Haddad. Besides, the Lebanese capital was nearing the brink of civil war, the kind of place where you needed the unequivocal protection of at least one local faction, preferably the most powerful, which Ramírez would not have.

A third alternative was Baghdad. Iraq had long been a loud supporter of Palestinian nationalism and its more radical fringe, and since the Ba'ath party had come to power in 1968, Iraqi embassies across Europe had been indispensable to the PFLP and Haddad's breakaway group, providing travel documents, weapons, 'drops' for secret messages and other logistic assistance. Five months earlier the plane carrying the attackers escaping Orly airport was allowed to land at Baghdad's international airport, and five months before that the Iraqi regime had hosted a summit of those who rejected Arafat's new pragmatic policies: the 'Front of Palestinian Forces Rejecting Surrenderist Solutions' or simply the 'Rejection Front'. But Ramírez had never been to Baghdad and could not be sure of his welcome there, given that Iraq was aligned with the Soviet Union and Moscow still officially disapproved of Palestinian armed groups that indulged in 'adventurist' attacks. Nor would the Iraqi regime want to anger the West gratuitously: Ramírez could not be certain that its security services, run by a fearsome and ambitious young Ba'athist official called Saddam Hussein, might not quietly hand him over to some Western power if it suited their immediate interests.

A final possibility was Algeria, a vocal and active supporter of the Palestinian cause, a centre for 'revolutionary activism' since gaining its independence from France more than a decade before, and long home to an eclectic range of militant organisers and exiled leaders. And yet President Boumedienne, for all his revolutionary credentials, had long tried to navigate an independent course between the superpowers and, for the same reasons as his Iraqi counterparts, might not be keen on harbouring someone like Ramírez. Nor would the Algerian president wish to imperil delicate but important relations with France for the sake of a fugitive Venezuelan who had just killed two policemen in Paris.

Faced with a difficult decision, Ramírez wavered. He had told the former lover he spent the night with on rue Amélie that he was heading for Beirut, but now he set off instead on a morning train to Brussels. At a kiosk he bought a copy of the *New York Herald Tribune* which, with his smart blue blazer, flannel trousers and white shirt, gave him the appearance of an international businessman. With his nose in the newspaper, he was not bothered by the police checking passports on the train. That evening, Ramírez called his lover again, probably from the apartment he had rented as a safehouse for the Popular Front–XO a year or so before. He asked her to pass on a message to someone who he said could arrange political asylum for him in Algeria.

But the next day Ramírez seemingly changed his mind again. He headed east, across the German border to Hamburg, a city he had visited repeatedly in the previous three years. Ramírez was now on the well-worn route for anyone looking to travel discreetly from western Europe to the Middle East. His next stop was West Berlin, where he arrived just over forty-eight hours since his departure from Paris. He then took the U-Bahn to Friedrichstrasse station where, after a thirty-minute wait, he crossed into East Berlin on one of the twenty-four-hour passes that the East German authorities made available to foreigners. He was so relieved at crossing the border that for a mad moment he considered embracing the border guards.

For the first time since the shooting, Ramírez relaxed a little and began to work out his next step. Without the right type of official invitation, he could not extend his day pass and the flight he wanted to take would not leave for seventy-two hours. Eventually, a diplomat from a friendly Arab country solved the problem by booking him a room in a hotel, a prerequisite for an extension but impossible for a casual visitor, and two days later, Ramírez was on board Interflug's twice-weekly flight to Baghdad. From there he set out on the final leg of his journey: to Aden, a far-flung, hard-scrabble former coaling station on the Red Sea, now the capital of the People's Democratic Republic of Yemen, the only avowedly Marxist-Leninist state in the entire Arab world.

It was an unlikely destination for a sybaritic young revolutionary who had spent much of his life in Knightsbridge and the Latin Quarter, but it was where his comrades in the Popular Front–XO were now based. The prospect of a reunion must have inspired even Ramírez with some trepidation. If he was unable to explain and justify his recent acts, it was very likely that he would be shot.

Back in 1970, when Ramírez had first travelled to the Middle East, the fedayeen had been at the centre of the Palestinian nationalist struggle, and the PFLP enjoyed international celebrity. Leila Khaled's picture had been splashed across newspapers around the world, Patrick Arguello had become a martyr of the global revolutionary cause, and Mahmoud Issa had been hosted in a suite at Cairo's Semiramis Hotel where he was sent flowers and chocolates by Gamal Abdel Nasser himself. Five years later, the contrast was stark. There had been no surge of revolutionary unrest across the Arab world, almost every ruler or regime in the Middle East remained in power, and the fedayeen had been expelled from Jordan and were now being drawn into a very nasty civil conflict in Lebanon. Arafat's shift towards diplomacy had pushed the PFLP towards the dissident margins of the Palestinian nationalist movement, which left Haddad's faction – with no official connection to the PLO at all – on the margins of the margins.

In May of 1975, as Ramírez had shuttled between London, Paris and other European cities, the CIA's research unit had circulated a study on the Middle East which highlighted what the agency saw as rare good news. The paper argued that 'in the past decade, the Arab world has seen a sharp decline in the importance of the rigid ideological dogma developed in the struggle for independence from foreign [i.e. colonial Western] control.' The pan-Arabist movement had lost most of its force and potential, in part because of the death of Nasser, 'its principal and charismatic spokesman' in 1970, but also because for 'most Arabs, the goal of liberation has been achieved and that of unification has lost its appeal'. The age of soaring ambitions to change the world was over. Instead, leaders across the Middle East were committed to 'particular, essentially local, goals'. Most significantly for groups like the PFLP, this turning away from grand projects of transformation was in tune with popular sentiment. Almost everywhere, the CIA said, leaders appeared to be 'not just leading, but riding, a tide of greater sobriety than their predecessors'. In short, the more important Arab countries were entering 'a post-revolutionary era'.

Though it significantly overstated its case, the CIA's analysis contained much truth. This was made amply clear by the distance Ramírez had had to travel to find Haddad and his breakaway faction. The band of ideological diehards had been banished not just to the political margins of the Middle East but to its geographic margins too.

In fact, Haddad had been building a base in Aden for some years, as the People's Democratic Republic of Yemen (PDRY) was an environment almost ideally suited to his brand of extremist violence. The short power struggle that followed the sudden ousting of British colonial control in 1967 had been won by a hardline leftist faction which had moved rapidly to push through radical reforms: nationalising foreign-owned companies and banks, passing a raft of laws to promote gender equality, abolishing the use of tribal names and forbidding the bearing of arms including the traditional *jambiya* dagger. At party rallies, crowds sang slogans enjoining patriotic Yemenis to burn the chador, reduce their salaries and reject the imperialism of the West. 'We want neither "hippy" nor bell-bottoms. We don't know if [they are] a boy or a girl. We want neither traitor nor reactionary . . . Our whole people is Marxist,' one chant ran.

Though its economy was in ruins, the PDRY was not without resources. The most obvious was its spectacularly strategic location at the tip of the Arabian peninsula and its deep-water port. From Aden, one could reach into the peninsula, whose oil reserves had suddenly become such a significant lever of geopolitical power, but also into the Horn of Africa and out across the Indian Ocean. A sleepy post-imperial backwater was thus transformed into a hub of intrigue and power struggles.

Foreign visitors who arrived at Aden's airport, a large cinder-block shed with booths for passport control hammered together out of rough planks, were directed by road signs and touts to the city's two functioning hotels. The Crescent had pretensions to oriental elegance, with spires, balustrades and an ornate clock with hands permanently stuck at five minutes to one; the Rock was a prodigiously ugly block of poured cement, though its balconies offered an astonishing view across the stunning blue waters of the Gulf with its vital, oil-bearing sea lanes. In their gloomy bars a thirsty traveller would find junior Western diplomats, East German intelligence officers, Soviet lecturers, Lebanese Communist intellectuals, Czech agriculturalists and European academics, all there to help and advise or at least observe the newly installed regime, and all sat shoulder-to-shoulder with their Seera beers, brewed nearby in the only officially-licensed brewery on the Arabian peninsula. Outside, little moved until late in the evening when temperatures dropped and the blinding light reflected by 'rock and dust and rubble, the white sky, the flat sea stretching all the way to India' dimmed. Then children played beneath dilapidated apartment blocks, women shopped for bolts of brightly coloured cloth, Somali immigrants played dominoes in coffee-houses beneath flickering TVs showing Egyptian soap operas, and men sat on streets chewing mildly narcotic *qat*.

Western powers had limited influence, or even presence, in the PDRY. The Soviets sent vast quantities of military hardware and thousands of advisers, as did the East Germans and Cubans. The Chinese too saw revolutionary potential in the new state, offering loans; every evening through the mid-1970s Beijing's diplomats jogged through the streets of the port city, chanting slogans from Mao's Little Red Book. By the same token, the rulers of the PDRY believed like Gaddafi and other leaders of the 'revolutionary' states in the Middle East that it was their ideological duty to support other leftist and nationalist armed movements, and the country had become a hub for the many small wars then being fought across half the region and much of the Horn of Africa. Guests at the Rock or the Crescent would soon run into 'men claiming to have liberated large swathes of southern Ethiopia or representatives of an underground grouping from Saudi Arabia', and insurgent factions from North Yemen, Iran and Iraq all enjoyed 'quasi diplomatic status' as well as financial or logistical support. Along with the People's Front for the Liberation of the Occupied Arab Gulf, which was largely focused on overthrowing the sultan of neighbouring Oman, and the Eritrean Liberation Front, which was fighting the ailing regime of Haile Selassie in Ethiopia, it was the Palestinian groups who enjoyed the greatest prominence and privileges.

The PLO had opened an office in Aden in 1973. On the mile-long avenue running through the centre of the city, apartment blocks that had once housed British servicemen's families were hung with placards lauding the achievements of the PFLP. The support it enjoyed went beyond street decoration. In 1971, Haddad had launched an attack from Aden on an oil tanker heading to Israel. A year later he directed the Lufthansa jet that had been hijacked in order to obtain the freedom of the surviving Munich attackers to land there. By late 1974, having become persona non grata among other Palestinian nationalist leaders in Beirut, Haddad was living with various aides and staff in a villa in the Khormaksar neighbourhood near Aden's airport. The PDRY had put other facilities at his disposal too: an office in Aden's centre, a series of supply depots and an old barracks known as 'Halma camp' an hour's drive east of Aden for 'military and political training'.

Situated among dry, scrubby hills and accommodating around forty people, the camp was 'not a particularly pleasant place', plagued by sandstorms and mosquitoes, and Haddad was 'a tough boss' who enforced 'strict and complete discipline', alumni remembered. The rudimentary shower block was infested by lizards and the only healthcare was provided by a Chinese homeopath who had somehow ended up in a nearby village. Breakfast was black tea, bread, canned jam and cheese, lunch was mainly rice and vegetables. Everyone was expected to help with cooking and washing up and there was no radio, let alone television.

The training regime was as demanding as the conditions. In the early mornings, before the heat became unbearable, recruits were drilled, pushed hard with long marches or runs, and practised hand-to-hand combat. Afternoons were spent on the shooting ranges and learning bomb-making and clandestine operations. Finally, there was 'ideological, psychological, and political training'. This did not mean passionate debates around campfires. Here, unsupervised political discussion was discouraged, there was almost no time for recreation, and trainees from different countries were banned from talking to each other without permission. To prove their commitment, new arrivals were asked to stand next to a block of plastic explosive as it was detonated in order to demonstrate their total trust in the instructors, who assured them that there was no risk of harm if the blast was not confined, directed or loaded with shrapnel.

This terrifying initiation was the start of a deliberate process of breaking down previous values and loyalties the better to build the type of fighters that Haddad wanted. Such rituals, the carefully controlled behaviour and the sheer isolation of the camp created a hothouse atmosphere equivalent to that of the West German communes that had incubated the RAF or the mountain retreats in Japan that had led to such extreme radicalisation there. 'The camp was our home, our stronghold, our world,' one trainee later remembered. 'Everyone who went [to the camp] knew why they had gone and that they were making [a] decision from which there was no way back.' The conditioning was effective. Life might have been tough but it was also deeply rewarding, the trainee said, offering 'the possibility of action . . . a sense of a common cause and camaraderie'.

Such solidarity was a double-edged sword. If you showed yourself to be loyal and obedient, then you could expect support, regardless of your aptitude. But those who displayed any tendency towards indiscipline were punished severely. With reports of the shooting on rue Toullier reaching Haddad in July 1975, Ramírez was destined to find himself in the second category.

When Ramírez finally arrived in Aden he was in poor physical shape, 'his face swollen like someone who ha[d] been [drinking and partying] for weeks' and so overweight he needed 'two chairs to sit on'. From the airport, Ramírez went straight to Haddad's office, where he was greeted with a blunt question: 'What have you done?' The facts did not look good. A relatively recent recruit, he had not only shot an experienced and valued member of the Popular Front–XO but had compromised dozens of other people and operations. If Haddad decided Ramírez had acted without good cause, everyone present knew what would happen: there were already shallow graves beyond the perimeter of the camp.

But Ramírez had two strong cards to play. For good reasons, Haddad was highly alert to the possibility of infiltration. By now he had learned the truth about Gunnar Ekberg, for example, and that others had betrayed him too. The Mossad, for one, had 'very good penetration' of many Palestinian factions, but more or less every actor in the Middle East had tried at some point to run informants or agents within the PFLP. The various fedayeen factions spied on each other systematically as well, and the PFLP had long been a particular target of Fatah, for example, who funnelled information to the CIA to reinforce Arafat's diplomatic offensive in Washington. Two of the senior men at the Popular Front–XO's Aden headquarters had been considered by the KGB to be at least 'assets/confidential contacts', if not full agents, for many years. Ramírez did not know this, but he was aware that there had been suspicions about Moukharbal's loyalty for some time. 'How many times did I tell you that André wasn't reliable? I had to kill him. If I hadn't done the same thing to the French cops, I wouldn't be here now. I would have been liquidated,' he told Haddad, using the dead man's codename. Haddad listened with his head in his hands, a habit that his close associates knew signalled deliberation and an imminent decision.

Ramírez's second card was equally potent. This was a sheaf of press cuttings that he had gathered during his travels over the previous weeks. Culled from dozens of magazines and newspapers from all over the world, they described not just the events in Paris, but the astonishing accomplishments and capabilities of the man now known as 'Carlos the Jackal'. Much of this was wildly exaggerated but the articles made amply clear that the murders had transformed the young Venezuelan into a propaganda weapon of awesome potential. Others had already recognised this. From Beirut, Bassam Abu Sharif, who was still spokesperson of the main PFLP, had issued an opportunistic press release that hailed Ramírez as the organisation's 'most brilliant agent and . . . chief international operative', who was 'outside the grasp of the police forces who are after him' but 'would make his presence felt in the months to come'. A second statement from Abu Sharif described Moukharbal as a martyr to the cause, a 'fighting comrade [who] took part in the planning and execution of numerous heroic and audacious actions' before falling victim to the merciless French police, and whose death was 'not the end but a new incentive to future struggle'. This fulsome praise left Haddad with little choice. To damn the murderer would be to damn the victim too; to spare Ramírez was to gain two heroes for the cause: a revolutionary military mastermind and a martyr.

So 'Carlos the Jackal' escaped the bullet in the back of the head and the shallow grave, and was embraced once again, literally and figuratively, by Haddad. Within days he was settling into a new routine at the Halma training camp. The exercise and spartan diet soon had an effect, and the weight Ramírez had gained in London and Paris disappeared. He was still only twenty-six and in relatively good health, despite all the cigarettes and alcohol, and the latter was in short supply in Aden.

Soon the events of the summer appeared to have been forgotten, and the young Venezuelan was back to his usual ebullient self: challenging the instructors, showing off his languages, announcing that the only useful weapon was a handgun, and making clumsy passes at women while 'correcting their aim' on the shooting range. When Haddad's deputy asked if he would undergo plastic surgery to disguise his identity, Ramírez refused point-blank, though he did enquire if a surgeon might be able to perform liposuction on his chest, where, he complained, he was developing 'breasts like a woman'. Few in the camp would have been party to such exchanges, and Ramírez was treated with respect and admiration by most of the trainees.

These came from a dozen or so countries on three different continents. There were Basques, Eritreans, Somalis and Omanis, Armenians, Iraqis, Syrians, as well as some from Latin America. Some came out of ideological commitment, others because they admired Haddad and hoped to replicate his tactics, many because there were few other places for them to go: in April 1975, when the June 2 Movement in West Germany kidnapped a local politician and forced Bonn to release five of their jailed comrades, those comrades were flown to Aden, taken in charge by Haddad and dispatched to the training camp. English was designated as the language of instruction but the trainees were so varied that Ramírez was often called on to translate.

The challenges were not merely linguistic. The newly arrived Germans decided that the main office and accommodation in Aden was unhygienic, so imposed a new cleaning regimen before eventually repainting half the rooms in pastel shades. Historic animosities resurfaced in new forms. There were angry confrontations between Egyptians, Syrians and Iraqis, while a group of Dutch trainees, annoyed at the German contingent's propensity to 'think they knew it all better', could not help remembering what their neighbours had done to the Netherlands in the Second World War. The Germans told the Dutch 'nerds' that their failure to observe basic security precautions en route to Aden had put everyone in the camp at risk. As in Jordan in the late 1960s, the frank and frequent sexual relations of Western trainees offended some Arab members of the group, while the Westerners viewed the religious faith of their more local counterparts as reactionary and repressive.

Ramírez saw something different. In late September, he had been appointed by Haddad to command a mixed group of Germans and Arabs in a forthcoming attack that would use the shoulder-fired Strela missiles that had been unavailable for the previous year's efforts in Paris to bring down an El Al plane as it came in to land at Nairobi. This was a far more complex operation than any Ramírez had previously been involved with. East Africa was almost totally unknown to him, the Strelas were untested, and escape would involve a nocturnal dash over hundreds of miles of dirt roads into Somalia. The attack would also be his first as a leader.

So when some of the more devout Muslims among the team suggested he might benefit from the protection of the Almighty, and that if he was going to lead them he should do so all the way 'to Paradise' if necessary, Ramírez saw an opportunity. He had repeatedly demonstrated an understanding of how to motivate or at least manipulate others and probably understood that this suggestion that he convert to Islam, or at least express his respect for the faith, was important to those he was charged with inspiring and directing in the forthcoming operation. So he learned the brief lines of the *Shahada*, the solemn and binding affirmation of Islamic faith, recited them in front of witnesses and so, in theory at least, became a Muslim.

This made no difference whatsoever to his lifestyle, and he paid no attention to the other four of Islam's five obligations – charity, pilgrimage, prayer and fasting during Ramadan. His conversion, like much else in his life, was opportunistic, pragmatic and cynical. But it was also perceptive. In the months after he arrived in Aden, he made trips to Saudi Arabia, Kuwait, Oman and the Emirates on various missions for Haddad. He probably visited Somalia and Iraq briefly too. This may have given him a better sense of what was happening across the region than was available to more distant observers. He may even have begun to intuit that the conviction expressed by the CIA in their report of May 1975 that the 'revolutionary era' in the Middle East had ended was true only in one, very narrow sense of the term, and that the faith he saw displayed wherever he went, even in states with aggressively secular regimes such as the People's Democratic Republic of Yemen, was not an obscure, obstinate legacy of an earlier time but had the potential to bring about as radical a societal transformation as any political movement.

By Christmas 1975, the CIA's optimism about the broad political situation in the Middle East was accompanied by a relatively sanguine view of the threat from terrorism too. The December edition of its monthly summary of international threats ended with an unusual warning. On the night of the 24th of the month, the agency said, a 'new organisation of uncertain makeup using the name The Group of the Martyr Ebenezer Scrooge' was planning 'to sabotage the annual courier flight of the Government of the North Pole'. Security precautions were being co-ordinated worldwide and the 'prime minister [of the North Pole] and chief courier S. Claus had been notified'.

Once Ramírez's Christmas plans took effect, there would be no such mood for jokes.

16

Christmas in Vienna

At the end of October 1975, almost four months after Ramírez landed in Aden, an envoy arrived in the port city with a proposal. A Syrian activist and poet based in Paris, he had been sent by a leader of one of the 'revolutionary' Arab states. This leader had heard much about Ramírez and wanted him to lead an operation in Europe against a dramatically new and high-profile target.

Ramírez was flattered and excited, but Haddad proved sceptical when he learned the details. The target was difficult, there was not time to prepare properly and the 'client' who was proposing the attack was not to be trusted. Negotiations followed, and when tens of thousands of dollars were offered as an advance payment along with weapons and detailed intelligence to facilitate the operation, Haddad was persuaded. It was agreed that the client's identity would be kept secret from the participants, and the operation was given a codename: 'The Striking Arab Hand'. The target was an event in Vienna set to take place shortly before Christmas.

Ramírez was told to drop his preparations for the attack on the El Al planes in Nairobi and focus his attention entirely on this new endeavour. The first task was to build a team and a support network in the Austrian capital. Haddad turned to the five Germans who had arrived in Aden seven months earlier. Among them was a twenty-three-year-old former sociology student who had been jailed for shooting at police when they apprehended her stealing number plates. She had been close to finishing her prison term when her comrades in the June 2 Movement had demanded her release, and she had wavered between joining the others on the plane to Aden or finishing her sentence and returning to something like normal life. In the end, she had chosen the plane. Haddad picked her for the forthcoming operation and gave her the *nom de guerre* 'Nada'. But he still needed at least one more German-speaking attacker. Ramírez was confident he could provide one.

From Aden, Ramírez got a message to Wilfried Boese, the founder member of the Revolutionary Cells whom he had met in Paris in March. Ramírez did not particularly like German activists, telling friends that he was put off by their greasy hair, dirty clothes and consumption of cannabis, but he and Boese had much in common and had got on well. Boese was a charming bon viveur who enjoyed 'sitting around drinking a glass of Franconian wine and eating Bratwurst from Nuremberg' or taking hour-long baths with a bottle of whisky and a record player within reach. Ramírez had also been impressed by his record of involvement in revolutionary causes. As well as his radical publishing business, Boese had founded organisations to support the Black Panthers, hidden American soldiers who had deserted from US bases, joined dozens of street protests and become a major participant in Frankfurt's 'Sponti' scene. More recently, he had been overseeing the forgery of documents on a massive scale, illegal fundraising activities and a non-lethal bombing campaign. The only thing that the carefully groomed Ramírez did not like about Boese was his habit of biting his nails and cuticles.

The man whom Boese recommended take part in the planned attack was Hans-Joachim Klein, or 'Schnitzel', the Revolutionary Cells member who had driven Jean-Paul Sartre to his meeting with Andreas Baader and worked with Ramírez in London on the aborted attempt to abduct the Emirati ambassador. Ramírez had asked Boese for someone who knew how to handle weapons and Klein was one of the few in the Revolutionary Cells who had not dodged his national military service. As a 'prolli' – one of the organisation's few members of proletarian or working-class origins – he was considered a man of action. Patronising as it was, this view was not unjustified. In mid-November, Boese took Klein for a walk in a wood outside Frankfurt, during which he sketched the outlines of the forthcoming operation in Vienna. Despite some misgivings, 'Schnitzel' agreed to take part.

When Ramírez learned that Klein was joining the team, he was delighted to be working with his 'serious and reliable' friend once more. From Aden, he travelled to Beirut for a series of meetings and then flew to Switzerland. At Zurich airport, Ramírez noticed a wanted poster bearing his portrait pinned to the wall behind the official who was then inspecting his false Ecuadorean passport. Once again, the combination of white skin, plausible documentation, smart business suit, leather

In September 1970, the Popular Front for the Liberation of Palestine hijacked four planes and flew three to a makeshift airstrip in Jordan. The attack was spectacular but almost bloodless.

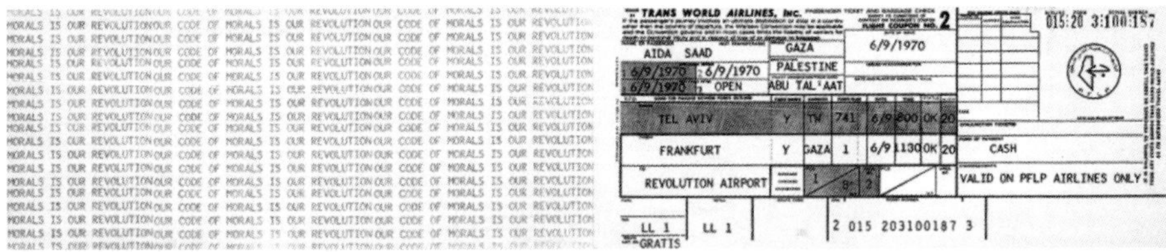

As part of their media campaign, the PFLP distributed fake airline tickets to 'Revolution Airport', telling bearers that 'OUR REVOLUTION IS OUR CODE OF MORALS'.

When the planes were destroyed with explosives, they were empty. The images of the fireball of jet fuel and smoke were viewed by tens of millions around the world within hours.

Yasser Arafat, founder and leader of Fatah and chairman of the Palestine Liberation Organisation, in 1970.

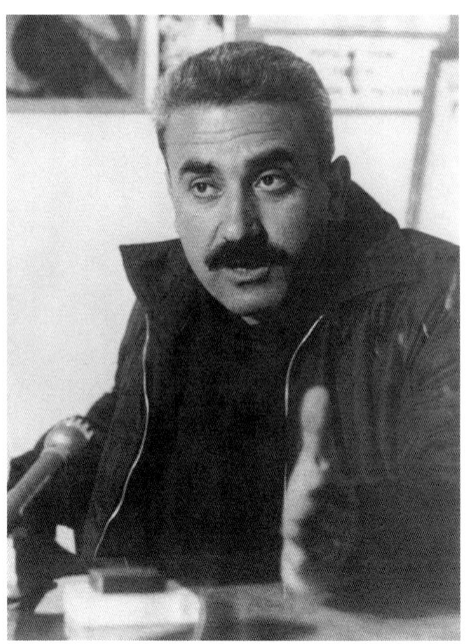

George Habash, founder and leader of the PFLP, also in 1970.

Leila Khaled after her second hijacking in 1970 and facial surgery. Khaled's image was carefully curated by Habash and others. Here Khaled is the very image of a modern young Arab woman. Note the PFLP insignia on her right.

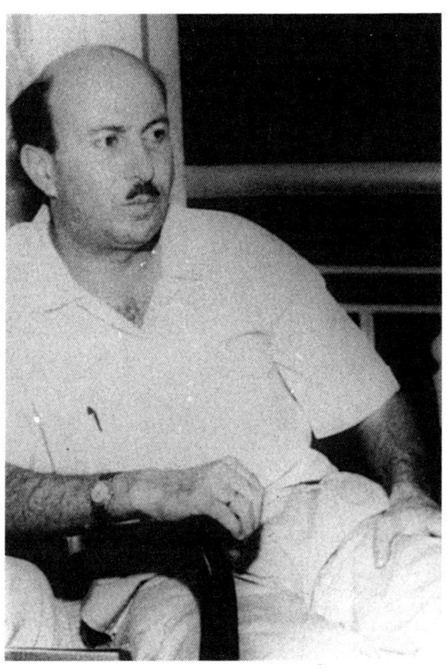

Wadie Haddad, a founding member of the PFLP and pioneer of the new hijacking strategy, who conceived and organised the September 1970 attacks but then broke away from the PFLP to run his own group in 1972.

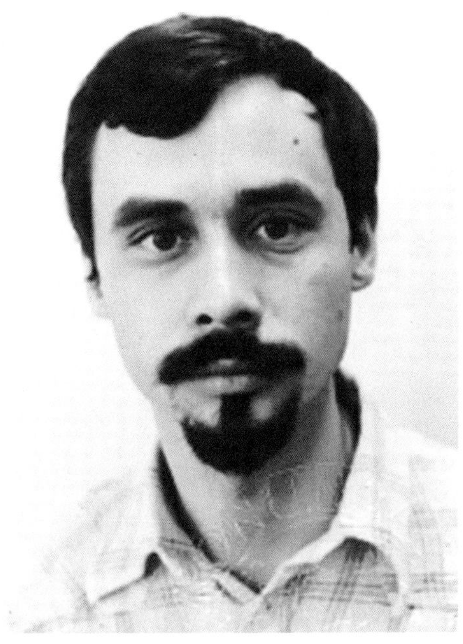

Gunnar Ekberg, the Swedish spy who infiltrated the radical leftist scene in Sweden and the PFLP on behalf of Swedish intelligence services and then the Mossad.

Fusako Shigenobu, a founder and leader of the Japanese Red Army.

Ali Hassan Salameh, also known as 'Abu Hassan'. Scion of a hero of the Palestinian cause, Salameh became a key leader of the Black September Organisation, a close aide of Arafat and a contact, but never agent, of the CIA.

Ulrike Meinhof, then a radical journalist, at a press conference in 1969 (*left*), and on a wanted poster a year later (*right*).

Andreas Baader and Gudrun Ensslin in court in West Germany in 1968 on charges of arson. Baader often intensely irritated other radicals; Ensslin frequently impressed them.

Mohammed Massalha gestures to 'Tony' (in black cowboy hat) during negotiations with West German officials outside the house in the Olympic village in Munich, where they were holding hostage eleven members of the Israeli Olympic team, on 5 September 1972.

One of the Black September attackers in Munich. Such powerful images had a massive impact, defining the Western perception of Palestinians and their cause for many years.

Photographers on a bank outside the Olympic village, only 100 m or so from the apartments where the Israeli athletes were held. The tunnel where German authorities planned an ambush is clearly visible.

The Mossad killed Mohamed Boudia, an Algerian radical activist who was key to a series of attacks in western Europe, with a car bomb on 28 June 1973 in Paris. A converted landmine was triggered as Boudia sat down to drive, his foot still on the road.

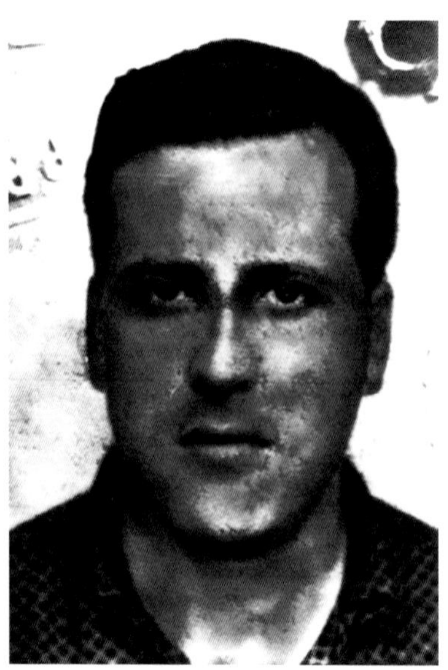

Boudia has been portrayed as merely a 'terrorist and womaniser'. But he was also a veteran of the Algerian struggle for independence from France, and an admired theatre director, actor, literary translator and talented playwright.

Hans-Joachim Klein, or 'Schnitzel' to his militant friends, drove Jean-Paul Sartre to Stammheim prison in Stuttgart to interview Andreas Baader in December 1974. In the back of the car is Klaus Croissant, Baader's lawyer.

Wilfried Boese, Frankfurt-based left-wing publisher, squatter, street-theatre organiser and founder of the Revolutionary Cells. Boese died at Entebbe in 1976.

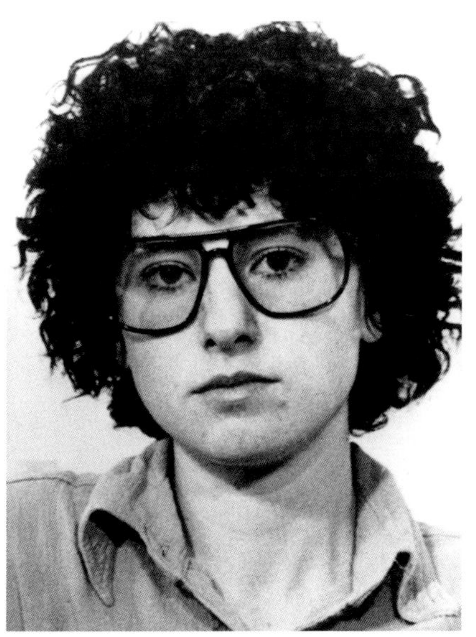

Gabriele Tiedemann, a former member of the anarchist June 2 Movement, who shot dead a policeman and an Iraqi bodyguard during the OPEC attack in Vienna in December 1975.

Ilich Ramírez Sánchez, or 'Carlos the Jackal', in discussion with the Algerian foreign minister at Algiers airport following the OPEC attack of December 1975. He is still wearing the Guevara-style beret he bought in Vienna.

briefcase and confidence ensured easy passage. One of the most wanted men in Europe then took a taxi to Geneva's main railway station and bought a first-class ticket to Vienna. Deeply absorbed in the American financial journals he had bought before departure and spread across the seat next to him, Ramírez had no trouble when police looked into his compartment at the border between Switzerland and Austria either.

Boese and Klein arrived on the same train as Ramírez, though they travelled in second class and, he said later with some disdain, were dressed 'like tramps'. Within days of arriving in Vienna, the pair unexpectedly ran into Ramírez outside an upscale department store in the city centre, whereupon he proudly showed them his purchases, which included a fashionable Che Guevara-style black beret and some designer clothes, and invited them to an expensive lunch in a nearby restaurant, where he brought them up to date on developments over the summer, including the regrettable incident in Paris. He shot Moukharbal not just because he was a traitor, he explained, but for his cowardice. First he had made no attempt to help him overpower the three policemen, then when the shooting started he had cowered in a corner, his hands over his face, and finally he had begged pitifully for his life.

That evening, Ramírez walked from his lodgings in the Vienna Hilton to the cheap hostel where the Germans were staying to tell them about the attack. The Organisation of the Petroleum Exporting Countries (OPEC), which between them accounted for eighty per cent of the world trade in oil, was to meet in just over a week. Around a dozen states would be sending their oil ministers at the head of large delegations. The plan was for the 'commando' to storm the OPEC offices in the centre of Vienna, take the ministers hostage and force the Austrian government to provide a plane. From there, the hostage-takers would fly to each of the ministers' home countries in the Middle East, obliging each of them to earn their freedom by declaring support for the Palestinian cause on arrival. The idea for this came from 'an Arab head of state', Ramírez said.

The six attackers, including two Palestinians, a Lebanese Popular Front–XO recruit and the German woman 'Nada' who had yet to arrive from Aden, would be amply equipped with weaponry and ammunition, provided by their sponsors. Anyone who resisted the attack or tried to escape or became hysterical or refused to obey an order – including Ramírez's accomplices – would be killed. Otherwise, the aim was to avoid harming the hostages, except for two: Sheik Yamani, the Saudi oil minister, and Iran's representative at OPEC, Jamshed Amouzegar. Both were to be executed at the conclusion of the operation.

For more than a week, the team waited. The materiel needed for the attack had not yet arrived, and 'Nada' had been delayed. Klein went to the cinema every afternoon, or simply walked the snowy streets. He was neither nervous nor excited, nor especially concerned at the thought of killing Amouzegar, who was responsible for Iran's internal security service, the Sazeman-e Ettela'at va Amniyat-e Keshvar, or the SAVAK, which had a well-deserved reputation for brutality. Yamani was a different matter, though. The Saudi oil minister was admired in revolutionary circles for his outspoken defence of the 1973 Arab oil embargo. When Klein tried to raise these concerns with Ramírez, there was an argument which ended inconclusively. In fact, Ramírez had his own reservations about such cold-blooded and public murders, and had complained to Haddad in Aden that the image of the Popular Front–XO would be irremediably tarnished. The response had been uncompromising. 'This is a war, not a boy scouts camp,' Haddad had said.

On the night before the attack was due to take place, the six members of the commando met in an apartment in the Viennese suburbs. 'Nada' had finally arrived from Yemen and brought a message from Haddad: the intelligence on the target promised by their client was insufficient and the operation should be aborted. Ramírez ignored this command and set out instead for a rendezvous opposite Vienna's opera house with Arab diplomats who had brought the weapons for the attack in their ambassador's car. The guns were brand-new, powerful and expensive. After a final briefing by Ramírez, the weapons were distributed and many of the team began drinking.

It was then that Klein realised it was his birthday. He felt suddenly very alone and dejected. He told himself that if he wore a mask and spoke only in his broken English, he would be able to return incognito to continue his life in the squats and protests of Frankfurt once the operation was over – assuming he made it out alive.

At around 11 a.m. on 21 December 1975, the six members of Ramírez's assault team loaded their weapons, ammunition, explosives and detonators into Adidas sports bags and took a tram into Vienna. It was a Sunday, and the streets were quiet. The air was chill under a clear blue sky, and carols piped over the speakers of the Christmas Market opposite the OPEC offices. Ramírez, who had grown sideburns, a moustache and a goatee beard, was wearing beige trousers and a blue polo neck under a brown Pierre Cardin leather jacket and a fashionable white trench coat, along with his new beret. 'Nada', whose real name was Gabriele Tiedemann, sported a long dress, a fur-trimmed jacket and a white ski hat. Klein wore a fur trapper's hat, corduroy jacket and matching trousers with a Tokarev pistol pushed through a belt. Still hoping to protect his identity, he had a balaclava stuffed in a pocket.

The group strode up to the modern seven-storey building on Ringstrasse, past a semi-circle of parked ministerial limousines, two plain-clothes policemen and a huddle of bored journalists, then rushed up the stairs to the OPEC offices on the first floor. Klein, now masked, shot two rounds from his Tokarev into the telephone switchboard, narrowly missing a terrified receptionist, while Ramírez and the others headed directly for the main conference room where the oil ministers and their aides sat in alphabetical order around a narrow U-shaped table, their places marked with miniature national flags in chrome holders. Throwing open the double doors, Ramírez fired five shots into the ceiling and walls, then shouted: 'Don't move . . . I am the famous Carlos. You may have heard of me.'

The little resistance they met with did not last long. Tiedemann killed the bodyguard of the Iraqi oil minister when he attempted to overpower her. She then shot one of the two plain-clothes policemen in the back of the neck as he tried to surrender, dragged the dying man into a lift and pressed the button for the ground floor. When the doors reopened below, his bloodied body rolled out in front of the reporters who had gathered in the lobby. Moments later, Ramírez shot dead an Iraqi economist who tried to grab the semi-automatic Beretta from his hands. It was his fourth murder in six months. There was a brief exchange of fire with Austrian policemen who rushed to the scene but then withdrew as Ramírez and his team threw grenades. One ricochet hit Klein, though, leaving him astonished that the small neat hole that suddenly appeared in his lower abdomen could cause him so much pain.

Very soon, more than sixty hostages had been separated into three groups: 'progressives and semi-progressives', 'criminals' and 'neutrals'. In the first category were Algeria, Iraq and Libya, which had all argued for maintaining the oil embargo as long as possible. The criminals were Qatar, the UAE, Saudi Arabia and Iran, which had all sought and secured its end after just six months. The neutral category included the non-Arab OPEC members and the local staff of the organisation. Explosives were wired around the room, and Ramírez sent out his demand for a plane and crew. He also arranged for Klein to be examined by a doctor, then taken off for treatment of what was clearly a serious wound.

With the building secured, his injured comrade now in an Austrian hospital and no signs of further resistance, Ramírez appeared to relax. He strode the congested office corridors distributing cigarettes, conversing in French, Spanish and English with his hostages, and ordering food for everybody from the Hilton. The ham sandwiches it sent were returned with an angry note pointing out that they were inappropriate for Muslims. Ramírez tried out his poor Arabic on some of the Middle Eastern delegates, upbraided the Kuwaiti oil minister for the mistreatment of Palestinian workers in the kingdom's petrochemical industry and made small talk laced with falsities about the Popular Front–XO, including the claim that Bonn was paying it around a million US dollars every year to prevent any violence within its borders. When one of the Palestinian gunmen struggled to adjust the wiring of the explosives, he quipped, 'Oh dear, I've told him a thousand times how to do it and he still can't get it right.' When an OPEC driver tried to persuade him to free the female hostages because women scare easily so 'might get hysterical', Ramírez demurred, indicating Tiedemann. The driver agreed that she did not seem the hysterical type. Ramírez laughed.

Tensions rose again in the early evening, as the deadline given to Bruno Kreisky, the Austrian chancellor, neared. None in the building knew that Kreisky, a moderate socialist who had long been sympathetic to the Palestinians' grievances and saw negotiation as the only viable strategy for avoiding further deaths, had already decided to accept all of Ramírez's demands. These included a broadcast on Austrian national radio of a lengthy 'communiqué' from the 'Arm of the Arab Revolution' written in elaborate French, which gave various clues as to the identity of the person who had commissioned the attack. It declared that oil resources should be used for 'the benefit of the Arab people and other peoples of the Third World', it denounced Saudi Arabia, Egypt and Iran for betraying the Palestinians by plotting with 'American imperialists', it demanded no negotiation with nor recognition of Israel, and it called for a new attack on the 'Zionist aggressors' by Syria, Iraq and the entire Palestinian resistance movement.

At sunrise, word came that a fully fuelled DC-9 aircraft had been readied at Vienna airport as Ramírez had requested. Shortly after 7 a.m., a bus drew up outside the rear entrance of the OPEC offices.

There was not enough room aboard for all the hostages, so the Austrian nationals and OPEC employees among them were released. The rest shuffled onto the boxy yellow vehicle which then drove slowly through the early morning traffic escorted by two police cars. Ramírez stood beside the driver, his beret on his head and his Beretta slung across his chest, waving to onlookers. The first part of the operation had been successfully, if bloodily completed. The second would not go according to plan.

As the DC-9 flew south across the Mediterranean towards the North African coastline, many of the forty hostages on board slept, exhausted by the ordeal of the previous twenty hours. The Saudi Arabian oil minister, Ahmed Zaki Yamani, was not one of them. In the very first minutes of the attack, amid the smoke and darkness, a torch had been shone in his face and a voice had said, 'This is him.' Ever since, he had been convinced that he would be killed. Twice during the afternoon, Ramírez had told the forty-five-year-old bureaucrat that he would be the first hostage to die. Yamani had recited verses of the Koran and, as the hours passed, grown resigned to his fate, writing a letter for his wife and two teenage children. The night had been long and uncomfortable. Yamani had been forced to sit on a chair rather than join the other hostages trying to sleep on the floor.

Now they were on the plane, the man who had promised to murder him was once more in a jovial mood, strolling confidently up and down the aisle, signing autographs, handing a letter for his mother to the Venezuelan oil minister, apologising loudly to the hostages for the murders in Vienna. Eventually he sat down in the seat next to Yamani and began to offer anecdotes from his youth, fictitious stories of combat in Jordan in 1970, boasts of sexual conquests, and his views on how political change might come to the Middle East. Yamani's suggestion that Ramírez and his comrades were mistaken in trying to impose 'revolution from above' rather than allowing it to 'well up from the masses' provoked a terse response. 'What do you know of the masses? You should talk to Algerians. They, not you, have made a revolution and know what it is all about,' Ramírez told him.

Despite their obvious differences, the two men had a surprising amount in common. Yamani was an Arab, born in Mecca, the son of a respected Islamic scholar, and a highly intelligent, educated technocrat whose unprecedented and meteoric rise through the ranks of the

Saudi bureaucracy had made him arguably the most powerful commoner in the kingdom. Since the oil crisis of 1973, he had also become a household name across the West. His urbanity, eloquence, command of detail and impish provocation both impressed and worried many of his Western interlocutors. Henry Kissinger had been charmed in their meetings. But outside the White House, Yamani had become something of a bogeyman, blamed personally for the soaring prices and economic chaos that had disrupted the lives of hundreds of millions of people. Cars with low fuel consumption were advertised as giving you 'A run for Yamani'. Editorials accused Saudi Arabia of daylight robbery under the headline 'Yamani or your life'.

As with Ramírez, his lifestyle added to his infamy. This 'simple bedouin', as he called himself, was in the habit of reserving a dozen or more rooms at The Ritz, wore Savile Row suits and his own personal blend of aftershave, enjoyed ski breaks in Switzerland and shopped in bulk at Harrods. Both men had been educated internationally: Ramírez in London and Moscow; Yamani in Cairo, New York and Boston.

If Yamani was the first ever celebrity oil minister, Ramírez could claim to be the first ever globally-recognised celebrity terrorist. By 1975 his fame was far greater than Leila Khaled's had ever been. The *New York Times* had used the term 'globalisation' for the first time in 1974 and the Venezuelan's lifestyle often resembled that of the new breed of international businessman – an identity he often used as a cover for his real activities. Both he and Yamani had recently holidayed on the Côte d'Azur. So it should have been unsurprising, as they sat next to each other on the DC-9, that the two men discovered an acquaintance in common: one of Yamani's younger assistants back in Riyadh had been a classmate of Ramírez at the private school he had briefly attended in London.

As they flew, Ramírez described the next phase of the operation to Yamani. The DC-9 would take them first to Algeria. This had not been in his original plan but it would have been wrong to turn down its invitation to set down there, which had been part of the deal done with Kre[illegible] in Vienna. Their real destination, however, was the Libyan capital Tripo[illegible] there a larger Boeing 707 with its longer range would allow them to carry out their Middle East tour, freeing ministers as they went. The first stop would be Baghdad. The last would be Aden, where any remaining hostages – apart from two – would be liberated. Ramírez wondered for a moment whether to ask Yamani for his watch as a souvenir but decided it would be inappropriate. Once on the ground in Aden, Ramírez then explained cheerfully, Yamani would be shot.

Ramírez and Yamani had two other points in common. One was that neither had ever met an Israeli. In an interview with Oriana Fallaci, the Italian journalist, in the summer of 1975, Yamani said he had once glimpsed Abba Eban, the veteran Israeli diplomat and former foreign minister, during his time as a student at Harvard, but otherwise had never known an Israeli in his life. The same was true of Ramírez. The other was that at the time of their conversation, both men were working for the leader of an Arab state: Yamani for King Khalid bin Abdulaziz al-Saud, Ramírez for Muammar Gaddafi.

There were many possible reasons why Gaddafi had dispatched an envoy to Aden in order to find and hire Ramírez that October. One was personal animus. Though vilified in the Western media, Yamani had always argued to restrain the demands of more radical Arab states who called for the wholesale expropriation of US businesses in their countries and an even tighter embargo. He had also successfully pushed to end the embargo in March of 1974, with the support of Iran, an ally of the US. As a consequence, Gaddafi saw both Riyadh and Tehran as traitors. More rationally, the attack on OPEC would be a powerful warning to all his enemies, reinforce Libya's revolutionary credentials and force up oil prices, simultaneously hurting the West once more and filling his own coffers. The operation led by Ramírez had achieved several of these objectives already. What remained unclear as the DC-9 approached Tripoli was whether Gaddafi actually wanted his hired attackers to go through with the second part of the plan, complete with the public executions of Yamani and his Iranian counterpart Amouzegar.

The stop in Algiers had taken much longer than Ramírez had anticipated, as local officials, led by the foreign minister Abdelaziz Bouteflika, had sought to negotiate the release of the hostages. Some had eventually been freed as a gesture of goodwill, and the DC-9 had taken off again. But when it touched down in Tripoli in the late evening, Gaddafi was nowhere to be seen. Libya's unpredictable head of state was thought to be out in the desert somewhere, but no one was exactly sure where, no one knew how or if he could be contacted, and he left no instructions behind for how to proceed. The prime minister who boarded the plane to solicitously welcome the high-ranking hostages had no idea who Ramírez was or why he was there.

This was a blow to Ramírez, and worse followed. Soon it became apparent that there was no Boeing 707 available, nor would there be. 'It is impossible to work with these people,' he shouted in frustration. After angry exchanges, the Libyans became increasingly unco-operative, then insulting. One of the two Palestinian attackers began vomiting in a corner of the plane. Tiedemann, who had been compulsively recounting to anyone who would listen how she had shot two men dead, began sobbing. Further acrimonious talks led nowhere. Reluctantly Ramírez decided that nothing more could be gained from the negotiations and gave the order to return to Algiers. It was now 4 a.m., more than forty hours since the crisis had begun, and it was clear that no one, neither the hostages nor the pilots nor the hostage-takers, could take much more.

Back in the Algerian capital, it was raining hard. The remaining hostages and attackers sat on the plane as Ramírez returned to the VIP lounge for a new round of talks with Bouteflika. Soon they were no longer talking about providing a larger aircraft but about the terms of a possible deal. As dawn broke, Ramírez returned to the plane, leering at his captives. 'I have a problem and I am unsure what to do,' he told Yamani and Amouzegar. 'You two are my problem . . . I am a democrat and you two do not know the meaning of democracy. I shall now meet with my colleagues and consult them on what to do about you both. I will inform you later about the decision that we have taken.'

In the final round of negotiations, Bouteflika had forcefully pointed out the weakness of the hijackers' position now that their sponsor and protector had disappeared into the sands of the Libyan interior. He had pointed out too that almost every Middle Eastern capital had closed its airspace to them, meaning that the grand tour was now impossible. Bouteflika had also suggested that Ramírez consider how difficult it would be for a minor power like Algeria to protect a man who had just executed senior officials of states as important as Saudi Arabia and Iran on its soil. But there might be a peaceful way out of the crisis that could be beneficial for everyone, Bouteflika suggested, which could include sanctuary in Algeria for Ramírez, for example, and a large payment in return for the lives and liberty of Yamani and Amouzegar. Maybe five million dollars, or ten million, or even more? Surely the Popular Front–XO would be pleased with this as an outcome?

So, in the DC-9's first-class cabin, Ramírez argued with his comrades in arms. The cash the Algerians were offering would be paid by the hated Iranian and Saudi Arabian governments and would fund further revolutionary operations, he told them. Moreover, they had completed most of the mission: they had got the hostages, and their communiqué had been broadcast. What else could they be expected to achieve? It was time to be realistic. Tiedemann and the Palestinians were incensed. The Lebanese member of the team appeared more supportive of the change of plan. The dispute continued, increasingly loudly, until finally Ramírez told the others that he was the leader, and Haddad's ultimate orders had been to obey him. 'Fuck you', shouted Tiedemann, but short of shooting Ramírez herself, there was little she could do to oppose him.

The Venezuelan then walked down the plane to where Yamani and Amouzegar were sitting. They would live, he told them, then made sure they were brought pillows, coffee and sweets. An hour or so later, Ramírez led his exhausted, angry team onto the Algerian tarmac, into the VIP lounge and eventually into a convoy of black cars that took them to the Albert Premier Hotel, a luxurious six-storey pile in the old colonial centre of Algiers. Some minutes later Yamani nervously followed down the steps from the aircraft. Ramírez had delivered a threat as he left: wherever you are, we will hunt you down and kill you. It was bluster, though Yamani could not have known that.

The mission was over and Ramírez had earned himself another difficult conversation with Haddad. After two weeks in Algiers, first in the Albert Premier and then a well-appointed government guesthouse, Ramírez set off again, taking Klein with him. Though doctors had said he would die from his wound if moved, Ramírez had insisted that his comrade be loaded into the DC-9 when the attackers left Vienna. A stretcher had been laid across the seats, connected to an oxygen supply, and a volunteer doctor sat nearby. Klein had regained consciousness only when the plane first landed in Algiers, where he had been removed. Though extremely weak, he now accompanied Ramírez back to Tripoli, from where a private jet arranged by Libyan authorities took them to Mogadishu, where they rested for several weeks. It wasn't until late January that Ramírez and Klein reached the People's Democratic Republic of Yemen.

Once more, Ramírez would escape with his life, but there would be no other reprieve. In Haddad's office in Aden, all those who had taken part in the attack underwent relentless interrogation. Every detail of the operation was picked over and criticised in meetings that lasted up to twelve hours. Why did Ramírez defy the command to abort the raid? Why did Klein not shoot the receptionist instead of the switchboard when they entered the building? Why did Ramírez ignore repeated instructions not to talk to the hostages and to keep his own identity a secret? What happened at Tripoli? Who negotiated what at Algiers and with whom? Haddad was 'beside himself with rage'.

Ramírez was irritable and defensive but if he was frightened he did not show it. 'If the operation got screwed up, it was because there wasn't enough money to prepare it properly,' he told Haddad, raising the issue that everyone knew was central to the debacle. After three days of interrogation and argument, nobody seemed able or willing to say where the ransom money paid by the Saudis and the Iranians had gone. It appeared that the Iranians had failed to honour the agreement when it actually came to wiring the funds, but several million dollars from the Saudis had somehow disappeared. Ramírez professed ignorance as to its whereabouts and swore that he had not profited in any way from the deal.

Haddad made his decision. The others could stay, but Ramírez must go. There was no place for 'stars' in his organisation, and particularly not ones suspected of embezzling such a large amount of money. The Venezuelan's time with the Popular Front–XO was at an end.

V

17
To Entebbe

Through the spring of 1976, a film crew was hard at work in the sandy dunes just north of Gaza in Israel. Their project was an unusual one: a farce depicting the amorous and other adventures of a group of military reservists.

There had been many films about the Israel Defence Forces over the previous decades, but none as irreverent as this. Everyone knew that it was reservists who had suffered the worst casualties in the conflict against Egypt and Syria three years earlier, shot and bombed in their trenches and bunkers as they tried to hold off the massive surprise attack. This did not deter the director, Assi Dayan, a famous actor and the son of Moshe Dayan, the former general and defence minister widely blamed for the debacle. Even the name – *Halfon Hill Is Not Responding* – was a provocation: an ironic reference to an earlier film about the final hours of a group of volunteers killed in combat during the conflict of 1948. The plot was as incendiary as the title, featuring a scantily-clad singer, a raid across the Suez Canal to rescue an Israeli soldier captured by an amiable Egyptian officer, a bid to discover oil, and climactic scenes on the frontlines in the Sinai involving a high loader-bulldozer, a conman, a jealous father and a portable toilet.

But the filmmakers believed its subversive and, to some, outrageous slapstick would also touch a chord. For most Israelis the war of 1973 had shown that the sense of invulnerability they had enjoyed following the victory of 1967 was misplaced. Israel's political and military establishment had self-evidently made a series of very serious misjudgements, not least in failing to heed obvious warnings that an attack was imminent. The effect had been to sow new doubt in their army, their leaders and their nation's future. At postponed elections held two months after the conflict, the Labour party, which in one manifestation or another had dominated Israeli politics throughout its existence, only just held on to power.

International isolation added to Israelis' general sense of insecurity and drift. The US military assistance that had been so important to their eventual victory in 1973 and the huge sums of money sent as aid in its aftermath underlined its worrying dependence on Washington. Elsewhere, many Israelis saw nothing but hostility. The oil crisis had made clear to western European leaders the advantages of courting Arab states, while the United Nations General Assembly had not only invited Yasser Arafat to address it in New York but had gone on to issue an unprecedented invitation to the PLO to participate as an observer in future sessions and activities. Then, in November 1975, the assembly declared Zionism to be 'a form of racism and racial discrimination'.

There was also plenty to worry about at home. The massive expenditure during the 1973 war had combined with the spike in oil prices to send the Israeli economy into a tailspin, and if anything it had encouraged Palestinians within Israel and the occupied territories to become more assertive. There were fierce protests over land expropriations in the West Bank and when municipal elections were held there it was nationalist candidates endorsed by the PLO who made massive gains, not the pliable leaders favoured by the Israelis. The mood was 'black, restive and very anxious', Golda Meir, the prime minister, said.

Meanwhile, attacks by Palestinian fedayeen within Israel continued. Even members of the army's specialist units whose job it was to counter such operations described it as a 'very scary time'. At the northern town of Ma'alot, gunmen held a hundred students and teachers hostage. When the special forces botched their assault, twenty-two children were killed, many when one of the attackers sprayed a classroom with automatic fire. In Tel Aviv, eight hostages and three soldiers died when attackers arrived by sea and detonated explosives in a hotel.

Israeli efforts to kill the individuals they held responsible for such operations failed. An attempt by Israeli warplanes to bomb a meeting in southern Lebanon of leaders of PLO factions linked to the Ma'alot attack and others failed due to poor weather. An abortive bid to capture George Habash by forcing a Lebanese passenger plane to land in Israel prompted global condemnation. 'We are perfectly conscious that such operations are against international law but we don't have any choice,' Moshe Dayan told reporters, an unusually frank admission that would echo over coming years and decades.

So too would the Israelis' tactics for attempting to deter their attackers. In 1974 alone, they conducted fifty-five air and 1,427 artillery strikes on training facilities and refugee camps in Lebanon. One attack on the Shatila camp in Beirut destroyed a fedayeen facility but also killed a sixty-five-year-old woman while wounding ten others. 'Casualties incurred in December 12 Israeli air raid were remarkably light, something which we attribute as much to luck as to professional abilities of Israeli air force,' read an acerbic cable from US diplomats in the city. 'We estimate that this latest attack, far from dampening fedayeen enthusiasm for terror operations against Israel, will whet their appetite for what they like to call "armed struggle" still further.'

One reason for the difficulties faced by the Israelis was a significant change among the attackers themselves: many of them now expected to die. Israeli experts had long believed that Arabs were not 'brave enough' to go down fighting and 'would always try to run away'. In 1972, the Sayeret Matkal's successful assault on the Sabena aircraft at Lod airport had only gone ahead because commanders were convinced the Black September hijackers would never actually set off their explosives as it would imperil their own lives. Dayan, who prided himself on his understanding of Israel's enemies, insisted that 'Arab fighters would never agree to [take part in] suicide missions' because they privileged their own survival over the success of an operation. Such ideas were not just profoundly prejudiced but increasingly outdated. When three gunmen took over an apartment block in the northern town of Kiryat Shimona in April 1974, killing sixteen civilians, the Israeli troops who eventually stormed the buildings found 'a booby-trapped bomb' strapped to one attacker and a prepared posthumous statement. 'Before, we told our combatants to fight up to the limits that would let them return safely. But [in this attack] . . . they were told to fight and die,' said Ahmed Jibril, the leader of a small but deadly breakaway group who claimed responsibility for the attack. David Hirst, the *Guardian*'s correspondent in the region, pointed out the psychological shift that was taking place: going 'right into the enemy's midst, with dynamite around one's waist, in the almost certain knowledge that one will have to detonate it' was dramatically different from undertaking a raid, even if the chances of survival were as little as one in ten. Frontline Sayeret Matkal officers recognised what was happening and told their senior commanders that they needed new ways to deal with these 'suicide operations' before they fundamentally altered the tactical balance against them.

But then, in 1976, there came an event that spectacularly revived Israel's confidence in its ability to protect its citizens from attack, even while it hardened its critics against it yet further. It revealed new opportunities offered to Israel's enemies by the shifts in power, attitudes and influence in the global South over the previous decade, but also the apparently unique capabilities of the country's armed forces and intelligence services. In its wake, the international divide between those who supported Israel's right to defend itself, whatever that might entail, and those who saw only a total disregard for international law, would turn into a gulf.

In January 1976, a team of three Palestinians sent by Wadie Haddad to Kenya disappeared without trace. They had travelled to Nairobi to carry out the attack that Ramírez had been preparing before he was redeployed to lead the OPEC operation: shooting down an El Al plane with Strela surface-to-air missiles on its approach to the city's international airport. There was no sign either of three young Germans who had been sent to Nairobi at the same time to play minor supporting roles. Word eventually filtered back to Aden that both the Palestinians and the Germans had been detained, though quite by whom was unclear.

Haddad immediately started planning a new attack on Israeli aviation in a bid to free them. Though hijacking an El Al plane had been made extremely difficult by the introduction of new security measures in previous years, other airlines serving Israel were much less robust, and some European airports remained very lax indeed. Haddad set his sights on an Air France plane that would be flying from Tel Aviv to Paris, and therefore certain to be carrying many Israeli citizens. The plan was to board the plane when it made a stopover at Athens. If his team arrived at Ellinikon airport as transit passengers they would evade any serious scrutiny of their belongings, Haddad calculated. The same trick had worked almost a decade earlier and there seemed no reason it should not again.

Haddad put together a mixed team to conduct the attack. Alongside four Palestinians, there would be two selected from among the dozen or so Germans then in the training camp in Aden. One was Wilfried Boese who had travelled directly to Yemen from Vienna after the OPEC attack and was keen to take a frontline role. Though he had helped build bombs and had briefly joined the team in London which had tried but failed to kidnap an Arab ambassador in the spring of 1975, Boese had never actually carried or used a firearm. Haddad instructed him to undertake intensified weapons training in preparation for what would be a very risky operation. The second German he chose was twenty-eight-year-old Brigitte Kuhlmann.

Kuhlmann had grown up in Hanover, studied pedagogy at the University of Frankfurt and worked as an educator with disabled children. Earnest, intelligent, a proficient forger and a talented amateur poet, she was among the earliest members of the Revolutionary Cells. Like Gudrun Ensslin, she was good at turning the more excitable ideas of the men around her into practical plans, impressing even Ramírez with her common sense and impatience with grandstanding or abstract Marxist theoretics. Four years before, Kuhlmann had organised the safehouse where Ulrike Meinhof had been arrested, and so felt responsible for the incarceration of one of her heroes. For her the attack offered the possibility of redemption, its aim being to free various high-profile prisoners, potentially including some in West Germany.

Haddad prided himself on putting together effective teams, and supporters admired his talent for choosing the right individuals. One former associate attributed this to Haddad's love of Arabic poetry, Shakespeare and the works of Charles Dickens, which supposedly gave the leader of the Popular Front–XO an 'instinct for human nature'. Others pointed to Haddad's extensive research and testing of candidates before an attack. One facet of Kuhlmann had remained hidden from Haddad, however. After his expulsion from the group, Ramírez had remained in Aden for several months, swimming with the convalescent Klein in the rocky bays nearby and enjoying days on the beach with Kuhlmann. Following their brief relationship, she was now four or five months pregnant with Ramírez's child.

The real problem for Haddad in the summer of 1976 was not finding the right personnel or the right location to hijack a plane, however, it was finding the right place to land it. The attack on the OPEC headquarters had shown how very few destinations now existed where the landing of a hijacked plane with 300 or so hostages would be even tolerated, let alone welcomed. Libya's Colonel Muammar Gaddafi had proved unreliable, and even the usually supportive authorities in South Yemen might balk at the unannounced arrival of such visitors. But there was an alternative.

Many of the stories told about Idi Amin since he had seized power in Uganda in 1971 owed more to racist stereotypes and European resentment than reality, but there was little doubt that the fifty-one-year-old was one of Africa's most impulsive, erratic and violent leaders. The former British army sergeant had displayed an impressive if unsavoury instinct for populist mass mobilisation and had cleverly exploited his country's many ethnic and religious divisions to entrench his power. But such tactics could only take him so far. After five years in charge, Amin's grasp on Uganda, and possibly on reality, was weakening.

This mattered. Though small and in itself strategically unimportant, Uganda was on an important frontline. In the middle years of the 1970s, swathes of sub-Saharan Africa were still being fought over in the last wars for independence, fuelled by support from both superpowers, who saw the developing world as an increasingly important zone of competition. Most of the newly independent African nations tilted towards Moscow. Others, such as the remaining white supremacist regimes in the south or Mobutu Sese Seko's Zaire, saw themselves as a bulwark against the spread of international Communism and were aligned with the West. This could produce unexpected alliances.

Since the 1950s Israel had pursued a foreign policy strategy of focusing on the 'periphery' of the Arab world, which meant cultivating non-Arab allies around the Middle East and in Africa, and local actors opposed to its enemies. During the 1960s, Israel had helped Kurdish peshmerga fighting for secession from Iraq and flown arms into Yemen to help the ruling imam fight Arab nationalist and Marxist insurgents, who were being assisted by Egypt. Efforts had been made to reach out to Iran and Turkey, as well as potential allies in Africa. Specialists from the Mossad were sent into south Sudan to help rebels fighting the pro-Palestinian, Arab nationalist regime of Gaafar Nimeiri, and weapons were sold to Emperor Haile Selassie's government in Ethiopia for use against separatist groups backed by the Soviets. In Kenya, Israel cultivated contacts in the Kenyan military, which would have important consequences for both Israel and the Popular Front–XO in the summer of 1976.

From the late 1960s, Uganda had been a particular focus of the Israeli effort. Israeli companies began investing heavily there with official encouragement while hundreds of Israeli instructors flew in to teach soldiers, security officers and farmers. Amin visited Israel several times, trained for weeks with its elite parachute regiment and repeatedly avowed his affection for his new allies. In a secret report, the Israeli defence attaché in Kampala told his superiors in Tel Aviv that the dictator's affection for Israel was due to a rumoured deathbed injunction from his mother to honour the Jewish people. It may also have been due to the private jet the Israelis sold him on very advantageous terms. 'Amin has an uncanny, animal sense of impending danger. Like many megalomaniacs, he has a devilish way of escaping death,' the report added.

Amin's relationship with the Israelis soon deteriorated, however. Faith may have been a factor. At least in public, Amin made a show of being an observant Muslim, ensuring that official photographers captured him visiting and praying in mosques at home and abroad. But above all Amin wanted to be a major leader in Africa and saw that the greater opportunity to boost his standing and resources lay through alliance with wealthy countries in the Arab world. He was also increasingly unable to pay his debts to Israeli companies or for the private jet, and the Arab states were offering generous aid.

After a little more than a year in power, Amin travelled to Tripoli for a meeting with Muammar Gaddafi, who offered massive financial and military assistance, even to send soldiers if Amin ever needed them. On his return, Amin expelled the Israeli advisers and investors, then, after the 1973 war, joined the thirty-one other members of the Organisation of African Unity in breaking off diplomatic relations with Israel. Anti-Israeli and anti-Zionist outbursts were accompanied by a series of virulent antisemitic statements and a new, vocal commitment to the Palestinian cause. The PLO was allowed to open an office in Kampala in the vacated Israeli Embassy. At Amin's lavish wedding, his fifth – this one to a nineteen-year-old dancer in the band of the Ugandan army's 'Revolutionary Suicide Mechanised Regiment' – Yasser Arafat served as best man. On another visit, the PLO chairman was offered land in northern Uganda as a training base for Fatah fighters. Amin claimed repeatedly that Palestinians were training with his own 'suicide units'.

Haddad was well aware of Amin's new orientation and ambitions. His first choice of destination for the plane they intended to hijack was Mogadishu, but that was unavailable because Somalian president Mohamed Siad Barre's ruling party would be holding an important international conference at exactly the wrong moment, and Haddad had no desire to embarrass a hitherto supportive leader by flying in with a plane full of hostages. Khartoum was an option, but would raise an identical problem for President Nimeiri. But there was no such concern with Uganda, and plenty of other advantages. Even if somehow Israeli special forces managed to travel the 2,000 miles from Israel, the thousand or so elite Ugandan troops based at Entebbe, the country's only international airport, should ensure that any attempt at rescue would end badly.

So on 6 July, the 'Basil al-Kubaisi Commando of the Che Guevara battalion of the Popular Front for the Liberation of Palestine', named after the PFLP intellectual and possible organiser killed by the Mossad in Paris three years before, seized control of Flight AF139 as it left Athens on its way from Tel Aviv to Paris. Two of the intended hijackers had failed to make their connection so the commando was under strength, but there was no resistance from the 240 passengers and crew, and the plane was secured without difficulty by Boese, Kuhlmann and the two remaining Palestinian hijackers. First they directed the pilot to take them to Benghazi in eastern Libya where the aircraft, a recently introduced Airbus, landed in the fierce heat of mid-afternoon and was refuelled. Then, after a six-hour wait, they took off again and headed south.

At roughly the same time, Haddad had sent two letters to Amin. One addressed the Ugandan leader in his capacity as president of the Union of African Nations and congratulated him on leading the organisation in 'denouncing racial discrimination in Israel, [the former British colony of] Rhodesia, and South Africa'. A second warned that he might find himself participating more directly in the battle against 'Imperialism and Zionism all over the world' in the very near future.

'Dear Commander,' the letter read, 'We believe that the people of Uganda and their President, famous for his brave positions against Israel and world Zionism and imperialism, will welcome our comrades ... with their hostages and the plane they have controlled [when they arrive] in Uganda ... We depend on the hospitality of the people of Uganda and on the courage, nationalism, and revolutionary positions the President of Uganda has taken. Salutations and our Best thanks, Your True comrades, the PFLP.'

At 6 a.m. on Monday 28 June, Flight AF139 landed on the main runway at Entebbe. Looking out through the windows, its passengers saw a vast expanse of water, swamp and long grass. They also saw a mass of heavily armed soldiers wearing camouflage fatigues and red berets, and a small group of Ugandan officials. Seven hours later, they disembarked and walked the short distance to Entebbe airport's 'old terminal'.

This long two-storey building with its square, squat control tower had been built in the late 1920s but had not been used since its replacement with a new complex just over a mile away the year before. The hostages were ordered into its 'huge ... dirty and dusty' departure lounge where they tried to make themselves comfortable among old armchairs and dirty mattresses heaped on the wooden floor. A lunch of bananas and potatoes was brought to them by airport staff. Later, Amin himself arrived, accompanied by his eight-year-old son, both resplendent in identical military uniforms. The Ugandan president made a speech, telling the hostages that it was thanks to his intervention that they had been allowed to leave the plane and to stay in his country.

Amin's talk of negotiations that appeared not even to have started made clear to the passengers that they were facing a lengthy stay. They pooled books and magazines to form a library, fashioned chess sets or draught boards out of cardboard boxes, played cards and dozed. Many wanted to know when they might get their hold baggage. Unexpectedly, a Ugandan television crew suddenly appeared, pointing lights and cameras through the windows of the terminal. A dinner of curried meat, rice and bananas followed, then the passengers tried to sleep, though the strip lights were left on, it was 'hot as hell' and there were swarms of mosquitoes.

On the second day in Entebbe, in the early afternoon and then in the evening, two developments transformed what had been a frightening and uncomfortable experience for the hostages into something genuinely terrifying. At around noon, children who had been allowed to play on the apron and terrace in front of the terminal were suddenly ordered back into the building. Boese now took a megaphone and read out for the benefit of the hostages the demands of the Popular Front–XO for their release. He spoke in English, which one of the passengers then translated into French. The list was lengthy, and clearly very difficult for any government to accept. The organisation wanted the release of fifty-three 'freedom fighters' held in five different countries. In Israel, these included the lone survivor of the Japanese Red Army attack at Lod airport four years before and a Greek Orthodox bishop convicted of smuggling weapons to fedayeen groups on the West Bank, among dozens of others. From Germany, the Popular Front–XO wanted Jan-Carl Raspe, a senior leader of the Red Army Faction, and six other jailed left-wing extremists from the June 2 Movement. Switzerland too was to release a jailed militant, and Kenya was to release 'one of our commando units' – presumed to be the Popular Front–XO team detained in January in Nairobi. France was to release the girlfriend in whose apartment Ilich Ramírez had hidden after the rue Toullier shooting and also to provide $5 million as ransom for the Airbus. If the money and the released prisoners were not flown to Entebbe within forty-eight hours, the plane would be destroyed with the passengers on board, Boese said. The official statement of demands that had been relayed to the French foreign ministry had spoken only of 'strict and severe punishment' of the hostages, but the hostages themselves did not know this. Boese's announcement raised a gasp and sobs from those listening in the crowded departure lounge.

Then, in the evening, the hostages were split into two groups. Some of the passengers had noticed a smaller hall, adjacent to the one they were occupying, and suggested that they be allowed to use this to relieve overcrowding. What they did not anticipate was the basis on which the hijackers would decide who went where. Amid anger, protests and fear, all those who were identified as Israelis were ordered into the smaller hall. These included passengers of other nationalities, such as six Orthodox Jews, whose passports plainly demonstrated their US citizenship but who had been sitting with the Israelis. Several Jewish passengers, and a few Israelis, were left in the larger hall and, after protests, some of the non-Israelis sent to the smaller one were eventually allowed to return. Later there would be much argument over how the hijackers divided the passengers but there is no doubt that for the many Holocaust survivors among them this 'selection' process revived appalling memories. So too did the need to stoop low, almost to a crawl, in order to access the smaller hall via a hole knocked in the partition wall, as well as the fact that there were Germans with assault rifles standing over them. 'The feeling is like an execution,' one hostage wrote.

The hostages were not as representative, socially and economically, of Israel's three million or so Jewish citizens as those at Munich had been, not least because air travel was expensive. Even so, they included a welder, a teacher and a nurse as well as a pharmacist, psychologist, doctor, lawyer, microbiologist, economist and computer engineer, and in many respects they reflected important new currents in Israeli society. Inevitably among them were some servicemen and many reservists, of whom several had fought in Israel's wars. All were in some sense globally connected – to France, the ultimate destination of the hijacked

Airbus – but also to the US, where many passengers were eventually headed. Several lived there, or had much of their family there and were travelling to attend weddings.

In fact, only a minority could be described as religiously observant. Some lit Shabbat candles in the terminal on the Friday night and sang the customary blessings, but this was a ritual in almost every Jewish home in Israel, as cultural as it was religious, and practised by many faithless and secular Jews. Others firmly considered themselves Jewish but were not Israeli, had never considered settling in Israel and felt little affinity for the country. Michel Cojot-Goldberg, for example, who acted as an interpreter for and representative of the hostages, had survived the Nazi occupation of France by borrowing the identity of a non-Jewish neighbour. His father had died in Auschwitz. Even after the Second World War, he continued to suffer the discrimination and abuse that had marked his childhood, and at one point had even set out on an obsessive quest to find and kill Klaus Barbie, the Gestapo functionary who had overseen massive deportations of Jews from France. But he was not an enthusiastic Zionist, saw himself as a patriotic Frenchman and had been in Israel with his thirteen-year-old son on a business trip. Nor had he, like most of the hostages, spent a huge amount of time or energy thinking about the Palestinians and their various grievances.

On the same day that the hostages were separated, the hijackers were joined by reinforcements – three Palestinians – bringing their total to seven. Their leader, nicknamed 'The Cruel One' by the hostages, was Fayez Abdul-Rahim al-Jabr, a veteran of the Arab Nationalist Movement of George Habash and then the PFLP. Tall, broad, with a black moustache, al-Jabr was from Hebron, the West Bank city which since 1967 had been under Israeli occupation. As a child he had slept with his brothers on thin mattresses on a cracked concrete floor. He had only a very basic education, but read voraciously: books by Marx and Stalin, a history of the Algerian revolution, much else. When as a teenager he disappeared from the family home at night without explanation, it was clear that he was becoming involved in some kind of banned political activity. This was something of a family tradition. His father, who sold wood, was a fervent nationalist, and a brother was deported to Jordan in 1970. Al-Jabr's story was one that many families in the West Bank could have told.

Al-Jabr had won his spurs with the PFLP by leading an attack on a luxury hotel in Amman shortly before the multiple hijackings of September 1970, and had then been picked by Habash to accompany him on a tour of North Korea. He fought in the battles in Jordan that followed the hijackings and had since travelled widely conducting clandestine missions for Haddad's breakaway faction. Fully aware of the risks he was taking, al-Jabr had told his younger brother that he wanted to be buried in Palestine, but if that wasn't possible, his body should be thrown into the River Jordan.

Al-Jabr's deputy had followed a very different route to Entebbe. Jael Naji al-Arja was a Christian from Beit Jala, in the West Bank just south of Jerusalem, though he claimed to be Peruvian, Colombian or Chilean, and spoke to some of the hostages in Spanish. They dubbed him 'Groucho Marx' because of his limping gait, cap and moustache. Cojot-Goldberg described him, half-jokingly, as a 'true member of the Fifth [Trotskyite] International', which was closer to the truth than the Frenchman knew. Al-Arja had represented the PFLP in Yemen and Latin America, where he had been in charge of relations with local left-wing activists and sympathetic governments. On joining the Popular Front–XO, he had been given responsibility for Haddad's global outreach effort, a post he still filled despite his deployment in a less diplomatic role.

The hijackers were sometimes harsh, sometimes less so. Though an increasing number of passengers were suffering from diarrhoea brought on by contaminated drinking water, medical care remained haphazard and restricted. Most of the lights were still left on overnight in the two halls. One young male hostage, wrongly suspected of being an Israeli soldier, was repeatedly beaten during an 'interrogation'. A father was hit with a rifle butt when he approached the hijackers with a request for a cushion for a baby. The hostages were also repeatedly reminded that their time was running out.

At the same time, hostages were permitted to hang laundry on makeshift lines strung outside the terminal, and sometimes to walk a few yards in the chill of an equatorial morning. There had been an opportunity to buy duty-free toiletries and cigarettes brought over from the new terminal complex, and the luggage was finally retrieved from the Airbus's hold. On one occasion, two of the younger hijackers, excited by a false rumour that Israel had accepted the Popular Front–XO's demands, brought bottles of spirits and wine to a group of French hostages who were more or less their own age and then sat with them, talking and laughing. The children were given another opportunity to play – though they were stopped from dancing.

Most of the hostages saw Boese as the most approachable of their captors. He had been talkative and solicitous on the flight from Athens, in stark contrast to Kuhlmann, who was aggressive and apparently exasperated by the passengers' indiscipline. On landing in Entebbe, Boese had given a short speech to explain their motives, telling them that an Air France plane had been deliberately targeted because, despite its ostensibly pro-Arab foreign policy, France was 'the historic enemy of the Arab nation . . . a junior partner prostrate in front of United States imperialism' which had supplied Israel with nuclear technology and weapons. He went on to explain that while the immediate aim of the operation was to free imprisoned 'freedom fighters', its broader objectives were to attract worldwide attention to the Palestinian cause, inspire revolutionaries everywhere to come together to fight for 'the oppressed' and 'defeat imperialism' and ultimately to liberate the whole of Palestine, expel almost all of its 'Jewish colonisers' and establish a 'socialist, secular democracy'. His lecture over, Boese expressed the hope that his audience now understood the mind of a 'crazy German revolutionary' and apologised for his poor English, which he attributed to a lack of sleep. 'I want to be human and I don't want to kill you,' he told them. 'But I am very tired and a little confused.'

With his long blond hair, blue eyes and generally cheerful demeanour, hostages later described him as 'cherub-faced', 'personable and sympathetic', like a 'kindergarten teacher with infants'. Perhaps unsurprisingly for a former sociology student, Boese spent hours in discussions about 'dialectics' with 'college-educated' American nationals, attempting to justify his actions and arguing repeatedly that he was 'not racist but anti-Zionist'. He also made some attempts to allow more Jewish hostages who were not Israeli to return to the larger hall. When a survivor of a Nazi death camp pointed to the number tattooed on his arm and told Boese that what he and Kuhlmann were doing to women, children and the elderly showed that nothing had changed in Germany, Boese 'blanched and trembled', and said that he had 'carried out terrorist acts in West Germany because the ruling establishment took Nazis and reactionaries into its service'. When a French passenger asked if he worried that his actions resembled those of the Nazis, Boese replied that both his objectives and means were different. 'We are very correct,' he claimed.

One night, those hostages who remained awake watched as Boese calmed a hysterical elderly Jewish woman who had escaped the Holocaust, leading her to a bench outside the terminal and sitting with his arm around her shoulders for two hours, talking softly in their shared language until she stopped sobbing and returned to the departure lounge to sleep. On another night, Boese made a prediction to one of the passengers: that the hijacking would end for him with 'many years in prison' or death.

It was now six days since Flight AF139 landed at Entebbe, and the situation for the men, women and children held at the airport had become considerably more perilous. Two batches of passengers had been released and less than half of those who had arrived on the Airbus now remained. On the third day, forty-eight elderly and ill passengers had been picked up by an Air France plane sent from Paris. Then, shortly before an extension to the deadline had been agreed, another one hundred healthy adults and children of a dozen different nationalities were allowed to leave, also on a plane sent from Paris. Among them was Michel Cojot-Goldberg, the Frenchman who had acted as a translator and intermediary between the passengers and their captors, despite a strong sense that he was abandoning the others when they needed him most. Hours before the new deadline, a second extension of forty-eight hours was agreed. There were now just over a hundred hostages left – seventy-eight holding Israeli passports, two Belgians, some US and some French nationals, and the flight crew, who were never given the option of leaving.

Throughout the crisis, there had been intense debate among the hostages over whether Israel would capitulate to the Popular Front's demands. Now these arguments were renewed. Many of the younger Israelis hoped their leaders would hold firm, so as not to hand the fedayeen a major victory and encourage further hijackings. Most of the older hostages favoured concessions. The mood was soured further by a new outbreak of diarrhoea and vomiting, probably caused by badly cooked meat. Most of the inadequate toilet facilities in the terminal were now unusable, and washing clothes was becoming difficult. The psychological state of the hostages was deteriorating. At least one wrote a letter of final wishes for their family, 'The Israelis' distress has increased as they have seen the planeloads of other passengers leave,' a US diplomat in Paris told Washington. 'They know that their chances of escape or rescue are nil.'

What the diplomat did not know was that over the previous forty-eight hours, Shimon Peres, the Israeli defence minister, and Mordechai 'Motta' Gur, the Israel Defence Forces' chief of staff, had not only drawn up a plan to rescue the hostages in Entebbe but now had hundreds of soldiers, medics, aircrew and technicians standing by to execute it. They even had a name: Operation Thunderbolt.

18
Operation Thunderbolt

Yitzhak Rabin and Shimon Peres were very different men, from very different backgrounds, and had followed different routes into politics. Rabin was a taciturn soldier who had played a key role in Israel's victory in the 1967 war. Born in Jerusalem in 1922, he was one of the exceptionally young military men who emerged to dominate the new country's defence establishment after independence. Peres had been born Szymon Perski in Poland, and was urbane, eloquent and charming, an effective administrator credited with building up the country's military and ever less secret nuclear programme. When Meir resigned in the aftermath of the 1973 war, both Peres and Rabin had hoped to become prime minister. After a bitter contest, Rabin had won, but his defeated rival was too potent a figure to ignore and had received the vital defence portfolio, recently vacated by Moshe Dayan. Throughout the first six days of the hostage crisis, the two had bickered like jealous siblings. Peres, safe in the knowledge that he did not have ultimate responsibility for any decision, had loudly maintained that giving in to the hijackers would be a devastating defeat. Rabin said Israel had no viable military options and therefore no choice but to negotiate.

With Gur and other senior military officers, Peres had spent much of the week trying to produce a workable plan that would win over Rabin and Israel's cabinet. Since the failures at Ma'alot and elsewhere, the commanders of the Sayeret Matkal had been training hard to launch exactly the sort of assault that would be required. Their commander was a thirty-year-old called Yonathan Netanyahu; like his brother Benjamin, he had been involved in several such operations before. But Entebbe posed challenges of a different order to anything the Israelis had previously encountered. The most obvious was the vast distance to the target. The Israeli air force's C-130 Hercules transport planes could just reach Uganda but would need to refuel before they could bring back the attacking force and anyone they rescued. Then there were Idi Amin's troops to deal with. No one could say if the elite parachutists the dictator had deployed around the old terminal would fight, and if so how fiercely. Finally, there was the lack of precise tactical intelligence. How many hijackers were there? With what weapons? Where were the hostages being held? And under what guard? No one knew.

As the days passed, these problems had been progressively resolved. Israeli intelligence officers got detailed information from freed passengers arriving in Paris, while a Mossad agent's flight over the airport in a light plane, along with news footage and archive photographs, provided further crucial details. Impractical plans – a massive parachute drop, an amphibious raid across Lake Victoria – were discarded. Night exercises showed that newly installed navigational equipment would allow the C-130s to land in poor visibility. An engineer at an Israeli company that had once tendered to build the new terminal at Entebbe provided plans of the old building. Former soldiers who had trained the Ugandan army were adamant that their former charges would not offer serious resistance. A critical piece fell into place when well-disposed Kenyan security officials quietly agreed to allow the Israeli force to fill their planes' tanks at Nairobi if they were unable to pump enough fuel from the tanks at Entebbe during the raid. Like most African nations, Kenya had broken off relations with Israel after the 1973 war, but the two states' intelligence services and militaries remained friendly. This was the payoff of Israel's longstanding 'periphery strategy'.

Finally, after days of brainstorming and discussion, all that remained were the operational details of the assault itself, and by the time the Popular Front–XO decided to extend the deadline for negotiations another forty-eight hours, these had fallen into place too. Four transport planes would fly almost 200 elite troops into Entebbe, landing on the main runway at night. Most of these would storm and hold the main terminal of the airport while a much smaller force from the Sayeret Matkal would drive to the old terminal in two Land Rovers led by a black Mercedes limousine of the type favoured by senior Ugandan officers. To reinforce the deception, they would wear Ugandan combat fatigues. This subterfuge would allow the assault team to get close enough to their target to kill the hijackers before they had time to massacre the hostages. Two refitted Boeing 707s would be sent as well: one to circle above Entebbe as a mobile command post and communications link with Tel Aviv, the other to set up a field hospital at Nairobi airport.

Senior officers deemed the operation feasible but doubted the politicians would accept the risks involved. Netanyahu, the Sayeret Matkal's commander, told his girlfriend he did not think the assault would happen, and few of his men believed that the plan would get the go-ahead either. Some had complained to their officers that they were inadequately prepared for such an ambitious operation. At dinner on Friday evening, Peres entertained a delegation from the US led by the hawkish Professor Zbigniew Brzezinski, tipped to be their next national security adviser, who had only withering criticism for the Israeli government's initial decision to consider negotiations with the hijackers. In response, Peres calmly listed all the many objections to the attack that he himself was trying to convince the prime minister to green-light, and which he had spent much of the previous forty-eight hours persuading Gur, the chief of staff, and other key ministers was likely to succeed. He had even driven across Tel Aviv to obtain the support of Israel's most famous, if most controversial soldier, Dayan, who was having dinner in a favourite restaurant with friends.

The next morning, a Saturday, Peres and Gur gave a detailed presentation to Rabin and a select group of senior officials. The prime minister still had reservations and expected significant casualties, both among the troops and the hostages, but decided to approve Peres' plan nonetheless. He called a meeting of the entire cabinet which, shortly after 1 p.m., voted unanimously to support his decision. Forty minutes later, the first of the transport planes carrying the attacking force took off.

The route taken by the Israeli planes illustrated quite how isolated Israel had become internationally. Maintaining strict radio silence and keeping very low, the four transport planes landed briefly at Sharm el Sheikh, the port at the tip of the Sinai peninsula, then flew down the Red Sea to avoid Egypt and Sudan. Having kept clear of both Jordanian radar and Soviet surveillance ships, and out of Saudi Arabia's airspace, they turned south opposite Yemen on a course that took them over Ethiopia – no longer a useful ally in East Africa but now under a new and unpredictable Marxist regime following the deposition of Emperor Haile Selassie in 1974 – and eventually over Kenya. After another hour or so following the Great Rift Valley due south, the heavily loaded aircraft turned west to fly over the vast waters of Lake Victoria, then turned again amid storm clouds before a slow and careful descent into Entebbe airport. The first plane landed very quietly with its lights out and taxied carefully to a halt. It was midnight, very still and very silent. 'I never felt such a loneliness . . . We really felt we were far, far from home and there was no one to rescue us and everything was on our shoulders,' one of the Sayeret Matkal men remembered later.

Then it began. The assault unit approaching the old terminal in Land Rovers and the Mercedes were spotted by a sentry and opened fire, earlier than planned, in order to silence him. Their cover blown, they jumped down from the vehicles and began sprinting for the building. Hearing gunfire, Boese moved to the front of the main departure lounge and took up a position next to Kuhlmann behind the large windows that faced the runway. Most of the Ugandan troops had fled or hidden at the sounds of the first shots but a handful had opened fire from the control tower at the men now running across the apron. Several witnesses described Boese turning to point an assault rifle at the hostages for a moment, then hesitating, shouting at them to 'get down', before finally swinging the weapon towards the oncoming Israeli soldiers. Yards from him, another hijacker was already shooting, emptying most of the magazine of his AK-47 at the figures illuminated by the spotlights outside. Boese pulled a pin from a grenade, looked again at the hostages, looked back outside – and decided to throw it at the soldiers. There was an explosion and a flash of light. An Israeli soldier entered the hall, firing short accurate bursts, then two more soldiers entered through a side door. Boese was shot dead, and Kuhlmann too. Within a minute, two more hijackers in the departure lounge had been killed. The remaining three died very shortly afterwards as the Sayeret Matkal cleared the rest of the terminal.

Three hostages were either dead or fatally injured, and three soldiers badly hurt. Less than half a mile away, the larger Israeli force had taken control of the new terminal without significant opposition. One of the injured soldiers was Netanyahu, the commander, who had been hit in the chest and arm, probably by fire from Ugandan soldiers in the control tower. Medics tried to save his life, but he died on the concrete beside one of the planes.

Soldiers checked the old terminal for stragglers and took fingerprints from the corpses of the hijackers. Some spent a moment looking for trophies, others made sure no Israeli equipment had been left behind. One detachment destroyed the eleven Soviet- and Libyan-supplied MiG jet fighters parked nearby, eliminating most of Amin's air force and fulfilling a promise made to the Kenyan officials who had offered the vital refuelling facilities. Just under ninety minutes after the raid had begun, the last Israeli plane left the ground.

The force returned to 'a welcome of pride and tears and carnival'. Peres, Rabin, senior soldiers, politicians, a vast crowd of well-wishers, ecstatic relatives and journalists met the planes as they landed at Israel's main international airport, recently renamed in honour of the nation's founding prime minister David Ben-Gurion. Under an improvised canopy, families were reunited and 'toasted their salvation in orange juice and Coca-Cola'. Across the country, there were 'scenes of rejoicing unparalleled in Israel since the Six Day War of 1967'. Businessmen offered free holidays to any soldier or airman who had taken part in the raid. Thousands of ordinary Israelis volunteered to contribute to the soldiers' welfare fund. In Jerusalem a solitary pilot traced the words 'All honour to the Israel Defence Forces' across the sky with a vapour trail. Newspapers printed hundreds of thousands of extra editions to keep up with demand. Menachem Begin, the firebrand opposition politician who led the right-wing Likud party and had supported Rabin's decision to launch the raid, told the Knesset that 'the message of Entebbe' was that Israel would come to the aid of anyone anywhere 'persecuted, or humiliated, or threatened, or abducted, or ... in any way endangered simply because he or she is a Jew'.

'The Entebbe operation has had a catalytic effect on the national spirit, replacing the post [1973] war sense of drift and passivity with renewed feeling of pride and confidence,' US diplomats cabled Washington from Tel Aviv. 'The lingering trauma of the October war, the sense that Israel no longer can control its destiny, has been replaced by a renewed sense of national confidence that the government and the army can act effectively in crisis situations', leaving Israel 'once again united, confident of its leadership and army, defiant of the terrorist organisations, and proud of its image and role in the free world.' Netanyahu, the only fatality among the attacking force, was grieved and honoured as a new national hero. In the US, his brother Benjamin, now studying for a doctorate in political science at Massachusetts Institute of Technology, drove for eight hours to his parents' home to tell them their eldest son was dead. Two days after welcoming the freed hostages, Israel's political and military leaders reunited for Netanyahu's funeral at the national military cemetery on Mount Herzl. Operation Thunderbolt would be renamed in the fallen soldier's honour.

Outside of Israel, the reaction to Entebbe was starkly and predictably divided in accordance with Cold War allegiances and ideology. US president Gerald Ford sent a letter to Rabin expressing the 'great satisfaction' of the American people at the Israelis' success in 'thwarting a senseless act of terror'. Many American commentators compared the raid with the dismal and chaotic evacuation of scared US Embassy staff from the roofs of Saigon only fourteen months previously, the final humiliating end to the superpower's failed war in Vietnam. Ronald Reagan, by contrast, the governor of California and aspirant presidential candidate, focused on the success of the Israelis' response rather than the need for it, describing the Israelis as 'acting like Americans used to act'. Other US journalists hailed a 'brilliant and heart-lifting victory'. A song about the raid did well in US charts, capitalising on a fortuitous coincidence of dates. 'It was early Sunday morning. Without a word of warning. Those big Israeli birds swooped from the sky,' Joe Glazer, a bluegrass balladeer, sang. 'A hundred years from now, I bet they'll still be telling how, That deed was done [on] the Fourth Day of July.'

In Europe, official reactions were more circumspect, at least in public. The German government had recently adopted a new policy of making no concessions to hijackers and had been extremely reluctant to release any detainees. Bonn now expressed 'profound relief' that a 'barbarous' act of violence had been foiled. Officials in London privately advised ministers that Britain had 'little to gain and possibly something to lose' by sending any congratulatory message to the Israelis, not least because the raid, 'however brilliant', was of 'doubtful legality' and 'has aroused strong feelings in Africa and the Middle East'. This highly political position shifted when it became clear that some days after the raid Amin's security services had murdered an elderly British-Israeli woman who had been among the hostages but had been taken to hospital in Kampala early in the crisis, whereupon London cut off diplomatic relations with its former protectorate.

The French government said little, partly because they were in the middle of delicate negotiations to obtain the return of the valuable Air France plane which was still parked on the runway at Entebbe. According to US diplomats in Paris, the French were also anxious not 'to be opposed to African opinion right after receiving criticism of [its] nuclear reactor sale to South Africa', despite the fact that the 'Israeli action was tremendously popular in France. French press was ecstatic in its praise.' But this last was not actually true. In contrast to the euphoric welcome in the US media, many western European newspapers, most but not all on the left, were critical of the raid. *Le Monde* worried that the raid would turn out to be a 'Pyrrhic victory' by redoubling Arab and African hostility to Israel, and the *Financial Times* pointed out that such operations would not alone eliminate extremist violence. This would only come, the newspaper said, when moderate Palestinian leaders could have a real hope of a negotiated solution to the problems of the Middle East.

It was at the United Nations that the divisions were most fiercely politicised. The US and its allies thought the UN should be discussing the various international shortcomings that obliged the Israelis to intervene militarily, and hoped to get a commitment from member states to fight 'international terrorism'. They saw clear evidence that Amin had colluded with the hijackers, and hoped such behaviour could be prevented. The view of the USSR, its satellites, China, Cuba, other 'revolutionary states' and almost the entirety of the developing and Arab worlds was altogether different: the Israelis had committed a flagrant breach of international law and no allegations of collusion by Ugandan authorities could justify the raid. 'The tragedy of Entebbe showed that Western powers manifested a fanatical solidarity against the blacks of Africa and against the browns of the Arab lands and lauded technical efficiency at the expense of honour and moral principles,' the Libyan ambassador told the assembly. The Egyptians described the Israeli operation as 'a terrorist demonstration of a theatrical nature', and when a special session was finally convened, its subject was 'the aggression of Zionist Israel against Uganda'.

Hostility to Israel did not necessarily equate to support for Haddad's attack, however. *Pravda*, the Soviet Union's official state newspaper, described Israel as 'bandits using the methods of gangsters' but did not condone the hijacking. In Beirut, George Habash told a reporter that the attack was the work of 'dissidents' and stressed that the PFLP had banned such operations four years ago. Though Yasser Arafat wrote to Amin expressing his admiration for the 'noble stand Uganda has taken against the barbaric Zionist raid', he had actually sent three senior envoys to Entebbe during the crisis to try to broker a peaceful resolution. Some weeks after the hijacking he asked French officials in Cairo to pass on to London secret information about imminent operations by Palestinian factions that would target British interests. Tunisian officials expressed public indignation at an attack that they said menaced all Africans but privately were happy to see Idi Amin 'trimmed down to size', and had been 'awed' by the professionalism and audacity of the Israeli special forces. Ilich Ramírez, the most wanted terrorist in the world, expressed enthusiastic admiration for their audacity and skill, too. 'When an enemy does something well, you have to be able to recognise the fact,' he told Hans-Joachim Klein when the two men learned what the Israelis had done.

For many policy-makers and security officials, the raid was indeed a revelation. As the CIA pointed out, 1976 had been the worst year on record for the sheer number of attacks. In Italy, the 'years of lead [bullets]' were entering their most intensely violent phase. The Irish Republican Army was now killing dozens of British soldiers a year and striking regularly on the mainland while retaining considerable popular support among Northern Ireland's Catholic community. ETA, the Basque separatist group, was still active and would remain so, as were various right-wing extremist groups who perpetrated much violence across the US, western Europe and Latin America, though they received far less political or media attention. Moreover, the violence continued to be conspicuously transnational. In 1975 a bomb at New York's La Guardia airport had killed eleven and wounded seventy-five – the most lethal attack in the US for more than fifty years. The list of suspects included Puerto Rican, Croat and Palestinian nationalists alongside the Jewish Defence League, a self-designated 'counter-terrorist group' founded to combat 'the sworn enemies of the Jewish people with hard-core violence' and whose leader had recently been charged with planning to kidnap a Soviet diplomat, bomb the Iraqi Embassy in Washington and ship arms from Israel. In Sweden, intelligence services uncovered a group led by a German citizen that included an Austrian, a Briton, a Greek, a Mexican and a Chilean as well as local Swedish activists.

This all meant, the CIA noted, that there was widespread frustration across much of the West with what was seen as a 'weak and ineffective' international response to 'international terrorism'. A 'major stumbling block was the controversy over justifiable vs illegal political violence', the agency commented. The raid on Entebbe suggested a new and less complex way forward, one that dispensed with legalism and compromise in favour of bold, violent action which, when successful, had the additional advantage of being popular with voters. 'Operation Thunderbolt marks a turn in the tide of the Free World's response to the new techniques of terror, [it] signified that some men and women have the guts to strike back, and it evoked a response from ordinary people that suggests the public is far ahead of governments in wishing to arm against this new danger,' wrote the American author of one of the several books published within months of the raid. A series of rapidly made feature films – the first announced by Universal Pictures five days after the hostages had been freed – reinforced the raid's mythic status in Western countries. Many Western governments rushed to reassure their publics that they too had troops who could undertake a similar mission – claims that were certainly untested, if not entirely untrue.

In Israel, the spectacular success of the raid was seen as the crowning achievement of the strategy its security services and army had adopted since the killings at the Munich Olympics four years earlier. Deterrence depended on the apparent certainty of an effective and probably lethal response to any perceived threat, and Entebbe had achieved exactly this. The Iron Wall had now been extended further than ever before, encompassing not just Europe and the Middle East but a significant portion of Africa too. In fact, as Begin made clear in his speech to the Knesset immediately after the operation, the Iron Wall was no longer restricted to any particular place, and thus, in theory, covered the entire world. A real durable peace remained elusive, and would almost certainly require concessions to the Palestinians that most found impossible to contemplate, but an acceptable degree of security, it appeared to many Israelis, was possible to achieve through force of arms alone.

US diplomats in Tel Aviv noted that the public mood had turned 'hawkish' and worried that the raid had 'reinforc[ed] deeply-held convictions on the intractability of Arab hostility . . . and the impotence of international bodies'. Of the many problems still facing Israel at home and on its borders, none were resolved by the raid on Entebbe: though 'its national psyche . . . [had] been profoundly altered', 'Israel's political situation' had not changed in the slightest. This did not bode well, they warned.

Indeed, one of the reasons that some in the West, and particularly the US, were so enthusiastic about the Israelis' success in Uganda was that they were avid for good news. Proliferating international terrorism was a consequence of much broader problems facing the 'Free World', they believed. The triumph of North Vietnamese forces in 1975, the takeover of Cambodia by the radical Marxist-Leninist Khmer Rouge, the presence of proudly socialist governments across much of South Asia, the stubborn resilience of the left in Latin America, not to mention the

USSR's military and nuclear capabilities, together convinced many that the titanic struggle against Communism was being lost. Within Africa, the crisis at Entebbe had made clear how few states could be relied on to support Washington or the western Europeans. Marxists in power in Ethiopia and Sudan remained resolutely aligned against the West, while Somalia appeared to be a staunch Soviet client. Further south, the white supremacist regime in Rhodesia was struggling in its war against insurgents backed by Moscow and Beijing. In Guinea-Bissau, Mozambique and Angola, Marxist guerrillas had all recently won bloody struggles for independence from Portugal. There were even flickers of new unrest in South Africa, regarded by many as a bastion of anti-Communism on the continent.

And yet the tension that had always existed – between the global struggle for 'revolution' that would liberate the masses as an international collective and the reality on the ground where this radical rupture was supposed to occur – was more evident than ever. The most successful of the organisations agitating for transformational change in late 1976 and early 1977 were those that were rooted in a profound, if sometimes newly discovered, sense of place, and which prioritised the immediate interests of that local community. In practical terms, the targets of the groups that had made the most progress were usually the nearest police outpost, army barracks, politician's office or landowner's residence. Their enemy was not 'imperialism' or 'capitalism' but the local regime. Their rallying cry was more often a call to fight for their country, not for the liberation of workers across the world.

If this was true of Angolan, Nicaraguan, Spanish or Irish groups, it was true of their Middle Eastern counterparts too. Like their enemies, Haddad and his associates sought to frame what had happened at Entebbe within their own narrative of struggle, heroism and sacrifice. In the weeks after the raid, posters bearing the insignia of the PFLP and portraits of the seven dead hijackers appeared on walls in Baghdad, where Haddad was now spending more time, and in Beirut. As part of the preparations for the hijacking, Boese and Kuhlmann had been photographed. They had known why. 'Hopefully I'll come back ... but it's a dangerous operation,' Kuhlmann had told a fellow trainee in Aden. The posters lauded the sacrifice made by the martyrs. 'With their sacred blood, our comrades have ... opened a new phase in the battle of the revolutionary movements of the world in the struggle against imperialism, Zionism and reaction,' the posters read. They had fought 'against ... racism, for international liberation movements, for Palestine' in 'the German armed struggle against Nazism'. On the poster, Boese had been renamed Mahmud, while Kuhlmann was Halima, a *nom de guerre* she had adopted some months before.

Few clear-eyed supporters of the Palestinian armed struggle were convinced that the raid was any kind of victory. The organisation founded by Boese and Kuhlmann, the Revolutionary Cells, had suffered a blow from which it would never fully recover, and Haddad's group had once more failed to live up to its now fading reputation as the elite of the armed struggle. It was also increasingly evident that neither they nor their West German allies could claim to be supported by anything resembling a mass popular constituency and that their violence had long diverged from any realistic political strategy. By late 1976, whatever their grandiose claims and ambitions, both Haddad's organisation and the Revolutionary Cells were little more than small, isolated groups whose few hundred members had somehow failed to see that their agendas were outdated, their means anachronistic and their resources inadequate.

In the immediate aftermath of the Entebbe raid, the remaining members of the Revolutionary Cells discussed a series of outlandish and unrealistic plans to exact revenge on the Israelis, including destroying passenger planes in flight. They planted bombs at two cinemas in Germany to force the withdrawal of the Hollywood films portraying the raid on Entebbe. These, they claimed, resembled 'Nazi propaganda movies that had mobilised the German people against the Jews'. One bomb was defused and those responsible were swiftly arrested. The other failed to explode. A plan to strike an airport on the Côte d'Azur ended abruptly when the attackers' arms and explosives were stolen from a safehouse in Rome, possibly by a rival faction. The bitter and very personal truth for the surviving German extremists, which nothing could disguise, was that the efforts of Boese, Kuhlmann and the five Palestinian hijackers had not ended in the pre-dawn of a bright new revolutionary era, but in a one-sided battle that lasted less than sixty seconds in a squalid, disused airport terminal in East Africa full of frightened and sick civilians whom they [illegible] held against their will for more than a week.

While the Soviets might be winning allies across the decolonising world, the reality was that these were often marriages of convenience. The new prominence of localised causes that had no real connection to Marxist-Leninist struggle suggested that the West was ultimately winning the intellectual battle, even if it was losing the territorial one. Western analysts welcomed the development. If identity was replacing ideology, that could surely only be to their benefit.

But such optimism rested on shaky foundations, or rather on a very narrow definition of 'revolutionary'. In fact, since the days of Western colonial rule, an alternative programme for radical social and political change had existed throughout the Middle East and in pockets of Asia and Africa. It had waxed and waned over the decades but now, in the mid-1970s, began to surge once more. Initially at least, its target was not distant 'capitalist exploiters', 'Zionist aggressors' or 'imperialists' in the West or Israel, but the 'unbelievers, apostates, hypocrites and tyrants' who were much closer to home.

VI

19

An Outrage for God

Even for a city as habitually febrile as Cairo, the first week of July in 1977 was unusually tense.

Six months earlier, news of drastic cuts in subsidies for bread, gas, sugar, rice and other basic necessities had prompted several days of rioting. These had left 171 people dead and were followed by waves of arrests. Hundreds of ordinary men and women had been picked up off Cairo's potholed streets, snatched in its markets or marched blindfold down the worn stairs of its dilapidated apartment buildings into waiting trucks under the eyes of fearful neighbours.

Now police and plain-clothes intelligence officers were sweeping through the city once more, concentrating principally on Cairo's outskirts and the industrial suburb of El Matariya to the north, where the riots had started, as well as the fast-growing satellite city of Giza by the Pyramids to the south, where a dozen of the notorious nightclubs that served visitors to the monuments had been burned to the ground.

The Egyptian capital's inhabitants were used to sporadic violence and the brutal reaction it provoked from the authorities. But this was different from the crackdown that had followed January's bread riots. Then, the authorities had blamed the unrest on 'criminals, traitors and extremists', whom they identified as socialists, Communists and supposedly 'dissident' intellectuals. Now the police were hunting a very different type of suspect.

The first sign of trouble had been a series of small bomb explosions in the final days of June. Several had gone off among crowds thronging Cairo's famous open-air cinemas. One had interrupted a concert at the Institute of Oriental Music in the wealthy neighbourhood of Zamalek. By a miracle, there had been no serious casualties. Then a senior Muslim cleric and former minister of religious endowments had been found dead with a gunshot wound to his head, five days after being abducted from his home. Such an act was unprecedented in Egypt.

Shortly afterwards those responsible issued a communiqué. They demanded the safe release of sixty 'imprisoned brothers', an amnesty for group members on the run, the sum of 200,000 Egyptian pounds in unmarked cash, apologies from five major newspapers and magazines 'for their lies', an official investigation into wrongdoings by Egypt's prosecutors and intelligence services and the publication of a statement of theirs in local and regional newspapers as well as the *New York Times*, *Le Monde* and the *Guardian*. Lastly, they wanted authorisation to publish a book entitled *The Caliphate* written by their leader. This last demand prompted intense speculation about the identity of its authors, as it seemed to rule out the usual suspects. Were they assassins hired by Libya, against whom Egypt had just fought a short war? Or were they actually Mossad agents? Maybe they were insane criminals escaped from a prison hospital? Whoever they were, they were not cowed by the Egyptian prime minister's rejection of all their demands outright and his vow to crush the miscreants with 'an iron first'. 'We will see who is forced to their knees first,' one told local news agencies.

The answer came swiftly enough. Around a week after the first bombings, the police called journalists to an impromptu press conference where they announced the success of their operations and presented a man detained the day before in a nondescript apartment in El Matariya. He was, they said, the leader of a group called Takfir Wal Hijra, which was responsible for the bombings, the murder and the demands.

Two years earlier, local newspapers had run a series of lurid articles about this same group of 'depraved Islamic militants' who had set up some kind of esoteric cult. The security services had been alerted to its existence by parents claiming that their daughters had been abducted and forced into marriages with its members. Subsequent investigations suggested that the young women had not been coerced, at least not sufficiently for criminal charges to be brought. Since then, Egypt's principal intelligence service, the Mukhabarat, had monitored the organisation's activities but had not seen them as a threat. This now looked like a misjudgement.

At the press conference, officials said that Takfir Wal Hijra, which roughly translated as 'Excommunication and Retreat', had around 2,000 members, recruited over the previous five or six years and comprising largely university students, mainly in technical or scientific disciplines, but also including a former policeman and a female engineer. The killer of the kidnapped cleric was a bricklayer. They considered their leader, who turned out to be an agronomist in his mid-thirties called Shukri Ahmed Mustafa, to be their 'emir' and described him as 'the chosen one, God's caliph on earth and the prince of the faithful'. The captured militant, who wore a dark jellaba and a full beard, was 'of imposing appearance' with 'eyes full of flames', *Le Monde*'s reporter wrote.

But Shukri's impressive appearance and apparent charisma only partly explained the existence of Takfir Wal Hijra and the violence of the previous days. In fact, the single most important influence on him and the group as a whole – whose real name was not Takfir Wal Hijra but Jama'at al-Muslimin, or Assembly of the Muslims – was a man who, by the summer of 1977, had been dead for almost eleven years.

Syed Qutb turned to Islamism relatively late in life. But the works and ideas he then produced were of such power that they not only had an enormous impact across much of the Muslim world but would continue to inspire extremists decades later.

Qutb was born in 1906, the son of a middling landowner in a village in Upper Egypt, and his education mixed the modern and the traditional: a state primary, an unhappy year at a Koranic school, three years at a government secondary, then Cairo's Dar al-Ulum, a prestigious teacher-training college which combined instruction in Islamic law with carefully selected Western subjects. During the inter-war years, Egypt went from being a British protectorate to a nominally independent kingdom, though frequent and bloody protests against British control continued. Qutb worked as a schoolmaster, inspector and Ministry of Education pen-pusher, spending his ample spare time writing literary criticism, poor poetry and trenchant texts that expressed profound concerns for social justice in Egypt and enthusiasm for anti-colonial struggles elsewhere.

Qutb's values were always profoundly conservative, coloured by a strong sense that many of Egypt's ills were attributable to Western influence. In 1948, having published a particularly vitriolic article that called for Egyptian society to return to its 'authentic' values, he was dispatched to the US, where he spent two years in Colorado studying educational curricula. If this close contact was meant to cure his anti-Western views, the effort failed. Instead, his time in the US convinced Qutb of the vacuity and inhumanity of American values, and on his return he published a book on 'The Battle between Islam and Capitalism'. This interest in a religious solution to political, economic and social questions intensified and, surer than ever of the threat to Egypt posed by a '[Western civilisation] operating at a crazed speed . . . without heart or conscience', he formally joined the Muslim Brotherhood.

The movement was a natural home for Qutb. It had been founded in 1928 by another Egyptian educationalist called Hassan al-Banna with the aim of resisting Western rule and cultural influence across the Islamic world. The movement attracted adherents avid to improve their lives and their nation with a coherent ideological framework that explained the chaos and repression of late colonial rule while drawing on apparently timeless Egyptian and Islamic values. But while the Muslim Brotherhood's opposition to imperialism and Zionism matched that of other secular nationalists in Egypt, their proposed alternative was very different. Al-Banna and his followers argued that the only solution was Islam.

Though they had supported the Free Officers coup, the Muslim Brotherhood's relationship with Egypt's new rulers soured very quickly and in 1954 the organisation was banned by Gamal Abdel Nasser and thousands of its members were detained. Qutb had risen quickly in the organisation, swiftly becoming one of its most prominent propagandists. Now, just short of his fiftieth birthday, this frail, melancholic, solitary, celibate thinker was arrested, roughed up and sentenced to fifteen years' hard labour. In prison, Qutb was joined by many more of the Ikhwan, as the Muslim Brotherhood called themselves. By 1961, 4,400 of the 6,600 detainees that British officials believed were held in Nasser's jails and camps were members.

Behind bars, Qutb's persistent poor health meant he spent much time in prison infirmaries where he saw at first hand the physical and psychological consequences of the brutal treatment of other prisoners. He was also allowed to write and, astonishingly, publish. For the first decade of his imprisonment, Qutb worked on a lengthy radical commentary on the Koran that was released in instalments. After that, he began a much pithier book called *Milestones*, a strident and uncompromising call to arms which laid out an argument across its ninety-three pages for an Islamic revolution in clear and dramatic prose. In it, Qutb argued that both the Muslim world and the West had returned to a state of *jahiliya*, the lawless chaos that had preceded the bringing of Islam and the establishment of a Muslim state in the Arabian peninsula by the Prophet Mohammed

1,300 years earlier. Over the centuries, the example and teachings of the Prophet had been 'buried under man-made traditions . . . false laws and customs'. Only when these innovations had been swept away could 'the call' to Islam succeed and the challenge posed by Western materialism or secular Arab nationalism or Marxism be successfully confronted. For this to happen, a vanguard of committed activists would have to overcome 'material obstacles' and so allow Islam to 'destroy the tyrannical forces, whether political or racial, or the domination of one class over another, in order to establish a new social and economic political system in which all men enjoy real freedom'. At stake was nothing less than the future of all mankind, now on the very 'brink of a precipice' and facing 'annihilation'.

Qutb's declared enemies were many and varied: not just the West and America, but Arab 'tyrants', Christians, and jazz music 'that the Negroes invented to satisfy their primitive inclinations', as well as 'World Jewry' with its 'financial institutions' and well-advanced plan to subvert global government. But the most dangerous foe was perhaps that closest to home: those ordinary people who called themselves Muslims but who had rejected the true values and practices of Islam. These were *takfir*, or apostates, and so worse than unbelievers, for they were not simply ignorant sinners but had been shown the way and turned from it. This was perhaps Qutb's most radical statement, and the one that would have the most lasting consequences over the decades to come. Traditionally, the punishment for apostasy was death, though Qutb did not appear to envisage such a fate for most of his countrymen, only their leaders.

Two years after *Milestones* was published in 1964, its author was hanged, having been convicted of plotting to assassinate Nasser by blowing up a train, ambushing a motorcade with automatic weapons or planting a bomb in the grandstand at a political rally. But if the Egyptian president or his advisers believed that his judicial killing and burial in an unmarked grave might somehow prevent the spread of Qutb's thinking, they were wrong. Even before the trial, *Milestones* had run through five reprints in six months. And if most of Egypt's Islamists rejected violence in favour of preaching and social activism, a smaller number of mainly younger members had been powerfully enthused by its call to arms. Among them was Shukri Ahmed Mustafa.

Like Qutb, Shukri had grown up in Upper Egypt, in the city of Asyut. He was twelve when Nasser became president. He lived with his mother and attended a school run by a Muslim charity, which was all the family could afford. Shukri's grades were mediocre, but sufficient to earn him a place studying agriculture at Asyut's university, which was undergoing massive expansion as Nasser sought to modernise a country where less than half the population could read and only a tiny proportion held a degree. Months after joining the Muslim Brotherhood, Shukri was caught in the same crackdown that saw Qutb hanged, and sent to Cairo's infamous Tora prison on charges of handing out subversive leaflets. Utterly convinced by Qutb's thinking, Shukri cleaved to the dissident fringe that was then forming among the incarcerated Islamists in Tora as it was in other Egyptian prisons.

Like other radicals they were riven by dispute over the correct method to bring about their envisaged revolution, and their debates mirrored those between left-wing activists who favoured the more immediate 'Foco-ist' approach pioneered by Che Guevara and those who favoured patient efforts to win over the masses before any violence took place. Shukri told the growing circle of young men who gathered around him in jail that the Islamist movement in Egypt was weak and so a direct attack on 'the tyrants' in power would be unwise for the moment. Instead, he said, true believers should *reculer pour mieux sauter*: temporarily withdraw from the impure, impious population and inspire them by example. Then, when eventually their compatriots recognised their error and returned to the true path of Islam, the vanguard that Qutb had envisaged would be able to seize power.

Shukri's reasoning was not entirely unfounded. As the 1960s turned into the 1970s, there was little sign that Egyptian society was ripe for an Islamic revolution. For most Egyptians, faith was not a political project. In the country's fast-growing cities, the poorly educated immigrants who arrived from the countryside struggled to maintain the conservative values that Qutb had associated with the 'authentic soul of Egypt'. Men and women spent more time together in the workplace and on public transport than ever before. Alcohol was widely sold and consumed, and even the mandatory fast in the holy month of Ramadan was routinely flouted by many. 'The veil has almost vanished from the streets of Cairo, and the students of Cairo's secular universities . . . now look like the students of any southern European university, free in their dress and easy in their relationships. The young women interviewers of Egyptian television might well commute between Cairo, Paris and New

York,' remarked one Western visitor. A religious scholar from Jordan complained that 'among 50,000 female students in Cairo University, there was [only] a single girl who wore proper dress, and that was Syed Qutb's niece'.

In the immediate aftermath of the 1967 war, observers noted a surge in the size of crowds at mosques and the 'lively sale by street vendors of plastic mottos inscribed "Allah" or "Allah with us"'. But this new interest in Islam and its teachings as people scrambled for answers and reassurance did not necessarily translate into a belief that religious texts were a template for modern government, let alone a desire for religious rule. At the massive demonstrations that took place in Cairo and elsewhere in those months, the demands and tactics of the student protesters resembled those of their counterparts in Paris or Berlin. 'The Islamic tendency was absent,' one witness remembered. 'The leftist tendency was influential but the majority consisted of students who advocated freedom and reform without an ideological approach.'

Instead, secular ideologies dominated the intense discussions of 'what should be done'. Many Egyptian intellectuals argued that Nasser's reforms had been insufficiently radical. 'People have decided to vent their spleen against socialism as being one of the causes of our defeat. But what we need to realise is that there has never been any genuine socialism in our lives,' says one character in Naguib Mahfouz's novel *Karnak Café*, published in 1971. In the same novel, the narrator recalls how 'The young folk . . . all started talking . . . about a new struggle on the broadest possible scale, a conflict on a world-wide level between progressivist forces and imperialism . . . they talked about radical transformations in the basic internal fabric of society.'

After years of fierce repression, even the Muslim Brotherhood's leaders believed the movement was 'not in a position or state of mind to envisage . . . a comeback'. But come the turn of the decade, that would abruptly change.

When the British writer Jan Morris visited Cairo some months after the bombings, abduction and arrests of July 1977, she described a city that was very different from the one she had known a decade before. 'President Sadat and I, separately considering the city, have arrived at the same conclusion: it is about to explode,' she told readers of *Rolling Stone* magazine.

When Nasser died in 1970, few had imagined that his successor had either the talent or the determination to remain leader of a country as important and unstable as Egypt for long. The fifty-eight-year-old vice president was seen by many as a bumbling sycophant. They gave him a few months, a year or so at best. Yet after a little more than a year in office, Sadat had launched a wholesale assault on his predecessor's legacy, imprisoning many of Nasser's most prominent loyalists, firing hundreds of army officers and bureaucrats and moving rapidly to distance Egypt from its alliance with the Soviet Union, signalling that he was prepared to swing the Arab world's most powerful state into the US-led Western camp. A new marketing campaign was launched to bring back the foreign tourists, restrictions on the media eased, the Interior Ministry's extensive collection of taped conversations was publicly burned and the sandbags protecting the Nile bridges that had so impressed the young Swedish spy Gunnar Ekberg on his visit a year earlier were replaced with shrubbery. Sadat even suggested he wanted to conclude some kind of durable peace with Israel, which was anathema in the Arab world.

No one had expected Sadat to reject the tarnished legacy of his predecessor so emphatically. As a young man he had shown no obvious ideological commitment beyond an ill-focused nationalism, flirting with fascists and monarchist militia, conspiring with Nazi spies in Cairo during the Second World War and being arrested for his alleged role in the assassination of a pro-British minister. His involvement in Nasser's seizure of power in 1952 was limited to the announcement of the revolution over the radio, a high-profile task but hardly a dangerous one. Under Nasser, he had been given posts where he could do little harm and his appointment as vice president had been something of an afterthought.

Sadat differed significantly from Nasser in several important aspects, however. If the former president had come from a modest background, his successor's was humbler still. Sadat was the grandson of an emancipated enslaved African and was notably darker-skinned than Nasser – a significant factor in Egypt's deeply discriminatory society. Nasser read European books on strategy, enjoyed chess and listened to Western classical music. Sadat was a fan of American potboilers and table tennis. Nasser was famously frugal. Sadat began acquiring palaces packed with priceless art and fake Louis XV furniture the moment he took over. Nasser had grown up in cosmopolitan, Mediterranean Alexandria and was the epitome of the young, progressive, urban Arab. Sadat made a point of travelling back to his native village in southern Egypt on his birthday, when he would be photographed in local clothes. His autobiography, written during 1977, was entitled *In Search of Identity*.

Another major difference between the two men was their attitude to religion. Though an observant Muslim and not afraid to invoke faith for political ends when it suited him, Nasser had seen the conservatism of the clerical establishment as an obstacle to his modernising project. He had closed religious courts, granted women the right to divorce, prohibited polygamy and made sure that Egypt's provisional constitution did not mention religion. Al-Azhar University in Cairo, the oldest, most prestigious Islamic educational institution in the world, was brought under government administration and forced to offer new courses including hard sciences and foreign languages. Nasser's attitude to the Muslim Brotherhood was very clear to everyone. In one speech in 1965, he joked about the impossibility of making Egyptian women wear a veil, one of the Islamist organisation's principal demands. Then there was what happened in Tora prison and police cells throughout the country to Qutb and his fellow activists.

Sadat broke with much of this. The new president saw Islam as not just important personally – he was proud of the mark on his forehead that supposedly came from repeatedly bowing to the ground in prayer – but central to any political or national project too. Sadat moved swiftly to introduce a new constitution which significantly enhanced the role of faith and called himself 'Ra'is al-Mu'minin', Leader of or Chief among the Faithful. To explain his abrogation in 1973 of the friendship treaty he had signed with Moscow just two years earlier and the expulsion of thousands of Soviet advisers, Sadat announced that he would 'kneel only to Allah' and not to Communism. When later that year, Egyptian troops marched into the Sinai Desert in their surprise offensive against Israel, they were issued with pamphlets telling them that they were 'soldiers of Allah' and their attack dubbed Operation Badr, after a famous military victory won by the Prophet Mohammed.

As for Egypt's Islamists, Sadat saw the movement as a useful auxiliary which could be deployed to reinforce his effort to counter the secular left in Egypt and establish a new constituency for his rule. Security services stepped up harassment of Marxists, Communists, socialists, followers of Nasser and dissident intellectuals, but allowed the Muslim Brotherhood to organise, recruit and campaign. Prisons were ordered to release the Islamists who had been jailed over the previous decade. A few hundred at a time, they stumbled out of Tora prison and the detention camps in the desert, blinking after years of appalling mistreatment and startled by the sudden change in their fortune.

By now Qutb had been dead for many years, but Shukri Mustafa was very much alive. When he was freed on 16 October 1971, Shukri had immediately returned to his scruffy, dusty, turbulent home town of Asyut to set about building up the community of believers that he had dreamed of in prison. His first followers were close relatives, including a brother and nephew, and a number of former cellmates. These in turn approached their own close associates and the more religious of the young worshippers at local mosques. By 1973, a hundred or so young men were living with Shukri, now aged twenty-nine, in caves in the arid hills outside Asyut, following as closely as possible their extreme interpretation of the teachings of Qutb and the Koran's teachings. Two years later, realising perhaps that their ascetic lifestyle was unlikely to inspire many followers from such a remote location, Shukri decided to move his group to Cairo.

In the aftermath of the bread riots of January 1977, most observers blamed the explosion of anger and frustration on the radical liberalisation of the economy launched by Sadat four years earlier. The 'Open Door' policy or Infitah sought to dismantle the statist socialism of Nasser and replace his paralysed, debt-ridden, inefficient economy with a dynamic, prosperous capitalist one that was integrated into the regional and the world economy. There were some successes. Very large sums of foreign money poured in and President Nixon made a successful visit, consolidating Egypt's new orientation. But administrative chaos, massive delays to construction projects and Egypt's soaring debts meant that the economic take-off Sadat hoped for never came. Instead, inequality became acute and obvious. Even the most obtuse government loyalist could see how a small number of entrepreneurs with government connections were getting very rich. In the nightclubs of Giza, businessmen from the Gulf stuffed wads of notes into the sequined gowns of fading divas. Meanwhile, few locals could afford meat more than once a month. 'This Open Door policy is . . . more than just economic. It is political, social, moral, historical, sexual. There is a libidinous, hedonist feel to it,' wrote Morris.

Officials spoke of hugely ambitious irrigation projects but two-thirds of the capital's inhabitants had no electricity and the stench in Tahrir Square was worse than ever. Cairene journalists noted the great quantity of imported goods that crowded Egyptian products off the shelves but which no one could afford. So when, in 1975, Shukri had abandoned the desert hills outside Asyut and installed his followers in a series of apartments in Cairo, he had made an inspired strategic choice. Soon Shukri's group was attracting new recruits in considerable numbers. For what it offered, along with its extremist ideology, were practical solutions to the problems that immigrant students from smaller towns or the countryside now faced in the brutally unforgiving environment of the city. Living outside of social convention and secular law, beyond the writ of neighbourhood clerics or petty bureaucrats, beyond the realm of parental authority, and paid for with funds sent by some of the many Egyptians now working in the booming oil economies of the Gulf, its young men were released from the battle for jobs or contacts, from military service and bribes and permits. There was no need for the diplomas so essential to social mobility. The terrific challenge of finding suitable housing and funds to buy furniture, which were the essential prerequisite for marriage and, thus, sexual relations, was resolved. So-called 'wives' were provided to them by the group from among the young women, usually relatives of members, who were persuaded to join. These would be allocated by Shukri, a marriage ritual concluded and the new 'couple' would be assigned a room, or sometimes simply a section of floor separated from that of other newlyweds by a curtain. It was the protests of these young women's parents that had alerted the police to the existence of the group, even while they failed to inspire sufficient curiosity or concern.

The young women were not the only victims of Shukri and his followers. The 'emir', as Shukri was known, ensured that leaving the group was almost impossible. Contact with non-members was banned unless express permission had been obtained. Any breach of its strict rules was punished, sometimes with a beating. Merely to express a desire to leave was enough to be declared an 'apostate', which brought the implicit threat of extreme violence. Days were filled with a gruelling timetable of worship, study, exercise or work as day labourers or hawkers to earn extra funds for the community. The barbarism and ignorance – jahiliya – of the rest of Egyptian society was discussed for hours on end in carefully observed group sessions. Even committed

Islamists were shocked by the group's implacable views. Members of the most extreme leftist communes in Italy or West Germany, those that had imposed rules on underwear or orgasms, would have been shocked too.

Despite the fervour of his followers, Shukri remained convinced of the need to avoid any violence that might endanger the Islamic community in what he maintained was its 'time of weakness'. The year before he moved the group to Cairo, a small group of extremists, several known to him personally, had attempted to overthrow Sadat's regime by seizing weapons at Cairo's military academy and then marching on the offices of the ruling party where Sadat was to give a speech. The conspirators believed the people of Egypt to be profoundly pious and had reasoned that either the removal of Sadat would trigger the Islamic revolution they sought or that their 'outrage for God', as they described their violence, would terrorise the unbelievers, inspire the unconvinced and mobilise the faithful. In the event, their ambitious attempt was a disaster. Eleven people died, the group was swiftly rounded up and their leader, a Palestinian who had come to Egypt from Jordan after 'Black September', was hanged.

Instead, Shukri played a long game. Despite the series of newspaper articles that portrayed the group as sex-crazed dropouts and some very public criticism from the establishment clerics of al-Azhar, the group continued to attract recruits through late 1975 and 1976. But with rapid growth came division. Factions emerged led by rival members, some of whom sought to challenge the authority of Shukri himself. These dissidents were threatened by Shukri and his loyalists and, in early 1977, several were killed, finally forcing the police to make arrests. And it was these arrests which in turn triggered the cinema bombings and the cleric's kidnap and murder that July, with the aim of freeing their now incarcerated fellow-members. When Shukri himself was then arrested and presented to the press, the group fell apart. By the end of July, several hundred members of Takfir Wal Hijra – or the Jama'at al-Muslimin, as it was more properly known – had been charged and faced lengthy prison sentences.

Shukri remained unrepentant to the end. In a makeshift courtroom set up in a former British military chapel on the grounds of Cairo's military academy, he told his judges that he remained 'the emir of this group' and so would 'inherit the earth and everything on it'. He called the prosecutors liars, threatened journalists and reiterated his intention to 'restore Islam' to Egypt. When, some months later, the judge read out a death sentence, he laughed loudly.

Egyptian officials were unable to blame the violence of July 1977 on either their usual suspects, 'leftist agitators', or the equally familiar machinations of Libyan intelligence agencies, and so were forced to admit that Islamist extremists were responsible. But sociologists who interviewed dozens of Shukri's followers shortly after their arrests were unconvinced by the government's claims that they were 'deviants', 'abnormals' or 'heretics' who knew nothing but the 'simplest elements' of the Muslim faith. Instead they described their subjects as people who would 'normally be considered model young Egyptians'. This was not what the authorities wanted to hear.

Diplomats in Cairo found the trial of Shukri and his followers worrying. They noted that the defendants had been allowed considerable time to expound their extremist vision in court, and that few respected scholars were prepared to publicly contradict their ideas, suggesting both 'pervasive support for fundamental Islam and fear for personal safety on the part of Muslim leaders'. Under Sadat's rule, the Islamist movement in Egypt had indeed recovered much of its strength and momentum, and while its slow return to health had not initially been obvious it was now reaching a point where it could no longer be hidden.

A series of police operations soon confirmed such fears. A month after Shukri's detention, security authorities arrested 104 members of a group calling itself Jund Allah, 'Soldiers of God'. Two days later, police broke up the Tanzim al-Jihad, 'Holy Struggle Organisation', detaining eighty people along with a large quantity of arms, explosives and ammunition. The arrests continued as the summer turned to autumn, all pointing to the presence of dozens of other similar networks in Cairo and pretty much every other city and town of Egypt. In a cable laconically entitled 'Yet Another Right Wing Group', US officials told Washington that local authorities were 'clearly attempting [to] give impression they [are] fully on top of situation . . . However, it seems apparent, despite official attempts to downplay importance [of] these groups, that this indigenous Muslim extremism is attracting an increasing number of Egyptian youth. Although the attraction of such groups [is] not yet fully clear, this trend in our view is potentially of real significance to Egypt's future stability.' The CIA station in Cairo came to a similar conclusion.

The same was true far beyond Egypt, almost everywhere Muslims lived. *Le Monde*'s correspondent in Cairo told readers that the violence of July 1977 revealed the growing strength of 'a phenomenon of Muslim revival' which was gathering strength 'across the Arab world'. Reports from Istanbul and Beirut noted the same trend, while in Algeria, a new 'National Charter' made Islam the state religion, obliging any president to be a Muslim and replacing Sunday with Friday as a day of rest. The Marxist academic Maxime Rodinson noted the 'application of Koranic law with some spectacular excesses in Libya and Saudi Arabia'. This was true on the more distant fringes of the Islamic world too. Gaafar Nimeiri, the ruler of Sudan, previously staunchly secular, was now reported to be making overtures to the leaders of the local Muslim Brotherhood. In Pakistan, a devout general with strong ties to the Islamist movement had taken power, and in neighbouring Afghanistan, a failed uprising had been launched by a small group of young Islamists led by a former Marxist engineer, a twenty-two-year-old admirer of Che Guevara and a professor of Islamic law who had translated Qutb's *Milestones* into the local Dari language.

Jan Morris wondered what eventual detonation 'the peculation, the high life, the emancipation of women, the moral permissiveness, the influx of foreign notions' might provoke. 'The revolution I find easiest to envisage in Cairo now would be neither communist nor militarist nor xenophobic,' she wrote. 'The more I think about it, the more I feel that the explosive feeling of Cairo comes chiefly from the arsenals of Islam.'

20
The Jackal at Bay

At least Ilich Ramírez Sánchez was comfortable. Baghdad in the summer of 1977 was not an unpleasant place to be, despite the atrocious heat. It was certainly better than Cairo: there was much less traffic and considerably less pessimism. Parks with gushing fountains provided respite from the blinding sun. The cafés on Rasheed Street served excellent *araq* or coffee, depending on the time of day. When the temperatures dropped at dusk, there was the recently reconstructed embankment of the Tigris where crowds gathered to eat fish cooked over wood fires and listen to local musicians. Alternatively, an excellent dinner for two in one of the city's four luxury hotels cost only six dollars including wine. At nightclubs such as The Auberge, The Select and The Embassy, foreign businessmen, aircrews, tourists and the rowdy scions of the local nouveau riche danced under glitter balls to Boney M, Abba, Demis Roussos and the psychedelic, electrified Arabic melodies of guitarist Omar Khorshid.

Nor was there much sign of the overheated politics of the region. Journalists described Iraq as a model of stability. There were no bread riots, and the security forces' persecution of anyone brave enough to oppose the ruling Ba'ath party was conducted with discretion as well as systematic brutality. Women in the city's poorer areas wore the abaya but downtown most shunned even headscarves. Around Baghdad's famous university, crowds of female students wearing uniforms of white blouses and short black skirts filled the light blue Volkswagen minibuses that served as collective taxis, ferrying them from lectures to home.

Yet Ramírez was not happy. The extraordinary self-confidence and assurance that had characterised his every moment since his late teens had been shaken. For the first time for many years, his mood was dark. 'I was at the bottom of a hole . . . I was like a zombie. It was the first and last time in my life that I thought seriously about killing myself,' he recalled decades later.

The year that had elapsed since Ramírez had been expelled from the Popular Front–XO had started well enough. He had left Aden in mid-May, almost six months after the OPEC raid of December 1975. He and his travelling companion, Hans-Joachim Klein, the German militant who had been shot during the attack in Vienna, had returned to Algiers where they had enjoyed a sybaritic early summer, living in a luxurious villa arranged for them by Algerian security officials, spending nights in 'men only clubs where English whores danced' and discussing Ramírez's plan to found and lead a new alliance of extremist groups. This was to be called the Organisation of Internationalist Revolutionaries, and it would bring together armed factions across the Arab world with, among others, the Red Army Faction and the Revolutionary Cells in West Germany, the Red Brigades in Italy and ETA in Spain. This force would rival, or even surpass, Wadie Haddad's group, Ramírez hoped. The head of the Algerian security service had already whispered that Houari Boumedienne, the Algerian president, would generously fund an effort to assassinate Hassan II, the pro-Western king of neighbouring Morocco, and this, Ramírez was sure, would be the first of many such lucrative commissions.

But as the weeks passed in Algiers, it became clear that realising Ramírez's new project would be far harder than he thought. Early efforts to reach out to various European groups were unsuccessful. Telephone and post from the Algerian capital was unreliable and heavily monitored, while travelling to meet any of their leaders posed obvious difficulties. But even when he did manage to get a message passed via a courier, the reaction was lukewarm. The respect he had been shown by the novice recruits at Aden was apparently not shared elsewhere.

A frenzy of speculation in the international press about his whereabouts offered some solace. In the space of three months over the summer of 1976, Ramírez was reported to have murdered the Bolivian ambassador on a busy street in Paris, blown himself up at Ben-Gurion airport outside Tel Aviv, travelled to Canada to disrupt the Olympic Games in Montreal, helped kill Italy's attorney general and masterminded the Entebbe hijacking, where he had apparently avoided death by having dinner in a gastronomic restaurant in Kampala on the night of the Israelis' raid. Ramírez scrupulously collected any press cuttings and was particularly pleased with one from *Der Spiegel*, which featured on its front page a decade-old passport picture in large glasses retouched in yellow, pink and brown, and the breathless lines: 'His name signals a new phase in the underground struggle: Ilich Ramírez, known as Carlos, head of the first fully internationalised terrorist group.'

Ramírez bought several copies of the article and had it translated by Klein but he could not avoid the fact that this sensational claim, however gratifying, remained utterly without foundation. The membership of the Organisation of Internationalist Revolutionaries was currently limited to its founder and his German bagman. Somehow Ramírez needed direct access to recruits.

Yugoslavia had long provided easy passage to and from western Europe for 'revolutionary' fugitives. The 'Socialist Republic' was theoretically non-aligned but had a long history of supporting 'progressive causes' around the world. In theory he could invite putative members of his new group to meet him there. Additional advantages included a beautiful coastline, cheap living, palatable wine and lots of sunshine. His ability to charm would do the rest.

A first effort was encouraging. A week or so after the publication of the *Der Spiegel* cover story, Ramírez and Klein flew into Belgrade in mid-July and spent four weeks visiting Split, Ploče, Mostar and Sarajevo. They relaxed, drank, ate, swam. They also met some Germans who had trained in Haddad's camps, and several other extremist activists from Europe and Latin America. Though none appeared particularly enthusiastic about joining his group, Ramírez had been able to spend a pleasant month on the European mainland without any major incident. Immediately on his return to Algiers, he began planning a second trip.

On 6 September, Ramírez set off again with Klein from Algiers, flying to Geneva and then on to Belgrade. Ramírez, wearing a silk scarf, an unbuttoned white shirt and dark brown leather jacket, calmly smoked a cigar as border control officers spent a very long time inspecting the two travellers' fake Dutch and Lebanese passports. Once finally allowed to enter Yugoslavia, he and Klein took rooms at the luxurious Metropol Palace Hotel in Belgrade's centre. Their plan was to leave for the coastal resort of Split the next morning, but within hours of checking in, they were approached by officials from the Služba Državne Bezbednosti (SDB), the principal Yugoslav security service, and firmly if politely told to pack their bags. They then spent a comfortable night in a secret and heavily guarded SDB facility in the otherwise pleasant suburb of Banjica.

Klein was not unduly worried. When he asked for German newspapers or coffee, he got both immediately. Ramírez, who had talked his way out of tighter situations, was still confident that an appeal to the Yugoslavs' revolutionary socialist solidarity would rally the authorities to his cause. But his hosts proved less sympathetic than expected. When Ramírez tried to convince his hosts that the aims of his nascent organisation were aligned with those of Yugoslav foreign policy, he made little headway. An offer of 'concrete co-operation' was rebuffed.

What he did not appreciate was that his presence had put his unwilling hosts in a delicate diplomatic situation. For Ramírez had been followed from the airport not only by SDB operatives, which was to be expected, but by a team of West German embassy employees, and the news that the infamous Carlos the Jackal was in Belgrade was now circulating among security officials across much of western Europe. Unsurprisingly, Belgrade was now under significant pressure to hand over one of the most wanted men in the world. To comply would inflict irreparable damage on the country's reputation as a 'progressive' state and its relations with Arab oil-producing countries. For all the Yugoslavs knew, it could also provoke revenge attacks by Ramírez's supposed followers and sponsors.

Belgrade had bought some time with an indignant statement explaining that Ramírez had been wrongly identified and that the man in question was in fact an Algerian history professor, but it was clear that this deception could not hold for long. A more sophisticated ruse was required. A recent bilateral agreement to co-operate with Bonn in 'the fight against terrorism' offered a potential solution. The Yugoslavs told the West Germans they would agree to hand over Ramírez and Klein if Bonn gave them several Croat extremists incarcerated in West German prisons in exchange, then made sure that their offer became public knowledge. As anticipated, this request was rejected, giving the Yugoslavs the excuse they were looking for to do nothing more than expel Ramírez and Klein.

This was not entirely straightforward either, as Algeria had denied any connection to the two men so they could not simply send them back. But another option presented itself. Saddam Hussein had visited Belgrade just months before and Iraq's deputy president had got on very well with Yosip Tito, Yugoslavia's veteran leader. So too had the senior officers of the two countries' respective security services. Less than seventy-two hours after arriving in Yugoslavia, Ramírez and Klein were hustled into a blacked-out car and driven to Belgrade's airport where, in part apology, they were offered champagne and caviar. Ramírez took the opportunity to explain to his companion the difference between strong Beluga and the finer Malossol varieties. Klein was obviously on better form than he had been a few months before: watchers from the West German Embassy observed a man 'about 180 cm, very athletic upper body, clean-shaven, [wearing] sand-coloured trousers, short turtleneck of the same colour and jacket'. Then the pair were put on a plane to Baghdad. Several of the men who had accompanied them to the airport shouted 'good luck' in Serbian, the West Germans noted grimly. By the late afternoon of 9 September 1976, Carlos and Klein were guests of the Iraqi government.

The principal reason there were no bread riots in Baghdad, nor raw sewage flowing from broken pipes in the city's own Tahrir Square, was that Iraq possessed the second largest oil reserves in the Middle East. The rise in oil prices since the war and embargo of 1973 meant that their exploitation now generated $8.5 billion in government revenues annually, fourteen times more than before the conflict. Under Saddam Hussein, the forty-year-old who had been a de facto ruler of Iraq for almost a decade, this geyser of money was being used to fund an audacious effort to transform the country into a prosperous, stable, powerful state. Iraq's extraordinary breakneck dash for development – described as 'a Great Leap Forward' by *Le Monde* – took the form of adult literacy campaigns that won accolades from the United Nations, a massive expansion of education and healthcare systems, huge hydroelectric power projects, the creation of hundreds of thousands of government jobs and much else. Astutely, Saddam made access to many of these new services and opportunities contingent on membership of the Ba'ath party. By 1976 half a million Iraqis – around one in every fifteen adults – had joined. At the same time, he brutally repressed any alternatives, reducing Iraq's Communist party, once a powerful force, to a shattered, traumatised remnant and unleashing tanks, helicopter gunships and security service torturers against new Islamist parties recruiting among the country's disadvantaged Shia, who comprised two-thirds of the population.

Though President Ahmed Hassan al-Bakr occasionally interfered, Saddam was also free to run Iraq's economic policies and foreign relations as he saw fit. These were intimately linked. Egypt's obvious problems and the profound anger generated by Sadat's outreach to Israel offered an opportunity to position Iraq as its replacement as the leading nation of the Arab world. On the one hand this meant seeking improved relations with the West. While Iraq would remain ostensibly a Soviet client, with a friendship treaty signed just a few years earlier that guaranteed huge quantities of grain and weaponry from the USSR, Saddam now encouraged trade with western European states, especially France which had promised in 1975 to supply a nuclear reactor 'for peaceful scientific research only', and the US. Increasingly large sums were also spent on arms from Western suppliers. A highly unpopular Soviet-style programme of collectivisation of Iraq's agriculture was abandoned, and lucrative infrastructure contracts given to British, West German and US firms.

On the other hand, to attain regional supremacy Saddam needed also to outshine his rivals – notably the Saudis and Muammar Gaddafi – as a leading champion of the Arab peoples against Western hegemony. Hence Saddam did not announce any dramatic 'Open Door' policy as Sadat had done, because in no way did 'Mr Deputy', as he liked to be known, want to unleash a new era of capitalism or shift Iraq definitively into the Western camp. Instead, he sought ways to burnish his anti-Western, anti-capitalist, anti-Zionist credentials. This was where Ramírez came in.

Iraqi embassies had provided essential logistic support for groups like the PFLP, Haddad's Popular Front–XO and the Black September Organisation in both eastern and western Europe since the early 1970s. The Euphrates valley west of Baghdad was now dotted with dozens of training camps used by armed Palestinian factions as well as an array of other Marxist or nationalist groups seeking to overturn regimes from the western Sahara to East Africa and the Persian Gulf. More recently, Saddam had begun building in Iraq a stable of individual operators who could carry out violent attacks across the region and beyond.

These could serve various purposes. Strikes on Israel or Israelis abroad might dissuade policy-makers in Jerusalem from threatening Iraqi interests or, more importantly, might provoke a reaction from the Israelis that could derail negotiations with other players in the Arab world that might be unfavourable to Baghdad. If Saddam decided to claim such operations openly, they reinforced his anti-Zionist credentials without risking any serious confrontation with the Israel Defence Forces or security services. Even if he didn't, the fact that Iraq was known to have the potential to deploy such actors could be useful. When in January 1977, Iraqi diplomats in Tokyo told local officials that they should stop the distribution of Hollywood films portraying the Entebbe raid or 'face the consequences', the movies disappeared from Japanese cinemas within days. Then there were those within the Palestinian nationalist movement whom Saddam wanted to intimidate, weaken or entirely eliminate: he was bitterly opposed to those who had signed up to the more moderate political strategy adopted by the PLO in 1974, partly due to his own hatred of Israel but also because an intransigent stance contrasted with the weakness shown by other regional rulers. Finally, there was Syria, ruled by the estranged other wing of the Ba'ath party and Hafez al-Assad, for whom Saddam harboured visceral personal animosity. The two states were already engaged in a dirty tit-for-tat war of bombings, shooting and sabotage. Saddam's actor in this conflict was a renegade former Fatah member called Sabri al-Banna, better known as Abu Nidal, who had been based in Baghdad for nearly three years and had acquired a reputation for loyalty to his immediate paymasters, efficacy and a total lack of scruples. Saddam had also encouraged Wadie Haddad to set up a base in the Iraqi capital, which by 1977 was fast replacing Aden as the headquarters of the Popular Front–XO.

Ramírez was now the latest addition to Saddam's boutique collection of 'terrorist masterminds', albeit one who was less enthusiastic about joining this select club than most other members. In many ways, Ramírez was a victim of his own celebrity. The Iraqis wanted him in Baghdad because they were impressed by his supposed capabilities, even if in reality his powers were considerably more limited than they believed. But the same conviction also encouraged prudence, and an array of polite or entirely unmentioned restrictions was imposed by Saddam's main security service, the Mukhabarat, on their new guest. Within moments of arrival in Iraq, Ramírez and Klein had been generously provided with 'bodyguards', who were also minders. It did not need to be made explicit, but there was no way either could travel through the international airport, or even Iraq's land borders, without the prior consent of his Iraqi handlers. Worse, international communications too largely depended on the goodwill of the Iraqi security services. Ramírez was installed in an attractive one-storey villa with high walls, three bedrooms, a garden and a black German shepherd on a leafy street of an affluent neighbourhood near the Tigris, surrounded by the family homes of doctors, dentists, academics and other members of the city's growing middle class. Here he could be easily watched, his movements tracked, any calls he made monitored and all his post read. The cook, cleaner and gardener all worked for the Iraqi security services. To assuage the injured pride of their new guest, the Iraqis provided Ramírez with a 'magnificent Volvo' and allowed him access to sufficient funds to pay for a new wardrobe of designer clothing as well as a considerable quantity of whisky.

Unsurprisingly, any new efforts Ramírez made to drum up support for his Organisation of Internationalist Revolutionaries from Baghdad met with limited success. In fact, its membership was about to be halved. Within weeks of their arrival, Klein had decided that he needed to escape not just from Baghdad, but from Ramírez, the Popular Front–XO, the German extremist scene and pretty much anyone involved in any form of violence whatsoever.

Even before they had been expelled from Yugoslavia, Klein, now twenty-nine, had tired of Ramírez's poor German, his arrogance and his obsessive personal hygiene routines that left Klein locked out of the bathroom for hours every day. When the Venezuelan threatened him with a pistol after discovering that Klein had told colleagues in Aden about their failure in Belgrade, he decided he'd had enough.

By now, Klein was deeply disillusioned with the life of an 'international terrorist', as he described himself. Though he enjoyed the luxury hotels, rides in limousines, dinners with ministers and international travel, it was hard to reconcile such indulgence with the radical activism that had propelled him into this world. Five years ago he was living in a squat, fighting the police on the streets, shouting slogans against Vietnam and driving Jean-Paul Sartre to Stammheim prison to see Andreas Baader. Now he appeared to have been corrupted. He thought the three murders committed during the OPEC raid had been entirely unnecessary. So too was much of the violence he had witnessed since.

In late 1976, after only a few weeks in Baghdad, Klein was allowed to leave the city by the Mukhabarat after Wadie Haddad interceded on his behalf. Haddad had always liked Klein and was short of experienced volunteers after the setbacks of that spring and summer. Klein had convinced Haddad that the wounds sustained in Vienna had healed and that he wanted to return to active duty. By the new year, Klein was back in the training camp in Aden. What he learned there only confirmed his alienation from the group and the cause.

Like so many others, Klein had joined the movement out of a conviction that fascism was on the march in West Germany once more and that it was his duty to join the struggle against 'a new Auschwitz'. His mistaken belief that his mother, a concentration camp survivor, was Jewish, made him considerably more sensitive than many of his comrades to the tendency of their anti-Zionism to shade into anti-Jewish prejudice. When Klein heard that the reports that Jewish passengers had been separated from others at Entebbe were true, he was reminded of 'what happened at the freight yards where the trains left' for the Nazi death camps and was deeply shocked.

He now saw his comrades very differently. Haddad, Klein realised, ruled over his miniature extremist state like a petty dictator, favouring some and exploiting others. 'The Master' was even served the best dishes at their supposedly communal dinners, which he consumed before others were allowed to eat. Klein saw how foreign volunteers generally received much better treatment than their Palestinian or Arab counterparts. Equally concerning were the plans now being made in the aftermath of the debacle in Entebbe. The dozen or so West German volunteers he knew from his previous stay in Aden had been joined by a fresh batch of extremists from home. Klein found their suggestions for new and spectacular attacks totally unacceptable. One wanted to hijack a plane with the Pope on board. Another proposed a missile attack on the Bundestag. A third wanted to assassinate Simon Wiesenthal, the well-known Jewish Austrian Holocaust survivor who had dedicated his life to tracking fugitive Nazi killers. This was apparently justified on the basis that Wiesenthal was a 'collaborator with Zionism'.

But the almost hallucinatory atmosphere offered Klein an opportunity. To deflect any suspicion that his revolutionary commitment might be fading, he came up with his own outlandish scheme: a kidnapping of Princess Caroline of Monaco. Though he fervently hoped this idea would not ultimately be pursued, it lent credibility to his request to be sent to Europe. Haddad, who held all trainees' passports while they were in Aden, reluctantly handed over Klein's travel documents after some weeks' delay. By late spring 1977, Klein was back in western Europe. Following to his instructions, he got in touch with other members of the Revolutionary Cells then made his way to a wood near Brussels to pick up weapons from a cache. This accomplished, Klein was given a second assignment: the reconnaissance of a passport office in Switzerland that was to be robbed. When at this point Klein began to raise the possibility of a permanent retirement from active duty, he was told that he 'knew too much to leave'. He had heard stories about what might happen to defectors and now feared for his life. In some haste, Klein abandoned his mission in Switzerland, skipping over the border with Italy to a remote mountain hut high in the Aosta valley that was used by extremists from a number of different groups as a place to lie low: the perfect place to hide from his former comrades and the police too. For the next three months, Klein, a high-school dropout, did something very unfamiliar. He wrote.

Klein's 100,000-word account of his time as a 'terrorist' was difficult to follow and far from profound. But it was powerful, emotional and full of detail about Ramírez-Sánchez, Haddad's Popular Front–XO and the mindset of western European radicals. Klein had worked on a cheap travel typewriter with a pistol within reach, sufficiently jumpy to have burned an initial thirty pages when he mistook the sounds of a cat outside his hiding place for the approach of a death squad sent by his former comrades. When eventually a car full of members of the Revolutionary Cells did turn up, Klein grabbed his gun and the manuscript, jumped through a back window and fled.

Klein was entirely unprepared for the situation in which he now found himself. He had been a follower not a leader. But he now decided that his rejection of violent extremism and his exit from the radical milieu required a dramatic and definitive gesture. From a hotel in Milan, he sent a resumé of the arguments in his book to *Der Spiegel* magazine's office in Rome. 'Silence is the greatest duty of a revolutionary,' he told readers, 'but so is speaking out when it is right to do so.' For good measure, he sent the magazine his pistol, a dozen cartridges, a set of his fingerprints to prove his identity and an account of a plot by the Revolutionary Cells to kill senior leaders of the Jewish community in West Germany. 'Many will certainly call me a traitor,' he wrote. 'I cannot change this. [But] I have not betrayed anyone or anything, but have acted only to prevent an insane act . . . I know what the guerrillas will say about this. They will be looking for me.'

It would take some time for Klein's book to be published, but when it finally got out into bookshops across Europe it sold 200,000 copies.

One of the reasons for its success was that its author's disillusion resonated widely. By the middle years of the 1970s, the 'New Left' was more fractured than ever, with traditional Marxist dialectics in further retreat, replaced with concerns about race, gender and sexuality, and many of even the most committed activists having fallen by the wayside, their former organisations weakened by internal dissent and lacking either charismatic leaders or popular support.

Klein's book had been distributed by a radical publishing house in Frankfurt with the help of veterans of the 'Sponti' scene who echoed and bolstered Klein's arguments. Danny Cohn-Bendit, for example, who had led protests in France in 1968 and played a leadership role in left-wing circles in West Germany and France through the 1970s and who had always opposed violent protest, wrote an introduction for Klein's book, arguing that it was possible to condemn the actions of the urban guerrillas without accepting the 'murderous logic' of government repression. A taxi driver and veteran organiser in Frankfurt's factories called Joschka Fischer also called on German terrorists to put down their weapons. In France, the intellectual and academic André Glucksmann, another veteran of the 1968 unrest and once a committed Maoist, began to talk about 'an opposition to extreme oppression of every kind, whatever its shape or cause' in place of anti-capitalism or anti-imperialism.

In the UK, such sentiments manifested in less intellectual fashion. In April 1977 the BBC had broadcast the first episode of a new sitcom depicting a feckless, cowardly and incompetent self-declared 'urban guerrilla' battling to free the inhabitants of a nondescript slice of suburban south London. *Citizen Smith* was a runaway success. Five years earlier, few would have mocked the fictional Tooting Popular Front quite so readily. In the US, meanwhile, an attempt in 1976 to relaunch the Weather Underground as the head of a grand coalition of radical leftist groups at the 'Hard Times Conference' in Chicago had been a humiliating debacle. 'I was almost lynched by a group of vegetarians . . . [and] constantly accused of being a racist,' remembered one organiser.

The turn away from violence and radicalism was partly a consequence of growing disillusion among a generation who were now a decade older than they had been when they first became involved in activism. But it was also because Western states were doing significantly better at countering the threat of violent and internationalist revolutionary groups. The learning curve had been steep but a combination of effective domestic legislation, new technologies such as computers, improved airport security and a greater degree of transnational co-operation all played their part. Better spying and sharing of intelligence also helped.

Other more drastic – and illegal – tactics were also under consideration. The CIA was in touch with an agent who they thought had access to Carlos and was willing to help arrange an attempt at abduction. French agents sketched out an elaborate operation in Venezuela designed to entrap Ramírez by poisoning his father. West German, British and French intelligence services sent representatives to their counterparts in Argentina, who ran a murderous secret campaign against dissidents and 'terrorists' known as Condor, 'to discuss methods for establishment of a similar anti-subversive organisation'. That Western security officials were tempted by such controversial methods was evidence that in their view the battle against 'internationalist revolutionaries' was far from over.

A final trial of strength would come sooner than expected. Haddad had suffered an undeniable setback in Entebbe but had not abandoned any of his aims, nor his strategy of violence. Just one successful hijacking or killing and everything could be put back on track, he believed. Fusako Shigenobu, the 'Mistress of Mayhem' who still led what was left of the Japanese Red Army, was also prepared to risk the future of her group on one last throw of the terrorist dice. In West Germany, the remainder of the Red Army Faction was now convinced that only by a significant escalation of violence could their incarcerated leaders be freed from Stammheim prison.

In the last months of 1977, these three groups joined forces in an extraordinary campaign that spanned western Europe, the Middle East, South Asia and East Africa. In time it would become known as the 'German autumn'. Those involved called it Offensive 77.

VII

21
Offensive 77

The afternoon of 6 May 1976 was unpleasantly hot across western Europe, a harbinger of the record-breaking drought that would last through the summer. In the northern suburbs of Stuttgart, where the Stammheim prison overlooked fields, a four-lane highway and a railway freight yard, temperatures rose steadily towards thirty degrees Celsius.

During the morning Ulrike Meinhof had joined the other three prisoners held on Stammheim's seventh floor to discuss Lenin, Gramsci and questions of 'revolutionary identity'. Later, she stayed in her cell, forgoing an opportunity to sunbathe briefly on the high-security facility's roof below the metal cage built to prevent escapes by helicopter.

Meinhof had now spent almost four years behind bars and was physically and psychologically much weakened by her incarceration. She had never fully recovered from the months she had spent shortly after her arrest in a whitewashed cell under a neon light, and her relationship with Gudrun Ensslin and Andreas Baader – both held in nearby cells – had deteriorated further. For two years she had refused to see her twin daughters and had recently begun chopping at her hair with scissors, which stood up in short irregular tufts. But what she did on 6 May 1976 was no less shocking for all that.

At some point between 10 p.m., when the guards heard the tapping of her typewriter cease, and around midnight the forty-one-year-old made a rope out of knotted strips torn from a prison towel and stood on her chair, which she had placed on her bed. She then hanged herself from the bars of a grating. Her body was found by guards at 7.34 a.m. when they became concerned that she had not come to the door of her cell as usual for her morning coffee. On a table, a work by Wittgenstein lay open. The cell's toilet was covered in black soot, as if Meinhof had been burning documents. A doctor gave the cause of death as strangulation. Meinhof's children learned the news from a radio bulletin.

Members and supporters of the RAF had long believed there was a campaign to kill incarcerated members of the group. They pointed to the 'assassinations' of Holger Meins, who had died in Stammheim after months of hunger strike, and that of Siegfried Hauser, who had been badly injured in the Stockholm embassy siege and died in a prison hospital shortly afterwards. Now they were convinced that Meinhof, 'the voice of the RAF', had been deliberately silenced too.

Despite the wave of outrage and anger her death provoked in Germany's far left, Meinhof's funeral prompted no major disturbances. Several thousand people filled the Protestant cemetery in West Berlin and then marched ten miles through the city. A very young Dutch activist gave a fiery graveside speech, which surprised her parents when it was televised on European networks, but better-known representatives of the revolutionary armed struggles stayed away. Both the Irish Republican Army and the Palestine Liberation Organisation declined an invitation to address mourners. Jean-Paul Sartre, Simone de Beauvoir and other left-leaning western European public intellectuals signed a letter which described Meinhof's death as a crime that recalled those of the Nazis but did not attend either. A series of small bombs targeted West German businesses and institutions in France, Denmark, Italy and Holland, and there were scattered protests in several German cities. In Frankfurt, the remnants of the 'Sponti' scene rallied to attack an American Express office and the US cultural centre, shouting 'Ulrike Meinhof is dead – let's rescue the living [prisoners]'.

This was easier said than done. By 1976 the Red Army Faction's networks comprised only three or four dozen active members of whom none had the intellect of Ensslin, charisma of Baader or acerbic eloquence of Meinhof. Not all of this 'Second Generation' of the RAF believed they would be able to use lethal force if called on to do so, and some hoped fervently that such a moment would never come. These networks were now under significant pressure, not only from the German police who were notably more professional and dynamic than they had been five years earlier, but from the imprisoned RAF leadership. Within months of their arrests in 1972, they had ordered swift, urgent and direct action to force their release. Baader had drawn up detailed plans for an all-out military assault on Stammheim and for a series of abductions to compel the government to grant their freedom. These had come to nothing. Now the pressure from the jailed leadership intensified.

Well aware of their own limitations and the weakness of other extremist groups in West Germany, the RAF sought help from further afield. When they contacted the Italian Red Brigades and sympathetic activists in France, Holland and Spain, they received fraternal revolutionary greetings but little in the way of significant assistance. There was an obvious alternative, however.

A month after Meinhof's death, a thirty-year-old lawyer who had represented Baader before going underground to escape an arrest warrant travelled from Germany to Beirut. One aim was to arrange instruction in the art of guerrilla warfare for his largely inexperienced and unskilled fellow extremists. But this was not his primary objective. The RAF was scattered across West Germany: two militants in Heidelberg, half a dozen in the so-called Black Forest group in Karlsruhe, four or five in Frankfurt and three slightly ineffectual young women known derisively as 'the Hamburg Aunties' in the northern port city. If members of all these factions could be brought together somewhere they could plan, organise and think, then a force capable of freeing his former client and the other prisoners in Stammheim might potentially emerge. There was no better place to bond than in a training camp in the Middle East, he reasoned.

The lawyer first sought out Yasser Arafat, but the chairman of the PLO and of Fatah had not revised his decision to forswear violence against third parties and so was unwilling to help. Arafat passed the lawyer on to George Habash, still the leader of the main body of the PFLP despite poor health, but he did not want to get involved either, and told his German visitor he needed to speak to Wadie Haddad.

The diminutive, balding, still frenetically active head of the Popular Front–XO was by now in Baghdad, busily organising the hijacking of the Air France plane that would end up at Entebbe some months later. He found time for the visitor and readily agreed to the German's request. Flying by circuitous routes, each of the different RAF factions in West Germany sent a delegation to Aden and were driven out to Haddad's camp in the desert where they were put through what was now a well-organised programme of basic guerrilla training. They had missed Ilich Ramírez Sánchez by some months and Wilfried Boese and Brigitte Kuhlmann, the two Germans who would be killed in Uganda, by a couple of weeks.

In long evening sessions, the trainees plotted a series of escalating attacks that they hoped would lead to the release of Baader and Ensslin, codenamed Operation Margarine, Operation Big Money and, most ambitious of all, Operation Big Breakout. Together, these successive strikes against the West German state would constitute 'Offensive 77', the biggest effort launched by the RAF for half a decade.

Around six months later, in February 1977, a woman called Brigitte Mohnhaupt was released from Stammheim having served five years for a series of offences ranging from assault to possession of firearms. Five feet three inches tall with straight blonde hair, blue eyes, a straight nose and square jaw, the twenty-eight-year-old was intensely committed and extremely capable. She had been groomed by Ensslin and Baader to take charge of the RAF 'on the outside', and within days of leaving jail she had reorganised the legal defence of the prisoners and instituted a new system to allow secure communications within the group. Mohnhaupt then travelled to an anonymous apartment in the Osdorp district of Amsterdam which had been rented by the RAF as a safehouse, where she found a twenty-six-year-old called Peter-Jürgen Boock.

Slender with lank, mousy brown hair and bad teeth, Boock was among those who had travelled to Aden the previous year and had been in Amsterdam since his return. He and Mohnhaupt spent their first evening in the apartment in animated conversation then in bed together. This was 'beautiful but sad' and 'sealed something' between the two extremists, Boock later remembered. Mohnhaupt was less sentimental. With typical efficiency, she rose early the next morning to begin organising the first of the attacks planned in the training camp in Yemen.

In late March, she and Boock travelled to find Haddad in Baghdad to consult on further operations. It was as they were returning two weeks later that they learned their comrades had just killed West Germany's most senior prosecutor in the south-western city of Karlsruhe. The killer had been riding pillion on a motorbike and unloaded half a magazine from an assault rifle into Siegfried Buback's car. The dead man was loathed by the Stammheim prisoners and a priority target. 'The general has to go,' Ensslin had written in an earlier message to her followers. Operation Margarine, the first of the planned series of attacks, had been a success.

Mohnhaupt had studied journalism and philosophy at university before being drawn to the RAF through the radical scene in Munich and then the Socialist Patients' Collective, a network of psychiatrists, carers and their charges based around Heidelberg who believed that mental sickness was the result of a diseased system and that its cure was the destruction of that system. She now sat down to write a communiqué. Boock, who had been a delinquent teenager at a reformatory school when he first met Baader and who had left school at sixteen to live on a commune in the Netherlands, urged her to remember that their audience were not well-versed in Marxist ideology and its lexicon. Mohnhaupt tersely replied that 'the masses' were sufficiently politicised to understand a properly revolutionary message and went back to typing. The statement they eventually released announced that Buback, a frontline fighter in a 'war' and so a legitimate target, had been 'executed' by the 'Ulrike Meinhof Commando' in retribution for her 'faked suicide'.

The next planned attack was Big Money, an attempt to kidnap Jürgen Ponto, a prominent banker with good political connections who had once advised the apartheid regime in South Africa. This went less well. The RAF gained access to the banker's spacious and well-protected villa in a wealthy suburb outside Frankfurt with the help of a recent recruit, twenty-six-year-old Susan Albrecht, who had inadvertently let slip that she was a family friend of the Pontos. The banker was packing for a holiday in Rio de Janeiro when Albrecht arrived holding a bouquet of red roses for 'Uncle Jürgen' accompanied by two friends: Mohnhaupt and another member of the RAF. When Ponto resisted, he was shot several times and fatally injured. Albrecht, who had been very reluctant to take part in the attack, was appalled by its outcome and suffered what others in the group called a 'nervous breakdown'. Mohnhaupt was angry at the failure, repeatedly cursing 'all this shit' as she was driven away from the scene of the murder by Boock. In Stammheim, Baader sneered that he wouldn't trust the RAF members then risking their lives to free him 'to buy bread rolls in the morning'.

A month after Big Money had failed, the immensely long trial of the RAF's founders finally came to a provisional close. Ensslin and Baader were convicted of five murders committed in 1971 and 1972, fifty attempted murders and dozens of bombings and bank robberies in the same period. With them in the dock was Jan-Carl Raspe, the thirty-three-year-old who had been arrested with Baader. The judgement stretched to more than 300 pages and took several hours to read. Despite the failure of prosecutors to establish exactly which defendant was responsible for which attacks, all were sentenced to multiple concurrent terms of life imprisonment. Their lawyers said they would appeal the verdict but did not have a chance to do so before events made any effort to overturn the judgement or reduce the sentence entirely redundant.

The West German government had hoped the trial would underline the resilience of the country's thirty-two-year-old democracy, but the measures taken to ensure the judicial process reached its desired end had the opposite effect. The question of individual versus collective guilt was only one problem. The defendants had been repeatedly denied permission to address the court and their lawyers' requests to call witnesses refused. Special laws were passed to allow legal representatives suspected of complicity in their clients' crimes to be excluded by judges, and the prisoners had been intermittently bugged. When medical specialists confirmed that the health of the defendants had deteriorated to a point where they could no longer concentrate on proceedings or even stand, new laws were hurriedly enacted to allow proceedings to continue in their physical absence on the basis that they had deliberately chosen to weaken themselves by going on hunger strike. This reinforced the fears of the far left that a new fascist regime was in power in West Germany, but it also concerned more moderate West Germans and organisations such as Amnesty International, much to the irritation of authorities in Bonn and the satisfaction of those in the dock.

This did not mean that the trial was a propaganda victory for the RAF. For a start, it made clear that the conditions they endured in Stammheim remained nowhere near as harsh as their supporters claimed. All the members of the RAF had larger cells than most prisoners, and Baader had two, totalling over 230 square feet. Prison authorities allowed them cigarettes, radios and electric blankets 'for back pain', as well as hotplates for making coffee and cooking. Ensslin had a cupboard full of rolled oats, different teas and spices, and both she and Baader had collections of make-up. The prisoners also had record players and hundreds of albums. Their library had expanded further and now numbered several thousand volumes and vast files stuffed with cuttings about the RAF. The prisoners were allowed to spend hours together almost daily and were able to converse without being overheard, as guards were not permitted within earshot.

It was not just messages that made their way in and out of the prisoners' cells. Legal documents for the Stammheim prisoners were exempt from search, which meant that box files could be hollowed out and then taped shut. This was how the components of three handguns reached the RAF's leaders in early 1977. Cannabis resin also made its way to the prisoners, along with a transistor radio and a miniature Minox camera. A series of portraits taken with this showed a smiling Ensslin and a relaxed-seeming Baader sporting aviator sunglasses, a shirt unbuttoned to the waist and a wide grin. The films were developed and printed but then languished in a lawyer's office. None were circulated. This was not how the RAF's incarcerated leadership wanted to be seen.

Instead, Mohnhaupt was briefed by Ensslin and Baader to tell followers that their leaders were psychologically fragile and the effort to secure their release more pressing than ever. The next attack – The Big Breakout – could not fail. Such news had the desired effect. 'I knew what was meant when [the leaders] said "If you can't make it work, we'll take our fate into our own hands,"' Boock later recalled. It meant using the handguns for the direst of outcomes. All the resources that the RAF could muster would be concentrated on the operation. Once again, the Palestinians would be asked to help.

In early August 1977 Mohnhaupt and Boock travelled once more to Baghdad. Haddad's office was a detached house in the quiet, expensive neighbourhood of al-Masbah, just a few hundred yards away from the slow-flowing waters of the Tigris river. Boock was impressed. On his first morning, he reached through his bedroom window to pluck a ripe orange from a tree outside. Eating the fruit was 'an animal pleasure', he later said.

The Germans' arrival was timely. In the aftermath of the Israeli raid on Entebbe, Haddad had been busy. He had organised an attack on Istanbul airport, where two of his men had opened fire on transit passengers waiting to board an El Al flight to Tel Aviv, killing four people and wounding over twenty. But this relative success had been followed by further setbacks: an attempt to assassinate King Faisal of Saudi Arabia had failed, and a planned hijacking of a passenger plane flying from Bombay to Tel Aviv had been aborted after a Dutch volunteer had been arrested by the Mossad at Israel's Ben-Gurion airport and revealed the entire plan. When the Germans had first come the year before, Haddad had 'made it clear that internationalism could not be a one-way street'. If he helped the RAF, they would have to help his organisation 'in a number of actions that [his] group alone would find difficult or impossible to carry out'. Haddad decided the time had come to call in the favour.

Over a copious meal of excellent Iraqi cuisine, Mohnhaupt and Boock explained their plan for 'Operation Big Breakout'. This entailed the abduction of Hans Martin Schleyer, the sixty-two-year-old president of two of Germany's leading business associations, friend of many politicians and unapologetic former SS officer who had served enthusiastically under Adolf Eichmann in Hungary during the Second World War. The RAF felt sure that the bonds of capitalism and fascism would impel the government of Chancellor Helmut Schmidt to free the Stammheim prisoners rather than allow Schleyer to die. Haddad wanted to know how much ransom money was to be demanded and what proportion his group would receive if he helped out.

Much of the ensuing discussion focused on how the RAF should handle the anticipated release of their leaders. Over the previous decade, hostages freed from European prisons following hijackings had been flown to various sympathetic countries, but by the summer of 1977, only Aden in the People's Democratic Republic of Yemen appeared a feasible destination for a planeload of triumphant German leftists with a long history of violent attacks. Egypt was now aligned with the West. Gaddafi had shown himself to be utterly unreliable. Algeria might balk at such an overt provocation. The enmity between the rival branches of the Ba'ath party in Damascus and Baghdad meant that Syria would not help anyone who had good relations with Iraq. And though Saddam Hussein had allowed Haddad to move much of his group's operations to Baghdad, he would not want to endanger warming relations with the US and western European powers. One option, Haddad suggested somewhat unhelpfully, was North Korea.

The Germans returned home with a commitment from Haddad to support their operation but without a firm decision on how it would end. By now there was only one way to find out.

In the first week of September 1977, a dozen or so young women and men met in a sixth-floor apartment in Junkersdorf, an unexceptional suburb of the West German city of Cologne.

The apartment was almost identical to hundreds of others used as safehouses by the Red Army Faction over previous years. Rented in a false name, with bills paid in cash well in advance, they generally featured a few cheap mattresses, some tools, firearms and ammunition, often left carelessly in a corner, suitcases and bags containing the occupants' scant belongings, and a telephone. Most were equipped with two radios, one tuned to the local police frequency, the other to news bulletins. Windows were covered with lengths of cloth with slits cut in them so the street outside could be monitored without detection. Ideally they would be situated on the middle floors of buildings that had unguarded underground car parks. If there was a motorway junction close by, so much the better.

The safehouse in Junkersdorf was more spartan than many. There was only one small light and no furniture. On the evening of 4 September the women and men sat in a circle around an upturned dustbin lid which they used as a communal ashtray, smoking heavily as they talked. Most were in their late twenties. Some had gone underground just months before, others had spent years on the run from the police.

Hours earlier they had received a message brought by courier from their leaders in Stammheim, over 200 miles to the south. This was a 'definite ultimatum', its bearer had explained, threatening those in the apartment with expulsion from the Red Army Faction if they did not act decisively within two weeks to free its senders. The ultimatum also made clear that if they failed to do so, their leaders in Stammheim would be forced to act themselves. All those in the apartment knew, just as Boock had known, that guns had been smuggled into the prison and hidden in their leaders' cells. These could be used by the jailed leaders in a final desperate bid to win freedom or, as likely, in a final act of spectacular suicide that would deny the 'fascist regime' its victory and inspire followers for decades to come.

The debate in the Junkersdorf safehouse that night hinged on a question that was of enormous importance to those gathered there – as it has been to so many who have used violence for similar ends over the centuries. Schleyer's abduction, which had been months in the planning, was scheduled for the next day. Proceeding with the operation would allow them to comply with the ultimatum they had just received. But for the operation to succeed, the attackers would almost certainly have to kill the businessman's bodyguards and driver. These were ordinary men, earning a living to feed their families – not major capitalists or former Nazis like the man they protected. An alternative would be to wait for another opportunity when the deaths of three ordinary 'proletarians' could be avoided, but this might mean a delay longer than the fourteen days specified in the ultimatum. So should the innocent men die, perhaps unnecessarily, to fulfil a deadline that some considered arbitrary? Or should they wait and so risk their expulsion from the RAF and the deaths of their leaders?

It was almost dawn by the time they reached a decision. Those who believed they should delay to avoid the bloodshed of innocent proletarians were in the minority. When one of the dissenters refused to take part in the attack, he was told to leave the apartment, and so effectively the RAF. This ended the discussion. The operation against Schleyer would go ahead.

Late in the afternoon of 5 September, a member of the RAF abruptly pushed an (empty) child's pram into the path of Schleyer's chauffeur-driven car as it cruised down a suburban street in Cologne, forcing the vehicle to a sudden stop. Others then produced weapons and began shooting. One jumped onto the car's bonnet and emptied the entire thirty-round magazine of a Heckler & Koch assault rifle through the windscreen. The driver and three police guards died of multiple bullet wounds at the scene. Schleyer himself was bundled into a waiting Volkswagen minibus, injected with a sedative and driven to an underground garage. There he was transferred to a Mercedes and taken to a carefully prepared 'people's prison': a cupboard in another safehouse, this one an apartment on the third floor of a totally anonymous modern tower block in the small suburban town of Erftstadt-Liblar, about fifteen miles away.

Twenty-four hours later, the RAF issued their demands: the freedom of two Popular Front–XO men held in Turkey for their role in the previous year's attack on Istanbul airport, an end to all efforts by West German authorities to pursue the RAF or locate the kidnapped businessman, the release of ten of the most senior members of the RAF from West German prisons with 100,000 Deutschmarks (worth approximately $50,000 at the time) each, and a plane to fly them to a destination that was not disclosed, largely because it had not yet been decided.

Chancellor Schmidt consulted with a new and possibly unconstitutional 'advisory group' on how to respond and decided they would not negotiate. 'The state will respond with all severity . . . Terrorists will not win in the long term . . . the entire will of the people is against them,' Schmidt told Germans in a televised address. There would be no repeat of the mass release following the abduction of Peter Lorenz, the West Berlin mayoral candidate, two years earlier. One senior official said later that to save the state Schleyer was sentenced to death. This was not quite accurate. Schmidt's intention was that the kidnapped businessman would be found by police and rescued: that, and not a deal, would secure Schleyer's freedom and his life.

None of this was made public, of course. Instead, officials stalled for as much time as possible so the search mission might succeed. The RAF demands were followed by a series of new communications. All were met with requests for clarifications, bureaucratic quibbles, apparently reasonable questions about procedure and demands for proof that Schleyer was still alive. Meanwhile, the federal police combed their new, secret and highly controversial database of five million potential suspects for clues, and strict solitary confinement was imposed on all RAF prisoners to prevent any orders reaching those outside. Schleyer himself refused a demand from his captors to appeal for concessions from the government. To pass the time in the safehouse, its inhabitants played chess and monopoly.

Weeks passed. Mohnhaupt and her associates realised they were losing the initiative. The tone of their communiqués changed from 'an almost superhuman confidence and control' to a petulant 'reiteration of previous (unmet) demands', commented a CIA analysis. In an attempt to regain the upper hand, the group stopped talking to the authorities altogether for a ten-day period and instead sent copies of Polaroid photos, ultimatums and declarations directly to journalists. Schleyer was put in front of a film camera, holding a placard with an RAF insignia, and told to appeal to authorities to spare his life. With this, they initiated an entirely new genre – the hostage video – that would proliferate dramatically over the coming decades.

When the police began combing residential areas on the outskirts of Cologne, with a particular focus on high-rise apartment blocks, the group moved their hostage over a hundred miles west, first to The Hague and then to Brussels. Frustrated and increasingly unsure of what to do, the RAF itself began to splinter. Some members went to ground in Hamburg, others sought safety and aid elsewhere.

To break the deadlock, on 25 September Mohnhaupt, Boock and several others flew back to Baghdad. Haddad welcomed them with 'hugs and brotherly kisses' and told them the abduction of Schleyer would 'certainly find its way into the list of the great revolutionary deeds of this epoch'. Then he outlined his concerns, telling them they had 'unleashed something . . . where defeat would not be limited to you as a group, but could affect everyone'. Finally, he suggested that his own organisation conduct an operation to ensure a victory for his 'allies' in

West Germany. They and the RAF would then issue joint demands: the liberation of the Stammheim prisoners and a very large sum of money. The RAF could keep the prisoners, the Popular Front–XO would take the cash. Two different attacks were already in an advanced state of preparation and could be set in motion very swiftly, Haddad said. The RAF just had to choose which they preferred.

The first option offered by Haddad was the takeover of a West German embassy in the Middle East by members of his own group. This was attractive as it would mean targeting an organ of the 'fascist regime' directly and would undoubtedly attract massive media coverage. On the other hand, among equivalent operations that had taken place over the previous five years there had been several spectacular failures, not least the RAF's own attack on the German Embassy in Stockholm just two years earlier. The second option, Haddad said, was to hijack a Lufthansa jet. This tried and tested alternative would certainly have the potential to force the German authorities into negotiations, but it would also mean targeting ordinary Germans, something that the RAF's leaders still sought to avoid wherever possible. Meinhof had told the Stammheim court that the 'actions of urban guerrillas are never, never directed against the people', only against 'the imperialist machine and the terrorism of the state'. It would be hard to argue that the operation Haddad was proposing struck a blow against either.

Both plans entailed a significant escalation of violence and offered as much chance of total, bloody failure as of success. The stakes for the RAF could hardly be higher. Mohnhaupt, Boock and the others wavered. Then the decision became much easier, thanks to the sudden and unexpected intervention of the RAF's Japanese counterparts, still led by the 'Mistress of Mayhem' Fusako Shigenobu.

Shigenobu, now thirty-four years old, was still based in Beirut. From here she attempted to run what she fondly imagined was a global network of 'revolutionary warriors'. In reality, the Japanese Red Army now constituted at most a few dozen members who lived precariously in a few semi-communal apartments nearby. With her was also her five-year-old daughter Mei, named to rhyme with May, the month of the Japanese Red Army attack on Lod airport in 1972 which killed twenty-six people and two of her followers.

Like the Stammheim prisoners, Shigenobu was acutely aware of her public image. From Beirut, she had written her life story for a popular Japanese magazine to publish in instalments, given an interview for broadcast on Japanese television and posed happily for pictures with visiting sympathisers. The death of Meinhof, the high proportion of women in the RAF's second generation and the saga of Patty Hearst, the American heiress turned gun-toting member of the far-left Symbionese Liberation Army, had prompted considerable interest in 'women terrorists' among journalists and academics. Much of it focused on their sexuality – they were often depicted as asexual, lesbian or libidinous harpies – and their psychological health. The *New York Times* described them as having an 'Amazon complex' which 'all started with Leila Khaled', pointing out that 'women, unfortunately, can be particularly fanatical'. *Der Spiegel* told readers that 'where guerrillas were most active, women have their finger on the trigger and unfortunately pull it again and again.' In referring routinely to the 'Baader-Meinhof Gang', journalists relegated the RAF's most accomplished thinker to a secondary role while excising the group's most effective actor, Ensslin, altogether.

Shigenobu was portrayed according to a different stereotype. A profile in the *Observer*, a British newspaper, described her as 'the lady terrorist with white gloves' who was less a 'cold theoretician of violence' than a 'political tender heart', and noted that she had worn a hat and lipstick to protests when young. One Japanese business magazine described her as a 'girl of extraordinary beauty' and wondered how Japan could produce such pitiless killers. Shigenobu did little to subvert such representations. Viewers of her 1973 TV interview saw an attractive young woman, speaking in 'unfailingly polite and feminine Japanese, brushing her long straight hair back from her modestly smiling face'.

In the same way that their seclusion from the rest of Germany allowed Ensslin and Baader to believe their cause enjoyed far more popular sympathy than it did, so the 6,500 miles between Beirut and Tokyo allowed Shigenobu to harbour equivalent illusions. In reality, any lingering support there might have been for the extreme left in Japan did not translate into the slightest endorsement of violence. When in early 1975, the JRA attacked an oil refinery in Singapore and the US consulate in Kuwait, the only evidence of approval in Japan was four posters stuck to the walls of Kyoto University.

Shigenobu saw things differently. If the revolution had yet to spread to Japan, her group had a duty to open new 'fronts' there themselves. To this end, over the course of 1977, a dozen or so JRA members were infiltrated back into Japan from Beirut. The next step was to recruit local reinforcements and get their hands on lots of money. There appeared an obvious way to provide both.

On 28 September, three days after Boock and Mohnhaupt had arrived in Baghdad, five armed men took control of a Japanese Airlines DC-8 with 156 people on board shortly after it took off from Bombay and ordered the pilot to fly east, not west, to Dacca, the capital of Bangladesh. This took the type of hijacking that had plagued the Mediterranean for a decade into an entirely new region. The JRA soon issued a communiqué which denounced the 'false international propaganda praising the Japanese economic miracle', described 'present Japanese history' as a 'pure and simple summary of treason, dishonour, avidity and aggression' and made no mention of any wider revolutionary struggle at all. From Beirut, the group demanded $6 million and the release of six prisoners, including three with no known connection to political violence but whom Shigenobu thought showed potential. There followed a forty-eight-hour standoff until Prime Minister Takeo Fukuda decided that 'the weight of a human life is heavier than the earth' and conceded all of Shigenobu's demands.

Fukuda's decision prompted a jubilant statement from the JRA, a 'storm of domestic criticism' and predictable derision from commentators in the US and Europe. In Baghdad, the RAF made their choice and told Haddad which of his two proposed attacks they preferred.

22
The Last Aktion

It is late afternoon. A light breeze blows in across the dunes from the Indian Ocean but barely stirs the thick humid air. Standing on the concrete of Mogadishu international airport, 200 yards from the squat control tower, is a plane, its tailfin painted in the blue and yellow of the West German national carrier, Lufthansa. On board there are almost one hundred people: four crew, four hijackers and eighty-six sick, exhausted, traumatised passengers.

Since the plane departed the Mediterranean island of Mallorca for Frankfurt, the German holidaymakers on board have been beaten, starved, subjected to mock executions and witnessed the captain of the plane shot dead. Many are tied to their stained, soiled seats. Now, after almost four days, they have twenty-five minutes left. If the German government does not agree to the hijackers' demands, the explosives wired across the cabin will be detonated.

The leader of the hijackers, a twenty-three-year-old Palestinian called Zohair Yousuf Akache, is talking to a German diplomat, Michael Libal, who stands in the control tower, easily visible from the plane. Alongside the diplomat are two Somalis: Mogadishu's chief of police and an air traffic controller.

Akache, who is calling himself Captain Martyr Mahmud, has been talking to Libal for several hours. The conversations, conducted in English, have been acrimonious. Akache calls Libal the 'representative of the imperialist fascist West German regime' and says he is only talking to him out of respect for the Somalis, who are fellow Arabs. Libal respectfully calls Akache 'Captain Martyr Mahmud' and receives a volley of abuse when on one occasion he uses 'mister' instead of his interlocutor's preferred honorific. Akache is violent both in word and deed, as the passengers have found out. Reluctantly, he has already delayed the destruction of the plane three times that day, most recently to allow

Somali ground staff to clear the area around it so that nothing else is damaged when the explosives are detonated. Akache, standing in the plane's cockpit, does not appear minded to extend the deadline again. The flammable contents of the on-board duty-free trolley – spirits and perfume – have been emptied over the cabin and splashed on passengers 'so that they burn better'. The passengers' passports have been thrown from a window to aid the identification of corpses that are certain to be charred beyond recognition.

Then the speakers in the cockpit crackle into life again and Libal delivers a simple message: the government in Bonn has capitulated, Chancellor Helmut Schmidt has agreed to the principal demand first submitted by the RAF when they kidnapped businessman Hans Martin Schleyer in Cologne five weeks earlier and reiterated by Akache and the Popular Front–XO when they seized the plane in Mallorca. Andreas Baader, Gudrun Ensslin and nine other RAF leaders will be freed and flown to the Somali capital Mogadishu. The $15 million they have requested will be delivered too. But all this will take some time, and the liberated prisoners may only arrive very early the next morning, Libal explains, so would Akache consider extending the deadline until then?

Akache is suspicious. It is 3,200 nautical miles from West Germany to Mogadishu. Why should he wait almost twelve hours? he asks. Libal is apologetic. A compromise is reached; the deadline is extended by ten hours.

No one relaxes. The consequences of any 'cheating' will be very serious, Akache warns. 'If you want to fool us or play games, I prefer to play games with explosives . . . We have already installed the explosives all over the plane and soaked all the seats and the floor of the plane with alcohol . . . If only someone lights a cigarette in the machine, it will all be over; it will explode into a thousand pieces,' he tells Libal.

'Captain Martyr Mahmud,' Libal responds, 'I can inform you on behalf of the government of the Federal Republic of Germany that we accept this extension of your ultimatum with gratitude. Over.'

There is a pause, and the Somali air traffic controller speaks, offering 'any help and assistance that you may need'.

Akache reciprocates, telling the tower that the hijackers 'have deep compassion in our hearts' and explaining that he was acting 'for the good of the people on board and for your government, the people and the president. Thank you, Mogadishu tower, thank you.'

But Chancellor Schmidt and his colleagues have not deviated from their policy of refusing to give way to blackmail. And while there is indeed a plane on its way to Mogadishu, it is not carrying Baader, Ensslin or any other prisoner.

Within hours of hearing the RAF's decision, Haddad had summoned two men and two women from the Popular Front–XO's training camp on the outskirts of Baghdad to his headquarters where they were instructed to hijack a plane. The oldest was Souhaila Sami Andrawes, a cherished child of wealthy Christian Palestinian parents from Beirut, who had studied English language and literature at the American University there and been recruited to the PFLP by the editor of a Palestinian magazine she worked for. Andrawes 'wanted to be a soldier' and so was happy to give up her 'luxurious and comfortable life . . . to share in such a thing'. She was also 'angry, angry with the world' and felt deeply honoured to have been chosen for the mission Haddad described.

The operation's aim was 'to free imprisoned compatriots from Israeli jails' and gain publicity for the Palestinian cause, 'the Master' explained. It was to be called Operation Kafr Qaddum, the name of a Palestinian town in the northern West Bank under Israeli occupation since 1967, and the team would be known as the 'Martyr Halima Commando', in honour of Brigitte Kuhlmann, the member of the German Revolutionary Cells who died at Entebbe. Andrawes already knew one other member of the team, Nadia Shehadah Yousuf Duaibes, a Lebanese Christian of the same age who had studied at the same time as her at the AUB. The two men, both slightly younger than her, were strangers.

One of them, a strikingly handsome twenty-two-year-old called Wabil Harb, was taking part in his first mission but Akache, the twenty-three-year-old who would lead the attack, was a veteran. He had grown up in a Palestinian refugee camp on the outskirts of Beirut, joined the PFLP in his early teens shortly after its foundation, and eventually become one of Haddad's most trusted young operatives. A year earlier, Akache had been sent to London tasked with killing a former prime minister of Yemen. Akache knew the city well, having spent two years studying aeronautical engineering there earlier in the decade, during which time he was twice arrested at pro-Palestinian protests. He completed his mission without difficulty, shooting his target dead in a car outside a hotel near Hyde Park along with the only close witnesses: the man's wife and a diplomat. Since Ramírez's departure, Haddad had been grooming Akache to lead the Popular Front–XO's most spectacular and complex attacks, swapping an 'adventurous internationalist' for a Palestinian whose dedication to the cause was unquestionable.

After almost a decade of organising such operations, Haddad had a well-worn routine. Andrawes, Akache and the others were given several days of intensive instruction as the last details of the attack were finalised. Then the four travelled separately on false Iranian passports to Mallorca. On the island, they checked in to two hotels and behaved as holidaymakers: going on excursions, eating out and taking photographs. A courier brought them a kilogram of plastic explosive, four plastic grenades and two handguns. The grenades were replicas and would not deliver more than a token blast but they were undetectable by security scanners. Haddad told the team in Baghdad that they should act ruthlessly to stamp out any spirit of resistance among their hostages but avoid killing anyone.

Then, following the Popular Front–XO's standard operating procedures, the attackers booked two seats in first class and two in economy on Lufthansa Flight 181 from Palma de Mallorca to Frankfurt on 17 October. The plane was a Boeing 737 that had been named the *Landshut* after a town outside Munich. Security checks were cursory and failed to discover the weapons and explosives that were hidden in make-up bags and a biscuit tin and inside a radio. Take-off was slightly delayed by the late arrival of a group of eight high-spirited young women who had taken part in a beauty contest in the Graf Zeppelin nightclub that had finished in the early hours.

At around one o'clock in the afternoon, the requisite twenty minutes of flight time having elapsed, the four hijackers stood up, each wearing a red T-shirt bearing a portrait of Che Guevara, and took control of the plane. The pilot, Jürgen Schumann, was ordered to plot a course for Cyprus. He demurred, pointing out that the Boeing 737 had insufficient fuel. Akache told him to head for Rome instead. So far, the attack resembled many previous such episodes.

But soon enough it became apparent that this was no 'ordinary' hijacking. The first victim of the Martyr Halima Commando's violence was a stewardess whom Akache struck hard on his way to the cockpit in the very first seconds of the attack. On arrival at Rome, the Italian interior minister refused a blunt request from his German counterpart to stop the aircraft leaving Fiumicino airport by 'shooting out its tyres', deciding instead that Italian interests were best served by refuelling the plane and allowing it to leave. The *Landshut* then flew to Cyprus, where

Akache angrily rejected requests by local officials to release women and children. When a representative of the Palestine Liberation Organisation tried to convince the hijackers that their actions would harm the Palestinian cause, he received an expletive-laden tirade. Cypriot authorities appeared more reluctant than the Italians had been to provide the fuel for onward travel, so Akache threatened to shoot crew members and passengers, holding a gun to the co-pilot's head as the terrified man pleaded with the control tower.

When the *Landshut* reached its next destination, Bahrain, Akache selected two of the teenagers who had taken part in the nightclub beauty contest and a twenty-three-year-old stewardess and told them they were to be executed one by one to force local authorities to comply with his demands for more fuel. They had been chosen, Akache informed them, because they had been identified as Jewish, which they were not. Diana Müll, nineteen, was told she would be the first to be shot and was forced to her knees in the open door of the aircraft. When the control tower frantically communicated the authorities' approval for the refuelling, Akache shouted in English over the on-board microphone: 'The three Jewish witches will not be shot!' The plane took off once again, aiming for Dubai.

As they flew between destinations in the Gulf, Akache's paranoia intensified. When he found a Mont Blanc pen in the luggage of one passenger, he mistook the distinctive design on its cap for the Star of David, and slapped and kicked the owner. A similar pointed star design on a watch led to the co-pilot being ordered to kneel for imminent execution. Only when Schumann, the pilot, calmly insisted that his colleague was a Protestant, not Jewish, did Akache calm down. When he saw that authorities had placed fire trucks on the runway at Dubai to prevent a landing, Akache pushed a gun into Schumann's neck and ordered him to put the plane down. At the last moment, as the *Landshut* approached, the fire engines were cleared. On the ground, Akache told the West German ambassador that his government should capitulate as the Japanese prime minister had done two weeks earlier, or the plane would be blown up at its next destination, wherever this might be.

After twenty-four hours, with the *Landshut* partly refuelled following further threats to execute hostages, Akache ordered a new departure. This time, the destination was the People's Democratic Republic of Yemen and Aden, an airport he knew well in a country where he expected a relatively warm welcome. His hostages were simply relieved to be flying, wherever they were headed. 'Every start was a new hope,' remembered Gabi Dillmann, another of the stewardesses who had been threatened with execution. 'In the air, there were moments of calm, phases of rest. It was known that at altitude . . . the terrorists would probably not shoot, because then they would endanger their own lives.'

At Aden, however, the runways were once again blocked and authorities adamant that there would be no landing. With almost no fuel, Schumann ignored the control tower's threats and managed to put the fifty-tonne aircraft down on sand and gravel parallel to the airport's main strip. Local authorities were unimpressed and told the *Landshut*'s crew that 'the plane must take off as quickly as possible'. Before complying, Schumann said he wanted to check the landing gear. Akache, angry and confused by the evident hostility of local authorities, reluctantly agreed. The pilot inspected the plane, which turned out to be serviceable, and then disappeared from sight. When he returned, having spent a few minutes trying to convince Yemeni officials to block the plane's departure, he found Akache incensed. Screaming that Schumann was a traitor, he forced the pilot to kneel by the open door and shot him in the face. There was a stunned silence, then other hijackers dragged Schumann's body down the plane's aisle before stowing it in a closet. They returned ashen-faced. For hours the plane stood in the sun as ground staff sought to find the correct equipment to pump fuel into its tanks. Finally, the co-pilot took the controls and prepared to execute Akache's new order to take off immediately, headed for Mogadishu.

The *Landshut* touched down at the Somali capital on the morning of 17 October at 6.34 local time. Akache told the control tower to pass on the message that he had extended the deadline given to the German government almost four days previously to three o'clock that afternoon, and Schumann's corpse was removed from the plane via an evacuation slide at its rear. For the next seven hours, a series of Somali officials tried without success to convince the hijackers' leader to release the passengers and crew for humanitarian reasons. 'West Germany . . . has had every opportunity to prove that it is not an opponent of humanity . . . But since the government has rejected our demands, we will blow up the plane,' Akache told them.

On the plane, both hijackers and the surviving crew were 'at the end of their tether'. Conditions on board were now appalling. In most previous such attacks, those who had taken control of aircraft had demonstrated some interest in the physical well-being of their hostages. This was not the case with the Martyr Halima Commando. From the first hours of the hijacking, terrified passengers were repeatedly threatened, struck with grenades or fists and abused. They were forbidden to use lavatories and some were told to defecate or urinate where they sat. Almost no efforts were made to provide sufficient fluids and food to the passengers – though in a bizarre episode at Dubai Akache ordered first a cake and champagne to be brought to the plane when he learned of the birthday of a stewardess, and then a consignment of toys for the children on board from the airport shop. When the on-board air conditioning failed due to lack of fuel, the plane became very hot and the stench appalling. When passengers removed clothing to ease swollen limbs or simply because of the extreme temperatures, the hijackers were angered by the apparent 'lack of modesty'. By the time they reached Mogadishu, there were almost no medical supplies, and several passengers appeared to have suffered heart attacks. Many more were showing symptoms of heat exhaustion and severe psychological distress. 'Time is running out,' Libal, who was at the airport, told his superiors in Bonn. The surviving pilot was convinced the plane would be unable to take off in any circumstances.

In the early afternoon the tower received over the plane's cockpit radio a message from Dillmann, the twenty-three-year-old stewardess. It was a final testament. 'We now know that we have to die . . . it will be very difficult, but we will try to die as bravely as possible. We are all too young to die, including the old among us. Please tell my family . . . that I have been brave. As brave as you can be. Please tell my boyfriend that I love him. . . . There are people in the German government who are responsible for our death. I hope you can live with this guilt on your conscience.'

What Dillman did not know was that the German government had a plan. Chancellor Helmut Schmidt had maintained his decision to refuse even to negotiate with hijackers, let alone make any concessions, but that did not mean a policy of inaction. In fact, throughout almost its entire journey the hijacked plane had been shadowed by a team from Grenzschutzgruppe Neun or GSG9, a new unit composed of well-trained and well-armed German policemen that had been created specifically to deal with hostage-taking situations following the German authorities' catastrophic failure at the 1972 Munich Olympics. Almost immediately after receiving news of the attack on Lufthansa Flight 181, Schmidt had ordered the unit to take everything they needed for an assault on the hijacked plane and set off in its pursuit.

Throughout the five days of the crisis, the hijacked plane had kept one step ahead of its pursuers. At Rome, it had departed well before the West Germans had even got underway. At Larnaca, in Cyprus, the GSG9 team arrived twenty minutes after the *Landshut*'s departure for Bahrain. In Dubai, the local ruler insisted that his own troops be included in any assault and by the time his soldiers had been prepared for such a demanding mission, the *Landshut* was gone. In Aden, authorities refused point-blank to allow the plane carrying the GSG9 team to even land. By the time the *Landshut* reached Somalia, it was clear that if there could be no rescue operation at Mogadishu, there would be no such operation at all.

Few West German officials expected President Siad Barre of Somalia, an authoritarian leftist with a long history of support for revolutionary causes and the Popular Front–XO, to allow the GSG9 team to deploy. Yet after a lengthy conversation with Schmidt, Barre agreed. It was then that Michael Libal, the chargé d'affaires and 'Mr Representative of the fascist imperialist West Germany', picked up the microphone in the control tower and told Akache that Bonn was prepared to exchange the prisoners but needed time to bring them to Mogadishu – a statement that was completely untrue but which bought the vital hours needed for the GSG9 force to fly in and get ready.

At 2.07 a.m. local time Libal was finalising arrangements for the transfer with Akache when the line went dead. The men from GSG9 had launched their assault. Libal saw a series of bright flashes and extremely loud explosions around the *Landshut*. A minute later came the sound of shooting and shouting from inside the plane, then, at 02.09, sudden movement.

Watching from the sand dunes, the GSG9 unit's radio operator transmitted a live commentary direct to a control centre in Frankfurt. 'The guys have control of the plane. The emergency doors are open now, and I can see six, seven, eight hostages rushing from the plane . . . They are running toward the control tower,' he told those listening 4,000 miles away in West Germany. At 2.10, he reported more passengers sliding down the 737's emergency chutes and being led away from the plane, then 'thirty-five, thirty-six hostages are out . . . More hostages.'

The radio operator watched until every passenger and the crew of Flight 181 had been led away from the aircraft, then spoke again to tell the control centre: 'The doors are closed. It is over. The operation is over.'

There was a pause, and then a question from Frankfurt: 'The Chancellor would like to know how many casualties there are.'

'Please wait. Will come back with the number.'

Another pause. Then: 'Frankfurt, this is Oscar X Ray. Three terrorists killed, one badly wounded.'

'Copied, OK,' came the reply, followed by a brusque order for the GSG9 men to return to their plane, load the freed hostages and fly back to Germany. Andrawes – the surviving hijacker – was left in the care of the Somalis.

In Germany, there was rejoicing. Radio stations blared Beethoven's 'Ode to Joy'. Newspapers' early editions sold out in minutes. A hero's welcome was prepared for the hostages and their rescuers, complete with bands playing the national anthem, flags and speeches. The British prime minister James Callaghan, who had sent two advisers from the UK's elite Special Air Service to join the GSG9 force in Somalia, said the Germans had done 'a superb job' on behalf 'of the whole world'. A headline in *France Soir* told Parisians to exult in a victory in a collective 'cause, drama [and] war'. The White House welcomed a major blow on behalf of all nations against the scourge of terrorism.

Many Germans felt that the successful raid had somehow redeemed them, either from the stain of Munich in 1972 or perhaps even from larger, more historic failings. One television commentator daringly told viewers: 'It feels good to be a German today.' *Der Spiegel* magazine marvelled at how the first overseas deployment of a West German fighting force since the Second World War had returned their country to the community of (Western) nations. Now, the magazine suggested, their often reviled country might have something to offer the Americans reeling from 'their catastrophes of Vietnam and Watergate', to the British whose once proud currency had been 'sold off to the sheikhs', to the Italians 'struggling with banditry and political failure', even to the French, indeed to 'all those . . . suffering a thousand humiliations [at the hands of] once despised colonial peoples, the military pressure of the Eastern Bloc, the gloomy future, the plague of terrorists: Irish, Basque, Corsican, Palestinian air pirates, Red Brigades, sundry Fascists'. The GSG9's achievement had shown that Germans can be both 'strong and human'.

The 'German autumn' was not over yet though. The elation lasted for a morning, before news came from Stammheim prison that Baader and Ensslin had committed suicide sometime during the night. Baader had shot himself in his cell. Ensslin had hanged herself with a loudspeaker cable from a window grille. Jan-Carl Raspe had also shot himself. Irmgard Möller, a fourth veteran of the group held in the same cell complex, was found alive with stab wounds to her chest, made with a table knife.

The deaths prompted profound shock – Chancellor Schmidt blurted 'That's impossible' when informed – and a flood of questions. How had the prisoners, supposedly in total isolation for several weeks, learned of events in Somalia? How had they got hold of firearms? Why had they not been under closer surveillance? Why had they ended their lives? Autopsies and a series of investigations provided few satisfying answers.

One discovery was that the prisoners had been listening to national news networks on makeshift transistor radios hidden in their cells, and so would have learned of events in Mogadishu when the first news was broadcast at 12.38 a.m. They may also have been able to communicate through a secret intercom system that Raspe had rigged up out of electric odds and ends or simply by shouting to each other, largely out of earshot of the guards. The firearms Raspe and Baader used were those that had been brought in earlier in the year. The autopsies were delayed to allow independent international experts to reach Stuttgart, which meant the exact time of death was impossible to establish. Those conducting the examinations were unanimous in concluding that the cause was suicide. None of them attempted to explain why Baader and Ensslin had taken their own lives.

One reason for Schmidt's shock at their suicides was that the RAF still held Schleyer. It seemed nonsensical that the RAF's leaders might end their lives before all possibility of liberation was exhausted. But this was to misunderstand what motivated Baader and Ensslin and what the RAF was really about. For both, violence was not practical or transactional as it was for the Popular Front–XO, the Japanese Red Army, the IRA, ETA and many others. It was performative and demonstrative. Baader's first radicalism had been artistic, in the bohemian circles of Munich and Berlin. From the start, the RAF had been steeped in the same late-1960s culture that informed the 'Spontis' with their happenings, agitational street drama and absurdist stunts. Baader and Ensslin's early violence had been as influenced by Guy Debord's situationism as by Marighella, Mao or Guevara. Their one attempt at serious military training – the trip to Lebanon in 1970 – had been a farce. Only much later, when Baader had been behind bars for many years, did the RAF begin to show a degree of professionalism and the body count begin to mount. Much terrorism is theatre, as the US political scientist Brian Jenkins had argued in 1974. Baader, once an aspirant actor, choreographed violence and eventually his own death too.

Ensslin, the pastor's daughter, understood the importance of propaganda by deed as well as Baader did, but was driven by something almost totally absent in her lover: a powerful if profoundly misguided sense of duty. Ensslin was determined not to remain silent when confronted with what she saw as evil. The West Germany of the 1970s appeared to her to present the same choice as the one her parents had faced a generation before and she was determined to take a different path. Ensslin's thinking was rigorously binary, a Manichean worldview typical of violent extremists but also of cult members. The arson, blasts, abductions and shootings of the previous eight years had been demonstrations of her absolute moral conviction. So too was her suicide, a 'martyrdom' that bore witness to her righteous belief.

In their own minds at least, the deaths of Baader and Ensslin provided a fitting end to the story they had created. But both also showed glimmers of an awareness that the RAF had strayed from its founding goals and ideals. Baader spoke most explicitly of 'mistakes' and miscalculations, explaining that the violence of the summer of 1977 was 'not the RAF's way of doing things'. If released, the thirty-four-year-old explained to two priests who visited him shortly before his death, the leadership of the RAF would certainly continue their struggle against the West German state, 'campaigning in the context of all international liberation movements', but to imagine they might 'fight as international terrorists' was absurd. 'Terrorism [against civilians] was not the policy of the RAF' and 'international terrorism' was not 'the RAF's scene' either, Baader said.

In such circumstances, the ultimate sacrifice might have seemed the only way to reassert not only the legitimacy of the project they had launched nine years before – with their symbolic, spontaneous arson in a department store in Hamburg – but their authority too. They had repeatedly threatened suicide throughout the year, promising they would 'take matters into their own hands' if their followers could not secure their release. The two leaders were now effectively faced with the consequences of their own ultimatum. Once the news from Mogadishu came through, there was only one thing left for them to do.

Baader and Ensslin were buried together in a single grave in Stuttgart nine days after their deaths. Raspe was laid in an adjacent plot. The funerals were not well attended. The city's mayor told foreign diplomats that there had been a thousand people in the cemetery, equally divided between media, police and mourners. In the Italian cities of Turin, Bologna and Leghorn, bombs were tossed into showrooms displaying German cars. Two unoccupied German tourist buses were set on fire in Paris. In Rome, police used tear gas to disperse a large crowd armed with Molotov cocktails, marching towards the German Embassy and the Lufthansa ticket office. A Mercedes-Benz showroom was incinerated in Limoges. In Athens, 'anarchists' took to the streets and an attempt to bomb a German-owned factory was narrowly averted. In London, protesters chanted 'Murder! Murder!' outside the German Embassy.

In Baghdad, a dozen or so RAF members gathered in shock in one of the Popular Front–XO's offices. Many wept, others made wild and entirely unrealistic plans for revenge. Mohnhaupt, uncompromising as ever, told the others to face a harsh truth. 'I suppose you lot can only suppose that they were victims. You didn't know them. They were not victims and never were,' she shouted angrily. 'You don't get made a victim, you have to make yourself a victim. They were in charge of their own situation until the last minute. What does this mean? They did it to themselves, not that it was done to them. Stop crying, assholes.' The suicides were 'eine Aktion' – an operation – Mohnhaupt insisted.

Among the many questions now facing the RAF, one was particularly urgent. What should they do with Schleyer, who was still being held in a Brussels safehouse? This too provoked fierce argument among those in Baghdad. About half now felt the abduction six weeks earlier had been an error, a higher proportion believed the businessman should be freed. Even Wadie Haddad counselled clemency, when asked for his advice. Mohnhaupt and the RAF members in Brussels did not agree, and argued that to free their prisoner without anything in exchange would be a humiliating demonstration of weakness. There was a brief exchange of telexes between Baghdad and the Belgian capital. Then, between twelve and twenty-four hours after the end of the hijacking in Mogadishu, Schleyer was driven to a forest on the border with France where he was shot dead.

A statement was then delivered to *Libération*, the left-wing French newspaper, and the German national press agency's Stuttgart office.

The group explained that they had ended the businessman's 'petty and corrupt existence', even if, given the group's 'pain and anger over the massacres of Mogadishu and Stammheim', this further death was 'without meaning'. Their victim's corpse could be retrieved from a green Audi 100 with a Bad Homburg licence plate parked on the rue Charles Péguy in Mulhouse, the group said, before signing off with a slogan: 'Freedom through armed anti-imperialist struggle!'

The RAF's defiance was born more of desperation than confidence. The violent campaign of 1977 had been a catastrophe for all concerned. The collaboration with Haddad's Popular Front–XO – the RAF's first truly international effort – had been disastrous. Nor had their allies fared much better. Even the Japanese Red Army's recent victory had been pyrrhic, merely tarnishing the reputation of the extreme left still further in Fusako Shigenobu's homeland.

This was not immediately obvious to outside observers. *Die Welt*, one of the largest daily newspapers in Germany, told its readers: 'Three suicides – a signal for new terror.' The more conservative analysts predicted further hijackings, assassination attempts and raids on embassies. Bolder ones suggested the use of biological, chemical and even nuclear weapons by terrorists.

Many ordinary citizens in the West took comfort in the new counter-terrorist capabilities displayed by the Israelis at Entebbe and the Germans at Mogadishu. Most of their governments now had similar units, many founded in the immediate aftermath of the Munich Olympics. The French Groupe d'Intervention de la Gendarmerie Nationale had recently freed a party of schoolchildren taken hostage in Djibouti by Somali separatists, while a Dutch counter-terrorist unit had successfully released a hundred passengers from a train that had been held for three weeks by armed Moluccan nationalists. Such successes offered for the first time the possibility of genuine deterrence of future attacks.

Inevitably, the violence of the German autumn also prompted a new effort to explain how well-educated, middle-class young men and women could commit such acts. The West German government launched a series of research projects, including an extraordinary effort to compile comprehensive biographies of hundreds of known extremists in a bid to understand what had led them to violence. On the political left, many pointed to a profound sense of injustice as an important motivation for extremism; on the right, there was talk of spoilt or immoral youths corrupted by films, rock music and contraception.

Much of the focus was on social, cultural, political and historical factors that were essentially local. As so often, the broader global context was either misunderstood or missed entirely. The fact that the extremist violence was far from being an exclusively German phenomenon continued to escape many observers. The deaths of a hundred people in December when a plane, almost certainly hijacked by Shigenobu's group, crashed shortly after leaving Kuala Lumpur received almost no attention whatsoever, despite the exceptionally high toll. When commentators in the West did recognise the geographic extent of the groups involved in the spasm of violence they had just witnessed, this was frequently taken as evidence of the existence of some kind of global network of terrorist groups led by a shadowy mastermind. Such thinking was closer to the plot of the recently released Bond film *The Spy Who Loved Me* than to reality, but it caught the imagination of many journalists, analysts and some politicians, particularly in the US. 'Is there an international organisation that coordinates hijacking and other acts of terrorism, the whole thing run by some warped mastermind out of a secret headquarters?' asked the *New York Times*. *Time* magazine even named the mysterious head of this secret network. The 'prime candidate' was Wadie Haddad, it said.

Yet if Haddad was indeed pulling all the strings, whether from some hidden desert hideout or even from a converted supertanker like Bond's latest adversary, then he was not doing so with much success. Since the OPEC attack of late 1975, he had enjoyed few unalloyed triumphs and two of the most ambitious operations mounted by his faction of the PFLP had been spectacular failures.

The reasons for this went well beyond the new competence of special forces units or the resolution of leaders such as Schmidt or Yitzhak Rabin. The outcome of both hijackings – at Entebbe and at Mogadishu – had been decided by choices made in places far away from either Israel or Bonn. Without the Kenyan offer to refuel the Israeli transport planes at Nairobi, the famous raid on Entebbe could not have taken place. Without decisions made by the leaders of the People's Democratic Republic of Yemen (PDRY) and President Siad Barre of Somalia, the outcome of the hijacking of October 1977 would have been very different.

The stops made by the *Landshut* in Cyprus, Bahrain and Dubai were diversions, aimed at ramping up the pressure on West German decision-makers. In fact, Haddad's plan all along had been to end the hijacking of the *Landshut* in Aden, where the hostages would either have been spirited away to his training camp outside the city or held on the tarmac at the airport by Popular Front–XO fighters until Bonn gave in to the group's demands. He did not warn local authorities in advance, but after almost a decade of close relations no doubt felt that he could count on their support or at least acquiescence. This was a miscalculation and it was only the skill of the pilot Schumann that meant the hijacked plane could land in Aden at all. Any remaining chance of success for Haddad's original plan then disappeared when PDRY leaders arrived at Aden's international airport and deployed troops to make sure that the sizeable contingent of Popular Front–XO fighters in the city could not get within half a mile of the hijacked plane, let alone secure the aircraft and its hostages.

There were many reasons for the change in geostrategic calculus, but the underlying sentiment was that the decade-old policy of backing 'revolutionary groups' was outdated. One reason was pressure from more moderate Arab states and the PLO, which had told Aden that supporting violence of this kind was not helpful to the Palestinian cause. A second was the recognition among leading members of the regime in Aden that their support for radical groups was an obstacle to better relations with oil-rich neighbours, who could be more generous with aid than the Soviet bloc or the Chinese and who were now potential sources of generous development funding thanks to soaring oil prices.

The situation could still have turned out favourably for the hijackers if it had not been for Barre, the dictatorial ruler of Somalia. Haddad told Akache before the operation that if something should prevent the hijacked plane landing at Aden, he should head for Mogadishu as a last resort. Like those in charge of the PDRY, Barre had long been a faithful client of the Soviet Union, a vocal member of the loose coalition of 'revolutionary' socialist states in the greater Middle East and a supporter of militant groups. The Somali president had allowed the Popular Front–XO to operate freely in Mogadishu for many years and had played a supportive role during the Entebbe crisis, personally ordering the Somali ambassador to act as a representative of the hijackers in negotiations. His delegate at the UN had subsequently been one of the fiercest critics of the Israeli raid, and not just due to ill-feeling towards neighbouring Kenya. But Barre too had radically revised his thinking in the few months before the *Landshut* landed unannounced at Mogadishu airport.

Barre's commitment to a domestic programme of development through nationalist 'scientific socialism' was waning, while shifts in regional politics had pushed him towards a definitive change in foreign policy too. The war Barre had recently launched against neighbouring Ethiopia, governed by a radical Marxist regime since the fall of Emperor Haile Selassie three years before, had forced Moscow to choose between its two major clients in the Horn of Africa. The Soviets had picked Ethiopia and, along with the Cubans, were now sending enormous quantities of men, materiel and money to their new protégés in Addis Ababa. Barre found himself in desperate need of a sponsor and so, like Anwar Sadat in Egypt, looked to the West. The arrival of the *Landshut* provided a fortuitous opportunity to send a powerful and timely message to Washington and other potential Western allies beyond West Germany. When Akache told Somali officials he and the Popular Front–XO admired Somalia because of its battle against 'fascist imperialists', he inadvertently revealed Haddad's error. For Barre, the US and its allies were now potential saviours. Coming after the failure in Aden, Haddad's lapse proved fatal to the attack.

The leader of the Popular Front–XO was not the only 'terrorist mastermind' named by Western journalists and politicians. Only a handful of security experts knew very much about Haddad outside the Middle East, and even in the region 'the Master' was hardly a household name. There was only one internationally active terrorist who enjoyed genuine celebrity in the middle years of the 1970s. And yet, while there had been thousands of mentions of his activities in newspapers, television documentaries, diplomatic cables and policy documents, the 'most wanted man in the world' had disappeared after the OPEC attack almost exactly two years earlier and no one had heard from him since. It was the death of the Master – in excruciating agony and in unlikely and highly suspicious circumstances – that would propel Ramírez back into the spotlight.

23
Carlos Redux

In the autumn of 1977, Ramírez was more unhappy than ever. The disappearance of Klein had not bothered him overmuch. The young German had only ever been a fairly tedious type of valet but Klein's departure did mean that the membership of the Organisation of Internationalist Revolutionaries was now reduced to its founder alone. Nor did it appear likely that Ramírez's career would be revived by a series of commissions from his hosts in Baghdad. His speciality was attacks on Western targets, which did not fit with Saddam's foreign strategy. Ramírez had dinner with Abu Nidal, his rival organiser of terrorist attacks, and discussed a series of possible projects, such as the assassination of Sadat, but nothing came to fruition. Meanwhile, a day-trip for a picnic at one of the lakes west of Baghdad ended in tragedy when a former lover, a daughter of an Iraqi general who had joined Ramírez, drowned in the river. Ramírez, a poor swimmer, had been unable to save her and felt partly responsible for her death. Bassam Abu Sharif, still the chief spokesman for the original Popular Front for the Liberation of Palestine, was shocked when he saw his Venezuelan acquaintance for the first time in some years. He knew Ramírez as ebullient, loquacious and charming. Instead, he found a man who was 'dejected, inattentive and monosyllabic'.

During his time in Baghdad, Ramírez had had little contact with Haddad or his organisation, even though their offices were just a short drive away in his Volvo. Nor did Ramírez encounter the leaders of the Red Army Faction on either of the occasions that they flew in – prior to the kidnapping of Schleyer and then again before the hijacking of the *Landshut*. Nor any other members of the group who later arrived, fleeing the crackdown in Germany that followed. But he did learn something of their presence from their one compatriot in the city with whom he had cordial relations. This was a well-dressed and precise member of the Revolutionary Cells called Johannes Weinrich.

Weinrich and Ramírez were old associates, though the last time they had seen each other was more than two years before. Weinrich had studied at Frankfurt University and helped run the city's well-known radical bookstore set up by other founder members of the Revolutionary Cells. There he had married an African American soldier, who had deserted while stationed in West Germany, in order to provide her with German citizenship. In late 1974, he had helped Ramírez in Paris, arranging the hire cars for the abortive attacks at Paris airport. When French police warned their West German counterparts about his role, Weinrich was arrested and sent to prison, where he fell seriously ill. The time he spent behind bars, and particularly a few days in the specialised high-security complex at Stammheim, hardened Weinrich's radical convictions. When the twenty-eight-year-old was released after eight months, close friends saw 'an extreme change in his whole behaviour: he seemed to be entirely focused on the struggle and everything else became secondary.'

In the summer of 1977, worried by the literary revelations of his former comrade in arms Hans-Joachim Klein and the West German authorities' hunt for extremists in response to the RAF's new offensive, Weinrich decided to flee western Europe. Baghdad was the favoured destination of West German extremists at the time and the obvious choice. Plausible and polyglot, he soon found a role as intermediary between Haddad's group and the RAF leaders arriving in the Iraqi capital. The latter mocked Weinrich for his fine suits, his ties and leather briefcase, but Haddad did not. Weinrich's reunion with Ramírez in Baghdad was emotional; the two men 'fell into each other's arms'.

Some months later, Weinrich decided he wanted to travel to Algiers, where he was thinking about living. Ramírez was allowed by the Iraqi security services to accompany him. From the Algerian capital, Weinrich phoned his girlfriend in Frankfurt, a petite, attractive and emotionally fragile photographer called Magdalena Kopp, and asked her to join him there.

K[illegible] found the offer tempting. The daughter of a postal worker and a hou[illegible] Kopp had never felt at home 'in her family and the petty bourgeoisie of south-west Bavaria' and was still at school when she moved in with an arts student at the local university, with whom she had a child. Kopp then studied photography in West Berlin before moving to Frankfurt, where she was drawn into the 'Sponti' squatting scene, helped out at the radical publishing house launched by Boese and came into contact with members of the Revolutionary Cells, one of whom was Weinrich. He had reminded her of the French actor Jean-Paul Belmondo, and the two had become lovers.

Though Kopp was concerned by Weinrich's deepening extremism, their relationship survived his frequent absences and his spell in prison. Partly to please him, she had ceded parental authority over her daughter to the girl's estranged father and became more involved in radical activism herself, deploying her photographic skills to help the Revolutionary Cells to forge passports and other documents. In early 1976 she went a step further, travelling to the People's Democratic Republic of Yemen to spend three weeks in the Popular Front–XO's training camp there. Weinrich had left for Baghdad shortly after her return and had only communicated since through couriered notes or hurried calls to public phone boxes at pre-arranged times. Kopp missed 'Hannes', as she called him, and while she did not quite understand what Weinrich was doing in the Algerian capital, she accepted his unexpected invitation to join him and agreed to bring some photographic equipment that he requested. At the airport, Weinrich was waiting for her dressed in a well-cut new suit. Outside stood a chauffeur-driven limousine provided by the Algerian security services.

Algiers impressed Kopp: the stunning light, the casbah where she was surprised to see so many women veiled, the dinners with senior officials, the soirées with ambassadors and the magnificent apartment on the outskirts of the city provided by the Algerian authorities. This was 'a strange and interesting world' that fascinated her. The presence of Ramírez, who shared the apartment, was less welcome. She had first encountered him in 1974 when the leaders of the Revolutionary Cells had asked her to travel to London to develop negatives and print photographs for Haddad's team as they planned their abduction of the ambassador of the United Arab Emirates. During the weeks spent there, Ramírez had made several clumsy advances and eventually grabbed at her in the darkroom she had set up. In the training camp in Aden two years later, Ramírez had used the pretext of correcting her aim with a handgun to manhandle her once more, though she had kept silent for fear of 'creating a scene'.

Now she was sharing a flat with him and her partner, who seemed in awe of this confident, arrogant man who went out every night, slept until almost noon and spent hours in the apartment's vast bathrooms. Everything about the situation was unpleasant and uncomfortable. Yet when Ramírez appeared late one morning wearing nothing but a towel and asked her to smear moisturising cream on his back, she agreed. She could not explain why, except to say that he had looked almost vulnerable, the most famous terrorist in the world, standing there, asking for a massage, and she had felt almost sorry for him.

Ramírez had other concerns beyond the seduction of his comrade's girlfriend. It was becoming clear that the hospitality he and Weinrich had enjoyed in Algiers was not going to last indefinitely. Algeria had come under increasing pressure from Western states to cut its ties with 'terrorists', and its president Houari Boumedienne was very seriously ill. At such a time, the country's security services would be wary of offering Ramírez the same welcome. To pre-empt any unpleasantness, he and Weinrich decided to return to Iraq, leaving Kopp to head back to West Germany, her job and her daughter alone.

But in Baghdad too, Ramírez's fine political antennae were picking up warning signals. Saddam was stronger than ever, his administration borne upward and forward by still surging oil revenues. Relations with Iran were deteriorating rapidly as well, which strongly suggested some kind of conflict in the not too distant future. To prepare, Saddam wanted to equip the newly expanded Iraqi armed forces with Western military technology to match that of their likely foes. Iraq's nuclear programme, which depended almost entirely on French assistance, took on a new importance and urgency. In this context, the various armed groups he was hosting, while useful in the short term, would soon become an inconvenience. Operators like Abu Nidal who did not target Westerners or Western companies were another matter; they could be allowed to stay in Iraq. But harbouring the infamous Carlos the Jackal, wanted for a string of murderous attacks across western Europe including several in France, was rather different.

This strongly suggested to Ramírez that it would soon be time to move on from Iraq, but his options were distinctly limited. He had just ruled out Algeria as a long-term base. The *Landshut* hijacking had shown the People's Democratic Republic of Yemen to be unreliable, Sudan was unpleasant, Lebanon unsafe, and his distrust of Gaddafi eliminated Libya too. He would be welcome in Damascus but to arrange a move to Syria from Baghdad would be delicate and dangerous. The very uncomfortable episode in Yugoslavia did not recommend it or any other supposedly socialist non-aligned states.

Then, unexpectedly, a range of new, exciting and seemingly inexhaustible possibilities opened up.

On 28 March 1978 Wadie Haddad died in a clinic in East Berlin. Some days later he was buried in Baghdad. The cortege of military vehicles was preceded by a vast wreath, a portrait of the deceased as a young man, masked but unarmed fedayeen and a guard of honour of Iraqi soldiers. Watched by crowds, the procession traversed the streets of the Iraqi capital to its main Christian cemetery where many of the most significant figures in the radical fringe of the Palestinian movement stood as the black casket was lowered into the ground. 'Let our enemies know that he did not die, but is alive in our hearts, and his name is organically bound to our people and to our revolution,' George Habash told the crowd. Nearby, making sure to avoid the lenses of newsreel cameras and international agency photographers, was Ramírez.

Haddad took many secrets with him, but the most significant of them was the true nature of his relationship with Moscow. Haddad's intimate associates all knew he had close connections with the security services of a dozen different 'revolutionary' or 'progressive' states and had been a regular visitor on the eastern side of the Iron Curtain for many years. This was barely noteworthy: thousands of fedayeen had received medical treatment or training in Soviet satellites. What few understood was the nature of their leader's links with the KGB, which had viewed Haddad as a 'secret working contact' since 1968 and a fully-fledged 'agent' from 1970, when he had been given the codename NATSIONALIST.

The recruitment of Haddad was a personal project of the KGB's 'chairman', Yuri Andropov, a dogmatic hardliner who had played a key role in the brutal repression of the Hungarian revolution in 1956 and was deeply committed to the prosecution of a 'global struggle' against capitalism and imperialism. Since taking command of the KGB in 1967, Andropov had encouraged numerous clandestine operations overseas, involving sabotage, blackmail, mass disinformation, covert efforts at regime change and, on rare occasion, assassination. Some were direct retaliations to supposed CIA efforts to harm Soviet interests, many of which existed only in Andropov's paranoiac imagination.

But Andropov's vision of a vast campaign of 'special actions' executed by KGB operatives all over the world soon ran into difficulties. Primary among them was the extreme sensitivity of senior Soviet officials when it came to the image of the USSR and the potential harm that the exposure of such activities might do to it. The belief in the supposed moral supremacy of Communists over their ideological enemies was not mere rhetoric. It was central to the worldview of many influential individuals in Moscow, just as the opposite was central to the worldview of their counterparts in Washington. It was also an important diplomatic and propaganda weapon. So even if clandestine operations could be justified in the great struggle for the good of mankind, they had to remain secret. As no one could guarantee this, most of the KGB's schemes were meticulously planned, found to be feasible and then, to the great disappointment of those involved, cancelled.

An obvious solution was to use proxies who could shield the USSR from scandal, and these were as diverse as the activities the KGB hoped they would undertake. The obvious candidates were allied, or at least aligned, security services. None were easy to deal with. Whether it was the Cubans, the 'revolutionary' regimes in Libya, South Yemen and Algeria or the satellite states in Europe, all had their own interests that at some point diverged from Moscow's. For this reason it was sometimes easier, or at least appeared so, to bypass local intelligence services and deal directly with violent leftist or nationalist organisations that might be interested in co-operation, including the various Palestinian armed factions – assuming, of course, that the KGB could still somehow maintain 'plausible deniability'.

When the fedayeen first emerged as a potent force after the 1967 war, the Soviets were wary of the disruption they might cause if left to their own devices. Soviet policy-makers and analysts repeatedly underlined the dangers of 'adventurism', the Foco-ism of Che Guevara and any efforts that were not rooted in a true understanding of Marxist-Leninist theory. Leonid Brezhnev was overtly contemptuous of the belief that a 'conspiracy of heroes could make a revolution'. But this did not mean the Soviets were not prepared to support the Palestinian armed groups at all, and by the early 1970s, shipments of thousands of small arms, artillery, mortars and even armoured vehicles were being sold or given to the fedayeen along with passports, disguises, printing equipment, darkrooms and communications kit, as well as instruction in espionage, bomb-making, urban warfare and many other useful disciplines, all via Soviet clients in the Middle East or through Moscow's satellite states in eastern Europe. The KGB were very unsure about the reliability of Yasser Arafat, whose desire for relations with 'reactionary powers' and constant manoeuvring they found unsettling, and much preferred dealing with groups that were closer ideological matches, such as the Democratic Front for the Liberation of Palestine or the PFLP.

The designation 'agent' was usually reserved for someone who consciously and willingly worked for the Soviet cause, whether for ideological or other less elevated reasons, and so dramatically overstated Haddad's commitment to the KGB. It was nonetheless a sign of the hopes the service had for its relationship with him. The service made it clear to Haddad they strongly disapproved of transnational hijackings but still offered to provide the often difficult to obtain weaponry that might well aid such operations. Though an initial shipment of arms to the PFLP in early 1970 consisted of just five rocket-propelled grenade launchers, those that followed were much more generous, containing hundreds of powerful assault rifles, 'special technical devices' such as technically advanced remote-controlled mines, fifty West German pistols including ten with silencers and much else. There was no possible doubt that the KGB knew what Haddad was planning to do with this large arsenal. Haddad had met the service's station chief in Beirut in April 1970 and described how he hoped to escalate violence against Israel and its 'imperialist supporters' with strikes against large oil-storage installations in Saudi Arabia, the Persian Gulf, the Asia-Pacific region and elsewhere, attacks on oil tankers and super-tankers, an operation against the diamond-dealing industry in Tel Aviv and direct 'actions' against US and Israeli representatives in Iran, Greece, Ethiopia and Kenya.

In reality, the KGB was keener for Haddad to carry out missions closer to home. Haddad's first task for them was to organise the abduction of the deputy head of the CIA station in Lebanon, who was to be sent to the Soviet Union for interrogation. The effort, which lasted for much of the summer of 1970, failed but Haddad's men did subsequently manage to abduct other less important targets, including suspected Mossad and CIA informers. The Soviets appeared happy nonetheless, and in the autumn of 1971 'Vadia Khaddad', as he was described in internal KGB documents, was invited to Moscow, staying with his wife, son and daughter in a KGB dacha.

Discussions with his hosts were not entirely cordial, however. Haddad balked at the Soviets' suggestion that the Palestinians should settle for a state limited to the West Bank, pointing out that this would leave Safed, his home town, in Israel, as well as Haifa and Jerusalem. Terrorism was central to the Palestinians' 'long term people's war', he argued, not least because other strategies had already been tried and failed. And yes, any civilian casualties were unfortunate, Haddad admitted, before pointing out that to defeat Nazi Germany the Red Army had destroyed much of Berlin.

Haddad was keen to work with the KGB, however, and agreed to help with hunting down Soviet defectors back in the Middle East. A year later, presumably as recompense, the KGB provided intelligence and advice that allowed Haddad to attack an Israeli-chartered tanker carrying oil through the Red Sea. The service had been unable to supply the miniature electric-powered submarines that the Popular Front–XO leader had wanted for the operation, mainly because they had none. Nor had they agreed to Haddad's requests for surface-to-air missiles. Such inconstancy irked Haddad. 'We have talked to our Soviet friends about this but they only help when it suits them,' he complained to Gunnar Ekberg, the Swedish spy, when the two met in Beirut that year.

Such disappointments may explain why contacts between the KGB and Haddad appear to have diminished through the middle years of the decade. But it is more likely that the relationship was hindered by the significant opposition in the USSR to Andropov's aggressive strategy of covert 'active measures' overseas. The Soviet political leadership was fully convinced of the utility of a well-timed, well-placed act of terrorism and had no compunction about terrorism as a tactic if circumstances demanded. But as detente between the superpowers broke down through the middle years of the 1970s, Soviet leaders sought increasingly to contrast their supposed revolutionary rectitude and respect for international law with the 'cowboy' attitude of the US in international fora like the United Nations. This inevitably meant prioritising the grand strategic goals of the Cold War rather than the immediate advantage that Andropov sought with his various plots and plans.

Above all else, the Soviet political leadership wanted to avoid being dragged into a greater confrontation with the US by some entirely unanticipated, uncontrolled 'adventurist' act. British officials observed how during the 1970s the Soviets largely kept away from areas of vital concern to the West and avoided anything that 'ran a risk of war'. Even Andropov recognised this. When in 1974 he briefed Brezhnev about the contacts between his service and Haddad, the KGB chairman boasted of his organisation's ability to 'exercise [a restraining] influence' on the Popular Front–XO that was 'favourable to the USSR'.

The spymaster may not have been entirely frank when making such claims, or Haddad may have been particularly duplicitous, for in the two years after Andropov made this claim Haddad organised both the mass abduction of oil ministers from OPEC and the hijacking that led to the raid on Entebbe. Either Andropov had hugely misrepresented his powers of persuasion, or he was ignorant of planned operations, or he did not seek to restrain Haddad. Whatever the case, the KGB gave little sign of being much dismayed by Haddad's international attacks, and in both 1976 and 1977 the KGB offered training to ten members of the group at the service's own specialised institute, and also invited Haddad to Moscow for 'operational discussions'. Here he was asked to broker an introduction for the KGB to the Irish Republican Army before being given $10,000 and a cache of sought-after West German pistols. Perhaps the KGB also took the opportunity to remind Haddad of the dangers of 'adventurism'. Perhaps it did not. The appalling violence of the autumn of 1977 followed shortly afterwards.

One thing that Haddad's relationship with the KGB certainly explained was the hospitality extended to him by the East Germans in his dying weeks. The veteran extremist, who was forty-nine, had fallen sick in the second week of January 1978, suffering severe abdominal pain after meals. He lost weight fast, suffered acute fevers and his hair began to fall out. Doctors in Baghdad initially diagnosed ulcers, then leukaemia, but suspected that their patient had been poisoned, though they could not tell how this had been done. Haddad was sent to a clinic in Algeria, but medics there could not help. An appeal was dispatched by Habash to East Berlin, and possibly Moscow too, asking for assistance. Shortly thereafter Haddad was moved to the Regierungskrankenhaus, a clinic usually reserved for senior members of the East German security establishment in East Berlin.

Among the various secret services that the KGB relied on to help deal with the fedayeen, the East German Ministry for State Security (MfS), or Stasi, was perhaps the most important. A series of agreements signed in the mid-1970s obliged the service to share the results of its 'political, military, economic, and scientific and technical' espionage with the KGB as well as open its files to the hundreds of officers working at the KGB's residency in Berlin. As a consequence, the Stasi's foreign intelligence division sent somewhere between eighty and ninety per cent of the material it gathered to Moscow.

The Stasi was particularly useful to the Soviets when it came to sensitive tasks that the KGB preferred not to undertake itself, which included dealing with Arafat and the PLO. Moscow's official position was that UN resolution 242 should be the basis for peace between Israelis and Palestinians. Public contact with Arafat, who continued to reject the resolution, was therefore delicate. The East Germans were free to go much further and did, entering into dozens of formal agreements of co-operation with Fatah. The Stasi was also useful to amplify strident propaganda against Israel (including much that was deliberately and explicitly antisemitic) and to manage relations with 'frontline revolutionary states' such as Sudan or the PDRY. Because the Stasi had effectively trained and equipped an entire security service in Aden, it was well placed in October 1977 to follow KGB instructions and tell senior officials in the city to prevent the Popular Front–XO's forces on the ground from reaching the Lufthansa plane once it managed to land. This had earned the GDR (and indirectly Moscow) grudging gratitude in Bonn but was entirely in line with the Stasi's own distaste for the dangerously destabilising 'adventurism' of attacks like Haddad's and a desire to preserve their own image as 'peaceable'.

But though Haddad had powerful friends in East Berlin, this did not mean he was guaranteed treatment there for his mystery illness. After no doubt considerable debate, the final decision, possibly taken in Moscow, was that any drawbacks were outweighed by the value of demonstrating to their allies and the developing world that those who fought against imperialism could expect to be looked after by the leaders of that struggle. The intercession of Habash, and later Arafat too, may also have played a role, and possibly suspicions about the cause of Haddad's deteriorating health. In the event, the East German specialists also proved unable to treat Haddad's worsening condition. All they could do was administer massive doses of tranquillisers and analgesics, then watch him die in appalling pain.

Ten years earlier Haddad had been virtually unknown outside a close circle of activists in Beirut, Damascus and Amman. In the aftermath of the 1967 war, he had a single, limpidly clear idea of how to prosecute a campaign of political violence in a dramatically new way. He had taken the 'guerrilla wars' of the 1960s into an entirely new dimension: the skies. This enabled the PFLP and then a host of imitators to win the initiative, effectively striking at will against a much more powerful enemy. For some years, this advantage had endured until Western authorities found ways to counter the new threat and the geopolitical balance tipped against it. This was because Haddad's tactical genius had never been matched by any commensurate sense of strategy; 'the Master', as some had dubbed him, never managed to harness his violence to a realistic political programme. His break with the PFLP and the PLO merely emphasised this fundamental failing, and by the time he died, Haddad was little more than a marginal actor, his group's survival dependent on the whim of Saddam Hussein and other brutal regimes, its links to the KGB tenuous and its capabilities put at the disposal of Western extremists in a desperate bid to raise funds. On Haddad's death, his organisation was without any popular constituency, realistic goal or ideology. In the weeks after his funeral, it became clear it was also without a future.

The moment its leader was gone, the Popular Front–XO disintegrated. Those former members who were prepared to work for Saddam remained in Baghdad and were rapidly integrated into the dictator's personal collection of mercenaries and misfits. Others found different patrons or attached themselves to other armed groups elsewhere in the region. A significant number decided their revolutionary days were over and disappeared into semi-retirement. Many of the Germans who had travelled to Baghdad to find Haddad a year earlier had already left. Some had sought a very uncertain haven in Aden. Others preferred Yugoslavia where they were swiftly detained. A few could not choose between the two and remained in Iraq, traumatised by the events of the previous year and, in some cases, addled by drug abuse. Saddam's security forces largely ignored them, correctly surmising that they were neither a threat nor of interest to anyone.

For Ramírez, however, his position and prospects were much improved. His first attempt to found an 'Organisation of Internationalist Revolutionaries' had failed. Now, instead of a coalition of armed groups led by him, he envisaged something less grandiose and ideological but much more practicable: not a formal group as such but rather a shifting cast of collaborators who were willing to work with him on individual operations and, crucially, acknowledge his leadership. Some might join him on a semi-permanent basis. Others just for a few months, weeks or even days. But with their assistance, he could offer any prospective sponsor a comprehensive, discreet and hopefully lucrative service. With Haddad's group now defunct, such clients would be numerous, Ramírez reasoned. Several Popular Front–XO veterans had already signalled that they would like to work with him. These included Weinrich.

Some six months after Haddad's funeral, Weinrich arranged for Magdalena Kopp to join him at Ramírez's villa in Baghdad. Kopp was enjoying a new job in the reproduction department of an advertising agency in Frankfurt and had been very reluctant to leave her child. But Weinrich told her that the German authorities were probably preparing to arrest her following the publication of Hans-Joachim Klein's book and that she had to flee. If she didn't, she would be under surveillance and so would have to cut herself off from all her former comrades in the Revolutionary Cells. Kopp reluctantly gave way to this flagrant emotional blackmail, travelled to Prague, where Weinrich met her, and then the two of them flew to Iraq.

At Baghdad airport, Ramírez was waiting with a large bunch of flowers for her and soon made clear that he hoped their relationship would progress further than a back rub. Weinrich appeared unbothered by their host's libidinous advances towards his long-term partner, and the three of them were soon installed in his villa. Though Kopp was initially excited by the roof terrace, palm trees, parrots, flowers and the prospect of exploring a new country, life in the Iraqi capital soon palled. Unused to the searing temperatures, she was reluctant to leave the house during the day, while there was not much a woman could do independently in the evenings. The two men had little to occupy them and the atmosphere in their shared home was claustrophobic. When Ramírez suggested that she spend two weeks at a holiday resort in Mauritius, ostensibly to steal passports from unsuspecting tourists, Kopp accepted with enthusiasm. On her return from a pleasant holiday that involved a fling with an entertainments organiser but little in the way of stolen identity documents, Kopp found much had changed.

To her surprise, Ramírez and Weinrich were preparing for a rapid departure from Baghdad. Torpid tedium had been replaced by feverish activity. Ramírez handed out new passports: well-prepared false diplomatic documents supposedly issued by the PDRY in a variety of Arabic names but carrying their portraits. He did not explain why the trio needed to leave, merely that their hosts 'had tried to put him under pressure'.

This was an understatement. While Kopp had been in Mauritius, he and Weinrich had been arrested and held for twenty-four hours in a cell. Here the Iraqi secret services had proposed that Ramírez undertake a series of overseas missions on their behalf. These were not particularly onerous, and the message was unmissable: it would be extremely unwise to refuse.

On 26 October 1978, Ramírez flew to Prague, the capital of what was then the Czechoslovak Socialist Republic, which had by then been under Communist rule for almost thirty years. His first task was to carry out a thorough reconnaissance of a building that housed offices frequented by Iraqi Communists who had fled Saddam's repression. The second was to visit Souhaila Andrawes, the surviving hijacker of the *Landshut*. Iraqi authorities had convinced the Somali government to allow her many injuries to be treated in Baghdad but, as with Haddad, found that they lacked the necessary facilities and so she had been dispatched to a clinic in Prague. Ramírez carried out this part of the mission with predictable enthusiasm. He brought flowers, impressed the twenty-four-year-old with his 'manners, rich lifestyle and thoughtfulness' and charmed her mother. The relationship rapidly blossomed to the point that the possibility of marriage was being discussed, though Andrawes eventually proved unwilling to make such a hasty and drastic commitment.

As he was travelling on a valid diplomatic passport, Ramírez had not been identified on entry to the Czech Republic. In Prague itself he switched hotels repeatedly, staying first at the Hotel Belvedere, then spending one night in the brand-new Interhotel Alcron, and ending up in room 328 of the Hotel Intercontinental. Though all these hotels were bugged and watched around the clock, Czech security services somehow failed to spot the most famous terrorist in the world, nor prevent his departure.

In any case, Ramírez was soon back. This time he met with an Iraqi embassy official who had been involved in a series of attacks on Iraqi dissidents in western Europe. Slightly sharper now, the Czech security service tapped a source who ran the intelligence operation of the Iraqi Communist party branch in Prague. The man revealed not only that Ramírez 'was working for the General Intelligence Unit at the Office of the Iraqi President' but that he had been sent to prepare and co-ordinate the assassination of an employee of the embassy of the PDRY, an Arab nationalist and former member of the PFLP. Quite why the Mukhabarat wanted the man dead was unclear.

Kopp knew none of this of course, and Ramírez was not likely to tell her. In January 1979, she, Ramírez and Weinrich left their villa in Baghdad for the last time, travelled to the international airport and boarded a plane. Once settled in his seat, Ramírez produced a briefcase full of neat stacks of dollars which he began counting in full view of astonished cabin staff and passengers. His duties performed, his freedom won, the money was a parting gift from Iraqi secret services. It totalled $200,000. Ramírez's return to the main stage of international terrorism could now begin.

Since Haddad's death, speculation had been rife about the mystery illness that killed him. Some months after his funeral, the PLO's weekly newspaper, the *Falastin al-Thawra*, announced that post-mortem examination by East German physicians had found that Haddad had not died of leukaemia, as publicly announced, but had been murdered by Saddam's regime with a slow-acting poison administered in Baghdad. The article pointed out that Haddad had fallen sick after a dinner with Saadoun Shaker, the head of the Mukhabarat, several weeks before his death.

The allegation was not implausible. Though the reporters for *Falastin al-Thawra* did not know it, the doctors who had been treating Haddad at the East Berlin clinic had already arrived at the same conclusion: their patient had been poisoned, and everyone knew the Iraqi security services had a long history of murdering those who became a nuisance or a threat. In January 1978 assassins sent from Iraq had killed the PLO's representative in London, whose moderation and loyalty to Arafat offended Saddam. There were many more attempted assassinations by Iraqi intelligence and its various agents that year and plenty of similar plots were still underway, such as those that had sent Ramírez to Prague. As for a motive, many reports said the Iraqis had decided to kill Haddad when he refused to tell them in advance of planned operations and so 'resisted their efforts to control him'.

But there were other obvious suspects. Haddad had long been near the top of the Mossad's list of potential targets and the agency had tracked him remorselessly throughout the decade, even once Yitzhak Rabin and Shimon Peres, who were much more concerned about the use of such controversial tactics than Golda Meir had been, were in power. By now even Israel's allies had made absolutely clear that such assassinations were neither welcomed nor condoned. A 1975 report by the Rand Corporation, commissioned by the US Department of State, had included such killings among its lists of 'incidents of international terrorism', just as the British had once done, echoing the CIA's use of the term 'counter terror', rather than 'counter-terrorism', to describe them. One solution was to keep such killings quiet, or at least not trumpet their involvement, as Israel had done before.

Later the Mossad would claim the assassination as theirs, achieved via a well-placed agent within the Popular Front–XO. The service certainly had recruited high-level individuals close to Haddad, and had displayed a ruthless ingenuity on multiple previous occasions. Accounts of how the poison reached its target vary: some say it was via spiked Cadbury's chocolates bought by Mossad agents in Belgium, which would have appealed to Haddad's famously sweet tooth, others via toothpaste, applied thoughtlessly morning and evening. Some in a position to know say it was the former. In either case, Haddad would have been exposed repeatedly to small amounts of the toxin over time, which would eventually have accumulated into a fatal dose that was almost impossible to detect. At the time, the Mossad did not advertise any involvement in Haddad's lingering death in the way they had done after earlier killings. There were no quiet calls to widows or the bereaved children of his victims, no background briefings for sympathetic newspaper editors. Even decades later, former officers directly involved with operations that targeted Haddad in the late 1970s would cast doubt on an Israeli role in his death, pointing out that 'terrorists get cancer too' and suggesting that their operation targeted a man who was already very sick, perhaps expediting his death, or perhaps having little real effect. Many close associates and family members came to a similar conclusion.

Besides, there were plenty of other targets on the Mossad's list, first drawn up in 1972, who had still not been crossed off. One was the man they had been trying to kill when they murdered an unsuspecting Moroccan waiter in front of his pregnant wife in Norway. This was Ali Hassan Salameh, the flamboyant philanderer with a taste for luxury hotels and fast cars who had once organised Black September attacks across western Europe before being recruited by Arafat to lead his personal security service. Though there was still no reliable evidence that Salameh had contributed in any meaningful way to the Munich

Olympics attack, the Mossad remained convinced that he was responsible for the deaths of the Israeli athletes. Regardless of whether this was true, they had lots of other reasons to want him dead.

If no one would ever be quite sure who or what had killed Haddad, there would be absolutely no doubt about who was responsible for the death of Salameh, nor how he died. The passing of the Red Prince, as some of his enemies had dubbed him, would be as spectacular and rapid as that of 'the Master' had been discreet and drawn-out.

24
'They are all mad'

On 29 June 1977, Ali Hassan Salameh married a woman once voted the most beautiful in the universe.

The wedding was modest, despite the wealth of the bride's family and the local taste for ostentatious display. One reason for restraint was that the thirty-six-year-old bridegroom already had one wife, who lived with their two sons not far from the well-appointed apartment in Beirut where this new match was celebrated. A second was that the terrible civil war that had convulsed the city over the previous two years did not encourage displays of gaiety. A third, perhaps, was the bridegroom's sense that he was living on borrowed time. It was always unwise to attract too much attention in the shadowy battlefield that had been his habitat for the best part of a decade.

The bride, Georgina Rizk, a twenty-four-year-old Lebanese model and socialite, wore a white dress with a white orchid in her red hair. Salameh replaced his usual unbuttoned black shirt and leather jacket with an immaculately tailored white suit, and for once was unarmed. The wedding, and the couple's unusual holiday in the US that had preceded it, were a testament to the charisma of Salameh, who had matured since his days as a young fedayeen leader in Amman in 1970, and to his status as the head of security for the chairman of the Palestine Liberation Organisation. Rizk was the child of an elite and relatively liberal family, and her parents would not usually have consented to such a match for their beautiful if somewhat rebellious daughter. It was also a testament to the resilience of Beirut. Salameh was a Palestinian and, at least nominally, a Muslim. Rizk was a Christian, her father being well known in the conservative Maronite community, and her mother Hungarian. Their union thus bridged a yawning and bloody intercommunal divide that threatened to bring great sorrow and loss to their country.

Since travelling to New York and the United Nations with Yasser

Arafat in 1974, Salameh had prospered, even if Lebanon had not. He continued to look after Arafat's personal protection, accompanying him on various global travels, and still commanded Arafat's personal guard, Force 17, now a unit of several hundred relatively well-trained, well-armed fighters who answered only to him. He also ran his own intelligence networks that targeted not just the PLO's obvious enemy, Israel, but other Palestinian factions, whether friendly or rivalrous, that might disrupt Arafat's own strategies. Salameh had no compunction about using lethal force when required. When one foreign interlocutor asked about the health of a Beiruti acquaintance, Salameh smoothly replied that he had ordered the man's death two days before. Some even spoke of Salameh as a potential successor to the PLO chairman.

But this capable, dangerous and influential man also recognised that violence had its limitations. By the mid-1970s, the PLO had become a chaotic but very extensive organisation with many of the attributes of a state. It contained welfare services running clinics and schools, representative assemblies, cultural associations, research institutions, unions and an Olympic committee. Businesses owned and managed by the PLO in Lebanon and overseas produced significant profits. Vast funds flowed in from donors ranging from oil-rich Gulf states to Western companies who paid what they hoped was protection money. Formal foreign relations had now been established with dozens of countries. Salameh understood the value of tact and diplomacy as well as brute force.

Being drawn into Lebanon's burgeoning civil conflict would imperil all of this. Harmony was the need of the hour, not further communal discord, and this was precisely why Salameh accepted an invitation to a soirée one evening in 1975, where he met Rizk, the former Miss Universe. Since receiving her crown four years earlier from a panel of judges in Miami Beach, she had acted in films, sung on Lebanese radio, appeared in television shows and been hired as chief hostess in the baccarat room at the Casino du Liban. To the gossip columnists of Beirut, Rizk was 'Lebanon's queen, Lebanon's goddess'.

It was at more or less the same time as their meeting that a spark set light to the Lebanese tinder, leading swiftly to the blazing chaos that would consume the country and its capital for the next two years.

In April 1975, a carload of men opened fire on a crowd at a church in central Beirut, killing several people. The leaders of Kata'ib or the Phalange party identified the Democratic Front for the Liberation of

Palestine (DFLP), part of the PLO, as the culprits and exacted revenge by ordering an attack on a bus full of Palestinians. The Phalange had been set up in the 1930s in emulation of fascist movements in Europe by Pierre Gemayel, a former captain of the Lebanese national football team and ambitious power-broker from the Maronite Christian community. It had since developed into a powerful militia dedicated to protecting Maronite political and economic dominance. Though initially supportive of the Palestinians' presence in Lebanon, Gemayel had come to see them as a significant threat. Inevitably the DFLP and its allies sought to avenge the attack, leading to further killings by both sides, which spiralled into eighteen months of violence that would destroy the centre of Beirut.

Arafat was very reluctant to formally engage the PLO in the growing civil war but events forced his hand. He owed much of his authority and legitimacy to his image as a protector of ordinary Palestinians and so could not resist demands for direct action to protect its community in Lebanon, which now numbered some 350,000 out of a total population of 3.5 million. In late 1975 the PLO joined a rough coalition of Communists, socialists, Nasserists, pan-Arabists and assorted groups of Muslims to fight the Maronites.

This coalition had been brought together by a 'gaunt, shambling politician-mystic' named Kamal Jumblatt, who was head of Lebanon's minority Druze community and a long-time supporter of the Palestinian cause. Jumblatt cut an eccentric figure among the warlords and power-brokers of Beirut. Now in his late fifties, he was a vegetarian and yoga aficionado which, as George Habash accurately noted, was 'quite rare in the Middle East'. He was also a personal friend of Arafat and the uncontested leader of Lebanon's hyper-active if fragmented left, having long pushed for radical reform of the Lebanese political system to favour the poor. Jumblatt saw the future of his country as a secular, pluralist, progressive democracy profoundly anchored in the Arab world, not a socially conservative quasi-oligarchy orientated towards the West. This too appealed to Arafat and so, by the end of 1975, the battle lines had been drawn: on one side there were the Maronite Christians' various militias and their conservative allies; on the other the 'Islamo-Progressives' or 'Palestino-Progressives' of Jumblatt's Lebanese National Movement and the PLO. Quite where an ideological contest ended and a sectarian one began was far from clear to anyone.

The first phase of the conflict lasted from autumn 1975 to the summer of 1977. One key battle was for control of Beirut's international hotels. This photogenic contest, with snipers firing from five-star rooms in thirty-storey towers and grenades hurled across wrecked restaurants, attracted global attention. It also devastated much of the heart of the city, definitively destroyed the tourist industry and prompted a massive flight of capital. Casualties were mercifully light, which was not the case in the next bout of fighting in which Maronite militias conducted a deliberately bloody campaign to clear Muslim and Palestinian neighbourhoods in Christian-dominated east Beirut. Some of the worst atrocities were committed during the Maronites' siege of Tel al-Za'atar, a Palestinian refugee settlement dating back to 1948, where somewhere between 1,000 and 3,000 people died from hunger, thirst, disease and artillery fire. Similar tactics were used to purge other settlements, prompting the PLO and its allies to commit massacres of their own. 'The guerrillas' revenge had been merciless,' commented a British reporter, after a Palestinian attack on the Christian coastal town of Damour, twelve miles south of Beirut.

After almost a year of fighting, the greater numbers and experience of the thirty or so factions that comprised Jumblatt's coalition began to tell and the Maronite-led alliance was forced back into its strongholds: east Beirut, the port of Jounieh and Lebanon's central hills. Arafat and Jumblatt now claimed to control more than four-fifths of Lebanon and victory appeared within their grasp. But this prospect did not please Syria's ruler Hafez al-Assad, who had been watching and manipulating the fighting from Damascus. Al-Assad first sent paramilitaries and then thousands of heavily armed regular Syrian troops with tanks and artillery to fight alongside the Christians. Among Assad's many strategic, personal and mercenary motives for fighting Arafat and Jumblatt was a concern to prevent the creation of a new revolutionary leftist state on Syria's doorstep. The intervention stunned the PLO leadership, which had been sure that the Soviets would protect them. Now Ba'athist forces from a client state of Moscow were supporting assaults on their positions by Maronites who themselves sought support from the US and saw Lebanon as an outpost of the West. Fighting flared again through the summer, causing further deaths and mass displacement.

Among those forced to move were Rizk's family, who swapped their leafy suburb on the outskirts of Beirut for the solidly Christian neighbourhood of Ashrafiyeh. Similar decisions taken by hundreds of thousands of people across Beirut further reinforced the divisions between religious communities. The city was now a series of sectarian cantons, guarded with checkpoints manned by teenagers with assault rifles. This did not mean all semblance of ordinary life had ceased. Many businesses remained open, children still went to school, stepping past debris and cartridge cases. Radio stations broadcast updates on potential flashpoints. At the Marble Tower Hotel, one foreign reporter watched as residents bombed out of their homes played an interminable game of bridge, continuing by candlelight when the electricity failed. Well-dressed women in heels walked on shell-scarred pavements to cafés and restaurants. The Casino du Liban remained open, and profitable.

The hostilities brought a whole new series of challenges for Salameh, but opportunities too. More than just an influential aide of Arafat, he was by now a powerful actor in the shadowy world of intelligence. He was a warlord too, spending his days and nights barrelling down Beirut's streets in vehicles loaded with his fighters or making calls on phones and radios. This made his information networks and personal contacts more important than ever, as it was these that allowed him to keep his men and his leader safe. For Arafat there was still some overseas travel but far less of it: his priority was the war in Lebanon – to win it, or failing that to exploit it, and ultimately just to survive it.

As a consequence, Salameh's aim was often to stop violence rather than start it. His relations with the commanders of the Christian militia were good. The important ones were men in their mid-thirties like him, also from prominent families in their respective communities and with similar tastes. When one day noisy shelling made conversation with a visitor impossible, Salameh picked up a telephone, dialled a number from memory and was put through to Bashir Gemayel, who had effectively inherited command of the Phalange from his father. Minutes later the mortars fell silent. On another occasion, the two men toured the frontline together, making show of their mutual respect in front of invited photographers. When Arafat wanted to negotiate a truce, it was his young protégé whom he sent to meet the Gemayels.

Salameh had a similar rapport with Dany Chamoun, the former president's son who led a smaller but also brutal militia called the Tigers. When Chamoun was captured by PLO forces, Salameh arranged for his release and then called in the favour when one of Arafat's favourite Fatah commanders was besieged by Christian forces. When there were fears of a massacre after fighters from one of the Shia Muslim groups allied with the PLO seized the famous St George Hotel from the Tigers and promptly locked all the Christian staff in its laundry, it was Salameh who 'in the middle of answering tens of phone calls' scribbled a note that obtained their freedom. Dean Brelia, the *Time* correspondent in Beirut, described Salameh successfully arranging a brief ceasefire on the frontline 'without raising his voice'. The shooting stopped, allowing each side to retrieve their wounded, and then 'almost at once, there was gunfire again.' Annoyed, Salameh turned to the reporter. 'They are all mad,' he said.

Salameh, his credibility reinforced by his public liaison with Rizk, also reached out to senior Christian community leaders beyond warlords like the Gemayels and Chamoun, seeking to convince them that the Palestinians were no threat to the stability of Lebanon, that the PLO did not want to take over their country and that the ongoing violence was without cause or justification. He told local reporters that 'ignorance breeds enmity' and that it had been a mistake to treat the Maronite hardliners or their allies 'as the enemy camp'. Such efforts intensified once Syrian tanks and soldiers entered the fray in May 1976. Though the PLO and Jumblatt's LNM put up a stiff fight, they were no match for the powerfully equipped professional soldiers sent by Assad and were forced to give up most of their gains. By the autumn, everyone was exhausted. An agreement negotiated by Saudi Arabia and backed by other major Arab powers gave a veneer of legitimacy to the Syrians' invasion and brought a moment of respite. There was some slim hope that the worst had passed.

For Salameh the fragile calm allowed a shift in focus. He installed Rizk in an apartment closer to his own and began to think about a wedding. And in advance of their nuptials, the happy couple enjoyed a holiday in the USA, travelling to Disney World, Hawaii and Washington. The PLO paid for the transatlantic flights, but everything else, from the hotel bills to their false identities and 'tourist' visas, would be taken care of by the CIA.

Unsurprisingly, Salameh's visit was controversial. Since the United Nations debate in 1972, the US had made innumerable public statements condemning terrorist attacks and criticising dozens of other states for their support for those responsible. In 1975, Henry Kissinger had secretly pledged to the Israelis that the US would never have any direct contact with the PLO. And yet now they were hosting a man who did not deny his involvement in precisely the violence the US deemed terrorism and who was reviled by the Israelis as a murderer of their citizens. Indeed, many within the CIA remained convinced that Salameh was the perpetrator of the Munich massacre and likely to undertake further similar acts. The presence of such a man on US soil was a 'diplomatic outrage', some officials believed.

On the other hand, over the course of his close relationship with the CIA since the late 1960s, Salameh had repeatedly shown himself to be both effective and trustworthy. He was also one of the very few channels anyone in the US had to the Palestinian leadership. In a cable sent by the US Embassy in Beirut in the months prior to his visit, diplomatic staff described Salameh as a 'moderate' and expressed their satisfaction at Arafat's choice of him rather than a 'hardline' senior official to represent the PLO at a delicate meeting with a Syrian general.

In December 1976, George H. W. Bush issued a formal if highly secret invitation for Salameh to visit. As US ambassador to the United Nations, Bush had previously put America's case for a sweeping definition of terrorism. In his new role as director of the CIA, he had apparently been converted to a more pragmatic view. Kissinger objected strongly to Bush's decision but his influence was waning and Cyrus Vance, the incoming Secretary of State of the new administration of President-elect Jimmy Carter, overruled his soon-to-be predecessor's objections, and so Salameh's visit got the green light.

This was partly the result of lobbying within the CIA by Salameh's long-term contact Robert Ames. The two men had stayed in touch since their meetings in Beirut three years previously to discuss Arafat's renunciation of international violence, and after stints in Tehran and Kuwait Ames had been brought back to Washington where, despite some controversy within the agency about his methods, he was given the much coveted position of overseeing all the agency's covert operations across much of the Gulf and Arabian peninsula. Despite his new seniority and salary, Ames, now forty-two, still wore his cowboy boots and aviator sunglasses.

One reason for the CIA's positive view of Salameh was the assistance he had provided to the US Embassy in Beirut. The security of American diplomats in the city was increasingly precarious and Salameh had become their 'principal contact' in the city. When senior US diplomats or dignitaries flew in and needed to move around the city or visit other parts of Lebanon, the PLO advised on possible threats and often provided armed guards too. In April 1976, Salameh learned that Haddad's PFLP–XO was plotting to kill Dean Brown, the US envoy to Lebanon, and surrounded the diplomat with Fatah forces, making it impossible for fellow Palestinians to carry out the assassination. When the US ambassador was abducted and killed three months later, it was Fatah's intelligence service that found his remains and car. Shortly afterwards, fighters from Arafat's personal bodyguard, led by Salameh, oversaw the evacuation of hundreds of US diplomatic staff and their dependents from the city. As the US Embassy was in west Beirut, which was controlled by the PLO, it was Salameh who provided a very unofficial 'security cordon' to protect the limited staff thereafter. Talcott Seelye, another senior US diplomat sent as an emissary to Lebanon, reported that Salameh provided a steady stream of intelligence about 'the plans of militia groups hostile to the US' which allowed the embassy to 'take evasive action' when necessary. This included a well-developed plan to target Seelye himself.

President Carter's arrival in office in January 1977 helped too. Unlike his predecessors, Carter was convinced that no real peace would be possible in the Middle East without concessions to the Palestinians. He even hoped to convene a major conference in Geneva to come to a final settlement. Aware of the opportunity this presented, Arafat had launched his own frenetic and typically indiscriminate diplomatic effort to establish contact with Carter's officials. He had long been convinced that, useful though Soviet support might be, the only real actors who could influence Israel were the Americans. So even while Salameh's extramarital liaison with Rizk offended his own conservative sensitivities, the PLO chairman was very happy to see the couple flown around the US by the CIA.

Salameh and Rizk flew separately from Beirut under aliases, met in New York and then travelled to Washington where Ames was waiting to give his friend a guided tour of the CIA headquarters at Langley and introduce him to colleagues. In New Orleans, Salameh spent several hours in a hotel exchanging intelligence with US officials, further proving his worth. Salameh did not enjoy his day at Disney World but adored everything about Hawaii, especially eating oysters, which he considered an aphrodisiac. The only disappointment was that a request from Ames to give Salameh a gun as a memento of the trip was vetoed by superiors at the CIA.

The next time Ames saw Salameh was in Beirut a month or so later, when the American flew in for a three-month assignment. Salameh gave him an effusive welcome and some gold prayer beads, then hosted a belated birthday party for the new arrival. The men met regularly during Ames' stay, spending evenings talking over the region's politics. Sometimes Bassam Abu Sharif, spokesman for the PFLP, joined them, occasionally helping Salameh read the more wordy English-language documents that Ames sometimes gave his friend.

Ames was shocked by the state of Beirut, no longer the freewheeling Mediterranean city he had known but fearful, dark and full of Syrian troops. It was spring, the season of thunderstorms: 'Lebanon needs the rain to wash away the ... filth,' he wrote to his wife. One of Ames' many concerns was that the PLO might return to the violent tactics of the early 1970s if they won nothing from the round of diplomacy that was now underway – a worry shared by diplomats in Beirut. But for now, progress seemed entirely possible. For it was not just in the US that Arafat's favoured envoy was making friends and influencing people.

In late November 1977, some five months after his US visit and second marriage, Salameh sat down at a table in Vienna with senior officials from the governments of Austria and West Germany. Salameh was travelling on false documents, but his interlocutors knew exactly whom they were dealing with.

Since the first hijackings of the late 1960s, almost every western European power had sought to mitigate the threat of such attacks by establishing some kind of relationship, if not an outright accommodation, with their perpetrators. As early as 1969, British diplomats in Amman had assured representatives of Fatah that they would make sure police at Scotland Yard understood the difference between their organisation, which had not yet joined the PFLP's campaign of hijackings, and those behind the attacks that had been hitting the headlines over the previous year. The Swiss had concluded a tacit agreement with the PFLP following a spate of violence there in the late 1960s. Italian authorities had long tolerated fedayeen activities to avoid being targeted, and the French followed a similar strategy: ten months before Salameh's trip to Austria, Mohammed Daoud Odeh, the self-confessed tactical commander of the Munich attacks, had been arrested in Paris but then swiftly freed, prompting almost universal Western outrage.

Austria's moderate socialist chancellor Bruno Kreisky had long sought to keep Austria safe from terrorism by seeking compromise and dialogue with Arab powers, as well as more controversial actors. The presence of a representative of the West German government at the table in Vienna was surprising, though. There had been no contact between the West Germans and the Palestinians since March 1973, when the German ambassador in Beirut had met with one of the founders of Black September and spoken of creating 'a new basis of trust' between the PLO and the German government, while other officials had sent messages to Arafat asking what they could offer to secure the exemption of West Germany and its citizens from attacks. In November 1977, however, West Germany was only just emerging from the worst public security crisis since the Second World War and a new wave of RAF revenge attacks was expected any moment, so Bonn had been pleased to receive Kreisky's invitation to join the very secret meeting he had convened with the PLO in Vienna.

Salameh was accompanied by Dr Issam al-Sartawi, a veteran PLO official who advised Arafat on international relations. The two men made no attempt to evade the PLO's responsibility for previous attacks in western Europe. Al-Sartawi explained that the organisation had been 'in a kind of state of war with all other countries outside of the Arab world' and such violence had been 'a necessity'. Salameh said 'he fully acknowledged all the actions during the PLO's phase of war', including those that 'he contributed to'. But circumstances had changed, the two Palestinians said, and so had the PLO's thinking. In recent years, Salameh observed, the PLO 'has found broad recognition and [is] closer to the goal of establishing [a] state'. This meant that the organisation was now opposed to other groups with 'nihilistic views' which sought 'the destruction of any kind of order'. For the moment, the PLO believed that bombings and hijackings targeting the West were counterproductive, Salameh said, and so, if given the right incentives, could be a very useful partner in the 'fight against terrorism'.

Like all good negotiators, Salameh and al-Sartawi first lowered their potential partner's expectations. 'Ali Salami', as he was named in a West German report of the meeting, said that the PLO would never hand over to Western countries any wanted individuals who were in Lebanon, even 'German terrorists', who should really be 'regarded as misguided children'. In addition, he pointed out, the sheer variety of actors involved made it extremely difficult to promise an end to all attacks on a country or its interests. Not only did the PLO have only 'a limited influence' on Libya or Iraq, for example, but there were plenty of Palestinian groups, not to mention those in Germany, France, Japan and elsewhere, which would contest any effort by the organisation to rein in violence, Salameh argued.

Then Salameh changed tack, issuing a warning. The PLO security services had 'an intimate knowledge . . . of the European terrorist scene', he explained. They even knew the whereabouts of all those wanted in connection with the recent wave of attacks in West Germany. Bonn should not delay a decision too long, Salameh advised. After recent setbacks, Palestinian 'terrorist groups' everywhere would be seeking to fight back and 'a new operation could be possible following thorough preparations in approximately three months'. It could even involve the 'Terrorist International' he had heard was in the making.

Finally, Salameh and al-Sartawi laid out their demands. These were modest, they suggested, being nothing more than 'a certain degree of recognition' and political support for Arafat. Unsurprisingly, this raised eyebrows around the table. Could Austria, or anyone for that matter, publicly recognise the PLO?, Erwin Lanc, the Austrian interior minister, wondered aloud. There were significant domestic political consequences that would need to be considered, especially if elections were close, not to mention the obvious foreign policy implications.

Al-Sartawi sympathised. The politics were indeed sensitive, and for the PLO too. The organisation had made its name as the standard bearer of the Palestinian armed struggle and its transition from a military to a political strategy was highly controversial among its supporters. But 'extremists who supported terror' were waiting to take over the PLO if Arafat and his allies failed, and nobody wanted to see them in charge. After all, any successful attacks would almost certainly benefit right-wing parties in Austria, West Germany or wherever they took place, al-Sartawi pointed out. In short, it was in the interests of 'progressive European governments' to help Arafat as much as possible.

The officials did not disagree. Lanc was so impressed with Salameh that he spent much of the following four days visiting him at the spa hotel where he was staying in Baden. Their conversation focused on what the Palestinians might do to gain more recognition in the West, and the shape of a future Palestinian state. Salameh followed 'an absolutely non-religious, secular line' and was very interested in how a 'more or less archaic peasant, artisan and nomadic society' could be 'transformed into a European-style state'. Lanc tried to steer Salameh towards social democracy as a model. The two men got on so well that when Salameh left Baden at the end of the week to go skiing with Rizk in the Tyrolean resort of Ischgl, Lanc was sorry to have to refuse an invitation to join the couple on the slopes due to prior commitments. The encounter left the minister reflecting on how a person could change dramatically over the course of their life.

The PLO had not given up all violence, however, and in Vienna Salameh had been careful to make clear that its attacks on Israel's armed forces and in the occupied territories would continue. But the truth was that the organisation's definition of what constituted a legitimate target was blurred, partly by design, and varied between its constituent groups. In March 1978, a team of Fatah fighters set out to land by dinghy on a beach in Tel Aviv with the intention of storming a hotel and taking hostages. Rough seas forced them onto a beach thirty miles north of their planned landing site, where they shot dead a photographer, then hiked to a main road where they fired on and hijacked several vehicles before eventually seizing a bus full of passengers to take them to the city. Police stopped the vehicle with a roadblock. Thirty-seven Israelis were killed, all but two of them civilians, and more than twice as many were wounded in what was the bloodiest terrorist incident in the country's history.

In response Menachem Begin, who had taken power a year before, sent tens of thousands of troops into southern Lebanon. These sought to drive the PLO fighters there who had been firing artillery and Syrian-supplied rocket launchers into northern Israel out of effective range. The incursion was short-lived but the Israelis left behind a proxy militia dominated by local Christians to secure the frontier zone. A United Nations force was deployed too, adding a new actor into the chaos of a now shattered country.

The invasion of southern Lebanon – known as Operation Litani, after the river that marked the northernmost advance of Israeli forces – was only one part of Israel's effort to eliminate the danger posed by the Palestinian presence to the north. The Israelis were well aware of Salameh's expanding influence in Beirut and had been informed by Kreisky of the meeting in Vienna. The Mossad knew too of Salameh's trip to the US, and Begin had by now been informed that the man his people blamed for the Munich massacre was the PLO's contact with the CIA. The Mossad's own sources within Fatah would almost certainly have kept them informed of Salameh's assistance to the US in Lebanon and its diplomats in Beirut. The Israelis may even have been aware that Salameh was due to return to the US for further meetings in early 1979. And the greater his proximity to and influence on the US, the more his value as a target increased.

Through the summer of 1978, the Mossad intensified their surveillance of Salameh. The service had hoped to obtain detailed information on Salameh's daily routines and location from Bashir Gemayel, but having initially agreed to help them the Maronite warlord clearly decided that his Palestinian counterpart's survival would be more beneficial than his demise and failed to do so. Instead, dozens of Mossad agents were infiltrated into the Lebanese capital.

With the pause in hostilities looking increasingly permanent, life in the battered city was slowly returning. Many shops, restaurants and hotels had reopened. On the Corniche, some wealthy Lebanese tried the new craze for jogging, recently imported from the US. Others went to gyms, a less novel pastime. Among them was Salameh, who enjoyed a daily workout at the International Hotel and drove there every day at the same time from the apartment near the rue Verdun in which he had installed Rizk. An Israeli operative struck up a conversation with Salameh in the hotel changing rooms and ended up playing squash with him. Other agents reconnoitred Salameh's office, his home and the apartment where his other wife lived with his children. Like the hotel, all were heavily guarded.

Salameh knew he was a target of the Israelis but had become lazy. He told one reporter that when his 'number was up, it will be up' and failed to vary his daily routine, an elemental security precaution. The Israelis were not 'supermen', he told friends. After all, had he not already escaped raids, attempted shootings, ambushes and letter bombs?, he asked them; but he ordered steel shutters for the windows of his apartment nonetheless.

In November 1978, a twenty-nine-year-old British woman arrived in Beirut and sought volunteer work at an NGO for Palestinian refugees called 'The House of Steadfastness of the children of Telesata'. Her name – at least according to her passport – was Erika Chambers. She spoke 'refined but energetically democratic English' and moved into a cheap eighth-floor apartment where she kept lots of cats. A keen amateur painter, Chambers spent much of her time before her easel, looking out over the rooftops of Beirut from her apartment's small terrace. The view was undoubtedly a good one: down onto the narrow rue Beqa'a, up across the city to the mountains beyond. She showed her work to some neighbours who expressed polite and insincere admiration.

A week later an utterly unremarkable British consultant – 'Gray suit. Gray hat. Glasses. One small suitcase', according to a witness – checked into the Méditerranée Hotel and rented a similarly coloured Simca car. Shortly afterwards, a Canadian businessman working in the catering trade took a room in the nearby Royal Garden Hotel and started handing leaflets advertising cutlery to local shopkeepers. He too rented a car, a Volkswagen. On 19 January, these two men met a third who had just arrived from Syria, carrying 100 kg of plastic explosives that he had been given by a team of Israeli special forces at a rendezvous in the desert just north of the Jordanian port of Aqaba a day or so earlier. With a detonator attached, these were placed into the Volkswagen which was then parked on Beqa'a street below Chambers' apartment.

Salameh had received several warnings that danger was closer than usual. In the summer of 1978, the Mossad had informally asked the CIA what kind of relationship the agency had with their target. There was no easy answer as Salameh was not considered an 'asset', having repeatedly rejected efforts to formally recruit him, and so had remained 'a liaison contact'. But this status offered only minimal protection to the Palestinian, who was now seen as a valuable resource for the agency. The obvious explanation for the Israelis' sudden curiosity was that they were about to kill Salameh, so the question posed by the Mossad prompted a heated debate within the CIA. Not everyone was keen to protect Salameh. Some senior staff still believed that even the current informal relationship with 'a wanted terrorist' was inappropriate. Others were concerned that instead of 'digging out secrets about Fatah's role in terrorism', the CIA were being used by Salameh as a conduit for the PLO to talk to policy-makers in Washington. Many were very critical of how Ames had handled Salameh, asking 'quite who had recruited whom'. A substantial number of senior officials felt that Salameh could be very dangerous if Fatah went back to conducting 'international terrorist exploits' in the future. The discussions dragged on for some days and the Israeli enquiry was eventually left unanswered.

Ames was not a party to these arguments but he heard about the Israeli approach. He had never had any direct contact with Israeli security services himself and so had no back channels through which to pass them a message. Instead, he sought to convince Salameh to allow the CIA to tell the Mossad that his friend was indeed their agent, even if this was untrue. This would make the Israelis think twice about any assassination, he believed, probably with some justification. But this elegant if mendacious solution did not appeal to Salameh. His refusal was motivated by both principle and pragmatism, as any such statement, even if untrue, would almost certainly leave him open to compromising blackmail or simply be leaked by the Israelis or other enemies with devastating effect on his reputation. Salameh preferred to take his chances.

On the afternoon of 22 January, at around three o'clock, Salameh said goodbye to Rizk and set out for his mother's home to celebrate the birthday of his three-year-old niece. His dented Chevrolet estate passed the parked Volkswagen at 3.35 p.m. After extensive tests, the Mossad had discovered that women were better than men at detonating bombs directed at moving targets. Chambers, watching from her balcony, did not disappoint. The Volkswagen exploded with terrific noise, hurling metal across the road, shattering windows for blocks around, killing four passers-by and injuring another eighteen. 'It was like Hell. It was incredible. I'd never seen anything like it, not even in Beirut. It was as if the whole of the city was on fire. So many people dead, burnt cars and young bodies littering the street,' a witness later told the BBC.

Salameh was dragged from the vehicle by his surviving bodyguards, loaded into a passing taxi and driven to hospital where he soon died of his many and severe injuries. His funeral in west Beirut's Martyrs' Cemetery was attended by as many as 100,000 mourners. 'We have lost a lion,' said Arafat as he delivered a graveside eulogy.

The killing of Salameh went largely unnoticed outside of Lebanon and the small circles in Israel and the US that took a specific interest in his career. In the West and across much of the Arab world, violence in Lebanon had become one more news item relegated to the category of 'more fighting in faraway country'. Besides, the dead man had lived his professional life well out of public view, so even those who did pay close attention to the civil war or the Palestinian cause were unlikely to know quite how significant an actor he had been in both. The implications of the assassination of Kamal Jumblatt, the leader of the Lebanese left-wing forces killed by the Syrians months earlier, were much clearer and so received much more attention.

But Salameh's death was far from inconsequential and signalled a profound change that would become evident with hindsight. The 'Red Prince' had been committed to violence and, at least in theory, the eventual destruction of the state of Israel. But he had also proved himself an increasingly mature political actor who was willing to compromise. An irreligious nationalist, Salameh was a tough opponent and negotiating partner but harboured no hatred for the citizens of Western countries, nor their leaders, nor their way of life. In fact, he repeatedly demonstrated an affection or even admiration for them. The terrorist attacks to which he had been definitively linked had caused few casualties. In almost every way, he was a far less intractable and lethal enemy than those whom Israel, the US and western European democracies would face in the Middle East in the coming years. These would display limited interest in seducing beauty queens, skiing in the Tyrol, snorkelling off Hawaii, discussing social democracy with Austrian ministers or sharing intelligence to prevent terrorist attacks in return for political recognition.

Another reason for the limited attention paid to Salameh's death was that this particular moment in the story of the Palestinian nationalist struggle was very swiftly overshadowed by seismic events elsewhere in the region – events that heralded a transformation of radical activism of immense consequence for the coming decade: a revolution, in fact.

VIII

25
The Red and the Black

At around 9 a.m. on 1 February 1979, forty minutes after his plane had landed at Tehran's international airport, Ayatollah Ruhollah Musavi Khomeini emerged from the cabin door into the low, chill sunlight. Supported by a dapper Air France steward, the elderly religious scholar made his way slowly down the steep steps to the tarmac, followed by his aides. The military policemen in light blue uniforms who stood to attention were barely able to hold back the crowd of clerics who had gathered on the tarmac to welcome, and who now threatened to crush, their frail seventy-five-year-old leader.

Khomeini was led into the terminal, where he gave a short speech denouncing colonialism, imperialism and Iran's ruler, the shah, and then set out in a convoy across the chaos of the Iranian capital. The tens of thousands of 'Islamic Police', arranged by his supporters to keep order, were soon overwhelmed. Khomeini's vehicle was separated from the bus that was supposed to forge a path for them through the surging crowds, and then broke down. To extract their leader from the crush, the crowd lifted and pushed the car and its passengers to a military helicopter 500 yards away.

Flying low over the rooftops of the city above the choked streets, the helicopter carried Khomeini to the Behesht-e Zahra cemetery situated amid the shanty towns and squatter camps of Tehran's southern outskirts. There, among the graves of victims of the unrest and repression of the previous years, Khomeini addressed a vast gathering.

Fourteen years earlier, when he had been sent into exile, Khomeini had been a controversial dissident cleric with a small but fervent following. Now he was returning as the leader of what was very obviously a revolution. 'This is only the first stage,' he told them.

In Tehran on the day of Khomeini's return as many as ten million people crowded the streets, some observers claimed, their estimates wildly inflated by wonder, excitement, fear and hope. Journalist Ryszard Kapuściński, covering events for the Polish state press agency, wrote: 'Everyone opposed the Shah and wanted to remove him. But everyone imagined the future differently.' For the vast proportion of them, this did not matter. Indeed, it may have been what was so attractive about the idea of revolution in the first place. Nothing was decided, everything was possible. Many had spent the night on the pavements. What were a few more hours after years of waiting? The shah was gone and whatever came next would be better.

Some framed the return of Khomeini in religious terms, quoting the fourteenth-century Persian poet Hafez: 'When the demon goes, the angel takes his place', or holding newspapers announcing 'Imam Amad', the imam has come, suggesting that the returning dissident was not just the leader of the nation, nor even of the world's Shia Muslims, but a messianic figure, chosen by God to lead believers into a new age of social justice and peace. Leftists saw a replay of the return of Lenin to St Petersburg in 1917 and felt sure that the ineluctable dialectics of history would soon consign the clergy to obscurity and so allow a true socialist state to be established. The many liberals and secular nationalists who had campaigned for years against the shah's regime hoped for a new constitutional and democratic order which would bring economic, social and political progress and make their country a great power. Some believed Khomeini would rule as a supreme and omnipotent leader. Others were convinced that he would retire from active politics, guiding the nation on spiritual matters alone. The US ambassador thought Khomeini would play a role similar to that of Mahatma Gandhi after India had gained its independence from the British almost exactly forty years earlier. He would be disappointed – as would almost everyone else.

The regime that had fallen had been seen as one of the most stable and powerful in the Middle East, a pillar of US foreign policy and a key Cold War ally, with a vast military and an infamous security service funded by massive oil revenues. Perhaps only a quarter or a third at most of Iranians had actively taken part in the upheaval, but there were few who did not celebrate the departure of the shah when he fled the country two weeks before Khomeini's return. The joy and optimism at that moment were authentic, and the idea that this elderly cleric and his close supporters would, within a relatively short span of time, be able to impose their extremist vision on a diverse and divided country of thirty-four million people seemed very far-fetched.

Yet this is what happened, and the consequence was that within months of the events in Iran of 1978 and 1979 a new and different energy surged through the Middle East. This broke old alliances and created new ones, dealt a swingeing defeat, both physical and ideological, to both superpowers, caused a war that killed at least half a million people and presented Israel with an unexpected and dangerous enemy. Perhaps most significantly, it accelerated and intensified the growing religious extremism across the Islamic world while simultaneously marginalising leftist forms of political activism that no longer appeared relevant to hundreds of millions of Muslims.

None of this was the work of one man, of course, but it did owe a very considerable amount to the ideas, pragmatism and persistence of Khomeini.

Born in 1902 amid the turmoil and insecurity of the last years of the rule of the impoverished Qajar dynasty, Khomeini was the son of a prosperous landowner and cleric in the small farming town of Khomein, 220 miles south of Tehran. When he was still an infant, his father was killed in a roadside ambush by brigands or rivals or both. Not long afterwards, male members of the household took rifles to the high towers of the family's compound to see off aggressors. Khomeini's mother died of disease when he was in his late teens.

From a young age, Khomeini showed a combination of outstanding intelligence, implacable determination and a willingness to stand outside the mainstream. An interest in traditional wrestling did not outlive his youth, but an attraction to the esoteric field of mystical Islamic enquiry and an affection for poetry did. He was initially schooled by relatives and family friends, then in seminaries where he had little difficulty completing the rigorous courses of logic, law and Islamic philosophy required to qualify as a *mujtahid*, a Shia Muslim scholar able to give a legal opinion, or *fatwa*. Tall, handsome and impressive, he was rarely seen dressed in anything but the long robes of a religious scholar and the black turban that signified his family's descent from the Prophet Mohammed. His personal life was irreproachable, appearance neat, habits ascetic. His teenage wife came from an impeccable, wealthy, devout Tehran family. In private he was warm and considerate, people close to him said. In public, he showed little or no emotion.

As a young cleric in the 1930s, Khomeini remained committed to the well-established tradition among Shia clerics of avoiding any direct involvement in politics. This was supposed to be a central principle of their minority branch of Islam. In reality, such quietism was never absolute. Having taken power in 1925, Reza Shah Pahlavi, a former commander of the Qajar king's elite Cossack brigade, had attempted to modernise and transform the lives of his largely poor and devout subjects in imitation of his Turkish near-contemporary, Kemal Atatürk, officially renaming the country 'Iran' and imposing new dress and secular legal codes. Senior Iranian clerics had spoken out against the changes, which appeared to threaten their status, privileges and traditions.

Khomeini was not among these dissident clerics, however, instead spending much of the next twenty years dedicated to his growing family and to the demanding stages of higher study at the shrine city of Qom, a burgeoning religious centre seventy-five miles outside Tehran, renowned for the intellectual brilliance of its scholars. But while he eschewed any overt political activities, he did follow current affairs closely. These were years of extreme turmoil, even by the standards of the new nation of Iran. In 1945, four years after Reza Shah Pahlavi had been ousted by the Allies, who suspected him of pro-Nazi sympathies, and replaced with his twenty-one-year-old son, Mohammad Reza Pahlavi, Khomeini made his first intervention in the world of politics. It took the slightly surprising form of an anonymous book aimed at secular, or at least non-clerical, readers. The work gathered together many conservative and nationalist complaints of the time: the misrule of the exiled former shah, the rise of anti-clerical sentiment, the spread of dance halls and wine shops, unsegregated education, contemporary medicine and even international time zones. Khomeini also took aim at modernisers who 'in ... European hats, stroll the boulevards, ogling the underdressed girls', enjoying themselves without a second thought for 'foreigners [who] were carting off the country's patrimony and resources'.

The link between moral decadence, 'Westernisation' and complicity in the exploitation of Iran by overseas powers or businesses would mark Khomeini's words and thinking until his death. So too would the connection between the restoration of Iran's fortunes as a national community and the protection of its authentic traditions and Islamic faith. Both would prove crucial in his popular appeal as the revolution neared.

But not just yet. After this sudden, intemperate outburst, Khomeini returned to teaching and silence. His next publication was a rather different type of text: 'a rigorous ... specific codification' of 'the way [a Muslim should] behave in every conceivable circumstance'. The work was mostly based on the many *fatawa* he had issued in response to questions from the faithful over the years. Well received by his peers, the work suggested that its author was content to follow the example of the most pre-eminent clerics in Iran who maintained that the best defence against the challenges of everyday life in a fast-changing country led by a strong-willed, autocratic leader was a redoubled effort to ensure the observation of the minutest detail of Islamic law, not confrontation with secular authority.

In the 1960s, however, this changed. By now Mohammad Reza was impatient for change. He had an ambitious vision of a modern, prosperous and powerful nation that would live up to its gloriously rich cultural and historical heritage – and believed that the moment was right to push ahead with far-reaching reforms. The privileges of absentee landowners which kept millions of peasants in share-cropping misery would be curtailed, massive swathes of land redistributed, key resources nationalised, the largely illiterate population taught to read and write, women allowed to vote, and much else. This new Iran would be an independent power in its own right, no longer forced to give way to the dictates of rapacious Westerners, and would, of course, submit to the shah's autocratic rule. Democracy, if it came at all, could come later. He called his programme the 'White Revolution', in deliberate contrast to those of other colours – the 'Red' of the leftists, the 'Black' of the clerics – that he saw as dangerous rivals to his own. 'If there is to be a revolution in this country, I will lead it,' the shah informed his subjects. 'Revolutions to advance the poor and underprivileged [are] not the exclusive field of Marxist or socialist-minded young colonels but [can] come from kings too.' In the Middle East of the 1960s, this was rousing and original rhetoric.

Unsurprisingly, many in Iran saw the shah's initiative very differently. Among them was Khomeini, who decided that it was impossible to remain silent in the face of such an assault on the interests of the clergy and what he saw as the most elemental values of the nation. For the cleric, this was yet another effort 'to rid Iran of Islam'. Had not the shah described his opponents among Iran's religious establishment as 'a stupid and reactionary bunch whose brains have not moved ... for a thousand years' during an impromptu tirade against 'Black reaction' at a ceremony in a village? Khomeini's call to defend Iran's religion and traditions masked more worldly concerns: many clerics, directly or through their religious foundations, were major landowners, and their influence as well as personal comfort depended to a considerable extent on the revenue their property brought in.

This time Khomeini did not restrict himself to an angry tirade in a book that few would read. Now a senior and respected cleric accorded the honorific of Ayatollah, Khomeini had other means of protest at his disposal. In June 1963, he delivered an incendiary sermon before loyal congregants in Qom in which he denounced alleged foreign domination of Iran, the foreign goods that were flooding its markets and shops, the foreign values that were corrupting the country's young people. If some of this was a reprise of his earlier material, the personal attack on the monarch was new. Khomeini denounced the shah's lack of respect for the Islamic faith, disdain for its scholars, obedience to the US, support for Israel and contempt for the Muslim world's grievances. Iran's ruler was a 'miserable wretch' who 'should listen to the clergy of Islam, not Israel', a willing accomplice of an 'Imperialist-Jewish conspiracy', whose 'inhuman acts' would divert the Iranian people from 'the great aim of Islam'. This aim, Khomeini maintained, introducing a new and provocatively activist dimension to his argument, was 'to prevent oppression, arbitrary rule, and the violation of the law . . . and to establish social justice'.

There was only one possible outcome of such a public outburst, as Khomeini must have known. Though an ayatollah, he was far from untouchable. There were dozens of other clerics of similar rank, and several more senior. Most saw him as a maverick and remained true to the broadly quietist Shia tradition. This left Khomeini exposed and within days of his sermon in Qom, he had been arrested.

What happened next was in part a consequence of the shah's failure to allow space for political dissent or criticism of his policies. Khomeini had tapped into a deep well-spring of discontent, whose existence had never previously been acknowledged, at least not in such explicit terms, by the religious establishment. Now that it had, religious students across Iran took to the streets to protest at Khomeini's arrest, often violently. Others joined them and in Tehran, huge crowds shouting 'Death or Khomeini' attacked police stations and ministries. Dozens, possibly hundreds, were shot dead by troops deployed to restore order.

Khomeini was held in relatively comfortable conditions until tempers had cooled, which took the best part of a year. Within months of his release in 1964, Khomeini made clear that detention had changed neither his views nor his determination to defend what he saw as essential to the lives of Iranians, delivering a series of new incendiary statements. This time he attacked the granting of immunity from law to members of the small army of US advisers, soldiers and diplomats sent to Iran as part of Washington's effort to bolster its key Cold War ally through economic and military development. All over the world 'colonial territories are bravely freeing the bonds that have chained them', but Iran was travelling in the opposite direction, bowing before a US president who took the Koran as his enemy, Khomeini told his followers. Once again, his rhetoric cleverly framed the challenges facing Iranians in nationalist as well as religious terms, ensuring it resonated with an audience well beyond the devout. He was now the de facto leader of the opposition to the shah, or at least its most prominent active figure.

This time Khomeini was not just detained but expelled. Some counsellors of the shah advocated a more extreme punishment – execution – but were overruled. Instead the scholar was loaded onto a military cargo plane and dispatched first to Turkey, where he stayed for several months as the house guest of an army officer, and then, in October 1965, to Najaf in Iraq.

In exile in Najaf, Khomeini lived in a house not far from the city's most important shrine: the tomb of Imam Ali. He was attended by his family and a small group of followers. His daily routine of study, teaching and writing was unvarying. When wealthy Iranian admirers offered to buy air conditioners that might mitigate the atrocious summer heat of the central Iraqi plains or pay for a car, he refused. Efforts by well-wishers to replace his battered furniture or repaint peeling walls met with similar disdain. Every night he walked the same route to the shrine of Ali to say his prayers and supplications.

Khomeini had not been well received by the renowned cleric-scholars of Najaf, many of whom enjoyed far greater prestige than he did. They had their own problems, and were concerned that the outspoken newcomer's political activism might cause them trouble with the Ba'ath party regime. This animosity was mutual and durable, so Khomeini kept to himself. He was sixty-three when he arrived in Iraq and in good health. Any return to his homeland seemed unlikely.

But if the shah and his ministers had believed they could isolate Khomeini by dispatching him to Iraq, they were wrong. Just as the 'Red' revolutionaries in Iran were connected to a broader international movement, so too were their 'Black' counterparts. Najaf was not just a historical centre of Shia scholarship and publishing but also the hub of a vast web of religious and cultural networks that spread throughout the region and beyond. When Khomeini's sons laboriously copied out his statements longhand, as they had done in Qom, it was not difficult to find someone among the thousands of students and scholars who passed through Najaf to carry them into Iran. Once there, they were copied with carbon paper and distributed further. Clerics could then relay Khomeini's views to their students and to worshippers in Iran's thousands of mosques and religious centres.

Thus the word was spread, but so too was the image. Khomeini was the beneficiary of a particular tradition within Shia Islam that enjoins believers to choose a senior scholar as their personal guide, known as a *marja-e taqlid*, or 'source of emulation'. The *maraji* numbered no more than a dozen at most, and, theoretically at least, were of such impeccable learning and character that each was obeyed not just by a huge number of followers but by more junior religious scholars too. Khomeini's authority owed more to his dissidence than his intellectual achievements, and not everyone agreed that he deserved such exalted status, particularly the followers of far more senior and moderate clerics such as Iran's Grand Ayatollah Kazem Shariatmadari, but no one doubted Khomeini's personal probity and even Shariatmadari's supporters saw Khomeini's word as law.

Exile helped. In Najaf, Khomeini was at a remove from the ferment of Iranian religious politics with its various rivalries and manoeuvres. The simple fact that he had been sent away by a secular ruler after raising his voice against apparent injustice resonated with powerful religious narratives known to every Shia Muslim from childhood. And while the opinion of other scholars was paramount to one's status in the informal hierarchy of the Shia clergy, popular opinion was important too. One traditional function of the Shia clergy was to articulate the feelings and opinions of the congregation. To some, Khomeini appeared to be doing this much better than many of his peers. Other more practical considerations counted too, such as a cleric's ability to access material resources. A marja's followers traditionally paid *khoms*, a religious tax that went directly into the marja's personal treasury. These often substantial funds not only gave Iranian clerics a degree of autonomy from the secular authorities but allowed for personal largesse which in turn brought new followers, initiating a lucrative cycle. The poor gave very small sums, though these were often a significant proportion of their income. Others gave much more. Merchants concerned to protect the practices of the traditional bazaar from the modernised capitalist system that the shah wanted to introduce often sent Khomeini very large amounts of money, for example. One estimate by US intelligence agencies described donations of $285,000 in just a few days as 'normal'. Members of the large Shia communities in Lebanon, Pakistan, Afghanistan, Yemen and the Gulf contributed too. For Khomeini, these funds were important in overcoming the practical challenges of exile, allowing the continued expansion of his networks of supporters within Iran.

The distance offered by exile allowed Khomeini to hone his ideas and strategies too. In 1971 he had given a series of lectures in which he outlined his idea of the Velayat al-Faqih or the 'stewardship of the jurisprudent': a regime in which clerics abandoned their traditional role as counsellors to secular rulers and exercised power themselves, on the basis that, until the return of the one true and infallible imam, only the most just and knowledgeable men were worthy of obedience, for only they could understand God's will on earth. This turned a traditional concept of the social responsibility of Shia clerics into an innovative and revolutionary political doctrine, shattering the heritage of centuries of quietism. A small book of Khomeini's new teachings was soon published. Largely incomprehensible to most Iranians, it circulated widely among clerics opposed to the shah's rule but appeared unlikely to mobilise much broader support.

Through the early and mid-1970s Khomeini honed the rhetoric and messaging, emphasising a much more socially radical message. Some of Khomeini's language now suggested the influence of the leftist ideologies that had made such a mark on the Middle East over previous decades – despite his own visceral contempt for their adherents. Having never previously admitted the existence of *tabaqeh* or 'class' as an analytic category, Khomeini begun using the concept in his speeches. Terms common to Marxists and pan-Arabists such as *enqelab,* revolution, and *jumhori*, republic, crept in too, as well as a series of familiar binary divisions. The poor were battling against the rich; the inhabitants of the slums against inhabitants of the palaces; the needy against the aristocrats. These oppositions mapped easily onto religious ones – belief against unbelief, virtue against vice, good against evil – and so contemporary social and economic grievances were explained through eternal truths, giving them immense appeal in a relatively devout country such as Iran. The same was true when Khomeini spoke against Iran's

Baha'i minority, claiming they used the shah's protection to exploit the Muslim majority, or the 'shrewd and energetic' Jews who were the real power behind imperialism, which they exploited in their bid to establish a 'world Jewish government', or the US, which was dubbed the Great Satan, *shaytan-e bozorg*: all attacks that could be understood through a religious paradigm or an economic one.

Even as late as 1977, neither Khomeini's steadily growing resources nor his new populist rhetoric seemed to matter very much. Though there was opposition to the shah, there was also considerable support for his rule. The White Revolution and the reforms that followed had undoubtedly made life much better for many tens of millions of Iranians. Factory workers' salaries had doubled or even trebled, thousands of schools had opened, housing projects provided cheap homes. There were free clinics, child welfare centres and libraries. Television bulletins showed the opening of an endless-seeming succession of dams, smelting plants, factories, power stations, roads and ports. The universities now offered 150,000 places, seven times as many as a decade before. The improvement of the lives of Iran's women, many of whom now enjoyed opportunities and freedoms denied for decades, was particularly marked. When the Shah and his glamorous queen went on tours to the provinces, to sophisticated Isfahan or to pious but moderate Mashhad, they were often feted. Overseas observers, including those in Washington, remained convinced that Iran was 'an island of stability' in a very troubled region. This meant that when its progress began to stutter, few outside the country initially noticed.

The immediate cause was economic. Iran's modernisation programme had been funded by the extraordinary sums earned from the sale of its oil. The shah was one of the greatest beneficiaries of the 1973 crisis. Amid soaring prices Iran's oil exports earned a spectacular $17.8 billion in 1975, three-quarters of all government revenue. But much of this immense sum was spent immediately and inevitably led to runaway inflation. Unfortunately for the shah, the sudden introduction of austerity measures intended to curb rising prices coincided with a fall in the value of oil as Western economies went into recession. Government revenues and subsidies reduced just as unemployment rose sharply. The construction industry ground to a halt and the wages of labourers plunged. Demand kept prices for basic foodstuffs and accommodation high. The economic machine built by the shah had been kept upright for the past fifteen years by the sheer momentum of its eye-watering growth. As this waned, its fundamental instability became obvious.

Many Iranians had tolerated their leaders' corruption and profligacy as a price worth paying for the improvement in their lives. Suddenly, as in Egypt at roughly the same time, the antics of the elite, with their St Moritz holidays, parties in five-star hotels, luxury cars, contemporary art collections and gaudy new mansions, were no longer seen as a distasteful but inevitable part of a 'modernising' process from which everyone would benefit, but as part of a broader assault on the supposedly authentic culture of Iran and thus incompatible with the interests and identity of the vast majority of its inhabitants. Suddenly, the presence of so many Western businesses and technicians seemed intolerable. And almost as quickly, the hundreds of statements Khomeini had been issuing from Najaf began to attract considerably more interest. No longer a familiar list of conservative complaints with limited relevance in a forward-looking Iran, they now offered potential solutions to very real and urgent problems facing millions of households across the country.

Through the early autumn of 1977, a growing number of clerics in Iran spoke out against the government in sermons and at increasingly frequent protests. The regime expected and for the most part tolerated the criticism, not considering it a significant threat. What was of much more concern were the calls for Khomeini to be allowed to return from exile. Few had mentioned the exiled cleric in public for many years. Now, the congregation of the largest mosque in Tehran offered prayers for 'our one and only leader, the defender of the faith and the great combatant of Islam, the grand Ayatollah Khomeini'.

The shah had never been very easy to like and did not get any more amiable as he aged. Mohammed Reza Pahlavi had taken power as a young man, a month shy of his twenty-second birthday, succeeding an overbearing, demanding father who had little time for his son's dreamier side. His expensive education had not prepared him for the complex tasks that faced him as monarch. In 1953, aged thirty-three, he had briefly fled the country, fearing for his safety amid a British- and US-backed coup that he had been persuaded to help mount against his own prime minister, Mohammed Mossadegh, who had sought to nationalise Iran's oil industry and who threatened his power. This brief experience left deep scars, compounding the insecurity of a man already lacking self-confidence. The shah's few genuine enthusiasms – military hardware, flying, adulterous sex with much younger women – were not endearing and his undeniable physical courage – proven in several assassination attempts – did little to offset his lack of charisma. Ascetic, autocratic and awkward in public, the shah inspired awe in some, sympathy in a few and affection in only a handful of close relatives and retainers. His well-meaning queen busied herself with good works and cultural patronage but could do little to address fundamental problems in the kingdom, and his continual failure to limit the ostentatious corruption and decadence of his relatives undermined any moral authority his crown might have conferred. The shah's smile, one journalist noted, was 'regal . . . brief and bleak'.

Among the few things the shah shared with his subjects was a deeply conspiratorial worldview. This was another consequence of the traumatic early years of his rule but was compounded by the opacity and violence of the Cold War during the 1970s, as well as the tendency of his own intelligence service, the SAVAK, to avoid telling him unpleasant truths. Mohammed Reza Pahlavi was convinced the USSR or its proxies were behind much of the opposition to his rule, both religious and secular, and believed that what the Soviets did not foment, Western imperialists did. He fought such subterfuge with equally underhand tactics, one of which was to smear his perceived enemies by placing scurrilous articles in newspapers.

On 7 January 1978 in a conservative newspaper called *Ettela'at*, alongside reports on a particularly virulent strain of influenza, a government plan to send students into factories, the activity of the Maoist Khmer Rouge in Cambodia and a piece entitled 'Turin, the Italian city that terrorists are destroying', there appeared an article about Khomeini. Headlined 'Iran and Red and Black Imperialism', the article described Khomeini as an ambitious opportunist 'without faith', a poet rather than a scholar, of non-Iranian origin, and paid by the British secret services to oppose the shah. It also suggested he might be homosexual.

Many readers ignored the article, which had been placed by the shah personally through his minsters. Others may have believed what they read. In Qom, however, there was outrage. To insult a marja and an ayatollah was to insult the clergy as a whole. Hundreds of students poured into the streets, attacking symbols of the regime and the modernisation it had sought to impose: banks, government offices, girls' schools, non-religious bookshops and the only two restaurants in Qom where men and women could dine in the same venue, if not actually at the same table. Security forces used live ammunition to restore order, and six students were killed. In Tehran, there was further unrest.

The protests might have died away but for a particular tradition carefully observed in Iran which offered an outstanding political opportunity to the more radical clerics, many loyal to Khomeini, who sought the end of the shah's rule. The Shia, like other Muslims, bury their dead as soon as is practicably possible but then observe a lengthy period of mourning before a final commemoration. 'On the fortieth day, family, friends, and acquaintances gather in the home of the deceased. Neighbours collect around the house – the whole street, the whole village, a crowd of people,' Kapuściński, the Polish reporter, wrote. 'If the death was natural, congruent with the usual human lot, this gathering consists of some hours of ecstatic, pathetic discharge, followed by a mood of dulled and humble resignation.' But 'if the death was a violent one, inflicted by somebody' then 'a thirst for revenge seizes the people [and] in an atmosphere of unfettered wrath and aggravated hatred, they pronounce the name of the killer, the author of their sorrow, and it is believed that, even if he is far away, he will shudder at that moment [for] his days are numbered.'

Exactly forty days after the deaths in Qom, there was a new wave of violence in Iran as thousands took once more to the streets. This time, the worst outbreak was in the north-western city of Tabriz. Once again, symbols of the government, as well as of 'decadent Westernisation', were attacked. More protesters were killed. From Najaf, Khomeini praised 'courageous and God-fearing' people for 'giving the [regime] a smash in the face' and called on all Iranians to 'expunge every trace of this anti-Islamic regime'. Once again a new forty-day period began, ending predictably in further protests and deaths. Only after six months was the cycle broken and a fragile calm returned.

Bombings, assaults and arson attacks, most the work of Khomeini's followers, continued but many Iranians had heeded a call for moderation from Grand Ayatollah Kazem Shariatmadari, still the most senior cleric in the country and the most popular. The anger of others had been assuaged by the shah's well-publicised pilgrimage to Mashhad, an announcement of further liberal reforms, the release of more political prisoners and the removal of the head of the SAVAK. The holy month of Ramadan began at the beginning of August, bringing daily fasts at the time of the year when nights are shortest and temperatures highest. Iran sweltered uneasily. Whether the growing discontent of many Iranians would evolve into a genuine uprising, or whether the shah, with his intelligence services, vast army, wealth and international support, would successfully quell or repress it was unclear. Then came the most lethal act of terrorism of the decade, indeed in many decades, anywhere in the world.

26

In the Name of the Oppressed

The city of Abadan, on Iran's border with Iraq just thirty miles from the Persian Gulf, was meant to be a model of what the shah's rule might offer a loyal citizen. A centre of the oil industry, surrounded by vastly expanded refineries, its 300,000 inhabitants were supposed to enjoy a prosperous and hygienic life among new parks and housing developments, with an international airport allowing visits from foreign music stars. Instead, Abadan was an example of how much had gone wrong with the headlong drive for modernisation. For weeks over the summer of 1978, power shortages had shut down water supplies in the city, and halted basic services. One of the few places to seek a respite from the heat, pollution and struggle to make a living was the cinema.

So the Rex theatre in the centre of Abadan was crowded on the evening of 28 August 1978. Its front rows were thick with rowdy young men in fashionable jackets and unbuttoned white shirts. At the back were women with their families or, much more rarely, fiancés. In all, more than 650 people had paid to watch a controversial film, very different to the escapist entertainment usually served up by Iran's booming film industry or the ageing Hollywood productions that were typically shown on its provincial cinema screens.

The Deer was a work of gritty realism that told a grim but entirely convincing story of contemporary Iran. Its hero was a fugitive bank robber who seeks refuge with a childhood friend, now a heroin addict, in a tiny room in a working-class neighbourhood of a major city. Despite their efforts, neither is able to help the other, and in its final tragic scenes, both are killed by police. Beyond the sheer subversive potential of such a work, the authorities feared that the exploits and violent death of its main protagonist might evoke those of the late Hamid Ashraf, one of Iran's most famous leftist militants and its answer to

Che Guevara. It had taken a year for the film's makers to get permission to distribute it.

About forty minutes after the film's start, there were shouts of alarm: a fire had broken out. Unsurprisingly in a city that was one of the biggest centres of the petrochemical industry in the world, much of the cinema's internal decor consisted of cheap and highly combustible plastics. Panicking staff failed to use an entirely inadequate pair of fire extinguishers. Emergency exits that would have allowed escape were blocked or locked or possibly opened inwards, which the crush of terrified men, women and children rapidly made impossible. When the fire brigade arrived, hydrants were either inaccessible or unusable. The heat was so intense that rescue workers could only enter the building several hours after the flames had died down. Victims were identified by jewellery or not at all. Quite how many people died was unclear, but only a fraction of the many hundreds inside survived.

The blaze sent a surge of horror through Iran. As terrorist attacks are meant to do, it forced its witnesses to make choices. Officials pointed out that the Abadan attack had come after a series of other violent acts committed by 'fanatics' directed against 'all signs of modern living and Westernization in Iran'. The country's official news agency blamed 'saboteurs' and 'unidentified protesters'. Moderate clerics said the perpetrators were 'hot-headed people with whom we have no links whatsoever . . . Nazi type people'. But such statements failed to convince. Many Iranians saw the Abadan fire as further proof that the shah had no interest in their welfare and that the bright new future that he had once offered them was nothing more than a mirage. Millions went further and were absolutely convinced that the shah himself had organised the burning of the cinema, either to smear his opponents or simply out of spite for the common man.

In fact, the man who had set the fire was a twenty-three-year-old drug addict and petty criminal called Hosain Takbalizadeh. He was very loosely connected to religious networks that were loyal to Khomeini, and was influenced by the thinking and rhetoric of the radical scholar in Najaf, but he did not take orders from him or anyone close to him. He did not need to.

Like those of all terrorists, Takbalizadeh's journey into extremism and violence was unique. But much about his life and upbringing was also representative of the experience of the millions of people who comprised

Khomeini's natural constituency. His parents had been among the vast number of illiterate migrants who moved to Abadan from surrounding rural areas to work in the oil industry. His father died soon after Takbalizadeh's birth in 1955. His mother earned a thin living selling soft drinks on the streets, while his stepfather was a heroin addict, like many other men in the city. Takbalizadeh attended a local school, which meant he could at least read, unlike between half and two-thirds of Iranians, and then trained as a welder. But work was hard to come by and from his late teens he earned enough to pay for his own narcotics habit with petty drug deals. A history of fighting and theft had resulted in several spells in jail.

Abadan had a long history of labour activism and support for the Iranian Communist party but by the mid- to late 1970s the new religious enthusiasm was evident here too, and was particularly pronounced in the poorer areas populated by rural migrants. One unforeseen consequence of the shah's radical reforms of land tenure had been to accelerate the flow of villagers into Iran's fast-growing cities, where they lived in squalid, overcrowded townships. These were the areas that suffered most when the economic boom slowed, and while religious faith had grown among all levels of Iranian society, it was here among this new urban underclass that it grew strongest.

In early 1977, Takbalizadeh had been introduced by mutual friends to activist clerics who had recently stepped up their efforts to find followers among the poor of Abadan. They did this by distributing copies of statements made by Khomeini and making speeches at private homes. Takbalizadeh promised to kick his addiction and was sent to the city of Isfahan for treatment. This was a failure but a second effort was marginally more successful, and when Takbalizadeh returned to Abadan in August 1978, he brought clandestine religious literature with him rather than a block of cannabis resin or paper bag of low-grade heroin. People he had met in Isfahan had mocked the inhabitants of Abadan for their lack of religious fervour and weak commitment to the revolutionary cause. Takbalizadeh had already decided that the efforts of the activist clerics in Abadan were insufficiently extreme, so this made sense to him. When friends from Abadan's bazaar found him at his mother's house and suggested an arson attack on a cinema, he readily agreed.

Torching a cinema was not a new idea. For years, conservative clerics had implicitly encouraged attacks on such venues, which they saw as a primary source of the corruption that was corroding the authentic culture and faith of the Iranian people. Even moderate clerics opposed the mixing of sexes in such relative proximity and the films' supposed (though in fact extremely rare) lasciviousness. The vast and often lurid billboards that advertised the films were enough to provoke a fire-and-brimstone sermon from conservative religious scholars, especially during Ramadan. The difference was that the dozens of cinemas that had been burned out over the summer of 1978 had been more or less empty.

On the evening of 27 August, Takbalizadeh and three friends, all of similar ages and backgrounds, attempted to set fire to another cinema in their city, the Soheila, but the solvent they poured over its lobby did not ignite, so they resolved to try again. The following day, the four men added cooking oil to their mixture. They bought seats at the Rex just before the screening was due to begin and walked up the narrow stairs to join the crowd in front of the screen, waited for the film to start and then made their way back to the lobby. This time, a single match ignited a fierce blaze.

Now barely thinking coherently, Takbalizadeh returned to his seat. 'I wanted to say something, but I did not have the strength,' he said later. By the time that others raised the alarm, Takbalizadeh was perhaps already halfway out of the building. Behind him, the flames had taken hold. Barred or obstructed doors prevented the escape of all but a hundred or so of the terrified crowd. Suffocated by toxic smoke, burned or crushed, somewhere between 400 and 500 were killed. Two years later, Takbalizadeh would stand trial in Tehran for his crimes. 'I am not a criminal and a murderer . . . I did what I did to get close to the people [who were] making a revolution. In my ignorance I made a great mistake,' he told the judges who sentenced him to death.

The horrific attack in Abadan was both a challenge and a chance for Khomeini. He had always been careful to keep a plausible distance from any violence. In the 1940s and 50s, though compliant in public with the Shia quietist tradition, he had in fact been close to networks of militant clerics and their supporters who called themselves the Fedayeen-e Islam and were responsible for the murder of anti-clerical intellectuals as well as senior ministers. At least one of these killings had followed an explicit call from Khomeini to physically eliminate a named wrongdoer for his alleged blasphemy. When the group was suppressed, its remaining members were swiftly integrated into a network of radical religious groups that sought the overthrow of the shah and the establishment of religious rule and which was responsible for further attacks in the 1960s. Khomeini had long warned against any generalised insurrection or 'armed struggle', believing instead that the regime in Iran would be overthrown when enough people understood that their salvation, spiritual and temporal, was to be found in faith and the laws of Islam. In the meantime, however, Khomeini did not condemn violence and made clear in his own teachings what targets might be considered legitimate. It was a very different strategy from the authoritarian and hierarchical approach of leftists with their vanguards and Foco-ism, relying instead on the slow spread of the ideas and principles that would motivate and guide adherents. It was to prove much more effective, too.

In the aftermath of the Abadan cinema fire, the exiled cleric maintained two contradictory arguments, both as disingenuous as they were opportunistic. First, to divert any blame, he told followers that as such an act was contrary to the laws of Islam, no opponent of the shah could have committed it and thus, 'only the authorities could have lit the ring of fire around the cinema and ordered the cinema staff to lock the doors'. But at the same time, he insisted that no one should be surprised if ordinary people decided to destroy cinemas in spontaneous acts of outrage. Most Iranians considered such 'centres for prostitution and training of misguided people' to be 'apt for destruction' and had no need of orders from their religious leaders to act, he said.

The reality in the weeks after the Abadan fire was that the actual identity of the arsonists no longer mattered. In a majority of minds, the breach of trust between the country's ruler and his subjects had become definitive. The royal family's reaction to the tragedy had shocked many Iranians. The shah had refused to cancel a lavish annual soirée with a banquet, two orchestras and hundreds of guests in the gardens of the royal palace at Saadabad outside Tehran, and when huge numbers marched in protest he declared martial law in the capital and eleven other cities. The groundswell of anger grew, now threatening to gather into a genuine rebellion against the regime.

On 8 September, often cited as the day when the Iranian revolution became inevitable, troops shot into a crowd of demonstrators who had gathered in the capital unaware of a newly imposed curfew. The soldiers may have been fired on first by gunmen among the protesters, and Khomeini's networks may well have set out to provoke such a reaction. But once again, rumours rather than fact established the reality for many Iranians. By the government's account, eighty-six people were killed; the opposition said more than 1,000, even 3,000, had died. The massacre of 'Black Friday', coming so soon after the Abadan fire, stripped the shah and his regime of the last vestiges of legitimacy.

Finally aware that his rule was now genuinely threatened, the shah made further concessions. These included the revocation of a decree replacing the usual Islamic calendar with a 'Persian royal' calendar, the closure of casinos, a new ministry of religious affairs, a code to deal with the corruption of the royal family and the abolition of the single political party he had sought to impose. Throughout his near three-decade reign he had consistently given away too little too late, and this was no exception.

To complicate matters further, Saddam Hussein now decided that Khomeini was no longer welcome in Iraq. Iraq's vice president was understandably unenthusiastic about the radical cleric's appeal to Muslims everywhere to rise up and overthrow ungodly tyrants, particularly given the growing unrest among his own Shia population. When in October 1977, Saddam ordered Khomeini to be placed under what was effectively house arrest with all communications cut, the elderly cleric, now seventy-five years old, decided to leave Iraq altogether.

When Kuwait refused him entry, Khomeini's aides and family briefly considered relocating to Lebanon, Syria or Algeria. The first of these options was considered too dangerous, the others would make Khomeini entirely dependent on the hospitality of unpredictable regimes. The US and the UK were rejected as supportive of the shah. In the end, they decided their best option was France. Though reluctant, their fractious charge consented to live among unbelievers. Quite how Khomeini was able to get through border controls in Paris has never become clear. One possibility is that he was the lucky beneficiary of the visa-free entry that France had offered Iranians in order to tempt their wealthy elite to the Côte d'Azur and Parisian boutiques; it may be that the authorities at the newly renamed Charles de Gaulle airport waved Khomeini through without fully understanding who he was or the implications of his arrival. Another is that the French president Giscard d'Estaing gave his consent to the arrival in response to a request from the shah, who assumed Khomeini would be muzzled by the French authorities.

The exiled cleric's first days in the City of Light were spent in a supporter's cramped apartment on its outskirts. Having assured a nervous French bureaucrat that he had no intention of causing trouble anywhere, least of all in Iran, Khomeini and his entourage then moved to Neauphle-le-Château, a village some thirty miles south-west of the French capital, beyond Versailles. Aides set about building a headquarters for the next phase of Khomeini's decades-long effort to depose the shah and bring about an Islamic revolution.

One of those summoned to Paris to help their cause was a twenty-two-year-old student living in Chicago named Mohsen Sazegara. Small, slight, bespectacled and bookish, Sazegara did not look much like the military commander he would soon become. Nor had his route into political activism prepared him for any such role. His upbringing in east Tehran had been unexceptional, and not particularly religious. His mother was a housewife who wanted her daughters to study to university level so as to be independent. His father was a shopkeeper, detested the 'mullahs' and rarely went to the local mosque. Their home was full of conversations about the latest political developments, but neither parent encouraged their son to become involved himself.

In his mid-teens, however, Sazegara had begun to study the Koran and read religious literature voraciously. He then decided he would pray five times a day. The sudden interest in faith coincided with an equally fierce attraction to politics. In Iran at the time – the late 1960s – the former increasingly implied the latter. Sazegara took his first steps towards illegal activism by laboriously copying and distributing to friends a book called *Westoxification*, or *Gharbzadegi* in Persian. Written by the literary intellectual and former Communist Jalal Al-e-Ahmad, whose thinking had been heavily influenced by Jean-Paul Sartre and Ernst Jünger, *Westoxification* blamed the ills of contemporary Iran on its slavish admiration of a mechanistic, materialist Western civilisation and its denigration of the country's own culture, traditions and faith. Cultural and political subjugation went together, becoming a virulent 'infestation' that had spread among Iranians, it argued. When parts of it were published in 1962, it proved immensely popular and was swiftly banned by the shah's censors, an entirely ineffectual act as evidenced by Sazegara's clandestine copying almost a decade later.

When in 1973 Sazegara had taken up a place to study engineering at the prestigious Aryamehr University, he had entered an institution convulsed by political opposition. Founded by the shah just under a decade before, the university's campus in western Tehran was the site of daily protests against the regime. Dozens of political organisations battled for influence and recruits on the campus. Sazegara was repulsed by the atheism of the Marxists but found the reformism of the moderate nationalists inadequate. The legacy of his father's antipathy toward the clergy and his own interest in modern science made the students who were loyal to the exiled Khomeini seem reactionary and ignorant. Instead, he formed his own small network, putting up posters at night that decried the shah's repression, leaving leaflets calling for resistance on tables in the canteen and attending secret screenings of Gillo Pontecorvo's classic revolutionary film, *The Battle of Algiers*.

All universities were closely monitored by the Iranian security services through informers among the students and staff, so even these discreet activities soon attracted attention. When in 1975 the SAVAK summoned his oldest brother for questioning, a common tactic of intimidation, Sazegara decided that there was little to be gained from following hundreds of others into Evin, the vast prison complex on the outskirts of Tehran built specifically for holding political dissidents in its gleaming new wings. A potential route of escape would have been to apply for one of the thousands of government scholarships offered to bright young Iranians for study overseas. The intention behind this massive and expensive programme was to foster a new generation of technocrats to run the modernised Iran envisaged by the shah. In reality, it gave the country's best students the opportunity to spend years in environments where they could escape the narrow strictures, ideological and practical, of their homeland. Many headed to western Europe, others to the US.

Much to the shah's irritation but to no one's great surprise, the substantial Iranian student community overseas was highly politicised. It appeared that generous government subsidies funded by oil sales bought neither loyalty to the throne nor affection for capitalism. Student protests against the shah's regime had been a feature of his trips to the West for many years, and these noisy demonstrations and the advocacy campaigns that accompanied them had by now ensured that opposition to Iran's ruler ranked among the principal causes that mobilised the New Left and its more violent offshoots. In fact, it had been a demonstration against the shah's visit to Berlin in 1967 that had triggered the radicalisation of the West German left and led, some years later, to the foundation of the Red Army Faction.

Sazegara did not want to accept subsidies from the regime, which ruled out a scholarship. Instead, he won a place at the Illinois Institute of Technology and worked for six months in a supermarket in Chicago before landing a research job there. He also joined the Muslim

Students Association, which was run by exiled leaders of the Nehzat-e Azadi-e Iran, or Liberation Movement of Iran (LMI). This was a group that had broken away from Iran's mainstream nationalist opposition in the political turmoil of the early 1960s to follow a programme that placed the Islamic faith and traditions at the centre of Iran's regeneration but without rejecting the technical advances that had assured the West's dominance. As such, its aims were roughly similar to those of the Muslim Brotherhood in Egypt and other Islamists across the Muslim world. Its principal founder, a former technocrat called Mehdi Bazargan, described religion as the 'engine behind [the LMI's] political and social activism' but was also a committed democrat who admired the United Nations and much of Western political culture. He had remained in Iran and largely true to his original moderate, non-violent ideas despite a series of lengthy prison sentences.

But severe state repression in the mid-1960s had convinced many of Bazargan's younger followers that non-violent activism was never going to rid the country of the shah. Some were arrested and incarcerated. Others had fled to Egypt, where they sought training and arms from the regime of Gamal Abdel Nasser, to France or to the US where by the mid-1970s many were living on or near university campuses. Inevitably, this had exposed them to the local intellectual and countercultural currents and encouraged a much more radical outlook. On their crowded bookshelves, works by major Islamist thinkers competed for space with Persian translations of the key texts of the New Left. Like so many others, they had read Che Guevara, Régis Debray, Frantz Fanon and other iconic theorists of the anti-colonial struggle, and believed the victories of insurgents in Cuba, Vietnam and Ireland showed the way to Iranians who dreamed of ousting the shah. In the apartment he shared with a friend in Chicago, Sazegara read and re-read a Persian translation of Carlos Marighella's *Minimanual of the Urban Guerrilla* and planned for the forthcoming insurgency against the shah's regime.

In the eyes of the LMI's overseas wing, it was the Algerians, fellow Muslims who had used the language of faith to mobilise millions against a powerful French colonial regime, who provided the ultimate example of what could be done by committed revolutionaries. And of the Iranian thinkers who influenced them most, one stood out above all others, a brilliant communicator and thinker called Ali Shariati. The son of a respected publisher and cleric, Shariati had studied Islamic philology and sociology before winning one of the new government scholarships, which had allowed him to pursue higher studies in Paris in the early 1960s. There he had become involved in the Algerian struggle, studied the works of Sartre and translated Fanon for Iranian readers. A devout Muslim, Shariati's faith was transformed by this exposure to the powerful currents of anti-colonial thought and revolutionary struggle. On his return to Iran in 1965, he began teaching again, first in his home town of Mashhad and then, from 1967, in Tehran.

Shariati melded the worldview of the global anti-colonial movement and the various ideological strands of the New Left with the egalitarian message of the Muslim faith, borrowings from contemporary political Islamism and Shia religious popular culture. This chaotic, intense and unconventional thinker also appeared very contemporary. Shariati wore a suit, was clean-shaven and used modern Persian which contrasted dramatically with the archaic language used by most clerics. His lectures were 'happenings' and hugely popular among educated young people on campuses across the country. Shariati had met al-e-Ahmad, the author of *Westoxification*, and shared the older man's conviction that no nation could be truly free if the cost was the rejection of its cultural identity and, in particular, its faith. But he went further, and with a much deeper understanding of that faith. Religion was not a reactionary force but a liberating one, Shariati argued.

In his lectures, Shariati spoke for hours, wreathed in cigarette smoke, covering an extraordinary range of topics, transforming the fundamental stories of Shia Islam – the murder of Ali, the long-suffering son-in-law of the Prophet Mohammed, and the martyrdom of the Prophet's grandson Hussein at the hands of Yazid, the corrupt Umayyad caliph – into parables of righteous social and political activism with a very real, urgent contemporary message. As Hussein had resisted the impious and repressive rulers of his day, so should the Iranians, Shariati told his listeners. For centuries, devout Muslims had fought on behalf of the *mostazafin*, a neologism that Shariati lifted more or less directly from Fanon's *The Wretched of the Earth* to describe the oppressed, the disinherited or the exploited masses, and so too should Iranians now. Only through a process of religious rediscovery could Iran face the challenges of 'world imperialism, including multinational corporations and cultural imperialism, racism, class exploitation, class oppression, class inequality and Westoxification', Shariati argued. In one lecture, Shariati suggested the replacement of the traditional formula 'In the name of Allah, the compassionate, the merciful', with 'In the name of the God of the oppressed'. This was radical, heady stuff, and deeply appealing. With Shariati, you could challenge your elders without being dismissed as a delinquent, be a revolutionary without being an atheist, a socialist while remaining devout, and support radical transformation while remaining a proud, patriotic Iranian.

Some of these young enthusiasts carried Shariati's ideas into provincial Iran or into urban working-class neighbourhoods, where they met with limited success. Others carried his texts onto campuses in western Europe or the US, and were better received. An increasing number of the young students who sought out Khomeini in Najaf were admirers of the maverick thinker. Khomeini himself was sceptical and mistrustful, particularly of Shariati's explicit anti-clericalism. 'I have read [his] books,' he told an aide in 1977. 'He should not have said what he did.' But Khomeini appeared nonetheless happy to adopt some of the concepts and rhetorical techniques Shariati favoured. Soon he too had begun to frame the struggle to depose the shah as just one part of a much wider global struggle pitting the mostazafin against their oppressors, while his followers adopted the Shariati-inspired slogan: 'Neither West nor East, but Islam.'

Unsurprisingly, the regime had taken a dim view of Shariati's immense popularity, particularly among the young educated middle classes in Iran whom the shah hoped would provide the vanguard of his modernising project. In 1973, Shariati was arrested and held in solitary confinement. On his release after a campaign by French intellectuals, he had not returned to lecturing and in 1977 he left Iran, having come under enormous pressure from the SAVAK either to recant or to reform his views. Shariati's death soon afterwards of a heart attack in the unlikely location of Southampton, a port town on Britain's south coast, prompted profound grief among followers in his homeland and overseas.

When Sazegara returned from Chicago to Iran for the summer vacations of 1977, he was encouraged by the changes he perceived. He noted with excitement that more students than ever before were attending mosques or religious meetings, and his own sisters had taken to wearing the hijab for the first time. A brother, once disapproving of Sazegara's views, helped to obtain a rare and extremely useful duplicating machine with which to reproduce the revolutionary literature Sazegara had carried through customs at Tehran airport in a suitcase with a false bottom. But though the unrest that had been growing since the economic downturn of 1975 was more obvious too, Sazegara returned to the US at the end of the break entirely convinced that the struggle against the shah's regime would take many years, if not decades, to bear fruit.

Two months later, the call came from Neauphle-le-Château. Sazegara did not hesitate. He borrowed $250 for the air fare and left immediately with $8 in his pocket.

In Neauphle-le-Château Khomeini lived first in a small, dilapidated villa lent by a supporter, then a larger rented house. Photographers from dozens of agencies and publications pictured the white-bearded, stern-faced cleric walking down wintry country lanes surrounded by fields and leafless orchards or leading his followers in prayer, ranked on carpets spread on the damp grass. So many visitors pressed to see Khomeini that a second house was rented with a spacious garden. The guests and supplicants waited in a hired tent for days for an audience or just a few moments with the ayatollah under an apple tree.

Sazegara had been summoned to Paris by Ebrahim Yazdi, a pharmacologist who had been a co-founder of the Liberation Movement of Iran and had fled to the US to avoid the shah's crackdown in the early 1960s. Half a dozen other young activists from the organisation were also on their way to France to help Khomeini, some from the US too, others from nearer by. The conditions they encountered were spartan. Breakfast was a modest chunk of bread with cheese, lunch was bread with traditional Persian lentil soup, and dinner yet more bread with some butter or a teaspoon of sugar. It was also very cold.

Like Sazegara, at least half of the new arrivals had lived for years in the West and saw immediately the opportunity now open to them to mobilise support for Khomeini, instigate further unrest and impose him as the leader of the entire revolutionary movement in Iran. Towards the end of Khomeini's time in Najaf, tape recordings of his speeches had supplanted hand-written copies but it had still been necessary to smuggle these to supporters in Paris, Berlin and Beirut for reproduction before sending them into Iran, where they were distributed by hand, sold in bazaars and circulated through Iran's thousands of mosques and informal religious associations. Such means had been effective – among the religious propaganda that the arsonist Takbalizadeh brought home from Isfahan the day before his attack were taped religious lectures – but the process of production and distribution was laborious and very dangerous. The SAVAK were continually seizing such material and couriers knew they were risking 'martyrdom' if caught.

In Neauphle-le-Château, Khomeini's young aides hit upon a much quicker and safer method. Telephone connections between Paris and

Tehran were good, in part due to the shah's recent purchase of a modern switching system from US contractors. Every evening a nephew of Yazdi who worked for the state telecom company in the Iranian capital opened a line to Neauphle-le-Château free of charge. Meanwhile, the mass manufacture of Western consumer goods in Iran now meant that audio cassettes were widely available there. Each evening, Khomeini's aides played a recording of their leader's statements down the line to Iran where they were re-recorded and then copied thousands of times on banks of connected cassette players. To speed the process further, calls were made from Tehran to other cities in Iran and new copies made in the same way. Within less than twenty-four hours, tens of thousands of cassettes would be in circulation. In time, Khomeini reduced his recorded statements to a weekly broadcast, made after evening prayers on a Sunday.

The impact of the tapes was greatest in the sprawling slums on the periphery of major cities. Though their inhabitants were aware of revolutionary struggles overseas – one neighbourhood where police fought repeated battles to clear unauthorised homes was known as 'Vietnam' – the slogans of university-educated, atheistic leftists either abroad or at home held little appeal and inspired considerable distrust here. By contrast, Khomeini's simple lapidary statements echoed the sermons they might have heard in their villages only a few years before. Huddled around a cassette recorder bought with their community association funds, they would listen to Khomeini explain the causes of their problems, and, in his typical blunt language and marked provincial accent, offer, repetitively and rhythmically, a single, obvious solution.

Through the late autumn of 1978, the rhythm of protest and violence in Iran accelerated, with scores of bombings or shootings every week. Everywhere, mobs of angry young men left a trail of chaos and destruction. Theatres, cinemas, police barracks, restaurants, banks, supermarkets, offices and ministries were reduced to charred ruins. Hundreds of thousands of public sector workers went on strike, plunging the economy into chaos and, when the oil industry shut down, depriving the government of most of its revenues. The white marble of the soaring Shahyad monument, built on the western edge of Tehran for the lavish celebrations of imperial rule in 1971, was covered in revolutionary graffiti.

In one typical incident, troops opened fire on thousands of students in Tehran as they were trying to tear down a statue of the shah. Five were killed. Hours later, banks, shops, cars, buses, luxury hotels, ministries and offices were in flames across the capital. Amid the rising sense of imminent and potentially apocalyptic change, there were reports of UFOs and on the night of 27 November a mass sighting of Khomeini's face in the moon. Later, some of those who took to their rooftops to search for the cleric's eyebrows among the lunar craters would talk of 'collective hysteria'.

The shah wavered between repression and further concessions, his indecision possibly exacerbated by the massive doses of drugs he was now taking to counter a rare form of blood cancer that had been diagnosed several years earlier but kept secret. He appointed a military government but then gave a speech on national television in which he told his subjects that 'as Shah of Iran, as well as an Iranian citizen', he could not 'but approve the revolution of the Iranian people'. This time, even loyal supporters saw the speech as evidence that their ruler was fatally weakened. The 'King of Kings, Sunlight of the Aryans' appeared desperate and incoherent, despite the make-up that disguised his physical deterioration. The contrast with the impassive, implacable ayatollah in Neauphle-le-Château escaped no one.

In the second week of December, between one and two million people – between a fifth and a half of the city's entire population – marched peacefully through Tehran calling for the shah to leave and Khomeini to return. Foreign observers noted that the demonstration comprised 'clerical leaders, shopkeepers and merchants in the bazaar, labour leaders, students' and was 'masterfully organised' by 'local religious leaders' who had 'mobilised small crowds around local mosques and then moved with these groups to join others to form a massive parade'. Khomeini, whose portrait was carried by many of the marchers, served as 'the focal point'. More marchers now were calling for an Islamic republic, and far fewer merely for reform. The crowd took eight hours to pass through the city centre. The sight of such a vast, dignified demonstration of a collective desire for change left no witness unmoved. Kapuściński described 'a human river, broad and boiling, flowing endlessly, rolling through the main street from dawn till dusk. A flood, a violent flood that in a moment will engulf and drown everything.'

The shah continued to waver, apparently 'bewildered' by events. By the end of December, he had decided that his sacred bond with the people of Iran was irreparably broken. Sixteen days into the new year,

Iran's ruler flew from Tehran to Cairo for an 'extended holiday', leaving behind a caretaker government of limited authority headed by a veteran nationalist politician and supposedly supported by the country's vast, superbly equipped but now leaderless armed forces. Khomeini was informed of this dramatic development by excited aides as he was performing his dawn prayer in France. He listened, asked if there was any other news, and knelt again without further comment. Just over two weeks later, he was driven to Charles de Gaulle airport and boarded a chartered Air France 747 for Tehran.

In Neauphle-le-Château, Sazegara had been given the task of managing the foreign journalists and had organised more than 200 interviews given by Khomeini to international media, generating massive newspaper and television coverage. One aim was simply to get as many Iranians as possible onto the streets. Another was to maintain Khomeini's image as the paramount leader of the Iranian opposition. A third was to allay the fears of overseas observers that Khomeini was a fanatic.

To this end, journalists were allowed four questions, which had to be submitted in advance. These received a written answer – usually penned by Sazegara or another of Khomeini's aides without reference to the leader. Only then would there be a short face-to-face interview with Khomeini himself, during which a single further question could be posed directly, though the response would be translated by a member of the media team. In these interactions, Khomeini was careful to avoid anything that might worry the moderates, liberals and leftists who made up the majority of the protesters on the streets, or their supporters overseas. One tactic was to assure interviewers that after the revolution all Iranians would be allowed the rights they were due 'according to Islamic law', a claim that could be made in the full knowledge that few of his questioners or their readers had much of a grasp of Muslim jurisprudence. Even Sazegara was unaware of his leader's real intentions. He would not realise until much later – almost too late, in fact – that he had been deceived along with so many others.

When the Air France 747 bearing Khomeini, aides and more than a hundred journalists entered Iranian airspace, the cleric was asked by a US television reporter to describe his emotions. 'Nothing, I feel nothing at all,' said Khomeini. This bleak reaction was also softened by his entourage. The ayatollah had 'no comment', an aide informed the reporter. After circling for some time over the mountains north of Tehran, the aircraft bearing Iran's most famous and most controversial exile began its descent to the city's international airport.

Sazegara had been among the passengers of the French 747 but there had been no space for him in Khomeini's car as it set out from the airport for the Behesht-e Zahra cemetery. Instead, having seen some of the international journalists who had flown in with him from Paris safely to their hotels, he decided to find his parents and so, just an hour or so after landing, knocked nervously on the door of the house where he had grown up. There were various reasons for his anxiety: the extreme lengths he had gone to over the previous days to organise Khomeini's return, the sleepless overnight flight and the fear that guerrilla war against the Iranian armed forces might break out any moment. But most immediately, Sazegara was worried about his parents' reaction to his sudden and unannounced arrival. He had barely communicated with them for more than a year and his father had never approved of his political activities. What sort of welcome would he get?

Sazegara was astonished. His father kissed him for the first time in many years. 'My son, I congratulate you,' he said. 'You succeeded in ousting the shah. I did not believe you could do it.' Sazegara spent the rest of the day and the night with his family before setting off early the next morning to rejoin Khomeini.

A month or so beforehand, Khomeini's supporters had taken over a private religious school funded by local merchants in a lower-middle-class neighbourhood in the centre of Tehran. This had become a hub of radical activism, attracting clerics and lay supporters from across the country. Khomeini now moved with his extended family into a larger educational establishment next door. In a sparsely furnished room on the raised ground floor, with a view through a large window of the jubilant throng in the schoolyard outside, he received the most important visitors and issued orders verbally or on scraps of paper. Loyalists, many armed, took up self-appointed guard duty in the streets around. To avoid overcrowding and enforce segregation, women who wanted to see the imam were ordered to come in the afternoon.

When Sazegara arrived at the radical clerics' headquarters he was told to continue the work he had done in France: attend to the numerous international journalists seeking information and comment.

Sazegara worked out of a classroom, briefing correspondents, arranging interviews where possible, explaining the revolutionary project to newcomers. There was much to do and the streets were unsafe, so at night he slept on the floor amid the tables and school chairs.

Four days after returning to Iran, Khomeini gave a press conference at which he named a prime minister of a new provisional revolutionary government. Sazegara welcomed the appointment of Mehdi Bazargan, the veteran nationalist politician and moderate Islamist who had founded the Liberation Movement of Iran almost three decades earlier. Bazargan's mild manners, Western-style jacket and wide striped tie also reassured the many Iranians who hoped for a return to constitutional and broadly democratic rule after the departure of the shah. His appointment raised hopes that Khomeini might be willing to seek a mutually acceptable compromise with other revolutionary forces, hopes that would prove utterly misguided.

More immediately, however, the effect of the pronouncement was that Iran had two governments: one under Bazargan, which according to Khomeini would be in charge until a new constitution had been ratified at a referendum, and the other installed by the departing monarch. No one knew which of the two governments would command the loyalty of the armed forces. The answer would come just under a week later, when the shah's tanks moved back into Tehran for a final battle with the revolutionaries.

27

'We are dealing with wild animals'

All revolutions contain many stories soon forgotten once the rupture they have brought becomes the new reality. Likewise, history consigns to oblivion possibilities that once appeared entirely plausible. The shah had long described two threats to his various projects for his realm: a 'Black reaction' from radical clerics such as Khomeini and their followers, but also a 'Red reaction' from the revolutionary left. It was the latter that was by far the more dangerous, he believed.

Though the shah was dangerously misinformed about many things, his view was understandable. Throughout most of the 1970s, at least up until the calls for Khomeini's return in the autumn of 1977, 'Red' activists had indeed been the most active and vocal opposition to the shah's regime, far more so than any religious dissidents, and had suffered most in consequence. These mostly young men and women continued to believe in their eventual victory for months, even for years, after the shah fell and Khomeini returned. They would be proved wrong, but it was never inevitable that their story would end with such decisive defeat.

One of them was Farrokh Negahdar, who at the time of Khomeini's return found himself the de facto leader of many of the most radical leftists and so plunged into the very heart of the conflict for the future of Iran.

When Farrokh Negahdar was very young, he often came home to his family's large house in north-west Tehran to find his aunts and uncles arguing in the kitchen. The heated discussions in the Negahdar household were wide-ranging: the waves of social unrest that swept Iran, the role of women in a socialist economy, the global class struggle and, above all, the Communist party's continuing underground efforts to bring about radical change.

In 1949, the shah had banned the party – known as Tudeh, the masses – and as many of Negahdar's relatives and neighbours were members, and an uncle sat on the party's central committee, this had an impact on the whole family. Negahdar's father, an accountant in government service, and his mother, a housewife, tried to shelter their children from at least some of the ongoing political turbulence but to little avail. In 1953, after nearly losing his throne in the power struggle with prime minister Mohammed Mossadegh, the shah had jettisoned any youthful liberal ideas acquired at his exclusive Swiss school and began to build a powerful administrative machine of repression. Communists faced a new crackdown and the National Front – Mossadegh's broad coalition of reformists – was outlawed too, along with much other political activity. It was then, with help from the CIA and the Mossad, that the shah had founded the SAVAK.

Though largely beyond the comprehension of the seven-year-old Negahdar, this episode marked him deeply. The idea that 'the government was the enemy of the people' would stay with him over the years of violence and struggle to come. When seven years later, the shah reluctantly agreed to grant greater political freedom in return for financial assistance from Washington, Negahdar became involved with the constitutionalist reformers of a newly-refounded National Front. Now a gawky, intensely curious teenager with straight dark hair, a square jaw, big ears and the beginnings of a moustache, Negahdar joined marches, helped with leaflet campaigns, circulated handwritten copies of banned Marxist histories, graffitied slogans on walls and recruited new members. These activities earned him expulsion from his prestigious school. Undeterred, Negahdar continued his activities at the new establishment to which he was sent. This was more conservative and, for the first time, he came into contact with young people who sought radical transformation of a rather different type.

Negahdar's attitude to those whose religious faith defined their political views was ambivalent. He was impressed by their fervour and their hatred of the shah but concerned by much of their agenda. None of the women in his neighbourhood or family had ever worn a headscarf, let alone followed the dress codes these young men wanted to impose. To depose the shah and fight capitalism was undoubtedly progressive, but so much else the religious students wanted appeared reactionary in the extreme. Should the leftists support them or not? Neither Negahdar, nor the older, more experienced activists who had taken him under their wing, were able to answer this question.

In 1964, the year of Khomeini's expulsion, Farrokh Negahdar graduated from his new school with sufficiently high grades to win a coveted place at the Technical Institute of Tehran University. Not only was it one of the best faculties in Iran for sciences and engineering, which he enjoyed, but it was where many of his friends were, especially those who were increasingly active in a clandestine organisation called the Sazeman-e cerikha-ye Fedai-e Khalq-e Iran, or the People's Fedayeen of Iran.

Like many other such organisations in the mid- to late 1960s, the Fedayeen-e Khalq was the creation of young people convinced that the radical transformation of society would only be achieved with violence. The reconstituted and relatively moderate National Front had been destroyed by internal division and pressure from the SAVAK. Tudeh, the Iranian Communist party, maintained a shadowy illegal presence but its strict hierarchy, reflexive obedience to Moscow and devotion to theory were off-putting to the young. As international news was well covered by Iran's newspapers, and copies of foreign magazines were readily available, it was inevitably the strategy and thinking of the leaders of recent struggles in Algeria, Vietnam and above all Cuba that were discussed by Negahdar and his band of activist friends on long hikes through the hills outside Tehran through 1964 and 1965. The repression following Khomeini's arrest had made very clear how the authorities would respond to any efforts at mass mobilisation. Led by an intellectual former advertising executive and Marxist called Bijan Jazani, the Fedayeen-e Khalq's few dozen initial members could see no alternative to launching 'the armed struggle' in Iran.

Negahdar had little experience of, nor aptitude for violence so was posted to the 'political and propaganda section' of the Fedayeen and told to focus on students. His best friend, a handsome and sporty engineering student called Hamid Ashraf, was given command of the armed section. Like so many others, Jazani decided the Fedayeen would replicate the famous 'Foco' tactics that had brought success to Fidel Castro in Cuba: as the 'objective conditions' for revolution did not exist, this small band of committed men and a few women would be forced to create them through violence. They would be the 'small motor' that would jump-start the 'big motor' of the revolution. The charismatic and committed Ashraf would be the 'Iranian Che Guevara', leading an intensive campaign of sabotage, assassination of public figures, attacks on police, kidnapping, bank robbery and bombing.

But much like their Latin American heroes, these aspirant guerrillas faced big practical problems. They had no experience, few of the necessary skills and almost none of the requisite materiel. For two years, Ashraf and the other leaders of the Fedayeen sent small groups of volunteers for 'military actions' into Iran's more remote mountains to harden themselves, only to watch with mounting anxiety as, one after another, their members were identified and arrested by the security services.

Ashraf's eventual solution was not a particularly original one, at least not in the late 1960s. The Fedayeen group had an extensive network of sympathisers in London who were in touch with representatives of the PLO's various factions there. The Iranian revolutionary leftists found natural partners in George Habash's PFLP and the dogmatic Marxists of the DFLP, but had good relations too with Fatah, which agreed to train some of them in camps in Jordan and then Lebanon.

Finally, in February 1971, nine young men attacked a police post in the small village of Siahkal, in the mountains of northern Iran. They were led by veterans of the overseas training and equipped with automatic weapons and explosives smuggled into Iran from Lebanon. Initially, the operation met with some success. The Fedayeen shot dead three gendarmes, freed two of their comrades arrested some days earlier and stole a quantity of weapons. At that point, Negahdar's comrades were supposed to melt into the surrounding forested hills, where they could lie low before striking again. Instead, they found themselves on the run from a massive force of soldiers and police equipped with helicopters. The total absence of support from local villagers, distrustful of the atheist, educated leftists from Tehran who asked them for food and shelter, did not help. Nor did deep snow. Within three weeks, the entire Fedayeen force had been captured or killed.

Negahdar had not been involved in the Siahkal operation, as he had been arrested on a relatively minor charge well before planning had begun and had been released only a month or two before it went ahead. Conditions behind bars had been bad, and his health had suffered considerably. But his commitment to the Fedayeen and their collective mission remained strong. Just weeks after the attack, Negahdar met his childhood friend Ashraf, now the leader of the Fedayeen's armed struggle and well on his way to becoming the Iranian Guevara as hoped. The two young men went on a long hike through remote rural areas some hours from Tehran where they could talk without fear of surveillance or betrayal. Ashraf had completed a lengthy report on the failure of the Siahkal attack, which he blamed principally on delays and the failure of the Fedayeen to win local support. Influenced by his idol Guevara, Ashraf concluded that their chances of success would have been much increased if the Fedayeen had used violence against civilians rather than just the state to prove their revolutionary commitment.

One evening the two young men stopped to rest in a workshop on the outskirts of a village. It was empty but for rusting machines, a donkey and a stove. Everything, including the animal, was filthy, a reminder of the deep poverty of Iran's rural areas. They ate a poor meal of boiled oats and talked. 'Our followers are students, professionals, educated people in the cities, women,' Ashraf said. 'Why did the villagers not help us in the mountains above Siahkal? Why did the rural masses not rise up? How can we get access to these people?' Then he pointed to the wall where someone had taken the trouble to tack a picture of a well-known elderly cleric. 'Why do the ordinary folk, in villages like this one, not support us but pin pictures of Khomeini in their homes and work-places?' Negahdar had no answer.

Ashraf suggested that Negahdar travel overseas to promote their cause. The Fedayeen's campaign was always meant to have 'two legs', one military and the other political, inside and outside Iran. A bid to travel via Iraq to London failed because of fighting between Baghdad's armed forces and Kurds, so Negahdar headed east instead. For eight months he used false identity documents to roam the towns and cities of Afghanistan and Pakistan, staying for weeks in Kabul, Peshawar and Karachi. Keen to report to his comrades and confident that he could return to Iran without detection, Negahdar hired a smuggler to take him across the border from Afghanistan but was betrayed. When he refused to recant his commitment to revolution in front of SAVAK interrogators, Negahdar was deemed a 'potential threat' and sentenced to first three, then five years in jail.

Conditions had changed since his first stint behind bars. Then, the cells had been filthy and the food appalling but newspapers were permitted and familial visits frequent. Now the new facilities were cleaner and healthier but inmates were held in almost total isolation. Negahdar was sent to a series of different prisons, finally ending up in Evin, recently constructed just outside Tehran to hold the SAVAK's hundreds of detainees. The only information about what was happening beyond the walls was brought in by new arrivals. None of the news was good.

For the radical left in Iran, the mid-1970s was 'a period of disaster'. Negahdar's comrades beyond Evin's walls managed to organise bomb attacks and even assassinations of senior officials, but there was no doubt that the regime had the upper hand. In 1974, almost the entire leadership of the Fedayeen had been caught in a single raid, then many of them were shot after 'trying to escape' prison. A year after that, Jazani, the founder and ideological leader of the organisation, was hauled from a cell and executed. Then, in the summer of 1976, Negahdar was called into the prison interrogation room and shown a picture of a corpse. Immediately, Negahdar recognised his friend Hamid Ashraf, who had killed himself with his last bullet after a shootout with police. Negahdar had known Ashraf since they were fifteen years old and had suggested him as a potential recruit for the Fedayeen. The two men had been very close. They had spoken about everything: hopes, fears, the revolutionary struggle, music, books, girls.

Though badly shaken, Negahdar still believed such sacrifice was justified to advance the cause of revolution in Iran, but victory seemed a long way off. So too did his own personal liberation: he had never been formally charged with any offence and his official release date had passed in early 1977 without anyone in authority offering the slightest justification for his continued detention. So it came as something of a surprise when, six months later, Negahdar learned that along with hundreds of other political prisoners, he was to be freed.

One reason for this sudden clemency was growing US pressure for Iran to improve its human rights record following the election of President Jimmy Carter. Another was a recognition among the shah's advisers that the tensions building in the kingdom could not be contained indefinitely. Indeed, when Negahdar walked out of prison, now thirty-one years old after most of a decade behind bars, he was astonished by what he found: the economic difficulties facing the country, the growing anger of many Iranians, but also what appeared to be an amazing new spirit of openness. The shah had dropped his demand that all citizens join the government-backed Resurgence party and had even begun to allow a modicum of public criticism of his rule. A trio of veteran National Front leaders tested the water with a mild letter calling for reform of 'a system of despotism dressed up as lawful monarchy', and evenings of poetry readings organised by the German government's cultural agency in Tehran attracted tens of thousands of ordinary people in a sudden and unexpected moment of relative freedom.

Now a figure of some authority within the Fedayeen, a senior leader who had spent many years in prison or on clandestine operations, Negahdar's personal circumstances had changed too. He had at last been able to marry a younger cousin, Nesrine, a student activist who was given the *nom de guerre* Saba by the Fedayeen. Neither he nor his wife were particularly keen on going underground again, not least because they wanted to start a family. Negahdar had also begun to believe, like so many of his counterparts in extremist groups around the world, that the theoretical arguments that had justified violence a decade earlier were out of date. Instead, the Fedayeen could now exploit the new, more permissive environment to mobilise 'the masses' through labour activism, peaceful protests and political organisation, he decided. Fewer people would die or be tortured, and the rural population would be won over by the example of their industrialised, urbanised comrades. But this brought him back to the questions he had faced as a teenager confronted by religious militants and that Ashraf had posed many years before in a dusty workshop under the portrait of Khomeini. What if the masses preferred the programme of an elderly reactionary cleric to the ideas of young progressive leaders like him? And if the religious extremists took power, what would become of leftists?

For Farrokh Negahdar and the Fedayeen-e Khalq, Khomeini's return forced them to again face questions for which they had so far failed to find answers. On the one hand, Khomeini had massive popular support and was a fierce critic of capitalism, Zionism and imperialism. On the other, there could be no doubt of the visceral hostility of Khomeini and his followers towards the leftists. After much debate, the Fedayeen decided that the cleric was an 'esteemed militant and Great Leader of the Shiites' who should be welcomed, and so Negahdar had joined the crowds lining the route from the airport to the Behesht-e Zahra cemetery. Alongside him stood comrades with celebratory placards and banners.

In these first hopeful months after the fall of the shah, Negahdar believed, much like Sazegara, that Khomeini's movement presented an opportunity to realise their dreams of radical reform and create something which both men believed could also become an inspiration for the oppressed and exploited across the world. In time, both would be disillusioned, and their goals would shrink from radical reform to mere personal survival, but this early optimism, though naive, was not without some justification. Negahdar and his fellow Fedayeen were immensely impressed by the huge crowds which celebrated Khomeini's return, which included so many who were clearly poor and uneducated.

Nine days later, Negahdar was in a meeting in a safehouse in the south of Tehran when he heard that his comrades were fighting and dying as they stormed police stations and military bases across the city. As de facto leader of the Fedayeen, he was surprised. His organisation had planned no uprising, and certainly no generalised offensive against Iran's security forces.

It took some time to piece together what had happened. First, hundreds of air force technicians at one of the biggest military bases in Tehran had refused to obey orders, then fired on their senior officers. Soldiers from the Imperial Guard, the shah's elite units, had been deployed but had been unable to restore order. News of the mutiny had reached tens of thousands of Fedayeen and their supporters who had gathered at Tehran University to commemorate the anniversary of the Fedayeen's attack on the gendarme post in Siahkal eight years earlier. Chanting 'We will turn the whole of Iran into Siahkal', they took a rapid decision to join the mutineers. Within hours, the Fedayeen had launched a series of assaults on military installations and police stations across the capital, which was when Negahdar first heard of this new violence.

On paper, Iran's armed forces remained very imposing. The shah had devoted up to a third of his government's total expenditure to the military and, even if as many as half of his forces were thought to have deserted over the previous year, this still left 200,000 soldiers beginning each day with a pledge to defend 'God, Shah and Fatherland'. But in the close quarters of Tehran's choked streets, the soldiers had been unable to bring their numbers and firepower to bear, and when Negahdar left the safehouse to venture into the city, he was amazed by what he found. The shah's Chieftain tanks, supplied by Britain, were being fought to a standstill by teenagers armed with petrol bombs. The police headquarters, national assembly, international airport and various palaces had been stormed, and the doors of the hideous Evin prison, where he had spent years, thrown open. When the radio station fell to the insurgents, millions of Tehran's residents were informed that a new network, 'The Voice of the Revolution', had replaced the national broadcasters. Hours later, the armed forces' most senior commanders decided that any further resistance was futile and issued a communiqué stating that the country's military would remain neutral and 'support . . . the wishes of the noble people of Iran'. Within twenty-four hours, the rival government left behind by the shah had collapsed. Soon afterwards Shapour Bakhtiar, the shah's prime ministerial appointee, fled Tehran in the first-class cabin of an Air France jet, hiding behind dark glasses and a copy of *Le Monde*.

In the fighting, the Fedayeen seized a swathe of the city, thousands of military-grade weapons and scores of regime officials, including many who worked for SAVAK, the hated intelligence service. The prisoners were held in a makeshift jail in the basement of the Fedayeen's headquarters. After hours of debate, Negahdar convinced his comrades that the Fedayeen should avoid any clash with the clerics. They needed time to grow their own membership and organisation, and they still shared many of the same enemies. As a fragile calm returned to Tehran, Negahdar ordered any armed Fedayeen to withdraw from the streets and hand over their prisoners to Bazargan's government, and so to Khomeini's radical supporters. At least one was shot almost immediately; the fate of the others was unclear. This did not bother the Fedayeen overmuch. Most, including Negahdar, called for supporters of the *ancien régime* to be treated with utmost revolutionary rigour.

Sazegara too had been in the streets during the fighting against the shah's army. A close friend had been killed. He had watched old women making food and Molotov cocktails for combatants, and his neighbours organising donations of blood for the wounded. It was an exhilarating moment, and in its aftermath, Sazegara was given a new task: to help collect the thousands of weapons that had been looted from military or police armouries. This took him away from Khomeini's central headquarters for long periods, and so he was fortunate to be at a remove from what was about to happen there.

In mid-March Khomeini took up the tool of many revolutionaries over the previous two centuries: terror.

The killings began almost exactly a fortnight after Khomeini's return and continued for several weeks. Their purpose was not merely the elimination of erstwhile enemies, though revenge was undoubtedly a factor and many of the executions were welcomed by Iranians. Deliberately spectacular, its aim was also to deter anyone who might seek to challenge Khomeini's authority and to radicalise his existing supporters and mobilise new followers. 'The execution of these executioners is not only to console those who have suffered. It is to infuse new blood into the veins of the revolution,' Radio Tehran told listeners, much as the mouthpieces of Robespierre and Lenin had done.

Detainees were brought before a 'revolutionary court' in a classroom at the school that continued to serve as Khomeini's main base. There they were sat on a school chair with their names on placards around their necks and were allowed neither witnesses nor lawyers. Their prosecutor and judge was a junior cleric whose self-regard was in inverse proportion to his religious knowledge. The sole journalist allowed to attend a trial was so disgusted that he left after half an hour. Found guilty of 'spreading corruption' and 'war against God', most of those brought before the court were shot almost immediately by firing squads assembled hastily on the school's flat roof. Photographs of their corpses were usually made available to all the newspapers and broadcast on television. It was advisable to feature such content prominently. *Ettela'at*, the newspaper that had published the scurrilous editorial that initiated the cycle of protests just over a year before, ran a special edition.

The first victims were all closely associated with the shah's regime, and included courtiers, generals and senior security officials directly implicated in torture. But soon Khomeini was signing off on the execution of people whose responsibility for the misdeeds of the previous decade or so was far less obvious: the only woman minister to serve under the shah; the former mayor of Tehran; a junior officer held responsible for the deaths at Abadan's Rex cinema; several freemasons, a Jewish businessman, and at least thirty members of the Baha'i sect, which had long faced persecution, particularly from conservative Muslims, despite having been founded in Iran. Similar killings occurred in the provinces as Khomeini's supporters hunted down fugitive officials, SAVAK agents, police officers and deserting soldiers. Many were shot after appearing before local versions of the revolutionary court in Tehran, others simply lynched. Protests from Bazargan, international human rights bodies and others were brushed aside.

Like Negahdar, Sazegara was not overly troubled by the executions, at least not the deaths of the royalists who had held senior posts. Those killings were to be expected in a real revolution, he decided. As for the deaths of those whose culpability was less clear, he had little information to go on and did not believe the rumours that detainees were being tortured. The religious nature of the revolutionary movement precluded such excesses, he believed. Anyway, Sazegara's work collecting weapons had evolved into a more difficult and distracting task, so he was very busy.

Khomeini had been impressed by a suggestion from Sazegara and others that the new regime needed its own force to defend the revolution, ward off any *coups d'état* and protect against foreign invasion. This would combine existing makeshift militias with recruits from his poorest supporters, thus rewarding the faithful while creating a powerful new weapon for the revolution. The commanders would be drawn from veteran activists, most in their twenties and thirties, who had suffered in the shah's jails or been active overseas. It would be called the Sepah-e Pasdaran-e Enghelab-e Eslami, the Islamic Revolutionary Guards Corps, and would answer only to Khomeini, not to Bazargan's provisional government.

As the radical clerics had never sought to prepare an armed insurgency against the shah's regime, few of Khomeini's followers within Iran had any military experience. But the radical wing of Bazargan's Liberation Movement of Iran (LMI) did. While in the US, Sazegara had been involved in organising the travel of some of its activists to Lebanon's training camps run either by factions of the PLO or by Shia groups newly formed to defend their community's interests against other local factions as well as the invading Israel Defence Forces. They were not the first to make this journey. Many dozens, possibly hundreds of Iranian dissidents had made their way to Lebanon over the decade. Relations between the secular, leftist nationalists who ran the PLO's camps and Iranian Islamist activists were rarely straightforward. The visitors were often shocked to see that 'none of the Syrian or Lebanese guerrillas said their prayers', that genders mixed freely and men even shook women's hands. Efforts to convince the 'Marxist Leninist' Palestinian fighters that the Koran was 'the only path to nations' and peoples' salvation, independence and dignity, and . . . to liberating Jerusalem' were entirely futile, one earnest LMI trainee complained. Relations with other Iranians in the camps – particularly the Marxist guerrillas from the Fedayeen or other Iranian groups – were often tense too.

But, as Khomeini's new Pasdaran could deploy only a thousand or so poorly-equipped novice fighters, the expertise of the LMI veterans was extremely valuable. Many were appointed to senior roles and were soon in action, leading the force on its first mission: helping local militia loyal to the new revolutionary regime crush nascent uprisings in regions of the country with large ethnic minorities. This had little to do with the global armed struggle against capitalism, imperialism or unbelief and everything to do with reinforcing the shaky authority of the revolutionary regime. Kurds, Turkmens, Arabs and others had been restive under the shah and often enthusiastically participated in the revolution in the hope of obtaining a degree of autonomy and more government resources. But Khomeini had no intention of indulging these wishes and instead thousands were killed in the north-west, parts of the north and Khuzestan, the oil-rich south-western province. When dozens of protesters were shot dead in Khorramshahr, Khuzestan's capital, Khomeini was unapologetic.

Fully committed to building the Pasdaran's intelligence capacities, Sazegara continued to work enthusiastically for the revolution.

Through the spring and into early summer, Negahdar also remained optimistic. Since the fall of the shah, more than 200 new newspapers had sprung up and there were open debates on every street corner and demonstrations by every possible political faction. By the early summer, the Fedayeen was holding mass rallies, with thousands signing up as new members, and the organisation's weekly newsletter was selling 300,000 copies. They had even been allowed to march on International Workers' Day on 1 May, a celebration that had been banned by the shah. Iran's Communists, the battered Tudeh party, were reviving, and smaller factions of Stalinists, Trotskyists and Maoists were emerging, blinking, from the long night of royal repression.

As the months passed, however, doubts grew about the Fedayeen's decision to engage with the revolutionary regime. Within days of withdrawing their fighters from the streets in February, the Fedayeen had been forced out of their base on the campus of Tehran University by a crowd of Khomeini supporters, losing most of the weapons they had collected during the battle against the army. Soon, Khomeini's clerics turned a new variety of thugs on the leftists, recruited from among the vigilantes who had exploited the almost total collapse of order across Iran to seize control of entire neighbourhoods. Known as Hezbollahis, or members of the Party of God, they had imposed their version of Islamic law, distributed food, patrolled the streets, raised 'voluntary' donations and settled local grudges. Now their violent energies were redirected against nationalists, constitutionalists, 'Western-style intellectuals', leftists and other 'counter-revolutionaries'.

In the face of this assault, the flowering of journalism and political debate that had followed the departure of the shah withered. Bookshops and publishing houses were attacked. The offices of leftist groups were ransacked. A new law banned around forty newspapers, almost all moderate, nationalist, pro-democracy or from the left. The cells in Evin prison were more crowded than ever. Khomeini had decided against withdrawing the right to vote from women, something he had advocated in the early 1960s, but paid no attention when huge numbers protested against an order that women wear the chador in public and annulling legislation that guaranteed them custody of children in the event of divorce. 'Those who did not participate in this movement have no right to advance claims . . . It was the mosques that created the Revolution, the mosques that brought this movement into being,' Khomeini told opponents.

Unlike most observers, Negahdar had some idea of what the cleric was trying to achieve. Once, following an interrogation in Evin prison, he had been able to steal a book that his questioners had left in a cell: a slim volume containing the series of lectures given by Khomeini in Najaf in 1971. Negahdar had read the work with equal interest and unease, learning for the first time of the cleric's radical reinterpretation of the Velayat al-Faqih as the absolute rule of a single supreme religious leader.

Though their contempt and hatred of the Fedayeen was now clear, Negahdar was still convinced that the project of the most extreme among the clerics would eventually fail. After all, the ineluctable laws of Marxist dialectics taught that the forces of religious reaction would eventually be defeated. But there was another reason for the Fedayeen to bide its time. Negahdar had a reputation within the Fedayeen of being a pragmatic strategist who coldly considered so-called 'objective conditions', and he was convinced that if the Fedayeen now took up arms to confront the regime, there would only be one winner: the forces of radical Islam. Patience, both individual and collective, would therefore bring a better future for all Iranians, he believed.

Sazegara did not last long with the Revolutionary Guards. Most of the men who filled its upper ranks were soon at ease with weapons, the violence of the revolutionary courts and the harsh reality of their new jobs. Sazegara had little taste for any of it. When he tried to use a handgun, he was laughed at. He was also worried by the continuing executions, and though he had not doubted the legitimacy of the killings of those first weeks, his commitment to revolutionary bloodshed began to waver. Would torture also be justified by the new rulers of Iran? Was inflicting pain on prisoners considered an inevitable part of revolution?, he wondered. When he put such questions to senior clerics close to Khomeini, the responses were far from reassuring. One told him that torture was justified by Islamic law; another that, right or wrong, it would be impossible to prevent.

By early autumn 1979, Sazegara had found more congenial employment. The National Iranian Radio and Television service was understaffed after purges of its employees and now run by one of the older activists from the LMI whom he knew well. Sazegara worked in the news department, overseeing the content and writing a daily analysis which he then read out live at noon. Millions of Iranians listened, including his neighbours and father. He found the work deeply satisfying.

A key theme of the network's reporting was the reaction of the international community to events in Iran. As the summer of 1979 unfolded, many in the West condemned the increasingly overt violence of the revolutionaries and expressed concern about authoritarianism. The Soviets remained supportive. Others were effusive in their praise: South Yemen's ruling National Liberation Front hailed a victory of 'patriotic and progressive forces', the Popular Front for the Liberation of Palestine welcomed a lethal blow struck against Zionism and capitalism, the Palestine Liberation Organisation saw Khomeini as having won a major victory for anti-colonial fighters everywhere, while Fidel Castro lauded the man who had defeated an arch-capitalist and US stooge. So too did Western leftists, such as Jean-Paul Sartre, who had once declared that if he was forced to choose a religion it would be 'that of [Ali] Shariati'. Michel Foucault was also a fan. The historian and theorist had visited Tehran in late 1978 and been impressed by the revolutionaries' effort to introduce a 'spiritual dimension' to politics.

Most Iranian listeners, though avid to learn how their revolution was perceived overseas, had other priorities. As the summer of 1979 turned to autumn, almost all faced great hardship as the government of Bazargan tried to restore order to an economy crippled by a lack of spare parts, hard currency and basic commodities. A crash nationalisation programme had wreaked havoc. Clerics had taken over hundreds of businesses whose owners had fled overseas and then proved incapable of running any of them. Shortages of fuel and basic foodstuffs led to protests that were often harshly suppressed. In the provinces, thousands of independent 'revolutionary committees' still ran entire towns. Successive deployments of the Pasdaran had yet to quell restive ethnic minorities. With Iran awash with weapons and without a functioning police force, violent crime soared. As the date for a referendum on the heavily revised constitution neared, opposition to the clerics' rule hardened. In response, the Hezbollahis went to work with their clubs and the country slid closer to total anarchy.

Khomeini's own mood had darkened considerably since the early spring. On the evening of May Day, a close aide and friend had been assassinated by a splinter group of anti-clerical Islamists. Khomeini had wept openly at the funeral, calling out the name of the victim in his grief, a very rare public display of emotion. This was only one of a half-dozen murders the attackers carried out, fuelling Khomeini's sense that the revolution was under siege. In an interview with the Italian journalist Oriana Fallaci in his home in Qom in September, he described the 'dark chaos' he saw everywhere, arguing that the revolution was a vulnerable infant that needed fierce and determined defence against 'those who call themselves Communists, or democrats, or God knows what'.

Khomeini was less restrained during the public audiences that he held, in emulation of the Prophet Mohammed, almost daily in Qom. When a group of religious Tehran University students described how they had been attacked by a stronger group of leftists, Khomeini told them to stop complaining and in future to 'hit first'. The days of clemency for the revolution's enemies were over. 'We thought we were dealing with human beings. It is evident we are not,' he said. 'We are dealing with wild animals. We will not tolerate them any more.'

Then a series of unanticipated events offered Khomeini a chance to impose definitively the authoritarian clerical regime he had outlined almost a decade before. He seized the opportunity with customary skill.

This 'revolution bigger than the first revolution', as Khomeini called it, started in the first week of November 1979, when a twenty-three-year-old supporter and activist called Mahmoud Ahmadinejad suggested to a group of fellow students that they occupy the Soviet Embassy to mark their opposition to the repression of Muslims within the USSR. A better target, Ahmadinejad's fellow activists suggested, would be the US

Embassy. Neither were particularly original objectives. On New Year's Day, a group of religious students had overrun the former, lowering the red hammer and sickle flag and hoisting the green of Islam. A month later, the latter had been stormed and Washington's diplomatic representative held captive for several hours. In both cases, the revolutionary authorities had dispersed the occupiers and order had been quickly restored.

Now, the students debated which should be targeted anew. In October, President Carter had reluctantly allowed the shah to enter the US to receive treatment for cancer. The students had no idea that the shah was dying and thought immediately of the US-led intelligence operation which had restored the same man to his throne in 1953. Televised images of a cordial encounter between Bazargan and US officials in Algiers just days earlier reinforced their suspicions that the US were plotting the return of the shah once more. A plan was rapidly formulated to take over the sprawling US Embassy compound in Tehran and hold its diplomats prisoner for a few hours, or possibly a day or two. This would be sufficient to 'transfer the voice of the students to the whole world', they felt, and confound Washington's counter-revolutionary conspiracy. To ensure no one mistook them for another faction, they called themselves 'Students Following the Line of the Imam'.

So on the morning of 4 November 1979, several hundred unarmed students chopped through the locks on the US Embassy gate and scaled the compound's walls. Most were young men from poor, rural backgrounds who were studying hard sciences at Tehran's Technical University, about a quarter were women, and their average age was twenty-two. The US Marines defending the complex fired tear gas but no live ammunition and no one was seriously hurt, though some of the Americans within were beaten or threatened. Soon, sixty-three embassy staff were captive. Pictures of them, blindfolded, bound and flanked by jubilant captors, ran on front pages around the world. Three others, including the acting chargé d'affaires, had been at the foreign ministry when the embassy was stormed and soon found themselves prisoners too. There had been many attacks on diplomatic representations through the 1970s – in Khartoum, The Hague, Bangkok, Stockholm, Kuwait City, Geneva and elsewhere – but nothing like this. Certainly, no previous such takeover had received the explicit endorsement of local authorities.

True to his habitual strategy of calling for violence but letting others reach their own decisions to act, Khomeini had been encouraging attacks on US interests since learning of the shah's arrival in New York. Most recently, he had put his name to a statement, probably written by one of the more radical members of his entourage, calling for unspecified 'actions' against America and Israel to force the return of 'the criminal shah' to Iran. For a few hours after the students stormed the embassy, Khomeini temporised. Then, possibly influenced by the enthusiastic crowds that had gathered as news of the attack spread and by the excited response of Iran's leftists, he offered his unequivocal support. 'This has united our people. Our opponents do not dare act against us. We can put [a new] constitution to the people's vote without difficulty . . . When we have finished all these jobs we can let the hostages go,' he explained to a close aide.

Khomeini's prediction proved particularly astute. Within days of the takeover, Bazargan and most of his cabinet resigned. This too was lauded by Iranian leftists who had seen the moderate prime minister and his cabinet as 'petit-bourgeois enemies of the proletariat' and 'imperialist stooges'. Thus emboldened, the Hezbollahis, Pasdaran and other paramilitaries associated with the regime now moved to destroy Bazargan's power base. At best, moderates found themselves ignored. At worst, they were beaten, blindfolded, pushed into trucks and disappeared into the prisons. To criticise the occupation of the embassy became very dangerous. Sazegara, who was upset by the trashing of international diplomatic norms as well as the attacks on Bazargan as a 'CIA spy', kept his concerns to himself.

As Khomeini had predicted, the occupation of the embassy rallied his existing supporters and attracted new ones. The pavements outside the embassy, along what had once been Roosevelt Avenue, now hosted a revolutionary carnival. Graffiti artists covered the outer walls of the occupied compound with cartoons depicting bloody, drooling Uncle Sam, portraits of recent 'martyrs' and quotes from Khomeini. Hawkers sold grilled corncobs, fresh walnuts and roasted beetroot – the favourite snacks of the urban poor – to the milling crowds. Booksellers offered texts of major Islamic thinkers, the ever-popular *Westoxification*, Shariati's lectures, badly printed translations of books describing US crimes in Vietnam and those of Israel against Palestinians. The Tudeh party sent a large bouquet of flowers to the front gate of the embassy every morning. When Farrokh Negahdar's Fedayeen held demonstrations under its walls to show their support for the takeover, the students within the complex applauded.

Internationally, the attack on the embassy brought Iran into firm alignment with those who opposed the 'hegemony of the imperialist, capitalist US' across the world. Even the conservative and risk-averse officials in Moscow decided to endorse the takeover, despite misgivings, in the hope that it might consolidate anti-US sentiment in Tehran and so improve the USSR's influence there. This was a forlorn hope. The radical clerics now in power were as opposed to the atheist USSR as to the US. For it was now clear above all to hundreds of millions across the Middle East that the slogan 'neither East nor West' was more than just rhetoric. Iran now offered a concrete example of a state that had responded emphatically to the desires and the everyday challenges of ordinary people not through the politics of the left but via appeal to the texts and traditions – albeit a radical, populist, revolutionary interpretation of them – of Islam.

28

Who Dares Wins

An overcast and chilly morning in west London. It is 30 April 1980. Outside 105 Lexham Gardens, a four-storey townhouse with bow windows and neoclassical portico, there is a small commotion. A group of young men have gathered on the pavement and are waving to the residents. Inside they have left a small mountain of luggage to be sent to an address in Baghdad.

After a month occupying flat 3 on the second floor they are saying goodbye. They may be off to the west of England, to Paris, or possibly returning to Iraq, none of the other residents is really sure. They have said different things to different people. But no one minds. The young men have been unobtrusive tenants, apparently living on a diet of Chinese takeaways, whisky and daytime television but disturbing no one very much. One of the young men blows kisses as they walk down the tiled steps to the pavement, turn left and walk away towards central London.

Ninety minutes later, the young men have gathered at the Albert Memorial in Hyde Park. The monument is only a thirty-minute walk away, but they have been slow on purpose. In their hands and at their feet are bags containing weapons – handguns, Polish sub-machine guns, Soviet grenades – and ammunition. Five of them wait while a sixth walks briskly a few hundred yards further east to Prince's Gate, a long row of whitewashed stucco houses with balconies, columns and pilasters, all much grander than those of Lexham Gardens. One is of particular interest: number 16, the Iranian Embassy. When the scout returns, there is a brief conversation, then all six pick up the bags and move off.

Much has changed at 16 Prince's Gate in the sixteen months since the revolution in Iran. The Rolls-Royce Silver Ghost has been sold and the vintage wines poured away. The SAVAK's offices are empty and the telex no longer chatters with intelligence reports on dissidents in

London. The elegant and sociable former ambassador has declined an invitation to return to Tehran and his replacement, a former university lecturer imprisoned under the shah, has sought neither to make influential friends among Britain's elite, nor win over other diplomats posted to the city. Instead, he has raised his concerns with London's Metropolitan Police at the potential counter-revolutionary threat to the embassy, and received a slightly disappointing response. A single officer, armed with a heavy .38 revolver, has been stationed outside the embassy.

But this morning, some minutes before 11.30 a.m., Police Constable Trevor Lock of the Diplomatic Protection Group is not at his post. He is inside enjoying a cup of coffee and so does not see the young men, faces masked and weapons drawn, rush the final yards from the street and up the stairs to the embassy's heavy door. There is a brief struggle, shots, flying glass that cuts Lock's cheek and no time to draw his own weapon. The attackers run through the embassy's rooms, up the stairs. There is confusion, more shots, screams, shouts, doors kicked down and eventually, a stunned calm. The twenty-six people in the embassy that morning are all now hostages. The leader of the young men explains who he is and whom he represents 'We belong to the Group of the Martyrs', he says, first in English, then in Persian. 'We belong to the Democratic Revolutionary Movement for the Liberation of Arabistan.'

The speaker, who is tall and burly with tightly curled hair, a moustache, a goatee beard and long sideburns, then outlines his straightforward and entirely unrealistic demands: the release of ninety-one prisoners held in Iran by the revolutionary regime and currently exposed to 'savage terrorism, torture and . . . liquidation', the revolutionary government's recognition of the legitimate rights of Iranian 'peoples', and a plane to fly either the freed detainees or the attackers themselves to an undisclosed location in the Middle East. The exact details of this last demand are unclear to the young man's captive audience. What is not unclear is that the Democratic Revolutionary Movement for the Liberation of Arabistan want whatever they want by noon the next day, or they will blow up the embassy, killing everyone within it, themselves included.

The statement read out to the shocked hostages at Prince's Gate provoked bewilderment as well as alarm among British officials. Arabistan had not existed in any formal way since 1925, when this semi-independent sheikhdom, once protected by London, had been forcibly incorporated into modern Iran by the former shah's autocratic father, Reza Shah.

Since, the dry plains in the country's south-western corner had been officially known as Khuzestan. This was one of the various wrongs that the young men who had just stormed the embassy wanted to put right.

In this sense, their motives were indistinguishable from those of tens of thousands of other young men committed to armed struggle in the cause of national liberation in previous decades. Khuzestan, the CIA had noted some months earlier, was 'economically and strategically the most important region in Iran', producing more than seventy per cent of the country's oil and much of its natural gas, as well as being the site of important ports. The region had never been fully integrated into the country constructed by the Pahlavis, father and son, and so remained its 'Achilles Tendon'. Around two-thirds of its 2.2 million inhabitants were Arabs, many with strong ties to Arab communities in neighbouring Iraq and other Gulf states, and about half of these were Sunni, not Shia Muslims. Under the recently deposed shah, the 'highland-dwelling Persians' had been overtly contemptuous of these poorer, less literate local Arabs who, unsurprisingly, 'resented both the Persians' attitude and their own lowly station' in the province, the CIA noted. The bureaucrats, technicians and managers sent from Tehran 600 miles away to run the region's booming oil business were viewed 'as carpet baggers'. Equally unsurprisingly, the marginalisation of Khuzestan's Arabs had led to a political movement seeking redress for their various cultural and economic grievances. This was firmly put down in the mid-1960s amid the shah's general repression of opposition, resulting predictably in a surge of extremist enthusiasm for the usual causes and familiar icons of the revolutionary left. Among the factions formed at the time was the Democratic Revolutionary Movement for the Liberation of Arabistan (DRMLA).

The trajectory followed by the DRMLA during the 1970s was a fairly familiar one too. For the first half of the decade, the organisation's leadership – mainly youngish men educated at universities in Kuwait, Cairo and Beirut plus a handful of older tribal chiefs – were based in Baghdad where they were part of Saddam Hussein's personal collection of assassins and dissidents. When relations between Saddam and the shah improved briefly from 1975, the DRMLA were forced to decamp to Syria. From there, like so many others, they sent fighters to train with Palestinian groups in Lebanon and to the camp run by the Popular Front–XO outside Aden. At the latter, some may have enjoyed instruction from Ilich Sánchez, aka Carlos, and they earned a namecheck a year later in the Popular Front–XO's statement justifying the hijack that led to the raid on Entebbe. Libya also played host to the DRMLA and offered support, holding a 'National Arab Festival of Solidarity with the people of Arabistan' in Tripoli in April 1978. By then, Saddam's relations with Tehran had begun to deteriorate and he had invited the DRMLA back, just in time to welcome a massive influx of recruits when the revolution came.

The man who would lead the attack in London and who first addressed the stunned hostages at 16 Prince's Gate was a twenty-seven-year-old schoolteacher from a middle-class family called Towfiq Ibrahim al-Rashidi. He had studied law and literature at Tehran University and so spoke good English. An activist since his teenage years, Rashidi had been detained and tortured by the SAVAK under the shah. Like many in Khuzestan, he had been initially supportive of the revolution, hoping that the Arab minority there would win greater autonomy, but was swiftly disillusioned. First, Rashidi sought unsuccessfully a personal audience with Khomeini to ask for the restoration of Arabic language tuition in his region's schools. Then he watched with dismay as Khuzestan's most prominent cleric and advocate was jailed. Through the spring of 1979 he took part in the widespread unrest in the region that was bloodily repressed by the Revolutionary Guards, and he was among the hundreds of young men from Khuzestan who subsequently fled to Iraq to escape arrest or execution.

Most ended up in Basra, the Iraqi port 150 miles away, where Saddam's security services kept a watchful eye on the new arrivals. Following the fall of the shah, Saddam ramped up support for Iranian dissidents, offering money, training and weapons to those fighting for the rights of 'Arabistan'. Some were sent back to their homeland to launch sabotage attacks on Iranian oil infrastructure or throw bombs into mosques and offices in a bid to destabilise the revolutionary regime's hold on the region. These operations were a nuisance rather than a strategic threat to the radical clerics in Tehran and only stiffened their resolve to bring the restive province under control.

In Basra, Rashidi fell in with a small group of other young exiles. One was Fowzi Badavi Nejad, the slim and strikingly handsome son of a civil servant in Khorramshahr. Nejad, who was twenty-two, had also fled to Iraq after the violence of the spring of 1979. Like Rashidi he had no intention of abandoning his activism now he was in Iraq, but nor was he tempted to participate in the suicidal missions into Iran being organised by the Iraqi security services. Exactly who suggested the attack in London is unclear. The idea may have come from the Mukhabarat, or from Rashidi and his friends, perhaps inspired by the PFLP's operations over previous years. At any rate, initial conversations about an operation went nowhere, leaving the young men in Basra frustrated and despondent.

But then new orders came. 'If you are serious we may have something for you,' Rashidi, Nejad and their friends were told by Saddam's security service. Six were selected and sent to different training camps across Iraq to receive rudimentary instruction in basic weapons handling. A handful of further recruits joined them over the following months and in mid-March a final selection was made. Those chosen were informed by their Iraqi handlers that an operation had been planned for them: to attack the Iranian Embassy in London. The young men were excited and happy.

By the end of the month, the six had arrived in the UK, travelling on Iraqi passports and posing as students. The youngest was nineteen. The oldest was Rashidi. Each had been given £700. They spent their first days in London getting drunk in pubs and shopping. Some brought sex workers back to their rented rooms and were evicted but an Iraqi Mukhabarat agent who had flown in separately was able to arrange new accommodation: the house in Lexham Gardens. This minder had instructed them not to launch the attack until his flight back to Baghdad had taken off – hence their intentionally slow progress to their target, involving leisurely circuits of Hyde Park, and hence their small stroke of luck, arriving exactly when PC Trevor Lock had just gone for a coffee, leaving the front door slightly ajar.

The 'Iranian Embassy siege', as it was known to the British media, was to last six days. After the initial shock had subsided and the first deadline for the destruction of the embassy and all within it had passed without incident, tensions eased, allowing attackers and hostages to establish a routine and a rapport. The seven women among the hostages were kept in one room; the nineteen men in another. Four were British: the policeman who had been on guard duty, a cameraman and a producer from the BBC who had been seeking visas for Tehran, and the embassy's caretaker. There was also a Pakistani educationalist and a Syrian reporter, who played a key role in calming their captors when they became agitated.

Over the 140 hours of the siege, there were moments of terror, relief, hope, even convivial celebration when it appeared that everyone would soon be freed. Sometimes Rashidi and his men proved solicitous, bringing water, warm clothes and snacks. At other times, their behaviour was violently aggressive. This left the hostages exhausted and disorientated. In the final hours of the 'siege', few of those behind the drawn curtains of 16 Prince's Gate expected to escape alive.

The Iranians among the hostages were a mix of the elite of the shah's Iran and the servants of the new revolutionary state. The personal assistant of the new chargé d'affaires was a glamorous and highly intelligent young woman who had been educated in international schools of France and Belgium, spoke four European languages fluently, drove a sports car and had already been threatened with dismissal for refusing to submit to new rules enforcing 'modest' clothing. In contrast, the chargé d'affaires, Ali Afrouz, was a dedicated servant and supporter of Khomeini who had served on the 'Revolutionary Committee' set up to ensure that students and staff at Tehran University complied with the demands of the new regime in February 1979. On taking up his post in London, Afrouz had purged the embassy of many staff whom he suspected of loyalty to the *ancien régime*. As yet, though, the building's expensive carpets, chandeliers and valuable paintings remained *in situ*, as did a number of colourful tourist posters advertising Iran as a holiday destination.

In the first moments of the attack, Afrouz had made an ill-fated bid to escape, jumping from a window, knocking himself unconscious and breaking his jaw. In pain from his injuries and unconfrontational by nature, Afrouz did not challenge Rashidi or his men during the siege. Nor did he argue with Iranian members of his staff who privately admitted that many of the grievances of Rashidi and his comrades were justified, even if their tactics were questionable. Abbas Lavasani, who worked in the embassy's press office, took a much harder line. Lavasani had been posted to London by the Revolutionary Guards, not the Iranian foreign ministry, and was known among the Iranian employees at the embassy for his fierce religious commitment. Former colleagues later described an intransigent and dogmatic zealot, though hostages remembered a small, quiet and dignified young man with a neat beard who 'had spent most of the time reading his personal copy of the Koran'. The two portraits were entirely compatible. Over the coming days, Lavasani would repeatedly clash with Rashidi.

One thing that struck the more perceptive of the hostages was that their captors appeared wholly unprepared for anything beyond the initial seizure of the embassy. Little thought had been given to the means by which Rashidi would communicate their demands, for example. He and the others had brought ammunition and a small quantity of Valium to help them sleep but no other supplies. This meant they were unable to feed either themselves or their hostages once the very limited stores of the embassy were exhausted. Within forty-eight hours, all those inside 16 Prince's Gate were entirely dependent on meals delivered by the British authorities. On the third day, one hostage was surprised to see the gunmen drying washing on a radiator. When hostages fell ill, it became clear their captors lacked not only spare underwear but medical supplies.

These failures of foresight went beyond simple incompetence. They betrayed the fact that the hostage-takers' Iraqi handlers had no interest in the outcome of the attack. Saddam had long coveted Khuzestan, with its Arab population, oil and agricultural potential, but his country's claim to the region was weak. An attack on a high-profile Iranian target by a group of young men from the province who demanded 'liberation' would be an extremely effective way to publicise opposition there to the rule of Khomeini and so help justify any outside intervention, particularly among other Arabs. The more drawn-out the hostage crisis, the more attention it would generate, but the duration of the attack was unimportant. The message had been sent the moment Rashidi and his men came through the embassy's front door, shouting and shooting.

Tellingly, the hostage-takers had also not been briefed in any serious way on how they might conduct negotiations with the Iranian regime. This was supposed to be left to Arab countries who would act as intermediaries. In the event, the radical regime in Iran proved utterly intransigent. There was no question of granting concessions to 'either superpowers or a small band of terrorists', the foreign minister Sadegh Ghotbzadeh said, adding that the hostages should be 'glad to die as martyrs for the Iranian revolution'.

The Iranian attitude surprised no one. Only days earlier, US special forces had launched an extremely ambitious and complex assault in order to free the dozens of US diplomats and other staff now in their sixth month of captivity in Tehran. Operation Eagle Claw had been a debacle, with the only saving grace being that the attacking force had never reached the Iranian capital as planned, thus avoiding what would almost certainly have been an even greater disaster. As it was, the Americans were obliged to abandon five helicopters, a burned-out transporter and the charred remains of eight servicemen in the middle of the Iranian desert. These were found by revolutionary authorities – along with an incinerated local petrol tanker and a bus containing thirty bewildered Iranian passengers. Quite what had happened was initially unclear but Iran's leaders drew the conclusion that the US had launched yet another attempt to restore the shah. Ghotbzadeh was not alone in seeing events in London as part of a concerted campaign to overthrow the revolution. Tehran radio blamed 'imperialists and international Zionists', and the foreign minister appeared convinced that the hostage-takers were agents of the CIA. When informed that Rashidi and his men were threatening to blow up the embassy, Ghotbzadeh shouted 'Let them do what the hell they like.' In reality, such a bloody and spectacular outcome to the attack was vanishingly unlikely as the hostage-takers had not been equipped by the Iraqis with any explosives.

Margaret Thatcher, who had become prime minister almost exactly a year before, was fully briefed on the attack late on the first evening. She agreed with the policies that her Home Secretary, William Whitelaw, and senior officials had drawn up during the afternoon. These stipulated that there would be no amnesty for anyone who had broken British law, under no circumstances would any of the 'terrorists' or their hostages be allowed to leave the UK, and the police would be allowed 'all the time they needed to resolve the crisis without bloodshed'.

London's police already had some experience of what they called 'siege' situations. In September 1975, three extremists on the fringes of Britain's Black rights movement had tried to rob an Italian restaurant in Knightsbridge and ended up taking its eight staff hostage. Three months later an 'active service unit' of bombers and bomb-makers sent to London by the Irish Republican Army were cornered in the home of a middle-aged couple. Both incidents were resolved without death or injury. But what was underway at Prince's Gate was very different. It involved the embassy of a hostile power, attackers about whom nothing was known, more than two dozen hostages and a five-storey building in the very heart of the capital.

The police could draw on significant new expertise, however. Case studies of other similar incidents over the previous decade had been carefully studied and lessons shared at a series of international seminars. These were now applied. To enhance the sense of isolation and pressure within 16 Prince's Gate, a cordon was thrown far across Hyde

Park so that almost no human activity would be visible from the building's high windows. All means of communication were cut off except a single phone line to police negotiators, which now became the captors' sole link to the outside world. Food was provided and occasional comforts were offered – cigarettes, clothes – but nothing else. No deadlines were given or admitted. Western European police forces, though not their US counterparts, had come to believe that the more time that passed, the weaker the position of the hostage-takers became.

Initially, this strategy brought some success. Several hostages were released – including one of the two BBC journalists, who provided much useful information about his captors. Listening devices pushed into walls and dangled down chimneys were unreliable but worked well enough to transmit conversations among the attackers, revealing that they were incapable of blowing up the whole building even if they had wanted to. It was also encouraging that Rashidi had steadily reduced his demands over the course of his conversations with the police's interlocutors, such that by the fifth day he seemed inclined to accept more or less anything that would allow him to end the attack without total capitulation.

But stalling the hostage-takers indefinitely held significant risks too. The attackers were increasingly tired as the days passed – which was good – but Rashidi appeared increasingly frustrated – which was bad. On the fifth day of the crisis, tensions increased notably after a fierce row caused by graffiti written on a wall by the younger attackers which insulted Khomeini, calling him a 'Shah in a Turban'. Another simply read 'Fuck the Ayatollah'. This outraged Lavasani, the devout revolutionary, and led to a heated argument. Lavasani had already told other hostages that he had prepared himself for death, saying that he had no family and welcomed the opportunity to die for the revolution. On the afternoon of 5 May, the sixth day of the attack, that opportunity came.

Rashidi had told the police he wanted to meet the Arab diplomats who were supposed to help negotiate the end of the siege. He gave them forty-five minutes to comply or he would shoot a hostage. The police did what they had done throughout the week: they stalled, explaining that there were all sorts of logistical challenges that prevented them from doing so. For once, this was true, as the Foreign Office was having enormous difficulty finding any Arab ambassadors in London prepared to mediate now that they were unable to offer safe conduct out of the UK. This time, however, Rashidi lost his temper. He found Lavasani, tied him to banisters in the basement and, with the line to the police negotiator still open, told the Iranian to identify himself aloud. Moments after the diplomat had said his name, there was a choked scream and shots. Everyone in the embassy, attackers included, was profoundly shocked. Five hours later, at 6 p.m., Lavasani's body was dumped on the embassy steps. Shortly afterwards, Rashidi told police he would shoot another hostage every thirty minutes until his demands were met. The British authorities recognised that a critical moment had been reached.

There were various reasons for Thatcher's insistence that no concessions be made to the attackers. One was the memory of the humiliating release of Leila Khaled nine years before. This had been portrayed as clever diplomacy at the time, but even the most obtuse observer could see that the UK's primary motive in releasing a woman who had just tried to take over a full Boeing 747 in British airspace and whose accomplice had nearly killed a crew member had been to avert future attacks on its interests. A second reason for Thatcher's obduracy was a set of new international laws which theoretically forbade any move to fly the attackers to a third country. A third was domestic: the British mainland and Northern Ireland had suffered years of attacks by the IRA which had caused hundreds of civilian casualties. The previous year a Conservative MP who was a valued friend and counsellor of Thatcher had been killed by a car bomb as he was leaving parliament, and Lord Louis Mountbatten, a cousin of the queen and one of the most prominent aristocrats in the country, had been killed on a fishing trip in Ireland when the IRA blew up his hired boat. Such attacks had prompted the new prime minister to promise 'a war on terrorism' that would be waged 'with relentless determination'.

But a final and perhaps deciding factor was that, unlike most of her predecessors, Thatcher had an alternative to negotiation or capitulation. The British army's SAS had been founded during the Second World War to carry out raids behind enemy lines that lived up to its regimental motto, 'Who Dares Wins'. Its troopers, as they were known, had seen action in various scrappy campaigns of Britain's imperial retreat, fighting in the 1960s in southern Yemen against the Arab nationalists and Marxists who eventually won control of their country, and then in the early 1970s in Oman, fighting similar enemies who didn't. When British officials had seen the fiasco that was the German police's attempt to resolve the attack on the Munich Olympics seven years earlier, they had decided, like many other governments, that they needed soldiers or police who could successfully undertake such a mission. The SAS had been given this role, and specialists from the regiment had usefully assisted Dutch security forces dealing with the hostage-taking on the train in 1977 and the West Germans when they launched their raid at Mogadishu the same year. The unit had been mobilised within an hour of the attack at 16 Prince's Gate and by the morning of the second day of the crisis dozens of troopers had been installed in a holding area in a barracks a five-minute drive away. There, they refined and practised an assault plan.

Thatcher and her officials had agreed not only that there would be no concessions but that they would order an assault to end the crisis if a hostage was deliberately killed. Shortly after Lavasani's remains were retrieved by armed police from the embassy steps, the SAS moved into their prepared positions. Thatcher had been warned the chances of getting the hostages out alive were about sixty per cent.

The operation was broadcast live. When at 7.23 p.m. the first explosions cracked and boomed across central London, the BBC interrupted coverage of the world championship snooker final and switched to the scene at Prince's Gate. Some sports fans later complained but not many. Instead, much of the British population watched in great excitement and some astonishment as the black-clad men of the SAS abseiled from the roof of the building and entered the embassy through its windows amid clouds of smoke and flames. There was a lot of gunfire, some screaming and many wailing sirens. It was very unclear what was happening and stupefied journalists could provide little clarity.

The assault lasted just over fifteen minutes and at its end five of the six DRMLA men were dead. Rashidi was killed first, having been dragged to the ground by an SAS man who had just come through the windows of the embassy and then fired several bullets into him from very close range. Another of the hostage-takers was shot running towards the room where the male Iranian captives were held. A third died as he prepared to open fire on Afrouz, the chargé, and his colleagues. One was killed while lying on the ground, having possibly surrendered, when the SAS soldiers thought he was reaching for a concealed weapon. A fifth tried to hide among the hostages as they were moved out of the embassy but was shot thirty-nine times when he appeared to raise a grenade. The only survivor among the attackers was Nejad, who was identified while lying face-down in the back garden of the embassy alongside many of the people he had helped hold captive for six days. He had been well liked by the female hostages, who had not immediately pointed him out to the SAS and so may have saved his life. The only casualties beyond the attackers were the Iranian diplomats who had been fired on by their guard before he was killed. Of these, one was dead and two were seriously hurt. Among the SAS, three men had been slightly injured.

The spectacular denouement to the 'Iranian Embassy Siege' provoked an almost ecstatic surge of national pride in Britain. The SAS had shown that Britain was still a superpower, newspaper columnists told readers. Despite decades of decline and years of strikes, inflation, power cuts and disappointments abroad, the spirit that had won the Second World War was still alive. That the British would take such risks to help a hostile regime, which was itself holding others hostage in appalling conditions: what more resounding evidence of the nation's sangfroid and spirit of fair play could one imagine? The novelist John le Carré commented acidly in the *Observer* that counter-terrorist feats had become a measure of national virility. 'The Israelis had scored at Entebbe, the Germans ... at Mogadishu. The French of course just barter and let everyone go. The Americans, who once put a man on the moon, could not even find six working helicopters to fly into the Iranian desert,' he wrote. 'It was a triumph ... That was the word everywhere. Not a victory but a triumph ... It was a police triumph ... a triumph for Conservatism and ... foreign policy and domestic policy and fiscal policy and for all the sunny spring of Mrs Thatcher's new Britain.'

There was much that could be celebrated, of course. The success of the SAS showed how far specialist police and military units had developed since Munich. While the raids on Entebbe and Mogadishu had made clear that no safe havens existed for hijackers, Prince's Gate was evidence that major Western cities, which had once seemed so vulnerable, were no longer so exposed. In short, the tide in the war between states and insurgent actors that had been taking place since the late 1960s had now definitively turned.

More than this, the SAS raid in London had provided the most arresting visual images of any episode involving terrorism and terrorists in recent memory. The sight of three aircraft going up in flames on the sand at Dawson's Field in Jordan in 1970 had been startling, and the live feed of the Munich attack nerve-racking. But nothing could compare to the balaclava-ed SAS gunmen clambering over the balconies of 16 Prince's Gate for sheer drama and immediacy. A decade earlier, the introduction of satellites, portable cameras and television sets in hundreds of millions of homes had allowed groups like the PFLP to win and manipulate massive public exposure almost without hindrance or challenge. Now, this vital arena had been at least partially reconquered. The 'theatre of terrorism' now had a rival: a 'theatre of counter-terrorism'.

Le Carré was not the only person in the UK to voice concerns about triumphalism, but those who worried about 'jingoistic self-congratulation' were few. And the claims of a victory over terrorism, insofar as a tactic could ever be defeated, were fair. But the real problem, which almost everyone missed at the time, was that the generals were fighting the last war.

The terrorism that was defeated in London in May 1980 was practised by an organisation that had been founded in the late 1960s. It was self-avowedly 'Democratic', 'Revolutionary' and sought 'Liberation'. Its ideology was profoundly influenced by Arab nationalism of the sort that had inspired Fatah and the PFLP. Its enemies, predictably, included imperialism, capitalism and Zionism. Its programme was, at least nominally, socialist. Its members, like so many others, had trained with factions of the Palestine Liberation Organisation. Its attackers wore the red and white chequered keffiyeh which, along with Che Guevara T-shirts, had been worn by revolutionary fighters since the late 1960s.

Nor did the DRMLA's attacks, whether in Khuzestan or London, aim to kill lots of people. Rashidi and the others had not carried explosives and their threat to blow up the embassy was empty. Before launching the attack, they had agreed among themselves that they would not kill anyone. They certainly did not expect to die, let alone seek death. The luggage they had sent back to Baghdad – nearly 100 kg between them – contained perfume, children's toys, jewellery and cocktail dresses for friends and family in Iraq, but also lingerie for girlfriends and expensive suits they intended to wear themselves. Their Iraqi handlers had told them that the unarmed British police would never try to retake the embassy by force, and, though they occasionally referred to themselves as the Group of the Martyrs, this was a reference to those who had already given their lives for their cause, not, as the internal Home Office report on the siege later erroneously concluded, a reference to their own aspirations. Shortly before the SAS launched their assault, Nejad and others discussed surrender. 'They wanted to live as much as I did,' one of the BBC journalists held hostage remembered. The only individual during the entire episode who spoke of desiring death as a statement and sacrifice was the man Rashidi shot dead on the last afternoon: Lavasani, the press attaché and dedicated supporter of Khomeini. Mrs Thatcher, her officials, the police and the SAS had indeed won a famous victory, but over yesterday's enemy.

Six months after the Iranian Embassy attack, the British Foreign Office began a review of the spread of 'so-called Islamic extremism or fundamentalism' across the Middle East and the wider Islamic world. British missions throughout the region were asked to submit memos explaining their sense of the extent of the phenomenon and its potential consequences. A similar effort in 1978 had reported that the 'Islamic revival' posed 'no significant danger . . . for British interests' and had no 'serious future implications'. Since then, however, there had been a number of events which prompted a potential revision of this sanguine view. The fact that 'Iran has become an Islamic Republic, [that] the Soviet Union has invaded Afghanistan', and that on 22 September 1980 Iraq had invaded Iran, meaning 'two major Islamic countries' were now at war with one another, were all good reasons to refocus the Foreign Office's attention on the issue of 'Islam', officials noted.

The responses received in Whitehall over the following weeks were varied. For British diplomats in the Middle East, the key consideration was the potency of the ideology that had mobilised Iranians against their shah. The British Embassy in Muscat warned that the personal appeal of Khomeini was not confined to Shia Muslims, citing conversations with Sunnis who had said that 'despite its shortcomings the regime in Tehran [stood] for Islam in a way no other regime did and deserved support on that score alone.' Diplomats in Pakistan, where General Zia-ul-Haq's Islamisation drive was intensifying, noted that 'among the less sophisticated, and also among those nearer the centre of power . . . Khomeini also enjoys the kind of prestige accorded by many Africans to Idi Amin.' The Iranian leader was not liked 'for what he is, but for the way he has succeeded [in] defying the West and in particular the Americans', they explained.

Others were less alarmist. In Turkey, British diplomats had noted inroads made by religious 'revivalist' parties on 'the extreme right wing of the spectrum' but thought it likely that these had been 'stopped in their tracks' by a recent military takeover there. Their counterparts in Riyadh appeared remarkably optimistic, and suggested that a useful course of action would be to emphasise 'the common ground [Britain] shared with Islamic revivalists' such as 'a healthy dislike of Communists and distrust of the Soviet Union'. It was of great importance not to be 'fatalistic in our acceptance that any Islamic revival must inevitably be anti-Western', the embassy in Saudi Arabia argued.

The longest contribution came from Cairo, however, where British officials expressed the opposite view. No common front could be found with the Islamists, not least because 'in the case of the hard-liners who set the pace, hostility to the West is central to their position and a main motive for it.' Though they admitted that Britain adopting a position of 'rigid hostility' to Islamic revivalists would 'no doubt be a mistake', the staff of the embassy in Egypt told Whitehall that as far as the revivalists were concerned, 'We in the West . . . are just as bad [as the Soviets] and . . . constitute the more present threat in the form of the demoralising and corrupting effects of Western economic penetration.'

Across the Atlantic, the CIA was inevitably preoccupied by Iran, which remained prominent on almost every one of the briefs it presented each morning to President Carter. A catastrophic failure of intelligence-gathering had led the agency to tell all major decision-makers in Washington that the shah was safe on his throne until only weeks before he was forced to flee, and the hostage crisis at its embassy in Tehran appeared far from any happy resolution. Having failed entirely to foresee either the fall of the shah or the rise of Khomeini, it now apparently sought to redeem itself with a small tsunami of analysis. An entire series of reports covered harvests in far-flung provinces, another listed in exhausting detail the various factions behind the ongoing regional revolts against central government. An eighty-page document on Islam in Iran included twelve pages on Ali Shariati. Despite the agency's almost total lack of sources on the ground, many of the predictions made in this slew of reporting were soon shown to be accurate. The death of the shah, when it came in Cairo in July 1980, did not make any difference to the plight of the hostages, as the CIA had advised some months earlier, and the border skirmishes initiated by Saddam Hussein through the summer did indeed presage a much broader attack on Iran. A month later, in August 1980, the agency bluntly warned Carter that Khomeini wanted to exploit the hostage issue to ensure the president failed to win a second term at the November elections. The Iranian regime wanted to humiliate the US further, the CIA said. This too was correct.

But the agency still stumbled frequently. Its analysts misread Saddam

Hussein's war aims, thinking they were initially limited to 'liberating' Khuzestan by attaching it to Iraq and redrawing the frontier. They underestimated the degree to which the offensive that came in September 1980 was both opportunistic and much more far-reaching, launched in the hope of exploiting a moment of Iranian weakness to ensure overarching regional supremacy. The CIA also completely misread how the Iranian population would rally to Khomeini's revolutionary regime in the face of the Iraqi invasion.

But perhaps their greatest misjudgement was the lack of attention they gave to the armed resistance Khomeini would face from within Iran. For the force that would come closest to unseating the clerics was not Saddam Hussein's Iraq, nor the Soviet Union nor even Farrokh Negahdar's Marxist Fedayeen-e Khalq, which remained stubbornly if uneasily aligned with the revolutionary regime. The final brutal and climactic battle to rule Iran in the aftermath of the fall of the shah was fought instead by a few thousand idealistic men and women, often students or educated professionals, mostly in their early or mid-twenties, whose language, ambitions and tactics recalled struggles fought a decade or so earlier, as well as the energies set loose by the Islamic revival that was reshaping the whole region.

The stakes in this contest were very high. Victory would bring the power to govern Iran without challenge, shaping its ideas and institutions more or less at will. Defeat would mean hurried flight or death.

29

'The most beautiful work'

During the chaos and excitement of the fall of the shah and its immediate aftermath, there had been pictures of the Ayatollah Ruhollah Khomeini everywhere. Portraits taken over the previous years and circulated clandestinely among supporters had been borne aloft above demonstrations. Grainy images had appeared on the fronts of newspapers newly liberated from censorship. And in the early months of the revolution a number of superb photographs were taken by foreign and local photographers given astonishing access to Iran's inscrutable, implacable new leader, capturing Khomeini outside his home in Qom as he was served tea by an aide or sweating as he addressed a press conference.

By the summer of 1980 no one was taking such images. The Western photographers had gone home or been expelled and most of their local counterparts had fled. No longer did Khomeini answer questions from journalists. Instead, he remained in his new residence in the village of Jamaran just north of Tehran, issuing diktats, managing the conflicts between his followers, crafting the final stages of the revolution and the radical regime he had imposed.

Many observers, abroad and at home, had expected the regime to last only a few months – at most, a few years. This was in part due to a belief that the clergy had no understanding of the contemporary world and would be incapable of running a modern state. Instead, by the time of the unsuccessful US effort to free its hostages and the assault by the SAS on Iran's London embassy, Khomeini had taken considerable strides towards realising his vision for Iran's politics, society and values.

Iran's new constitution had been adopted in December 1979 following a referendum. Now that the nature of the new regime had become all too clear, many boycotted the poll in sensibly mute protest and the turnout was much lower than when the country had voted almost unanimously to replace the monarchy with 'an Islamic Republic' six months earlier.

Iran's new political system retained some of the elements of the constitutional, democratic system that Bazargan and his supporters had once tried to construct, and that many if not most Iranians still wanted. A legislature, judiciary and executive remained. There was a president and a prime minister. Torture was outlawed, freedom of association and speech permitted. But onto this recognisably democratic system a second had been superimposed, with clerics given an all-encompassing oversight role, and the supreme leader granted sweeping powers. This was not exactly the Velayat al-Faqih that Khomeini had outlined in his 1971 lectures, but as close as anyone was likely to come anywhere in the world in the first year of the penultimate decade of the twentieth century.

The constitution had also cemented the central role of the Pasdaran or Islamic Revolutionary Guard Corps, which had expanded exponentially following the outbreak of war with Iraq. A new paramilitary group known as the Basij-e Mostazafin – the militia of the oppressed or disinherited – now provided a further counterweight to the suspect regular army, which had been weakened by a series of bloody purges. From the ruins of the SAVAK a new internal security service was slowly being created, while across the country, revolutionary tribunals continued their bloody work. The radical clerics' hold over the country's religious establishment was stronger than it had ever been. So too was their grasp on control of the courts, national assembly and bureaucracy.

In addition, the regime now controlled much of the mass media, from the national television and radio networks to the Friday sermons delivered in tens of thousands of mosques by regime-appointed clerics. The appropriation of the Pahlavi Foundation, a sprawling network of businesses and banks run by the royal family supposedly for charitable purposes, had given the regime huge wealth and power, not least in the opportunities it bestowed for patronage. So too did the seized assets of the tens of thousands of affluent Iranians who had fled the country or been executed. On the basis that 'all the problems of the last fifty years' were the fault of 'liberals, academics and other intellectuals', Khomeini had shut the country's 'colonial and Westernised' universities. 'Most of the deadly blows which have been delivered to [Iranian] society have been due to the majority of these university-educated intellectuals who have always regarded – and still regard – themselves as being great and have always said things – and still continue to say things – which only their other intellectual friends can understand, regardless of whether the people understand them or not,' the Ayatollah had told his countrymen. Finally, a raft of new laws introduced Koranic *qisas* or retributive punishments, and further reduced women's rights.

Yet Khomeini knew that, despite the widespread support of much of the urban and rural poor, his authority was still contested. To move too far too quickly as he consolidated his power would be counterproductive. This meant that the democratic provisions of the new constitution needed to be obeyed at least in form, even as their spirit was traduced. In the spring of 1980 Iran had elected a new parliament and its first president. Neither process was anything close to being free or fair. Groups of young men armed with clubs and iron bars were sent to disrupt opposition rallies, candidates were disqualified on spurious grounds or threatened, some voting took place in mosques, ballot boxes were stuffed and electoral registers manipulated. The resulting parliament was dominated by the radical clerics' political vehicle: the Islamic Revolutionary Party. But to most observers' great surprise the president who took power was much less subservient.

Khomeini, exercising his new constitutional powers, had ruled against a cleric standing for election as president, perhaps believing that it would be better to distance the religious establishment from the messy business of day-to-day administration and aware that many Iranians were wary of clerical overreach. The supreme leader calculated that Abolhassan Bani-Sadr, a forty-seven-year-old Islamist economist who had been an adviser to him since before the revolution, would in no way challenge his own hold on power. In this, Khomeini had made a rare but serious miscalculation and so set the stage for a final, climactic battle for political supremacy in revolutionary Iran.

Bani-Sadr was the son of an ayatollah, but his view of the world owed less to Shia faith and traditions and more to the anti-colonial ideas current in Iran in the 1950s and the *élan révolutionnaire* he had seen in the 1960s while studying part-time at the Sorbonne. He was a theoretician of revolution rather than a practitioner and, for all his undoubted commitment to Islamism, was something of an anarchist aesthete. He had appreciated the 'popular effervescence' on display during the unrest in Paris in 1968 and believed revolution was 'the most beautiful work a generation can conceive or realise'. Self-assured, loquacious and faintly absurd with his swept-back hair, square glasses, dapper moustache and beautifully cut suits, the new president was also considerably more popular than any of the clerics close to Khomeini.

Bani-Sadr had studied law and theology at Tehran University but spent much of the 1960s and early 70s in Paris developing an 'Islamic concept of economics'. This attempted to combine the radical redistributive mechanisms of socialism with the fundamental tenets of the Muslim faith and so resembled the thinking of Ali Shariati. Yet, despite the differences between his intellectual approach and that of Khomeini, Bani-Sadr had fallen under the spell of the elderly cleric on a visit to Najaf in 1972. His admiration grew during the following years, and in October 1978 it had been Bani-Sadr who welcomed Khomeini to Paris, evicting his own teenage daughters from his small suburban apartment to make room for the fugitive cleric until more suitable accommodation could be found. In Neauphle-le-Château, Bani-Sadr had been an invaluable aide and adviser to Khomeini, and this earned him a place on the semi-secret revolutionary council in Tehran that later worked to translate Khomeini's will into political reality. Even so, Bani-Sadr had never enjoyed good relations with the radical clerics around the supreme leader, as few of them shared his relatively liberal outlook or belief in the individual's right to interpret sacred Islamic texts. When Bani-Sadr won the election, Khomeini offered him limited and grudging support, calling on Iranians to obey 'as long as he acts according to the principles of Islam and helps the poor and the downtrodden and avoids *taghuti* [idol-worshipping, satanic or, in this context, secular] behaviour'.

In the event, Iran's first president never even had a chance to prove himself. During the electoral campaign, Bani-Sadr had promised to fight against censorship, the regime's thugs and the 'power monopolists'. This led more or less immediately to confrontation. There was much to argue over: the appointment of cabinet ministers, the right way to restore some semblance of order to the economy, the recent subversion of electoral process and the continued detention of the US hostages seized in November 1979 which, Bani-Sadr believed, was isolating Iran on the world stage and depriving it of military parts much needed for the war against Iraq.

That war had been described by Khomeini as a 'gift from heaven' for the opportunity it offered to rally the nation behind the regime, but its conduct proved another flashpoint. Bani-Sadr, who had also been appointed commander-in-chief of the armed forces, spent much of his time at the front, driving from base to base in a mud-daubed Land Rover, and exploited the profile this gave him to win considerable popular support. Iran's military forces had forced Iraq onto the defensive through 1980, but, despite strenuous and costly efforts, failed to retake any ground from Saddam's forces.

This led to fresh clashes between the new president and the clerics. Bani-Sadr opposed the increasingly important role being given to the Pasdaran and the creation of a brigade of religious 'commissars' whose job was to ensure that all troops displayed 'correct Islamic ideas', as well as other initiatives that he saw as having ideological rather than military aims. The clerics suspected that Bani-Sadr was more interested in winning domestic support than the war and sought to portray him as weak, or even an outright traitor. One potent weapon in the hands of Bani-Sadr's opponents were the hundreds of shredded documents taken from the US Embassy, which had been painstakingly reassembled by teams of young volunteers. One revealed a clumsy attempt by the CIA in early 1979 to convince Bani-Sadr to become an informant in return for a monthly payment of $5,000. Though he had indignantly refused the offer, Bani-Sadr was hurt by the revelation.

Through late 1980 and into the new year, the confrontation between the hardline clerics and Bani-Sadr grew. The release of the US hostages on 20 January 1981, the day of Ronald Reagan's inauguration as president, ended the 444-day crisis but brought little improvement in relations with the superpower or relief within Iran from internal tensions. Two months later Khomeini tried to reconcile Bani-Sadr and the clerics, but the effort failed because the supreme leader so obviously favoured the latter. Realising that he could expect nothing from the Supreme Leader, Bani-Sadr began to look for allies elsewhere.

The obvious candidate to join him in a coalition against the clerics was the biggest and best-armed opposition movement in Iran at the time: Mojahedin-e-Khalq-e-Iran. The final confrontation that followed was between two powerful movements, each representative of broader revolutionary ideologies still battling for primacy across the Middle East. Both had their origins in the thinking and practices of the 1960s. Both had been forced to adapt to rapidly changing circumstances during the 1970s. Only one would survive to dominate the decade that followed.

*

The Mojahedin-e-Khalq-e-Iran, the Iranian People's Mojahedin or simply the Mojahedin, had been founded in the middle years of the 1960s by a dozen recent graduates from Tehran University and so was very much part of the great wave of radicalisation and mobilisation taking place across so much of the developing world at that time. They had the same heroes as their New Left counterparts elsewhere – the Vietnamese, the Cubans, the Algerians and the Palestinians – and had read their Mao, Marighella, Debray, Fanon too. Their understanding of history and economics was Marxist, their strategy Leninist, their tactics derived from the Foco-ism of Che Guevara and the urban guerrilla campaigns of Latin American groups like the Tupamaros. Like so many others, they dispatched a delegation to Jordan to train in the camps of Yasser Arafat's Fatah. Arriving in July 1970, the delegation from the Mojahedin was there at the same time as the Red Army Faction and their visit too was managed by 'Abu Hassan', or Ali Hassan Salameh, who distributed the Iranian visitors among Fatah's camps, made sure they received the training they hoped for and flattered one with the rank of 'commander'.

Yet, in one key respect, they differed markedly from the rest of the international revolutionary movement of which they were a part. As Mojahedin, 'those who strive on the path of holy struggle' or jihad, they believed, like Ali Shariati, that Marxist-Leninist ideas and theory were inadequate if they were not supplemented by the traditions, values and outlook of Shia Islam. They did not call themselves Communists or socialists but 'revolutionary Muslims'. 'We say "no" to Marxist philosophy, especially atheism. But we say "yes" to Marxist social thought, particularly to its analysis of feudalism, capitalism, and imperialism,' the Mojahedin told potential recruits, following Shariati more or less word for word. 'After years of study . . . our organisation has reached the firm conclusion that Islam, especially Shiism, will play a major role in inspiring the masses to join the revolution.'

The Mojahedin's first effort at revolutionary action was nothing if not ambitious. Learning that the shah planned to celebrate 2,500 years of monarchy in Iran (and Persia) in October 1971 with a spectacular and hugely expensive festival that would be attended by hundreds of foreign dignitaries but no ordinary Iranians, the group set about formulating a strategy to disrupt the event. A direct attack on the 160-acre tent city erected opposite the ruins of Persepolis appeared impractical. Instead, the Mojahedin decided to strike at electrical transmission stations in Tehran with the goal of plunging the celebrations into darkness, and then to hijack an Iranian aeroplane.

This was a disaster. To obtain explosives the Mojahedin approached a former Communist who had recently been recruited as a police informer. Hours before their operation was due to begin, some seventy Mojahedin were rounded up, around half of the group's active strength. The shah – and hundreds of heads of state, celebrities and billionaires – enjoyed the vintage wines, gourmet food flown in from top caterers in Paris, parades and ball without disruption. Eleven of the Mojahedin's founders and members of its central committee were executed and the few who remained alive were tried and given long prison sentences.

Though this was a heavy blow, the organisation had still been able to recruit new members, mainly on the restive, overcrowded campuses of Iran's new universities. The Mojahedin won particular support among science undergraduates from clerical families and teachers, though they did far less well among women and humanities students who tended to favour the Fedayeen-e Khalq. The influx of enthusiastic recruits was sufficient to continue sporadic acts of violence against the shah's regime over the following years. There were gun battles with police, shootings of US civilian technical advisers, arson attacks on Western hotels. Bombings were usually designed to avoid civilian casualties, with warning often given to authorities before a blast. One device exploded at the tomb of the shah's father forty minutes before President Nixon was due to arrive there. 'Death to America by blood and bonfire . . . is the cry of the Iranian people,' ran the uncompromising words of the Mojahedin's marching songs. 'May America be annihilated.' It was a sentiment shared with both its right-wing and left-wing rivals.

With the SAVAK focusing its efforts on suppressing the Fedayeen-e Khalq through the middle years of the 1970s, the Mojahedin escaped relatively lightly. In the gruesome contest between opposition groups over who could claim the most 'martyrs', they lost out to their purely Marxist rivals, and though the release of hundreds of their members from prisons in 1977 provided a welcome boost, the Mojahedin had played only a peripheral role during the final years of unrest that led to the shah's fall. But once the Pahlavi regime was gone, they proved adept at navigating and exploiting the chaos of revolutionary Iran. The Mojahedin had contributed significantly to the defeat of the armed forces in the street battles in Tehran in February 1979. This, coming after a decade of attacks and sacrifice, won the organisation much popular admiration, as well as tens of thousands of weapons looted from government armouries.

The group now set out to mobilise as a mass movement, offering Iranians an apparently more progressive and leftist alternative to the reactionary populism and traditionalism of the radical clerics but without the secularism of the purely Marxist groups. In the chaotic liberty of the early months after the flight of the shah, this proved particularly attractive among relatively devout but educated young people from a lower middle-class background. Soon enough the Mojahedin's rallies were attracting attendances as large as those of the Fedayeen, its newspaper too was selling hundreds of thousands of copies and the party's candidates were winning massive support in elections to the constitutional assembly that sat during the summer of 1979.

Initially, the Mojahedin saw themselves as playing the role of a loyal opposition to the clerical regime. This was partly because their leaders recognised that the appeal of the Ayatollah Khomeini among Iranians was 'greater even than Stalin's among Comintern Communists or the Pope's among Roman Catholics' and that open contestation would be counter-productive. It was only when it became clear to even the most obtuse and dogmatic observer that Khomeini and the men around him were not only uninterested in sharing power with them or anyone else but were aiming to obliterate all resistance to their authority that the Mojahedin moved towards direct confrontation.

Khomeini loathed the Mojahedin and had long looked for an opportunity to destroy them. A first wave of repression through the summer and autumn of 1980 weakened the organisation and warned of what was to come. In response, the Mojahedin stepped up recruitment among soldiers, students and factory workers and stockpiled weapons. Editorials in *The Mojahed* now accused the 'medieval-minded' clerical regime of widespread corruption, violating human rights, failing to manage the economy, imposing seventh-century tribal laws and repressing women. Such slogans resonated among the millions of Iranians increasingly concerned at the direction the revolution had taken, or simply sick of continuing unemployment and soaring inflation. 'As Muslims, we have a sacred duty to resist tyrannical behaviour,' announced Massoud Rajavi, the organisation's charismatic but wildly over-confident thirty-year-old leader, to his increasingly numerous followers. Khomeini, appealing to his working-class political base and religious conservatives, did not mince his words either. The Mojahedin were 'hypocrites' who were 'more dangerous than unbelievers', he said, adding that 'anyone who speaks against the clergy, must of necessity be against the whole of Islam.'

By now, of course, the most prominent new ally of the Mojahedin was Bani-Sadr, who increasingly saw them as the only force capable of resisting the radical clerics. A deal was done: Bani-Sadr promised to use the power of the presidential office to shield the group from the regime in return for rallies in his support. In February of 1981, Bani-Sadr told a mass meeting that a 'new despotism' threatened to drag Iran back to 'the dark days of the past'. A month later, he repeated his warning to an enthusiastic crowd of more than 100,000. The rally was protected by Mojahedin who physically detained dozens of thugs sent by the radical clerics and then paraded them as evidence of the regime's misdoings. In April, an even bigger protest filled central Tehran. The regime's supporters attacked but were beaten back and for a moment it looked like the Mojahedin might take control of the streets. Events then accelerated. All further demonstrations were banned by the chief prosecutor. Bani-Sadr called for a national referendum on the direction Iran was taking. The Mojahedin threatened a return to 'the armed struggle' and organised a new, even bigger rally in his support. For two days, huge numbers chanting 'Long live freedom, down with despotism' flooded towns and cities across the country. Bani-Sadr then called for a nationwide uprising. Khomeini responded with an address on national television, describing the protests as a war on God and the Islamic Republic led by Communists, nationalists and hypocrites. Those who broke the ban on protests would be shot, he said. Bani-Sadr denounced a clerical '*coup d'état*'.

The climactic trial of strength came on 20 June. Vast protests erupted across the country. In Tehran, more than half a million people marched against the regime. This time, however, demonstrators were met by thousands of armed Revolutionary Guardsmen who fired at them indiscriminately, quickly clearing streets. In the immediate vicinity of Tehran University at least fifty were killed and hundreds injured. This was probably a fraction of total casualties. The use of violence by the authorities – as bad as anything seen under the shah – ended the protest movement overnight. On 21 June, Bani-Sadr was impeached and went into hiding in a Mojahedin safehouse. Massoud Rajavi was already underground.

The rebels were not quite finished yet, though. A week after the bloody end to the attempted uprising, seventy members of the Islamic Revolutionary Party died when a massive explosion almost levelled its Tehran headquarters. The casualties included dozens of the regime's most senior officials, among them several of Khomeini's closest collaborators. Further attacks followed. Eric Rouleau, the veteran correspondent of *Le Monde*, reported from Tehran that 'the bombings were the first sign of a civil war, or at least bloodbaths.'

Such predictions underestimated the brutal power the revolutionary regime had by now acquired. The bloodbath came, but not the civil war. Even before news of the bombing at the IRP offices had been announced to the nation, militiamen spread out to secure strategic positions in Tehran and round up suspected supporters of Bani-Sadr and the Mojahedin. In the prisons, hundreds of detainees from opposition groups were taken from their cells and shot. The tempo of extrajudicial murder accelerated through the rest of July and into the autumn as thousands more were rounded up in mass arrests. Entire families were hanged, including teenagers and grandmothers. Around a tenth of victims were women, including many high-school students and some who were pregnant. A similar proportion were under eighteen and included an eleven-year-old boy and a fifteen-year-old girl, both executed for 'waging war on Allah'. Those who were not immediately put to death were packed into atrociously overcrowded cells and periodically subjected to appalling torture. Children of prisoners were frequently taken hostage to pressure their parents to confess. Khomeini told anyone opposed to the regime to 'repent before it was too late', saying that those who 'swam against the waves' would 'be smashed'. This was exactly what happened.

The Mojahedin was no match for this massive, focused, relentless violence and it crumbled. Some of its more senior members were able to escape, including Rajavi, who fled Tehran for Paris. 'Though we were successful at first in shaking the regime to its very foundations, the brutality of its methods surprised us,' Rajavi admitted shortly after his arrival there. Bani-Sadr quickly lost his distinctive moustache and escaped Tehran in a plane piloted by a sympathetic air force colonel, also to France. Speaking to reporters from the picturesque village of Auvers-sur-Oise, Bani-Sadr issued a call for a new uprising that 'shall succeed again, and conquer, like we succeeded in conquering the old regime'. It went almost entirely unheeded.

The flight of these two leaders marked the end of the second phase of the revolution. The first had seen the shah forced from his throne by a broad coalition of opponents. The second saw the consolidation of Khomeini's regime and the elimination of almost all alternatives. The third would last until almost the end of the decade, and Khomeini's death. From the late summer of 1981, the radical clerical regime in Iran would face many further challenges but none with genuine potential to end its rule.

Neither Bani-Sadr nor Rajavi could be described as moderates. Both were extremists in their own ways and much of their rhetoric and some of their thinking overlapped with that of their enemies in the new regime. But they were also steeped in the ideological activist culture of the revolutionary international of the late 1960s and early 70s, and overall it was this that influenced them most. Their categorical defeat was yet another sign of the exhaustion of this older wave of activism and radicalism and the advent of something altogether different.

Mohsen Sazegara had steered a careful course through the political and administrative chaos of 1980 and 1981. His relative radicalism and outspoken anti-Americanism, as well as a capacity for hard work and talent for quickly mastering a complex brief, had won him favour with the radical clerics around Khomeini and in early 1980 he left his post at Iran's national radio service to begin working as a key political adviser for Mohamed-Ali Rajai, the blunt, outspoken former teacher and Khomeini loyalist who had just been named prime minister. Sazegara found the role exciting and interesting, even if an initiative he launched to reconcile Iran's various political factions was thwarted by extremists on both sides. Professional fulfilment was matched by personal happiness. Sazegara had recently married and on 20 June 1981, the day of massive protest and street battles between regime militia and the Mojahedin across Tehran, his wife was delivered of their first child.

Just over two months later, Sazegara was in his office in central Tehran when the building shuddered, shaken by a huge bomb blast. Unharmed, he rushed down three floors to find that Rajai, who had been elected president in polls held following Bani-Sadr's impeachment, had been killed. Sazegara was summoned for interrogation by investigators who suspected the bomb had been planted by a government insider. He narrowly evaded arrest but a friend was taken off to Evin prison, which seriously frightened him.

For Farrokh Negahdar, the annihilation of the Mojahedin through the later summer and autumn of 1981 marked the beginning of 'the most frightening time' of his life. Since the fall of the shah, he had held the Fedayeen-e Khalq to their strategy of avoiding confrontation with the clerical regime. As a result the organisation's newspapers had continued to publish and the Fedayeen had been exempted from a wide-ranging ban on political parties and even invited to participate in lengthy televised debates with senior clerics. The anti-imperialism and anti-Americanism of Khomeini and his acolytes still aligned with the Fedayeen's worldview, and the war against Iraq called for solidarity among all Iranians. Negahdar remained hopeful that eventually circumstances would allow a more representative government to emerge in Iran. Early in the year, he had warned the leaders of the Mojahedin that an effort to overthrow the radical clerics' regime was premature and would lead to 'a massacre'.

But in the aftermath of the summer's violence, the costs and risks of Negahdar's strategy became starkly apparent. It was now an obvious possibility that once they had definitively destroyed the Mojahedin, the radical clerics would turn on anyone else with the potential to threaten their absolute power. Members of the Fedayeen were already turning up dead in mysterious circumstances or simply disappearing as they sought to spread the organisation's message in the provinces. Negahdar's organisation had avoided explicit endorsement of either the Mojahedin or Bani-Sadr but they were becoming targets nonetheless. Within six months, he would begin organising escape routes that would allow members of the Fedayeen to flee Iran. One would take fugitives to Kurdish enclaves in Iraq, another east to Afghanistan and a third over the northern border to the Soviet Socialist Republic of Azerbaijan. He hoped they would never be used, but if the battle within Iran was lost, they would at least allow the leadership to continue the struggle from elsewhere.

Khomeini did not publicly applaud the repression of the Mojahedin in the late summer and early autumn of 1981 but he made absolutely no attempt to curtail the bloody crackdown either. Dozens of his own aides and associates had died violently in the thirty months since the shah had fled. In public, he remained as undemonstrative as ever, but the sheer number of these losses cannot but have affected him. The darkness and belligerence of his public statements during this period suggested real fears. Not for his own personal safety – this never appeared to concern Khomeini – but for his revolution.

These fears would quickly pass. Better news arrived from the frontlines, where a well-coordinated offensive involving regular troops and the massed battalions of the Pasdaran succeeded in breaking the Iraqi siege of Abadan, a key strategic objective. On 20 October 1981, despite continuing violent efforts at disruption by surviving Mojahedin networks, new elections were held to fill the vacant post of president. Khomeini had dropped his ban on clerics holding the office, clearly believing that concessions to public concerns were no longer necessary nor wise. The winner of the poll was an articulate, elegant and ambitious forty-two-year-old protégé of the supreme leader called Mohammed Ali Khamenei. Since committing himself to Khomeini's cause fifteen years earlier, Khamenei had made up for his lack of scholarly credentials with absolute loyalty to the supreme leader and total dedication to the revolutionary project. Three months prior to the election he had been badly injured while speaking to a congregation at a mosque in Tehran by a bomb concealed in a tape recorder. On taking office, Khamenei told Iranians that he would spare no effort to rid Iran of 'deviation, liberalism, and American-influenced leftists', setting an agenda that would endure well into the next century. In reality, following the clerics' victory over the Mojahedin and Bani-Sadr, there was little opposition left to eliminate.

Like most revolutionaries, Iran's new rulers saw their ideology as a universal panacea to the suffering of mankind. It followed therefore that their duty, once their power was consolidated domestically, was to spread their ideas internationally. In mid-1980, Khomeini had told Iranians that the 'export of our revolution to the world' was both a religious duty – 'because Islam is the supporter of all the oppressed people and does not regard . . . Islamic countries differently [from non-Muslim ones]' – and a strategic imperative: 'all the superpowers and all the powers have risen to destroy us [so] if we remain on the defensive we shall definitely face defeat.' Several clauses of the new constitution underlined the wider ambitions of Iran's new rulers, pledging the nation's support to all those fighting 'the just struggles of the deprived and oppressed . . . in every corner of the globe'.

In truth though, this universalist ideal was more rhetoric than reality. The Islamic revolution's ideology inevitably appealed almost exclusively to Muslims, including often distinctly unobservant ones. In the early months of the revolution, representatives of Islamic organisations from all over the Muslim world had travelled to the Iranian capital, where they were enthused and inspired by what they found. In Libya, little-known radical preachers won popular followings by advocating the 'Iranian model'. In Pakistan, the veteran thinker Abul A'la Maududi, one of the most influential Sunni Islamist ideologues of his time, spoke of his excitement and joy. Pan-Islamists like the leaders of Hizb ut-Tahrir, a transnational organisation committed to the restoration of a caliphate to unite all Muslims, even announced that the Ayatollah Khomeini could potentially fulfil the role of caliph. From Morocco to Malaysia, young men were avidly reading new translations of the writings of Iran's new leader – as well as the works of Ali Shariati and other radical Iranian thinkers. Since the late 1960s, Islamists had been promising that their ideas were a solution to the problems faced by their fellow believers and countrymen and that they had the power to overturn established rulers. At last Khomeini had offered proof for those claims.

Nonetheless, the project to 'export the revolution' soon ran up against the same difficulties that so many others had faced. The first foreign leader to visit Tehran after the fall of the shah was Yasser Arafat. The chairman of the Palestine Liberation Organisation celebrated the change in Iran in fulsome terms, embracing Khomeini for the cameras. The Iranian revolution was a 'new dawn and a new era' which had 'turned upside down' the balance of power in the Middle East, he told reporters, promising that what had happened today in Iran would happen tomorrow in Palestine. The new rulers of Iran promptly handed over the ransacked building of the former Israeli mission in Tehran to the PLO to serve as an office. Further mutual support was promised. 'The Iranian revolution can be safeguarded only if we remember to send assistance to freedom fighters all over the world,' The Voice of the Islamic Revolution radio said. 'Certainly, in sending men to fight side-by-side with the fighters on Islamic fronts, the PLO will hold a special position.'

Yet the relationship swiftly soured. One reason was that the tactile, effusive Arafat failed to build any real rapport with the taciturn Khomeini. But there were other much more significant differences. Arafat was a nationalist, who understood the cultural importance of faith to many of his followers but was very far from being an Islamist in the mould of the radical clerics in Tehran. When Khomeini lectured him on the dangers of secularism, arguing for the PLO to be transformed into a faith-based movement, Arafat demurred. Worse, the PLO chairman insisted on making a gesture of solidarity with Iran's Arabs, opening an office of the PLO in Khuzestan. Mediation by Arafat had led to the release of thirteen of the hostages seized at the US Embassy but when Fatah delegates arrived in Tehran to attend a conference of World Liberation Movements in January 1980 some of the same tensions that had bedevilled relations between Fatah and Iranian trainees in the camps in Lebanon surfaced. The Palestinians saw their hosts as both over-zealous amateurs and amateurish zealots. 'Strategically, the changes in Iran have been very important for us. [But] the trouble is that there are some real nut cases over there,' a PLO official admitted. For their part, the Iranians were shocked at the Palestinians' decadent behaviour. 'None . . . were religious. Most of them drank alcohol, and they wanted to watch films,' complained an Iranian official. When the war between Iran and Iraq broke out, the PLO said it would remain neutral but clearly favoured Saddam. Arafat then re-established contact with the Mojahedin, which it had supported throughout the 1970s. All this further angered the radical clerics in Tehran.

If the effort to build a relationship with the Palestinians failed, there were plenty of other opportunities to build support among Muslim communities abroad. The tens of millions of Shia Muslims in Iraq, linked so closely to Iran in so many ways, were obvious candidates. Yet here too, the new regime in Tehran was to be disappointed. Events in Iran did prompt a wave of protests and some violence by Shia activists in Iraq in May 1979 and then again in 1980 but these were swiftly suppressed. Despite Iranian efforts, there would be no mass uprising of Iraq's Shia majority, let alone of Iraqi Sunnis. Just as the war with Iraq united Iranians to their national cause, so the conflict rallied Iraqis to their own. Instead of being a platform for the expansion of the Islamic revolution, Iraq turned out to be an irreducible obstacle.

The same was true of Saudi Arabia. In December 1979, violent protests had broken out in Qatif, the province with its largest oil deposits and highest concentration of Shia. The unrest suggested to the more imaginative among Khomeini's entourage that the entire kingdom was on the point of insurrection, even if only ten or fifteen per cent of Saudi Arabian citizens identified as Shia. Certainly the thousands of young Shia who took to the streets, some waving placards showing portraits of Khomeini, others chanting Iranian revolutionary slogans, believed that the more confrontational approach of Khomeini and his followers might win more concessions from their rulers than had been achieved by the quietist approach their community had hitherto favoured. But as in Iraq, any revolutionary fervour remained restricted to a relatively small number of people, and there was no mass uprising. The unrest in December 1979 was undoubtedly significant – such open defiance of the kingdom's rulers was unprecedented – but the security forces were able to crush the ill-equipped and unprepared movement rapidly and brutally. 'What are you going to fight them with – your sandals?', one eighteen-year-old heading out to a protest in Qatif was asked by his grandfather. A few superficial concessions and much heavy policing ensured there was no repeat of the protests the following year, and, as in Iraq, there was no sign that the regime was seriously threatened.

The only places where Iran's effort to export the revolution gained much purchase were those where the state was so weakened or absent that it was unable to crush any nascent opposition, though even there the results were disappointing. In Afghanistan, Iran attempted to support a fragmented coalition of Shia groups who were fighting the radical Marxist government in Kabul and who would soon be fighting Soviet troops too, but it met with only limited success. In time Lebanon would become the site of the most successful of revolutionary Iran's overseas interventions, but a series of efforts to establish a presence in war-torn Lebanon from early 1979 brought inconclusive results and as the bloody summer of 1981 drew to a close there was little prospect they would improve.

The reality was that the Iranian revolution had not ignited the chain reaction across the Islamic world that the clerics in power in Tehran had anticipated. The fall of the shah might have encouraged and inspired many individual activists but it had not prompted a single successful effort to seize power elsewhere. Instead, once the seismic geopolitical shock of the revolution had been registered, it was the reaction of fearful rulers across the region and beyond that often had the most significant immediate consequences, not the decisions of the new regime in Tehran or the power of their ideas. One reason the Soviets had dispatched massive forces to Afghanistan was fear that events in Iran might inspire a similar upheaval there. Saddam Hussein had attacked Iran because he believed it had been so weakened by the revolution that its armed forces could offer no serious resistance. Neither of these outcomes were anticipated by the radical clerics in Tehran. The forces generated by the revolution largely escaped their control.

Over the coming decades, the Iranian revolution would contribute much to the growing wave of religious extremism across the region:

new tactics, a particular emphasis on martyrdom and a new readiness to attack Western interests such as the US directly. But the greatest immediate upheavals would come not from the Shia extremists of Iran but from their sectarian rivals. Drawing on their own powerful and pre-existing currents of radicalism, it was Sunni extremists who would most effectively export their ideas and practices in the years to come, not Khomeini and his followers, and it was they who would build the revolutionary international that would eventually take violent Islamist extremism out of the Middle East and across the world.

IX

30
The Black Flag

Very early on the morning of 9 January 1980, six men were taken from prison cells in Riyadh, the capital of Saudi Arabia, and brought to al-Adl Square in the centre of the city. Soldiers posted on the rooftops watched as the blindfolded captives, shackled at the wrist and ankle, waited in the pre-dawn half-light. From a balcony, so too did the city's governor, Prince Salman, and a small group of officials and government ministers. The captives offered no resistance or even complaint, prompting onlookers to wonder if the condemned men had been drugged.

They had not, as soon became clear. The first of the captives was brought before the tall executioner, one of the governor's guards, and pushed to his knees. An assistant stood by with a long spiked rod, used to ensure the posture of the condemned man was sufficiently erect that his head could be cleanly removed with a single arcing stroke of a razor-sharp three-foot sword. Such inducement was unnecessary. Raising his chained wrists high, the man looked upwards and called out loudly and without any trace of fear. 'Bismillah, al-Rahman, al-Raheem, in the name of God, the Compassionate, the Merciful. You know what they have done. You have witnessed their sins and corruption. May their end be most horrible!' Then the man threw his shoulders back, braced and exposed his neck to the descending blade.

In all, sixty-three men in eight cities in every corner of Saudi Arabia would be decapitated that morning. Two months before, they had joined a hundred or so others and seized control of the Great Mosque in Mecca, the holiest site in Islam and the spiritual centre of the faith. Their aim was not just to end the reign of the al-Saud dynasty and transform Saudi Arabia, but to trigger the coming of a new messiah and so usher in a new era of justice and peace for all humankind. Armed with no more than light weapons and an implacable belief in their sacred mission, they had then held the kingdom's defence forces at bay for more than two weeks.

The movement to which all the condemned men belonged had already been defeated, its most prominent members either killed in the fighting or captured and condemned to death. The revolution that they had sought would never come. Like so many others who hoped and fought for radical change in the 1960s and 70s, they had failed. But that they had made the effort at all was evidence of a singularly important phenomenon: the resurgence over the previous twenty years of religious faith and revolutionary violence not just in Iran but across the entire region and broader Muslim world. Indeed, the attack on the Great Mosque went well beyond anything seen in Tehran, not just because it involved Sunni Muslims but because it drew so literally and directly from apocalyptic traditions that even the most excitable of the Ayatollah Khomeini's supporters did not advocate in practice. Likewise, the movement's ambitions were certainly international but had little to do with a global uprising of the oppressed against capitalism or imperialism. The transformation of the world they sought and believed in was one of divine – and apocalyptic – intervention.

At the centre of this new ideology was a vision of a global community of Muslims under attack, and so in desperate need of redemption but also active defence through deeds of bravery and violence. This was a matter of principle and duty rather than political strategy. And while the attack in Mecca appeared to be an outlier in terms of the extremist activism at the time, many of the ideas and practices of those who launched it were far more widespread than almost all but the most perceptive contemporaries realised.

Among those who died under the sword in Riyadh on that January morning was Juhayman al-Utaybi, the forty-two-year-old leader and mastermind of the attack. He came from Sajir, a very poor village in the arid, isolated Najd region of the Arabian peninsula, one of scores of such settlements founded by a minor tribal leader called Abdulaziz al-Saud around the turn of the twentieth century. They had been home to the warriors al-Saud recruited from the desert Bedouin tribes to spearhead his campaign to overcome his rivals and unite their dominions into the kingdom that bore his name: Saudi Arabia.

Juhayman's grandfather, like most of the men of the al-Utaybi tribe, followed the extreme and reactionary teachings of an eighteenth-century revivalist cleric called Ibn Wahhab, who believed in a return to the foundations of Islam, an absolute rejection of anything considered *bida*, innovation, and violence towards those who disagreed with him. The flags of Ibn Wahhab's followers reflected the singular importance their leader placed on *tawhid*, the fundamental Islamic idea that God, the world and a single code of worship and life are all one and indivisible: they bore the *Shahada*, the statement of Islamic faith that there is no God but Allah and Mohammed is his prophet, in white lettering on a black or green background and nothing else. Few outside al-Saud's growing domains were particularly enamoured of the illiterate desert warriors who followed this intolerant, puritanical creed, and many contemptuously referred to them as 'Wahhabis'.

Among these uncompromising fighters were many men from Juhayman's village, including his grandfather. Children in Sajir were raised on stories of faith, blood and betrayal. None were allowed to forget how, once his rule had been successfully established over much of the Arabian peninsula, Abdulaziz al-Saud had offered the Wahhabi fighters who had fought for him a deal: while he and his descendants would retain temporal power, the Wahhabi clergy of his new realm would have authority over his subjects' spiritual well-being and education, advising the royal rulers and receiving much of the kingdom's wealth. Many accepted this pact, but some did not, and when thousands of his former fighters rebelled, al-Saud deployed loyal forces equipped with machine guns mounted on trucks and crushed them in open battle. Survivors included Juhayman's father, whose son had continued the family tradition of implacable loyalty to Wahhabi teachings and resentment towards the House of al-Saud.

Juhayman's childhood and youth were indistinguishable from those of hundreds of thousands of other young Bedouin, and so was his deeply conservative, patriarchal, religious view of the world. He attended a government school for only a few years but learned to shoot, ride and hunt. A basic religious education was provided by the local cleric. Some time in his late teens, around 1955, Juhayman joined his tribal levy in the National Guard. This paramilitary force served two main purposes: to offer moderately lucrative and undemanding jobs to men from potentially restive communities like Juhayman's and to act as a counterweight to the kingdom's regular army if its officers became infected by the new ideologies of Arab nationalism and pan-Arabism surging through the Middle East at the time. Juhayman remained a guardsman for eighteen years, never rising beyond the rank of corporal but building a dense network of familial and tribal connections during his service that would be important later.

In 1964 King Faisal bin Abdulaziz al-Saud, the third son of the founder of Saudi Arabia, took power after a rude struggle with his brother, who had ruled for just over a decade. Oil, discovered in 1938, was now earning the kingdom's rulers large sums, but the profligacy of Faisal's immediate predecessor meant royal finances remained precarious. Almost immediately, the new monarch cut the stipends paid to thousands of princes, halted a series of extravagant building projects and began professionalising the kingdom's bureaucracy. One initiative was the promotion of talented young bureaucrats who had been educated in the West on government-funded scholarships. A beneficiary of this policy was Ahmed Zaki Yamani, the flamboyant oil minister who was to intimidate and charm western Europe and the US a decade later. Another initiative was a new deal with the US companies that owned and ran much of the oil industry which secured King Faisal a much greater proportion of its profits. The wealth of the al-Saud family now began to reach authentically extraordinary levels.

When Juhayman left the National Guard in 1973, the ninth year of Faisal's reign, Saudi Arabia was in the middle of one of the most extraordinarily rapid economic, social and cultural changes occurring anywhere in the Middle East, with the sole possible exception of Iran. Accelerated by the energy crisis that followed the October or Yom Kippur war, which doubled Saudi Arabia's GDP more or less overnight, oil revenues reached $22.5 billion in 1974, almost twenty times the total earned four years earlier. Stories of the Saudi Arabian royals' excesses became a trope across the West at this time. Some of these tales were exaggerated. Others – such as tips of ten thousand dollars to sex workers in London hotels or an attempt to purchase an iceberg – were not.

It was not just members of the royal family in Saudi Arabia who became stupendously wealthy. So too did a new class of contractors, businessmen, fixers and property speculators. As hundreds of thousands of villagers poured into cities in search of employment, entire neighbourhoods were torn down to make space for new construction. Office blocks rose, airports were extended or built from scratch, ports enlarged and international phone lines connected. Eric Rouleau, the indomitable *Le Monde* correspondent, was astonished that the vast four-lane highways being built all over the country were frequently blocked by traffic jams 'that would have outraged even the most jaded Parisian'. A reporter from *Time* marvelled at the same phenomenon, commenting that such congestion was all the more surprising in a country where women were forbidden to drive.

As in Iran and Egypt, the rapid cultural change was exacerbated by a massive influx of businesses, products and visitors from overseas. Many were from the US, drawn in by lucrative contracts to build swathes of the new infrastructure. Labourers from Egypt, Yemen, Pakistan and elsewhere in the Islamic world were less obviously alien but much more numerous. By 1975, half a million foreign workers were resident in the kingdom. These vast changes posed a dramatic challenge to the predominantly rural, illiterate and deeply conservative population who had been living until that point in almost total isolation from the rest of the region, let alone the world.

King Faisal was aware of the problems this could bring and believed that economic development required the gradual evolution of his subjects' often far from progressive views towards something more 'modern'. To this end, he introduced television and pushed through measures ensuring Saudi Arabian women could receive adequate education. The king told critics that 'revolutions can come from thrones as well as from conspirators' cellars', an almost exact echo of the words used by the Shah of Iran about his own effort to 'modernise' his country a decade earlier.

Faisal's effort did not end well, though not quite as badly as the shah's. In 1975, the king was assassinated by a relative whose brother had been shot dead in protests against the education reforms. The king's killer was a playboy prince without obvious faith whose motives remained obscure but the murder underlined the violence that change could bring. To many conservatives in Saudi Arabia, it also showed the dangers of rapid Westernisation. King Khaled, who succeeded Faisal, was elderly and infirm so effective executive power passed to Crown Prince Fahd, a large man with expensive tastes who had spent the summer of 1974 gambling away huge amounts of money in Monaco. Fahd continued his predecessor's strategy of combining rapid economic development with incremental moves to nudge Saudi Arabians away from the harsh rigour of Wahhabism. This too brought mixed results.

The exact circumstances of Juhayman's departure from the National Guard were never clear, even to those who knew him best in subsequent years. On occasion, he referred to mistakes he had made, suggesting some kind of disgrace. Another possibility is that Juhayman became involved with one of the revivalist religious movements that were emerging in Saudi Arabia in the 1960s and decided to devote himself to study and *dawa*, preaching. What is clear is that by late 1973 Juhayman, no longer a guardsman, had travelled to Medina, the major city to the west of his native al-Qassum province, to begin a new life.

Medina was the most important site for the Islamic faith after Mecca and one of the great civilisational centres of the Muslim world. Its inhabitants had offered a haven to the Prophet Mohammed and his followers when they had been forced to leave Mecca by powerful local enemies, an event so significant that its date, 622 CE, became year zero of the Islamic calendar. Medina had then become the launchpad for the Prophet's successful return to his native city and of the astonishing series of political and military victories that followed thereafter. In the 1960s, the city had become a centre for a new wave of more activist Islamist thinking and teaching, which may have been what attracted Juhayman.

Not far from where the former guardsman settled in a small whitewashed house in the scruffy eastern outskirts of Medina was a purpose-built two-storey cinder-block building known as the Beit al-Ikhwan, the House of the Brotherhood. This was the headquarters of a movement founded by a small group of religious students around a decade earlier and committed to a radical social conservatism. The name Ikhwan was a reference to earlier Wahhabis, who had also called themselves 'brothers' and dreamed of an Islam purged of the supposedly erroneous practices that had crept in over the centuries. One of the group's first acts was to march through the streets of Medina hunting for pictures, photographs and other images which breached a supposed Koranic injunction against depicting living beings. Shop windows displaying female mannequins were smashed. More controversially, so too were portraits of the king.

Many of these new 'brothers' had studied at the Islamic University in Medina, an institution founded in 1961 on the initiative of the then Crown Prince Faisal, and sought support for their new group from the dean of the institution, Abdulaziz bin Baz. A scholar of undisputed erudition, bin Baz was a known conservative with a history of standing up to the rulers of the kingdom on matters of religious principle. Blind almost from birth, his disability added to his air of otherworldly authority.

Many saw him as the conscience of a country that was losing its moral compass. Others saw him as an arch reactionary. Bin Baz accepted the request of the 'brothers' for sponsorship for their new group, which they had named al-Jamaa al-Salafiyya al-Muhtasiba, meaning 'the congregation or organisation of the Salafiyya', the first generations of Muslims. The final part, al-Muhtasiba, was added on his express recommendation and was a reference to the Wahhabi belief that all Muslims must work to 'forbid evil and encourage good'. Thus titled, the group thrived and expanded.

Juhayman learned of it from a friend and rapidly became a fixture at its main office. The former guardsman had found he could earn a halfway decent living in Medina refitting and reselling the Cadillacs, Pontiacs and Oldsmobiles that were being imported in vast numbers at the time, leaving him ample time to pursue his religious ambitions with his new friends. Mainly this meant preaching among the residents of poor neighbourhoods, such as the one that Juhayman inhabited, filled with recent migrants from rural areas who, like their counterparts in Tehran, had yet to benefit from Saudi Arabia's economic boom. Here in the rubbish-strewn 'sordid alleys', between half-built tenements, huts of wood and mud or even tents, the slightest rain created stinking swamps of sewage. Healthcare was non-existent, drinking water unsafe, and the power supply unreliable. Above all, the values and worldview that had structured the migrants' narrow but predictable village lives were of little use in the face of the dizzying complexity and chaos of urban existence.

In this environment, Juhayman thrived. More than six feet tall and rail-thin in his white traditional *thobe* and headdress, with his long hair, intense gaze, straight nose and full lips above a beard allowed to grow unchecked, he looked every bit the desert Wahhabi and commanded instant respect. He was also older than most of those he spoke to and came from a well-known tribe. Juhayman's anecdotes about his father's struggle to follow the right religious path added to his authority. Above all, he spoke simply and directly in the blunt Bedouin dialect of many of his listeners, appealing to them much as Khomeini had done with his use of folksy, uncomplicated language delivered in the accent of an increasingly distant but comforting rural past. With other preachers, Juhayman went door to door, mosque to mosque, telling the faithful that only a return to 'true' religious principles would bring remedy to the challenges they faced.

In reality, the interpretation of the Islamic texts that informed their ideas was highly questionable. Juhayman's attempt to enrol in a course of lectures at Medina University had been rejected, and most members of the group had little formal training. He and his 'brothers could not find religious education in the schools' so had been obliged to educate themselves, he later wrote. Untrammelled by any established authority, the group decided that identity cards and passports were haram, forbidden, because they suggested the existence of an authority that was not God's. So too were bank notes, as they carried an image of the king. Soon mainstream religious leaders in Medina began to get concerned.

In the late summer of 1977, a delegation of senior clerics arrived at the Beit al-Ikhwan. An acrimonious meeting took place on the roof after evening prayers. Many of the more senior members of the group abandoned their activism following the confrontation. Others, mainly the younger and more radical, remained committed to what they saw as their mission to return the faithful to the true path. Juhayman was particularly strident in his rejection of the criticisms levelled against the group. Under his leadership, they now jettisoned the unwieldy name they had been using and simply called themselves the Ikhwan.

In the early autumn of 1977, authorities finally raided the group's premises in Medina. They rounded up a dozen or so young men, but Juhayman was not among them. Tipped off by a policeman from his al-Utaybi tribe, he had left the building minutes earlier, heading out into the desert in a pickup truck with two others and driving for several days until he reached remote settlements where he knew he would be safe. For the next two years Juhayman remained far from Saudi Arabia's towns and cities, moving through the more remote areas of the country's north, sheltered by Bedouin communities who shared his background and many of his beliefs. Hiding in the expanse of the desert rather than the anonymity of the modern city as young recruits of the Red Army Faction or the Revolutionary Cells had done, Juhayman had gone underground.

The environment was very different but the challenges were much the same. The members of Juhayman's group were scattered across several towns and cities or living in remote villages in what were effectively communes. All needed to be motivated and organised. To do this, Juhayman recorded sermons on cassette tapes – the technology that had served Khomeini so well during his exile – and compiled a series of pamphlets, which became known as the 'letters of Juhayman'. These were printed in Kuwait by a left-wing publishing house which believed its clients were leading a proletarian uprising against the Saudi monarchy. Passed hand to hand among sympathisers, their distribution prompted a further wave of arrests.

Juhayman's prose was fairly amateurish but the concern his twelve 'epistles' inspired among Saudi Arabia's rulers was real. In one, he accused them of '[exploiting] religion to guarantee their worldly interests, paying allegiance to the Christians and bringing evil and corruption to Muslims'. In another he said the al-Saud family was guilty of 'putting an end to jihad', a claim that resonated especially with those who remembered how the founder of the dynasty had shot down his Ikhwan warriors rather than allow them to extend their military campaign against the Shia and beyond the peninsula. Such transgressions meant that the personal oath of allegiance or *bayat*, sworn by all Saudi citizens and enjoining obedience to any member of the ruling family, was invalid, Juhayman argued. It followed from this that the House of al-Saud had no claim to authority over their subjects. Nor did any of the kingdom's clerics who remained loyal to its current rulers.

Juhayman also addressed another problem that his followers had been struggling to resolve. The desperate condition of the kingdom was clear, as was the solution, which was for all mankind to live according to the correct interpretation of the Koran and the Islamic texts. What was less clear was how the radical transformation they desired might actually come to pass. How could all believers be compelled to follow the righteous path? How would the evil-doers be cleared away? How could the idols be struck down?

There had long been talk within al-Jamaa al-Salafiyya al-Muhtasiba about a Mahdi, or messiah. In the Sunni Muslim tradition, the idea of a saviour whose coming would usher in a new era of social justice had resurfaced episodically, often in times of upheaval and conflict, but was otherwise marginal. The same was not true of the Shia, for whom the tradition was central, but Juhayman abhorred such heretics and had paid little attention to recent events in Iran. In his remote desert camps, he may even have been wholly unaware of what was happening on the other side of the Persian Gulf. Instead, Juhayman arrived at the idea via his own means, drawing inspiration from the religious texts he kept in a steel trunk he had welded to the chassis of his favourite pickup truck. These taught that the Mahdi would come at a time of great discord, when the Muslims were divided among themselves. He would be pale-skinned, bear the Prophet's name and belong to his lineage, the Qurayshi. In late 1978, Juhayman told his excited and frightened followers that the Mahdi was among them: a dreamy and handsome twenty-four-year-old member of the group who apparently fulfilled all these criteria. His name was Mohammed al-Qahtani.

This unexpected news prompted some to quit the group entirely. But others spoke of dreams that confirmed their leader's claim. Even al-Qahtani, who had initially been reluctant to assume the intimidating status bestowed on him, accepted his new role. 'Better to be a false Mahdi than a false imam,' Juhayman told him to steel his nerves.

The conversation within the group now shifted to practicalities: how would they create the conditions in which the Mahdi could come into full possession of his powers? According to Juhayman's interpretation of the texts in the steel trunk, al-Qahtani had to be consecrated at a particular spot beside the Kaaba, the stone structure at the centre of the Great Mosque in Mecca, at the beginning of a new century. Fortuitously, this momentous date fell in almost exactly twelve months' time. Through the rest of 1978 and the first ten months of the following year, Juhayman continued to traverse Saudi Arabia's northern desert, visiting the small communes where his followers were based, organising makeshift military training in remote Bedouin settlements and arranging for the acquisition of a considerable stock of weapons. These ranged from eastern European-made AK-47s to antique Spanish shotguns and Yemeni swords. By the morning of 20 November 1979, according to the Western calendar, or the first day of the fifteenth century according to the Islamic one, everything was ready.

One of the five duties that all Muslims should perform at least once in their lives is the pilgrimage to Mecca. This is known as the hajj if performed over ten days during the twelfth and final month of the Islamic year or the umrah if undertaken, less meritoriously and more rapidly, at other times. For many centuries, the pilgrimage involved lengthy, expensive, uncomfortable and often dangerous travel. Those who completed the journey were honoured and respected. Over the course of the twentieth century railways, steamers and eventually passenger planes made the voyage safe, swift and affordable to millions. In the 1960s and 70s, pilgrims, like revolutionaries, were able to take advantage of the same processes of globalisation that were shrinking the world for everyone. In 1974, 600,000 non-Saudis came for hajj; a year later, the total was 900,000, of whom sixty per cent arrived by air.

This was a boon to the rulers of Saudi Arabia, and not just because the pilgrim trade generated a lot of money. The House of al-Saud was desperately short of religious credentials: they were descended not from the Prophet's own tribe, the prestigious Quraysh, but from a canny and ruthless minor warlord. Excluded from the domain of the clergy by the very pact that secured their family's control of the kingdom, they could not boast of even a single renowned Islamic scholar among their numerous ranks. As so often, the House of al-Saud deployed their most obvious resource – money – to make up for deficiencies elsewhere. Since the 1950s, they had expanded the Great Mosque five times over, allowing it to accommodate hundreds of thousands of pilgrims at any one time. High, elegantly colonnaded galleries surrounded a huge precinct around the Kaaba, while vast walkways allowed pilgrims to perform the rituals of hajj without risk of overcrowding. Prayers from the complex were beamed live and almost without interruption on Saudi Arabian television networks, reaching listeners on radios across the Islamic world, literally amplifying the protective power of Saudi Arabia's rulers. The Great Mosque was a stage on which the al-Saud could demonstrate their piety, competence and leadership. In the wrong hands, of course, other players could use it to broadcast a very different message to an equally large audience.

But in the late 1970s, there appeared to be little threat to the rule of the al-Saud. Fears that Arab nationalism would inspire a wave of revolutionary agitation, as had occurred elsewhere in the Arab world, had proved unfounded. Occasional scares over Communist agitation, especially among the kingdom's Shia minority, had never been very convincing. A Ba'athist plot went nowhere. This and the sheer wealth pouring into the country led to a degree of complacency. 'The level of restlessness among young Saudis appears to be well below the boiling point,' a *Time* correspondent wrote in 1976, noting that unlike in most other places in the region the word 'revolution' was never uttered in the kingdom. A year later, Rouleau told readers of *Le Monde* that 'after a long period of turbulence, the Saudi monarchy is today one of the very rare regimes in the Middle East which faces no organised opposition, public or clandestine.'

In fact, the regime did face opposition – simply not of the sort that anyone was expecting. The loudest and most obvious domestic critics of the al-Saud were the conservative clergy. Senior scholars like bin Baz recognised that the kingdom's rulers, however flawed, offered an effective defence against the atheist ideologies that had done so much damage elsewhere. But this did not stop them from continually and stridently complaining about the progressive reforms they sought to implement. As the impact of Western culture grew from the mid-1960s and through the 70s, these reproaches increased in pitch and volume. On 31 December 1978, for example, as Juhayman set about convincing his followers that the Mahdi was among them, bin Baz issued a fatwa arguing that the recently introduced game of table soccer was contrary to Islamic principles because the miniature human form of the players was suggestive of idolatry. Six months later, as Juhayman began to ready his followers to take control of the mosque in Mecca, bin Baz complained vociferously to the kingdom's rulers about a series of 'blatant violations of Islamic practice', such as 'foreign women eating in public places and appearing unsuitably dressed in the markets', Christians wearing crosses 'prominently', shops 'playing raucous Western music', the use of foreign names for Saudi businesses, and Saudis 'loitering outside mosques and stores at prayer time and openly neglecting to pray'. The tirade led US diplomats to tell Washington that 'the violations of tradition listed [by bin Baz] are perhaps not so much un-Islamic, as . . . contrary to the values of the fundamentalist Wahhabis within the Saudi establishment who are trying to maintain their own version of Islamic orthodoxy in Saudi Arabian society.' Though perceptive, this was irrelevant. In the kingdom, bin Baz defined what was or was not 'Islamic', and its rulers, without their own religious credentials, could not afford to ignore his views.

Bin Baz made more direct interventions too. When the authorities arrested more than thirty members of al-Jamaa al-Salafiyya al-Muhtasiba in the aftermath of the rooftop argument in Medina in 1977, the cleric had used his influence to secure their release. The young men now languishing in the police cells were misguided but not fundamentally ill-intentioned, bin Baz told the interior minister, Prince Nayef, who promptly set them free. When a year later, some of the followers of Juhayman, by then a fugitive, sent a selection of their leader's incendiary epistles to bin Baz for review, the scholar said he approved of many of their conclusions even while he warned against any specific criticism of Saudi Arabia and its rulers. This very mild rebuke was much too little too late.

Shortly after 5 a.m. on 20 November 1979, as the new Muslim century dawned, Juhayman and his men took control of the vast mosque in Mecca. Around 200 of them had entered the complex through the night, concealing weapons under shrouds on the litters more usually used to carry the dead for blessing before burial. A volley of shots fired into the air was sufficient to end any thoughts of resistance among the few policemen who patrolled the complex. Juhayman, flanked by three heavily armed men, a green band holding back his shoulder-length hair, seized the imam's microphone while his followers barred the mosque's fifty-one gates. Close to panic, the tens of thousands of pilgrims now confined within began to chant 'Allahu Akbar', God is Great, and the unexpected chorus reverberated around the mosque and out into the waking city.

Once the shouts had faded away, Juhayman gave orders in his Bedouin dialect, instructing men to take up firing positions in the minarets that towered above the complex, then handed the microphone to a follower who was able to speak the classical Arabic suitable for important declarations. For the next hour, those now captive in the complex listened to the grievances of the Ikhwan. The al-Saud were corrupt and beholden to their Christian masters, Western ways had polluted the pure spring of Islam in the land of the Prophet, soccer was a pagan scourge. These were not demands, merely a list of complaints, and most were familiar to anyone who had listened to or read the statements of the kingdom's more conservative clerics over the previous decade. The radicalism of the rebels lay in their astonishing audacity, and their belief in their messiah: the slim, fresh-faced al-Qahtani.

Many onlookers were astonished by his apparent youth and gasped audibly or stared in shocked silence when the crowd of militants parted to allow al-Qahtani to walk unimpeded to the very spot supposedly designated for his consecration. 'In the name of Allah, the most gracious, most merciful, here is the awaited Mahdi,' Juhayman called out. The Ikhwan lined up to kneel and offer their allegiance to their unlikely deliverer, then spread out around the mosque to prepare their defences for the battle that was sure to come. The Islamic texts that Juhayman had consulted – a mixture of well-known traditions relating the words and acts of the Prophet, known as Hadith, and esoteric, often centuries-old commentaries – were clear: an army from the north 'made up not of Jews or Christians but of Muslims' would soon arrive to 'besiege the Mahdi in the Great Mosque', then be scattered by angels.

In fact, it was the police who made the first attempt to stop the messiah and his followers. The army would come – but only after a lengthy delay caused by the need to get a fatwa from bin Baz and other senior clerics on the propriety of using violence within the mosque. This was not a straightforward matter as the Prophet himself had banned the use of any weapon in the sanctuary. The clerics, recognising that a protracted crisis would threaten the stability of the entire kingdom, eventually agreed that a military operation to expel the rebels was justified. They did not deliver the outright condemnation of Juhayman and his men that had been asked of them, however, refusing to speak of 'religious deviants' as the authorities had done but referring to them merely as an 'armed group' instead. The angels never turned up at all.

The first assaults launched by the Saudi soldiers were unsubtle, extremely costly and achieved little. Only when armoured personnel carriers advanced into the mosque through the main gallery and anti-tank missiles were deployed against the snipers in the minarets did the rebels give ground. A turning point came on the third day of fighting when shrapnel from a grenade killed al-Qahtani, the supposed messiah. Unsurprisingly, this delivered a significant blow to the morale of the Ikhwan, though the fighting continued.

The frightened government soldiers fought their genuinely fanatical enemies among shattered pillars and on broken floors slick with blood and littered with bodies. After five days, the soldiers had cleared the mosque above ground, but not the labyrinth of corridors and study rooms below the complex. An attempt to flood the basement and electrocute the defenders there was a fiasco. Tear gas fired down its narrow passages blew back into the faces of the ill-trained troops. Body armour provided by a small team of French special forces who had been flown in to advise the Saudis proved ineffectual, though the canisters of paralysing gas they also supplied had a greater impact. Even so, the battle remained a desperate one.

Finally, on 4 December, two weeks after the takeover, Saudi soldiers broke through a last barricade deep underground to find a group of shattered, shell-shocked young men gathered around an older man with long hair and wild eyes. Juhayman was marched from the shrine, beaten, imprisoned, interrogated. Hundreds, possibly thousands, of soldiers and pilgrims had died. Much of the mosque had been reduced to rubble, and almost no part of it was left undamaged.

There was no trial, just another fatwa, this time less equivocal, delivered by the kingdom's most senior clerics. King Khaled was able to issue a terse decree. 'God almighty has ordered us to kill those who fought us at the . . . mosque and tried to revolt and to divide us,' it said.

When Juhayman was led out to the executioners, he did not resist or cry out in defiance but died without a word. Over the next few weeks and months, most of the other adult rebels who had been captured met a similar fate. The executions took place in secret and totalled around 170, including about twenty women.

It suited a significant proportion of observers to believe that the attack on the Great Mosque in Mecca was a local affair and that its causes and consequences were limited only to Saudi Arabia. A classified research note by the Foreign Office in London referred to 'the stresses and strains' of 'rapid development over the last 40 years' in the kingdom but explicitly denied any international significance. There were problems with such an optimistic analysis. One was the support for Juhayman's organisation beyond Saudi Arabia's borders, specifically in Yemen, where the group had an active if small following, and Kuwait, where hundreds of young men had been recruited and the infamous epistles first published. A second problem was the appeal those epistles had outside the kingdom. Copies of them soon began turning up in Egypt and Algeria among other places, some imported by former members of the group, others smuggled in by admirers. All told, they were now reaching thousands of new readers. Finally, there were Juhayman's followers themselves. Among those executed were ten Egyptians and six Yemenis, as well as Pakistanis, Kuwaitis, Iraqis and, possibly, one Afghan. In all, foreigners constituted about a third of those sentenced to death. If this was representative of the rest of Juhayman's followers, it meant that hundreds of recruits were from overseas. There were even two African Americans who had found their way to Saudi Arabia having converted as part of their engagement with radical civil rights groups such as the Nation of Islam.

Most of Juhayman's foreign followers were migrant workers, part of the vast population of foreigners from around the Muslim world who had travelled to Saudi Arabia in recent years to work in its booming economy. A considerable number returned home rich, having made the equivalent of decades of earnings in the space of a year. But of those who did not, many remained in conditions of near slavery and destitution. Illiterate, often on their first trip beyond their village let alone their country and utterly disorientated, they were attracted by the combination of a simple explanation of all that was wrong with the world and a clear programme for its transformation.

Saudi Arabian radio and television networks told their audience none of this. News bulletins simply announced that control had been re-established over the mosque complex by 'soldiers of the faith seeking martyrdom' who had defeated the 'renegades'. Prince Fahd said that any negative media coverage of a 'domestic incident' was the work of 'world Zionism, which was seeking to harm the Saudi Arabian kingdom'. The rebels' overseas connections were used as a way to deflect attention from the kingdom's own problems. In hastily arranged interviews, Saudi officials told foreign reporters that Juhayman was 'sponsored by international organisations, probably Russians', and his men had trained 'in camps in Marxist South Yemen'. This was entirely untrue.

Other public comments were equally misleading. In one interview shortly after the attack in Mecca, Fahd compared Juhayman and his followers to the 900 members of the People's Temple, a cult founded in the US among mainly poor African Americans, who had been coerced into taking their own lives at a commune in Jonestown, Guyana in November 1978. Juhayman's group had many aspects of a cult, and his supposed revelations were devoid of sense or foundation, but there was no evidence that anyone was ever prevented from leaving or threatened in any way. And while the ideology of the People's Temple was soon forgotten, Juhayman's message of radical transformation through apocalyptic violence was not. On the contrary, it would reverberate for years to come in the Middle East and eventually further afield too. Among those it would one day inspire was a young Saudi scion of a very wealthy family whose name would become infamous across the world some two decades after Juhayman's head rolled on the paving stones of Riyadh's al-Adl Square.

31
A New International

Just over thirty-six hours after the final battles in its basement, King Khaled entered the Great Mosque in Mecca through one of its few gates that remained unobstructed by barricades or rubble. Illuminated chandeliers shone in the dusk, their lights reflected by the shining white walls of the colonnade that surrounded the main precinct. Here the king and his entourage performed the ritual circumambulation, walking seven times around the Kaaba, before kneeling in prayer.

The next day thousands came. The Friday sermon and service was broadcast live, reaching tens of millions once more and sending an emphatic message to the world's Muslims that the al-Saud were back in control of the most sacred shrine in Islam. Over the following days and weeks, the perpetual flow of worshippers through the galleries and around the Kaaba recommenced and a semblance of normality returned, although there were few pilgrims from overseas, most of the visitors being residents of Mecca itself or other nearby towns and cities.

Among them was a shy, tall, slender twenty-two-year-old from Jeddah, a port city fifty miles away. Osama bin Mohammed bin Awad bin Laden was a devout believer and had been a frequent visitor for many years. No doubt he felt a powerful personal bond with the mosque. An aspirant member of the Muslim Brotherhood, he took an active interest in the more political aspects of contemporary Islamic teachings and had followed the violent events of the previous weeks closely. Like most Saudi Arabians, he would have been keen to gauge the potential threat the rebels posed, whether to himself and his young family or to the dynasty whose relatively stable rule over Saudi Arabia he had known all his life. It was possible he also felt some sympathy for the men who had risked their lives in the name of their faith.

Arriving after his two-hour drive from the Red Sea coast, through the craggy coastal mountains, into the city and eventually to the Great

Mosque itself, bin Laden must have been shocked at the sight before him. The marks left by the tracks of bulldozers and fighting vehicles on the building's once pristine marble tiles seemed to him a desecration. Nothing bin Laden said or did at the time suggested that he supported Juhayman and his rebellious followers, though to have made any public comment in support of the 'misguided renegades' and 'deviants' would have been extremely imprudent. But just a few years later, he was able to speak more freely, and he did, expressing his regret at the deaths of the rebels, whom he believed to be 'true Muslims . . . innocent of any crime . . . killed ruthlessly' by the descendants of a 'tribal chieftain'. Their example was inspiring, he would say, as they had courageously followed the right path in the face of almost insuperable odds and had been afraid neither of shedding the blood of unbelievers nor of dying themselves. They had lived 'in the way of jihad' and this, he explained, was how he tried to live too: in the hope that God would be good enough to grant him martyrdom.

Bin Laden was a child of the 1970s – at the beginning of the decade, he was twelve – which meant that Black September and the death of Gamal Abdel Nasser, the 1973 war with Israel and the oil crisis that followed, the outbreak of the Lebanese civil war and the roughly contemporaneous assassination of King Faisal all took place during some of his most formative teenage years. In his first years as an adult he lived through even greater turbulence: the Iranian revolution, a peace agreement between Israel and Egypt and, two weeks before Juhayman's execution, the Soviet 'special military operation' in Afghanistan. Each of these changed the kingdom of Saudi Arabia, the Middle East and the Islamic world irrevocably. They also changed bin Laden's view of the world and the course of his life. None of this turned him into an extremist, still less a terrorist, but without these events it is inconceivable he would have followed the path that led him eventually to such infamy.

Typically for a port city, the Jeddah of bin Laden's childhood and youth was a melting pot. There, for decades, the various currents of Westernisation, consumerism, conservatism and faith had combined and sometimes clashed. As Saudi Arabia's commercial and diplomatic hub and the capital of the Hejaz, a coastal province with a distinct and proud identity and one of the last areas of the Arabian peninsula to be conquered by Abdulaziz ibn al-Saud's forces, Jeddah had remained more outward-looking and tolerant than the conservative, xenophobic Nejd up on the desert plateaus of the interior. Jeddah was still profoundly religious though, with gender segregation strictly enforced in public spaces and the few women on the streets appearing as black silhouettes in their billowing abaya robes. Even so, the religious police kept a relatively low profile, sporting associations thrived, and heavily censored Western films were shown in the city's single cinema. Much later, bin Laden would highlight his Hejazi heritage to underline and partly explain his rejection of the legitimacy of the House of al-Saud.

Bin Laden grew up in a modest two-storey villa on the outskirts of the city with four younger step-siblings. He was one of fifty-four sons sired by an uncouth, ambitious immigrant who had come to Jeddah from Yemen with nothing in the 1930s and gone on to build an enormous construction conglomerate, the Saudi Bin Laden Group. Mohammed bin Laden practised polygamy and kept four wives, the last being a fairly temporary position of limited status. Osama's mother, a Syrian teenager, had filled this junior role for around four years before being divorced in 1960. Her former husband had then arranged for her to marry a middle-ranking manager in his company and installed the couple in a home some distance from the main bin Laden family residence. Osama would later refer to his mother as a 'concubine'. Even so, he venerated the memory of his father, who died in a plane crash when he was ten. Osama's share of the family fortune did not make him enormously wealthy, at least by Saudi standards, but it meant an annual income that guaranteed a very comfortable life.

When he was eleven, in 1968, bin Laden was enrolled in the al-Thagr Model School, a prestigious local establishment organised along Western lines and funded and staffed by the government. Gifted poorer children got places if they passed stiff entrance exams, but most students came from the city's elite who could easily afford the relatively modest fees. Students wore smart blazers, ties and trousers and followed a Western curriculum adapted to provide many hours of Islamic studies. Bin Laden took up his place at al-Thagr a year after the 1967 war, which had led to 'many of the children wanting to get on buses' to join the fight against Israel and much subsequent debate about the reasons for the Arabs' defeat. Former teachers remembered a quiet, courteous and studious boy entirely unremarkable but for his exceptional height and piety.

By his early teens, bin Laden's commitment to his faith had begun to attract attention, at least at home. He fasted twice a week in imitation of the Prophet Mohammed, woke for the optional midnight prayers and reprimanded his less-committed siblings for their lack of devotion. Following the example of the kingdom's most senior clerics, bin Laden's adherence to a strict and literal interpretation of Islamic practice was matched by an effort to purge his personal life and environment of Western influences. He stopped wearing trousers and shirts and replaced them with the traditional Saudi thobe, and when he played soccer for a local side in the scruffy, half-finished neighbourhood of Musharifah where he lived, he demanded that his teammates wear loose shorts rather than the tight ones that were fashionable at the time. He avoided the cowboy or action films he had once enjoyed and made sure that his friends did too. Bin Laden's mother, who was not particularly observant, was worried by this new religious rigour and wondered what had caused it.

Bin Laden had always been a serious child and relatives believed that his new interest in religion had been prompted by his father's death. But whatever his need for spiritual reassurance or comfort following the bereavement, the most obvious religious influence in his teenage years was exposure to an ideology and organisation that had built a significant presence in Saudi Arabia over the previous decade, with significant consequences for all its inhabitants and hundreds of millions across the Islamic world: the Muslim Brotherhood.

Though King Faisal was committed to incremental steps to 'modernise' his subjects, their purpose was not to weaken religious observance but to reinforce it and so inoculate the population against atheist ideologies like Ba'athism or Communism. The massive expansion of education from the mid-1960s onwards was designed to produce young subjects who were devout and respectful of authority, and who shared the king's own sense of Islam's profound importance in the world. To this end, Faisal founded dozens of religious secondary schools as well as a series of higher institutions teaching and researching all aspects of the faith.

The physical construction of such institutions was easy. Saudi Arabia had plenty of money and could hire contractors such as Mohammed bin Laden to build them with astonishing rapidity. Finding staff was harder. The kingdom's clerics were profoundly knowledgeable about the most recondite corners of traditional Islamic scholarship but had only a very limited understanding of the contemporary world. Faisal wanted the graduates of the new institutions to be ambassadors of his vision of 'Islamic development', not unthinking religious reaction. Recruiting teachers from the small but growing 'intelligentsia' in Saudi Arabia was out of the question as their sympathies often lay with the nationalist and secular ideologies that Faisal wanted to counter. The obvious solution was to import teachers and academics from elsewhere in the Islamic world.

Almost by default, this meant members of the Muslim Brotherhood, which had been founded in Egypt forty years earlier with the express intention of ensuring that Islamic nations and communities could benefit from the technological, military, legal, political and other advances of the West without abandoning their own culture or faith. The Muslim Brotherhood had long recruited from among the Middle East's professional, pious middle classes and already had a strong presence in schools and universities throughout the region. As a result its members were socially conservative and devout yet modern in their outlook and approach, exactly the combination that Faisal sought. Through the late 1960s and early 70s, hundreds of Muslim Brothers arrived in Saudi Arabia to fill newly created teaching posts. Around 1971, one of these joined the staff at al-Thagr Model School where he greatly impressed the young bin Laden.

To engage his young charges, the newcomer set up an after-school sports and study club – a standard recruitment tactic of the Muslim Brotherhood everywhere – offering extra soccer practice to entice students to join. When it became clear that members would spend more time learning Islamic texts, listening to the semi-dramatised retelling of legends from Islamic history and resolving the problems of the *ummah*, the world's Islamic community, than perfecting free kicks or beating an offside trap, many left. Bin Laden remained, spending hours after school with the teacher, the Koran and a very partial view of the politics of the Middle East.

Such interests did not entirely preclude more familiar adolescent pursuits. Bin Laden enjoyed horse-riding in the desert as well as powerful US-manufactured cars which he drove very fast, crashing at least one. He was interested in the opposite sex, too. Other wealthy teenagers in Jeddah, including his half-brothers, accompanied unchaperoned girls to private house parties. Bin Laden, who reprimanded his half-siblings when he suspected them of flirting with a maid, kept any amorous activities well within extremely restricted bounds. In 1974, aged seventeen, he married a tall, pretty fifteen-year-old cousin he had met while visiting his mother's family near Latakia, the Syrian coastal city. The wedding followed puritanical Wahhabi traditions with none of the singing or dancing his in-laws usually enjoyed at such celebrations. His over-awed young bride donned an abaya, the full veiling cloak favoured in Saudi Arabia, for the first time on the plane back to Jeddah.

The trips to Latakia were not bin Laden's only foreign excursions. Elite families in the kingdom were now sending children overseas for education as a matter of course. Even so, bin Laden was better travelled than most young Saudi Arabians. He had spent several months in Lebanon at a boarding school before starting at al-Thagr, and he had visited Beirut with relatives several times through the early 1970s. Though he did not join a major family outing to Sweden, he did go on a safari in East Africa. He also visited the UK to receive medical treatment for an eye condition, and returned a year later to spend several weeks learning English at Oxford, from where he made trips to London and, on one occasion, the home of William Shakespeare in Stratford-upon-Avon. The 'loose morals' he encountered in Britain were shocking and distressing, bin Laden later said.

Though his family stipend was sufficient to cover his everyday expenses, bin Laden would have the opportunity to work at a relatively senior level within the family business once his formal education was complete. This was encouraged among the bin Laden sons – though not, obviously, the daughters – and bin Laden was happy to put his shoulder to the corporate familial wheel. To gain the professional skills needed, he enrolled in the economics and business management faculty of King Abdulaziz University, a broadly secular institution founded in Jeddah eight years earlier as part of King Faisal's expansion of education.

And so there he was in 1976, on the cusp of adulthood, a pious and shy young man living in a couple of rooms of his stepfather's house in a fast-growing, noisy Middle Eastern city, planning a family with his teenage wife and heading for a life working in the family firm. Little at this stage marked bin Laden out as exceptional among his peers.

The success of a propagandist in the 1970s, as at any other period, depended less on the originality of the views they expressed than on their ability to speak to and coherently articulate the pre-existing, if unformed and unspoken, ideas of large numbers of people. This is what Khomeini did for poor, conservative Iranians. It is what Yasser Arafat had managed with the disorientated, disillusioned Palestinians a decade earlier. Abdallah Azzam, a Palestinian scholar and Muslim Brother in his late thirties, had the same gift. At the beginning of the decade he was almost unknown. By its end he would be one of the most influential and important of the Sunni Muslim voices proposing radical solutions to the problems of the region and the Islamic world. He would also become a mentor of bin Laden.

Born in the far north of what was later the occupied West Bank, Azzam had watched as Israeli troops marched into his village during the 1967 war. His radical turn had come two years later, when he was working in a secondary school in Jordan. At the time, he was no more than a devout, disciplined young teacher with modest ambitions to one day become a respected Islamic scholar. But late one night he was woken by a group of leftist fedayeen fighters who were camping nearby and singing a nationalist a cappella chant, or *nashid*. A member of the Muslim Brotherhood since his early teens, Azzam despised the singers' secular, socialist ideas and resented the hold such ideologies had on Arabs, young and old, across the region. Indeed, he attributed the Arabs' crushing defeat two years earlier to their lack of Islamic devotion and rejection of what he saw as their own culture. But now a realisation seized him with a jolt. Azzam had done little to fight the occupation since it began, nor much to redress his sense of humiliation. The leftists, by contrast, singing so earnestly of their Palestinian homeland, were all actively involved in an armed struggle against Israel. As the echo of the song reverberated through the darkness, Azzam regretted bitterly his inaction and 'decided that instant to begin the jihad, at whatever cost'.

Some months before, Islamists from the Muslim Brotherhood had opened a series of small training camps and bases in the north of Jordan, not far from where Leila Khaled would train with the PFLP that same year. Azzam sought out 'the bases of the sheikhs' or *al-qawa'ed al-shuyukh*, as they were known, and joined the few hundred fighters from around the region he found there. Though nominally part of Yasser Arafat's Fatah and thus comrades in arms of the type of fedayeen that Azzam had heard singing, relations between the Brotherhood's trainees and the other factions of the PLO were poor. Azzam and his fellows were incensed when the leftist factions celebrated Lenin's birthday, and were disgusted by the sight of women 'beguiled in the name of Palestine' who hung around their bases 'wearing tight trousers, sleeping . . . and waking to oud strings mixed with Beatles and Hippies music'. Summoned before a 'revolutionary tribunal' by Fatah officials to face the charge of publicly insulting Che Guevara, Azzam was unrepentant, telling his judges that, as a Muslim, he reviled their hero.

When King Hussein moved to crush the Palestinian fedayeen in Jordan in September 1970, the local branch of the Muslim Brotherhood declared their loyalty to the crown. Azzam was demobilised and played no role in the bloody battles of 'Black September'. Instead, he set about advancing his career as an Islamic scholar, finishing his master's studies in Sharia law at Damascus University. Though he made little secret of his dismay at the continued dominance of leftist and secular ideologies across the Arab and Muslim worlds, his vocal tirades had no discernible impact and in 1973 he left Syria for Egypt to study for a PhD at al-Azhar University.

In Cairo, Azzam was able to befriend a series of major Islamist figures. Many had recently been released from prison by Anwar Sadat, now in the third year of his rule, and these included several members of the family of Syed Qutb, whose hugely influential writings and example as a 'martyr' Azzam deeply admired. Like Qutb and many of his new companions, Azzam was far from convinced by the argument of the mainstream leaders of the Egyptian Muslim Brotherhood that victory for the Islamist cause would come only through non-violent outreach, social activism and propaganda. But this did not mean Azzam supported the wilder thinking of the most radical among Cairo's Islamists at the time either. When he met a member of Takfir Wal Hijra, the extremist group led by Shukri Mustafa that would unleash a wave of bombings and murder a senior Egyptian cleric and minister in the summer of 1977, Azzam was shocked to be told that his own 'lack of religious rigour' made him a backsliding 'infidel' who did not faithfully follow the true teaching of Islam. 'I had never met a young man of such conviction,' Azzam remembered some years later.

Once his doctorate in Islamic law was complete, Azzam returned to Amman where he began teaching at the University of Jordan. His job was a good one, providing a salary that allowed his now large family to live decently, the prospect of promotion, time to study, contact with students, which he enjoyed, and the opportunity to further the Muslim Brotherhood's agenda in the kingdom. By now in Jordan, the ideological tides were turning in favour of the Islamists, as they were throughout the Middle East, and in 1976 the Brotherhood took over the country's biggest student union. Overseas interest in Azzam's work and activism increased. New connections were being made between Islamist activists across the Islamic world, facilitated by new and cheaper flights, the spread of fax machines and telephone exchanges and the myriad processes of globalisation. Azzam was an effective orator with an impressive physical presence: lean and handsome, with high cheekbones, a broad forehead and straight nose. When he spoke he was energetic but authoritative, making coherent arguments about what he believed were the most pressing issues of the day for Muslims everywhere.

His growing reputation as a scholar and speaker attracted invitations to the conferences, seminars and lectures that easier travel and communications were making possible. Some came from the US and western Europe, where Muslim communities were growing more politically aware, wealthy and assertive, helping to consolidate the sense of a genuinely global community of believers. In 1977 Azzam flew to Bloomington, Indiana to talk to a conference of local student groups associated with the Muslim Brotherhood. US officials were unconcerned by the presence of Islamist ideologues in the country, not least because the FBI and other agencies were almost entirely ignorant of their agenda. The same was true in Europe when Azzam set off for Perugia, Italy, to address a Muslim audience there. Most invitations were from the Middle East, however, and many came from Saudi Arabia, which he visited repeatedly. In 1975, Azzam had spoken at a conference held during the hajj in Mecca on the evils of polytheism, a theme likely to please the local Wahhabi crowd. In 1977, he visited Jeddah to deliver a series of lectures on Islamic culture.

Though comfortable in Jordan, Azzam remained outspoken, perfectly prepared to criticise King Hussein if he felt it justified. Inevitably, local authorities took a dim view of this, as they did of much Palestinian activism, and in 1979 they expelled their increasingly troublesome guest. This caused Azzam no great hardship, as almost immediately he was offered a job at King Abdulaziz University in the Sharia department. In early 1980, he arrived in Mecca with his family and moved into an apartment a twenty-minute walk from the Great Mosque. He would spend the next year writing, teaching and preaching.

In just over a decade, Azzam had gone from being a minor, marginal figure, spitting in the Arab nationalist wind, to a respected public intellectual at the very centre of the Muslim world. The post in Mecca allowed further opportunities to build his reputation and network of close contacts. This would soon include the wealthy and pious young man who had recently walked, shocked and dismayed, through the rubble-strewn galleries of the Great Mosque.

That Azzam ended up living, albeit fleetingly, in Mecca was not particularly surprising. By 1979, the city – along with Jeddah and Medina, 120 miles away – had become an unprecedented hub of activity dedicated to the formulation and dissemination of a new vision of the Muslim faith. This vision fused populist politics with a radical Wahhabi conservatism and was to be as transformative of the Muslim world as the Iranian revolution – though it received much less attention and provoked no alarm whatsoever at the time. The populist element came from men like Azzam, but the equally important radical conservative component was largely the consequence of decisions taken by successive Saudi rulers.

These decisions pre-dated the attack on the mosque in Mecca by almost two decades and had all been made with one aim: to protect and advance the interests of the al-Saud dynasty. They were the international counterpart to King Faisal's promotion of 'Islamic development' among his subjects, at the heart of which lay a sprawling semi-autonomous organisation called the Muslim World League. Established by Faisal in 1962 when he was still crown prince, and managed by the Saudi clerics and imported Muslim Brotherhood technocrats, the League's purpose was to promote Muslim solidarity through the spread of the Islamic practices that were then current in Saudi Arabia. From its Mecca offices, it mounted a massive outreach effort across the entire Arab world, supporting preachers, building mosques, organising conferences and sponsoring the publication of immense quantities of literature supportive of Wahhabi Islam, as well as paying for millions of Korans, establishing schools, creating charitable foundations and working 'to cleanse the Muslim media generally of elements alien to the spirit of Islam'. In 1977, the League organised conferences in Mauritania, New Jersey and Trinidad, and established offices in Karachi, Paris and Dakar, Senegal. A weekly *News of the Muslim World* was produced in English and Arabic, along with a monthly edition. Thousands of scholarships were offered to allow students to travel to Mecca, Jeddah or Medina to attend the new universities there, and teachers were sent out to distant countries. By 1980, the League's budget was $12 million, six times that of 1972. Nor was it alone. Important auxiliary roles in this effort were played by the Organisation of the Islamic Conference, founded in 1969 in Jeddah, and the World Association of Muslim Youth, headquartered in Riyadh from 1972.

The impact of all this on the practices of Sunni Muslims around the world was massive. The same technological advances that allowed Islamists like Azzam to build connections from Indiana to Islamabad helped the Saudi government's proselytisation effort too. The distribution of texts was immeasurably easier than it ever had been and, after several decades of concerted efforts to raise literacy rates in states across the Islamic world, hundreds of millions of people could now read them. For those who remained illiterate, there were audio cassettes. It was not just radicals like Azzam, Khomeini or Juhayman who could exploit such technology to ensure their views reached a much wider audience. Governments could too.

Most important of all was the timing of the Saudi effort, which intensified and expanded at exactly the same time as the Islamic revival of the 1970s began to gather its momentum. It did not create the surge of interest in faith, but it did influence the form it took. This was to the great detriment of pre-existing traditions of Islamic observance everywhere, many of which had their roots in the earliest days of the faith, when Islam had fused with local religious practices to produce something diverse, supple and relatively tolerant. But many such traditions were already suffering from a perceived lack of relevance to communities who had left the village and were now struggling to cope with the challenges of life in crowded towns and cities. Now they faced a Saudi campaign that, like the Wahhabi fighters who once rode across the Arabian peninsula, specifically targeted the shrines, rituals, tombs, music and mysticism on which they depended. It was an unequal contest with only one likely winner.

During his international lecture tours in the late 1970s, Azzam drew on ideas that would eventually furnish two books published shortly after he moved to Saudi Arabia. The first, *Red Cancer*, gave voice to Azzam's antisemitism and longstanding hostility to Marxism and its various offshoots. Echoing Nazi propaganda that had been widely spread in the Middle East over previous decades, Azzam asserted that the Bolshevik revolution was 'Jewish in ideology, planning, funding and execution' and that since 1917, 'all Communist revolutions in the world are Jewish'. The other work, *Islam and the Future of Mankind*, argued that Islam was the only faith that could rescue humanity from the 'misery from which it can no longer find an escape'. Clearly influenced by Qutb, the book portrayed Western civilisation as empty materialism that had achieved nothing but global conflict, 'alcohol addiction, drug abuse, sexual promiscuity, incivility, venereal disease and suicide'. Over the centuries, the West had 'sucked up the blood of Muslims, plundered its homelands, trampled its sanctities and violated its [women's] honour'. Defeat at the hands of 'Western Crusaders, the Eastern atheists and Global Zionism' was inevitable because Muslims had abandoned jihad. Only jihad could provide the spark that would ignite the energy of the ummah and so return Islam to its rightful power and glory. Only through violence would come renewal.

Both books proved extremely popular, selling thousands of copies and running eventually into multiple editions. The reason was simple: such ideas were already widespread but had rarely been expressed with Azzam's verve and coherence. The books drew on the anti-imperialist rhetoric that had been a central part of the Muslim Brotherhood since its foundation but combined it with the core message of the massive Saudi effort to export its version of Islam to the rest of the Islamic world.

In early 1980, the secretary general of the World Muslim League told the faithful that, with 'sacred shrines under the Zionist occupation in Palestine [and] millions of Muslims suffering suppression, oppression, injustices, torture and even extermination campaigns [all over the world]', their enemies were clear: 'Zionists, Communists, Freemasons, Baha'i and Christian missionaries.' He too had a solution to offer, one that was familiar to readers of Azzam: a 'jihad'.

The hajj season of 1980 fell in October. Once again a million or so people came to Mecca to worship. In the Great Mosque, all traces of the previous year's violence had been erased. Among the dignitaries invited to enjoy the city's traditional hospitality, offered by the great families of the kingdom, were several dozen distinctive figures wearing heavy, embroidered robes and long wound turbans. They were the commanders of the 'mujahideen', now fighting on the newest frontline of the Islamic world's 1,300-year-old battle against the forces of unbelief: Afghanistan.

By the time the hajj was underway, King Khaled, Crown Prince Fahd and their advisers had become convinced that Moscow's invasion of Afghanistan was the precursor to an aggressive bid to reach the warm waters of the Persian Gulf. Coming so soon after the destabilising episode at Mecca and the revolution in Iran, this new threat placed the

Saudi rulers in an invidious position. On the one hand, it was clear that they needed the support of the US more than ever. Washington had guaranteed the security of their state for thirty-five years, and now was definitely not the moment to abandon the relationship. On the other, the attack on the mosque at Mecca had dramatically demonstrated the continuing dependence of the House of al-Saud on the kingdom's clerics, who were viscerally anti-American. This was why through the early months of 1980 King Khaled had authorised a series of measures to reverse the greater personal freedoms of previous years, thus fulfilling many long-standing demands of the kingdom's most conservative religious scholars. Women disappeared from television and the workplace. Huge new resources were handed to the religious police, now empowered to take a much more active role in regulating the personal and public lives of their fellow subjects. In Jeddah, cinemas shut and sporting activities were restricted. In Riyadh, a state-of-the-art $140 million opera house finished just months earlier was permanently shuttered. The effort to export 'Wahhabism' overseas received even greater funds.

The invasion in Afghanistan offered a way to reconcile, at least partly, these two conflicting imperatives. Moscow's apparent aggression was viewed with as much concern in Washington as it was in Riyadh. Coming so soon after the Iranian revolution, it had reinforced the sense among Carter's senior officials that they were facing another major strategic defeat in the Cold War and that an effort was needed to rally Muslim leaders and communities to their side in this gigantic struggle. Just months after the Soviet invasion, the president had committed the United States to going to war in the Persian Gulf if its national interests there were threatened – the so-called Carter Doctrine – but more active measures were needed too. There was already some small and discreet US assistance reaching Afghan rebels. Now senior Saudi defence and intelligence officials suggested to the US that the kingdom could match their funds dollar for dollar, as well as solicit further funds from other donors within the Islamic world. The kingdom's senior officials pledged to liaise with the government of Pakistan and facilitate the travel of any volunteers seeking to join the struggle against the Soviets. This new initiative did not entirely resolve the dilemma facing the rulers of Saudi Arabia, but it helped.

The presence of dozens of mujahideen leaders in Mecca for the hajj was one consequence of this new policy. Many had been personally invited by the Saudi authorities or had flown in knowing they were likely to return to Afghanistan or Pakistan with substantial amounts of cash, funds gifted by wealthy princes, rich merchants or the charitable institutions of major companies. Some of these donors were genuinely devout and acted out of a sense of religious duty, others gave in order to maintain their personal standing or that of the business they represented within the kingdom. The money would rarely be handed over directly, but usually through an intermediary. Often this would be a pious relative of a senior royal or a junior son of a wealthy family. When senior directors of the Saudi Bin Laden Group looked for candidates to act as their ambassador to the Afghan jihad, as it was now increasingly called, one of its young executives appeared particularly well-suited to the role.

Osama bin Laden had been working almost full-time for his family's firm for more than a year when he was tapped for his new role in the summer months of 1980. Much of that time had been spent overseeing the levelling of ground for construction projects in and around Mecca. To the surprise of the workers, this young, educated, rich man rose early and worked hard, returning from the sites covered in dust. He even drove the heavy trucks and bulldozers himself, as his father had done. Few wealthy Saudis ever performed manual labour, or much labour at all for that matter, and even fewer showed such evident pleasure when they did.

This did not mean bin Laden had abandoned his interest in the more extreme and politicised fringes of the Islamic faith, nor in asceticism as a proof of conviction. As a father, he was occasionally affectionate but more often distant and demanding. Toys were not allowed in the spartan family home. Air-conditioning was not permitted either. On family outings drinking water was restricted, despite the often intense heat, on the basis that good Muslims needed to be tough for the trials they would face in life. Bin Laden had also plunged deeply into the works of the most radical thinkers of Sunni revivalism. As a student, he had read with admiration the major works of Syed Qutb and discussed them with friends. He had also attended lectures by Qutb's brother, Mohammed, who was briefly based in Jeddah, and the course given by Abdallah Azzam when the activist scholar had visited Abdulaziz University in 1977.

But even as he reached his mid-twenties, there was still little to suggest that bin Laden's commitment to the Islamist cause would go beyond rigorous personal practice, a passing acquaintance with some radical intellectuals and several hours a week devoted to Islamic study.

Employees remembered later that bin Laden never demonstrated the slightest hostility to the US as a country nor to the Bin Laden Corporation's many US, European or non-Muslim employees.

This began to change in the summer and autumn of 1980. As ambassador of the family firm to what was now widely known as the 'Afghan Jihad', Osama began to spend an increasing amount of time with the leaders of the mujahideen. Some had begun fighting well before the Soviet invasion and had been fundraising in the Gulf for several years. Others were newly mobilised. Many were political entrepreneurs who undoubtedly believed in their cause but also sought to advance their own personal interests. Several of the most prominent were senior clerics of the reactionary South Asian Deobandi school, which had much in common with the Arabian peninsula's most conservative traditions. These tended to be from rural areas and have deeper links with Afghanistan's powerful tribes. Others were more contemporary in their approach, more highly politicised and so closer to the Muslim Brotherhood in their thinking. Often such men had emerged from the revolutionary ferment of Kabul University in the late 1960s and several had taken part in the abortive Islamist uprising there in 1975. As bin Laden's personal views chimed with both the traditionalism of the clerics and the activism of the political Islamists, this split posed no particular challenge and he was able to build relations with both. In this, the twenty-three-year-old was entirely representative of tens if not hundreds of millions of other young men across the Muslim world at the beginning of the new decade.

In the last months of 1980 or early 1981, bin Laden travelled to Pakistan, where Islamist forces had continued to gain ground with the enthusiastic personal and political commitment of General Zia-ul-Haq, now in his third year in power. Bin Laden went nowhere near the fighting just across the country's border with Afghanistan, or even to Peshawar, the anarchic western frontier city where the embryonic mujahideen factions were based. Instead, he travelled to Lahore, on the eastern border with India, to deliver funds for the mujahideen into the hands of the senior officials of Jamaat Islami, the local mass organisation that was close to the Muslim Brotherhood. There was no great epiphany and bin Laden spent only a few weeks in Pakistan before flying back to Jeddah where, in between driving bulldozers and the demands of his growing family, he continued his outreach work with visiting Afghans.

Others too were rallying to the cause. One of the most prominent among them was Abdallah Azzam. Bored by his comfortable teaching post in Mecca, the thirty-nine-year-old had thrown himself into a packed schedule of writing, public speaking, travel and lobbying to promote the cause of the mujahideen in Afghanistan. Bin Laden had admired the older scholar-activist for some time, and even if the reverse was not true, the advantages of a relationship with a representative of a very wealthy family close to the Saudi Arabian royal family would not have been lost on Azzam. There were also many genuine interests and ambitions that the two men shared and, though the gap in age, education, wealth and experience was wide, they rapidly became close associates and, to some extent, friends. This union – of the Saudi Arabian scion's access and funds with the Palestinian's talent for propaganda – would prove remarkably effective in the years to come.

In early 1981, Azzam took a teaching post at the International Islamic University in Islamabad, an institution recently founded in Pakistan's capital with $30 million donated by the World Muslim League. A week after arriving, he travelled the seventy-five miles along the crowded, chaotic road to Peshawar to meet the leaders of the mujahideen, and thereafter he continued to visit the frontier city whenever possible. 'I came here to do jihad . . . I did not like being a lecturer,' he explained to one of the commanders. Bin Laden continued to make trips to Pakistan through the spring and summer of 1981, ferrying increasingly large sums collected from his Rolodex of donors in Saudi Arabia. The amount of gold and cash handed over by the kingdom's businessmen and their wives was now so great that the Bin Laden Group built a dedicated vault in Jeddah to hold it all.

Despite the efforts made by Azzam and others who had recently arrived in Pakistan, the war in Afghanistan was far from being a preoccupation of the Islamic world's violent extremists, let alone most Muslims. But over the coming years, this would change and the war would come to generate tremendous centripetal force. Azzam would soon move permanently to Peshawar, where he set about organising those who arrived hoping to help the Afghan resistance or even fight themselves. These volunteers had often been persuaded to do so by the propaganda that now circulated with such ease and in such volume around the Islamic world. Entirely convinced that the world's Muslims were under attack, they followed Azzam's teaching that Afghanistan was the first of many battles to be fought to defend the ummah from atheists, Communists, Zionists, Jews and the Americans. Some, like bin Laden, were well educated, having attended the new universities founded across the Middle East over the previous twenty years. Others belonged to the displaced, deracinated constituency that had provided many of Juhayman's foreign followers. Together, they would eventually constitute a new movement that would prove as revolutionary as anything seen for decades in the region.

The forces that drove this process were layered and various, but one factor that undoubtedly played a crucial role over the decade to come was the increasingly harsh and effective repression faced by Islamists, moderate and radical, almost everywhere in the Muslim world. And one reason for this was what had happened in Egypt in October 1981.

32
Death on the Nile

After a decade in power, Anwar Sadat had established a daily routine. He would wake for dawn prayers, then sleep again until late morning. A servant would bring him the day's newspapers, a cup of tea and a spoonful of honey mixed with royal jelly. He would do some light exercises and bathe. A massage would be followed by a breakfast of cheese and bread.

For two or three hours, Sadat would then be available for meetings and memos. There might be calls from foreign leaders and a visit from a speechwriter or his tailor. Now sixty-three years old, his broad forehead increasingly lined and his wiry black hair turning grey, he was still slim and he still liked his made-to-measure Savile Row suits.

After a late lunch of cold meats and salad, Sadat would rest until dusk. Following the Maghrib or evening prayers, he would meet officials, sign orders prepared by his staff and discuss with senior journalists the headlines that would appear in the next day's carefully monitored newspapers. Sometimes these visitors would find him at his official presidential residence in Cairo or a palace renovated at immense cost in Alexandria, sometimes at his villa on the Mediterranean coast, or at a favourite government rest house in the Sinai or one of many other residences. Later in the evening he would dine, often alone, occasionally with his wife Jehan, and then ask what new films were available. As both foreign and local productions reached the president's office before the government's censors, there was usually a wide selection. Two were chosen even if the single member of the audience was usually dozing by the time the second of them had finished.

That Sadat sought the simple escape of Hollywood was perhaps understandable. His authority was now weaker than it had been at any time since the immediate aftermath of his accession when he had moved to crush his predecessor's supporters and other opposition groups. Challenges were accumulating, each more intractable than the last. The Infitah or Open Door economic policy launched in the aftermath of the 1973 war against Israel still offered foreign firms and well-connected Egyptians opportunities to make serious amounts of money while bringing little benefit to anyone else. As a consequence, the nine million inhabitants of Cairo – three million more than a decade earlier – continued to struggle with appalling pollution, crumbling roads, extortionate rents and soaring food prices. Government propaganda could boast of growth rates touching eight per cent and the restaurants serving haute cuisine in the new five-star hotels were full, but the sewers in Tahrir Square were as malodorous as ever.

Simmering resentment at home was made worse by audacious initiatives abroad. Nasser's foreign ventures had been repeatedly ruinous but had at least fitted a broader story about Egypt's place in the world that resonated with its citizens. By contrast, Sadat's vision of the country's future ran counter to the idea many Egyptians had of themselves, individually and collectively. The continuing rapprochement with the US was not unpopular but the treaty he had concluded with Israel in 1979 was much harder for many of Sadat's countrymen to accept. Egypt had suffered massive losses in the wars against Israel, and though peace and the return of the Sinai were welcome, these came at great cost: the apparent betrayal of the Palestinians and Egypt's expulsion from the Arab League, which withdrew its headquarters from Cairo. The Nobel Peace Prize subsequently awarded to Sadat and Menachem Begin, the Israeli prime minister, brought him little gain at home. Nor did the full state funeral that Sadat ordered for the former Shah of Iran, reviled by many Egyptians, when he died in a Cairo clinic in July 1980.

Hollywood films were not his only refuge. Another was celebrity. Sadat's close aide and adviser Mohammed Heikal later mocked the president for his name-dropping. There was 'my friend Giscard [d'Estaing], my friend [Helmut] Schmidt, my friend [Aristotle] Onassis'. When Elizabeth Taylor visited for filming, Sadat called her the queen of Egypt and placed a presidential helicopter at her disposal for the duration of her stay. Frank Sinatra sang to hundreds of foreign tourists at the foot of the pyramids, then joined prominent Egyptians at a private party at the president's residence. Julio Iglesias, the popular crooner, was flown in from Spain to perform at a televised festival of song, also below the pyramids. As in Iran, such events pleased the elite but deepened ordinary Egyptians' concerns about an invasion of Western culture. Sadat brushed away such complaints, allowing a full third of national TV networks' prime-time programming to consist of imported US soap operas such as *Dallas*. In August 1981, he personally hosted a sunburnt Prince Charles and his wife Diana Spencer at Port Said as the couple travelled through the Suez Canal aboard the royal yacht *Britannia* on their honeymoon.

In the final weeks of the summer of 1981, even the usually supportive Americans were anxious. With the fall of the shah two years earlier they had lost one hugely important ally in the Middle East. Now worried about Saudi Arabia and the invasion of Afghanistan, they could not afford a second such blow. US diplomats reported to Washington that Sadat displayed an 'unusual flair for the dramatic' while being 'supremely self-confident', a disconcerting combination. The Egyptian president rarely consulted with others, and was now 'risking isolation from reality', having 'surrounded himself with those who are reluctant to report unpleasant developments frankly'. One of these was the growing strength of Egypt's Islamists who, in the view of some foreign observers, posed an increasingly direct threat to the president's life.

The surge of religious sentiment and observance in Egypt through the middle years of the 1970s had reached a tipping point by the end of the decade. In one way or another, it was a revival that now touched almost the entire population. Millions joined Sufi brotherhoods, attracted by the mystic traditions of the faith. Similar numbers began attending meetings of the Muslim Brotherhood. Mosques were being built everywhere, visitors reported. Most congregants were content with authorised sermons by government-appointed preachers but others preferred the fiery rhetoric of less compliant clerics who called for a total overhaul of Egypt's society, politics and economy. A growing number joined so-called 'Salafist' groups which sought to impose the rigorous traditions of Saudi Arabia on the traditionally more tolerant and diverse Egyptians. Some of these received funds from the kingdom, and many recruited among returning migrant workers who had lived there. A series of huge prayer meetings took place in cities across Egypt in 1980 and early 1981. One, held opposite the presidential palace in Cairo, drew a crowd of half a million.

This massive rediscovery and reinvention of faith was most evident in the universities, which Islamists had turned into bastions of support. In the vanguard of this campaign were not the cadres of the Muslim

Brotherhood, which had yet to fully recover from the brutal repression of the 1960s and was still committed to change through peaceful means, but those of al-Gama'a al-Islamiyah, or 'The Islamic Groups', a new movement led by much younger activists that had similar aims but was far more confrontational. In 1977, al-Gama'a al-Islamiyah won a series of landslide victories at student elections across the country, purging any remaining Marxist, revolutionary socialist and pan-Arabist leaders from the student bodies. The organisation's success owed much to the practical solutions it offered young Egyptians, often from conservative rural backgrounds, as they sought to navigate overcrowded educational institutions and the social, economic and physical chaos of the country's cities. Packed public taxis were uncomfortable for everyone and meant systematic sexual harassment of female students, so the Gama'a al-Islamiyah provided their own segregated but free transport. Clothes were expensive, especially for the huge numbers of penurious students who now crammed into hostels and halls, so the group created their own subsidised dress for women. Books were not cheap either, so it distributed affordable photocopies of textbooks and set up bookshops where religious works could be bought at a discount. When such initiatives did not yield the desired results, the young leaders of the organisation were not afraid to use more muscular methods. Bans on films, concerts, evening dances and other events that violated 'Islamic morality' were enforced with fists, clubs and iron bars.

Then there were those who were impatient with both the Muslim Brotherhood and al-Gama'a al-Islamiyah. Following the trial of Shukri Mustafa and the other members of his group in late 1977, security services had exposed dozens of other extremist networks and organisations. Like their counterparts elsewhere, Egyptian officials systematically blamed such activism on regional enemies such as Libya or Iraq, or dismissed their conspiracies as the work of yet another 'fanatical sect'. This was inaccurate and unhelpful.

In December 1980, a pioneering article appeared in an academic journal in the US describing the motivations and backgrounds of Egyptian Islamist extremists. Though much thought and ink had been expended on exploring the social origins and views of western European violent activists over the previous decade, there had been little equivalent research into their counterparts in the Middle East, and almost none at all by academics living in the region. The article was the work of Egyptian researchers who had been able to spend some 400 hours interviewing thirty-four imprisoned Islamist extremists, all convicted of serious crimes over the previous six years and who represented 'a significant variant of social movements that have been proliferating all over the Third World in recent decades'.

One aim of the study was to establish the views and aspirations of the militants. These were fairly obvious. The interviewees believed that Islam provided a complete vision for a healthy society on earth and for heavenly paradise hereafter. As all the problems of Egypt (and other nations in the Muslim world) were attributable to deviations from the correct path embodied in the Sharia, it followed that the only solution was the full implementation of Islamic law. This much would have been familiar from the works and words of the Ayatollah Khomeini, Juhayman al-Utaybi, Abdallah Azzam and many other conservative clerics across the Islamic world. 'Other factors – overpopulation, scarcity of cultivable land and other natural resources, the burdens of defence, and the war efforts – are not considered causes of Egypt's present economic difficulties,' the article's authors noted.

Most of those interviewed had been students or professionals, a few were civil servants. Apart from the odd shopkeeper and very occasional skilled manual worker, the majority were graduates. They were all male, with an average age of twenty-seven. Their 'social profile' was strikingly similar to that of their leftist counterparts in Egypt and Iran, wrote Saad Eddin Ibrahim, the sociologist at Cairo University who led the research. Many of their grievances were the same too, even if their proposed solution was very different. The Islamists spoke of fighting on behalf of the poor and the dispossessed against the rich and the capitalists. They, like the leftists, appealed to a body of canonical texts, used the same vocabulary, sought to emulate iconic individuals, understood history through a specific and selective prism and saw all those who disagreed with them as enemies. So why, Ibrahim asked rhetorically, were young men in Egypt and the Arab world joining militant Islamic movements more readily than leftist or Marxist groups?

The answer lay in the significant advantages enjoyed by Islamists in Egypt, Ibrahim decided. One was years of state propaganda dismissing leftist and Marxist opposition as atheists or agents of foreign powers that were bent on destroying Islamic and authentic national heritage. In practical terms, this meant there was little protest when 'leftist elements' were rounded up but an outcry when Islamic groups were targeted. A second was the recent historical setbacks suffered by 'quasi-socialist

Brigitte Kuhlmann, a teacher and Revolutionary Cells member, who died at Entebbe in June 1976.

A passport photograph of Ilich Ramírez Sánchez, aged around nineteen. This and other images were used repeatedly by newspapers and media throughout the late 1970s and 1980s, becoming iconic.

A pilot of the transport planes which flew Israeli special forces to Entebbe on their successful rescue mission is carried by celebrating hostages upon their return to Israel.

Brigitte Mohnhaupt, the utterly committed and highly effective leader of the Red Army Faction's second generation.

Johannes Weinrich, whose elegant clothes and manners inspired derision among his fellow West German leftists but who became Ilich Ramírez Sánchez's indispensable right-hand man.

The kidnapping by the Red Army Faction in September 1977 of Hans Martin Schleyer, a senior industrialist and unrepentant former Nazi, led to the hijacking of the *Landshut* Lufthansa plane in Mallorca and marked the climax of the Red Army Faction's violence. Schleyer was killed days after this image was taken.

The *Landshut* on the ground at Dubai on 15 October 1977. One of the two male attackers is visible at its open door, wearing a Che Guevara T-shirt. The hijackers forced the crew to fly the jet with eighty-six passengers to Aden the following day, where the pilot was shot dead.

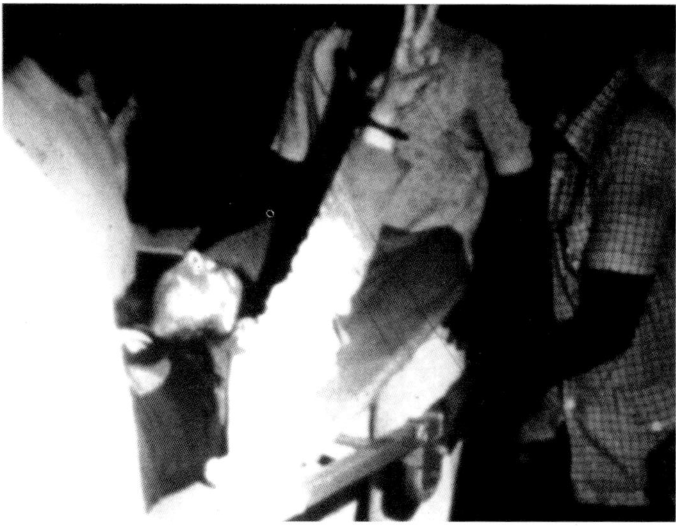

The sole surviving hijacker of the *Landshut*, a badly injured Souhalia Andrawes, gives a V for victory sign as she is stretchered away from the plane after it was successfully stormed by West German special forces. She, too, is still wearing her Che Guevara T-shirt.

Followers and reporters surround the Ayatollah Ruhollah Khomeini in Neauphle-le-Château, a small village near Paris, in January 1979, shortly after he announced his intention to return to Iran within days.

Thousands of Iranian women, guarded by Fedayeen-e Khalq militants, march in Tehran on 12 March 1979, the fifth day of protests against loss of freedoms under Iran's new radical clerical regime.

Supporters of the Mojahedin-e-Khalq, opposing the government, prepare to shoot a member of the security forces during a bloody riot in Enqelab (Revolution) Street in Tehran, 7 November 1982.

Farrokh Negahdar, leader of the Fedayeen-e Khalq, during a televised debate including Communists and clerics in April 1981.

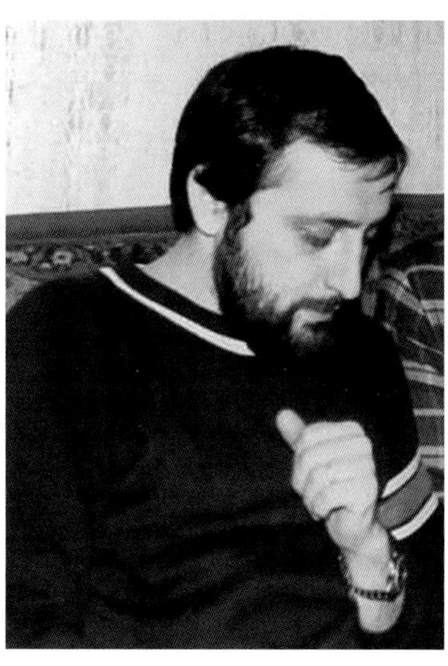

Mohsen Sazegara in Tehran in mid-1979.

The assassination of President Anwar Sadat in October 1981 in Cairo by Islamic militants.

Ayman al-Zawahiri stands behind bars in an Egyptian court in 1982 during the mass trial of militants. Convicted of membership of an illegal Islamic group, he spent three years in jail, then fled overseas, eventually joining other extremists, such as Osama bin Laden, in Pakistan.

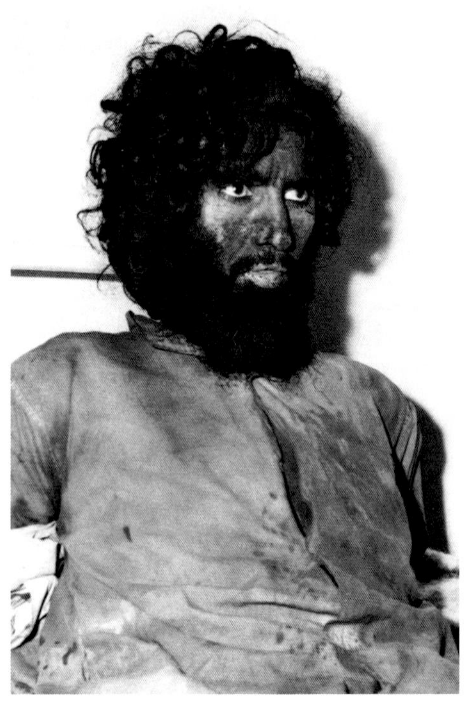

Juhayman al-Utaybi, the leader of the men who took over the Grand Mosque in Mecca in December 1979, pictured after the bloody battle to reclaim the site. He was executed within weeks.

Magdalena Kopp in around 1978, shortly before her relationship with Ilich Ramírez Sánchez began and four years before her arrest in Paris.

Bruno Bréguet, the Swiss militant who was recruited by Ramírez Sánchez into the Organisation of Internationalists Revolutionaries not long after his release from an Israeli prison.

A policeman stands next to a victim of a car bomb explosion in rue Marbeuf, in Paris on 22 April 1982 outside the office of *al-Watan al-Arabi*, an anti-Syrian newspaper. The attack killed one and injured sixty-three.

British special forces end the six day 'siege' of the Iranian Embassy in London on 5 May 1980. For once, the theatre of counter-terrorism replaced that of terrorism.

Israel's invasion of Lebanon caused international outrage, even before the intense and deadly bombardment of Beirut throughout weeks of the summer of 1982.

In April 1983, a massive suicide bomb destroyed much of the US Embassy in Beirut, killing sixty-three. Most victims were Lebanese, but included Robert Ames, the most senior CIA analyst working in the Middle East. Worse was to come.

A poster from 1983 of wanted RAF leaders. All those of the 'first generation' have been crossed off, and also Brigitte Mohnhaupt, who had been arrested the previous year.

experiments' in Egypt and the Arab world, of which the defeat in 1967 was the most obvious. Finally, there was 'the deep-rootedness of Islam in the entire Middle East'. The Marxists had first to overcome negative cultural stereotypes of Marxism and then teach its precepts from scratch, Ibrahim noted. The Islamic extremists did not. Half their task had been achieved for them by the environment in which they had grown up. All that remained was to 'politicise consciousness' and turn enthusiastic recruits into disciplined actors.

Other advantages, which did not take a professor of sociology to discern, included the tacit practical support of the Egyptian authorities for the best part of the last decade, the deep resentment inspired by the peace treaty with Israel and, perhaps most importantly, the example of the Iranian revolution. From 1978, the Muslim Brotherhood in Egypt had been republishing the speeches of Khomeini, whose highly personal attacks on the shah's economic policies, pro-Western foreign policy, sympathy for Israel, supposed betrayal of the Palestinians and alleged failure to care for his subjects all resonated with Egyptians. When Khomeini railed against the cronies, relatives, senior officials and other *kravatis* (tie-wearers) in Iran, Egyptians knew exactly who was being described. If an Egyptian reader substituted the local Coptic Christian community for Iran's Baha'i, Khomeini's attacks on minorities became instantly relevant too.

Nor was Khomeini the only Iranian whose words and ideas influenced Islamists in Egypt. Al-e-Ahmad's 1960s bestseller *Westoxification* was well known along the Nile, and the men who had taken part in the military academy attack in 1974 had been admirers of Ali Shariati. Egyptian militants continued to describe the poor as *al-mustada'afin fil-ard*, an Arabic translation of the Persian term used so often by both Shariati and Khomeini to describe the oppressed and 'wretched of the earth'. They also shouted the Iranian revolutionary slogan 'Neither East nor West: Islamic Republic.' *Al-Dawa*, the Muslim Brotherhood newsletter, boasted that the fall of the shah showed 'that God's party is victorious regardless of the power of tyrants and the forces that support them', and a book entitled *Khomeini: the Islamic Alternative* that called for Islamic revolutions across the Middle East sold 10,000 copies in two days.

There were practical lessons to be drawn from events in Iran too. Egyptian Islamists copied their Iranian counterparts' tactics, using cassettes to disseminate their message and launching a series of new magazines that copied the format of those published by the protest movement in Iran. They also began to use tactics such as sit-ins and wildcat street protests. Some decided the failure of the shah's armed forces to crush the revolutionaries was owing to the successful recruitment by Khomeini's networks of large numbers of military officers. The obvious conclusion was that their own efforts should henceforth be concentrated on Egyptian soldiers.

One of those working towards the overthrow of the government of Sadat in Egypt in 1980 was a tall, slim, bespectacled and very intense young doctor called Ayman al-Zawahiri, who fitted the profile drawn by Ibrahim from his prison interviews with impressive exactitude. Al-Zawahiri was twenty-seven, the average age of the extremists in the study, and a successful educated professional. His father had been a pharmacology professor and his upbringing in Maadi, a comfortable suburb of Cairo, was typical of Egypt's new middle classes. His family could boast more prestigious members than most of its neighbours – one grandfather had been the rector of al-Azhar University, another a diplomat and leading pan-Arabist intellectual – but otherwise neither their conservative nationalism nor their practice of a moderate if devout Islam was in any way exceptional.

Zawahiri's interest in radical Islamist activism had come early, shortly after the death of Syed Qutb, whose execution in 1966 had enormously impressed him. 'Humankind stands on the brink of a precipice,' Qutb had famously stated in the first line of *Milestones*, and so Muslims had a duty to act urgently to prevent the imminent catastrophic fall. Zawahiri, an introverted and somewhat otherworldly young man, did just this, joining school friends and neighbours in a clandestine group dedicated to overthrowing the regime of Gamal Abdel Nasser.

By the time Zawahiri graduated in 1974 from Cairo Medical University, Nasser was long gone and the small band of teenagers had evolved into a network of several dozen members whose commitment went well beyond adolescent enthusiasms. Now serious adult men, they were in no hurry to launch their bid to transform Egypt, recognising sensibly that, for the moment, not one of them had any practicable idea of how they might achieve their aim. But they continued to meet, recruit, talk, learn and, above all, stay out of the way of Egypt's brutal security services. Zawahiri wore Western clothes like most other urban Egyptian professionals and, when he left university, spent three uneventful years as an army surgeon. He then opened a clinic in the neighbourhood where he had grown up and married a pious young woman from a respected Cairene family. Their wedding was a sombre affair, one guest noted, much as the roughly contemporaneous nuptials of Osama bin Laden had been.

In early 1980, Zawahiri took a temporary job in one of the many medical facilities in Cairo run by the Muslim Brotherhood as part of its outreach programme. One evening, during a long shift, he was approached by its director. Many of the refugees fleeing the new war in Afghanistan were arriving at the hastily erected camps in Pakistan in need of medical attention, Zawahiri's senior colleague said. The Muslim Brotherhood were recruiting doctors to treat them. Would he go?

Zawahiri needed little convincing. For years, he had been arguing that all Muslims had a duty to help alleviate the suffering of fellow believers wherever they were in the world. Events in Afghanistan had been widely reported in Egypt, with many prominent religious personalities calling for ordinary citizens to lobby their government to send help to the mujahideen and their communities. In addition, the trip might allow him to observe 'the jihad' first-hand and learn valuable lessons that might serve on his return. No one would doubt his motives for the trip, least of all the security services. Zawahiri was on his way east within weeks, travelling with a plastic surgeon and an anaesthesiologist. He arrived around seven months before Osama bin Laden's first trip to the country and just over a year before Abdallah Azzam moved from Mecca to Islamabad.

Zawahiri spent four months in Pakistan, working at a clinic in Peshawar set up by the Muslim Brotherhood. Conditions in the refugee camps were harsh, and medicine in short supply. When antiseptics ran short, Zawahiri sterilised wounds with honey instead. He was lonely, and anxious about making mistakes as he tried to treat hundreds of patients, some with appalling injuries inflicted by the Soviets' indiscriminate air strikes. 'May God erase my ineptness . . . despite my offences [against him],' he wrote to his mother.

But the experience, though stressful, had been exhilarating. Zawahiri was astonished by the stoicism of his patients and their families. At one point he had even managed to cross the border into Afghanistan, and so had witnessed the mujahideen's courage at first hand. Back in Cairo, Zawahiri took new risks, wearing Pakistani-style clothes and a long beard. He gave discreet talks on university campuses, telling stories of the 'miracles' he had witnessed. Zawahiri remained convinced however that it was Egypt, not Afghanistan, Iran or even Saudi Arabia, that remained 'the heart of the Islamic world, and where the fundamental battle for the future of Islam was being fought'.

Zawahiri's role among the loose network of extremists in Cairo was as a form of 'cultural officer', whose main responsibility was providing ideological or religious advice or justifications for their collective decisions. Its leader was an officer in an armoured unit called Essam al-Qamari who had an elaborate if unoriginal plan to seize power and install a truly Islamic government. First, a campaign of assassinations would wipe out the current political leadership of Egypt, then militants would seize control of all government media to broadcast a call to arms that would, he believed, inspire a mass uprising that would sweep the remnants of Sadat's regime away. In the absence of any better plan, Zawahiri and other members of 'al-Jihad', as the group called itself, set to work and through the autumn of 1980 and into the winter, built up at least some of the resources necessary for its execution. They recruited more manpower, got hold of weapons and rented apartments in poor areas of Cairo as safehouses. The surge of Islamist activism, popular piety and discontent helped them, but also meant greater scrutiny from increasingly worried security agencies.

In January 1981, around six months after Zawahiri had got back from Afghanistan, Egyptian intelligence services moved to break up extremist networks in Cairo and Asyut, the southern city which had long been a centre of radical religious activism. Several such sweeps had been launched since the hot summer of 1977 but warning lights were now flashing red across Egypt. This new operation was larger in scope than any other and hundreds of suspected Islamist extremists were detained. Though Qamari and Zawahiri escaped unscathed, one of their couriers was intercepted with a bag full of maps, ammunition and weapons. Qamari immediately cut off all contact with his fellow conspirators and disappeared. Zawahiri halted his own clandestine activities, devoted himself solely to his medical practice in Maadi for a month and then flew back to Pakistan.

But this time Zawahiri stayed just a few weeks in Peshawar before returning to Cairo in the belief that the immediate threat to him – and to the Egyptian president – had passed. He was wrong on both counts.

In September 1981, Sadat ordered yet another wave of arrests. The crackdown was anything but discriminate – evidence of the increasing desperation of the authorities – and the 1,500 people detained by security forces this time included prominent leftist academics, former judges, nationalist politicians, mildly critical journalists and wealthy businessmen. Among the Islamists were the supreme leader of the Muslim Brotherhood and a twenty-seven-year-old student named Mohammed al-Islambouli who had been caught defacing a poster of the president some months earlier. It was the arrest of the latter that was to prove most consequential.

The Islambouli family came originally from Mallawi, a town 180 miles from Cairo, but like so many other Egyptians in recent decades they had forsaken their provincial ancestral home for the capital. Like the Zawahiris, they were relatively prosperous, and also had some illustrious ancestors. Islambouli's father was a lawyer who worked for a government-owned sugar manufacturing company while his younger brother Khaled had done well enough at school to win a lieutenant's commission in the army. The two boys and their two sisters had been brought up to be conservative, nationalist, pious and law-abiding.

Both the Islambouli brothers had been drawn into the more radical fringes of Egypt's religious revival. Mohammed had got involved with the Gama'a al-Islamiyah at Asyut University, where he was studying commerce. In 1979 he had spent several months in Saudi Arabia, studying at Medina University and performing a pilgrimage to Mecca. He may have been in the city when the Great Mosque was attacked but either way had been sufficiently impressed by the rebels to smuggle a copy of Juhayman al-Utaybi's 'twelve epistles' back to Egypt when he returned. This he passed to his brother.

Khaled was two years younger than Mohammed and followed a different route into extremism. Broad-faced and stocky, he was a promising young soldier, though his intense devotion and hardline views had been noted with some concern by brother officers. His personal faith was catalysed into something more active by his friendship with an Islamist extremist writer called Abdelsalam Faraj whom he had met by chance in a mosque in 1980 while looking for an apartment in a slightly down-at-heel neighbourhood of Cairo.

Faraj, who was then twenty-six, had studied engineering at Cairo University, and also came from a relatively prosperous middle-class family but, like many other graduates in Egypt, had been unable to find a job beyond the manual trades and worked as an electrician. This brought in just about enough to eat and rent a two-room home in the poor part of Cairo where he had met Khaled Islambouli. Faraj devoted most of his time to reading Islamic texts, writing, and the al-Jihad group. Thin-faced, intense, an energetic and convincing public speaker, he also gave frequent lectures in unregistered mosques in Cairo's slums – an environment and a practice that would have been familiar to Juhayman al-Utaybi and to many of Khomeini's followers too. Such lectures were a good way of gathering new sympathisers and it may have been at one of these that he identified Islambouli as a potential recruit.

Despite his total lack of formal Islamic training, Faraj had compiled his somewhat incoherent thoughts into a short book called *The Neglected Duty*, in which he argued, fairly predictably, that the parlous condition of the world's Muslims was a consequence of their failure to follow the injunctions of the Koran and specifically to fulfil their obligation to violently confront Muslims' own corrupt rulers or the usual overseas enemies. The former had to be defeated before the latter – the US, imperialists, the Zionists, Communists, 'Crusaders' et al. – could be dealt with. 'Verily the main reason for the existence of Imperialism is these rulers. Therefore to begin with the destruction of the Imperialists is a waste of time. We have to concentrate on our Islamic state,' he wrote. This required jihad, the 'neglected duty' of the title, which Faraj said was as important for a Muslim as prayer, charity or the hajj.

Such views had a familiar ring in Egypt in 1981. They were frequently expressed, in only marginally more moderate terms, in the Muslim Brotherhood publications read by hundreds of thousands or voiced by propagandists such as Abdallah Azzam, whose texts were increasingly well known in the country. Along with the work of Qutb, a key influence on Faraj was the work of Taqi al-Din ibn Taymiyya, an uncompromising and reactionary thirteenth-century revivalist theologian whose voluminous teachings had been widely distributed in Egypt by the World Muslim League and other major Saudi organisations. Faraj's insistence that active personal involvement in jihad was as important as prayer for any true Muslim was borrowed directly from Ibn Taymiyya, as was his view that obedience to un-Islamic authorities was itself apostasy and so punishable by death.

But Ibn Taymiyya was far from the only influence on Faraj, who also mentioned in his book the return of a Mahdi for the final apocalyptic battle against the unbelievers. This may well have owed something to Utaybi's epistles, which Faraj had almost certainly read. His insistence that a Muslim did not have to obtain the prior consent of ruler, cleric and father before participation in violent jihad could well have been influenced by contemporary sources of a rather different nature: rebellion against established authority and particularly the older generation had been one of the most widely shared themes of the 1960s and 70s pretty much all over the world. His call for a new vanguard of militant believers to create the conditions for radical political and social transformation had unmistakable echoes of secular revolutionary thinking, too.

Not every reader of Faraj's work was impressed. Some of his extremist associates found it excessively derivative. One dismissed the book as 'pubescent'. Others worried that the existence of the text might attract attention to their networks. A military intelligence officer among the groups' leaders in Cairo told Faraj to destroy all 500 copies. The author reluctantly complied, though only after he had given one to Khaled Islambouli who kept the volume safe among his belongings at the family home in Mallawi, where it was found by investigators after his violent and extremely public death.

When Islambouli found out that his elder brother Mohammed had been arrested in Sadat's latest crackdown in September 1981 he broke down sobbing. Eventually, he led his equally distraught mother around government offices across Cairo and even to the dreaded Tora prison on an ultimately fruitless search for information about the fate of her other son. Angry, anxious and humiliated, the twenty-four-year-old wrote a quote from Faraj's book in his diary: 'The greatest prize for a believer is salvation, and to kill or be killed in the cause of God.'

Just under three weeks after the arrest of his brother, Islambouli was presented with an entirely unexpected opportunity to put Faraj's ideas into practice when he learned that his unit had been chosen to participate in the annual Victory Day parade. Three days later, Islambouli contacted Faraj and told him he needed three volunteers, a handgun and ammunition. The requested materiel was obtained from released Islamist extremist prisoners who had established a commune in the Nile Delta. The manpower came from among the many military recruits of the Islamist groups. One was a former officer who had given up his military career to open a religious bookshop, a second was a sergeant known as the best marksman in the entire army, while the third was a reserve engineer officer. All were summoned to Faraj's small home where they listened to Islambouli explain his plan. They were enthusiastic, even when it became clear that their participation implied almost certain 'martyrdom'.

Over the next few days, Islambouli arranged for two of the soldiers in his artillery unit to be sent away on leave and special duties. A third fell sick, which was useful. Word was passed to Faraj who told the volunteers to shave their beards, put on their uniforms and present themselves at the army base on the outskirts of Cairo where Islambouli was based. Islambouli, who had provided the fake papers that enabled their entry, greeted them coolly, sent them off on fatigues, and then made sure that they were assigned to the truck which he would command.

On the eve of the parade, orders were given to render harmless all the weapons belonging to Islambouli's unit by removing their firing pins, a standard precaution before every such event to protect the president. As a further precaution, all ammunition was locked away too. During the night, Islambouli, who knew this would happen, replaced the missing firing pins in four weapons with substitutes stolen earlier from army stores. He then marked the lethal rifles with a small strip of cloth to allow his three comrades to pick them out when they went to collect their weapons for the parade the next morning. Finally Islambouli hid the ammunition and the handgun supplied by Faraj in his command vehicle. The unit assembled in the pre-dawn, hitched their twelve heavy artillery guns to the six-wheeled trucks and then drove through the silent streets to their assembly area.

On Monday, 6 October 1981, Sadat woke at his residence in Giza and followed his usual routine of light exercise, massage and breakfast. At around 10.30 a.m., now wearing a spectacular navy blue dress uniform, he was driven across Cairo to the new suburb of Nasr City. There a broad road alongside a soaring memorial to Egypt's war dead was to be the venue for its Victory Day parade, an annual demonstration of Egypt's military might commemorating the 1973 war. The president had decided against wearing body-armour, which would have spoiled the careful cut of his new jacket and undermined the authority he sought to project.

At 11 a.m. sharp the parade began with the national anthem and the placing of bouquets at the Unknown Soldier Memorial. Diplomats and carefully selected reporters had been informed that for the first time the parade would feature more Western weapon systems than Soviet ones. French Mirage jets flew overhead, trailing multicoloured smoke above

US-made armoured personnel carriers, a handful of much older tanks of uncertain eastern European manufacture, military bands and serried columns of infantry. Then came the camel corps with its turbaned soldiers, and the cavalry, mounted on sleek Arabian horses. A rocket was fired into the air and on exploding rained Egyptian flags and portraits of the president hanging from tiny parachutes onto the ground below.

Islambouli and his unit had been waiting for several hours when they received the order to start their vehicles and take their positions in the long column making its slow way onto the parade ground. When eventually their truck was level with the president, Islambouli pointed his loaded handgun at the driver and told him to stop.

Most of the onlookers who saw the truck slew to one side and then halt thought it had broken down. Even when four soldiers carrying assault rifles jumped down and began running towards the viewing stand, no one quite realised what was happening. Sadat, standing alone in front of nearly a thousand dignitaries, the massed ranks of Egypt's political and military elite, continued his stiff salute. Moments later, the men opened fire. The president collapsed, hit in the neck, chest and abdomen. Islambouli stood over the mortally wounded Sadat and shouted, 'I have killed the Pharaoh and I do not fear death' before being overpowered. For a minute or more the shooting continued. By the time it had ended, a general, a bishop and five others had been killed and dozens of others injured. Sadat was driven to a waiting helicopter and airlifted to Maadi military hospital but was pronounced dead by doctors after an hour of frantic efforts to save his life.

Most Egyptians first learned that something had happened at the parade when the live television coverage of the event abruptly stopped. The state radio continued to broadcast live for a few minutes until a voice was heard shouting obscenities. It was swiftly replaced by readings from the Koran and old reports of the president's finest moments: the reopening of the Suez Canal, the post-war parade of 1973, the Nobel Prize won jointly with Menachem Begin for the Camp David Accords. After five hours, the vice president Hosni Mubarak announced 'the death of fighter and hero, Anwar al-Sadat' to the 'Egyptian nation, the Arab and Islamic countries and the whole world'. Mubarak would take power within a week and not relinquish it for thirty years.

In the aftermath of the killing there was sporadic violence but no sign of the mass uprising that the assassins had hoped to provoke. In Asyut, a local extremist group seized control of a police station and almost took over a second but were all killed after a battalion of paratroopers was deployed against them. In Cairo, a bid to take over the state media's broadcasting facilities was an abject failure. But nor were there any public demonstrations of grief as there had been for Nasser or for the singer Umm Kulthum six years earlier. For all the adulation he received in the West, the 'pious president' died unmourned by his compatriots.

The Egyptian security services did not take long to identify and apprehend those responsible. Islambouli and two accomplices had been held at the parade ground and the fourth gunman was swiftly found at his home in Cairo. In the massive sweep after the assassination, thousands more were detained. The trials of those involved in or linked to the killing of the president began in December 1981 and lasted more than a year. On the first day of hearings, twenty defendants stood in a metal cage to hear charges against them. Photographs in Egyptian newspapers showed Islambouli, defiant in a white cloak and a prayer cap with the Koran in his hand. Faraj, eyes sunk in his narrow face, stood at his side. Neither expressed the slightest regret. 'Do not be sad because I will be joining my God. We are free and you are the prisoners,' Islambouli told his mother, who sat through the trial in the courtroom. Both men were hanged in April 1982, along with the three others who had killed the president.

At the end of the year a much larger trial got underway, with a total of 302 defendants. Many were minor figures whose connection with the assassination of Sadat was tangential at most. One attracted particular attention however: a well-known southern Cairo physician whose confidence, simmering fury and vitriolic eloquence marked him out from the other accused.

Zawahiri had no prior knowledge of the plot to kill Sadat. After returning from Pakistan in late spring of 1981, the thirty-one-year-old had given his talks at universities and grown a beard but not been particularly active otherwise. Many of his associates in the clandestine Islamist movement had been detained or gone to ground and he had only learned of what Islambouli and Faraj were planning on the morning of the parade. The plan astonished Zawahiri and, convinced that it would fail, he refused demands to launch action in support, arguing that such efforts would be useless and dangerous. Later that night, when it was clear that Sadat was dead, Zawahiri changed his mind and began plotting an attack on the president's funeral with two associates but this fizzled out when one of them was arrested. Zawahiri was detained two weeks later.

Neither Zawahiri's social standing nor the prestigious history of his family was any protection against the humiliated and fearful security services. Detainees suspected of Islamist extremism were stripped, beaten, electrocuted, sexually assaulted, starved, denied medical treatment and packed into overcrowded cells. Their captors made sure they could hear the screams of other prisoners. Relatives of those reluctant to 'confess' were threatened, imprisoned, raped or assaulted. Under torture Zawahiri betrayed his close associates, who were then detained, tortured in turn and deliberately put in his cell so he would learn what had happened to them.

At the very beginning of the trial, Zawahiri made a statement to the court. He stood tall and erect at the bars of the cage containing the packed defendants, almost rigid with anger as he described the mistreatment they had received, detailing the specific techniques of torture, listing the names of those who had died in agony in jail and shouting in English a series of questions: 'Where is democracy? Where is freedom? Where is human rights? Where is justice? We will never forget! We will never forget!'

Zawahiri then began to speak of the mission of the most violent extremists, but also of al-Gama'a al-Islamiyah, the Muslim Brotherhood and all the other groups whose members stood or sat in the cage behind him.

'Now we want to speak to the whole world,' he shouted. 'Who are we? Why do they bring us here, and what do we want to say? We are Muslims! We are Muslims who believe in their religion . . . both in ideology and practice, and so we tried our best to establish an Islamic state and an Islamic society.'

This was unprecedented. Language such as this had been in use for a decade or more but always confined to extremists' safehouses, their squalid shared apartments, desert hideouts, unregistered mosques and rooms in run-down shantytowns. This was true not just in Egypt but everywhere in the region. Such rhetoric had been present on the streets in Iran, but only as part of a much broader movement of opposition to the shah and tempered by the pragmatic calculations of the clerics. When voiced in Syria or Iraq or over the loudspeakers of the Great Mosque in Mecca, it had been ruthlessly, bloodily crushed. But now it had been heard, loud and clear, in a courtroom, before judges, the public and television cameras in Cairo, a city that served as the cultural and political capital of the Sunni Muslim world.

'We are ... the only true Islamic opposition against Zionism, Communism and imperialism ... We are here [behind bars] because they are trying to abolish this true Islamic movement,' Zawahiri told the judges, the lawyers, the security forces and, via the journalists present, the world. 'We have sacrificed and we are ready to make more sacrifices.'

The assassination of Sadat prompted a predictable array of reactions. In Israel, Begin said Sadat had been 'murdered by the enemies of peace', while Ronald Reagan, who had been in the White House for nine months, called the assassination 'an act of ... cowardly infamy' that deprived America of a close friend and the world of a great statesman. Official Saudi media barely mentioned events in Cairo, preferring to report a speech by King Khaled addressed to hajj pilgrims.

The Soviets sent a cool message of condolence while Moscow Radio blamed the killing on 'the discontent of Egyptians with Sadat's foreign and domestic policies, especially the peace treaty with the Israeli aggressor and military co-operation with the United States'. In Beirut, Palestinian guerrillas shot streams of tracer ammunition into the air in celebration. One of Yasser Arafat's closest aides declared that the PLO wanted to 'shake the hand that fired the bullets'. In Tehran, state media described Sadat as 'a treacherous and mercenary pawn of Zionism and imperialism' who deserved what he had got. From Paris, exiled former Iranian president Abolhassan Bani-Sadr said the late Egyptian president had 'abandoned the deep internal problems of his country to devote himself to external affairs, and he paid for it'.

Many of the first reports on Sadat's assassination blamed Libyan agents – a reasonable if unjustified speculation. Now in his thirteenth year in power, Gaddafi had long seen his Egyptian counterpart as an unworthy successor to Nasser. He had fought a short war with Egypt in 1977, was outraged by its peace deal with Israel and had been trying to have Sadat killed for some time. Gaddafi had not chosen Islamic militants as his preferred instrument, however. Instead, his secret services had commissioned a thirty-two-year-old self-styled revolutionary of some notoriety, offering a large advance payment, considerable logistical assistance and $4 million on successful completion of the contract. Predictably, Ilich Ramírez Sánchez, by now much better known as 'Carlos the Jackal', had accepted with no little enthusiasm.

X

33
Carlos in the East

Ilich Ramírez was asleep in a villa in Budapest when the BBC began broadcasting news of Sadat's assassination at around 1 p.m. local time. When he awoke, his reaction was loud and extremely angry. Ramírez shouted a series of imprecations against 'double-crossing bastard Libyans' and expressed vehement regret that he and his organisation had 'just lost out on four million dollars'. His fury soon subsided into petulant frustration. 'Everything was ready!' he complained.

The pyrotechnic display of irritation – captured by listening devices placed throughout the house – may well have bewildered the Hungarian secret services who overheard it. They knew a great deal about the world's best-known terrorist and, as far as they could see, Ramírez had every reason to be pleased with his current circumstances. Since leaving Baghdad in January 1979, he had successfully realised his ambition, first formulated on his expulsion from the PFLP in 1976, to create his own group, available for hire by any 'revolutionary' state which cared to put up sufficient funds. By late 1981 the 'Organisation of Internationalist Revolutionaries' (OIR) comprised only half a dozen core members but it had a network of reciprocal alliances with other extremist outfits that stretched from Beirut to Bilbao. The money Ramírez earned from his violent trade had funded a lavish lifestyle. He had a comfortable home in Budapest, boltholes in at least three other capitals in eastern and central Europe, and there was a new woman in his life.

Yet these achievements were more fragile than they looked, and Ramírez may well have sensed that the assassination of Sadat in October 1981 marked a turning point not just for the Middle East but for his newly revived fortunes. If so, his instincts, proved uncannily accurate over the previous decade, would be proved so again.

*

It had been nearly three years since Ramírez's arrival from Iraq, each involving different phases of activity for the OIR. In the first months and through much of 1979, Ramírez had been primarily occupied with building up his network and capabilities and selling his services to potential clients. The second phase, which lasted through much of 1980, saw the OIR developing its tactics and fulfilling a range of relatively undemanding missions for its new sponsors. Through 1981, a third phase involved a series of increasingly ambitious missions that offered a chance to secure massive wealth and prestige, but also risked catastrophe for the organisation. This last had continued up to the moment when Ramírez learned of the killing of Sadat.

The two people who played the most significant roles in Ramírez's successes in eastern and central Europe were Johannes Weinrich, the West German extremist who had teamed up with Ramírez in Algiers in the summer of 1977, and Magdalena Kopp, the timid and unassuming former photographic technician who had reluctantly ended up giving the Venezuelan a massage during her stay there. Weinrich and Kopp had been lovers for many years and had lived with Ramírez as a rather uncomfortable *ménage à trois* in Iraq. Though the departure from Iraq had offered the opportunity for a clean break, Weinrich had had no second thoughts about joining Ramírez on the flight to Budapest, and Kopp had few concerns about following Weinrich.

This was to Ramírez's advantage. Weinrich was a formidable logistician, making him a valuable asset given the Venezuelan's habitual inattention to detail. Slim and bespectacled, with straight sandy hair, a small moustache and a wardrobe of expensive suits with matching ties, Weinrich looked more like a fastidious and slightly seedy corporate lawyer than the chief operating officer of a globally-feared terrorist network. The thirty-two-year-old was not only talented and ambitious but had a wide range of contacts in Europe derived from his long association with the Revolutionary Cells. Weinrich's responsibilities in the OIR would soon become extensive: to manage the group's money, organise accommodation, arrange the transfer of weapons across borders, set up flights and trains, sort out visas and passports and frequently act as an unofficial emissary of Ramírez himself when difficult clients needed to be convinced or placated. Quite what Kopp offered Ramírez was initially less clear.

Weinrich's first task on arrival in Budapest was to find a convenient base in eastern and central Europe. His solution was a sprawling two-storey villa in the exclusive neighbourhood known as the Hill of Roses. The house was hidden by tall trees. The neighbourhood, much favoured by senior Communist party apparatchiks, diplomats and businessmen, was quiet. Citizens of the Hungarian People's Republic wryly described their country as the 'happiest barracks' behind the Iron Curtain, and residents of the big houses lining the Hill of Roses' pretty streets above the Danube were among the most content of all. Here, there was little chance of nosy neighbours causing trouble, or unwanted attention from the local security services who were still unaware of their new arrival. Kopp and Weinrich moved in to the villa, while Ramírez continued to enjoy the pleasures of bachelor life in luxury hotels in the city centre.

One evening shortly after their arrival, Kopp and Weinrich dined with Ramírez at an expensive local restaurant known for its high-quality Hungarian cuisine. Ramírez enjoyed a crepe stuffed with minced meat in a paprika and cream sauce, then a faux-filet with ratatouille. Weinrich chose mushrooms followed by a steak. All three ordered apple tart and when Kopp could not finish her serving, Ramírez ate what she had left. He then informed Weinrich that he wanted him to go to Prague and then to East Berlin in order to establish contacts with local security services and gauge how Ramírez might be received were he to pay a visit to either city. These appeared reasonable requests and Weinrich set off a day or so later without questioning his mission.

Ramírez had ulterior motives for dispatching his faithful and effective aide far from the Hill of Roses. Mere hours after her boyfriend had left for Prague, Kopp was surprised to open the door of the villa to find Ramírez, holding two bottles of wine. Kopp had been with Weinrich for almost a decade and sacrificed much for their relationship, leaving her now twelve-year-old daughter in West Germany and moving first to Baghdad and now Budapest to be with him. She had given no previous sign of being attracted to Ramírez and had previously rebuffed his clumsy advances. As well as the episode with the massage in Algiers, Ramírez had harassed her in London and Aden, physically and verbally. On one occasion he had complimented her 'nice legs and pretty breasts'. On another he told her that he found her attractive because she washed regularly, 'unlike a lot of leftist girls'.

There are contrasting accounts of what happened that night in Budapest. Ramírez has described being 'seduced'. Kopp, in stark contrast, has spoken of something that she did not initiate, desire or enjoy in any way, and that although she 'would have liked to forget the incident' Ramírez subsequently made perfectly clear that she should henceforth consider her relationship with Weinrich over. When Kopp informed her boyfriend what had happened, Weinrich was upset and angry, telling her simply that 'this man will not make you happy'. But he did not argue with her decision to follow Ramírez's instructions and eventually moved into a spare bedroom in the villa, leaving the master bedroom to Kopp and her new partner.

With his personal relations now arranged to his satisfaction, Ramírez started travelling himself. Between February and August 1979, he made three trips to Prague, which Weinrich had deemed safe for him to visit. The city had many attractions: shops stocked with Western goods, theatres, concert halls and a very good Indian restaurant. There was also its strategic location at the heart of Europe, hard against the frontier between East and West, with Vienna four hours by train and Frankfurt reachable in a long afternoon's drive.

Ramírez went to see Souhaila Andrawes, the PFLP hijacker who had been injured during the German special forces' storming of the plane in Mogadishu two years previously and who was still in hospital after further operations to remove a West German bullet from her leg. Then he set about finding new recruits for the OIR. The Czechoslovak Socialist Republic had a long history of government support for radical factions in the Middle East, particularly Yasser Arafat's Fatah and the main body of the PFLP, and had for years welcomed dissidents from across the region. This meant there were plenty of disaffected, highly motivated and under-employed activists there who might be persuaded to join his new group.

Among these numerous veterans were several old friends. One was an experienced Palestinian called Kamal al-Issawi who had been a key aide to Wadie Haddad and was well known to Ramírez. Al-Issawi was swiftly recruited to the OIR and given the codename 'Ali'. But others proved harder to convince. Ramírez spent hours in the café of Prague's Intercontinental Hotel with Mohammed Daoud Odeh, who had led the Munich Olympics attack in 1972 and then fallen out with the PLO leadership over its rejection of international violence, but their discussions were inconclusive. A mutual friend put Ramírez in touch with people close to Salah Khalaf, the head of Yasser Arafat's security and intelligence services, but this contact too went nowhere. Talks with representatives of western European extremist groups such as the Basque nationalists of Euskadi Ta Askatasuna (ETA), the Italian Prima Linea and an arms dealer whom the local security service, which bugged many of these conversations, believed was 'Carlos's [contact] man' in the Irish Republican Army were cordial but none were keen on actually joining the OIR.

As well as recruits, Ramírez sought new clients. Everything he did and intended to do was wholly dependent on the regular arrival of large sums of money. Only states could provide the kind of funds Ramírez required, so their representatives in Prague were the obvious people to approach. Relations with the Iraqis remained chilly so alternatives needed to be found. One evening in August 1979 Ramírez met a group of Syrian diplomats at a celebrated Czech restaurant. The famous Venezuelan recounted his career and, as the hours passed and levels of inebriation rose, described a new but apparently profound admiration for the foreign policy of president Hafez al-Assad. A few days later, while drinking with his new Syrian friends at the cocktail bar at the Intercontinental Hotel, he loudly criticised Baghdad's policy towards Communists and ostentatiously refused to shake the hand of an Iraqi diplomat. When one of his drinking partners joked that he should kill the snubbed official, Ramírez appeared to consider the suggestion seriously. Suitably impressed, the Syrian diplomats later made a formal offer of collaboration.

Around the same time, Ramírez snared another big client. Despite his personal dislike of Muammar Gaddafi, Ramírez was aware that the unpredictable Libyan leader personally handed out tens, possibly hundreds, of millions of dollars of his vast oil revenues to dozens of different 'revolutionary' organisations every year. Recipients of the Libyan leader's largesse ranged from authentic resistance movements to those, like the OIR, whose motives were more nakedly mercenary. The Libyans had two possible jobs for Ramírez: to kill dozens of 'stray dogs' – Libyan dissidents who had fled the country and taken refuge in western Europe – and to transport weapons to groups that Gaddafi wanted to support in places like Spain and France. They were offering a substantial amount of money and the use of their diplomatic bags to move arms or anything else into or around Europe. A deal was done in the late summer of 1979.

So when Ramírez, Kopp and Weinrich spent Christmas Eve of that year dining and drinking in the top-floor restaurant of a luxury hotel in

Budapest that overlooked the Danube, they had much to celebrate. The first phase of building and selling the OIR had gone well. They were flush with weapons, money, new partners and clients. Ramírez was particularly happy about the prospect of obtaining a recently developed guided missile with an effective range of nine miles which he hoped would be included in a large shipment of arms and ammunition that was supposed to arrive soon from Libya, having travelled via Moscow and East Berlin. In order to manage the logistics of the transfer, Weinrich flew to Tripoli on Christmas Day.

True to form, however, Gaddafi proved a demanding and inconstant client. On arrival in the Libyan capital, Weinrich discovered that the chances of receiving any state-of-the-art weapons in the immediate future were slim. In fact, the OIR would be lucky to receive anything at all. The group's Christmas celebrations had been premature. In a tense meeting, a senior officer in Gaddafi's intelligence service told Weinrich that the Libyans had so far been disappointed by the group. A $3 million advance paid to the OIR was not meant 'to fund a luxurious existence in expensive hotels . . . but . . . to eliminate enemies of Libya in Europe', Weinrich was warned. The Libyans imposed a deadline, threatening to cancel the contract and turn to 'another more reliable group' if they did not see results within a month. For the moment, Ramírez was not overly concerned. In the new year – the first of a new decade – there would be plenty of opportunities to prove to the Libyans and everyone else what he and the OIR were capable of.

As Ramírez, Weinrich, Issawi and Kopp moved around eastern and central Europe, they left confusion and concern in their wake. No officials in Budapest or Prague welcomed these troublesome visitors, but none could do much to prevent their arrival or enforce their departure. Even tracking the OIR members' movements was a serious challenge. Ramírez and his comrades travelled on genuine diplomatic passports in fictitious Arabic names given to them by supportive Middle Eastern states – primarily Iraq, Syria, Libya and the People's Democratic Republic of Yemen. This meant not only that identification of the OIR's members at a frontier depended on visual recognition by a sharp-eyed official but that any delay, let alone detention, of the passport-holder in question risked offending countries that were in theory aligned with the USSR and thus allies.

As a consequence, Ramírez and Weinrich could disappear almost without trace for weeks and then surface unexpectedly thousands of miles from their last known whereabouts. If either had forgone the conspicuous luxury hotels stuffed with listening devices and informants and opted instead for anonymous two-star suburban pensions, they might have stayed undetected for much longer than they did. But neither saw the need to moderate their behaviour or avoid attracting attention. In Prague, Ramírez waved huge stacks of dollar bills at a hotel receptionist who dared to request an advance payment by credit card and later ran down a corridor angrily waving a pistol after locking himself out of his room. The professional spies of the Czech security services sniffily described how male members of the OIR failed to observe even the most basic laws of espionage, having repeated 'contacts with unreliable and unscreened persons', such as the dozens of women they paid for sex, despite the obvious likelihood that their temporary companions were working for, or at least known to, local security services. When Ramírez needed a vehicle in Budapest, he bought himself a large Mercedes from an Arab diplomat which he promptly resprayed gold. At the opening night of a new casino for foreigners in the city, he behaved so objectionably that management were forced to call the police to break up a brawl.

But the real problem for the authorities in Prague and Budapest was not practical but political. The presence on their territory of the most wanted terrorist in the world and his close associates presented a new and acute version of the dilemma that had faced all Soviet satellites over the previous decade whenever other extremist groups had arrived uninvited in their capitals. Every regime in eastern Europe recognised that such actors could be useful. They were potential sources of important intelligence, rare Western-made weapons or other technology and they could even be used to carry out sensitive operations. Many such organisations were also seen as allies in the great campaign against imperialism and capitalism, and their leaders had been offered education, medical care and holidays for decades. Thousands of those involved in 'liberation struggles' around the world had been trained behind the Iron Curtain, often returning to their countries full of enthusiasm for the socialist revolutionary states who had hosted them and, not infrequently, as informants. At the same time, such relationships were not without risk.

The first was the threat their exposure posed to the Soviet satellites' claim – and by extension the claim of the Soviets themselves – to moral superiority over the duplicitous, warmongering 'cowboys' in Washington, an essential element of their legitimacy at home as well as abroad. A second major risk was to relations with western European countries that supplied credit, technology, consumer items and much else on which faltering eastern European economies relied.

But the most significant reason for the reluctant hospitality offered by the Czechs and the Hungarians was the widespread belief that Ramírez and his followers could be very dangerous if crossed. All officials in eastern Europe were mindful of the attack Ramírez had launched on OPEC in Vienna four years previously. The liaison officer charged with managing Hungary's relationship with the OIR was convinced that if any of its members were expelled or detained, 'the whole terrorist group would have declared Allah's revenge on Hungary [and] all our embassies abroad would [be] exposed.' For their part, the Czechs were certain Ramírez was a 'very dangerous terrorist' who, though 'a progressive individual in agreement with the politics of socialist states', was a serious threat to them too.

Such fears were misplaced but entirely understandable. Regimes across eastern Europe deployed immense resources to spy on their own citizens and could use these to gather information on visitors too. At least some of the time, they were able to watch or listen to even the most intimate moments of the OIR's senior leadership. As well as Ramírez's outburst after Sadat was killed, the Hungarians recorded him having sex with Kopp in a hotel room after delivering a long lecture about the political history of the Middle East. But while they learned a vast amount about the OIR's day-to-day activities, its members' personal desires and disappointments, analysing this mass of data to produce a reliable picture of the whole was much harder. For their wider understanding of the OIR and its history, services across eastern Europe relied much of the time on cuttings from often sensationalist Western media, recycled information from other Soviet satellites and unreliable or fragmentary reports from informants among Arab extremist circles at home or abroad. All tended to portray Ramírez as possessed of near-superhuman powers.

Many of the Western accounts should have stretched credulity. Journalists, politicians and other commentators routinely claimed that 'Carlos the Jackal' had participated in more or less every terrorist attack that had occurred in the previous decade, including the Munich Olympics attack of 1972, the hijacking that led to the Entebbe raid and the wave of violence in the summer of 1977. Ramírez was supposed to have masterminded the seizure of the US Embassy in Tehran in 1979, organised the fatal shooting of Nicaragua's former dictator Anastasio Somoza in Paraguay a year later and led a team of Libyan assassins from Mexico across the Rio Grande into the US. An Italian magazine reported that Ramírez had links variously to the Italian Red Brigades, 'neo-Fascists', the Palestinians and a network of Freemasons. In one of the more spectacularly irresponsible reports of this sort, the weekly magazine *New York*, recently bought by the up-and-coming Australian businessman Rupert Murdoch, described in detail what might happen if 'the most dangerous man in the world' used a small nuclear bomb against an American city.

Meanwhile, a series of cinematic blockbusters depicted an often thinly disguised version of Ramírez as an omnipotent mastermind of violence, as did books with names like *The Carlos Complex* or *Brothers in Blood*. Some accounts declared Ramírez dead; others said he was a master of disguise and very much alive. All placed him at the heart of an international terrorist network, and this is what the eastern European services duly described to their political masters. In one memo, Czech analysts reported that the OIR comprised 100 or 120 hardened extremists. The true total was around ten.

Even when officials decided that the costs of hosting Ramírez and his colleagues outweighed the benefits, it was extremely difficult to persuade them either to leave or not to visit in the first place. When Ramírez, Weinrich and Kopp were asked to avoid travelling again to the Czechoslovak Socialist Republic a few months after their first visit to the country, they simply refused outright. Just under a year after they arrived in Budapest, the Hungarian State Security police broke into the villa on the Hill of Roses and soon after sent cars to follow its new occupants when they went to meet someone at the airport. The aim was to intimidate them and so precipitate their departure. The operation did neither. Spotting the vehicles late at night, Ramírez opened fire with a handgun, narrowly missing a policeman. The next day, he turned on agents who were following him and marched one at gunpoint to the nearby police headquarters where he lodged an official complaint about the surveillance. In the meeting with officers from the State Security police that followed, it was suggested that Ramírez might consider leaving Budapest relatively soon. Ramírez expressed bewilderment that a supposedly socialist country was not prepared to help him in his struggle on behalf of the world's oppressed masses and proposed a bargain instead. 'In return for adequate compensation and security', he would be more than happy to 'undertake actions abroad in the interests of Hungary'. The officials refused this offer and turned down a series of requests made by the OIR over the following months for weapons and explosives. But the OIR's base in Budapest stayed open.

The problem of what to do with Ramírez was particularly acute for the secret services of the German Democratic Republic. When in March 1979, a Palestinian informant reported to the Stasi that Ramírez had just checked in to a thirty-seven-storey luxury hotel above Alexanderplatz, in the centre of East Berlin, there was consternation. Erich Honecker, the leader of the GDR since 1971, wanted to expel the visitor immediately. If the West discovered that Ramírez was on East German soil, the consequences would be costly. But the Stasi warned that such a move could provoke reprisals from the OIR and was very dangerous. Many senior Stasi officials pointed out that their visitor was a potential ally against 'imperialism, racism, colonialism and all other reactionary forces'. Others disagreed, noting that though 'Carlos defines himself as a "Marxist" and a "Communist"', the views he expressed were 'simplistic and in part erroneous'. In the end, Honecker decided to allow the OIR a presence in East Germany, but with the proviso that Ramírez himself stayed away.

Over the next three years, therefore, Weinrich, who had given himself the codename 'Steve' in homage to the actor Steve McQueen, would spend much of his time in East Berlin, representing the OIR on Ramírez's behalf, enjoying fine restaurants and expensive female company and attending regular meetings with his Stasi liaison officers. Requests for a doctor, then a house to rent with a prized external phone line and finally a sporty if sturdy Lada 1500 were all granted. In return, when the East Germans needed a favour the OIR complied. When the Stasi demanded an assurance that a visit to Bonn by the ailing Soviet president Leonid Brezhnev would not be disrupted by any terrorist attack, Weinrich obliged. The agreement worked well for all concerned, except possibly Ramírez, who expressed frustration at being denied access to one of his favourite cities.

It was not the only city beyond his reach. Through 1980 and into 1981, Ramírez would make several efforts to visit Moscow but was never granted a visa. The Soviets' attitude to actors like Ramírez was similarly complex and contradictory. On the one hand, such individuals and their groups had obvious uses, and the harm they caused to the West advanced the USSR's overall interests in the great struggle against capitalism and imperialism. On the other, the OIR and its like were unpredictable, unreliable and prone to the 'adventurism' detested by good Marxist-Leninists.

A factor exacerbating this tension was the recent and drastic deterioration of relations between the superpowers. The 'Detente' of the early 1970s had collapsed long before Ronald Reagan came to power in 1981, but the commitment of the new US president to a much more explicitly hostile stance towards the USSR considerably raised the stakes of any relationship with people like Ramírez. Convinced that they now faced a final, all-out confrontation with the US, the ageing and ill-informed leaders of the USSR prepared for nuclear war and sought any means they could to win advantage over their rival, all while seeking to preserve their regime and avoid Armageddon.

The rhetorical tone of the new administration in Washington had been set almost immediately. On 28 January 1981 Alexander Haig, the hawkish former general appointed as Reagan's Secretary of State, used his first press conference to announce that 'international terrorism will take the place of human rights [as a priority] in our concerns' and that the USSR was 'training, funding and equipping' the world's main terrorist groups. Haig was not alone in this conviction. Many of Reagan's senior security officials sincerely believed that the KGB was using violent extremists to spearhead a clandestine offensive against Western democracies and their allies on a global scale.

Such ideas were at the heart of a new and powerful current of thinking among resurgent right-wing circles in the US and western Europe. For decades the KGB as 'terrorist mastermind' had been a trope in popular culture, during which time US policy-makers had often ascribed adverse events, particularly violent ones, to the 'hidden hand' of Moscow. The grain of truth contained within the exaggerated claims of Haig and his kind allowed their more outlandish assertions to gain traction, exactly as the Stasi and the KGB had feared.

The peak of such rhetoric came in early 1981 with the US publication of a book called *The Terror Network*. This described how Moscow supported the violence of the Red Army Faction, the Italian Red Brigades, ETA, the IRA and around 140 other groups. Its author, a Rome-based American journalist called Claire Sterling, claimed also that both 'Carlos the Jackal' and Gaddafi were piloted by the KGB.

The fact that such charges were unfounded did nothing to harm the book's commercial success, nor its influence. A bestseller in the US, *The Terror Network* not only received massive coverage in mainstream US media but even won fulsome reviews in respected publications like *Foreign Affairs*. Emboldened, Sterling went on to make a further series of wild assertions. When the fiercely anti-Communist Pope John Paul II was shot and injured in May 1981, she attributed that attack to the KGB too.

Somewhat awkwardly for the Reagan administration and Sterling's most enthusiastic supporters, the CIA simultaneously produced a series of assessments that offered a different analysis. In May 1981, at the height of the media frenzy provoked by *The Terror Network*, the agency oversaw a National Intelligence Estimate on 'Soviet Support for International Terrorism and Revolutionary Violence' which took very deliberate aim at Sterling's thesis. Her book was 'well-written and extensively documented', the CIA said diplomatically, but was 'uneven' and relied on sources of widely varying reliability. The agency's analysts were well placed to make such a judgement because they had detected some of their own disinformation among Sterling's source material, such as the idea that Ramírez had been recruited by the KGB while at Lumumba University in Moscow and then trained by the Cubans. They may also have recognised falsehoods fabricated by the French foreign intelligence service, which identified Ramírez's supposed KGB handler, or by their British counterparts, which claimed he had been taught both sabotage and karate in Moscow in 1974. None of this had any foundation in fact.

Having made quite clear what it thought of *The Terror Network*, the CIA went on to make a series of more nuanced points. It was true that the Soviets had had no 'scruples' about using 'terrorist tactics' to advance their interests, the agency said. Moscow had always provided significant help to 'national liberation movements', and many of these employed 'guerrilla tactics' which included terrorism. Even if the Soviets avoided any direct contact with 'nihilist groups' such as the Red Army Faction or the Italian Red Brigades, Moscow could be considered guilty at least of the lesser charge of offering 'substantial support' to terrorists, the CIA said. But while the Soviets exploited such opportunities, they rarely instigated them, the crucial point being that the 'problem of revolutionary violence [was] more significant and broader than its terrorist component per se'. A decade or so earlier this would not have been a particularly controversial statement. In the early 1980s, with Reagan in power, it caused a tremendous row and led several US intelligence agencies to withdraw their support for the assessment. So too did the CIA's new director, the hawkish Bill Casey, who made little secret of his virulent anti-Communist views.

A second influential work published in the summer of 1981 was an edited volume of speeches that had been made at a conference in Jerusalem two years earlier, organised by a young Israeli special forces veteran, lobbyist and aspirant diplomat called Binyamin or, when anglicised, Benjamin Netanyahu. The conference, named after Netanyahu's brother Yonathan who had been killed leading Israeli troops during the raid on Entebbe, had been attended by a number of prominent US conservatives, several British right-wing public intellectuals and an array of hawkish Israeli academics, diplomats and former security officials. For three days, speakers had described the support offered to terrorists by the USSR, Libya and other Arab states. Many claims were typically sensational – that 'Carlos the Jackal' was a KGB spy or that the USSR and the PLO had played a major role in the fall of the shah. But others described more or less accurately Moscow's active, if indirect, support for a variety of regimes and factions around the world which frequently employed or condoned terrorist tactics. George H. W. Bush, the former US ambassador to the UN who had recently completed a stint as Director of the CIA, spoke at the conference of the dangers of 'state terrorism', by which he meant that fomented by the Soviets. Others described the importance of 'rallying the democracies of the world to a struggle against terrorism' as part of a larger conflict pitting the forces of civilisation against those of 'savagery and violence' and 'barbarism'.

Above all, the book appeared most concerned to convince readers that there was no connection between 'revolution' and terrorism. 'What we see is quite a new breed of fighter against the established order of things, one who styles himself a revolutionary, but who differs radically and fundamentally from all revolutionaries known to us from the past,' Benzion Netanyahu, an expert in medieval persecution of Jews in Europe and Benjamin's father, wrote in the book's introduction. 'Terrorism' was 'a moral evil' that 'infects not only those who commit such crimes, but those who, out of malice, ignorance or simple refusal to think, countenance them' or subscribe to 'the easy moral relativism' of the idea that 'one man's terrorist is another man's freedom fighter'.

Like *The Terror Network*, the Netanyahus' book, entitled *International Terrorism: Challenge and Response*, was reviewed extensively and positively by conservative media in the US and elsewhere. 'The first political task at hand . . . is to cut the idea of terrorism loose from the connection it now has in many Western liberal minds with notions of national liberation and social justice,' as 'only then can terror be viewed plainly as a crime and a threat,' enthused the *Wall Street Journal*.

As the alarm was being raised in Washington and the West about the civilisational threat posed by terrorism, the leadership of the OIR were enjoying their most hopeful period in Europe, with extensive and highly lucrative plans for operations finally coming to fruition. And yet, this was also the moment when the inherent weaknesses and ultimate fate of Ramírez's operation began to become clear.

The first unwitting steps towards the OIR's eventual collapse were taken in August of 1980 when Ramírez and Weinrich travelled to Bucharest. There they engaged in five days of talks with the security service of the Socialist Republic of Romania, perhaps the most brutal and repressive of the eastern European regimes at the time. On the table was a very attractive deal. Negotiations dragged but after multiple visits through the autumn, an agreement was reached.

The Romanian Departamentul Securității Statului – known as the Securitate – had two tasks for the OIR. The first was the murder of five Romanian dissidents who had fled to western Europe; the second was the bombing of Radio Free Europe, a network based in Munich that was partly funded by the US, highly critical of President Nicolai Ceauşescu's incompetent regime and extremely popular in Romania. In return, the Securitate would provide the OIR with weapons and explosives, a bank account and a stack of professionally forged western European passports. Most valuable of all for Ramírez, given the irritating conditions placed on the OIR's stays in East Berlin and the pressure from the Hungarians and Czechs to leave or avoid their countries, was the offer of a house in Bucharest and a guarantee that the group would be protected there for as long as they wanted. Ramírez's mother was invited to spend several weeks at a celebrated Romanian spa resort and Weinrich's parents were hosted too.

This generosity surprised its beneficiaries, who could not help but notice the poverty in which most Romanians lived, but it was motivated by the same exaggerated view of the OIR's capability that skewed the analysis of so many other secret services. Some years previously the Securitate had opened a file, unoriginally entitled 'Jackal', in which they had compiled reports of its subject's various alleged exploits, many culled from Western media. Thanks to this the Securitate's senior officials were convinced not only that the OIR was the ideal candidate for tasks that no one else was prepared or equipped to execute but, like their counterparts elsewhere, that they risked serious consequences if they offended their touchy but hugely capable new hire. When Ramírez initially appeared wary of any collaboration, this only reinforced the Securitate's beliefs. In reality, his frosty attitude was owing to Ceauşescu's well-known relations with Israel and his fear that it was a set-up by the Mossad who would seek to abduct him.

Once the deal was signed and the requisite toasts drunk, it naturally fell to Weinrich to plan the logistics of the attacks. With typical thoroughness, he first drove to Munich to reconnoitre the Radio Free Europe headquarters in person and then drew up a highly detailed eighty-page plan for the attack. A Swiss veteran of radical left-wing extremism was recruited to carry out the bombing itself, while other associates across western Europe were tasked with sending letters packed with explosives to the targeted dissidents. Neither job should have stretched the experienced members of the OIR and their more numerous collaborators overmuch, yet both turned out to be beyond their capabilities.

In January 1981, the letter bombs were delivered to two addresses in Paris. Neither was fatal: one dissident was seriously injured, the other was unharmed. There was no follow-up, and the remaining targets never knew they had been in danger. The attack on Radio Free Europe, dubbed 'Operation Munich Tango' by Ramírez, went ahead regardless. At 9.47 p.m. on 21 February the twenty-kilogram bomb detonated in front of the network's offices. The blast shattered windows hundreds of yards away and was heard across the city. Eight employees were injured, at least one seriously, and a huge hole torn in the building. The network's broadcasting was interrupted, though only for a few hours.

Ramírez was elated at what appeared to have been a spectacular success and gave everyone involved in 'Operation Tango' a ten-day holiday. Some flew to the Middle East, while two members of ETA who had played a peripheral role headed to the beaches of Bulgaria. Ramírez, Kopp and Weinrich returned to Bucharest, where they were driven to a large villa near the city's Otopeni airport to meet their Securitate contacts for a debriefing.

The ensuing conversation put a rapid end to the celebrations. Initially, Ramírez's clients had been very pleased with the attack on RFE.

Then they learned that instead of planting the bomb adjacent to the Romanian section of the radio network, the OIR's operatives had inadvertently targeted the Czechoslovak section instead, and this made them very angry. Ramírez sought to placate the Securitate but even his considerable powers of persuasion proved ineffective. The meeting in Bucharest concluded on an unhappy note. The Romanians would honour much of the deal but would withhold some of the payment. Worse, the OIR would not get any business from them in the future.

This was a significant problem for the group, so Ramírez turned to the Libyans in a bid to drum up some business. In March 1981, a month after the attack in Munich, Weinrich was on the road again, meeting representatives of the People's Revolutionary Struggle in Athens, a local coalition of violent left-wing extremist groups, to organise an overland shipment, probably of weapons or explosives, to Greece via Budapest and Belgrade. This was almost certainly a new commission from Tripoli. Though such jobs would not in themselves generate enough income to cover the OIR's outgoings, they were a useful way of proving the group's capabilities to their clients. Sure enough, Gaddafi's intelligence officers were soon back in touch with a more lucrative proposal.

There had been much talk among extremists across the Middle East of killing President Anwar Sadat since his definitive realignment of Egypt with the West and his efforts to secure a bilateral peace deal with Israel following the 1973 war. In 1977, commissioned either by the Libyans or the Syrians, Haddad's faction of the PFLP had made a desultory effort to assassinate the 'pious president', probably in Cairo. A year later in Baghdad, Ramírez discussed Sadat's murder with Sabri Khalil al-Banna, better known as Abu Nidal, his fellow mercenary and terrorist. Shortly after his arrival in Europe, he had then made some kind of bid to recruit an Iraqi Communist in Prague to the same project. In the spring of 1979, word had reached the Stasi that an effort was underway to kill the Egyptian leader, apparently involving Ramírez, and when he had turned up unexpectedly in East Berlin a few months later they asked him not to carry out any such project. A year after that, the Czech security service officials charged with watching the OIR told their Hungarian counterparts that the group had sent someone to Cairo to assess whether a plan to bomb one of Sadat's residences from the air was feasible or if a 'kamikaze-style' attack was preferable.

But in the late spring of 1981, the plan appeared to be up and running again. In May, the vigilant Hungarian security services were reporting that 'the Carlos group set up a plan for further operations [and] intend to carry out attacks against Sadat – in this case Libya is interested.' A month later, negotiations had advanced sufficiently for Kopp to fly to Tripoli. Ramírez and Weinrich decided that the best opportunities to kill the Egyptian president were likely to be found outside the Middle East. A state visit to West Africa mooted for later that year was attractive. Sadat would be more vulnerable as he toured chaotic and poor countries where security arrangements were likely to be haphazard.

From Tripoli, Kopp flew to Freetown, the capital of Sierra Leone, one of the likely stops on the Egyptian president's putative tour. While she scouted for possible locations for an attack, planning for the assassination began in earnest in Budapest. Then, in October, came the news, broadcast during Ramírez's siesta on the Hill of Roses, of Sadat's assassination on the parade ground in Cairo by Khaled al-Islambouli and his accomplices. Immediately, the leader of the OIR concluded that the Libyans had double-crossed him, giving the same mission to someone else too. The idea that the attackers were Islamic militants acting independently of any state evidently did not occur to him, or if it did it seemed too far-fetched to be credible.

So, the explosion of anger and disappointment overheard by the Hungarian eavesdroppers was not entirely an expression of Ramírez's bruised ego. Significant sums had been spent on the effort to kill Sadat, and the group now badly needed more money. The meals of stuffed crepes, steaks, carp and apple tart were not cheap. Nor were the flights, vintage wines, high-class escorts, luxury hotels and the villa in Budapest. Without the gifts of weaponry and explosives that Gaddafi or the Romanians supplied, the assistance of western European extremist groups could no longer be purchased. If there were no blank diplomatic passports being handed out, no diplomatic bag to use, no safehouses with phone lines, then movement around the continent became impossible. In short, the system that supported the OIR as a whole, and Ramírez personally, could not function.

But the OIR were not finished yet. Ramírez had been sensible enough to hedge his bets, which is why he had made such efforts to win favour with the Syrians back in the summer of 1979. Since recruiting him almost two years earlier, the regime of Hafez al-Assad had not made much use of the famous 'Carlos', commissioning only minor surveillance on

Islamist dissidents who had fled repression to eastern Europe and a few critical journalists and other 'enemies of the Syrian people'. Ramírez's principal reward had been to be welcomed on several visits to Damascus, where he had been wined and dined by senior officials close to Assad.

Fortuitously for Ramírez, the Syrians now needed his expertise for an ambitious and potentially difficult task. Assad had long been angered by criticism in most Western and some regional media. A plan to bomb the famous complex on the banks of the Seine that was home to France Radio, which had been among the more strident of those critical voices, had been rejected for fear of the diplomatic repercussions. Now, inspired by the attack against RFE in Munich early in the year, the Syrians were considering a similar operation against an Arabic-language newspaper in Paris.

Al-Watan al-Arabi was a sharp and irreverent publication that was both widely read and outspokenly critical of Damascus. On the outbreak of conflict between Iran and Iraq in September 1980, the newspaper had published a series of vituperative editorials aimed at Tehran and its allies, which included Syria. More recently, its journalists had revealed that Assad's security services were planning the murder of the French ambassador in Lebanon, who was shot in his car by unidentified gunmen only days later. The Syrians had already made one abortive effort to close the newspaper by planting a bomb in a transistor radio at its offices on the rue Marbeuf, close to the Champs Élysées, in December 1981. Immediately after this failure, Ramírez was summoned once more to Damascus where the Syrians made him an offer. Given the accumulating problems faced by the OIR, it must have seemed very attractive. In fact, it was the beginning of the end for the group, and for Ramírez.

34
Carlos in the West

Magdalena Kopp had not wanted to go to Paris to kill on behalf of a distant Middle Eastern regime, but Ilich Ramírez had decided that she had a specific role to play in the grand drama he had planned for the French capital, and she had no choice but to play it.

Kopp had already agreed to wear the clothes Ramírez wanted, smarter and more expensive than anything she had worn before. She had learned to avoid any confrontation with him, never challenging his authority and ignoring his frequent infidelities. Whenever he asked her, as he often did, whether she had enjoyed their first, unsought night together, she lied and said yes. When once he blamed her for a venereal infection he had contracted, then admitted without any embarrassment that it had probably come from 'another woman', she did not complain. Now, Kopp decided, she had an opportunity to prove that she could be the 'ideal fighter for world revolution and submissive wife' that he wanted her to be. Ramírez's self-confidence and 'power' fascinated her, she admitted. When he promised to marry her after the operation in Paris, she was happy.

So, at eight o'clock on the evening of 16 February 1982, Kopp found herself in an underground car park off the Champs Élysées, sitting in a green Peugeot 504 packed with explosives. Next to her was one of the newest and most committed recruits of the Organisation of Internationalist Revolutionaries, a thirty-one-year-old Swiss Italian called Bruno Bréguet. Thus far, her mission had been plagued with minor mishaps but no serious incident. Ramírez had directed Kopp and her accomplice to a hotel in the relatively scruffy eleventh arrondissement, a neighbourhood far removed from his preferred haunts on the fashionable Left Bank but which was 'full of Arabs' and so safer. On arrival they discovered that the chosen establishment had long since closed, forcing them to find hastily an alternative. Then Kopp's handbag, which contained her fake passports and $50,000 in cash, was stolen in a bar, almost certainly by a petty thief whose surprise and delight can easily be imagined. Finally, there was no sign of their contact from the Basque separatist group ETA who was supposed to deliver the explosives needed for the attack, nor of the Corsican responsible for the vehicle they needed. In tears, Kopp telephoned Ramírez in Budapest, pleading for the operation to be called off. She should stop snivelling and get on with the job, he told her. Everything they needed would soon arrive.

About this, at least, the leader of the Organisation of Internationalist Revolutionaries was right. The ETA contact eventually turned up with exactly what had been ordered and so did the Corsican. Bréguet drove through Paris to a private car park near their target, the offices of the *Watan al-Arabi* newspaper, where he left the vehicle. In the boot was a bomb made of an alarm clock, plastic explosives, two grenades and two large containers of cooking gas. Twenty-four hours later, he returned with Kopp.

But just as they were preparing to drive off, they were approached by security guards whose curiosity had been piqued by its incongruously new number plates. Would they mind showing their papers?, the guards asked. Or those of the car? The ticket for the car park perhaps? If this was not possible, would they mind waiting while the police were called?

Bréguet had no intention of doing any of these things, and reached for the 9mm automatic pistol under his jacket.

The two individuals Ramírez had sent to Paris were very different. Kopp was a small, slim, diffident thirty-one-year-old German, her pale, sharp features topped by dark brown hair with tints of red. Bréguet was tall, handsome and looked like an 'investment banker after a cycling holiday on Mallorca', in the words of one observant journalist. Kopp had been drawn into violent extremism through a series of poor decisions, emotional pressure, delusion, vulnerability, a leftist political outlook that was radical but far from uncommon among her peers, and chance. Bréguet, by contrast, was a true believer from his teens, fiercely intelligent and dedicated to what he saw as the cause of global revolution, as best exemplified by the struggle of the Palestinians. On the walls of his bedroom at his parents' modest home in Ticino in southern Switzerland, he had pinned a portrait of Che Guevara, pages from Jean-Paul Sartre's preface to Frantz Fanon's *The Wretched of the Earth*, a large colour map of South America and a bronze plaque depicting Palestine and a guerrilla fighter, with an inscription in Arabic and English: 'We will fight the enemy everywhere.' While still at school in the late 1960s, Bréguet had been involved in New Left campaigns 'for the liberation of all the peoples oppressed by imperialism' and in 1969 may well have set fire to a department store in Locarno. The target in the unconfirmed attack was selected because the owner 'was a Jew', he pointed out to a friend.

Unenthused by studies in economics and a career in accountancy, Bréguet joined the several thousand young western Europeans who headed to the Middle East seeking adventure, political engagement and stories for their friends back home. He was nineteen, it was 1970 and so he travelled to Lebanon, making his way to Beirut and to the offices of *al-Hadaf*, the Popular Front for the Liberation of Palestine's newsletter.

From there he was sent on the standard tour of the miserable camps where the Palestinian refugees lived, which had the intended effect. Powerfully moved, the teenager accepted a series of missions for the PFLP, then in the middle of the first wave of its international offensive. Bréguet was an amateur, wildly out of his depth, and was detained in June 1970 as he tried to enter Israel by boat, probably with the intention of placing a bomb in the toilets of the Shalom Tower, a thirty-four-storey skyscraper in Tel Aviv. He may have attracted suspicion by wearing a heavy overcoat to hide explosives strapped to his body on a hot summer's day. More likely, Israeli security services had been warned by an informant within the PFLP of his imminent arrival. Tried and convicted by an Israeli court, Bréguet was given a long sentence to dissuade any other western Europeans who might be tempted to follow his example.

Despite the harsh conditions in prison, Bréguet refused to repudiate the Palestinian cause in return for a reduced sentence or release, and angrily rebuffed efforts by Israeli intelligence services to recruit him as an informer. Instead, he learned Arabic and English, and tried to understand the lives, values and views of his fellow inmates. Freed in 1977 after a lengthy campaign by western European intellectuals including Sartre, Bréguet gave a defiant press conference in Zurich, telling reporters: 'I feel determined and single-minded. I have learned to live without hesitation and without compromise. There is no such thing as grey: only black or white.'

Unsurprisingly, given such sentiments, Bréguet was soon in contact with extremists in Switzerland, including some who had connections behind the Iron Curtain. When Ramírez Sánchez learned of a polyglot Swiss national who had been involved with the PFLP back in the good old days, spent years in an Israeli prison and was still dedicated to the revolutionary cause, he saw immediately a potential recruit for the Organisation of Internationalist Revolutionaries. Sometime in 1979 or early 1980, an invitation to join the group was extended and enthusiastically accepted. Bréguet had recently moved to West Berlin where he was studying for a degree in Arabic studies and so was perfectly placed to act as the group's agent in the city. His first task was organising the distribution of weapons and other materiel sourced by the OIR in the Eastern bloc for distribution among the various armed factions in the West which were its clients.

Three months later, Bréguet took part in the attack on the offices of Radio Free Europe in Munich. His job was to detonate the bomb. This lethal task caused him no moral or ethical qualms and once it had been accomplished, albeit in the wrong location, he then devoted much of the rest of the year to building a home in the Bavarian countryside for his West German girlfriend and their very small child. On a card to an acquaintance, Bréguet wrote: 'I have a son, and this gives my life a new meaning.'

By early autumn 1981, Bréguet was active again for the OIR. He travelled to Budapest for a week in September to meet Ramírez and then, the following month, stayed at the Metropol Hotel in East Berlin with Kopp, where the Stasi recorded their conversations. They discussed moving arms around western Europe and obtaining a particular type of detonator via a radical network in Switzerland and France. In November, he flew to Bucharest to see Ramírez once more, then in December spent time in Belgium with the Cellules Communistes Combattantes, a local violent left-wing extremist network. A month later, he was back in East Berlin, where he was briefly detained on arrival at Schönefeld airport before the OIR's Stasi contact intervened. After spending Christmas with his family in Bavaria, Bréguet returned to Budapest, where a new task was presented to him by Ramírez Sánchez: the mission in Paris.

For all their differences, there were some things that Kopp and Bréguet had in common. Having been attracted to the New Left in the mid-1960s, by the end of the decade both had become involved with its increasingly radical and violent fringe and then persisted in their engagement with it well past the time when most of their contemporaries had moved on. Both clung to a simplistic binary worldview, born from an idealism that may have been misplaced but was genuine. Crucially, progressive exposure to violence diverted neither of them from their path. If they had any doubts, neither Luca nor Lilly – their codenames within the OIR – were troubled by them sufficiently to reconsider their approach over nearly fifteen years of activism.

But the reality, which neither of them fully grasped, was that, by 1982, in working for the OIR they were risking lengthy prison sentences or worse not in the name of some utopian solution to the problems of the 'oppressed', but for reasons that were sordid and cynical.

The enthusiasm with which Ramírez had accepted the job of bombing *al-Watan al-Arabi* was explained not simply by the large sums of money the Syrians were offering.

Two years earlier, the newspaper had run what purported to be an exclusive interview with the man they called 'Carlos the Jackal'. At the time, no one had seen or heard from Ramírez since 1975 and many thought he was dead. This made its lengthy interview with the world's most wanted terrorist a major scoop.

Nor did the content disappoint. Ramírez described his youth in Venezuela, London and Moscow, then gave detailed and convincing accounts of his abortive effort to murder the chairman of Marks & Spencer in 1973, the rue Toullier shootings two years later, the OPEC attack and much more. He offered tips on which weapons an aspirant assassin should use and some noisy opinions about Middle Eastern politics. He swore that his 'religion' was 'Marxism' and admitted that despite his bloody record he did not consider himself 'a professional killer'. After all, he told readers, 'I like good food, to drink, and good cigars. I like to sleep in a bed that has just been made. I like surprise parties and dances . . . and theatre from time to time.' Ramírez was also quick to assure his interviewer that of course he would happily renounce such worldly pastimes for the struggle, insisting that he remained 'a revolutionary Marxist whose duty was to support revolution everywhere and anywhere'.

The revelations in *al-Watan al-Arabi* were reprinted word for word in newspapers and magazines worldwide. The problem with the scoop was that the interview had never taken place, or at least not in the way suggested to millions of readers. The journalist responsible was Assem al-Jundi, a Syrian dissident, poet and writer who had befriended Ramírez in Baghdad and taken extensive notes towards writing his biography. After one drunken evening together Ramírez had jokingly threatened him with a gun to the head. The book was never completed or published. Then, two years later, al-Jundi had evidently sold the repackaged material as an 'exclusive interview' to *al-Watan*. Ramírez had been incensed, less at the betrayal and more at his portrayal. An image as a publicity-seeking sybarite whose ideological commitment could charitably be described as superficial was not likely to endear him to his new sponsors in Damascus. After the initial publication of the first part of the interview, threats of extreme violence against the newspaper had successfully prevented further revelations. For good measure Ramírez had arranged for al-Jundi to be shot in Beirut. The writer had only just survived, whereas *al-Watan* had thrived on its new-found celebrity. Ramírez had privately sworn revenge. The Syrian contract to bomb the newspaper nicely combined personal gratification, pecuniary gain and political advantage.

On 2 January 1982, Bréguet arrived in Paris and started work. His first task was to gather intelligence on the principal target: *al-Watan al-Arabi*'s ebullient forty-four-year-old editor-in-chief, Walid Abou Zahr. Early impressions were not encouraging. Staff at the newspaper were keenly conscious of their security: Abou Zahr's chauffeur-driven dark green Mercedes was always preceded by a powerful Land Rover crewed by bodyguards, and the newspaper's offices were heavily guarded. In the last week of January, Bréguet flew back to Budapest to tell Ramírez and Weinrich that they might have to abandon the mission.

Neither agreed, and instead added a new dimension. Over the previous decade, several of the most extreme and violent Palestinian groups had extorted vast sums by threatening violence against victims as diverse as Lufthansa, Lebanese businessmen and wealthy Gulf monarchies. The OIR was already involved in a variety of purely criminal rackets including illicit arms dealing, trafficking black-market oil and much else, so the step to straightforward blackmail with threats of violence was a small one. Anyway, such acts could easily be justified as 'revolutionary expropriation'. So Bréguet was told to plan for an attack on Kuwait's embassy in Paris, too, which would be followed by a demand for an enormous amount of money which the wealthy kingdom would have to pay if it wished to avoid further such attacks in the French capital or elsewhere.

Of course, Bréguet had messed up the placement of the bomb outside the RFE headquarters, so Ramírez had decided he needed someone else involved as well, and specifically someone who could be relied upon to execute this aspect of the forthcoming operation successfully.

Few members of the OIR could travel without risk in western Europe but Kopp was still more or less unknown to local security services and would be able to evade suspicion, at least until it was too late to stop her. Ramírez Sánchez decided that Bréguet would build a bomb to be used either against *al-Watan al-Arabi* or the Kuwaiti Embassy, and then Kopp could deliver it to the target. Which was how Lilly and Luca found themselves in an old green Peugeot 504 in an underground car park off the Champs Élysées on a cold February night in 1982, arousing the suspicions of its security guards and being asked either for their papers or for their patience while the guards called the police.

It was at this point that Bréguet drew a gun from under his jacket, pointed it at the guards and shouted at Kopp to flee. There was a click as the weapon misfired. Kopp sprinted through the car park, out from under the flickering neon and into the bright lights of the centre of Paris. Behind her were shouts and rapid footsteps.

Now panicking, she ran on, hoping to find a Métro station or somewhere she could hide, forcing her way blindly through the evening crowds. Then, without warning, she found herself flat on the pavement, pinned 'by strong arms'. Minutes later, her accomplice was also overpowered by police. 'I am a soldier of the Organisation of Internationalist Revolutionaries . . . [and] you'll be hearing from them by this evening,' he told his captors. Kopp showed no such defiance. Terrified, she wet herself. 'I knew I had done wrong and now it was over . . . It played over and over again like a movie; my escape, how they threw me to the ground and put me in the car,' Kopp remembered later. 'I was afraid of what was to come next.'

Ramírez's reaction to their arrest was brutally simple and entirely in character. On 28 February, a letter was delivered to the French Embassy in The Hague. Signed 'The Organisation of Armed Arab Struggle – Arm of the Arab Revolution', it warned of the consequences of keeping its members in prison and demanded their freedom within a month. 'Our organisation will not ever abandon its members . . . We are not at war with Socialist France . . . and, I pray you in all sincerity, not to force us to be. We hope for a rapid and happy end to this affair.' Under a signature that read 'Carlos' were two thumbprints to allow reliable identification of the author. There was no need to spell out to the French government what those consequences might be.

The OIR had sustained significant losses over the previous year but much of the trans-European network that Ramírez had built up over the previous three years was still very much operational. Reserves of explosives and weapons were transferred to where they would be needed, vehicles stolen or bought, false documents distributed and orders issued. Very quickly, members of the group who were largely unknown to local security services were moving across the continent by car and train, slipping without great difficulty across frontiers. On 29 March, the day the ultimatum expired, a bomb in a suitcase placed on a luggage rack exploded on a train travelling from Paris to Toulouse, killing five and injuring twenty-seven. Over the next month, there were more attacks: multiple bombs were defused but one detonated at an Air France office in Vienna. In Beirut, where Ramírez's contacts and caches were still intact, a French diplomat and his pregnant wife were shot dead at their home. Within moments of the trial of Kopp and Bréguet opening in Paris at 9 a.m. on 22 April, explosives packed into an orange Opel Kadett detonated outside the bistro Chez Bébert almost exactly opposite the offices of *al-Watan al-Arabi*. The tall apartment buildings lining the narrow street channelled the blast, which killed a thirty-year-old woman instantly and injured dozens, including a teenage boy who lost most of a leg. Debris was strewn over a 200-yard stretch of the street.

There was no follow-up to this last attack and the Kuwaitis escaped unscathed. But the Syrians' commission had been fulfilled, and Ramírez had made his point.

During their brief trial, Kopp and Bréguet were defended by a well-known radical lawyer whose charm, eloquence, tailored suits, cigars and taste for antique lacquerwork masked an implacable ideological commitment. The son of a Communist French doctor and a Vietnamese mother, Jacques Vergès was an inveterate provocateur whose world-view had been shaped by his active role in the anti-Nazi struggles of the 1940s and the anti-colonialist ones of the 50s. In the late 1960s, he had written a book explaining his strategy of '*défense de rupture*', the legal equivalent of Guevara's form of guerrilla warfare whereby a single lawyer could subvert an entire criminal justice system by aggressively and audaciously challenging the legitimacy of a trial. The idea was very much of its time and had considerable influence though limited practical effect. Naturally, this was the strategy Vergès adopted to defend Kopp and Bréguet.

The lawyer began by blaming the bombing in the rue Marbeuf on the Mossad, and went on to describe Ramírez as 'a man of audacity and courage'. The two defendants sitting silently behind bulletproof glass screens were 'soldiers, prisoners of a noble cause' and so 'beyond this court's judgement'. Vergès then reiterated the threats made by Ramírez in his letter to the French government, in which he had explained that he and other friends of Kopp and Bréguet would 'not rest as long as they are in prison' and that the amount of 'blood to be shed' depended merely on whether the pair were released after '48 hours, a month [or] three months'. Finally, the lawyer suggested that France had reneged on a secret deal with 'certain revolutionary movements' and was therefore to blame for any violence. Here, Vergès touched a raw nerve.

The longstanding French policy of offering a home to dissidents from across the Middle East and well beyond had survived even the wave of terrorist violence in western Europe of the late 1970s. These had included the Ayatollah Khomeini and his fiercest opponents, maverick leftist Ramírez's onetime bagman Hans-Joachim Klein, as well as an assortment of Latin American and African revolutionaries. France had also offered a haven to a motley collection of semi-repentant hijackers, Basque separatists, members of the Italian Red Brigades who renounced violence and nationalist extremists including Armenians, Turks, Syrians and Palestinians. As in eastern Europe, there was no formal deal with any of these actors, but a tacit agreement that such 'guests' would do no harm to French citizens or interests. Even those who targeted nominal allies of France were usually treated with leniency, and requests from overseas to extradite such fugitives were routinely refused. In Washington, the more sober analysts attributed this to a French tendency to be simultaneously 'idealistic and egotistic', a local 'tradition of revolutionary democracy that . . . inclined most Frenchmen to be sympathetic to those who profess to share the same ideals' and to French officials' desire to 'shield their country from violence'. Others in the US used stronger and shorter words.

But by the time the socialist administration of President François Mitterrand won power in May 1981, attitudes within the French security establishment were changing. France was now a signatory of a number of recent international agreements aimed at toughening the global response to acts of transnational violence such as hijacking or assassination, and so under pressure to take a firmer position on international terrorism. The previous year, meanwhile, there had been a particularly bloody attack on a synagogue in Paris, the first such violence against the French Jewish community since the Second World War. As the first left-wing president for decades and the leader of an administration committed to a series of progressive legal reforms, Mitterrand understood that he was vulnerable to accusations of being soft on political violence. In the first half of 1982, the French police and security services launched a new investigation into a fresh terrorist incident more or less every week. This led even the most jaded French security officials to wonder if a new approach might be a good idea.

But not just yet. The ultimatum issued by Ramírez and the bloody attacks that followed prompted poisonous disputes between Mitterrand's most senior officials – the president, typically, kept his own views to himself – but the consensus was that the time for a firm stand against terrorism had not quite come. Even as the trial was underway, Vergès was secretly meeting with representatives of the French prime minister. The results were soon evident. Bréguet was tried only for possession of an unlicensed weapon and explosives, despite having attempted to shoot a security guard and to plant a bomb in central Paris. For his accomplice, the public prosecutor requested only a 'moderate' punishment. In the end, Kopp and Bréguet were sentenced to five and four years in prison respectively, just sufficient to demonstrate the court's independence but an extraordinarily mild punishment given what they had been trying to do. The man who had supplied the battered Peugeot got just eighteen months, with six suspended.

If anyone in the French government thought such leniency would end Ramírez's efforts to free his fiancée and subordinate, they were wrong. When he learned of their prison sentences, he told his followers to be 'ready to do anything necessary', then ordered further attacks in France and in Lebanon. On 24 May 1982, a bomb was attached to the car of a secretary at the French Embassy in Beirut, who then drove the vehicle to work. When it exploded, it killed twelve people, mainly Lebanese staff, and injured many more. There was no longer much pretence that this violence was 'revolutionary'. Weinrich for one was honest about what Ramírez was doing. It was a 'private war', he told his contacts in the Stasi in East Berlin a month after the Beirut attack.

With the French clearly unwilling to release Kopp or Bréguet, Ramírez now found himself committed to a risky, expensive and possibly lengthy campaign of violence against an enemy that was not of his choosing. For once, his personal feelings had trumped his political instincts, with significant consequences for the future of the OIR. All the eastern European security services that had tolerated or hired Ramírez since he had arrived from Baghdad three years earlier were well aware of his role in the attacks in France and against French interests elsewhere. For most, bombing the trains or embassies of a Western power crossed a red line. By mid-1982, the Czechoslovaks had finally managed to convince Ramírez to stop using Prague as a base but by now the Hungarians had decided there was no way they could permit their bumptious guest and his associates to stay in Budapest. Even the Stasi and the Romanians were forced to reconsider their relationship with a man who was certainly useful but also unpredictable, reckless and infamous across the entire globe. Once a significant asset, Ramírez's notoriety was becoming a fatal weakness.

Nor was there any relief for Ramírez in the Middle East. The Syrians were less than enthused by their new hire's personal campaign of violence, even if the primary target was a mutual enemy, and were distracted by events closer to home, where security services were bloodily repressing an Islamist uprising, and in Lebanon where the civil war ground on intermittently. The OIR's relations with the Libyans had remained chilly since the assassination of Sadat, which Ramírez still believed was a double-cross. There was nothing to be expected from the Iraqis either, who continued to favour rivals that were more pliable and effective. The Algerians showed no interest in restoring relations severed years earlier. Nor did the Marxist-Leninist leaders of the People's Democratic Republic of Yemen, who were now cleaving closer to Moscow and so sharing the Soviets' generally dim view of any direct involvement in the OIR's brand of 'revolutionary violence'.

The effect on the OIR's meagre resources was catastrophic. The campaign against France sucked in more and more money and people, while simultaneously driving sponsors away or drastically reducing their support. In June 1982, not even two years after the sumptuous Christmas Eve dinner in Budapest where he, Kopp and Weinrich had feted their success, Ramírez Sánchez ordered all members of his group to restrict their spending. Everyone needed to 'be very modest in [their] expenses [and] avoid unnecessary travelling', he told Weinrich, noting that their collective funds now totalled a mere $39,000. A week or so later, Ramírez bought himself a Cartier watch when travelling through Damascus airport. Such retail therapy might have provided a moment of comfort but could not disguise a harsh reality: for Ramírez and his close associates, the days of good living in Europe were soon to end.

In mid-April 1982, ten days before the trial of Kopp and Bréguet was due to start, a second ultimatum had been delivered to the French government. It threatened 'powerful measures' if the government did not immediately release the two OIR members. 'Our task is to stand by our comrade prisoners because where states persecute democracy through imprisonment, resistance becomes a duty,' it read. 'The revolution will triumph.' The authors of the ultimatum were senior members of a group thought by many in Europe to be largely defunct: the Red Army Faction.

Like Ramírez and the OIR, the Red Army Faction still existed but by now in much diminished form, even if its rhetoric, like the Venezuelan's taste for luxury, had yet to catch up. Certainly, any revolutionary victory was a very distant prospect indeed.

Its leader, Brigitte Mohnhaupt, was now thirty-three years old and as ferociously committed to the RAF's original aims as ever. When the RAF's contingent in Baghdad had been forced to leave the Iraqi capital after the debacle of the 'German autumn' and the hijacking of the Lufthansa passenger jet in 1977, Mohnhaupt had led her now homeless comrades to the training camp outside Aden run by Haddad's faction of the PFLP. This had proved only a temporary respite. When Haddad died in March 1978 the facility was shut down by local authorities and the group scattered. Some returned to western Europe, others tried the Balkans, one or two remained in the Middle East. Mohnhaupt ended up in Yugoslavia where she was detained for months and only narrowly avoided extradition to West Germany. On her release, she probably crossed from Yugoslavia into Italy and so returned to western Europe.

Mohnhaupt had two aims, one easier to achieve than the other. The first was simply to stay ahead of the authorities. In the late 1970s, security services and police in countries like France and West Germany were significantly more capable than they had been a decade earlier, but it was still relatively straightforward for a fugitive to avoid detection if they took basic precautions, avoided all contact with the state and were not unlucky enough to be recognised. Mohnhaupt's second aim – to rebuild the RAF as an effective force – was more challenging. Its limited funds aside, the group had negligible support even among radical leftists and its remaining active members were deeply demoralised. Some were living underground in Amsterdam and Namur, protected by Dutch and Belgian extremists. Others had ended up in Paris, where a small and increasingly overcrowded apartment had been rented. A few remained in West Germany itself, though the pressure from authorities was intense and police arrested a senior member every few months.

One obvious option was to reach out to other groups for assistance. The RAF had never liked doing this, but the circumstances meant it had little choice. The results were mixed. The remnants of the June 2 Movement had raised significant funds through a series of lucrative kidnappings and were happy to merge their few dozen members into the RAF, which was useful. But there was little to be gained from closer relations with the Revolutionary Cells, whose most notable revolutionary achievements of recent years had been to sprinkle weedkiller on the gardens of industrialists and push stink bombs through their doors. Efforts to reach out to Italian militants, who had their own acute problems, stumbled on an unexpected obstacle. When Mohnhaupt travelled to Italy to talk to counterparts in the Red Brigades, the (male) militant she was supposed to meet at Milan station failed to identify her. He had been told that the 'leader of the RAF' would be sitting on a particular bench reading a crime novel but had abandoned the appointment when the only person he saw doing this was a woman.

Despite these and other setbacks, Mohnhaupt had eventually been able to rally sufficient members to ensure the RAF did not disappear entirely. Moving from safehouse to safehouse across a swathe of northern France, the Low Countries and the Rhine valley, she cajoled, encouraged and organised the few dozen remaining members into action. An early strategic decision was to invest in an ambitious high-profile attack in order to signal that the chaotic violence of 1977 had not been the end of the group. This took some time to organise but finally came in June 1979 when the RAF attempted to kill Alexander Haig, then NATO's supreme commander in Europe, by detonating a massive bomb under a bridge in Belgium as his official car drove across it en route to NATO headquarters. Haig was unharmed but the RAF had made its point.

But it then fell more or less quiet for eighteen months, preoccupied by a series of hunger strikes among its prisoners in West Germany which led to the death of one participant. Most observers decided the group had now disappeared for good. The *Guardian*'s correspondent in West Germany described a new 'atmosphere of peace and relaxation' in a report headlined 'the terror that died more with a whimper than a bang'. In August 1981, the RAF managed a series of small attacks and a bomb that injured twenty people at the US and NATO European air command centre in Ramstein. A month later, a rocket-propelled grenade was fired at the car of another senior US general in Heidelberg, though it did no serious harm. A further pause followed. When a year later, the RAF threatened 'powerful measures' to free Kopp and Bréguet, few French officials paid much attention.

One of the biggest challenges facing Mohnhaupt was managing the departure of those who wanted to leave the RAF. These were numerous – perhaps a dozen or more out of a total active strength of only thirty or so – and their motives for doing so varied. Even within the group, the offensive of 1977 was now widely seen as profoundly misguided. Some members had also been badly affected by the accidental murder or maiming of innocents during more recent attacks. An oft-cited example was the killing of a fifty-eight-year-old woman in an exchange of fire with police when the RAF robbed a bank in Zurich in November 1979. Others simply felt the group had lost its way or argued that the 'urban guerrilla' could never succeed in achieving radical change in western Europe because there was no 'fascist dictatorship with a population . . . ready to revolt'. A few were terrified by the prospect of the long prison sentence that no doubt awaited those of them who managed to avoid a violent death. Jail would be 'a living grave', one said, in stark contrast to members of the first generation of the RAF who saw incarceration as an extension of the struggle. Others had developed depression or dependencies on drugs. Mohnhaupt's former lover Peter-Jürgen Boock, who had supported her in Baghdad when she had decided to accept Wadie Haddad's offer to hijack the Lufthansa jet, had become addicted to painkillers and was placed under a form of house arrest by the rest of the group at the RAF's safehouse in Paris. Boock eventually escaped but was traced by West German authorities to an apartment in Hamburg, where he was found in January 1981 living with a divorced teacher, two forged passports and thirty-three carefully tended cannabis plants.

Mohnhaupt was contemptuous of those who wanted to quit but did not seek to retain them. Instead, she sought to mitigate the potential threat they posed once they had left. If tracked down and detained by the West German government or its allies, former members would face trial and heavy prison sentences. It was inevitable that some of them would be tempted to give up sensitive information to the authorities, or even appear as state witnesses. Mohnhaupt was well aware that in Italy the increasingly successful campaign to put leaders of the Red Brigades behind bars had been greatly aided by former militants. So any member who left needed to be hidden, for decades if necessary, from West German or other security services.

Relocating the defectors within western Europe was clearly impractical – they were too numerous and too easily recognised – and no state in the Middle East would take them, so Mohnhaupt and her closest collaborators turned to other regions of the world. The group needed somewhere that was remote but run by a sympathetic 'progressive' regime. Discussions went on for several months. One possibility was a country in Latin America, though it seemed unlikely anyone could hide effectively in Cuba or Nicaragua, and the rest of the continent looked distinctly less promising. Sub-Saharan Africa appeared attractive and soon the choice was narrowed to Mozambique or Angola, both distant, newly independent and fiercely anti-Western. Some of the retiring RAF members started learning Portuguese and thinking about how they might earn a living as expatriates. Then a very welcome alternative was suggested much closer to home and by a very unexpected ally.

The Stasi's attitude to the RAF had always been ambivalent. When Ulrike Meinhof had sought the service's support 'to organise the resistance in West Berlin' in the aftermath of Andreas Baader's dramatic liberation in May 1970, the response from the East Germans had been frosty. Relations had not warmed greatly over the following decade. Official East German media followed the dictates of Moscow and were often critical of the 'adventurist' efforts of the armed groups across the frontier to the West, describing the RAF as young people 'who do not represent the true interests of the working class and are not part of the genuine Marxist-Leninist revolutionary struggle'.

Nonetheless the Stasi took a keen interest in the activities of extremists in West Germany and worked hard to gather information on them, always hopeful that they could somehow be used against their shared ideological enemies while ensuring that they posed no threat to East Germany itself. This led to pragmatic and somewhat inconsistent policies throughout the 1970s. Members of the RAF and other violent factions were allowed to traverse East Berlin on their way to the Middle East, but were then often intercepted on their return and thoroughly interrogated before being allowed to continue their journey home, for example. In 1977 the Stasi had made sure that the authorities in Aden refused to help the hijackers of the Lufthansa jet when it landed there against their will, thus forcing the detour to Mogadishu that allowed the West German authorities to mount their spectacular and successful assault that saved the plane, its crew and passengers.

Towards the end of the 1970s, however, as policy evolved in Moscow, the Stasi's attitude to extremists in West Germany had become more benign. In 1978, a group of RAF escapees from a prison in West Germany were allowed to transit East Berlin and so reach safety. On at least two occasions subsequently, the Stasi used its influence to obtain the release of RAF members detained elsewhere in eastern Europe. An internal Stasi memo approvingly noted that the RAF's main enemy was 'US imperialism and its henchmen and supporters' in West Germany and that the group's 'main method of confrontation with imperialism is armed struggle'. When the Stasi learned that Mohnhaupt had travelled from Baghdad to Yemen in early 1978, it informed the local authorities there but recommended that no action be taken that might lead to her arrest by 'imperialist security organs' and that the 'loyal attitude' of the RAF be rewarded.

Then, in the spring of 1980, the Stasi had learned from a veteran RAF member who was in touch with the head of its Department XXII, responsible for counter-terrorism, that the group had a problem with a number of members who wanted to leave and retire. Any plan to send the defectors to sub-Saharan Africa was very rash, the Stasi counselled, as the risk of swift identification pretty much anywhere on the continent was very high. However, the Stasi had an alternative proposal: if the defectors came to East Germany they would be given new identities, homes and jobs, and no one would be the wiser.

In late summer 1980, eight former RAF members made their way from France to a rudimentary lodge in a forest near the East German border with Poland. There, after a celebration dinner with champagne, they received new names, dossiers of documents to prove their entirely fictitious new biographies, and certificates of East German citizenship. A year later, the Stasi organised two short sessions of military training as a 'confidence-building measure'. This was fairly rudimentary – mainly consisting of firing handguns on a makeshift range – but it did also involve a German shepherd dog being chained into the seat of a Mercedes in order to test the effect a rocket-propelled grenade might have on its passengers.

This shift by the Stasi to more proactive support for the RAF coincided with its decision to offer at least some assistance to Ramírez and his group, and greater support for various Palestinian factions that were once again active in western Europe at this time. The motivation was different, however. Though the Stasi undoubtedly saw the Venezuelan as committed to their own ideological agenda, they sought to control and exploit him. By contrast, any advantages derived from the hospitality offered to the RAF defectors were likely to be negligible compared to the risks of hosting them. Instead, the decision to offer them a home was rooted in a genuine – if uncharacteristically sentimental – sense of revolutionary solidarity. Subordinates reported that Erich Mielke, the veteran head of the service, saw the young West German extremists as participants in a struggle against a common enemy, whose violence recalled that of his own days as a Communist underground activist fifty years earlier.

But any such view was an anachronism. It was more difficult than ever to explain the terrorism that occurred in western Europe at this time with reference to the binary ideological divisions of the Cold War. Almost half of all acts of international terrorism in 1982 took place here but few could be described as a direct consequence of superpower conflict. Activists on the left were now as likely to turn to violence to fight for the rights of indigenous peoples or against the sale of graphic pornography on the high street as in support of distant anti-colonial struggles. A newly re-energised squatting movement drew in thousands of young people, of whom a handful directed occasional bombings against efforts at gentrification. In late 1981, in one of their last jobs for the Libyans, Weinrich and Ramírez Sánchez had organised the delivery of a brace of rocket-propelled grenade launchers to a Geneva-based network of militants in return for a set of remote-controlled electronic detonators. The grenade launchers were used six weeks later not against a NATO general, Israeli aviation or even a newspaper critical of a repressive Middle Eastern regime, but were fired into the concrete shell of a new 'Super Phoenix' nuclear reactor under construction on the Rhône. The aim, a spokesperson told Agence France-Presse, was 'to reopen the debate on nuclear power in France'.

*

The most consequential terrorist attack in western Europe in 1982 involved neither the RAF nor Ramírez and his OIR. It also did not kill a single person – at least not directly. When he was shot in the head on the pavement outside the Dorchester Hotel in London's West End in early June, Shlomo Argov, the Israeli ambassador, suffered massive brain damage but survived.

The attack was the work of Ramírez's competitor and occasional dining partner in Baghdad, Sabri Khalil al-Banna, aka Abu Nidal. From a villa just outside Warsaw, where he lived with his family for much of the year, al-Banna organised violent operations across Europe on behalf of his longtime paymaster and protector, the Iraqi Mukhabarat. Several of the targets had been moderate members of the PLO who had been outspoken about the necessity for a political solution to the conflict between Israel and the Palestinians. Al-Banna had also launched a wave of attacks against Jordanian officials and almost certainly provided some of the weapons used by the attackers in the 1980 siege of the Iranian Embassy. In the late spring of 1982, acting on a new commission from the Iraqis, he sent an assassin to London to shoot the Israeli ambassador.

That Argov did not die did not matter. The aim of the effort was to provoke the Israelis, and in this al-Banna and his sponsors were entirely successful. The shots fired on Park Lane would lead to an immense outpouring of violence in Israel's northern neighbour Lebanon over the summer of 1982. This in turn would catalyse the developments of the previous fifteen years, ultimately creating a new form of political and religious extremist violence that would be tragically and instantly recognisable four decades later.

XI

35
Yasser Arafat's Last Stand

Despite the ravages of seven years of war, Beirut in early summer of 1982 still retained some of its charm. There was the sundeck at the Sporting Club and the restaurant Chez Jean-Pierre, with its view of waterskiers and speedboats on the Mediterranean. The campus of the American University remained a haven of arboreal, academic calm and the Commodore Hotel's pet parrot still squawked the first bar of Beethoven's Fifth Symphony to the amusement of visiting journalists. The city's once numerous newspapers had been reduced to a hardy handful but these were still published regularly and read widely, and though Middle East Airlines had been forced to sell its prized 747 to Saudi Arabia, other planes bearing its distinctive Cedar Tree logo still flew around the region from Beirut's battered but functioning international airport. Buses packed with the uniformed children of the elite drove through the city to expensive schools on its outskirts. Mothers shopped at markets, grandfathers played chess in cafés, families walked to mosques and churches for festivals or to more secular celebrations in each other's homes.

But no visitor – even those considerably less observant than the best-selling novelist David Cornwell, better known as John le Carré, who spent several weeks in the city in 1981 and early 1982 – could fail to notice the city's scars. Martyrs' Square, once its centre and one of the few places where its multiple communities mixed, was now a no man's land, blocked at each end by barricades of burned-out buses, shipping containers and oil drums. Anyone wanting to cross the frontline between largely Muslim west Beirut and the Christian-dominated east had to use one of three main crossing points. Power supplies were intermittent, refuse rarely collected, clean water scarce and the phone network virtually unusable. Among the most popular programmes broadcast by local radio stations were special bulletins offering news of missing relatives.

And, as Cornwell noted in his journals, Beirut remained extremely violent. The tactics of the many militias active in the city had evolved to include car bombs, mortars fired at hospitals and peremptory executions at barricades. Victims ranged from the entirely innocent – children caught in a crossfire – to the obviously guilty: criminal gang leaders murdered in a brutal competition for rackets, influence and territory. Divining exactly who was killing or abducting whom required an encyclopaedic knowledge of every regional power and all their local proxies. Even masters of this arcane art admitted their understanding was, and could only ever be, partial. Sensible visitors admitted their ignorance. On one of his first nights in Beirut, Cornwell watched from his top-floor room at the Commodore as illuminated tracer rounds and flares lit up the night sky, failed to work out who was firing on whom and then decided just to enjoy the spectacle.

After an extremely bloody power struggle, Bashir Gemayel, son of the Phalange's founder Pierre, had overcome the other Christian Maronite warlords and now sought to consolidate his control over east Beirut and a swathe of Lebanon along the coast to the city's north – as well as what remained of Lebanon's formal government and administration. In sullen opposition, too weak to take on Gemayel's forces or the Syrians but too strong to be forced from the field entirely, were the remnants of the coalition of leftists, pan-Arabists and Palestinian factions who had fought together since 1975. Fighting was desultory, with long breaks as all protagonists stocked up on ammunition and made money, but it was also an ever-present risk. The most vulnerable were the refugees packed into apartment blocks that housed fifty or sixty people before the war but were now home to hundreds. Many ended up even more exposed to shot and shell, living in parks, on rubbish-strewn waste ground or in cramped shacks in Sabra and Shatila, the two Palestinian refugee camps in the city's south.

Also in Beirut, left like sea-wrack on a shore as the tide of leftist internationalist extremism had gone out, were veterans of the 'revolutionary international'. Cornwell never got to meet any of these people, though they would undoubtedly have interested him given the subject of the book he was in Beirut to research. Scattered across the city were a dozen or so collaborators of Ilich Ramírez, mainly friends or associates of the veteran Palestinian militants whom the Venezuelan had recruited into his Organisation of Internationalist Revolutionaries. Fusako Shigenobu, the leader of the now more or less defunct Japanese Red Army, lived with her infant daughter in a quiet neighbourhood of the city along with a dozen or so of her followers. Then there were the Italian, Dutch and Danish exiles, veterans of violent activism in western Europe who had been forced to flee east to avoid arrest. A single member of the Red Army Faction had made a home there too, following their expulsion from Baghdad in early 1978. She was now married to an Iraqi bomb-making specialist she had met in Aden. Few of these were particularly active or violent any more, and most had little contact with the Palestinian armed factions they had once so enthusiastically supported.

Notably absent were any new recruits from overseas. A decade earlier hundreds of volunteers from all over the world had flown in to see at first hand the armed struggle against Zionism, capitalism and imperialism. Now, Lebanon was an unattractive destination for all but fugitives with nowhere else to go, a faction of Armenian separatist extremists and a handful of West German neo-Nazis. There were no Parisian students or squatters from Hamburg or errant Italian idealists in search of an adventurous few weeks in the Middle East, some small-arms training, a book of poetry and a sun tan. Those days had long gone.

Cornwell was fascinated by Yasser Arafat, now in his thirteenth year as chairman of the Palestine Liberation Organisation, and sought to meet him while in Beirut. The author ended up waiting at the Commodore for some time before finally being granted an interview with 'the elusive, wily, terrorist-turned-statesman' whom he found in a 'bullet-pocked apartment house with empty windows and no lights' somewhere in the city. After emotionally embracing Cornwell in front of dozens of young fighters, Arafat asked his guest why he had come to Beirut. On hearing that Cornwell was seeking the heart of Palestine, Arafat cried 'It is here, it is here,' and thumped the left chest pocket of his khaki shirt. The PLO's chairman smelt of baby powder and his beard was surprisingly soft, the writer noted.

Arafat ordered that his visitor be given a tour of the quasi-state that the PLO had established in Lebanon over the previous decade. For several weeks, Cornwell drove around Lebanon, guarded by teenage Palestinian bodyguards and a series of official minders. He joined a PLO parade of 'hospital nurses, war crippled kids in wheelchairs . . . girl guides and boy scouts and fighters' in the southern city of Sidon, toured Fatah's bases in Lebanon's south and was invited to tumultuous New

Year celebrations in the hills east of Beirut where he watched Fatah's 'high command, camp followers, ecstatic children as well as an entire convocation of spies' dance a frenzied *dabke* during a loud rendition of Palestine's national anthem.

Colourful as this was, it revealed little of the PLO's actual situation in Lebanon in the first half of 1982, which was precarious. The organisation's sponsors in the Arab world were increasingly disillusioned with it, funds were short and efforts to transform lightly armed guerrilla fighters into a conventional force capable of taking on the hugely superior Israeli military had made little progress. At the rallies attended by Cornwell, speakers still called for 'Revolution until Victory', but neither appeared close.

Much of this was the fault of the PLO's leader. Since the fedayeen had been forced out of Jordan and to Lebanon eleven years earlier, Arafat had told supporters and critics alike what they wanted to hear, or whatever would gain him immediate advantage. He had used his vast powers of patronage to buy off any threats to his authority and to deliberately aggravate competition between his rivals. He had refused to acknowledge the racketeering, bullying and outright predation that had cost the Palestinians the sympathy of communities in Lebanon that had once been supportive of them, particularly in the south. His habitual mendacity and opportunism had infuriated the major Arab states, and relations with Damascus were especially bad, which was a significant problem given that Syrian troops occupied half of Lebanon. Cornwell noted that while poor Palestinians were crammed into insalubrious refugee camps, senior PLO functionaries enjoyed comfortable apartments, generous expense accounts and luxury chauffeur-driven cars.

On the other hand, any objective observer would be forced to admit that it was largely thanks to Arafat's dedication, intelligence, pragmatism, charisma and capacity for hard work that the PLO not only still existed, no mean achievement, but had gained its observer status at the UN, diplomatic relations of varying degrees of formality with more than a hundred countries and substantial wealth. The organisation's sprawling bureaucracy in Lebanon was certainly corrupt and inefficient but nonetheless administered a vast range of clinics, schools, training camps and cultural institutions that had simply not existed a decade before. This had been achieved amid great instability and violence, and despite the strenuous efforts of powerful enemies throughout the region and beyond.

As ever, the question of the use and abuse of violence posed the most difficult decisions, which Arafat typically sought to avoid. To have explicitly abandoned the 'armed struggle' in all its forms, as some in the West demanded, was inconceivable. It was the *raison d'être* of Fatah and all the other PLO factions and had been written into the PLO's constitution almost fifteen years earlier. To do so would mean explaining to the pre-teenage recruits that Cornwell had seen march in Sidon that they would never get the chance to join their older brothers waving assault rifles aboard the dented pickup trucks at the head of the PLO's parades. It would mean changing the words to the songs sung in its schools, on its posters, in its poems and in most of its speeches. It would mean too that Palestinians in Lebanon would be defenceless before Christian militia with a long track record of atrocities. And if there was no evidence that any of Israel's leaders were inclined to make the slightest concession to the Palestinians as a consequence of the PLO's or anyone else's violence, there was also nothing to suggest that diplomatic pressure had much effect on them either.

It had been almost a decade since Arafat had renounced attacks against third parties in the Palestinians' conflict with Israel, and this ban remained in place. But he was also well aware that the possibility that such operations might be perpetrated by disobedient elements of the PLO usefully concentrated the minds of western European powers, as well as leaders in eastern Europe and the Middle East. Nor had Arafat ever forbidden attacks against Israeli targets around the world. Such violence was not without costs, of course, but it had multiple uses too. So when in 1981 and early 1982, Arafat faced pressure from subordinates to launch a campaign of bombings in western Europe, he sought merely to moderate their enthusiasm but not to stop them.

At the same time, though, Arafat sought to bolster the PLO's credentials as a force *against* terrorism. The Israelis' assassination of Ali Hassan Salameh in 1979 had not closed Arafat's channels to Washington, despite the ongoing ban on direct dealings with the PLO that Kissinger had conceded to Israel in 1975. The CIA continued to rely on the PLO's intelligence services to protect the US Embassy in west Beirut, keep an eye out for US diplomats in the city and warn of potential threats elsewhere in the world. In 1981, Arafat had alerted the CIA to a wave of attacks planned by minor or breakaway PLO factions against US embassies in Kinshasa and Rome, and when the agency got wind of a plot among Palestinian hardliners to assassinate Menachem Begin, the Israeli prime minister, during a visit to the United Nations

General Assembly in September of that year, Arafat ensured the attempt was aborted. Five months later, the CIA paid its dues, warning the PLO chairman of what appeared to be a Syrian plot to ambush his motorcade.

Everyone involved worked hard to keep this quiet, of course. Other assistance that Arafat offered Washington was trickier to conceal. Indeed, Arafat had no intention of doing anything of the sort. During the US Embassy siege in Tehran he had won considerable goodwill within the highest levels of the Carter administration by negotiating the return of the bodies of US servicemen killed during the failed rescue mission of April 1980 and then arranging for the release of thirteen of the hostages. Though Ronald Reagan was convinced that Palestinian factions were 'all terrorists', the new president had nonetheless personally given a green light to informal and indirect contacts between the US and Arafat to discuss possible peace agreements in the Middle East. The PLO chairman was not the only leader making compromises when faced by complex and dynamic challenges, it seemed.

Reagan's officials had also made repeatedly clear to Israel that they did not want the country to intervene in Lebanon. Menachem Begin had won a second term as prime minister in June 1981 shortly after ordering a risky but successful attack on an under-construction nuclear reactor in Iraq. His victory had been followed by a particularly intense bout of cross-border shelling and rocketing of northern Israeli towns and kibbutzim by the PLO and retaliatory attacks by the Israelis. After a bloody Israeli air strike on southern Beirut, the US had negotiated a truce which Arafat worked hard to maintain, limiting the PLO's attacks into Israel and using the months of relative quiet to build up his forces. Begin was less enthusiastic about the pause in hostilities, and made clear that, despite US concerns, he hoped to use the massive power of the Israeli military to achieve a more definitive end to the threat posed by Palestinian factions in southern Lebanon as soon as possible. By the time Cornwell left Beirut and his PLO hosts in the spring of 1982 and set about writing his new novel, Arafat was fully convinced that an Israeli invasion was imminent.

An invasion of Lebanon to crush the PLO was precisely what Israel's controversial new defence minister and former general had in mind.

Ariel Sharon, then fifty-three, was a legendary and polarising figure. Born and raised in Palestine on a moshav, a cooperative farming community, he had fought in every one of Israel's conflicts. His career had been marked by a series of spectacular military exploits but also bitter controversy. In 1948, Sharon had been praised for his leadership when wounded in fighting to open a road to Jerusalem, and was subsequently picked to lead a newly founded special forces unit. Five years later, men under his command killed sixty-nine villagers during a raid on the West Bank that had been ordered as retaliation for the murder of an Israeli woman and her two children. In 1956, Sharon fought in the Suez campaign, helping Israel win key engagements but also ordering a rash attack that led to heavy Israeli losses. In 1967, 'Arik', as he was known to his troops, commanded an armoured division in several key battles, and then was deployed to newly-occupied Gaza where he methodically uprooted the Palestinian armed factions there by detaining hundreds without charge and using bulldozers to clear lanes through built-up areas to allow his troops to patrol. In the war of 1973, after being accused of paying more attention to the journalists he wined and dined in his headquarters than to the enemy, Sharon had personally led Israeli forces across the Suez Canal and deep into Egypt in a counter-offensive that was, and still is, lauded as one of the most audacious and effective commands of armoured forces in modern military history.

The impetuosity, tactical acuity and evident lack of concern for the human cost of his decisions that Sharon had displayed as a general brought similar praise and criticism when deployed in service of a political career. Broadly secular in his outlook, Sharon did not share his prime minister's almost mystical vision of the destiny of the Jewish people. He did however enthusiastically embrace Begin's maximalist vision of the extent of Israel's potential territory and, as minister of agriculture during Begin's first term, had sought to consolidate Israel's hold on the occupied West Bank by supporting the Jewish settlements there. Sharon's appointment to the defence portfolio was described as rash even by his own fans.

From the moment Sharon took up his new post, he had begun planning a major military operation in Lebanon. Since 1973, the Israeli army had been reformed and re-armed – largely with cutting-edge US technology. With the threat of Egypt removed by the peace treaty recently signed by Begin and Sadat, this powerful force could now be deployed in a new and different way. Some of Sharon's ambitions were extreme – for example, to force the transfer of the Palestinians in Lebanon to Jordan. Others, such as establishing a friendly regime in Beirut, had been part of Israeli strategic thinking for decades. But his overriding and immediate aim was the definitive destruction of the PLO and an end to the threat its various factions posed to Israel. It was not just the organisation he wished to eradicate but the ideas it espoused and represented. For that to be achieved, Sharon was convinced that Arafat, the individual who incarnated the Palestinian nationalist cause more than anyone else, would have to be killed or somehow incapacitated.

When Sharon sought the approval of the Israeli cabinet for an invasion of Lebanon in late 1981, there was little support from other ministers, despite Begin's own enthusiasm. Years of bloody raids into Israel by Palestinian factions had had substantial emotional and political impact on the nation, and the recent scenes of tens of thousands of Israelis fleeing rocket attacks on their homes along Israel's northern border had been traumatic to behold, but this did not necessarily justify a major and apparently unnecessary conflict. Between 1980 and 1981, the Palestinian armed factions' attacks in Israel, the West Bank and Gaza had killed a total of sixteen people and wounded 136 more, and while their violence around the world was spectacular and often lethal – ten people died and more than 130 were hurt in three attacks on synagogues in Vienna, Paris and Antwerp over the same period – it could hardly be considered an existential danger.

Where persuasion failed, duplicity might succeed. Through the spring of 1982, Sharon tried to convince his fellow ministers that he merely wanted to push the PLO far enough from the border to prevent any further bombardment of Israel's north. This more limited objective was harder to oppose. Then came the shooting of Israel's ambassador outside the Dorchester Hotel in London on 3 June.

Within hours of hearing of the attack, Begin ordered air strikes against PLO targets across Lebanon, breaking the truce arranged the previous summer by the US. The PLO responded, as everyone knew they would, with a barrage of rocket fire on northern Israel. Though this was aimed into empty fields and so caused no casualties, it allowed Begin to ask his ministers to approve an attack that would take the IDF only twenty-five miles into Lebanon, not even half the distance to Beirut. Sharon insisted this would take only forty-eight hours, even just twenty-four, and enable the IDF to force the PLO back beyond artillery and rocket range of Israel. Specialists from military intelligence told Begin and the cabinet that those who had tried to kill the Israeli ambassador in London had nothing to do with Arafat or any of the

Palestinian groups based in Lebanon, but had instead been dispatched by the Baghdad-based Sabri al-Banna, well known to their audience as Abu Nidal. Though they pointed out that al-Banna had left Fatah almost a decade before and for years had targeted PLO moderates on the orders of Saddam Hussein, the information made little difference. 'Abu Nidal, Abu Schmidal,' Rafael Eitan, the blunt-speaking chief of staff and Israel's most senior soldier, said. 'They are all PLO,' agreed Begin.

At 11 a.m. on 6 June 1982, some 55,000 men, 800 tanks and 1,500 armoured personnel carriers crossed Israel's northern border, swept through the lines of the small United Nations peacekeeping force established after the incursion four years earlier, and advanced into Lebanon. 'Operation Peace for Galilee' had begun. Facing them were the 15,000 lightly-armed fighters and sixty ageing tanks of the PLO.

The Israeli armoured columns made rapid progress but, despite the massive superiority of the forces under his command, not everything went Sharon's way. At Beaufort Castle, a former Crusader strongpoint just a few miles into Lebanon, Israeli special forces suffered heavy casualties. In Sidon and Tyre rapidly-formed local militias and PLO fighters held off Israeli assaults for days, even after their senior officers fled. The Israelis destroyed almost all Syria's Soviet-supplied missile batteries and about a third of its air force for virtually no loss in a one-sided aerial battle, but elsewhere Syrian troops fought hard before eventually falling back.

The twenty-five-mile limit initially set by Sharon was soon left far behind but by the time anyone in Jerusalem expressed concerns, Israeli forces were even further north. On 13 June the Israelis reached the outskirts of Beirut and ten days later cut the highway from the city to Damascus after more fierce clashes with Syrian troops. Once the encirclement of the Lebanese capital was complete, Arafat and other PLO leaders like Habash and their fighters had no way out.

This posed a dilemma for Sharon. Israel had identified the Maronite Christians as a useful partner inside Lebanon several years earlier. Though well aware of the Phalange's appalling record of ethnic cleansing, killing and systematic use of torture, it had given them weapons and funds in an effort to build up their capabilities. Such assistance increased under Begin, who had a romantic and entirely ahistorical view of the Maronites as a persecuted minority that the Jews of Israel had a historic duty to save from a threatened genocide. In January, Sharon had met with Bashir Gemayel and won what he thought was a promise to use the Phalange to force the PLO out of Beirut. Yet, when resistance from Arafat's forces and their Lebanese allies stiffened on the outskirts of the city, Gemayel showed limited interest in offering any significant assistance to the Israelis at all. A canny political operator despite his youth, Gemayel was aware that to do the Israelis' work for them would not be viewed at all well by his compatriots, and could jeopardise his presidential ambitions in elections due to be held within weeks. Sharon knew that if he sent Israeli soldiers into Beirut, they risked appalling casualties in urban fighting where their tanks, air power and artillery would offer little protection against agile defenders. This left him with a significant problem which, characteristically, he decided to solve through the application of overpowering force.

Within days of Israeli forces taking up positions around Beirut, their artillery and planes had begun to bombard parts of the city. Sharon would later say that his men had 'tried as much as possible to strike at selective targets', and it was true that the PLO had placed at least some of their anti-aircraft guns, command posts, stores and bunkers in close proximity to schools, markets, medical facilities and mosques. But the sheer intensity of the Israeli attack and the nature of the weapons deployed made large numbers of civilian casualties inevitable – a cost that was clearly acceptable to senior Israeli military planners.

Many deaths came through Sharon's single-minded and ruthless pursuit of Arafat. The PLO chairman spent most of his time underground in bunkers like the one visited by Cornwell months earlier. Several were underneath apartment blocks in Fakhani, the west Beirut neighbourhood that was the PLO's stronghold, and so attracted Israeli strikes that sometimes destroyed entire buildings. One bombing raid 'literally flattened' a seven-storey building, killing or wounding hundreds. Arafat had so many narrow escapes that his followers began to wonder if he had his own informants among the Israelis. The civilian death toll mounted daily. With many hospitals badly damaged and an acute shortage of medicines, help for any casualties was often rudimentary at best, increasing the toll on human life yet further. The Israeli use of bombs containing dozens of smaller bombs – 'cluster bombs' designed to cover an area indiscriminately – was common. Cars and even donkeys exploded in a series of mysterious and bloody bombings in Fakhani and other Palestinian strongholds. To increase pressure on the PLO, the

Israelis cut off power and water to much of the city, then restricted the supply of food.

Estimates of how many died varied greatly and the chaos, hasty burials, ongoing combat and poor record-keeping made any definitive count impossible. Most observers simply gave up. The few Israeli soldiers who challenged their orders made no appreciable difference, nor did dozens of short-lived ceasefires. In early September, the respected Beirut newspaper *An-Nahar* reported 17,825 persons killed and another 30,203 wounded during the invasion of Lebanon, according to police and hospital records. Though it was hard to track the precise proportion of the casualties who were fighters, the stacked bodies of women and children in morgues made it clear to anyone on the ground that a very high proportion were not combatants. The Palestine Red Crescent said that civilians comprised more than four-fifths of the 5,500 dead they had counted in Beirut alone. Sharon said that there had been only 2,000 casualties, mostly military.

In previous conflicts, Israel's military had been able to operate without any serious international scrutiny. This was not the case in Lebanon in 1982. The images taken by Western newspaper photographers in Beirut showed dismembered civilian corpses, teenage fighters wide-eyed with fear and adrenalin, a march by desperate foreign nurses demanding the Israelis lift their blockade, a row of burning apartment blocks along the Mediterranean shore, a woman who had just lost four children, and Israeli fighter jets streaking through the blue sky over the smoking city. The hundreds of journalists who flew into Beirut were able for the first time to cover an Arab–Israeli war without censorship by either side, and new satellite technology meant major television networks could broadcast scenes filmed just hours earlier to huge audiences. That the Christian parts of the city had escaped more or less unscathed went largely unreported, but that was beside the point. 'Five hundred thousand people live [in the area being targeted],' John Chancellor pointed out to his viewers on NBC's nightly news. 'One in a hundred is a PLO fighter. The Israeli planes just never stopped coming.'

Arafat recognised the public relations opportunity the siege offered, and managed to give multiple interviews, including to the editor of a left-wing Israeli magazine, all while moving from bunker to bunker. PLO spokesmen offered correspondents daily briefings in their hotels too. His message was one of continual defiance, echoed by other PLO officials like Habash, who told an interviewer in Beirut that he thanked

God for allowing him to see 'the day that a Palestinian Army fought an Israeli Army' and called for the city to become an 'Arab Stalingrad'.

Almost from the beginning of the war, the question was when not if the PLO would be defeated. One night several weeks into the siege, Janet Lee Stevens, a young activist and freelance journalist whose commitment to the Palestinian cause had earned her the nickname 'the Little Drummer Girl', which may have given Cornwell the title of his new book, sought out Arafat. She found him in yet another bunker deep under Fakhani and implored him to 'hold out to the bitter end', because 'the people of Beirut are with you.'

In reality, the people of Beirut were not with him. Most inhabitants of the Christian-dominated east loathed the PLO and all it stood for, and though some residents elsewhere had rallied around the Palestinians, leaders of almost every significant political party in the country, including most nominal allies, had been working hard since the earliest days of the siege to convince Arafat to leave the city. Quite soon even those who were broadly favourable to the Palestinian cause came to understand that the Palestinians' leaders were holding out against the Israelis primarily in the hope of gaining better terms for their eventual departure and so they could boast of their prolonged resistance to vastly superior forces. This prompted bleak jokes. One ran: Arafat is called from a meeting to be told by an aide that 450,000 west Beirutis have gathered outside his headquarters to say goodbye. 'Why?' Arafat asks the aide, 'Where are they going?'

The siege of Beirut reached its climax in the first two weeks of August, with hundreds of air strikes accompanied by massive artillery bombardment pummelling Fakhani almost every day. Along with the growing outrage outside the US, this prompted direct intervention from the only individual the Israelis could not afford to ignore. Having sought to restrain the Israelis before the invasion, the Reagan administration had then been broadly supportive through the war's early stages. Now, even if striking further heavy blows against Syria, a Soviet ally, and the PLO both remained attractive prospects, there were deep concerns in the White House and particularly at the Department of State at the course of events. One worry was that the bloodshed and chaos of the war might eventually provoke Soviet intervention. Another was that the US would be blamed for Israeli excesses. After a particularly murderous eleven hours of shelling and air strikes on 12 August, Reagan called the Israeli prime minister and, choosing his words carefully, described what was happening in the Lebanese capital as 'a holocaust' which seriously threatened future relations between their countries. Begin, much of whose family had been killed by the Nazis, replied coldly that he knew exactly what a holocaust was but nonetheless told Sharon to ease, if not end, the bombing and shelling. A day later, Arafat agreed to a US proposal that his fighters would leave Beirut and be dispersed among seven different Arab countries. A principal condition of the deal was that the PLO's forces would be able to march out of the city with their weapons. A second was that their departure would be overseen by a multinational military force led by the US which would then stay behind for at least a month to prevent the Israelis entering west Beirut and attacking the now defenceless Palestinian civilians left behind.

This ended the siege, and over the last ten days of August 1982 between 8,000 and 10,000 fighters from Fatah, the PFLP and all the other factions that made up the PLO drove through Beirut to its battered port, now secured by recently arrived detachments of the French Foreign Legion, Italian Bersaglieri and US Marines. One reporter described 'trucks and jeeps ablaze with colour, the multi-coloured Palestinian banners trailing in the breeze, the scarlet banners of Marxist organisations . . . the men wrapped in checkered keffiyehs brandishing their guns; around them, the mind-jarring chatter and boom of thousands of guns being fired into the air and a circle of middle-aged Palestinian women all crying together, "Revolution, Revolution until victory".' Others described shouts of Allahu Akbar, God is Great. A reporter from *Libération*, the radical French newspaper, spoke to a young and defiant PFLP fighter. 'They call us terrorists?', the teenager told him. 'Fine. Soon our hour of revenge will come.'

The Palestinian fedayeen were feted as they rode in their ramshackle convoys through west Beirut on their way to the waiting ships, and some onlookers had wept, though, as more than one observer commented acidly, it was hard to tell whether they were shedding tears of pride, joy or simple relief. No one cheered the 6,000 Syrian regular soldiers who simultaneously headed out of the city east along the road to Damascus, or shed tears at their departure. Israeli soldiers shouted insults as the Syrian army trucks drove through the hills east of the capital and the sentiments of most inhabitants of Beirut were equally unflattering. During the siege, Arafat called on Arab leaders to offer 'their swords' not 'their prayers', but his appeal had fallen on apparently deaf ears. 'Tell your children what Israel has done. Tell your children what the

Arabs have done. Tell your children what the world has done,' read the writing on one wall. Finally, on 31 August, dressed in his trademark fatigues and keffiyeh, Arafat himself walked up the gangplank of a waiting Greek freighter, flashing a Churchillian V-sign. Once aboard, he stood at the railing at the stern, watching the coast recede as the ship headed westwards, explaining to hand-picked journalists that the war had proved that 'no one can annihilate the PLO'.

Pleased at this outcome and wary of a Vietnam-style 'quagmire', Caspar Weinberger, Reagan's defence secretary, then ordered the US troops it had sent to Beirut to withdraw. This broke the promise made to Arafat. As the US Marines boarded the landing ships that would take them out to their offshore flotilla and thence home, they waved banners bearing the words 'Mission Accomplished'. The president himself used similar words when he explained his actions to the nation a day or so later on TV.

Arafat had come much closer to death than he knew. An Israeli sniper had had Arafat in his sights at the port but had been told not to fire on orders that almost certainly came from Begin, who was fearful of the reaction in Washington that such a killing would provoke. The presence off Beirut of the US Sixth Fleet, sent by Reagan to discourage Soviet meddling in Lebanon some weeks earlier, prevented any Israeli attempt to capture or kill at sea the most famous Palestinian in the world. When his freighter docked in Cyprus, the first stop en route for Tunis, its ultimate destination and Arafat's agreed place of exile, Mossad agents got to within three feet or so of the PLO chairman on the quayside. They could have killed him without difficulty, and no doubt would have done if offered such an opportunity a week or so earlier. Instead, their mission was simply to identify and photograph members of Arafat's entourage so that headquarters in Tel Aviv knew exactly who among the PLO's leaders and hangers-on had left Beirut.

The list of these was long. One of the reasons so many senior Palestinian officials had maintained close relationships with certain Arab regimes was to make sure they always had a bolthole – a strategy now revealed as prudent. Many now decided that exile with Arafat was unattractive. Habash headed to Damascus, with Bassam Abu Sharif, the PFLP's ebullient spokesman, in tow. So too did the leaders of the DFLP, and other left-wing factions.

Some left more discreetly than others. Shigenobu and her JRA followers took advantage of the PLO's massed departure to slip out of the city unnoticed by any media or security officials, possibly on a Greek ship headed for South Yemen, which had also agreed to take some of the new refugees. Leila Khaled, who had been in west Beirut through much of the Israeli siege and was heavily pregnant, went to Syria, but from there she would eventually make her way with her second husband to Amman, the place where she had arrived from Kuwait as an aspirant frontline fighter for the PFLP almost a decade and a half earlier.

That Arafat escaped alive was a disappointment for Sharon but not a serious concern. Even before the PLO chairman had left Beirut, Sharon boasted in an editorial published in the *New York Times* of 'the crushing defeat' inflicted on the PLO. 'The kingdom of terror that the PLO had established on Lebanese soil' had been destroyed, 'international terrorism dealt a mortal blow' and the 'whole infrastructure of violence and revolution . . . broken', Sharon, or whoever wrote the article on his behalf, told readers. The language was carefully chosen to frame the Israeli campaign as a Cold War battle – and a rare one that had been unequivocally won. Just in case readers had not understood either this point or the significance of Israel's achievement, Sharon spelled it out for them. It was, he wrote, 'a victory for peace and freedom everywhere'.

One reason for such triumphalism was that, four days before his NYT editorial was published, Bashir Gemayel, the leader of the Phalange and Israel's main ally in Lebanon, had won the country's presidential elections. No one pretended these were free or fair, nor was there any way they could have been, given the fighting at the time and the prevailing political circumstances. But the result meant that, in addition to dispatching Arafat to distant lands and dispersing the PLO, Sharon appeared to have achieved one of his main secondary objectives: the installation of a pliable, pro-Israeli leader in Lebanon. Israeli intelligence officers were reported to have joined Phalange gunmen emptying their magazines into the air in celebration.

But such jubilation did not last long, mainly because the new political dispensation in Lebanon displeased some of the more powerful local actors who were still smarting from the sharp reminder of Israel's military superiority received during the summer. On 14 September, just two weeks after the departure of Arafat into exile, Gemayel died when a Syrian agent planted a bomb that demolished the headquarters of the Phalange. As had so often been the case over the previous decade and a half, this precise and well-timed use of lethal violence would have just as transformative an effect on the course of events as the indiscriminate use of force favoured by Sharon. The assassination forestalled the possibility of a serious regional setback for Damascus, removed the keystone of the political settlement Sharon wanted to impose on Lebanon and sent the war there spiralling into a new and unpredictable phase.

This much was clear even before what was left of Gemayel had been definitively identified by his distinctive hexagonal wedding ring. The morning after the bombing of the Phalange headquarters, Israeli troops moved into west Beirut where they secured key buildings, roads and intersections. This was supposedly to prevent general chaos in the city but was a further flagrant breach of the deal brokered by the US in August and put Israeli forces in a position to control access to the Palestinian refugee camps of Sabra and Shatila. Shortly afterwards, at Israel's request, the Phalange agreed to secure them both. Sharon attempted to reassure US diplomats who were worried by this, saying: 'Nothing will happen. Maybe some more terrorists will be killed. That will be to the benefit of all of us . . . So, we'll kill them. They will not be left there . . . You are not going to save these groups of the international terrorism.'

On the morning of 18 September, journalists entered Sabra and Shatila camps to find piles of bodies blocking narrow alleys, mutilated corpses of women and children lying in pools of blood inside their own homes, infants with their skulls smashed, evidence of gang rape, barely concealed mass graves and traumatised survivors. The number of the dead was unclear, but may have reached around 1,400, though some said half as many and others said three times that total. Nearly all were women, children and old men. There was little evidence that any were 'terrorists', let alone international ones. The attackers had met with very limited resistance from a few lightly-armed teenagers in the first minutes of their operations, but that was all. There was also very little evidence that watching Israeli troops had made any effort whatsoever to restrain the Phalange during their thirty-six-hour murderous rampage, and much that suggested their most senior commanders' complicity in the killings.

The reports of the massacres caused global outrage. Reagan described his 'revulsion', acutely aware that the US would now be blamed for the massacre. Anxious to deflect criticism at home and abroad, he also ordered US troops back into Beirut. So too did his equally penitent Italian and French counterparts, who had followed Washington's lead two weeks earlier.

For Israel, the killings in Sabra and Shatila marked an important turning point. Exactly a decade earlier, in the aftermath of the Munich Olympics attacks, the country had been seen as the victim of indiscriminate violence against civilians, not a perpetrator. Now, Israel was seen as a bullying aggressor, clumsy with its great strength, truculent, bellicose and bloodthirsty. 'Israel had transformed itself from underdog to overlord in the Middle East,' said *Newsweek*, the US magazine. The Palestinians, on the other hand, had gone from being troublesome refugees with a taste for spectacular aerial violence to long-suffering subjects of a great and ongoing historical injustice that needed urgent attention and just resolution. The siege and its aftermath rehabilitated Arafat as a statesman.

There was more bad news for Israel, or at least for Israeli hawks. A peace plan announced by Reagan even before the massacres called for a degree of Palestinian 'self-government' in the occupied territories in association with Jordan and an end to the construction of Jewish settlements there, effectively putting paid to Sharon and Begin's hopes that the war in Lebanon would somehow allow the rapid and total integration of the occupied territories into Israel proper. To rub salt into this particular wound, Reagan also reasserted the 'legitimate rights of the Palestinian people', pointedly adding that 'while Israel's military success in Lebanon [had] demonstrated that its armed forces are second to none in the region, they alone cannot bring just and lasting peace to Israel and her neighbours.' The succession of Amin Gemayel to the post of his late brother Bashir did little to raise Israeli spirits either. The new president of Lebanon was much closer to Syria than his sibling had been, distinctly wary of Begin and his government and absolutely committed to Maronite Christian dominance of his homeland. He was not the friend of Israel that Sharon and the Israeli prime minister had, at least in part, launched their war to put in power.

In Israel itself, there had been growing protests against the war for several weeks before the Sabra and Shatila massacres. Now hundreds of thousands took to the streets in some of the biggest demonstrations the country had ever seen. One bereaved father, a former Jewish resistance fighter in the Second World War whose only son was among the 420 Israelis killed in Lebanon that summer, wrote to Begin: 'Remember: Your deeds will be a warning and a verdict for generations to come ... May my great suffering – the suffering of a father whose entire world has been destroyed – pursue you forever, during your sleeping hours and when you are awake. May it be a mark of Cain upon you for all time.'

*

From Cyprus, the cruise ships bearing the PLO's fighters headed for Greece. On his arrival at Piraeus, Arafat was greeted warmly at dockside by Prime Minister Andreas Papandreou as a row of sailors stood at attention for review and a small crowd of mostly Greek Socialist party members chanted pro-Palestinian slogans. When the PLO reached Tunisia some days later, President Habib Bourguiba and his cabinet were likewise waiting at the quayside in Bizerte to welcome their guests. An invitation soon arrived from the French foreign minister for Arafat to visit Paris. Arab heads of state sent their own similar requests and much money.

A month later, Arafat set off on a tour of the Middle East, starting with Amman, from where his forces had been bloodily expelled almost exactly twelve years earlier. On his first night in the Jordanian capital, he spoke at a rally. 'We lost 5,000 in Sabra and Shatila and we are ready to lose 50,000 to liberate our homeland,' the PLO chairman told an enthusiastic audience. A day later, Arafat enjoyed a lengthy and apparently convivial audience with King Hussein.

The PLO's new headquarters was the five-star Salwa Beach Hotel, a modern and elegant white building among the dunes on the outskirts of Tunis, reached via a long and pleasing drive lined with palm trees. Arafat and his followers had soon filled all of its 200 rooms. Weeks earlier, they had been in the thick of the only real military confrontation that had taken place between Israelis and Palestinians since the battle of Karameh in 1968. Now, 1,500 miles from Jerusalem, Arafat's aides and dozens of Fatah's most experienced military men sat in beach chairs, admiring the peacocks, playing on the miniature golf course and ordering innumerable cups of coffee from elegantly-attired waiters. 'In Beirut, we were in exile,' one senior PLO official told a visiting American reporter. 'Here we are in exile from exile.'

Arafat himself remained as buoyant and busy as ever, with his notepad in the breast pocket of his freshly pressed uniform, holstered pistol at his hip and keffiyeh. But when Cornwell flew in for an interview, the British author was not allowed to exchange a single word with the PLO chairman. There was no interview, or frenzied dancing of the dabke, or parades in the rain. Instead, Cornwell was permitted to watch as Arafat exercised at a stables in Tunis, riding a white Arab stallion around a ring of beaten white sand again and again and again.

36

The Bloodiest Year

On a wet morning in November 1982, five months after Israel's invasion of Lebanon and three after the departure of Yasser Arafat from Beirut, a small car carrying a large bomb exploded outside an Israeli military headquarters in the southern Lebanese port town of Tyre. The eight-storey building collapsed, detached from its supporting columns by the massive blast, and was reduced to rubble. Seventy-seven Israelis, mainly soldiers or paramilitary police, and a dozen or more Lebanese prisoners were killed.

There had been many attacks on Israeli troops in southern Lebanon since the summer but none so lethal. Most had been claimed by minor armed groups whose names few recognised. But what bewildered investigators in this case was that whoever had organised the bombing had given their own driver not even the slightest chance of survival. For all the talk of 'martyrdom' over the previous decade, only a vanishingly small number of attacks had involved the almost certain death of the perpetrator. Military officials decided this information was far too unsettling to be shared with Israel's news media or the bereaved. Instead they blamed the explosion on a gas leak.

Over the next year, attacks against Israeli, US and French troops in Lebanon escalated rapidly. One caused the most powerful non-nuclear explosion since the Second World War and the highest number of casualties sustained in a single day by the US military since the 1968 Tet Offensive in Vietnam. A second inflicted the worst single-day loss on French forces since the end of the Algerian war of independence twenty-one years earlier. A third hit the Israeli headquarters in Tyre again, causing dozens more casualties. These were unlike almost any previous attacks. They destroyed very large buildings, killed hundreds of people, injured thousands and forced decisions in Washington and elsewhere that had major strategic implications for the region and the world. All took place in Lebanon, which had become the crucible in which this radically new form of terrorism was being forged.

A decade or so earlier, when the Popular Front for the Liberation of Palestine had hijacked three planes and landed them at their makeshift airport in Jordan, they had carefully evacuated the aircraft before destroying them. Now, attackers sought to maximise loss of life. Not only did they seek mass casualties, they also targeted Western powers much more directly, no longer treating them as third parties to Middle Eastern conflicts but as participants and enemies. In their aftermath, no press conferences were held to explain their cause, justify their actions or issue any demands. Indeed, often nothing very clear was said at all. It was as if the violence was meant to speak for itself.

The departure of Arafat and the PLO in the wake of the Israeli invasion did not bring peace. Instead it left a vacuum which others swiftly filled. The bombing in November 1982 had been the work of one of several new forces which had stepped in to organise resistance to occupying Israeli troops. Like its various counterparts, it was acting with the backing of one of the many regional powers which now sought to exploit the new situation. In the face of this complexity and chaos, the US 'peacekeepers' sent into Lebanon to stabilise the country and reinforce Washington's influence in the Levant proved unable to achieve either end. And yet their underlying problem was not a practical one. It was their failure to grasp where this unprecedented wave of violence sprang from and why.

For, despite the beliefs and insistence of Benzion Netanyahu and others in the US and Israel, there was in fact a link between 'revolution' – in the sense of a project of radical social, political or economic transformation – and terrorism, and had they seen this connection they might have stood a chance of understanding their enemy far better than they did. Instead, over the course of 1983 and into the following year, they stubbornly pursued a misconceived strategy that made a bad situation very much worse.

The 'gas explosion' at the Israeli headquarters in Tyre received little international attention. Foreign TV crews had returned to Beirut to cover the aftermath of the Sabra and Shatila massacres in September, but then moved on to other stories. The US, French and Italian troops which had redeployed in the city brought a measure of calm, allowing its inhabitants to recover a little from the horrors of the preceding months. New palm trees were planted along the seafront, fishermen reappeared on the Corniche and the most popular restaurants were booked solid days in advance. The airport welcomed diplomatic missions and business delegations. Princess Anne, the Queen of England's daughter, flew in to visit a medical clinic run by an international NGO. Investors arrived too. In east Beirut, the Jet Set Disco offered the opportunity to party 'all night, all day, every day'. The Israelis had withdrawn from the city and, awed by the military might of the Western forces, the local warring militia had stowed their weapons. The 'bad days' were over, residents said.

But by the early spring of 1983 any hopes of peace, let alone prosperity, were fading fast. Bombs exploded in Beirut every other day, targeting political leaders, ordinary civilians who happened to be from a different community and, increasingly, the international forces stationed there. In mid-March, a dozen patrolling US Marines were injured by hand grenades dropped from houses, and further attacks followed. The troops' primary task was to support Lebanon's central government and they had just started joint patrols with the Lebanese army. They had not anticipated becoming targets themselves. As with the bombing at Tyre, quite who was responsible for such attacks was troublingly unclear. Robert Fisk, *The Times* of London's correspondent in Beirut, reported that they had been claimed by an organisation called Islamic Jihad, which no one had previously heard of. Other reporters thought the claim was a hoax.

By March, even those with long experience of the dangers of Beirut and the region were alarmed. Robert Ames, the CIA officer who had befriended Ali Hassan Salameh in Beirut fifteen years earlier, was now the agency's most senior Middle East analyst. Based at its headquarters in Langley, Virginia, Ames regularly briefed senior US officials including President Reagan, and his reports headed the agenda of meetings of the National Security Council. When it was decided that he should visit the city, colleagues at the CIA warned him that 'things were getting pretty dangerous there'. Ames believed that the US might be able to bring together warring parties in the region with its new peace plan and decided the trip was worth the risk.

Ames arrived in Beirut on 17 April, checked in to his favourite hotel and went to dinner with colleagues. The next morning, after breakfast with a contact, he headed to the US Embassy for a meeting of senior CIA staff that was scheduled to last all day. Just after 1 p.m., a black pickup truck turned sharply off the Corniche and into the open entrance of the embassy. The seven-storey block with two angled wings had been built less than a dozen yards from the wide road along the seafront, a spectacular location offering views of sunrise over the mountains and sunset over the sea, but also very vulnerable.

The driver of the pickup truck swerved past the ambassador's parked armoured limousine, accelerated, rammed the pickup through the embassy's double glass doors into its central lobby and then detonated approximately 1,000 kg of explosives that had been hidden under a tarpaulin behind the cab. The blast sheared away a third of the front of the building, in which Ames and his colleagues were meeting. A vast mushroom cloud shot through with flames rose hundreds of feet into the sky. This was the first major bombing of 1983, which would soon be known as 'the bloodiest year'.

The man who would eventually be blamed for the attack on the US Embassy in Beirut, as well as many other attacks over the coming years, was a Lebanese Shia Muslim, around twenty-one years old, called Imad Mughniyeh.

At the time of Mughniyeh's birth, Lebanon's Shia community comprised around a third of the country's population and was concentrated in the south and the Beqa'a valley. Oppressed by their own semi-feudal landowners, exploited by the country's wealthier Sunnis or Christians, 'impoverished and quiescent', their levels of education were a fraction of those enjoyed by other communities, half their villages had no water and only one in twelve had electricity. Per capita income in the south was a fifth of that in Beirut. Sometime probably in the mid-1960s, Mughniyeh's father did what many other Lebanese Shia Muslims were doing and moved to the capital in search of a better future.

Like most of the Shia who moved to Beirut through the 1960s and early 70s, the Mughniyehs ended up in the sprawling southern neighbourhoods, known as Dahiye. Planes landing at the international airport flew low over their two-roomed cinder-block home with a deafening roar. Sewage and rubbish clogged open gutters and children played in the dirt. To put food on the table, they sold vegetables from a barrow. Around them, thousands of other Shia families tried to make ends meet, few with much success.

The new arrivals tried hard to continue the village customs and obeisances of their faith in their new surroundings. In this, they were similar to the crowds of migrants then filling shanty towns in Tehran, Cairo or Jeddah. Religious community centres and mosques were built or expanded, family rituals and festivals carefully observed, the deep and historic ties joining Shia communities in the Levant to the great centres of Shia learning thousands of miles away were maintained and reinforced. Many Lebanese Shia followed marja'iyya in Iraq or Iran and their clerics continued to travel to Qom, Mashhad or Najaf, where many had studied.

When he was old enough, Imad spent his evenings in the Sheikh al-Kobeissi mosque near his home, learning the Islamic texts and dreaming of travelling to study at one of the great religious seminaries. This was not unusual. Plenty of young men in Dahiye aspired to be clerics. Some were caught in an adolescent moment of religious fervour and enquiry, but for an intelligent Shia teenager in Lebanon in the early 1970s, a career as a religious scholar was one of the few routes to respect, authority and a modicum of prosperity.

Mughniyeh was also living through a profound cultural and specifically ideological transformation that was taking hold among the Shia in Lebanon, just as it was among hundreds of millions of others across the Islamic world. For many years, it had been secular and leftist ideas – those of Arab nationalism, Syrian socialism, Communism and the Ba'ath – that had captured the imagination of Shia intellectuals, appearing to offer a solution to the marginalisation and poverty of their community in its homeland, as well as the challenges facing the broader Middle East. But after the shock of the 1967 war, the death of Gamal Abdel Nasser and the arrival of Palestinian armed groups from Jordan, new influences had begun to gain ground. Some claimed that the 'revolution' had not been prosecuted with sufficient commitment, but more had begun to argue that faith held the answer.

A key figure in the religious and political resurgence of the Lebanese Shia was Musa al-Sadr, a young Iranian cleric who had moved to Lebanon in 1959. Sadr had been educated in Qom and Najaf and was related to a respected family of Shia scholars so possessed traditional religious authority. But he was also a brilliant communicator who saw how traditions of devotion and faith could be turned to political ends. Not only a highly effective public speaker, Sadr was completely at ease with new technology such as cassettes which allowed him, like Khomeini, to reach a large illiterate audience. Very tall, with startling green eyes, he had a charisma even enemies and rivals did not deny, and by the early 1970s he had become the pre-eminent political and religious leader of the Shia in Lebanon. For the poorest and most pious, Sadr was 'the imam', even if the wealthier and more educated often disdained his populist approach.

Unsurprisingly, Sadr drew on radical thinkers in Iran, both lay and religious, to inspire and attract followers. Following the example of Ali Shariati, the Iranian intellectual who was then at the height of his popularity, he told his audience about the exploitation of 'the disinherited' or 'dispossessed' by tyrants and capitalists, turning accounts of the deeds of the greatest figures of the Shia faith into stories of social and political activism as well as sacrifice. Above all, he upended the quietist tradition among the Shia in Lebanon, as Khomeini had sought to do in Iran. 'From today we will no longer complain or cry . . . We are men who revolt against all tyranny, even if this costs us our blood and our lives . . . What does the government expect . . . other than rage and revolution?', Sadr told a mass meeting in 1974.

Though Sadr recognised the central significance of the Palestinian cause to Arabs and Muslims, he resisted any temptation to side with the PLO and Lebanese leftists as the country slid towards civil war, reaching out to Christians and Sunnis in an effort to reduce sectarian tensions. At the same time, he recognised the dangers the Shia would face in the event of outright conflict and so founded a Shia militia to provide the community with its own means of self-defence. This he called the Afwaj al-Muqawama al-Lubnaniyya, the Lebanese Resistance Forces, or, by its catchier acronym, AMAL, or 'hope'. This new force soon gathered much support, particularly among young Shia men in Beirut's southern suburbs.

But Mughniyeh was not among AMAL's new recruits. When civil war broke out in 1975, the teenager abandoned his plans to study Islam and, like most peers in his neighbourhood, began spending his days assisting the fighters from the various leftist factions who now occupied the narrow streets around his home. He helped build barricades to shield civilians from snipers, acted as a bodyguard for leaders and joined patrols of his neighbourhood. Such employment offered the same prospects of eventual status and wealth as a career as a religious scholar, and considerably more excitement. Mughniyeh fought for Syrian socialist nationalists, Communist factions and several Lebanese leftist groups. Such promiscuity was far from uncommon and suggests only that his motivation was more practical or personal than ideological. Eventually, however, sometime in 1976 or early 1977, Mughniyeh found a more permanent home with Fatah, which controlled much of the frontline close to his home and recruited heavily among his Shia and Palestinian neighbours. This marked a significant turning point in Mughniyeh's life, setting him on the course that would lead eventually to the bloody bombings of 1983.

In 1978, Mughniyeh was sent by his Fatah commanders for three weeks of training in a camp near Damour, the coastal town twelve miles south of Beirut that had been the site of a massacre after Palestinian fighters seized it from Christian militia two years earlier. The camp was run by a Lebanese Sunni called Anis Nakkache who had joined Fatah in 1968, fought in Jordan two years later and then been recruited for the organisation's intelligence services. Nakkache was one of the most experienced clandestine operators in the Middle East, with a talent for extremely dangerous undercover work. He had been based in Paris during the Mossad's assassination campaign after the Munich Olympics and provided the rocket-propelled grenades used by Ilich Ramírez Sánchez and others in the abortive attacks on El Al planes at Orly airport a year or so later. Nakkache's most spectacular exploit had been to infiltrate the PFLP on behalf of Fatah's intelligence service and take part in the attack on OPEC in Vienna led by Ramírez in December 1975. On his return to Lebanon, Nakkache was made the PLO's contact man for the many Iranian dissidents who were arriving in Lebanon seeking training.

In Damour, Nakkache noted that, unlike almost all other young Lebanese trainees, Mughniyeh showed an interest in tactics rather than 'just shooting guns' and took careful lecture notes. The veteran recommended the teenage Fatah fighter for enrolment in the Fatah Students Brigade, a unit which acted as a reservoir for promising young recruits. Mughniyeh excelled once more and was selected for missions with the elite Force 17 led by Salameh. When Salameh was killed by the Mossad in January 1979, the command of Force 17 passed to a senior Shia official who had known Mughniyeh back in the mid-1970s when he was in charge of Fatah's operations in southern Beirut. Once more Mughniyeh impressed his superior.

But they were not the only ones to have noticed the young man's military talents. Even as he made his mark among the secular radicals of Fatah, Mughniyeh was also in contact with their Shia equivalents, now increasingly active in Lebanon, some supported by Iran. These included members of the local branch of the Islamic al-Dawa organisation, which claimed responsibility for a huge bomb that levelled the Iraqi Embassy in Beirut in 1981, and many younger clerics who fervently admired Khomeini. Others were veterans of decades of Islamist activism in Lebanon and elsewhere. On several occasions, Mughniyeh acted as a bodyguard for a senior Lebanese religious scholar who had recently faced a series of assassination attempts. This brought him into further close contact with those who were committed, at least in general terms, to the vision of Khomeini and earned Mughniyeh a pilgrimage to Mecca.

This was not the only travel he undertook at this time. When Israeli tanks crossed the border in June 1982, Mughniyeh was in Iran visiting the holy shrines in Mashhad. He returned at once, narrowly avoiding abduction by Maronite Christian fighters from the Phalange as he drove from Damascus and then across the central Lebanese mountains. For the next two months, Mughniyeh fought with Fatah in Beirut. None among his comrades in arms appears to have doubted his commitment, and some accounts suggest he was among the Force 17 fighters picked to guard Arafat in his bunkers as the Israelis pounded the city, a task given only to the most trusted. One witness describes seeing Mughniyeh at the meeting of Arafat and Janet Lee Stevens, the Little Drummer Girl, as she implored the PLO leader to remain in Beirut to fight. Yet when the crucial moment came and Arafat agreed to leave the Lebanese capital, Mughniyeh chose to stay.

It is possible that Mughniyeh remained in Lebanon on the orders of senior Fatah officials who hoped he would lead other men from the PLO against Israel once their main force had left. Much more probable is that the Israeli invasion finally forced Mughniyeh to make a choice between Arafat's idea of what a revolution might be and that of the Shia activists and clerics with whom he was now spending much of his time. He would maintain close relations with many Fatah leaders and former comrades in the months to come and remain deeply committed to the Palestinian cause for the rest of his life, but his departure from the organisation was definitive.

Whatever the personal reasons for Mughniyeh's decision to abandon Fatah in favour of a religious movement that appealed to identity as much as ideology, the decision itself was very much in keeping with trends across the Middle East at the time. The religious resurgence of the 1970s, the predatory behaviour of the Palestinian factions in southern Lebanon, the cynicism displayed by almost all actors in the civil war: all had combined to undermine the attraction of secular, nationalist and leftist movements. The situation for someone like Mughniyeh was complicated further when in 1978, Sadr disappeared while on a trip to Tripoli to seek support from Muammar Gaddafi, almost certainly murdered by the unpredictable Libyan dictator. His replacement at the head of AMAL was a secular former lawyer called Nabih Berri whose moderate and pragmatic views enthused the more educated and better-off but were considerably less attractive to the poor, ill-educated young men who had filled the lower ranks of the militia. Then came the extraordinary, inspiring events in Iran.

Many of the Shia fighters within Fatah had long struggled to reconcile the PLO's broadly progressive agenda with the more conservative values of their community. At first, when Arafat had been seen as a close ally of the Iranian revolution, the tension was manageable. But when the PLO chairman's relationship with Khomeini soured, the evident personal and vast ideological differences between the two men became impossible to ignore. For those who supported the radical regime in Tehran this was a serious problem. Arafat made a belated attempt to recruit more Shia Muslims into the PLO in Lebanon but his outspoken support for Iraq in its war against Iran, coming even as Saddam Hussein was torturing and executing revered Shia clerics, prompted a wave of defections. In late 1981, tensions between Shia in the south and Palestinian factions there flared into open clashes, with many killed. By the spring of 1982, the violence had spread to Beirut.

The deaths of hundreds of Lebanese Shia in the massacres in Sabra and Shatila that September further underscored the need for a force to protect Shia families, faith and culture. AMAL was still the dominant force representing and defending the Shia community and, despite the disappointments of Berri's leadership, attracted the lion's share of PLO defectors and new volunteers. But some sought out the more radical networks that were closer to Tehran, both organisationally and ideologically. One of these was the deputy commander of Force 17 who had promoted Mughniyeh. Others came from Fatah's Students Brigade, including several of Mughniyeh's comrades in arms. Anis Nakkache had by now adopted Shia Islam, travelled to Tehran, been recruited into the regime's nascent security service and then dispatched to Paris to kill Shapour Bakhtiar, the last prime minister appointed by the shah. Reporters in Beirut described 'an influx' into the city of bearded young men wearing headbands advertising their willingness to die. In reality, there was no influx, just a transference of allegiance of men who had long been living and fighting in its streets.

Within weeks of the PLO's departure, such men were playing an increasingly prominent role in the violence against Israeli troops and international 'peacekeepers' in Lebanon. Initially, these attacks were relatively limited in ambition, restricted to ambushes, sniping or lobbing mortar shells onto Israeli bases. Others assaulted or killed Lebanese who 'collaborated' with the Israelis or targeted merchants selling the Israeli products that had poured into Lebanese markets in the aftermath of the summer's invasion. Some called themselves the Islamic Resistance, or the Hussein Suicide Squadrons, others used the name Islamic Jihad. Given their lack of any formal structure, it is unsurprising that, as Fisk reported, no one could say exactly who they were. For the moment, neither the Israelis nor Western security services paid them much attention.

For some months, Mughniyeh had been in contact with members of a newly formed organisation that had broken away from AMAL in the summer of 1982. Many of its leaders were militant young Shia clerics who wanted to turn Lebanon into an Islamist state along the lines of revolutionary Iran. More immediately, they wanted to fight against invading Israeli forces, which AMAL was not doing with much enthusiasm. Led by a former chemistry teacher and autodidact Islamic scholar called Hussein al-Moussawi, their first major act was to seize a military base in Baalbek in the Beqa'a valley, close to the Syrian border, in November 1982. The reason for the operation became clear when, shortly afterwards, the site was occupied by a force of several hundred Islamic Revolutionary Guards recently dispatched to Syria by Tehran.

Within days of the arrival of the Iranians in Baalbek, new posters were glued to walls across the town denouncing Israeli and Western imperialism or displaying the implacable features of Khomeini. A four-star hotel was requisitioned to become a rudimentary clinic. Local children were instructed in the Koran, while older boys got military training. Local women were advised in no uncertain terms to cover their hair. A thirty-five-foot mural of Iranian women 'shrouded in black robes' urged modesty.

Many of the new arrivals in Baalbek were veterans of brutal street battles in Tehran or the recent mass offensives along the Tigris against Iraq, where Tehran's forces had just begun to deploy 'human wave' attacks involving tens of thousands of very young soldiers mounting frontal assaults on Iraqi positions. When Fisk drove across the hills from Beirut to Baalbek, he found a propaganda office with a notice on the front door describing its occupants as 'lovers of martyrdom' and young Iranians who spoke of the need to spread their revolution around the world.

The Baalbek base was not only useful for propaganda and outreach but also offered a secure headquarters, defended by machine gun posts and hundreds of hardened fighters. This, along with the money and training the Iranians could provide, proved very attractive to young men such as Mughniyeh who was one of many who now travelled to Baalbek to join the rough coalition of local 'Islamic revolutionary committees', radicalised study groups and committed individuals that the Revolutionary Guards were building there. This was soon sufficiently distinct and cohesive to be considered something approximating an organisation of its own. A message was sent to Khomeini in Tehran. The 'imam' had initially opposed the deployment of Revolutionary Guards to Lebanon on the grounds that the Shia were insufficiently educated and politicised to justify the diversion of such fighters from the war with Iraq. Now, perhaps convinced of the project, he blessed the effort. It would be more than a year before the new organisation would adopt the name Hezbollah, the Party of God.

Another reason for Khomeini's reluctance may have been the long-standing opposition of Hafez al-Assad to any intervention in Lebanon by the new regime in Tehran. But, despite his visceral hatred for and fear of Islamists, Syria's brutal ruler was a realist. With the relative weakness of his own forces made clear during their confrontation with Israel that summer, Assad now saw the potential benefits of having a force of highly motivated, radical fighters such as those Tehran wanted to send and recruit in his fight against the wide array of actors – including 'the Zionists', the US and the French, the Maronite Christians – who opposed Syrian influence in Lebanon. Assad, as prudent as ever, refused access to a full division of elite Revolutionary Guardsmen, only allowing a few hundred to enter Lebanon on the strict condition that they avoid any fighting and restrict their activities to training and logistical support.

In March 1983, a meeting took place – possibly in al-Zabadani, a town just across the border with Syria, or possibly in Damascus itself – of senior Iranian security officials and the Lebanese militants who were responsible for the bombing of the Israeli headquarters in Tyre five months earlier. Mughniyeh may have been there. Some Syrian officials may also have been. On the agenda was a new attack, planned for the following month, this time in Beirut, though not against the Israelis. The logistical challenges of such an operation were obvious. Someone needed to find a large and more or less roadworthy truck, identify a potential driver, source or smuggle large quantities of explosives, assemble a bomb, reconnoitre the target and much else. With his contacts and intimate knowledge of the city, Mughniyeh would have been an obvious candidate to carry out many of these tasks.

Sixty-three people lost their lives in the bombing of the US Embassy in Beirut in April 1983, and hundreds more were wounded. Only seventeen were Americans, but they included Ames, who died along with seven of his CIA colleagues, effectively wiping out the agency's bureau in Beirut and decades of accumulated knowledge and contacts. Another was Lee Stevens, the Little Drummer Girl, who had been meeting a US official to discuss assistance to Palestinians in Sabra and Shatila. Most of the casualties were local Lebanese: translators, advisers, secretaries and cleaners, as well as pedestrians on the Corniche. Witnesses described bodies hurled out to sea by the blast, rescuers scooping body parts into buckets and a deafened, temporarily deranged security guard walking through the wreckage shouting 'It's gonna blow, it's gonna blow' again and again.

Once again, responsibility for the attack was claimed by Islamic Jihad – or at least by someone purporting to represent them – in a telephone call to the Agence France Presse. 'This operation is part of the Iranian revolution's campaign against the imperialist presence in Lebanon . . . We will continue to strike at the imperialist presence in Lebanon, including the multinational force,' a man said in classical Arabic and then hung up.

Investigators from the CIA later traced several individuals who had apparently played key roles in the attack. One was a senior former Fatah intelligence officer married to the daughter of a prominent Shia politician. Another was a veteran of the Black September campaign of violence in western Europe. A third was Mughniyeh.

Nothing much improved in Lebanon through the summer of 1983. The apparently random violence on the streets of Beirut intensified, with assassinations and bombings blamed on a variety of factions, including – and with some justification, as it later turned out – Israeli intelligence services. Visitors described the sound of 'staccato bursts of automatic fire as Palestinian and Lebanese leftists were rubbed out by . . . Maronite Christian militia gangs'. Every month the list of foreigners and local Lebanese bundled by armed men into battered vehicles never to be seen again grew longer. Travelling any distance involved tense, frightening negotiations with any of dozens of militia or regular forces. Returning to Beirut from Baalbek, Fisk drove through checkpoints successively manned by Iranians, fighters from the PFLP, Syrian troops, Syrian intelligence agents, the Israeli army, the Phalange, Lebanese national soldiers, French paratroopers and US Marines.

Any hopes raised by the possibility of a US-brokered peace deal between Israel and the government of Amin Gemayel were soon dashed. The Lebanese president had been lukewarm about the whole agreement while Assad, who had received a massive transfusion of weapons from Moscow, was unwilling to withdraw his troops from Lebanon, a prerequisite for Israel doing the same. Not that Menachem Begin ever appeared likely to do so either. When Israeli forces retreated from the central Chouf mountains, they did so unilaterally, and bloody clashes immediately broke out there between Christians and Druze militia led by the young warlord Walid Jumblatt, who usually appeared in public wearing a leather jacket and biker boots. In one of those shifts of allegiance that marked the entire civil war in Lebanon, and which US and other policy-makers in distant capitals had great difficulty tracking, the Druze, whose military capabilities made up for their relative lack of numbers, were now aligned with the Syrians, despite the fact that it was they who had killed Jumblatt's father Kamal in 1978.

Down at the international airport, where their main base was sited, the US component of the international peacekeeping force in Lebanon was having a torrid time, subjected to constant mortar fire and sniping. These attacks caused limited casualties but were unsettling. Which of the many possible perpetrators was actually responsible was often unclear. Most were blamed on the Druze, not unfairly, but various other factions acting as Syrian proxies were also involved, as well as some of the few Palestinian armed groups who had retained a presence in Lebanon.

The Marines themselves were increasingly frustrated by strict rules of engagement that prevented them from responding to the incoming bullets, shells and mortar rounds with their far superior firepower. Those further up the chain of command, including senior White House officials and Reagan himself, persisted in the belief that the US could somehow save the Lebanese from themselves. In reality, their forces were seen as merely another actor in the chaotic struggle for power, and thus another legitimate target.

By late September, the Americans at the airport were receiving a dozen warnings every week of new threats. 'One day they said we should look out for dogs with TNT strapped to their bellies,' a Marine posted at the airport remembered later. 'For a few days we were shooting every dog around.' Senior officers knew their men faced a greater threat than exploding canines, but any information received from the Lebanese intelligence services or other sources was maddeningly imprecise. Many such warnings mentioned car bombs, and in mid-October there was an attack on a Marines convoy with a vehicle packed with explosives, but none suggested the sheer scale of the threat they faced. 'A pickup truck, ambulances, UN vehicles, myriad types. Those ... things we had taken appropriate countermeasures toward. But never the sheer magnitude of [a] dump truck going ... 60 miles an hour with an explosive force from 12,000 to 16,000 [pounds of TNT]. When was the last time you heard of a bomb that size?', Colonel Timothy Geraghty, the commander of the thousand or more Marines based at Beirut's airport, explained much later. For that was what was being planned.

A weak point in the Marines' defences at the airport was the nineteen-tonne tanker which brought them water every day. A team organised by the new arrivals in Baalbek and their Lebanese allies had been carefully watching the truck and had built an exact replica in an underground garage in Haret Hreik, a once mostly Christian neighbourhood close to the airport that had been largely taken over by Shia displaced during the war. On 22 October, the real water truck was seized at gunpoint and hidden. A day later, at around 6.20 a.m., the substitute vehicle, filled with a huge quantity of explosives, twice circled the parking lot of the old airport administration block, which was being used by the Marines as a barracks, then crashed through a chain-link fence and barbed wire barrier, swerved past a wall of sandbags and accelerated towards the building. A stunned guard remembered a smiling, bearded, dark-haired young man at the wheel, a pause, an orange flash and a vast explosion.

This blast was even greater than the one that had destroyed much of the US Embassy six months earlier. It razed the forty-foot-high concrete and steel structure, leaving a crater twenty feet deep. The Marines had been ordered to sleep in their barracks because of the constant shelling of their bunkers on the perimeter of the airport and this, combined with the early hour of the attack, raised the death toll considerably. In all, 241 US servicemen died. According to some accounts, Mughniyeh watched the attack through binoculars, though quite what part he actually played in the attack is still unclear.

Minutes after the explosion at the airport, there was another huge blast on the other side of Beirut. Another truck had detonated at the base of the French contingent in the capital, a few miles north. Guards had managed to shoot the driver but not prevent him from triggering a massive bomb which demolished much of the nine-storey building, killing fifty-eight soldiers, mainly French paratroopers.

Both attacks were claimed once more by Islamic Jihad in telephone calls to news agencies. Two days later, the group published a statement in Beirut newspapers describing itself as 'soldiers of God [who] crave death', ready to turn Lebanon into another Vietnam. The group stressed its patriotic as well as religious credentials. 'We are not Iranians or Syrians, or Palestinians. We are Lebanese Muslims who follow the dictates of the Koran,' the statement read.

The question in Washington and Paris was how to respond. Few there had any clear idea. Thirteen years earlier, when decision-makers in the US and Europe had been confronted by the PFLP's simultaneous multiple plane hijackings, followed by the standoff in Jordan, they had had little real understanding of the threat they then faced, so dramatically different as it was from anything faced previously. And so it was again: not only did they lack strategic, legal or indeed moral certainties to guide them, they had not even the vocabulary to describe the new threat. Journalists, soldiers and spies alike fell back on stereotypes, referring to 'kamikaze' fanatics and zealots, or simply 'Mysterious Death Warriors' driving 'flying truck bombs'.

Badly rattled, the commanders of the international forces in Beirut took new precautions, reinforcing protection of their bases with concrete blocks and barriers. Anti-aircraft batteries were installed on the roof of the US facilities in the city to protect against 'Shia suicide pilots', and the ships of the Sixth Fleet were warned that they might be targeted by flying planes loaded with explosives. The CIA complained of a mass of disinformation and false alerts but then added to both by warning that Shia militants in the Middle East were likely to join forces with Ilich Ramírez Sánchez in order to launch attacks in Europe. Congressmen in Washington predicted a wave of terrorism in the US. George H. W. Bush, now vice president, flew in to Beirut to make clear that the US would not 'let a bunch of insidious terrorist cowards shake the foreign policy of the United States'.

The overwhelming military firepower that the US had amassed in or near Lebanon offered the most obvious way of retaliating against the shadowy force who had attacked them. 'I cannot get it out of my head that some F-14 warplanes coming in at about 200ft over the Marines and blowing hell out of a couple of artillery emplacements . . . would deliver a message to those gun-happy middle east terrorists,' Reagan had written in his diary shortly before the bombing. The president had also signed a directive allowing the use of the F-14 fighters aboard the USS *Independence*, which was then cruising a mile or so off Beirut. In the aftermath of the bombing, these offered a potential means of reprisal – but against whom?

Hours after the attack at the airport, Reagan told Margaret Thatcher that 'the Iranians did it and they are the same ones who blew up our embassy.' The president used similar words in a televised address four days later, informing Americans that 'circumstantial evidence' suggested that the 'hideous, insane . . . act was performed by a group of Iranian radicals, the same ones that destroyed our embassy last April'. This was broadly true, and though US intelligence agencies pointed out that there was 'no smoking gun', intercepted communications between Tehran and the Iranian ambassador to Syria strongly suggested Iranian knowledge and sponsorship. Reagan also told Americans that he held responsible a 'tyranny of forces hostile to the West' led by the Soviets, who had encouraged violence in Lebanon, where they 'provided direct support through a network of surrogates and terrorists'. There was no evidence to back up this wildly misleading allegation.

The US joint chiefs of staff drew up a plan for bombing military targets in Iran, the headquarters of the Revolutionary Guards in Tehran and critical infrastructure for its oil industry, but any such attack would have been difficult to justify internationally and would have sent the price of oil soaring. An internal row between senior officials stymied a joint raid with the French against the bases of Hezbollah and the Iranian force in the Beqa'a. While Washington prevaricated, the Israelis did not hesitate to launch a series of air strikes when a suicide bomber killed twenty-eight Israelis and more than thirty Lebanese prisoners in another attack on an intelligence service headquarters in Tyre. These targeted some Palestinian camps and other facilities, as was customary, but were aimed primarily at 'pro-Iranian Shiite Moslem radicals just three miles from the Syrian border', the *Washington Post* reported. As on so many previous occasions, these attacks had little effect, merely continuing a failed and failing strategy.

Next it was the turn of the French, who had tired of waiting for the squabbling US officials and their indecisive commander-in-chief to act. Eight Super Étendard fighters were launched from the aircraft carrier *Clemenceau* against the main Hezbollah base at Baalbek. Officials initially claimed that the raid had inflicted heavy casualties and destroyed the residence of the organisation's presumed leader. Further investigation by French media revealed that any damage had been negligible and no casualties inflicted at all, not least because the base had been evacuated following a warning of the impending attack from an embittered senior French official.

Finally, in early December, the US launched an air strike against Syrian anti-aircraft batteries in the Beqa'a valley. This was an attractive target because Damascus was believed to have supported the bombing of both the Marines' barracks and the US Embassy and was also seen as a Soviet proxy. The first suspicions had some foundation in fact, while the latter was incontrovertible, though the relationship was more complex than many in Washington thought. Syrian batteries were also bothersome to US planes over Lebanon. The raid did not go well, however. Two F-14s were shot down, one pilot killed and his co-pilot captured. Further escalation was now inevitable.

For several months, American warships in the Mediterranean had been firing on Lebanese targets. In August, they had bombarded Druze militia who were then pressing the Christian-dominated Lebanese national army of Amin Gemayel's regime back towards the eastern outskirts of Beirut. Later, the warships targeted Palestinian factions too. These strikes were loud and intimidating but largely ineffective.

On 12 December, a suicide attacker detonated a massive truck bomb inside the US Embassy in Kuwait, causing extensive damage and killing five, though no Americans. The French Embassy had also been targeted, as had Kuwait's principal oil refinery, electricity distribution hub and desalination plant in what appeared to be a bid to collapse the country's basic infrastructure. Once more, Islamic Jihad claimed responsibility. Within hours, Reagan had been informed that the group, though 'little known', was probably 'a cover for Iranian agents or Lebanese Shia connected with Iran'. Later it would become clear that Mughniyeh's cousin and brother-in-law, another veteran of Fatah and Force 17, had been the leader of the attack in Kuwait, with the al-Dawa organisation – the backbone of Shia Islamist opposition in Iraq to Saddam's regime – providing most of the manpower. The possibility that the attacks might have been inspired by the increasingly vocal and generous support offered by both the US and France to Iraq in its war against Iran seems to have escaped US analysts and policy-makers, at least immediately.

The US now reached for, literally, its biggest guns. Since late September, the USS *New Jersey*, built in the Second World War for service in the Pacific and last in action during the Vietnam war in 1968, had been cruising the eastern Mediterranean. The battleship had recently been brought back into service as part of Reagan's effort to expand the US military at a moment of the most extreme Cold War tension for decades. The vessel was enormous, displacing 45,000 tonnes, with a crew of nearly 2,000 and armed with nine sixteen-inch guns, the largest of any naval vessel afloat.

When, on 14 December, the *New Jersey* began firing at Syrian positions east of Beirut, journalists stood on the roof of the Associated Press bureau to watch. Though hardened by years of conflict, they were awestruck. 'It was like a spell,' Fisk wrote later. 'The barrels would bloom fire, a big tulip of golden flame as long as the battleship, a gaseous sunlit balloon that would evaporate in the evening sky . . . Then the concussion wave would swamp us as the wind might slam a dungeon door in a great castle . . . And then the little, tell-tale harmless reverberation far across the mountains.' For an hour or so, the vast ship sent shells weighing as much as a small car hurtling over the city to land up to twenty miles inland. Quite what damage they did on impact was less clear. In Damascus, officials said one Syrian soldier was injured but mentioned no other casualties or damage to Syrian anti-aircraft guns or missile emplacements.

The *New Jersey* maintained an intermittent bombardment of Syrian and Druze targets over the following ten days. Then the routine was broken. It was nearly Christmas and famous visitors from the US had arrived. On 24 December, Bob Hope, the eighty-year-old veteran entertainer, was joined by eighteen-year-old actress and model Brooke Shields for a show on the battleship for 400 Marines flown in from their airport base. The two stars sang carols, played jazz standards and told jokes. Hope raised a laugh with his praise for the Mediterranean weather and the views from the ship, then made a few mildly suggestive comments to Shields, who was wearing a close-fitting, silver lamé dress. The comedian also delivered a special edition of a local newspaper from Long Beach, California, the USS *New Jersey*'s home port, composed of letters from families and friends, along with 140,000 giant chocolate chip cookies, weighing a total of 3,000 pounds, donated by a cookie company.

The battleship continued shelling targets in Lebanon over the following two months, on one occasion firing for more than nine hours, delivering one of the most intensive artillery bombardments by US forces anywhere since the Vietnam war. No one now pretended this would do much to advance the US goal of creating 'an independent, sovereign Lebanon, free of all foreign forces'. On 18 January, Malcolm Kerr, the popular and respected president of the American University of Beirut, was shot dead by gunmen from Islamic Jihad. The international forces could no longer keep their own citizens safe, let alone help the Lebanese.

At the end of the month, Reagan ordered the Pentagon to draw up plans for a withdrawal of the US peacekeeping contingent. A week later, Professor Frank Regier, an American academic in Beirut, was kidnapped, the first victim of a series of such abductions, most by Iranian-linked groups, that would continue for years. In mid-February, the gunmen of AMAL, which had largely stayed out of the fighting over the previous eighteen months, surged into west Beirut, easily routing the Phalangists in a few days of vicious street fighting. Much of the south of the city was already in their hands. Gemayel's government was now close to collapse.

On 26 February 1984, the last Marines boarded landing ships as more giant shells from US warships barrelled through the air overhead. Within hours, Shia militiamen had taken over their now empty bunkers at the airport. The British, the French and the Italians were soon gone too. The national army that the US had spent more than a year trying to build into a coherent force began to disintegrate. In Washington, State Department officials were phlegmatic about the future of Lebanon and the region. 'We're waiting to see what emerges,' one said.

37
The Revolutionists

In the spring of 1984, analysts at the Rand Corporation were putting the final touches to a new report on trends in international terrorism. The California-based think tank earned huge sums from its contracts with the US government but frequently sought to challenge the assumptions of its principal client.

Since the early 1970s, governments had become more proficient at combatting terrorism, the analysts wrote. It was now much harder to smuggle weapons aboard planes, embassies had become like fortresses and there were dedicated military or police units with specialised skills developed for use in hostage situations. Diplomats now travelled with bodyguards or in armoured vehicles.

Yet terrorist activity had risen inexorably over the last ten years, they warned. There were now three to four times as many terrorist attacks every year compared to the late 1960s, and each of them was generally bigger, more lethal and more indiscriminate. Even before the bombing of the US and French barracks in October, 1983 had qualified as 'the bloodiest year' since Rand had started recording casualties of terrorism a decade and a half earlier. Also, terrorists were now more likely to be 'suicidal' and their violence more frequently directed against 'ordinary citizens – bystanders who happen to be in the wrong place at the wrong time'.

The report's conclusions were stark: 'Often overshadowed by events of grander scale – the Soviet invasion of Afghanistan, the war between Iran and Iraq, the declaration of martial law in Poland – terrorists have continued to wage a hundred little wars on the boulevards and back streets from Beirut to Bogota.' Terrorism remained 'a worldwide problem' which showed 'no sign of abating and every sign of becoming less discriminate and more bloody'.

As terrorism had evolved, so too had the thinking about its nature and causes. Inevitably, both were a reflection of their times. Plane hijacking had once been a problem almost entirely limited to the US, but between the late 1960s and the mid-1970s, a new era of international terrorism had dawned in which it had become a global phenomenon. During this period, ideas about terrorism had evolved dramatically and a broad consensus had emerged among both experts and elected officials in the West that individuals and groups committed terrorist attacks because they sought radical transformative change – in other words, a revolution. Terrorist acts were routinely treated as criminal by the state, even if the idea that terrorism was an extension of politics went largely unquestioned. In West Germany, enormous state resources were invested in a (fruitless) effort to identify the social, economic, cultural or other factors which led an individual into violent extremism. In many countries, academic experts in the new field of terrorism studies examined the same question at great length in a multitude of seminars, conferences and lectures.

By the early 1980s, however, a new thinking had emerged and a gap between the policy-makers' approach and that of the experts – not just of academics but often of analysts within their own intelligence services – had widened. Books like those published by Binyamin Netanyahu and Claire Sterling in 1981 had argued that there was no link between politics – or at least 'revolution' – and terrorism. Instead, they said, extremist violence was a product either of state sponsorship or of individuals who were mad, bad or misled. To propose that terrorism had anything to do with broader social, political or economic factors was seen as a moral failure, even cowardice. Despite its flaws and the many dissenting voices who opposed it, this new analysis rapidly became very influential in policy-making circles.

It was attractive for many reasons, but one was that it implied a simple solution to a difficult and complex problem: if states could be made to cease their support, and wayward individuals eliminated, there would be no more terrorism. Even better, the most powerful states could act pre-emptively to head off the danger before getting involved in the messy and complicated business of trying to retaliate after being attacked.

Five weeks after the last Marine had left Beirut, President Reagan issued National Security Decision Directive 138, ordering all major departments and security agencies of the US government to significantly increase their efforts to 'attack the pressing and urgent problem of international terrorism'. The initiative was the most ambitious and wide-ranging effort yet by a US administration to tackle 'a frightening challenge to the political stability of friends and allies' that had, officials stressed, killed 6,500 people, including 2,500 Americans, in the past decade and 720 in the previous year alone. Quite what form this threat would take was unclear – experts had speculated recently about the use of nuclear, biological or chemical weapons and one had even raised the possibility of 'hijacked planes trying to crash into major buildings' in the United States – but few doubted that it was clear and present. The US, Reagan ordered, must 'work intensively ... to eliminate the threat of terrorism to our way of life' and so would ensure that 'states that practice terrorism or actively support it, will not be allowed to do so without consequence.' It was obvious to Reagan which state could be blamed above all others for providing 'support and perhaps guidance directly or indirectly' to terrorists: the USSR.

Hawks within the US administration and Congress criticised NSDD138 and the accompanying legislation for being overly bureaucratic but some analysts pointed to a different problem. Brian Jenkins, the prominent expert who had said that 'terrorism is theatre' a decade earlier, emphasised the risks of 'a declaration of war against an unspecified terrorist foe, to be fought at an unknown place and time with weapons yet to be chosen', and pointed to the mission in Lebanon as an example of an effort that had once been about 'combatting' terrorists but had evolved into a much wider war 'against terrorism'. Such an effort would be 'long' and politicians would 'struggle to persuasively claim victory', Jenkins warned.

Any objective survey of international terrorism would have reinforced such a conclusion. By 1984, continental western Europe offered the most positive example of what might be achieved in the fight against domestic extremist violence. Democracies like West Germany and Italy had been seriously destabilised by terrorism in the 1970s, but a combination of increasingly effective counter-terrorist tactics, a greater degree of international co-operation and a refusal to make immediate concessions to attackers, as well as consumerism, economic growth, wide-ranging reforms on crucial social issues, and careful if sometimes questionably constitutional use of legal process, had eventually contained the challenge posed by groups like the RAF, Revolutionary Cells or Red Brigades. The fading attraction of Marxist-Leninism, the end of the Vietnam war, the rise of alternative causes such as environmentalism and the genuine repulsion at so-called 'revolutionary violence' felt by most citizens helped too, as did the steadily diminishing support offered to violent extremists by Moscow and its satellites, particularly from 1981 onwards.

Western democracies still had much to worry about, of course, even in 1984. Deadly and determined separatist groups were very active in some countries, a motley set of home-grown right-wing extremists were an important danger, and attackers dispatched by often distant hostile states such as Iraq and Libya remained a problem. But by the time the Rand Corporation published its report on 'Trends in Terrorism' the threat from the extreme left that had once seemed so significant had faded.

In the Middle East, there was no similar victory to boast of. Here, every form of terrorism had flourished: that deployed by states against other states, by regimes against their own populations or parts of them, and by those seeking radical change against governments or their supporters. The CIA noted in an internal report in early 1984 that ninety-nine per cent of acts of terrorism in the region remained domestic, but pointed out that this was no comfort. Though most such violence was indeed rooted in 'localised political, ethnic or religious conflicts', most international terrorism was 'a spillover' from these smaller struggles. This in turn suggested that 'the battle between democracy and totalitarianism', shorthand for the Cold War, was unlikely to have any impact on terrorism in the West. Instead, it would be 'developments . . . around such issues as the Palestinian problem, pan-Arabism and Muslim Fundamentalism' that would determine not only the level of 'indigenous terrorism' in the Middle East but also of its international variant too.

The reality was that almost nowhere in the Middle East had any leaders made significant reforms or concessions that might have diverted individuals or groups from violence, whether domestic or international. European strategies in the 1970s and early 1980s to reduce extremist violence had succeeded because force had been combined with social, economic and political reform that had drained support for terrorists, leaving them isolated and, eventually, vulnerable. This was impossible for authoritarian regimes across much of the Middle East, as any intimation of weakness could lead to their fall from power. Nor could they point to any achievement that might have advanced the Palestinian cause, wasting much of their time and treasure, and frequently their subjects' blood too, on fighting each other.

Instead, any discontent was dealt with by manipulating divisions between communities, buying off potential dissidents with sinecures or lucrative contracts, the promotion of an aggressive nationalism and, above all, through coercion, fear and control. Leaders of movements calling for radical change were killed, tortured and incarcerated for decades, their writings banned, their speeches prohibited, but no serious effort was actually made to answer their criticism, let alone redress their grievances. The consequences were inevitable: a radical minority among the alienated and angry found extremist ideologies attractive, a small number of these turned to terrorism and this, as the CIA pointed out, prompted violence across the region and the world.

Simultaneously, many of the same rulers who were threatened with domestic terrorism turned to its international variant as a strategy to advance their own interests. Muammar Gaddafi, Saddam Hussein and Hafez al-Assad were perhaps the most notorious, but others such as the radical regime in Tehran used terrorism as a tool of statecraft, sending assassins thousands of miles to conduct spectacular killings of high-profile enemies or abducting dozens of civilians in a bid to gain advantage over the US. The combination of domestic 'spillover' from the Middle East and intentional use of terrorist violence as a continuation of diplomacy (or war) by other means was behind much of the continuing rise in numbers of dead and wounded outlined by the Rand Corporation.

In the case of Israel, the concessions that might have answered some of the Palestinian grievances and thus eased, if not ended, that particular conflict were simply inconceivable given the mindset of leaders at the time. For decades Israeli strategists had made security their primary objective, not peace. The former appeared attainable with the means at the country's disposal and fitted perfectly with the idea behind its creation: a place of safety for a persecuted people. The latter meant making painful compromises and taking significant risks. Just a decade later, an Israeli leader would be prepared to argue for both. In the early 1980s, with first Begin and then the equally intransigent Yitzhak Shamir in power, neither appeared conceivable.

Yet, this was the moment when the failure of Israel's strategy for its protection and defence against terrorism was becoming starkly apparent. The invasion of Lebanon in 1982 had been the culmination of almost twenty years of Israeli efforts to destroy the PLO. In the narrowest sense, 'Operation Peace for Galilee' had been successful. In 1983, the number of attacks in Israel by the PLO's various factions dropped precipitously. The organisation had called for revolution and victory, and won neither. Yasser Arafat had been forced into exile, his aides scattered, his fighters disarmed and dispersed, and Fatah was rent by a bitter and bloody internal battle which further degraded the capacity of either its leaders or its fighters to cause Israel harm. However, none of this had made Israel safer in anything other than the shortest of short terms. The vacuum left in Lebanon by the PLO's departure had soon been filled by a more intractable and dangerous enemy.

This was true elsewhere in the region too. Those rulers that had successfully targeted secular, leftist and Arab nationalist groups which sometimes used terrorism had rarely won more than a Pyrrhic victory. The left-wing groups that had led the violent opposition to the shah had been destroyed by his security services well before the revolution of 1978, but this had allowed the radical clerics to take a much more prominent role in the campaign against his rule and eventually seize power. In Egypt and Iraq, any activists suspected of genuine commitment to Marxist-Leninist ideologies had been the focus of brutal repression while Islamists had been tacitly encouraged, until President Sadat had been killed by them.

Even in so-called 'revolutionary states', including Algeria, Syria or Yemen, opposition to supposedly socialist or outright Marxist regimes had been co-opted or destroyed. The Arabian peninsula had been effectively purged of the few leftists or Arab nationalists who had survived the 1960s, while an intolerant and implicitly revolutionary strand of religious observance was deliberately strengthened. In Libya, Colonel Muammar Gaddafi forged his own idiosyncratic, autocratic path, allowing no dissent while sponsoring scores of 'revolutionary groups' and commissioning scores of terrorist attacks. He too would reap the Islamist whirlwind.

The early and mid-1980s saw further expansion of Islamic militancy which would soon mount direct challenges to these regimes. As Islamists in prison in Egypt had told interviewers shortly before the assassination of Sadat, they enjoyed natural advantages in societies where most people were raised as Muslims, particularly following the resurgence of faith from the late 1960s. Communism and socialism offered social justice but ignored identity. Political Islam, and its violent fringe, offered both. This was true in Lebanon, where the coalition of Shia groups now known widely as Hezbollah continued to grow in strength and would soon oust the more moderate AMAL to assume the leadership of the Shia communities of the country. It was true in Gaza, where Islamists were fast making inroads, including the ostensibly quietist activists who would eventually form the armed and violent Harakat al-Muqawama al-Islamiyya, or Hamas, before the decade was over. It was true too in Jordan, Turkey, Afghanistan, Sudan and more or less everywhere else from northern Nigeria to the Philippines.

Western media continued to portray these 'Islamo-fascists' or 'fundamentalists' as a curiosity, either romanticising them as defenders of tradition or dismissing them as crazed fanatics. Within Western security agencies, attitudes varied. In 1984, even as they ramped up support for the mujahideen fighting Soviet troops in Afghanistan, US agencies produced lengthy reports on those in the Islamic world who were turning 'to militancy and terrorism to unseat unpopular secular leaders or "impure" Muslim leaders' and highlighted the threat they might pose to US allies. But there was little sense in London or Washington of any danger to their own citizens, at least those who stayed at home. The Islamists might become a local threat, it was generally believed, but not an international one. When in 1984 Mossad specialists who had long exchanged information with Britain about Palestinian factions began warning their British counterparts that the UK could be a target, they were met with scepticism and some suspicion. Like most Western intelligence services, their focus remained elsewhere: on the latest radical leftist splinter groups, nationalist separatist organisations and specific teams of assassins or bombers sent by Middle Eastern regimes, including the few veterans of the 1960s or 70s who somehow remained at large and active.

By the summer of 1984, the bloody campaign being waged against France by Ilich Ramírez Sánchez had reached a stalemate. His fiancée, Magdalena Kopp, arrested two years previously on the Champs Élysées, remained in a high-security prison on the outskirts of Paris, with at least thirty months of her sentence left to serve. So too did Bruno Bréguet, her Swiss accomplice in the effort launched by the Organisation of Internationalist Revolutionaries (OIR) to bomb the offices of the *al-Watan al-Arabi* newspaper and the Kuwaiti Embassy in the French capital.

There was no indication whatsoever that President François Mitterrand was prepared to risk the political opprobrium at home and abroad that the premature liberation of either of them might bring. The subtle manipulation of a trial to ensure relatively lenient sentences was one thing; freeing convicted members of a group now conspicuously responsible for killing and maiming French men and women in France was entirely different.

The toll of the OIR's campaign to free Kopp and Bréguet had mounted since the first months after their arrest. In August 1983, the group had placed a bomb on the third floor of the French cultural centre in West Berlin. It had caused extensive damage and killed a young protester hoping to hand in a petition against the Mitterrand government's programme of nuclear testing in the Pacific. Five months later, on New Year's Eve, the OIR bombed a high-speed train travelling through the Rhône valley and the principal rail terminus in Marseille, killing five and injuring dozens more. In a communiqué claiming responsibility, Ramírez said these attacks were retaliation for the (ineffective) French air raids in Lebanon's Beqa'a valley. This bid for broader legitimacy for a 'dirty private war', as Johannes Weinrich, Ramírez's right-hand man, had described the OIR's campaign just two years earlier, fooled almost no one.

Though the French security services undoubtedly found it extremely difficult to protect their citizens from Ramírez and his associates, the OIR was nowhere close to being able to generate the kind of violence that might conceivably have forced Mitterrand to make the concessions they were seeking. In reality, the group's international reach was patchy and the competence of its key operatives far from assured. A series of ambitious plans – to bomb a luxury hotel on the French Riviera, to assassinate a French general and to attack several French embassies – had all failed. French police had seized a van full of weapons destined for Basque separatists at the Italian border, and when the OIR were commissioned by Libya to assassinate the Saudi Arabian ambassador to Greece, they killed a driver but left the principal target unscathed. Funds were running even lower than a year or so before. In a letter to Weinrich in August 1983, Ramírez complained that the expenses of the Berlin bombing had left just $15,000 in reserve and warned once more that no unnecessary expenditure would be tolerated.

The most obvious challenge for the OIR was diplomatic. Relations with the regimes in central and eastern Europe that had once offered grudging but vital hospitality to the group had soured further. Czech and Hungarian authorities had both made clear that a short stay by the leaders of the OIR might be tolerated, but not residence. The villa on the Hill of Roses in Budapest had been vacated and Ramírez's prized Mercedes sold. The Prague safehouses had long been shut. Weinrich's boast at a meeting with Salah Khalaf, the PLO's head of security, that Ramírez and he were 'everywhere and nowhere' and would only be 'tracked down [when] in our tomb', was grotesque braggadocio.

The only regimes which remained supportive of the OIR were Romania and East Germany – and even these were hardly reliable. The Securitate had never got over the OIR's imprecise bombing of Radio Free Europe in Munich, while Nicolai Ceauşescu, Romania's mercurial, dictatorial ruler, now hoped for closer relations with the West. The Stasi, meanwhile, were increasingly fearful that Western intelligence services would learn of their support for the most wanted, most famous terrorist in the world. This would not only be intensely embarrassing but could have significant economic consequences. Flagging economic growth already threatened the East German model of 'consumer Communism' and had led to rising discontent. If Western countries halted transfers of technology, ended the discounted loans from Western banks and blocked investment, the results could be devastating.

The OIR's activities in 1983 confirmed for the Stasi's director, Erich Mielke, that 'the ratio of [potential] political damage to operational benefit' of shielding or supporting the OIR had changed. His officers had been appalled by a plan Ramírez and Weinrich had hatched to free Klaus Barbie, the ageing Nazi official responsible for dispatching tens of thousands of French Jews to death camps, who had been extradited from Bolivia earlier in the year and was then being held in a French jail awaiting trial on charges of committing war crimes. The bombing of the French cultural centre in West Berlin had been carried out using rare, high-powered explosives that the Stasi had confiscated from Weinrich a year earlier and then handed over to the Syrian Embassy, which had promptly returned them to Weinrich. This meant that only one intermediary separated East German security services from lethal terrorist violence against a Western European government. When called in by the Stasi for a stiff reprimand, Weinrich was entirely unrepentant, warning the service that the OIR had the capacity to strike where and when it wanted, independent of East German support.

By the spring of 1984, the Stasi was convinced Western intelligence services had finally learned about the OIR presence in East Germany. Detailed accounts of OIR operations in East Germany had started appearing in West German media. These appeared to be based on the revelations of a defector from the group, who had turned himself in to Swiss authorities a year earlier, and on information provided by an agent run inside the group by West German security services. The Stasi asked the KGB for advice but, as ever, received none. The East Germans were well aware that the Soviet authorities had refused the Venezuelan's multiple requests for entry between 1980 and 1984, which should have told them all they needed to know about the KGB's attitude towards him. If they were going to continue their support for Ramírez and his OIR, they would be on their own.

The new and ambitious security directive issued by Reagan in April may also have helped the Stasi to their decision. The directive explicitly ordered that 'state-sponsored and organised terrorism should be appropriately exposed ... in every available forum' and sanctions imposed on those responsible. Senior US officials would soon be dropping heavy hints to east European diplomats indicating that Washington knew much more about the Stasi's relationship with the OIR than had been revealed hitherto. Weinrich's year-long multiple entry visa to the GDR was promptly cancelled, and in September he was turned away at East Berlin's Schönefeld airport. Back in Budapest, Weinrich was placed under heavy and obvious surveillance, prompting his rapid departure from Hungary too. Cash was now so tight that Weinrich borrowed money from his elderly parents, whom he had not seen for so long that he had to check if they were still alive before tapping them for a loan.

For several months in 1983, Ramírez had lived incognito in Belgrade, where he had rented an apartment and spent much time in the luxurious Hotel Yugoslavia. Detected by the local authorities in the early autumn, he had been forced to move to neighbouring Bulgaria, before once more being sent on his way. Ramírez had then spent much of the winter and spring of 1984 in Damascus, where he had built close ties with members of Assad's inner circle. The Syrians had been impressed with at least some of the operations the OIR had carried out for them in western Europe and were happy to offer a haven. They had uses for men like Ramírez in Lebanon, where there were plenty of people they wanted either scared or killed. Ramírez did not like the Syrian capital particularly, but at least it was relatively safe. At the end of the summer of 1984, Weinrich flew to join him there.

Kopp spent much of her time at Fresnes high-security prison in the institution's hospital, confined to a spacious cell on the top floor painted in pastel shades and with a large window through which she could see the sunrise and sunset. Unaware of much of what was happening in the world outside or of the relatively privileged conditions in which she was being held, the thirty-four-year-old spent long days knitting sweaters, practising yoga and meditating. On Sunday afternoons she watched children's TV programmes with other inmates, and regularly saw her lawyer Jacques Vergès who brought newspapers and made sexual advances. Ramírez told his followers that he was not worried about his fiancée because he knew she was fed decently and guaranteed a bed for the night, which he said was more than any other member of the OIR could expect. When Kopp was freed just over a year after Ramírez arrived in Syria, she was deported to West Germany and, following a lengthy interrogation by the police, ended up at her mother's home near Ulm. Ramírez called her there only a few days after her arrival, saying just 'Hello, how are you?' before hanging up. Kopp understood she was being summoned and flew within days to Damascus. She would not return to Germany for many years.

The first day of the trial of Brigitte Mohnhaupt in February 1984 did not go as smoothly as the German authorities had hoped. A crowd of around a hundred supporters stood outside the high-security prison complex at Stammheim chanting 'Solidarity with political prisoners of the Red Army Faction', their words clearly audible within the fortified courtroom. Shortly afterwards, the judge was forced to clear the packed public gallery after formal submissions by the lawyers were drowned out by loud, co-ordinated coughing. Eventually, after Mohnhaupt and her co-defendant, a thirty-one-year-old RAF veteran called Christian Klar, started shouting obscene abuse, leading to scuffles with police officers, the hearings were suspended for several days.

As leader of the RAF in 1977 Mohnhaupt had overseen the fiasco of Mogadishu and the abduction and murder of businessman Hans Martin Schleyer in a forest on the border between Belgium and France. Her subsequent years on the run had come to an abrupt end when West German police got a lucky break in the early autumn of 1982. Two men hunting mushrooms in a wood south of Frankfurt found some carefully buried plastic bins which turned out to be full of weapons, false identity papers, wads of cash and an archive of RAF documents meticulously documenting the group's past operations. Specialists quickly cracked a code based on the names of RAF members and so were able to read maps that indicated the location of another seventeen similar caches. These were all placed under surveillance by a total of 3,000 police officers.

Three weeks later, two women carrying shoulder bags and folding shovels were seen approaching a suspected cache in woodland on the outskirts of Frankfurt. One, wearing a blue duffel coat against the October chill, was a twenty-seven-year-old RAF militant called Adelheid Schulz. The other, in a lambskin leather jacket with her long blonde hair cut short and dark rings of exhaustion around her eyes, was Mohnhaupt. Armed officers from GSG9 – the unit that had been formed after the debacle of the Munich Olympics – were watching from hideouts among the trees and bushes.

Mohnhaupt was armed too, but the Polish-made machine pistol she carried was in her shoulder bag and wrapped in protective plastic. When the police shouted at her to surrender, this left her about as much time to decide whether to obey or to fight as Ulrike Meinhof had had twelve years earlier when faced with the choice between giving herself up or following Andreas Baader out of the window of a Berlin library. Mohnhaupt decided that to reach for her gun would have been suicide. Instead, she and Schultz were swiftly immobilised and transferred to high-security prisons. Klar was detained five days later when he approached another cache near Hamburg.

Thirty-four years old at the time of her trial, accused of blackmail, kidnapping, attempted murder and nine counts of murder, Mohnhaupt could expect to spend much of her future life back behind bars. Most of the charges related to the terrific violence of 1977. This now seemed a long time ago, almost another era. 'As the last two RAF protagonists are put on trial in Stammheim, this much is certain: the concept of the urban guerrilla as an underground army is dead. In the Federal Republic of Germany, there will no longer be a new terrorist organisation along the lines of the old RAF,' *Der Spiegel* told readers in its report on the opening of Mohnhaupt's trial.

By now almost all of the second generation of the RAF were either incarcerated or in East Germany as guests of the Stasi or inactive. There were plenty of protest movements still active in West Germany, as in most of western Europe, but the various mobilisations against nuclear weapons, nuclear power, US foreign policy, environmental issues or mainstream politics rarely spilled over into genuine violence.

The RAF and other extremist groups were not entirely without support. West German security services believed that although there were only a couple of dozen members of the group who were prepared to commit violence themselves, there were 'concentric circles' of more numerous supporters who willingly provided logistic help – as they had done at the very beginning of the RAF's campaign – and this allowed a small amount of relatively amateurish activity to continue.

In mid-December 1984, more than nine months after Mohnhaupt's trial had begun, a car loaded with explosives was discovered near the NATO Officers' School in Oberammergau, in Bavaria. A faulty timing mechanism meant the bomb did not detonate but as the RAF pointed out to authorities: 'We only have to be lucky once, you have to be lucky always.' This was a quote from the Provisional Irish Republican Army, which a few months earlier had failed – but only just – to kill Margaret Thatcher. The RAF could pull off no such feat, however, and a month or so later there were two incidents in which bombers blew themselves up before they could do any harm.

In a statement read out in the courtroom at Stuttgart-Stammheim high-security prison – the same place where the leaders of the first generation of the RAF had been tried and sentenced – Mohnhaupt admitted that 'the West European guerrilla' confronted 'especially difficult conditions'. The years of struggle had brought both 'mass casualties and critical defeats' for revolutionaries everywhere, she said. The enemies of the proletariat – 'counterrevolution, war, and fascism, on the one hand, and the different methods of social democracy, consumption, and the state on the other' – remained strong.

Yet, there was hope, she insisted. Making references to Che Guevara and Jean-Paul Sartre, who had died in 1980, Mohnhaupt argued that, as the bitter struggles fought and won in Algeria, Vietnam, South Yemen and Latin America had mobilised revolutionaries across the world twenty years previously, so too would her and her comrades' struggles then taking place in western Europe, Nicaragua, Mozambique, Angola and Cambodia. In Lebanon, for example, the failure of 'the heaviest bombardments since the Vietnam war' to bring about an American victory revealed that the whole imperialist 'machine' was now facing a level of resistance that would cause its 'power to collapse'. A new international alliance would eventually bring victory, Mohnhaupt promised. Fifteen months later, she and Christian Klar were sentenced to five life sentences each, disappearing into German prisons for twenty-two and twenty-three years respectively.

By February 1984, more of Ayatollah Ruhollah Khomeini's revolutionary vision had been realised than anyone had thought remotely possible when the elderly cleric had stepped from the Air France jumbo jet onto the tarmac of Tehran's international airport five years earlier. In a speech to the nation to commemorate the anniversary of his return to Iran, the country's supreme guide and leader described the survival of his revolutionary regime as a 'miracle'.

The war with Iraq, now in its fourth year, had allowed a massive expansion of the state. The government's authority was now established across most of the territory of Iran, and there were now 850,000 bureaucrats managing the daily life of some 45 million Iranians. The Islamic Revolutionary Guards Corps could boast 150,000 fighters, the pick of new imported weaponry and its own ministry. Even if the economy was still in an appalling state, surging oil prices brought in $23 billion in 1983, not much less than the revenue enjoyed by the shah in his last years, which was enough to fund massive subsidies of basic essentials. The 'Cultural Revolution' that had purged the universities of enemies of the regime had been deemed a success, and students had returned to their campuses. 'Alcohol, cosmetics, Western music and Western entertainment are forbidden. Even the ubiquitous Muzak has been banished from the elevators of the Tehran Hilton, which has been renamed the Freedom Hotel,' one Western correspondent reported. Few now contested strict segregation of women and men and rules imposing a conservative religious order, though there was still much grumbling among the educated and more Westernised upper middle classes. The war had cost as many as 120,000 Iranian lives and immense sums of money but, for the moment at least, it still enjoyed significant popular support, especially among Khomeini's political and social base.

In the spring of 1983, the regime had moved to destroy the Communist party in Iran, known as Tudeh. Its leaders, guided by Moscow, had remained convinced that, as taught by the laws of Marxist historical determinism, the reactionary regime would eventually give way to a socialist state, and so had avoided confrontation with the radical clerics, supporting them in their anti-imperialist or anti-capitalist initiatives and ignoring much else. Seventy senior officials were arrested and then Tudeh was proscribed, with all its remaining members ordered to report to the office of the prosecutor general. Soon, the party's leader appeared on live television confessing his 'espionage, deceit and treachery', and telling viewers that his mistakes deserved 'the most severe punitive actions that the Islamic Republic may decide to mete out'. Britain's most senior official in Iran suggested 'half in jest' to London that 'perhaps the Islamic Republic's torture was more effective than that of the Shah.' The executions would begin within weeks.

When Farrokh Negahdar, now thirty-six and still the leader of the Fedayeen-e Khalq, heard of the raids against the Communists, he convened an emergency meeting of its politburo. It was now clear that flight offered the only hope of survival. Soon, dozens of Negahdar's comrades had left their hideouts in Tehran and other cities and headed north on the clandestine routes he had plotted for this eventuality a year earlier. Travelling more than 500 miles in cars or by motorbike, staying with trusted members of their organisation, they made their way to the frontier with the Azerbaijani Soviet Socialist Republic. In theory safety lay across the mountains and the border, though it was often difficult to learn much of what happened to those who successfully made the crossing, and now a rumour was circulating that Moscow had done a deal with the radical regime in Tehran and would send back any such fugitives.

When Negahdar's turn came, he left the secret safehouse that for months had been his home in Tehran and headed north with his wife, Saba, and fifteen-month-old son. Close to the frontier, they joined up with another family and continued on foot. It was dark, cold and frightening. The two families had been told by local guides to hike to the top of a pass and then take a track which would lead them, after fifteen minutes, to the border. But Negahdar slipped into a stream and the fugitives were separated. He stumbled on alone, clutching his swaddled child to his chest, slipping and falling on the wet rocks. Then he saw a hut with light in the windows. Arriving at it he knocked and heard dogs barking. The door was opened by border guards, who pulled him inside. The other family and Saba were found not far away.

It was now midnight. The border guards contacted their superiors. None of the fugitives had received any news of those who had fled before them, nor had any contacts in the USSR, as only Tudeh had a relationship with Moscow. Negahdar still did not know if the rumour was true and whether the regime in Tehran had convinced the Soviets to return anyone trying to escape its borders. An hour later, a senior officer arrived and, to everyone's immense relief, announced that not only was Negahdar known to the KGB but that Moscow had ordered that he should be 'received as a guest'.

In the morning, Negahdar was driven down from the border with his family. The journey allowed him his first view of the Soviet Union. He had committed his life to Marxist-Leninism in his teens, seen his best friend killed and spent the best part of a decade in prison as a result of his activism. The USSR, or this particular corner of it at least, looked 'poor and dirty and very underdeveloped' compared to Iran, Negahdar decided. The ersatz chocolate he was given was inedible, the road bad, the uniforms of the frontier guards frayed. It was a bitter disappointment.

Mohsen Sazegara, in contrast, appeared to be thriving. Since leaving the Revolutionary Guards and his work at the national broadcasting service, the thirty-year-old had enjoyed a rapid rise through the ranks of the new regime's bureaucracy. He was now head of Iran's Industrial Development and Renovation Organisation, founded in the 1960s as part of the shah's push for modernisation. Sazegara, despite his relative youth and lack of experience, was in charge of tens of thousands of workmen at hundreds of different sites, producing everything from family cars, pipes and boilers to bridging equipment for the armed forces. Yet he was still vulnerable. Powerful men within the regime were convinced that Sazegara had been complicit in the attack that killed President Mohamed-Ali Rajai three years earlier. His own influential sponsors had protected him but in the acrimonious factional manoeuvres that characterised the revolutionary regime, they might not be able to do so forever. In March 1984, just after the birth of his second son, Sazegara was placed under arrest on suspicion of being a traitor, in league with the Mojahedin-e-Khalq. If found guilty, he would be executed.

Sazegara was ordered to report to Evin prison for questioning, where he was left alone in an interrogation room for several hours then led down a long corridor where he saw lines of cowed, immobile prisoners, male and female, waiting for questioning. In a second corridor, he saw more terrified young people. There was shouting. 'Guard, take this [bitch] to be beaten more,' an interrogator called. When the woman pleaded that she could stand no more lashes, she was told that her sins meant she would face worse punishment 'in the next world'. This glib reference to divine justice by an official of the Islamic Republic stunned Sazegara. Twelve hours later, after the intervention of the minister of industry, his direct superior and a personal friend, he was released.

The next morning, Sazegara obtained an appointment to see Khomeini in person at the ayatollah's residence in northern Tehran. Iran's supreme leader remembered Sazegara from the months they had spent together in France some five years previously and listened carefully to his account of what he had seen in Evin. The prosecutor who had ordered the arrest of Sazegara was fired a week later, but Sazegara's faith in the revolution had been profoundly shaken. He began re-reading the books that had once inspired him in a new light. Now, Sazegara decided, the teachings of Ali Shariati, or of Khomeini himself, were not a call to freedom and liberation but to authoritarianism and violence. Eventually, Sazegara too would flee Iran, though only after further harrowing returns to Evin.

Despite his growing infirmity, Khomeini's own commitment to a true Islamic revolution in Iran and across the Muslim world remained as solid as ever. In his address in February 1984, he told Iranians that criticisms of his government were attacks against Islam and called for new resolve. 'I am nearly eighty-five years old,' he said. 'I am very weak, and I am more affected by fatigue and complaints than you. If anyone is to leave the arena, it should be me. But we have all entered an arena, and a retreat, even by as much as one step, would result in our defeat.'

Such statements were aimed particularly at the huge numbers of Iranians who were fighting and dying at that very moment on the marshy battlefields of the banks of the Tigris river. Khomeini had rejected a ceasefire offered by Saddam Hussein in 1982, deciding instead to seek regime change in Iraq, which he believed would allow for the creation of a new Islamic state there based on the country's Shia majority. In January 1984, Iran launched a vast offensive, with more than 500,000 troops mobilised in what was supposed to be a 'final blow' to end the conflict. To counter the superior weaponry and defensive advantages of Saddam Hussein's troops, the Iranians drew on their greater numbers to deploy 'human waves' of tens of thousands of poorly-trained and under-equipped fighters in a bid to overwhelm Iraq's defences.

Since the beginning of the war, the Iranian regime had sought to foster a culture that promoted martyrdom. Murals on walls in major cities depicted the Supreme Leader saying, 'Our leader is a twelve-year-old who throws himself under the tank with a grenade in hand.' Films showed mothers raging against their cowardly children who refused to fight and die. A Martyrs Fund dispensed generous welfare payments to bereaved families. In Tehran's Behesht-e Zahra cemetery, where Khomeini had made his first major speech on his return to Iran, water coloured red with dye flowed from a 'spring of blood' through pools and channels among the rows of graves.

Though 'human wave' tactics had brought some success in 1982 and 1983, the offensive of spring 1984 was an enormously costly failure. Iraqi generals, initially caught by surprise by Iran's amphibious attack through terrain they had considered impassable, quickly recovered using massive bombardments, chemical weapons and a high-tension electric power line diverted into the marshes to inflict appalling casualties on their enemies. In choking clouds of mustard or nerve gas, as many as 30,000 Iranians were killed or injured. Thousands of bodies floated in the fetid water of the marshy battlefield. Collected by earthmovers, they were dumped in mass graves so big they formed permanent landmarks.

As the offensive wound down, a reporter for the *Guardian* reached a small Iranian town, Behbehan, 150 miles from the frontlines, where a school had been hit by one of the Soviet-made Scud missiles that Iraq fired periodically at population centres in Iran. Mourners at the funeral for the seventy-two children killed in the strike called for 'jihad' against 'the unbelievers', meaning the Sunni leaders of Iraq. In the town square, buses were ready to ferry new volunteers to join the war despite the carnage. Leaning through the buses' windows, passengers raised their fists and shouted 'death to America' when they saw a Western journalist. Hamdollah, forty-seven, said he was not too old to fight but 'young and strong' and 'had such a strong faith' that he was willing to die. Ali, fifteen, said he was looking forward to meeting his older brother, already under arms, and that Iranians would 'fight for God until we win'.

Sometime in the spring of 1984, as Mohnhaupt's trial was getting underway, as Ramírez was settling into a new life in Damascus and as Sazegara was recovering from his day in Evin prison, the wealthy scion of a well-known Saudi Arabian family made a decision. Despite many trips to Pakistan since his first visit to the country more than three years before, Osama bin Laden had never visited Peshawar, the city thirty-five miles from the border with Afghanistan, let alone actually crossed into the neighbouring country. Now the time had come to see the mujahideen's war against Soviet forces and their Afghan auxiliaries at first hand.

The twenty-seven-year-old Saudi was not the only young Arab Muslim who sympathised deeply with the Afghan resistance but who had hitherto showed limited enthusiasm for any personal risk in its support. Since the Soviet invasion five years earlier, only a few dozen Arab volunteers had reached Peshawar and even fewer had actually seen combat. They came for various reasons. Some arrived with the sole intention of working as humanitarians. Others were simply fugitives, fleeing the wave of repression triggered across the Middle East by the killing of the Egyptian president. One was Mohammed al-Islambouli, the brother of the man who had led Sadat's assassins. Many of the most committed and radical came from Syria, where Assad continued to jail, torture, shoot and bomb Islamists, even as he supported them in neighbouring Lebanon. One or two had been living in western Europe.

A substantial number were inspired by the ideas of Abdallah Azzam, the scholar and propagandist who had moved from Saudi Arabia to Pakistan in 1981 to take up a university post in Islamabad. Azzam's books, which excoriated Marxism and called for a renewed commitment to 'jihad', continued to sell thousands of copies and complemented the vast and increasingly effective outreach effort funded by the Saudi Arabian government. Azzam's latest work was a compilation of stories of martyrdom and miracles supposedly witnessed by participants in the Afghan conflict. These had been collected in Peshawar, where the forty-three-year-old now spent most of his time, but may also have been influenced by the promotion of martyrdom that was then occurring in Iran. Entitled *The Signs of the Merciful in the Afghan Jihad*, it described armies of angels putting Soviet infantry to flight, birds intercepting bombs in mid-air and an exploding Koran that destroyed a tank, as well as multiple examples of the spectacular self-sacrifice of the mujahideen. It was an immediate bestseller.

Azzam had also continued to travel extensively around the Middle East and to the US to deliver lectures in which he exhorted Muslims to support the mujahideen in Afghanistan and the cause of the Palestinians, and in which he expounded on the importance of Islamic education, as well as the broader effort to resist the atheist Communists, the morally rotten West and the nefarious 'capitalist' Jews. Often, he spoke in local mosques, deploying straightforward language and wearing traditional

Afghan dress, complete with round *pakol* hat and grizzled beard. But he also lobbied the wealthy and powerful, and made a point of travelling frequently to Saudi Arabia, always for the hajj pilgrimage, but at other times too.

In the spring of 1984, Azzam was working on two major projects that would both have enormous impact. One was a text that he had been preparing for some time. This argued that an attack on a particular Muslim community anywhere constituted an attack on all the world's Muslims; that fighting in defence of any Muslim community was a religious duty for all believers wherever they were in the world; and that Muslims should defy anyone, even Islamic scholars, local governments or their fathers, who sought to stop them from fulfilling this obligation. Though many of these ideas had been advanced in some form by more mainstream Muslim thinkers or by Sunni militants in Egypt or Saudi Arabia, Azzam's extension of them to implicate all Muslims in armed struggle, combined with his rejection of local authorities, made his argument authentically revolutionary.

The second project was the founding of an office that would be able to manage the logistical needs of the many volunteers he hoped his argument would attract to the battle against the Soviets. The obvious location for the new office was in Peshawar, and preferably in Hayatabad, the more modern western part of the city closer to the frontier and the refugee camps where millions of Afghan refugees were now sheltering. But rents were high, and fuel, food and flights for the new international legion would be very costly. The magazine Azzam wanted to launch would not be cheap either. He needed a donor. And there was one obvious candidate.

When in Saudi Arabia, Azzam often stayed with bin Laden at his home in Jeddah, where he lived with his two wives and many children. The two men had remained in contact since their initial meetings some years earlier but were not close. Nonetheless, it was a convenient base for visits to both Mecca and Medina, and bin Laden deeply admired his famous guest, organising hunting trips in the desert outside the city and even agreeing to his visitor's request to turn on the air conditioning in his sparsely furnished house.

On his trips to Pakistan to deliver funds, bin Laden had often visited Azzam in Islamabad, where the older man still taught at the Islamic University. In the spring of 1984, his host suggested he travel to Peshawar and even over the border into Afghanistan. Bin Laden initially demurred, saying he was 'nervous of [such a trip]' as 'some wise people had advised against it'. This may have been a reference to cautious members of his family or to Saudi royals he knew or even to the Saudi security services, but it may simply have been an excuse for genuine fear. Azzam appears to have had little difficulty overcoming such objections. 'Do not listen to anyone,' he told bin Laden, following the anti-authoritarian logic of the fatwa he was in the process of formulating, and then offered to arrange a trip to Jaji, a mujahideen stronghold a few miles inside Afghanistan that had been the site of fierce clashes between the Afghans and the Soviets in recent years. Bin Laden agreed.

Reaching Peshawar from Islamabad was straightforward, involving a short flight from Islamabad or, more likely, a drive up the main highway, where the only real danger would have been a potential collision with one of the many garishly painted trucks and overloaded coaches decorated with dozens of mirrors that sped along the road. From Peshawar, a rough dirt road led further west through the foothills of a spur of the Hindu Kush and up to the small, scruffy town of Parachinar, a major supply hub for the Afghan mujahideen. From there, a track would have taken him up to the rocky mountain ridge that marked the unguarded frontier, then through pine forests and steep defiles scattered with desperately poor villages, some now reduced to rubble by Soviet bombing, and on to a cluster of tents and shelters surrounded by trees and boulders. There, bin Laden was hosted by the Ittehad-e Islami, the Union of Islam, a mujahideen faction led by Abdul Rasul Sayyaf, who was close to the Saudi authorities and whom bin Laden had met several times in Mecca.

The destination had been carefully chosen. In April 1984, when bin Laden visited, Jaji was relatively quiet, though there was much fighting elsewhere on the winding, broken frontlines across eastern Afghanistan. To counter criticism that his forces were doing little while other factions fought hard against the occupiers, Sayyaf had launched a media campaign to present his faction in a slightly more combative light, commissioning an amateurish documentary about his men's relatively insignificant activities and hosting Western journalists in Jaji – as well as influential Middle Eastern visitors like bin Laden.

But this did not mean there was no fighting at all. At this time the Soviets were using their as yet unchallenged air power to interdict the supply routes from Pakistan that allowed ammunition, medicine and much else to reach the mujahideen, and early one morning the base was attacked by Soviet jets. Bin Laden and his hosts scrambled into trenches as explosions around them drowned out the mujahideen's few, outdated anti-aircraft guns. 'The mountains were shaking from the bombardment, the missiles making a huge noise,' bin Laden wrote later. 'I felt closer to God than ever.'

Bin Laden later claimed that four Soviet jets were shot down during the attack. This is unlikely, as none were recorded as lost in April 1984, or anytime between February and December, and only five such aircraft had been lost to enemy fire since the war began. But such stories expressed what the experience meant to a still relatively young man who had been insulated from any physical danger or real discomfort since birth. The few days spent at the frontline had been uncomfortable, exhilarating and life-changing. Bin Laden was 'very moved', he told others, and particularly affected by the poor conditions and equipment of the mujahideen. Most importantly, the trip had convinced the young Saudi that he had found his vocation. He expressed deep regret at his failure to venture into Afghanistan earlier, saying that such a 'sin' could only be 'atoned for through martyrdom in the cause of God'. This meant a return to Afghanistan, and not simply for a short stay on a relatively quiet front.

In the meantime, there were other ways to help. When Azzam asked bin Laden if he could find the funds for his new ventures – his magazine, calling for Muslims worldwide to participate in the Afghan jihad, and an office in Peshawar to manage the volunteers – the Saudi was enthusiastic, agreeing on the spot to 'finance the presence of fifty or sixty Arabs as well as their families', a total of many hundred people. Within weeks, he had come up with between five and ten million dollars. Within months, the volunteers were arriving in Peshawar as Azzam had hoped.

Unlike those who had arrived in the early years of the war from various places and for various reasons, most of these new volunteers came with the same ambition. Like bin Laden, they wanted to join the battle against the Soviets, but this was not all. Convinced by Azzam's new global vision of the campaign to save the Islamic world from the forces of unbelief, many saw the jihad there merely as the first of many battles in a much greater armed struggle, one that would last decades, possibly centuries, maybe even millennia. Once victory had been achieved in Afghanistan, there would be other enemies, far away, who would have to be faced and fought.

Epilogue

Osama bin Laden returned to Jaji in 1987 with a small force of Arab fighters and fought a short pitched battle against Soviet special forces. A year later, he founded al-Qaeda. In 1990, a year after the end of the war against the Soviets in Afghanistan, Saudi Arabia's rulers refused bin Laden's offer to lead a force of Islamic militants to defend the kingdom against Iraq. He then travelled to Sudan, where he continued his extremist activities before, in 1996, returning to Afghanistan first as a guest of local warlords, then of the Taliban after they took control. In 1998, bin Laden oversaw the bombing of two US embassies in East Africa, and on 11 September 2001 an attack using hijacked planes against targets in New York and Washington that killed 3,000. Al-Qaeda's actions and the US-led response to them, such as the war in Iraq of 2003, triggered a wave of violence across much of the world. In 2011, bin Laden was shot dead by US special forces in a compound in northern Pakistan where he had been living for several years with domestic staff, two wives and many children and grandchildren.

Abdallah Azzam's celebrity grew through the 1980s as he continued to travel through the Middle East and the West, recruiting and raising funds. His tract *The Defence of Muslim Lands* was published in 1985 and proved immensely influential. Azzam was killed in 1989 by a car bomb in Peshawar blamed variously on Soviet, Israeli, US and Pakistani secret services.

Ayman al-Zawahiri was released from prison in 1984, just two years after his fiery speech from the cage in a Cairo courtroom, possibly as a reward for further co-operation with local authorities. He left Egypt almost immediately, travelling first to Jeddah, then reaching Peshawar in 1986 where he rebuilt the Egyptian Islamic Jihad group. By the summer of 2001, this had merged into bin Laden's al-Qaeda, which

Zawahiri led from 2011 until he was killed by a US drone strike in Kabul in September 2021.

Khomeini died in 1989, shortly after agreeing to end the Iran–Iraq war, a decision which he described as 'drinking a cup of poison'. He was succeeded as supreme leader by Ali Khamenei, who remains in power at the time of writing.

Farrokh Negahdar did not linger in Azerbaijan and spent most of the 1980s in Uzbekistan, then part of the Soviet Union. In 1990, his wife and son reached the UK. Negahdar joined them shortly afterwards, and now lives in west London.

Mohsen Sazegara was imprisoned in Evin for his opposition to the regime three more times after his short detention in 1981. He left Iran in 2004 and now lives in a suburb of Washington, DC, where he is a researcher and activist.

Ilich Ramírez Sánchez lived in Damascus until 1990, working primarily for the Syrian intelligence services, but was then expelled when Hafez al-Assad opted to support the US in the war against Iraq of that year. Refused entry to Libya, Ramírez used a diplomatic passport to enter Sudan, where he stayed until 1994 when he went into hospital in Khartoum for minor surgery on a testicle. Sudanese authorities allowed French secret services to abduct Ramírez while he was unconscious and bring him to Paris for trial for his 1975 triple murder in the city. Convicted at separate trials of throwing a grenade into a Rive Gauche café in 1974 and masterminding the series of bloody bombings in Paris and Marseille in 1982 and 1983, he is currently detained in Fresnes high-security prison.

Magdalena Kopp married Ramírez in Damascus in 1985 and gave birth to a second daughter in 1986. When forced with her husband to leave Syria in 1990, she travelled to Venezuela with their child. Kopp eventually returned to Germany, where she lived in the Bavarian town of Neu-Ulm until her death in 2015.

Hans-Joachim Klein fled to France, where he remained underground for twenty years. In 1998, married with two children, he was arrested and extradited to Germany where he served two years of a nine-year sentence for his role in the OPEC attack before being released on parole. Klein then returned to France where he lived in some poverty in a rural community in Normandy until his death in 2022.

Johannes Weinrich's movements in the 1980s and early 90s are unclear. In 1995 he was arrested in Yemen and extradited to West

Germany to stand trial for multiple terrorist offences. He was jailed for life five years later for his role in the bombing of the French cultural centre in Berlin, though acquitted of involvement in the wave of violence in France in 1982 and 1983.

When Bruno Bréguet was released from his French prison in 1985, he went back to work for Ramírez's Organisation of Internationalist Revolutionaries, travelling across western Europe and the Middle East to meet contacts from other extremist groups or to broker arms deals. In the spring of 1991, he walked into the US Embassy in Berne and offered to spy for the CIA. The agency enthusiastically accepted, putting Bréguet on a monthly salary of $3,000 and giving him the codename FDBONUS/1. Bréguet told the agency all he knew about Ramírez and his organisation, as well as many extreme leftist groups, and for the next four years he appears to have supplied information, possibly indirectly contributing key elements to the French operation to seize Ramírez in Khartoum in 1994. A year later, Bréguet disappeared while on a ferry in the Mediterranean. He drowned in what was probably an accident.

Fusako Shigenobu returned to Japan sometime between 1982 and 2000 and lived undetected until an off-duty policeman identified her by her particular manner of smoking cigarettes. In 2006, at the age of sixty, she was sentenced to twenty years in prison for her role in the 1974 attack on the French Embassy in The Hague. Diagnosed with stomach cancer in 2008, she was released in 2022. 'It's half a century ago ... but we caused damage to innocent people who were strangers to us by prioritising our battle,' she told reporters when free. 'I want to continue to reflect ... and live more and more with curiosity.'

Imad Mughniyeh became Hezbollah's most notorious clandestine operator, accused of masterminding the hijacking of a TWA passenger jet in 1985, organising the abduction of dozens of foreigners in Lebanon on orders from Tehran and conducting multiple other attacks, including many against Jewish or Israeli targets beyond the Middle East. In 1991, Mughniyeh attended a conference in Khartoum where he met bin Laden and offered training in bombing techniques to al-Qaeda members. He was assassinated by the Mossad in 2008.

Mohammed Daoud Odeh or Abu Daoud – the self-confessed tactical commander of the Munich attacks – was sidelined within Fatah after his jailhouse confession to Jordanian authorities in 1973 and spent increasing amounts of time behind the Iron Curtain. He was shot and badly wounded in Warsaw in May 1981, probably by an assassin sent by Sabri Khalil al-Banna, aka Abu Nidal. He published his memoirs in 1999, and died in Damascus in 2010.

Al-Banna survived until 2002 as an appallingly cynical, brutal and increasingly paranoiac gun for hire but was eventually killed in Baghdad, probably on the orders of Saddam Hussein.

Salah Khalaf – Abu Iyad – accompanied Arafat to Tunis in 1982 where he was killed by the Abu Nidal Organisation nine years later.

Bassam Abu Sharif was expelled from the PFLP in 1987 and joined Fatah, where he became a key adviser of Arafat and an earlier convert to what was then known without irony as 'the peace process'. He published several books, including his memoirs, and now lives in Jericho.

Mahmoud Issa fought with the PFLP in Lebanon through the 1970s. He lived in Canada from 1987 to 2013 when he was deported for failing to disclose on arrival his previous activities. Issa died of cancer in Lebanon in 2015.

Arafat escaped an Israeli raid on Tunis aimed at killing him in 1985 but his distant exile weakened both his personal authority and the PLO. The outbreak of the first Intifada or uprising in 1987, which was initially led by grass-roots activists, underlined this growing marginalisation and provided opportunities to new actors, notably the newly-founded militant Islamist group known as Hamas. The collapse of the USSR and an ill-considered decision to side with Iraq in the Gulf War weakened him further. In 1993, he stood alongside Bill Clinton and Yitzhak Rabin, Israel's prime minister, on the White House lawns for the signing of the Oslo Accords, by which Israel recognised the PLO, which in turn recognised Israel's right to exist and renounced violence. A year later, Arafat shared the Nobel Peace Prize with Rabin and moved to Gaza to run the newly created Palestinian National Authority, which was supposed to lead within five years to a Palestinian state in the occupied territories of the West Bank and Gaza. In 2000, a US effort to bring Arafat and Ehud Barak, the former special forces officer and then Israeli prime minister, to agreement over outstanding issues failed, and a new uprising, the second or al-Aqsa Intifada followed. This was very violent, with multiple suicide bombings and gun attacks in Israel and a fierce Israeli military campaign in the West Bank. In 2002, Arafat's compound was surrounded by Israeli forces. In 2004, seriously ill, he was airlifted to Paris where he died, aged seventy-five.

The second Intifada broke out immediately after a high-profile visit to Jerusalem's most fiercely disputed holy site, the walled Old City compound known to Muslims as al-Haram al-Sharif and to Jews as the Temple Mount, by Ariel Sharon, then leader of the opposition in Israel. Sharon had been forced to resign as defence minister following a judicial commission of inquiry into the 1982 Sabra and Shatila massacres but remained active in politics. He eventually took power as prime minister in 2001. Incapacitated by a stroke in 2006, Sharon died in 2014.

Once the furore caused by his espionage activities had died down, Gunnar Ekberg enjoyed a successful career in advertising and as an author. He still lives in Malmö where he continues to dive.

Leila Khaled remained an active PFLP official after arriving in Jordan following the Israeli offensive in Beirut. At the time of writing, she still travels frequently, if controversially, from her home in Amman to promote the Palestinian cause.

Expanded notes on sources

The Revolutionists is based on more than a decade of research. Among its most important sources are the dozens of interviews I conducted with those who participated in the events it describes. Sometimes these conversations lasted many hours; sometimes only a few minutes. Not all those I spoke to are named, or even appear in the book, but all influenced to a greater or lesser extent my understanding of what happened and why, and how it felt to be there when it did.

I held many of these interviews quite late in the research process so that I was able to test my interviewees' accounts, claims and descriptions against a sufficient mass of other primary and eye-witness source material, including film footage, postcards and a vast array of contemporary literature. Speech uttered several decades ago is almost impossible to corroborate or confirm without contemporaneous recordings. When speech is quoted, it comes from a participant in a conversation or a witness or an account that I think is reliable.

My other primary sources include many thousands of contemporary media reports in several languages. These not only provide surprisingly accurate accounts of past events but reveal, sometimes unintentionally, how those events were viewed at the time they occurred. Dozens of so-called 'instant' books that were common then but are rarer now – often published just weeks after major events – were frequently very helpful too. So too was archival footage and photographs, parliamentary inquiries, judicial reports and thousands of declassified government documents (some released at my request), ranging from diplomatic cables to intelligence agencies' reporting.

Among the most useful material were interrogation reports and memos by police and secret service. Many had not been released by any government but were leaked, sometimes inadvertently. Other useful official material came from the files of other specialists who were kind enough to share. Transcripts of court hearings provided much detail too, as did documents from a handful of legal cases. Unpublished memoirs by key actors were often more useful than their publicly available counterparts.

The secondary literature, both popular and academic, covering the various conflicts described in these pages is vast. Some languages – French, for example – I can read myself. But the combined miracle of specialised internet search engines, e-publishing and online translation (plus generous friends) allowed me to work in a dozen more. I tried to use as many Arabic sources, usually neglected, as possible.

In my first draft manuscript, references ran to a full third of the overall length. In their place, I offer the following expanded notes and suggestions for reading. These should guide the reader to most, if not all, of my sources. I have used some abbreviations for repeatedly mentioned publications. Books are given their full title on first mention and then referred to by author's name, with, if necessary, an additional word or two of the title to distinguish from other works. Full details of publisher etc. will be found in the select bibliography.

Any reader seeking more precise details of sourcing can contact me via my publisher or agent and I will do my best to provide.

PROLOGUE

The account of the early moments of the hijacking of El Al 219 is based on multiple sources. A twenty-seven-page secret Mossad report that was circulated to western European intelligence services describes the organisation of the attacks, and gives details of participants, weapons and more. It also corroborates much of the account given by Khaled in several hours of interview I conducted with her in 2021 and 2023. Khaled also describes the attack in her 1973 book, *My People Shall Live*, written with George Hajjar, pp. 92–4. Multiple other accounts published in newspapers and magazines at the time and since were useful, but particularly *Leila's Hijack War*, by Peter Snow and David Phillips, pp. 1–17. It is worth noting that when I spoke to Khaled in 2021, she denied carrying live grenades.

The Mossad report gives fascinating details of the Algerian network – mainly former members of the Front de Libération Nationale – in Paris which provided much crucial logistic support for 'Skyjack Sunday', underlining the important ideological and organisational links between anti-colonial North African and later Palestinian armed groups.

1. 'WHERE ARE WE GOING?'

Khaled's biographical details are based on interviews I conducted with her as well as accounts in her book, in Sarah Irving's *Leila Khaled: Icon of Palestinian Liberation* and Eileen MacDonald's *Shoot the Women First*. For broader historical context on the 1948 war, the 'Nakba' and Palestinian identity, I found very useful Ian Black's *Enemies and Neighbours*, Rashid Khalidi's *The Iron Cage*, Yazid Sayigh's *The Armed Struggle* and Nur Masalha's *Palestine*. Masalha argues that many inhabitants had long described themselves as 'ahl e filisitn', or people of Palestine. Both Ilan Pape's *The Ethnic Cleansing of Palestine* and Benny Morris' *1948* were also helpful. On the history of Haifa, I enjoyed M. Yazbak and Y. Weiss, *Haifa Before and After 1948*, and Yfaat Weiss' *Wadi Salib and Haifa's Lost Heritage*, a fascinating account of Leila Khaled's neighbourhood, which I visited in November 2024. Menachem Begin memorably describes the seizure of Haifa in *The Revolt* and Salah Khalaf, writing as Abu Iyad, describes his family's flight from the city in his memoirs *My Home My Land*.

My account of the early years of the Arab Nationalist Movement was helped by John Cooley, *Green March, Black September*, pp. 135–6; Shafiq al-Hout, *My Life in the PLO*, p. 24; Georges Habash, *Les Révolutionnaires ne meurent jamais*, pp. 23, 33; and Yezid

Sayigh, 'Reconstructing the Paradox: The Arab Nationalist Movement, Armed Struggle, and Palestine, 1951–1966', *Middle East Journal*, Vol. 45, No. 4, 1991, pp. 608–29. On the impact of the 1967 war in Egypt, there is an entire library or ten to read. These references come from Fawaz Gerges, *Making the Arab World*, pp. 294–6. On Kuwait in the 1960s, Gowers and Walker, *Arafat: Behind the Myth* is good, as were the diplomats I spoke to who had worked there then. Biographical details of Haddad are primarily drawn from Ghassan Charbel, *Asrâr al-sundûq al-aswad* (*The Secrets of the Black Box*), pp. 141–2, the most authoritative account as it relies on interviews with the subject's associates and friends, not merely his enemies.

On the innovative strategy of the PFLP, see Charbel, p. 116, and Sayigh, pp. 160–61, 214–15. For hijackings at the time, read Brendan I. Koerner, *The Skies Belong to Us*. On Arguello, I was helped immensely by the work of Marshall Yurow who interviewed Arguello's family members, friends, Sandinista associates active at the time, and almost all of the surviving members who trained in the Middle East, as well as tracking down personal letters and many relevant documents. Other sources used here include an online biography at www.Sandinovive.org and the 2006 PBS documentary *The American Hijacker*. I interviewed Dorothy Brown, Arguello's fellow Fulbright scholar in Peru. Declassified CIA documents on Nicaragua and the PLO were also helpful, as were British Cabinet Office archives on the restitution of Arguello's remains. Régis Debray's *Revolution in the Revolution* is widely available, as are the works of Guevara himself, particularly the influential *On Guerilla Warfare*, and Carlos Marighella's *Minimanual of the Urban Guerilla*.

My description of the Palestinian training camps in Jordan is based on interviews with Gunnar Ekberg, Khaled and Palestinian veterans who trained in them or ran them, most conducted in Ramallah, Jericho and Amman in 2023–24. Further sources included John Amos, *The Palestinian Resistance Movement*, pp. 167–70; Sayigh, p. 233; and Gérard Chaliand, *The Palestinian Resistance*, pp. 96–8. The camps seem to have closely resembled those I saw in Afghanistan in late 2001, which is interesting if not surprising.

Much has been published or broadcast about the hijacking of TWA Flight 840 from Rome. My account is informed by interviews with Khaled, and the accounts she gave to MacDonald, p. 109, and Irving. Also useful were detailed Italian newspaper reports of the time, especially 'Per un giorno a Roma gli arabi del commando', Livio Zanotti, *La Stampa*, 31 August 1969 and those of Milziade Torelli in *Corriere della Sera* on 30 August 1969. See too 'This is your new captain speaking' in *Life* magazine of 18 September 1970, and testimony published online by the US-based Association for Diplomatic Studies and Training. The details of the aftermath of the attack, the publicity effort and the surgery come from Khaled directly, but also Irving, p. 47 and MacDonald, p. 118.

2. SPIES ACROSS THE JORDAN

I conducted several hours of interviews with Gunnar Ekberg between 2020 and 2025 online and in Malmö. I also drew on his memoirs published in Swedish as *De ska ju ändå dö: Tio år i svensk underrättelsetjänst*. Swedish government reports were useful to corroborate his account. An official inquiry into the infiltration of left-wing and pro-Palestinian organisations by Swedish security agencies confirms that Ekberg had asked about obtaining passports for Palestinians in September 1970, for example. Interviews with former Swedish and Israeli security officials serving at the time also helped in this regard. Archive photographs show the appearance of many key locations in both Beirut and Amman, such as the office of Ghassan Kanafani, and there are multiple other descriptions in memoirs such as Bassam Abu Sharif's *Tried by Fire*, al-Hout, and Robert Fisk's *Pity the Nation*. The Eighth World Spearfishing Championship did indeed take place off the Cuban island of Cayo Avalos in 1967.

Details of different PLO factions in Jordan can be found in Amos, John Cooley's *Green March, Black September*, and Sayigh, as well as the voluminous contemporary reporting by news media, and that of diplomats and spies, much now declassified. See, for example, the CIA's October 1968 report: 'Anti-Israeli Arab Terrorist Organisations'. The DFLP actually started as the Democratic People's Front for the Liberation of Palestine, and so DPFLP, underlining its origins as a breakaway group from the main PFLP.

Some details from Cairo were taken from 'The Painful Presidency of Egypt's Nasser', *Time*, 16 May 1969 and Eric Rouleau's entertaining *Truth and Lies in the Middle East*. Eugene Rogan's *The Arabs* is typically good on Nasser's Egypt. The best evocation of the city at the time is Sonallah Ibrahim's pioneering modernist novel, *That Smell*, published in 1966 and immediately banned.

3. THE FEDAYEEN

An interesting question is how much Haddad was drawing on other thinkers within the PFLP for his 'forests to the skies' strategy. Sayigh quotes documents that suggests the answer is a lot. See *Armed Struggle*, pp. 209–16. Also useful on the new strategy of the PFLP was Charbel (again), p. 116 and Abu Sharif, *Tried by Fire*, pp. 59–63. George Habash explained the PFLP's strategy to journalist Oriana Fallaci in *Life*'s June 1970 edition. All references to Mahmoud Issa come from his book, *Je suis un Fedayin*.

My account of international networks linking the PFLP and DFLP with Latin American radicals draws on Federico Vélez, *Latin American Revolutionaries and the Arab World*, pp. 105–07 and Tricia Bacon's *Why Terrorist Groups Form International Alliances*, as well as Marshall Yurow's research. Also see Bruce Hoffman: 'The PLO and Israel in Central America, the Geopolitical Dimension', Rand Corp, March 1988, pp. 4–7.

For the early days of Fatah, see Sayigh, p. 195, Amos, Cooley, Rouleau, Barry and Judith Rubin's *Revolution Until Victory*, and Black, pp. 170–75. My interviews with Fatah veterans helped too. Useful memoirs include those of Abdel Bari Atwan's *A Country of Words*, Fawaz al-Turki's *Soul in Exile* and al-Hout. I also took details from 'A New Vow Rouses the Arabs: al-Fatah', *Life* magazine, 20 December 1968.

Arafat's real name was Mohammed Abdel Rahman Abdel Raouf al-Qudua al-Husseini, according to Said Aburish on p. 7 of *Arafat: From Defender to Dictator*. See also Abou Iyad, *My Home My Land*, pp. 19–25; Gowers and Walker, p. 12; Abu Daoud's *Palestine*, pp. 48–9, among many others. Below I refer both to Mohammed Odeh and, when referring to his book, Abu Daoud. These are the same person, of course.

The account of the first Fatah attack on Israel is based on interviews with Fatah and PFLP veterans, Michael Oren's *1967*, Eric Rouleau's article 'The Palestinian Quest' in *Foreign Affairs* in January 1975; David Hirst's *Beware of Small States*, p. 83; Helena Cobban's *The PLO*, pp. 32–5; and inevitably Sayigh, pp. 84–91.

Reasons for Arafat's failure to raise the West Bank will become immediately obvious to anyone who drives from Hebron or Jericho to Jerusalem: this is no country for insurgents.

My description of Amman in 1970 and the fedayeen cross-border attacks draws on interviews with Ekberg and on Sayigh, pp. 203–05; Abu Daoud, pp. 184–5; Abu Iyad, pp. 57–60; Gowers and Walker, pp. 59–60; and Ronen Bergman's *Rise and Kill First*, pp. 112–13. Also useful was 'The Violent Men of Amman' by Eric Pace in the *New York Times* (NYT) of 19 July 1970 and a February 1971 National Intelligence Estimate compiled by the CIA, 'The Palestinians and the Fedayeen as Factors in the Middle East Situation'.

The section on Karameh and its consequences draws on interviews with Khaled and on Sayigh, p. 180–81; al-Turki, p. 110; Atwan, p. 73; Abu Sharif's *Tried by Fire*, p. 57; and Abu Iyad, p. 60. Also useful was *Time* magazine's report, 'The Arab Commandos – A Defiant New Force in the Middle East' from December 1968, and *Le Monde*, 'El Fath domine au nouveau conseil de l'Organisation de libération de la Palestine', Rouleau, 5 February 1969. See also Hirst, p. 435 and *Time*, 'The Fedayeen Revisited', 13 June 1969. A good account from the perspective of the Israeli attackers, who included one Benjamin Netanyahu, can be found in Muki Betser's *Secret Soldier*.

The excellent site https://www.palestineposterproject.org/ offers an insight into the fedayeen's world view, and graphic talent. It is also worth reading Mahmoud Darwish's poetry, especially the 1964 work 'Identity Card', and the writing of Ghassan Kanafani who, in addition to editing the PFLP newsletter *al-Hadaf* and being the group's chief spokesman, was a gifted novelist. A personal favourite is his short story *Men In The Sun*, published in 1962.

To tell the story of the Athens attack, I used Issa's account, corroborated by press reporting at the time. I spent way too much time on architectural historical websites for the interior decor of Athens airport, sadly cut from the final text. For the aftermath of the Athens attack, see Charbel, p. 372; the CIA report, 'The Palestinians', cited above and Khaled's *My People*, p. 92.

My account of Arguello's movements until the week before the attacks relies on Marshall Yurow again, who obtained a passport copy under the FOIA and interviewed Arguello's sister Cila in 1989. Also useful were Charbel, p. 71; Bacon, pp. 77–81; PBS's *Hijacked*; and Vélez, pp. 105–07.

Many of the details of the last days and hours before the TWA attempted hijacking come from interviews with Khaled, who stressed that she and Arguello had stayed in separate hotels. In large part, these are corroborated by the lengthy Mossad report. For the camels, see *Hijacked*. The details of Arguello's itinerary and transcript of the letter were kindly provided by Yurow.

4. REVOLUTION AIRPORT

A gripping account of the hair-raising landing of Pan Am Flight 93 in Cairo can be found in David Raab, *Terror in Black September*, with this amazing quote at p. 25. See also Associated Press, 'Guerrilla Hijackings Deadline at Dawson's Field', broadcast 23 September 1970.

For the events aboard El Al Flight 219 and in the UK on its landing, I used my interviews with Khaled, also Irving, pp. 49–51; *Leila's Hijack War*, pp. 11–17; *Tried by Fire*, p. 81; Raab, p. 18; MacDonald, p. 123 and much contemporaneous press reporting.

For the PFLP's demands, see the useful SitRep 'as of 0600 Hours EST' by the Department of State's Operations Center in Washington and an FCO cable Amman to London FCO/469, both prepared 7 September 1970. For the preparation of the landing strip, see Issa, and Charbel, pp. 366–7. The account of Abu Sharif's role is based on *Tried by Fire*, pp. 82–4, and his brief comments to me in 2023. The scene in Jordan was brilliantly captured by Eric Pace in the NYT on 19 July 1970. For the BOAC hijacking, *Tried by Fire*, p. 85 and declassified FCO documents were useful. For the subsequent negotiations: see *Le Monde*'s 'Berne, Bonn et Londres sont disposés à accepter les conditions des ravisseurs, Israël se refuse à toute négociation', 9 September 1970; Raab, p. 102; Snow, p. 69; and the useful account in Kai Bird, *Divided City*, pp. 263–4. My depiction of the press conferences and the ordeal of the hostages is based on contemporary reporting in UK and US newspapers, mainly the *Guardian* (GDN) and NYT. Useful details can be found in Bird's *Divided City*, pp. 260–67. Also helpful, particularly on the release of some hostages but not others and otherwise differing treatment, were Raab, pp. 80–81; Rouleau, p. 205; PBS's *Hijacked*; and *Time*, 'Drama of the Desert' of 21 September 1970. See also Sharif, *Tried*, p. 87. The quote is from Henry Kissinger's fascinating *The White House Years*, pp. 601–02.

Habash's quotes are from a lengthy and controversial interview with Oriana Fallaci, published in *Life* magazine, cited above. The hours before the planes were blown up are described in *Tried by Fire*, pp. 86–7 and Raab, p. 109, also in *Time*'s reporting. The Associated Press's twenty-six-minute film broadcast 23 September 1970 and cited above has interviews with released passengers and images of the explosions. What happened immediately afterwards is described in Bird, pp. 264–5; Issa; Charbel, p. 117; and Raab, p. 118. My account of the liberation of the hostages relies on Issa, and further reports in the NYT, GDN and other publications; you can find footage of the PFLP press conference on YouTube. For the incapacity and ignorance of the US and its allies, see Raab, p. 121; Kissinger's memo to Nixon, 12 September 1970; and Nixon's morning intelligence briefing of 18 September 1970. All such briefings for these weeks are easy to find at the CIA's website and, though redacted, offer a fascinating view of what was literally crossing the president's desk on any one day.

5. BLACK SEPTEMBER

One of the reasons I wrote this book was the incongruity of Leila Khaled in a police station in west London in 1970, with reporters queuing ill-temperedly for nearby phone boxes to file their copy and burly coppers holding back crowds on west London pavements.

My account of Khaled's time in British custody is based on interviews with Khaled, her *My People Shall Live*, p. 56, and UK government archives, including the letter she sent home from Ealing. Also useful were local newspapers from the time, such as the *Middlesex County Times*, news photographs and BBC archive footage.

My account of Ekberg's second trip to Jordan relies on interviews with him, as well as references from Rouleau, p. 202, and a useful report from, again, Eric Pace in the NYT, headlined 'Amman, From the Inside', published 21 September 1970. For the final days of the hijacking crisis, UK government documents are useful, such as the draft government legal advice to FCO (Cabinet Office 484B/5. 19.9.1970) and the SitReps of 29 September 1970 (FCO 17/1057 NEJ 1/10). The account in Raab is good, pp. 215–29. For Khaled's departure from the UK, see Irving, pp. 60–61; the *Birmingham Post* of 1 October 1970; and *Leila's Hijack War*, p. 175. For Khaled's return to Beirut, I have relied on interviews with her, Irving, pp. 68–9; and MacDonald, p. 130. For Khaled's celebrity, see Colin Smith, *Carlos*, p. 46, as well as 'Revolution is Not Just for the Single', NYT on 27 November 1970, and the letter from Gerald E. Zuriff, Cambridge, MA, published a week later. The smaller faction whose members were released by the Germans was Issam al-Sartawi's short-lived Action Organisation for the Liberation of Palestine, which was backed by Iraq.

For the reaction to Khaled's release, see *Daily Mirror*, 11 September 1970 and Bird, *Divided City*, p. 266. The quotes on skyjackers and the ghetto come from *Time*, 21 September 1970, 'Drama of the Desert'. The idea of examining bags before boarding planes can be found in GDN, Letters: 'Ways to beat hijackers', 12 September 1970. For the Habash quote, Hirst, *Gun and Olive*, p. 432, quoting *Stern* magazine. The full interview with Fallaci can be read in the June 1970 issue of *Life*, which can be found online.

The parcel bomb that brought the Swissair flight down was the work of a group sponsored by Syria known as the PFLP-GCC. It was probably aimed at an El Al flight and remains the bloodiest crime in modern Swiss history.

Issa describes his ordeal in his book, and his description of harsh treatment is entirely plausible. The fake air tickets were reproduced in Ekberg's book. Abu Sharif discusses his own experience in *Tried by Fire*, p. 88. I found some details of the identification and repatriation of Arguello in *Leila's Hijack War*, p. 18; FCO SitReps 14, 15 September 1970 (7/1056 NEJ 1/10/A) and a Cabinet Office advice note (B03145) dated 14 September 1970.

6. THE GERMAN CONNECTION

For details of Germans' journey to Jordan see Stefan Aust, *The Baader Meinhof Complex*, pp. 65–6; Mario Krebs, *Ulrike Meinhof: Ein Leben im Widerspruch*, pp. 216–18; and *Spiegel*, 'Bis irgendwohin', 14 June 1970. The report of the interrogation of one of the group, Hans-Jürgen Bäckers, questioned by the Stasi in East Berlin on his way back to West Berlin, is available online at the Stasi Mediatech. The United Arab Republic – with whose passports the Germans travelled – was dissolved by Anwar Sadat a year later as part of his efforts to distance himself from Nasser's legacy.

For the evolution of the left's views on Israel in western Europe and the US, see Dave Rich, *The Left's Jewish Problem*, pp. 53–4; Jeffrey Herf, *Undeclared Wars with Israel: East Germany and the West German Radical Left, 1967–1989*, pp. 83–4, among many other works. Maxime Rodinson's influential *Israel: A Settler Colonial State?* was first published (in French) in July 1967.

Eric Hobsbawm bemoans the proletariat's preference for consumer goods rather than the barricades in his 1973 book *Revolutionaries*, pp. 323–4. For links between African American activists and the Palestinian cause see the excellent Michael Fischback, *Black Power and Palestine*, especially pp. 112–14.

On European sympathisers' trips to Jordan see Cooley, pp. 188–9; Colin Smith, *Carlos*, pp. 42–3; Thomas Skelton-Robinson's contribution to Wolfgang Kraushaar, pp. 117–22, and Herf. On the recruitment of some among them, see two reports by the FBI: 'The Fedayeen Terrorist', June 1970 and 'The Fedayeen Impact – Middle East And United States', June 1970, as well as Ian Black and Benny Morris, *Israel's Secret Wars*, p. 68; Adrian Hänni, *Terrorist und CIA-Agent: Die unglaubliche Geschichte des Schweizers Bruno Bréguet*; Ekberg interviews and book. On their unpredictability, see John Follain, *Jackal*, p. 138; also *Turning Money into Rebellion* by Gabriel Kuhn, p. 66, and Peter Øvig Knudsen: *Blekingegadebanden – Den danske celle*. Also: Abu Daoud, p. 573; Neaman, *Free Radicals: Agitators, Hippies, Urban Guerrillas, and Germany's Youth Revolt of the 1960s and 1970s*.

There are a few books about Ensslin, Baader and Meinhof in English, but very many in German. On Ensslin, I consulted Karin Bauer's *Everybody Talks About the Weather*; *Vesper, Ensslin, Baader: Urszenen de deutschen Terrorismus* by Gerd Koenen; and *Gudrun Ensslin: Die Geschichte Einer Radikalisierung* by Alex Aßmann. Gillian Becker's *Hitler's Children* is ideological and dated but full of detail. On the scene in Berlin, see Aust, pp. 25–7 and Jeremy Varon, *Bringing the War Home*, p. 32. For Baader, I found *Andreas Baader: Das Leben eines Staatsfeinde* by Klaus Stern and Jörg Herrmann very helpful, as well as passages in Bauer, pp. 59–60; Koenen, p. 21; Becker pp. 76–8; and Neaman. The relevant chapters in Michael Burleigh's *Blood and Rage* offer a good overview.

The 'fuck-ups' quote is from the inimitable Norman Mailer, in *A Fire on the Moon* of 1970, which, with the slightly earlier *The Armies of the Night*, gives a fabulous insight into both the USA of the time and the New Left.

For Baader and Ensslin in France and Italy see: Aust, pp. 51–2; Becker, pp. 102–03; Neaman, loc 2603. See too Astrid Proll, *Hans und Grete: Pictures on the Run 1967 to 1977*, Zurich, Scalo, 1998, which is full of images of the pair smoking and drinking in French bistros. Most of the time, they look very happy.

Ulrike Meinhof is perhaps the most interesting single character I encountered writing this book. For these pages, I consulted Alois Prinz's *Liber wutend als traurig sein: Die Lebensgeschichte der Ulrike Meinhof* and Jutta Dittfurth's *Ulrike Meinhof*. I also looked at many German press reports, including writing by her daughter Bettina Rohl in *Der Speigel* and elsewhere, as well as English newspaper commentary, such as Neal Ascherson, 'A Terror Campaign of Love and Hate', the *Observer*, 28 September 2008. There is useful material in a host of documentaries too. The resistance quote is from 'Vom Protest zum Widerstand', *Konkret*, No. 5, May 1968. Richard Vinen's *1968* is very good on broader context, and especially pp. 180–84 which deal with Germans. Other references from Aust and Becker, 'An Interview with Ulrike Meinhof's Sister Wienke', 9 May 2016, Kersplebedeb.com; 'Extra-Drill für verwöhnte Bürgerkinder', *Die Welt*, 20 June 2020; Bauer; and Katherina Karcher, *Sisters in Arms*.

The question of whether Meinhof intended to follow Baader into clandestinity remains unanswered. Dittfurth, pp. 11–13 suggests she had made up her mind long before jumping out of the institute's window. Others disagree. That no arrangements for Meinhof's new underground life appear to have been made suggests they are right.

On the Germans in Jordan see Aust p. 66; *The Red Army Faction, A Documentary History, Vol. 1: Projectiles for the People*, p. 57; Horst Mahler interview in the 2002 BBC

Four documentary *In love with Terrorism*; Khaled, *My People*, p. 55; Daoud, p. 267. On the culture clashes between European volunteers and the Palestinians, Colin Smith, *Carlos*, pp. 42–3; Rich on drunk British Maoists, pp. 50, 85; also Cooley pp. 135, 186. The Khaled quotes are from my interviews with her. On the specific tensions between Baader et al. and their hosts see Butz Peters, *Tödlicher Irrtum*, pp. 201–03 and Aust, pp. 68–75. The foundational communiqué – 'Die Rote Armee aufbauen' – can be found with many other useful documents at socialhistoryportal.org.

7. ARMED STRUGGLE IS THE REALITY

The 'Call to World Revolution by PFLP – Japanese Red Army' can be viewed online and is well worth watching. The English-language literature on the Japanese Red Army is not extensive, sadly, though there are some very interesting blogs online. I found William Farrell, *Blood and Rage: The Story of the Japanese Red Army* useful, as was Patricia Steinhoff's work, especially 'Portrait of a Terrorist', *Asian Survey*, Vol. 16, September 1976. 'Global Revolution Starts with Palestine', by Jeremy Randall, *Comparative Studies of South Asia*, 2023, was helpful, as was Yoshikuni Igarashi, 'Dead Bodies and Living Guns', *Japanese Studies*, September 2007, pp. 119–37.

On communes, see Julia Lovell, *Maoism*, pp. 292–3, 294; Brian Burrough's excellent *Days of Rage*, pp. 77–8; Varon, pp. 58–9 and much other literature. The Red Brigades is from MacDonald, pp. 174, 182–3, the Swedes from Ekberg's book. See Aust, p. 11 for Meinhof's pig quote. The Hobsbawm reference is from *Revolutionaries*, p. 316. Charbel describes relations between the PFLP and the JRA, p. 151. The obsession of left-wing extremists of the period with occupying and redefining spaces – homes, houses, fields, training camps, campuses, hostels, lecture halls, etc. – is striking. People confined in small apartments was a common starting point for many radical filmmakers, some connected to violent groups. Ensslin acted in an experimental arthouse film in the mid-1960s, in which she and a male actor, not Baader, stayed, more or less naked, in bed in an apartment for an undetermined but clearly very long time.

My account of the 1972 Lod airport attack draws on reporting in *La Stampa* from 31 May 1972; a lengthy report on the JRA in a CIA 'International Issues Monthly Review', February 1978, pp. 43–50; *Spiegel*, 'Weißer Kreis', 4 June 1972; 'Israelis Say They Have Traced Route of 3 Terrorists From Japan to the Tel Aviv Airport Massacre', NYT, 6 June 1972; 'The Tel-Aviv Massacre in the Making' in the GDN on the same day; 'Wanted Japanese Red Army Member Maintains 1972 Airport Attack Wasn't Terrorism', in *The Mainichi Shimbun*, published on 31 May 2017. Also court documents filed in CALDERÓN-CARDONA Et Al. vs The Democratic People's Republic of Korea, US District Court For Puerto Rico, March 2008. Among those whose freedom was demanded by Black September during the Sabena hijacking were the French and Moroccan citizens recruited by Mohammed Boudia in France and then jailed in Israel in 1971 after being detained with explosives on or shortly after their arrival there.

The discussion of suicide attacks is based on my interviews with Ekberg and his book, p. 168; Sharif's *Tried by Fire*, p. 75; a CIA trace request form on François Genou, a wealthy and connected Swiss neo-Nazi, made in October 1985, that mentions an exploding chianti bottle. See also Charbel, pp. 51–2 and a Shigenobu interview in online edition of *The Mainichi Shimbun*, 30 May 2021. For broader context, Sayigh, p. 197.

Some sources suggest that shortly after the PFLP's expulsion from Jordan, Haddad had begun to experiment with operations that would almost certainly result in the deaths of any attacker, such as flying a plane packed with explosives from southern Lebanon to Tel Aviv and into Israel's tallest building, the Shalom Tower. Haddad may also have placed liquid explosives hidden in a rustic-looking chianti flagon, complete with red wax seal, creating a bomb that was to be carried through Lod airport and detonated there by its courier. It is more likely the aim was only to transport the explosives. This is certainly what happened on a later occasion when an effort was made to bring explosives into France in 1974 for Ramírez's bombing campaign by concealing them in this way.

Okamoto explicitly denied to Steinhoff that his own death was an integral part of the Lod attack plan, suggesting instead that the shooting in the luggage retrieval hall was unforeseen. Instead, the aim may have been to attack planes on the runway, or the control tower, or both. For the aftermath of the operation, see 'Arab Commandos Show No Remorse', 4 June 1972, NYT.

Margrit Schiller gives a useful glimpse of both the thinking and interpersonal dynamics behind the Red Army Faction's campaign in 1972, in her *Remembering the Armed Struggle*, especially pp. 31–7. See also Bauer, p. 107; Varon, p. 199. For life underground, Schiller, p. 48; 'Terrorist ohne Führerschein', *Spiegel*, 18 October 2007; and 'Rote Armee Fraktion: So kam die RAF zu ihrem Namen', *Die Welt*, 25 February 2021. Bommi Baumann's book, *Terror or Love?: Personal Account of a West German Urban Guerrilla*, 1980 is an entertaining read. If you have never watched Gillo Pontecorvo's *The Battle of Algiers*, a very good film that was politically and creatively very influential in its time, you now have an excellent excuse.

On sexism, see Tony Judt, 'Revolutionaries', *New York Review of Books*, February 2010; *Projectiles of the People*, p. 86; Lovell, pp. 287, 289; 'Man kann nur zurückbrüllen', *Spiegel*, 6 February 1972; MacDonald, pp. 209–10; Karcher, p. 108; 'Frauen in der RAF', Gisela Diewald-Kerkmann, *Bundeszentrale fur politische Bildung*, 20 August 2007; Aust, pp. 116, 130.

For the 1972 RAF campaign see Aust, pp. 157–60; Becker, p. 254; and Neaman.

There is gripping footage of Baader's arrest available online, and multiple accounts.

For a real sense of the atmosphere at the time in West Germany, and particularly the role of the media, read Heinrich Böll's 1974 masterpiece, *The Lost Honour of Katharina Blum*.

8. MUNICH

The meeting in Rome and other preliminaries to the Munich attack are described in Abu Daoud, pp. 577–82; Abu Iyad, pp. 107–10; the useful Simon Reeve, *One Day in September*, which drew on extensive research for the award-winning 1999 documentary of the same name, pp. 47–8; Peter Taylor, *States of Terror*, p. 13. Abu Daoud is frequently unreliable and quite how advanced the plot to attack the Olympics was at this point is unclear. Sayigh, *Armed Struggle*, p. 309, points out that it is also unclear if Arafat knew or not.

On training camps in Libya, see a cable of December 1972 from UK Tripoli embassy to FCO (p. 16 of FCO 17/1624 NE 1/5); also *Stern*, 'Wir unterstützen jede Aktion der Gureillas', 12 November 1972.

There is a good account of the ceremony and other events in Large, *Munich 1972* and *The 1972 Munich Olympics and the Making of Modern Germany*, by Kay Schiller and Chris Young. For the Israeli athletes: Henry Hershkowitz, *People*, 15 July 1996; *Munich Memoir*, Dan Alon, pp. 15, 46–8, 57–8; *A New Shoah: The Untold Story of Israel's Victims of Terrorism*, Giulio Meotti, pp. 47–8; Shaul Ladany, *King of the Road*, p. 16; 'The Munich Massacre: A Survivor's Story', CNN, 5 September 2012; *Gazeta Sporturilor*, 12 February 2017; 'Survivor Relives Munich Horror', Dave Hyde, *South Florida Sun-Sentinel*, 29 September 2000; Simon Reeve, *One Day in September*, pp. 68–9.

The Israeli accommodation at 31 Connollystrasse was very close to the perimeter fence of the Olympic village. I paced the distance in February 2025. The eighty-odd yards would have taken the attackers across a small entry ramp, and onto a narrow cobbled alley which would have taken a maximum of thirty seconds to traverse.

For the background of Massalha and 'Tony', see 'An extensive investigation reveals new details about the Munich massacre', Shay Fogelman, *Haaretz*, 31 August 2012; and Reeve, p. 55. On preparations in Munich see Abu Daoud, pp. 621–4; Reeve, p. 9; 'Septembre Noir: Aucun Mal Ne Devait Être Fait Aux Otages Sauf En Cas De Légitime Défense', *Le Monde*, 9 September 1972; *Irish Times*, 'Massacre in Munich', 21 January 2006. The question of where the weapons came from is still debated.

My account of the day of the Munich attack relies on Reeve; Large; much contemporary media reporting, for example: *Time*, 'Horror and Death at the Olympics', 18 September 1972; Odeh's own testimony before a Jordanian military tribunal on 24 March 1973, which I found in a CIA internal memo entitled 'Propaganda Perspectives from April 1973'. There is good archive news footage, such as that used in Al-Jazeera's documentary, *Israel's Hunt for the Red Prince*, 2018. The excellent 'digital memorial site for the 1972 Olympic Massacre, Fürstenfeldbruck' has transcribed interviews with many key actors. For the debacle at the airport, see Large, pp. 220–21; Klein, pp. 71–81; Reeve, p. 136; interviews and witness accounts on the digital memorial site and 'When the Terror Began', Don Yaeger, *Sports Illustrated*, 26 August 2002. Adrian Hänni, research director at the official German historical investigation of the attack, offered much guidance and made useful suggestions too.

There has been some debate over whether the attackers had been told not to shoot to kill other than in defence. Their claim that this was the case is reinforced by the fact that when two athletes fled in the early minutes of the attack, their captors fired in the air or not at all when other lethal options were obviously available.

The well-established idea that Massalha was alerted to the preparations for the police assault by images broadcast by TV networks that he saw on a television set inside the Connollystrasse house is an excellent demonstration of the extraordinary power and novelty of live television at the event, but is a myth. German investigators meticulously documented all the items and furniture in the building, down to each item of cutlery and an apple. There was no television or even television connection. See 'Munich Olympics Attack: The TV That Never Was – or Why the Liberation Attempt in the Olympic Village was Aborted', Adrian Hänni, Dominik Aufleger, Lutz Kreller, Leibniz Institute for Contemporary History Munich-Berlin, April 2025.

9. THE BLACK SEPTEMBER ORGANISATION

For the aftermath of the Munich attack, see 'Heroes' Burial Held For 5 Arabs In Libya', NYT, 13 September 1972; 'Leaders Around the World Express Horror at the Guerrilla Attack at Olympics', NYT, 6 September 1972; Daoud, pp. 634–5 and 644; British FCO cables from Algiers and from Tripoli to London, both 13 September 1972, in FCO 17/1740 and FCO 17/1741. See also Reeve, pp. 156–72; police statement on digital memorial site cited above, and Dan Alon, *Munich Memoir*, p. 45.

Habib Bourguiba was the first Arab leader to request the remains of the attackers for burial in Arab soil. The Tunisian president stressed that a refusal would seriously harm relations between Germany and the Arab world, already strained by the German 'betrayal of the fedayeen' at Fürstenfeldbruck and the public criticism of Arab governments by German officials during and after the attack. Israeli quotes here are in Rouleau, *Truth and Lies in the Middle East*, p. 158; Amos Elon, *The Israelis*, p. 184; and Amos Oz, *Under This Blazing Light*, (CUP, 1990) p. 92. For Israel and the Holocaust, see discussion in Daniel Gordis, *Israel*, pp. 238–57. For Israel's immediate reaction to the Munich attacks: Taylor, p. 9; The President's Daily Brief of 9 September 1972; US cables from Tel Aviv and Beirut; and 'Du Drame de Munich Aux Représailles Israéliennes', *Le Monde*, 1 September 1972. There are several biographies of Meir, but few are very critical. A reader of, say, Elinor Burkett's *Golda* or Francine Klagsbrun's *Lioness* would do well to read the relevant chapters from Avi Shlaim's *Iron Wall* for a different perspective. The same book would be useful too for anyone interested in Vladimir Jabotinsky and his concept of an 'iron wall of bayonets' to defend Israel.

I discussed the Mossad's failures before and at Munich with former Mossad officials in Tel Aviv 2024, and with Yossi Melman, the veteran and informed author and journalist.

For Black September, I quote here from the CIA's report, 'The Fedayeen – Politics of Spoiling', of 26 October 1972, and *Time*, 18 September 1972, 'Black September's Ruthless Few'. Also useful were interviews I did in Tel Aviv and Ramat Hasharon in late 2023 and 2024 with former Mossad officials and in Ramallah with the men they once hunted. I also spoke to former CIA officials in 2021.The letters on the note handed to the Germans at Munich actually spelled out IBSO: International BSO.

This brief description of Ali Hassan Salameh is based on contemporary media reporting; and an FCO memo on Black September of 11 October 1972 in file FCO 17/623, 'Acts of Violence by Arab Terrorist Organisations'. Kai Bird's authoritative and readable *The Good Spy* was very useful. Other sources include Bar-Zohar, Haber, *Massacre in Munich*, pp. 91–5; Al-Jazeera World, *Israel's Hunt for the Red Prince*, 2018; Paul O'Neill, 'The Charming Assassin', *Life*, April 1979; Taylor, pp. 42–5; and my interviews with former associates of Salameh, Ramallah, 2023, 2024. Salameh's right-wing connections are detailed in 'The New European Right', *Mother Jones*, May 1987, as well as in 'Der "rote Prinz" zwischen CIA und Mossad, Ali Hassan Salameh', Marcel Gyr, *Neue Zürcher Zeitung*, 3 September 2020.

For Salameh's father, see Hillel Cohen, *Armies of the Shadows*, pp. 138, 149; Bird, p. 85; Bar-Zohar, p. 28; Taylor, pp. 30–34. For his youth, Bergman, *Rise and Kill First*, p. 21; Al-Jazeera World interview with Nidal Salameh, a sister; Abu Daoud, pp. 147–8. For Salameh as a young man: Paul O'Neill, *Life*, April 1979; Bird, p. 89; Abu Daoud, pp. 149–51; Taylor, pp. 34–5. In Egypt: Abu Daoud, pp. 207–13. In Jordan: Amos, p. 135; Abu Daoud, pp. 247, 271; Al-Jazeera, interview with Murid al-Dajani, 2018; Sayigh, pp. 224, 254; Abu Sharif, *Arafat and the Dream of Palestine*, pp. 34–5; and Diagonalthoughts.com. Godard's text was originally published in *El Fatah* magazine in July 1970. On Trieste: Al-Jazeera World, interview with Ghazi al-Husseini; author interviews, Ramallah, 2023–24; Sayigh, p. 307; Charbel, p. 335; Abu Daoud, p. 593; 'Une Française impliqué dans l'attentat commis en 1972 contre un oléoduc a Trieste', *Le Monde*, 14 March 1973. References on Salameh's alleged role in the Munich attacks include the Department of State's 'Directory of Leaders of the Palestinian Resistance Movement', Research Study, 9 January 1973. The briefing I mention was partly based on an 'authoritative' article in a German magazine, *Quick*, which the authors of the document said was based on Israeli intelligence. For a British official perspective, see FCO 17/623, 'Acts of Violence by Arab Terrorist Organisations', 11 October 1972. Ilich Ramírez told Eugene Casey, an FBI agent who interviewed him in prison in 2012, that Salameh was not responsible for Munich; Casey told me this when we spoke in 2021.

10. THE SHADOW WAR

Oriana Fallaci's persistence, charm and self-belief won her a series of extraordinary exclusive interviews in a time when some of the most important people in the world would find several hours to talk to a single journalist, and without media advisers. The contrast with today is striking. Fallaci's *Interview with History*, published in 1974, includes her interviews of Henry Kissinger, Yasser Arafat, Indira Gandhi and the Shah of Iran, inter alia. That with Meir is on pp. 88–122. See also Golda Meir's *My Life*, pp. 141, 334.

On Western services' description of Israeli tactics: FCO 17/1622, 'Acts of Violence by Arab Terrorist Organisations', pp. 28–30; also FCO 93/489, 'Israel Terrorist [*sic*] Activities'.

For the attacks on Kanafani and Abu Sharif, see Black and Morris, pp. 191–201; Bergman, *Rise and Kill First*, pp. 69–73, 143; and 'Les Palestiniens soupçonnent des agents d'Israël d'avoir assassiné Ghassane Kanafani', *Le Monde*, 11 July 1972. More than fifty years later, in his home in Jericho, Abu Sharif angrily and bitterly described to me the bombing that maimed and half-blinded him.

For the letter bombings and shooting in Brussels: Meir, *My Life*, pp. 333–4; Christopher Dobson, *Black September*, p. 105. For Zwaiter's murder: Eric Salerno, *Mossad Base Italia*, pp. 167–79; Bergman, pp. 154–5; Reeve, pp. 196–7; Taylor, p. 18; and *Le Monde*, 'Le Représentant Du Mouvement Palestinien En Italie A Été Assassiné', 18 October 1972. On al-Kubaisi: Bergman, pp. 157, 180; Klein, pp. 54–5, 137–8; 'Le Professeur Tué A Paris Était Dirigeant Du F.P.L.P.', *Le Monde*, 7 April 1973; 'Iraqi on a Guerrilla "Mission" Shot and Killed in Paris Street', 7 April 1973, Associated Press. Bird raises the intriguing possibility that al-Kubaisi could have been a CIA contact. The details of Kilowatt are from

Aviva Guttmann's very useful *Operation Wrath of God*. See p. 54 for Zwaiter, and p. 85 for Hamshari.

On the Mossad campaign: Gowers and Walker, p. 99; Bergman, p. 146; and author interviews, Israel, 2023 and 2025, including with members of the assassination teams. For the killing of Baruch Cohen: Reeve, pp. 204–05; Taylor, pp. 55–61; Patrick Seale, *Abu Nidal*, pp. 156–8; Abu Iyad, pp. 112–14. On the bereaved: Reeve, pp. 218–19; Black and Morris, p. 274.

My account of Ekberg's final trips is based on his book and our conversations.

There are many accounts of the Springtime of Youth operation – one of the most famous in Israeli military history. I used Klein, pp. 157–65; Reeve, pp. 206–10; Bergman, *Rise*, pp. 162–7; Sayigh, pp. 308–10; Taylor, p. 22; Betser, pp. 166–74; Guttmann, pp. 154–9. Also *Time*, 'Most Probably We'll All Die', 23 April 1973. I also spoke to veterans of the attack when in Israel in 2024. On the reaction of the Lebanese and the West Germans, see Letter From Permanent Representative of Lebanon to President of UN Security Council, S/L0911, 11 April 1973, and 'Germany's Secret Contacts to Palestinian Terrorists', *Spiegel*, 28 August 2012.

11. THE RED PRINCE

On Salameh in 1972, I have used, among other sources, Thomas Riegler's useful article on Black September in western Europe ('Das Spinnennetz des internationalen Terrorismus: Der Schwarze September', published in 2012); Mohammed Odeh's testimony in April 1973 and his book, pp. 549–63, 593, 666; Pierre Pean, *L'Extrémiste: François Genoud, de Hitler à Carlos*, p. 339; 'The Black September Guerrillas: Elusive Trail in Seven Countries', NYT, 12 October 1972; 'Israel Fights Terror With Terror', *Washington Post* (WP), 15 October 1972. For Khartoum and Israeli reprisals, see Hirst, *Gun and Olive Branch*, pp. 446–8; David A. Korn's *Assassination in Khartoum*, pp. 1–2; 'Political Kidnappings 1968–73', US Congress House Committee on Internal Security, 1 August 1973, p. 36; CIA Intelligence memo June 1973, 'The Seizure of the Saudi Arabian Embassy in Khartoum; Memo of Conversation, Sec of State Kissinger and Foreign Minister Abba Eban, Washington, 12 May, 1973'; 'Les Israéliens attaquent, en débarquant, deux camps Palestinians au nord du Liban', *Le Monde*, 22 February 1973; Sayigh, pp. 310–11; Barry Rubin and Judith Colp Rubin, *Yasir Arafat*, pp. 77–80; Letter From the Permanent Representative of Lebanon to the UN to the President of the Security Council, S/10885 of 21 February 1973; Jewish Telegraphic Agency, 'Tekoah: Lebanon's Reaction to Raid is One of Distortions, Lies', 23 February 1973.

On Salameh and Bob Ames, see the inimitable Bird, *The Good Spy*, pp. 127–37 and 146–9, where you will find an excellent description of contacts in 1973. See also 'CIA Memo To Ambassador Helms From Robert Ames: Contacts With The Fatah Leadership', 18 July 1973. The quote is from US National Intelligence Estimate, 'The Palestinians and the Fedayeen as Factors in the Middle East Situation', February 1971. Salameh's Sudan trip is described in Gowers and Walker, p. 104. The 1969 reference is from Yevgeni Primakov, *Russia and the Arabs: Behind the Scenes in the Middle East from the Cold War to the Present*. Aburish is typically good on Arafat's thinking at the time, see p. 93. Odeh's testimony has been already discussed above. On 'turning off' Black September see *The Atlantic Monthly,* December 2001, 'All You Need is Love: How the Terrorists Stopped Terrorism', by Bruce Hoffman. On how Salameh was a marked man, see Bird, pp. 137–8 and Bergman, p. 179.

Boudia has been reduced to a 'womanising terrorist' in many accounts. This misses a very great deal. Boudia is in many ways a much better example of the violent extremist of the time than many other much more high-profile individuals. I was helped by these sources: Mohamed Boudia, *Oeuvres*, Premier Matins de Novembre, Toulouse, 2017; *El-Moudjahid*, 'Mohamed Boudia: dramaturge militant', 11 August 2024; Thomas Reigler, 'Das Spinnenetz'; my interview with a former CIA officer active in western Europe in the early 1970s, January 2022; Bondyblog.com: 'Mohamed Boudia, l'Algérie combative', 15 January 2020; Mohamed Boudia, 'Le théâtre est une arme', *El-Moudjahid*, No. 97, 13 October 1962; John Follain, *Jackal*, pp. 37–8; and *Le Monde*, 'Un témoignage sur Mohamed Boudia', 6 July 1973. Guttmann found material circulated by Kilowatt that adds much to our understanding of how Boudia operated – and how he died. See pp. 178–205. The Mossad report into 'Skyjack Sunday' in September 1970 in my possession reveals not just Boudia's vital role in supplying the missing weapons that forced the attack to be postponed but that the courier sent to Beirut to smuggle them back to France was an assistant at his theatre whom he had recently seduced. The account of how the Mossad picked up the supposed trail of Salameh comes from Klein, p. 186.

On PFLP and other armed groups' activities in Scandinavia, see Gabriel Kuhn, pp. 25–7, 75, 105, and *Tried by Fire*, p. 94. Ulf Bjereld, *Övervakningen av den Svenska, The Monitoring of the Swedish Palestinian Movement, 1965–1980*, 2002, pp. 72–3 gave further details, as did interviews with former Israeli and Swedish security officials. See also Guttmann, pp. 211–12, and for the picture from MI5, p. 218.

On Lillehammer, see Bergman, pp. 180–82; a biography of Sylvia Rafael by Ram Oren and Moti Kfir; Norwegian contemporary press reporting; the English translation of the judgement of the Oslo court, February 1974, in FCO 93/489, 'Israel Terrorist Activities'; 'The Man Who Took the Fall for Mossad Breaks His Silence', Yossi Melman, *Haaretz*, 29 October 2021. Also my several interviews with two former Mossad agents active at the time in western Europe, Israel 2023, 2024 and 2025.

Ekberg described the end of his espionage career to me and the affair was widely, if sometimes inaccurately, covered in Swedish media at the time.

On the Berlin festival, see Paul Chamberlin, *The Global Offensive*, p. 174; a film made by the Deutsche Film-Aktiengesellschaft (DEFA); Kay Schiller's 'Communism, Youth, and Sport: The 1973 World Youth Festival in East Berlin', in *Sport and the Transformation of Modern Europe, 1950–2010*, Routledge, 2011; 'Yasser Arafat in Berlin', *Journal of Palestine Studies*, Autumn 1973, pp. 166–8; US DoS cable from Berlin, Arafat At World Youth Festival, 16 July 1973. Meinhof's quotes are from Becker, *Hitler's Children*, pp. 339–43; also see Herf.

Helms sent his memo on Significant Area Developments on 8 October 1973. It is available in CIA online archives.

12. CARLOS!

For a sense of the UK at the time of Ramírez's first attack, see Andy Beckett's *When the Lights Went Out*, Alwyn Turner's *Crisis? What Crisis?* and Dominic Sandbrook's *State of Emergency*. All are good books.

For the attempted murder of Sieff, see Follain, pp. xvii–xviii, 41; Smith, pp. 102–05; 'Bomb Blast Rocks Bank in London', *Liverpool Echo*, 24 January 1974, 'Le Front Populaire Pour La Libération De La Palestine Revendique L'attentat Contre M. Sieff', Agence France Presse (AFP), 2 January 1974; and Laszlo Liszkaï, *Le Monde Selon Carlos*, p. 67.

David Yallop's *To the Ends of the Earth*, Follain, Smith and others all give comprehensive accounts of the childhood and youth of Ramírez. 'My Son The Guerrilla: Carlos', the *Observer*, 15 February 1976 was useful too, and my correspondence with Ramírez in March 2023.

For context on Ramírez in the USSR, see 'The Lumumba University in Moscow: Higher Education for a Soviet–Third World Alliance, 1960–91', Constantin Katsakioris, *Journal of Global History*, 2019, and the CIA's October 1968 intelligence assessment of the Soviet programme to provide academic training to students from less developed countries and its report in July 1989, 'Moscow's Third World Educational Programme'. On the KGB and Ramírez, see Follain, pp. 17–18; Yallop, pp. 29, 326; Christopher Andrew, *The Mitrokhin Archive, Vol.* 2, pp. 254–6.

For Ramírez's first trip to Beirut: Bassam Abu Sharif, *Wadi' Haddad*, pp. 177–80; *Tried by Fire*, p. 72; Smith, pp. 44–5, Yallop, pp. 326–7, 330; and my interviews with Ekberg.

For Ramírez, back in London, then in France: Yallop, pp. 328–40 and also Nydia Tobón, *Carlos: terrorista o guerrillero*, Grijalbo, Barcelona, 1978.

On Haddad's break with the PFLP and the appointment of Moukharbal, see Charbel, pp. 130–32, 371; 'La scission au sein du Front populaire pour la libération de la Palestine est consommé', *Le Monde*, 13 March 1972; and 'Moukharbal était responsable du réseau de soutien logistique d'une organisation d'extrême gauche', *Le Monde*, 16 July 1975. Also, author interviews with former PLO, Fatah and PFLP officials, Ramallah and Amman, 2023–24.

For Ramírez's semi-successful attacks in Paris, see Sophie Bonnet, *Salutations Révolutionnaires*; and for the Japanese Red Army, Farrell, pp. 158–9; CIA report of November 1974, 'The Emergence of the Japanese Red Army'; there are useful accounts too in Follain and Smith.

For the drugstore bombing, the most comprehensive current resource I found were the summaries and transcripts of the ten days of hearings of Ramírez's unsuccessful appeal in March 2018 against his conviction for the attack, provided to me by the Fédération Nationale des Victimes d'Attentats et d'Accidents Collectifs (FENVAC). Also useful were *Le Monde*, 'L'OLP dément être mêlée à l'attentat de Saint-Germain-des-Prés', 17 September 1974; '38 ans après l'attentat du drugstore Saint-Germain, un rescapé raconte', *L'Express*, 15 May 2013; also Follain, pp. 46–55, Smith, pp. 2–3.

13. THE REVOLUTIONARY CELLS

Footage of Sartre's visit to Stammheim is easy to find online, so too is the contemporary media reporting of the event. On the details of his conversation with Baader, see *Spiegel*, 'When Sartre Met RAF Leader Andreas Baader', 6 February 2013; US cable from Stuttgart, Sartre Seeks Support For Baader-Meinhof Gang, 6 December 1974; and *Libération*, 'La Mort Lente d'Andreas Baader', Jean-Paul Sartre, 7 December 1974. Fanon's *The Wretched of the Earth* and Sartre's introduction are essential reading to understand the ideas of many people in this book, whether right- or left-wing, religious or secular.

Meinhof's comments are from *Die Tageszeitung*, 12 February 1990, 'Ulrike Meinhof: Briefe aus dem toten Trakt'. Some – such as biographer Judith Dittfurth – have denied she was subjected to such harsh attacks by the others but Aust, pp. 214–17 and Margrit Schiller, pp. 91–2 seem convincing. For court appearance and other details, as well as the death of Holger Meins, see Aust, pp. 202–03 and *Everybody Talks About the Weather*, and Butz Peters, *Tödlicher*, pp. 329–31.

On the Weather Underground, see Burrough, *Days of Rage*, p. 159. On the abortive collaboration between the BSO and RAF see Margrit Schiller, p. 77, and Thomas Skelton-Robinson, in Kraushaar.

My account of Klein's story relies on his memoirs, *La Mort Mercenaire*, and interviews with journalist Marcel Bouguereau published in 1981 as *The German Guerilla: Terror, Reaction and Resistance.* He also participated in a 2005 documentary: *De Terrorist Hans-Joachim Klein*. The Adorno quote is from Kay Schiller, 'Political Militancy And Generation Conflict in West Germany During the "Red Decade"', *Journal of Contemporary Central and Eastern Europe*, 11, No. 1, 2003. The discussion of Spontis in Paul Berman's *Power and the Idealists: Or, the Passion of Joschka Fischer and its Aftermath* is useful. See also *The Red Army Faction, Vol. 1: Projectiles for the People*, pp. 43, 264–6; Varon, p. 46; and Magdalena Kopp, *Die Terrorjahre*, pp. 47–9.

On the Revolutionary Cells, I used Klein, *La Mort*, pp. 191–2, 256–7; Karcher, pp. 58, 124–5; Oliver Schröm, *Im Schatten des Schakals: Carlos und die Wegbereiter des Internationalen Terrorismus*, p. 131; Robert Wolff is the authority, see his contribution on pp. 281–305 in Adrian Hänni, ed., *Über Grenzen hinweg, Transnationale politische Gewalt im 20. Jahrhundert*; *Die Zeit*, 'Der Terrorist, der Sartre chauffierte', 9 January 1976; and Schiller, p. 80.

Klein described his meeting with Ramírez in court in Paris in 2011 (for this I used the FENVAC's transcript) and in Bouguereau, loc 589. On the Orly attacks: Follain, pp. 51–5 and Charbel, p. 314. On the London kidnap plot: Klein, *La Mort*, pp. 70–71, 250–52; Yallop, pp. 127–30 and 448–9; Schröm, pp. 11–13 and 38–42; Klein's 2011 court testimony, during which he also spoke of his admiration for Ramírez.

On US views of RAF violence: US cable from Stuttgart, Baader Meinhof Developments, 5 February 1975 and a report in NYT, 'West Germany's Leftist Guerrillas Reawaken Sensitive Political Issues', 4 March 1975.

On the Stockholm attack: Varon, pp. 236–7; 'German Radicals Flown To Mideast', NYT, 4 March 1975; Jens Nordqvist, *Baader Meinhof: Terrorismens årtionde*, pp. 107–08; Butz Peters, *1977: RAF gegen Bundesrepublik*, p. 127; and *The Red Army*

Faction, Vol. 1: Projectiles for the People, pp. 325–36. I also found several online interviews with Karl-Heinz Dellwo, a participant.

14. WINTER IN NEW YORK, SUMMER IN PARIS

Many of the details of the scene in the rue Toullier apartment come from 'Carlos: The Most Dangerous Man in the World: Profile of a Terrorist', *New York* magazine, 7 November 1977, p. 36. Other sources include Jacquard, *Carlos: Le Dossier Secret*, pp. 18–23; Smith, pp. 150–60; Follain, pp. 58–66; 'Trois morts rue Toullier à Paris: un carnage signé Carlos', *Libération*, 27 June 1975; and Ramírez's own account in his supposed interview published in *al-Watan*, reprinted in *Le Figaro*, 15 December 1979. The building still stands though, as I discovered on a recent trip to Paris, the neighbourhood is no longer quite as cheap and cheerful as in 1975. There are certainly fewer student parties.

Also useful were: *Le Monde*, 'L'Enquête Sur L'affaire De La Rue Toullier Prend Un Caractère International', 4 July 1975; *Le Monde*, 'Michel Moukharbal Était Inconnu Des Services Français Au Moment De Son Arrestation', 11 July 1975; Bernard Violet, *Carlos: Les réseaux secrets du terrorisme international*, p. 135; Daniel Burdan, *DST – Neuf ans à la division antiterroriste*; Casey notes on conversations with Ramírez.

On the radical scene in Paris: Brendan I. Koerner, *The Skies Belong to Us*, pp. 222–3, 227; *Le Monde*, 'Soixante-douze personnalités ont signé l'appel en faveur d'Eldridge Cleaver', 7 August 1973; Julia Lovell, p. 279.

On US frustrations with the French, my interview with a former CIA official posted to western Europe 1971–75, in 2022 was informative. At a counter-terrorism conference, French intelligence services demanded that any aid to their counterparts overseas be kept secret for fear of annoying either armed groups or Arab governments. See Foreign Office File 17/623, 'Acts of Violence by Arab Terrorist Organisations', minute of meetings of the political directors, 24 October 1972.

On Italian arrangements with the PLO see *La Repubblica*, 'Nelle Carte Dei Servizi: L'Accordo OLP-Andreotti', 30 July 2023 and Hänni, *Terrorism in the Cold War, Vol. 2*, pp. 153–73. For the release of Boese see Schröm, pp. 41–2. The Swiss authorities have denied making any deals, which makes the following useful: Hänni, *Terrorism, Vol. 2*, pp. 63–88, and Marcel Gyr's *Schweizer Terrorjahre: Das geheime Abkommen mit der PLO*, NZZ Libro, 2016. Ramírez described the raid in his *al-Watan* interview. For the clumsy British surveillance operation see Aldrich and Cormac, *The Black Door* (Kindle references: loc 5742, 638). On Kilowatt, see Guttmann, as cited above.

On Salameh's renewed contacts with the CIA see Bird, *The Good Spy*, pp. 149–52 and US government Office of the Historian, Department of State, *Foreign Relations of the US, 1969–75, Vol. XXV*, 'Memorandum of a conversation, Washington, August 3, 1973', as well as the CIA's declassified Memorandum to the NSC of August 1973. On Arafat's other outreach efforts: Memo On The Reactions Of The Americans To The Suggestions Relayed On Behalf Of Yasser Arafat, 5 December 1973, Sectia Relatii Externe, Romanian National Central Historical Archives file 284/1973, pp. 2–3, cited Eliza Georghe of the Wilson Center; also, FCO to Cairo, 21 December 1973, FCO 93/180; FCO to Cairo, 21 September 1973, FCO 93/180.

On the PLO shift in strategy see Gowers and Walker, p. 123; Cobban, pp. 61–2; and 'The Palestinian Quest', *Foreign Affairs*, Rouleau, January 1975. On the terrorism debate at the UN, Resolutions at United Nations, A/RES/3034 (XXVII), 18 December 1972; Bruce Hoffman, *Inside Terrorism*, pp. 23–4; Chamberlin, *Global*, pp. 181–2; 'U.N. to Debate Terrorism Despite China and Arabs', NYT, 23 September 1972; Bernhard Blumenau, 'The UN and the Struggle against International Terrorism in the 1970s', *Journal of Cold War Studies*, 2014, and cable from UK Mission to UN on 6 September 1972, FCO RE2/7 17/740. The twenty-two per cent I refer to is of course of the territory of the historic British Mandate excluding Transjordan. Arafat's efforts to open new channels to the US were successful quite quickly. On 8 March 1974, Vernon Walters, a retired US general and polyglot diplomatic troubleshooter who was deputy director of the CIA, met Khaled al-Hassan, the PLO's de facto foreign minister, in a royal guesthouse in Fes, Morocco 'in [a] real Arabian nights environment' for an informal discussion. See Backchannel Message From the Deputy Director of Central Intelligence (Walters) to the President's Assistant for National Security Affairs (Kissinger), Rabat, 8 March 1974.

Details of Salameh's row with the exasperated US diplomats can be read in two US DoS cables from Beirut, both titled PLO Delegation to UNGA, 11 and 12 November 1974.

On Arafat's UN speech and Salameh's meeting with the CIA, see: al-Hout, pp. 124–5; BBC Witness, 30 September 2012 with Nabil Shaath; Gowers and Walker, pp. 131–6; 'Dramatic Session', NYT, 14 November 1973; United Nations record A/PV.2282: Palestine question/Arafat statement, UNGA debate, 13 November 1974; Associated Press, 12 November 1974, 'Palestinian Delegation Under Guard at the UN'; 'Advance P.L.O. Contingent Is Rushed to Waldorf', NYT, 12 November 1974; Taylor, p. 44; Bird, pp. 154–5; and David Ignatius, 'The Secret History of U.S.-PLO Terror Talks', WP, 4 December 1988.

The angry quotes from Habash can be found in 'La participation de l'O.L.P. à la conférence de Genève équivaudrait à la reconnaissance de l'entité sioniste, nous déclare le Dr Georges Habache', *Le Monde*, Rouleau, 6 February 1975.

For the shooting on the rue Toullier: Ramírez interview with Casey; Follain, pp. 62–7; *Libération*, 27 June 1975, 'Trois Morts Rue Toullier À Paris'; *Le Monde*, 'Les enquêteurs croient à la culpabilité de "Carlos" dans les affaires de La Haye et du drugstore Saint-Germain', 8 July 1975; *New York* magazine, 'Carlos: The Most Dangerous Man in the World', 7 November 1977; *Libération*, 'Carlos refait la fusillade de la rue Toullier', 19 December 1997; *Libération*, 'Rue Toullier, le crime était presque signé', 23 December 1997; Bouguereau; Liszkaï, p. 88. Most accounts vary in details only. Ramírez also described the shootings in his famous *al-Watan* interview, published in 1979, and told Casey he had hesitated before shooting Herranz because he did not think the policeman was armed.

For the first stage of Ramírez's escape: Yallop, p. 365, Follain, pp. 67–70; Tobón later told a French court that Ramírez never called her. In London, see GDN reporting: 'Arms Found in London Flat', 2 July 1975; 'Mystery Man With the Black Bag: the Trail That Led From Latin America to a Flat in Bayswater', 3 July 1975; and 'Carlos the Jackal "in London"', 8 July 1975.

15. SAND, SEA AND KALASHNIKOVS

The French authorities were still using identikits, which used sketched features to create a likeness of a wanted individual, as opposed to the newer photofits, an assembly of photographic images, which speeded up the process of creating a likeness. Technology was not the main problem though. Carlos told the FBI in 2012 that the reason he had escaped capture for so long was that customs officials were looking for Arabs, not a pale Latin American.

For the scene at the Air France offices: Follain, p. 68; Smith, pp. 160–61; *Le Monde*, '"Carlos" avait indiqué à l'une de ses amies qu'il allait se rendre au Proche-Orient', 25 July 1975.

Ramírez told a former lover who had allowed him to stay the night that he would travel to Beirut via Brussels and Berlin, according to German police reports based on shared intelligence from other European services. In Swiss documents there is the testimony of a Belgian taxi driver who saw Ramírez in Brussels, according to investigative journalist Marcel Gyr. A US cable from Brussels, Carlos Not Caught In Brussels Raids, 4 March 1976, confirms the existence of safehouses set up by Ramírez in the Belgian capital and mentions a sighting by a cleaning lady.

Ramírez gave a full account of his escape to both Sophie Bonnet, see *Salutations Révolutionnaires*, and to Laszlo Liszkaï, *Le Monde Selon Carlos*, pp. 92–3. There are flaws in his account however. He describes staying at the Hotel Metropol in East Berlin, which only opened in 1977, for example, and is vague about who helped him there.

The 'post revolutionary era' CIA study is available at DI/OCI, Job 79T01022A, Box 1, Folder 40.

I enjoyed my plunge into 1970s Aden immensely. My envious reading of contemporary visitors' accounts included Neil Brehony, *Yemen Divided*, loc 1541, 1832; Fred Halliday, *Revolution and Foreign Policy: the Case of South Yemen 1967–1987*, pp. 8–33, 175; Joe Stork, 'Socialist Revolution in Arabia: a report', *MERIP Reports*, March 1973; and 'Aden in the Time of the Red Star', Franck Mermier, *Transeuropéennes*, 6 April 2010. The CIA's report, 'Problems In The Persian Gulf', of 7 June 1973 noted that 'radical regimes in Iraq and in the People's Democratic Republic of Yemen (PDRY) – aid the Popular Front for the Liberation of Oman and the Arab Gulf (PFLOAG), an umbrella group dedicated to the overthrow of all monarchies in the region.' See also 'PFLO and the subversive threat to the Gulf', 16 October 1975, in FCO 8/2485 NBN 1/3.

On Ramírez's arrival in Aden see Follain, p. 76; Demaris, p. 61; Schröm, pp. 51, 131; Yallop, p. 379; Liszkaï, *Le Monde Selon Carlos*, p. 93; Charbel, p. 94.

Senior Mossad officials told me that their penetration of fedayeen groups during the period was 'very good' but agents' access to information was often limited and few could communicate in a timely fashion. Often intelligence was offered voluntarily. In an internal circular in December 1974, the CIA mentioned a warning from Fatah of a potential attack by a rival armed group in West Germany, for example.

My description of the PFLP camp and its offices in Aden, as well as the experiences of the trainees, is based on Charbel, pp. 53–6, 212–13; Schröm, pp. 94–8; 'Sag mal S'ch', *Spiegel*, 3 October 1977; a transcript of the interrogation of a Dutch extremist who had recently spent time in the camp by Israeli intelligence officials who detained her in 1976; and *TP* magazine, Frans Dekkers and Daan Dijksman, 'Desert Rats, The Game is Over', June 1988, which likewise includes first-hand accounts. Also, Leena Malkki, *How Terrorist Campaigns End*; 'In jeder zweiten Nacht kommen die Gespenster', Peter-Jürgen Boock, *Die Zeit*, 21 November 2020; Kopp, pp. 97–8. Bouguereau, loc 727; Klein, *La Mort*, p. 272.

On Ramírez's conversion: Sophie Bonnet, *Salutations Révolutionnaires*, and Liszkaï, ibid., p. 95. Ramírez described it to Bonnet as a joke but Bonnet, who spent hours in his company, does not believe this to be the case as any levity on his part would have been grossly insulting to those who had suggested the conversion. See also 'Carlos: Ma Vie Avec les Médias', in *Médias*, No. 25, 2010 in which Ramírez explained he had converted at the urgent request of the Muslim fedayeen under his command, who wanted him to lead them, if necessary, to paradise.

You'll find the CIA's humour here: CIA Weekly Situation Report on International Terrorism, 17 December 1974.

16. CHRISTMAS IN VIENNA

The man who brought the request from Gaddafi was Kamal Kheir-Beik, a Syrian Alawite and former senior official in the Syrian Social Nationalist Party once close to the Assad family who had fled to Paris in 1962, probably after the coup attempt of that year. In France, he studied modernist Arab poetry and was active in the Palestinian and Arab nationalist movements, though closer initially to Fatah. Considered the inevitable successor to Mohammed Boudia after his assassination in 1972, many were surprised when Haddad appointed Michel Moukharbal instead. See Charbel, pp. 57, 224; undated FBI memo on Kamal Kheir-Beik, author collection.

For the preparations for the OPEC attack, I used: Liszkaï, *Le Monde Selon Carlos*, pp. 63, 99–102, and Charbel, pp. 81–93 and a summary of Ramírez's interview with Casey. Ramírez has said repeatedly that Gaddafi was responsible for the attack, telling Casey in 2012, French filmmaker and author Sophie Bonnet in around 2015, and me in a letter in 2023. Charbel, pp. 219–21 states categorically that the Libyans both commissioned the operation and supplied the materiel for it.

On Ramírez and the Revolutionary Cells: see Bouguereau, loc 326, 698; Liszkaï, p. 100; Saul David, *Entebbe*, pp. 47–8; Kopp, p. 47; Wolff, in ed. Hänni; Klein, *La Mort Mercenaire*, p. 75; Schröm, pp. 12, 35–6, 60–62; Charbel, pp. 218–21; Skelton-Robinson, in Kraushaar; Schiller, loc 1709; interview with Gerd Schnepel in *Jungle. World*, No. 2000/48, 'Dossier: The Carlos Haddad Connection', 29 November 2000; Follain, pp. 79–80; Bonnet, loc 1893.

On the days before the attack: Bouguereau, pp. 391, 404; 'When modern terrorism began: The OPEC hostage taking of 1975', Thomas Riegler, in *Handbook of OPEC and the Global Energy Order*; Klein, pp. 79–91; 'Account of the debriefing of Carlos', internal document of the PFLP–XO, presented at the trial of Hans-Joachim Klein in 2000; *Face à Carlos le Chacal*, France 2, 2018; also my correspondence with Ramírez Sánchez.

For the attack itself: Colin Smith, pp. 191, 200–12; Schröm, pp. 61–70, Yallop, pp. 383–97; Charbel, p. 243; *Le Monde*, 'Vienna, 1975: Je suis Carlos!', 21 September 2001; 'Terrorists Raid Opec Oil Parley In Vienna, Kill 3', NYT, 22 December 1975; US DoS cable from Berlin, Terrorist Attack Against Opec HQ In Vienna, 23 January 1976.

On Yamani and in the plane: Smith, pp. 229–31; Jeffrey Robinson, *Yamani: The Inside Story*, Kindle edition loc 3683; Schröm, pp. 70–75; Riegler's chapter in the *Handbook of OPEC and the Global Energy Order*; US cable from Tripoli, Additional Details On Opec Attack, 24 December 1975. US DoS cable from Algeria, Release Of Opec Terrorists, 31 December 1975; Robinson, loc 3725, 3730; and US DoS cable from Kuwait, Opec Kidnapping, 4 January 1976 which describes the Kuwaiti oil minister's complaining about Ramírez's poor Arabic.

For events in Tripoli and Algiers: Yallop, pp. 397–409; Schröm, pp. 83–7; Robinson, loc 3835; Charbel, pp. 243–9; Smith, pp. 229–40; and 'Freeing Of Raiders Upheld In Algiers', 2 January 1976, AFP. See also the interview with Klein, who refused an invitation to meet Gaddafi because he was still shocked by the killing in Vienna, in the documentary *De Terrorist Hans-Joachim Klein*, 2005.

Back in Aden: Charbel, p. 59; Schröm, pp. 91–3; Yallop, p. 411; Bonnet, loc 2370, 2502; Follain, p. 104; Casey's notes of interview with Ramírez, 2015. Leila Khaled says that many within the PFLP were unclear about what had happened to the money until around 1978, when they were told by Algerian secret services that Ramírez had stolen some or all of it. Liszkaï, pp. 115–17, says Ramírez and Klein flew in a jet provided by Gaddafi to Mogadishu, where they rested for several weeks and saw Haddad, before returning to Aden.

17. TO ENTEBBE

Halfon Hill Is Not Responding can be watched online and is very funny even if you do not speak Hebrew. My thanks to the Jerusalem Cinematheque for the correct location of where it was filmed.

Meir's quote is from *My Life*, p. 382. Shimon Peres describes Israelis as 'unnerved' and having lost 'self-confidence' in *No Room for Small Dreams*, pp. 112, 139.

On Palestinian attacks and Israeli reprisals, see: Sayigh, p. 358; Betser, pp. 263–78; 'Israelis bomb camps after kidnappings', GDN, 8 August 1974; 'Un raid de représailles Israélien fait douze morts', *Le Monde*, 23 August 1975; 'Le général Dayan: ces opérations sont contraires aux lois internationales mais nous n'avons pas le choix', *Le Monde*, 14 August 1973; US DoS cable from Beirut, Further Details Re Israeli Air Raid On Beirut, 13 December 1974; Smith, p. 93; 'Tactics Shift in Guerrilla Warfare', David Hirst, GDN, 12 July 1974; also Hirst's *Gun and Olive Branch*, p. 458. The statement was a letter to Yasser Arafat explaining that they had 'given their lives in confidence that our sacrifice . . . will not be sold for surrender solutions'. Ahmed Jibril, who sent them, said: 'The trio accepted the instructions quite willingly . . . This is the point in the case of Palestine. It is a big challenge . . . It shows there is a people ready to fight and die rather than surrender.' The Israelis were not entirely unaware of the threat. Writing in 1975, Golda Meir described how the Libyan airline shot down by Israeli fighters in 1973 was thought to be packed with explosives and aimed at Tel Aviv. Meir, p. 347.

On the abortive Nairobi attack: *Die Zeit*, 'Den Haien zum Frass', Holger Stark, 24

January 2018; 'Schwarze Kapuze', *Spiegel*, 27 May 1979; thanks to Thomas Skelton-Robinson for making his research available to me.

On planning of Entebbe attack, I was helped by an unpublished interview by Saul David with Gerd Schnepel in 2013; Liszkaï, p. 121; Bouguereau; Wolff, pp. 281–305; David, p. 48; Kopp, p. 64. See Charbel, p. 30 for Haddad's literary and sporting interests. Ramírez told me that Kuhlmann was pregnant with his child in a letter in 2023 and told Bonnet too.

On Israeli periphery strategy see Yossi Alpher, *Periphery: Israel's Search for Middle East Allies*, 2015.

For Amin, I was helped by: *Idi Amin: The Story of Africa's Icon of Evil*, Mark Leopold, pp. 154–5, 169–71. Also helpful were 'Uganda Expulsion a Blow to Israelis', NYT, 22 April 1974; 'Amin Praises Hitler for Killing of Jews', NYT, 13 September 1972; 'Libya's Military Largesse Feeds Idi Amin's Anti-Zionism', WP, 26 February 1977; 'Amin says War Confirms his View on Hitler and the Jews', NYT, 11 October 1973. US cables from Kampala, Soviet Plans To Get Second Military Foothold In East Africa, 16 October 1975 and Amin Meets Local PLO Representative, Reiterates Support for Palestinian Cause, 1 September 1973. Also, US cable from Bonn, Conditions In Uganda, 16 October 1975.

Amin's involvement in the PFLP's plot has been much debated but it seems clear to me that the Ugandan president only learned of the plan after it had been launched. See Liszkaï, p. 119, and Charbel, p. 108, where a letter from the PFLP to Amin sent as the hijacking was underway is reproduced. Also US cable, Ugandan Role In Air France Hijacking, 7 July 1976 and British FCO memo, FCO 93/913 on Collusion Between Idi Amin and the PLO Hijackers, 6 July 1976.

The hijacking itself has been described many times. The most balanced and readable is the account in Saul David's *Entebbe*. Goldberg-Cojot's extraordinary book, *Namesake*, Claude Moufflet's *Otages à Kampala* and William Stevenson's *90 Minutes At Entebbe* are all useful too. Other sources include Yehuda Avner, *The Prime Ministers*, and *Operation Thunder: The Entebbe Raid: The Israelis' Own Story*, by Yehuda Ofer. I also consulted much contemporary media reporting as well as US DoS cables from Paris: Air France Hijacking, 3 July 1976; Highjacked Air France Aircraft, 1 July 1976; Hostage Discussions Uganda Hijacking, 8 July 1976; and Jonathan Freedland's 'The Raid on Entebbe, 40 Years On', GDN, 20 March 2017. The argument over the alleged 'selection' of Jewish passengers continues to this day.

For the stories of the attackers, I used Laura Blumenfeld, 'Brothers in Arms', WP, 9 March 1997; George Habache, *Les Révolutionnaires*, pp. 88, 93; Bassam Abu Sharif's book on Wadie Haddad; Cojot, p. 109; a footnote on p. 211 of Abu Daoud's *Palestine*, as well as interviews in Ramallah in 2023 and 2024 and letters from Ramírez to me.

Details of Bose's speeches and deteriorating conditions at Entebbe can be found in Moufflet; David, pp. 66–7, 69; Herf; Cojot, p. 111; a US DoS cable from Paris, Air France Hijacking, 3 July 1976; and FCO documents in file FCO 93/913.

Several sources suggest Haddad himself travelled to Kampala, or even Entebbe, to manage negotiations with Amin. This is plausible, though it would have been a very risky thing to do. That Haddad used Mogadishu as a forward base, as several other sources recount, is also possible.

18. OPERATION THUNDERBOLT

To avoid being influenced by the many cinematic – and often semi-fictionalised – versions of events described in this book, I watched (or rewatched) most of them only after finishing a first draft. Those showing the Entebbe raid offer a good example of how representations on the screen have a determining influence on the popular memory of this kind of event.

For this account of the debates among Israeli decision-makers, I have relied on Avner, pp. 308–09 and 323, Peres, pp. 121–2, 127 and 134. David is very good, pp. 248–56.

For the flight of the Israeli special forces, see David and Stevenson. Amir Ofer's public lecture on being 'The First Israeli Soldier in Entebbe Airport' is available online. Listen to *Covert* podcast 10: 'Entebbe: Hostage Rescue, Part 2', 24 July 2018. See too Iddo Netanyahu, *Yoni's Last Battle*, pp. 168–71.

For the short firefight at the airport and its immediate aftermath, Ofer, pp. 121–2; Netanyahu, pp. 182–93; Moufflet, loc 2334; Simon Dunstan, *Israel's Lightning Strike*, p. 116; Betser, p. 333. See also: Ynet.Com, 'Operation Entebbe: Heading to Uganda', and 'Storming the Terminal', 28 and 30 June 2016, by Ronen Bergman and Lior Ben-Ami.

That Bose hesitated is well documented by multiple witnesses. The shout of 'get down' comes from NYT, 'Drama in Hijacking of Jet to Uganda', 11 July 1976, and other accounts.

For the reaction in Israel: 'Israelis Jubilant as Amin Laments', GDN, 5 July 1976 and Avner, pp. 314–16. Also, David, pp. 336–7 and Anshel Pfeffer, *Bibi*, p. 175. In the US: 'Folk Song on Entebbe', Jewish Telegraphic Agency, 19 August 1976; Amy Kaplan, *Our American Israel*, pp. 132–4. In the UK: see FCO cables from London and from Kampala on 5 July 1976, both in in FCO 93/913, and Leopold, p. 273. In Germany: US DoS cable from Berlin, Uganda Hijacking: Release Of German Prisoners, 3 July 1976. At the UN: 'For and Against Amin – the Africans Divided', GDN, 6 July 1976; US DoS cable from UN, Uganda Rescue: Egyptian FM Fahmy's Statement, 10 July 1976; US DoS cable from New York, Security Council – Entebbe Events, 15 July 1976; 'La Pravda: un raid de bandits et des méthodes de gangsters', *Le Monde*, 12 July 1976. For reaction in the Middle East see *Le Monde*, 'Le détournement à eté réalisé par des dissidents du F.P.L.P., affirme M. Habache', 13 July 1976, among much other media reporting. Also DoS cable from Tunis, Bourguiba Message to Idi Amin Dada on Entebbe Raid, 12 July 1976 and from Rabat, GoM Hits Hijackers, Criticizes Israeli Commando Operation, 9 July 1976. Finally, for reaction of Ramírez: Bouguereau, loc 681, 682; Yallop, p. 418.

The CIA's report on 27 September 1977 entitled: 'International Issues Regional And Political Analysis' gives a sense of views among spies and policy-makers in the US and Israel and elsewhere. See also Stevenson, p. 9 and US DoS cable from Tel Aviv, Israel After Entebbe, 14 July 1976.

The poster with Kuhlmann and Bose is reproduced in Herf, location 9570; the references to the photographs taken of the German attackers prior to the operation come from David's unpublished interview with Schnepel.

My account here of the reaction of the Revolutionary Cells is based on multiple sources, but particularly Schröm, p. 130; David, pp. 363–4; and press reporting at the time.

For the broader context, see the entertaining and informed Thomas Borstelmann, *The 1970s: A New Global History From Civil Rights To Economic Inequality*, and relevant parts of the very good Paul Chamberlin, *The Cold War's Killing Fields*.

19. AN OUTRAGE FOR GOD

For the summer of 1977 in Cairo, Gilles Kepel's *Muslim Extremism in Egypt: The Prophet and Pharaoh*, pp. 73–101 is hard to beat. Details also came from reporting in *Le Monde* and the *Guardian*, and US cable from Cairo to DoS, Further Atonement (Takfir) Society Developments, 11 July 1977.

I have been reading about Qutb for twenty-five years but here I used Jonathan Calvert's *Sayyid Qutb and the Origins of Radical Islam*, Fawaz Gerges, *Making the Arab World: Nasser, Qutb and the Clash that Shaped the Middle East*, and Esposito and Shahin, *The Oxford Handbook of Islam and Politics*, pp. 159–68.

Learning about Qutb's enthusiasm for the anti-colonial causes worldwide of the immediate post-war years and even left-leaning Third Worldism of the 1950s was exciting and important. See pp. 116–18 in Calvert, who makes the excellent point that Qutb had 'absorbed the revolutionary discourse' so ubiquitous by the mid-1960s 'by osmosis'.

There is no doubt that Qutb saw both Zionists and Jews as enemies and made little distinction between the two. A tract from the early 1950s was entitled 'Our Struggle with the Jews', who he describes as a perpetual enemy of Muslims, naturally selfish, and without a sentiment of connection to the rest of humanity. Herf has pointed out that not only does Qutb argue that Jews are enemies of Islam, and have always sought its destruction, but also that they have deserved punishments inflicted by Allah and, in one instance at least, carried out by Hitler. See Paul Berman et al., 'Islamism, Unveiled: From Berlin to Cairo and Back Again', *Foreign Affairs*, Vol. 89, No. 5, 2010.

The detainees statistic is from FCO memo, The Muslim Brotherhood Since 1954, 7 November 1963, FCO 464/60. In his book *Karnak Café*, finished in 1971 and published in 1974, probably because the political climate was more conducive to a controversial work, Naguib Mahfouz describes prison conditions and torture of suspected Communists and Islamists.

My account of Qutb's imprisonment is drawn from Kepel's *Prophet*, pp. 236–9 and *Princeton Readings in Islamist Thought*, pp. 129–35, 322–3; Jeffrey Kenney, *Kharijites and the Politics of Extremism in Egypt*, pp. 119–22; and Alison Pargeter, *The Muslim Brotherhood: From Opposition to Power*, pp. 32–4, among other sources.

For Shukri's ideas and practice, see Kepel, pp. 74, 90–91; Rogan, p. 503; Hegghammer's *The Caravan*, pp. 30, 75; and Gerges, p. 321. There is also the brilliant article by Saad Eddin Ibrahim, 'Anatomy of Egypt's Militant Islamic Groups: Methodological Note and Preliminary Findings', first published in the *International Journal of Middle East Studies*, Vol. 12, No. 4, 1980, and reprinted in *Egypt, Islam, and Democracy: Critical Essays* twenty-two years later.

The 'Allah' quote is from Dina Rezk, *The Arab World and Western Intelligence: Analysing the Middle East, 1956–1981*. The witness is in Gerges, pp. 304–13. On Sadat and the Islamists see Kepel, p. 76; Eddin, 'An Islamic Alternative in Egypt: The Muslim Brotherhood and Sadat', *Arab Studies Quarterly*, Vol. 4, No. 1/2, 1982, pp. 75–93; Abdullah al-Arian, *Answering the Call: Popular Islamic Activism In Sadat's Egypt*, p. 84; and Jan Morris, *Destinations: Essays from Rolling Stone*. Sadat's assumed title was a compromise between the secular *el Rais* – the chief or president – and the religious *emir ul Momineen* – the leader of the faithful.

Details of the military academy plot come from media reporting at the time, such as 'Eleven Killed During Sabotage Attack on Cairo Army Academy', GDN, 20 April 1974, as well as Kepel, pp. 92–4; Ibrahim's articles and Montasser al-Zayat, *The Road to al-Qaeda*, p. 26. Salih Sirriya, its leader, may have been a former member of the PFLP and veteran of the 1970 fighting in Jordan. He had arrived in Egypt in around 1971, was rapidly drawn to the 'Qutbist' fringe of the Islamist movement but was not convinced that ordinary Egyptians were corrupt and decadent, only their leaders.

For the trial of Shukri and its aftermath see 'Death Sentence for Minister's Killers', Reuters, 1 December 1977 and US cables from Cairo: Takfir Trial Opens, 24 August 1977, Yet Another Right Wing Group, 30 August 1977 and Takfir Drags On, sent 11 November 1977. See too the astonishing Associated Press footage of Shukri's male followers arriving in court in army trucks, chanting defiantly, and of his female followers looking utterly cowed and miserable. Search for 'SYND 051077 Court Scenes in Cairo'.

There is vast academic literature on the Islamic resurgence during the 1970s around the region and beyond. Kepel's *Jihad* is probably still the best, along with Olivier Roy's work, see for example his provocatively entitled *The Failure of Political Islam* of 1994, and *The Search for a New Ummah*, 2002. Kim Ghattas' *Black Wave* is a readable recent addition. I read much contemporary press reporting, which showed that many observers were well aware of the phenomenon. See 'Où Dieu n'est pas mort', Maxime Rodinson, *Le Monde*, 6 December 1978, for example.

20. THE JACKAL AT BAY

Recreating life in Baghdad in the mid- to late 1970s was a great pleasure. I had done some groundwork when reporting from the city in the late 1990s and in 2003 but contemporary travel guides and postcards as well as online archive footage, specialist social media (such as Old Iraqi Pictures @IraqiPic on X) and blogs on the history of popular music in the Middle East all helped. French reporters did some good work there at the time. See Mark Yared's 'Iraq: Parti Dirigeant, Appareil D'état Et Armée', *Le Monde*, 18 July 1977 for an example.

The quote on Ramírez's emotional state is from Liszkaï, p. 131. His jet-set lifestyle and ambitions are based on Liszkaï, pp. 110, 121; Klein's interview in Bonnet's film; and *Tel Quel*, 'Carlos "le Chacal" et le régime algérien voulaient-ils assassiner Hassan II?', 29 June 2017. For the multiple sightings: Bouguereau, loc 608; US cables from Mexico, Whereabouts Of 'Carlos', 12 October 1976 and from Algiers, Terrorism: Whereabouts Of Carlos, 30 September 1976. Also, see *Spiegel*, 'Carlos: Der terror Wird International', 25 July 1976. Smith talks about Ramírez at Entebbe enjoying a meal in Kampala during the Israeli assault, p. 250; Hänni, *Terrorism in the Cold War, Vol. 1*, pp. 1–21 gives an excellent overview of the media frenzy.

On Yugoslavia as a potential base: 'Yugoslavia, Carlos "The Jackal" And International Terrorism During The Cold War', Gordan Akrap, in Hänni, ed., *Vol. 1*, pp. 173, 178; Liszkaï, p. 130; Cable from DoS to embassies, Alleged Planned Terrorist Attacks By Ilich Ramírez Sanchez Aka Carlos, Hans Joachim Klein And Others, 6 September 1976.

For Ramírez's truncated stay in Yugoslavia, I have relied on Akrap's article, and Polona Balantič, 'Jugoslavija in mednarodni terorizem v sedemdesetih letih. Dva primera neizročitve teroristov Zvezni republiki Nemčiji' (Yugoslavia and international terrorism in the 1970s. Two cases of non-extradition of terrorists to the Federal Republic of Germany), in *Contributions to Contemporary History*, 1/2015, pp. 146–87; also Schröm, pp. 119–35; much German media reporting; Liszkaï, pp.130–31; and Aburish's *Saddam Hussein: the Politics of Revenge*, p. 118.

On Iraq's Shia, Faleh A. Jabar, *The Shiite Movement in Iraq*, Saqi, 2002 stands out for its detailed analysis of the rise of radical Islamism there, and how it was closely related to the repression and decline of Communism, pp. 213–15.

For the training camps etc., see the CIA's 1982 report 'Iraq: The Uses Of Terror', and a US cable from Baghdad, Terrorist Activities Supported By Iraq, 30 November 1976. Further details are in a 1981 note filed by officials from Romania's Ministry of the Interior on Palestinian organisations in Iraq: see translation by the Wilson Center. For Japan reference: US cable DoS to Tokyo, Terrorist Threats Against US Movie Distributor, 27 July 1977. On the appalling Abu Nidal, see books by Patrick Seale and Yossi Melman.

Details of the arrival of Ramírez in Baghdad and arrangements made for him are in Liszkaï, *Le Monde Selon Carlos*, pp. 110, 121–3, and Kopp, pp. 120–21.

My account of Klein's desertion of Ramírez and the cause is based on his accounts in *La Mort Mercenaire*, especially pp. 266–70, interviews with Bouguereau and the FENVAC transcript of Klein's testimony during Ramírez's trial in Paris, November 2011, for the bombings in France in 1982 and 1983. For further details of his reaction to Entebbe and other schemes, see Schröm, p. 137; 'Pope Faced Kidnap Plot', GDN, 7 August 1978; Follain, p. 105; and Kopp, p. 109. For Klein's writing retreat in the Aosta valley, see Schröm, pp. 139–41; the 2005 documentary; Bouguereau; and *Jungle.World*, 29 November 2000, 'Mit Angie im Aostatal'. Also, Kopp, pp. 107–08.

The planned abduction is mentioned by Duane Clarridge in *A Spy For All Seasons*, pp. 230–32. For the South American collaboration see GDN, 'Operation Condor', 3 September 2020.

On general context and turning away from violent extremism, see Berman, p. 67 and Burrough, pp. 367–8. 'Whatever happened to Leon Trotsky, [or] dear old Lenin?' asked the Stranglers, a British band in the vanguard of the new disruptive musical style dubbed punk, in 1977 before concluding there were 'no more heroes anymore'.

21. OFFENSIVE 77

My description of Meinhof's last months and death is based on diverse sources, including Dittfurth's biography, Becker's *Hitler's Children*, Aust, Butz Peters' *Tödlicher Irrtum*, and others. Other details came from Bauer, pp. 81–2, 86; *Die Welt*, 'Warum sich Ulrike Meinhof wirklich das Leben nahm', 8 May 2016; 'Ulrike Meinhof's Dance of Death', GDN, 10 May 1976; and an interview with Bettina Rohl in the documentary, *Children of the Revolution*.

For Meinhof's funeral: media reporting at the time, Dittfurth, p. 445; Aust, pp. 262–3. US diplomats also noted that the 'reaction of average citizen to funeral activities ranged from indifference and curiosity to outright hostility on part of many'. The plan to break Baader et al. out of Stammheim is mentioned in Schiller, p. 80. The Dutch activist is here: *Trouw*, 'Ik voelde me een desperado', Antoine Verbij, 18 October 2007.

For my account of the events of the summer and autumn of 1977, the following works were essential: Butz Peters' *1977*, Aust and *Stern* magazine's reporting. The latter was happily not merely compiled into an 'instant book' but one translated into English as *Assault at Mogadishu*, by Peter Koch and Kai Hermann. Bernard Volker's *L'Affaire Schleyer* is similar, but in French. *Spiegel*'s archives are very useful too, not least because many are automatically translated into English online.

On the new trips by German extremists to the Middle East, see Thomas Skelton-Robinson in Kraushaar; Peters, *1977*, pp. 132–4, 153–6, 334–6; Aust, pp. 268–71, 276–7; and Peter-Jürgen Boock's interview with *Die Zeit*, 'In jeder zweiten Nacht kommen die Gespenster', 21 November 2020.

For the killing of Siegfried Buback, see Aust, pp. 286–8; Michael Sontheimer, 'Tödliche Salve an der Ampel', *Spiegel*, 4 May 2007; Koch and Hermann, p. 17. The codename was a reference to the victim's initials. SB was also the name of a well-known brand of margarine.

For that of Ponto, see Peters, *Tödlicher*, pp. 389–90; also 'Red Roses from Roter Morgen', *Time*, 15 August 1977; and Boock's *Die Zeit* interview. Ponto had been executed 'according to Stammheim guidelines', announced a statement written by Mohnhaupt.

For the trial, references include a US DoS cable from Bonn, Baader-Meinhof Trial Jeopardized By Stammheim Bugging, 22 March 1977 and Amnesty International's annual report of 1977, pp. 249–53. The German government was sufficiently concerned to send Amnesty a very long and detailed rebuttal of its allegations of mistreatment and mistrial.

For conditions in Stammheim for RAF inmates and the RAF leader's ultimatum, see Aust, pp. 313–14; Neaman; and Varon, p. 221; 'So kamen Schusswaffen in den Hochsicherheitstrakt', *Die Welt*, 17 June 2021; Peters, *1977*, p. 516; Aust, p. 297. Ensslin read *Le Monde* and deputed Mohnhaupt, who spoke some English, to scan the British newspapers.

For Mohnhaupt and Boock in Baghdad, see Aust, pp. 287–8; Volker, p. 103; Malkki, pp. 60–61; Aust, pp. 287–8; Skelton-Robinson in Kraushaar; *Spiegel*, 'Sie haben Schach gespielt und Gesellschaftsspiele', 6 September 2007. Curtis, *The Middle East*, p. 242 for the Saudi plot.

The extraordinary, intense debate in Cologne is described in Butz Peters, *1977*, pp. 533–5 and Aust, pp. 301–02. The abduction of Schleyer is narrated in some detail by Koch and Hermann, pp. 21–2; also see Aust, pp. 308–09; Peters, *Tödlicher*, pp. 397–8. For the reaction of the German government, see US DoS cable from Bonn, Schleyer Case Enters Its Eighth Day, 13 September 1977; Peters, *Tödlicher*, pp. 402–10; Koch and Hermann, pp. 26–35. On conditions for Schleyer, see Schiller, pp. 121–2 and Peters, *1977*, p. 249. On negotiations, see 'Sie haben Schach gespielt und Gesellschaftsspiele', *Spiegel*, 6 September 2007; 'The Verbal Component of Terrorism Strategy: A West German Textual Case Study', CIA, May 1984; Aust, p. 343; Koch and Hermann, pp. 35–6; Volker, pp. 38–51. For the RAF's choice of which attack offered by Haddad: Skelton-Robinson; Peters, *1977*, pp. 249–52; Varon, p. 236; Aust, pp. 350–52; Sigrid Sternebeck, *Spiegel*, 'Dann sind bald alle tot', 12 August 1990.

It is worth pointing out quite how controversial for the RAF a hijacking of a Lufthansa plane would have been. When Heinrich Böll described the RAF as 'six against sixty million' many years before, Meinhof had objected, arguing that inhabitants of West Germany were never the group's enemy.

For Shigenobu and her image in the media, see Szendi Schieder, *Coed Revolution: The Female Student in the Japanese New Left, 1957–1972*, pp. 115, 207; 'Women Active Among Radicals In West Europe', NYT, 14 August 1977; 'Lady Terrorist in White', the *Observer*, 9 February 1974; Hanshew, pp. 187–8.

When the German federal police analysed forty profiles of wanted RAF suspects in 1977 they counted twenty-four women, and that of 112 'anarchist' or 'terrorist violent criminals' of the RAF and the J2M combined, fifty-four were female – just under forty-eight per cent. See 'Frauen im Untergrund', *Spiegel*, 8 August 1977; 'Worte der Wut', *Spiegel*, 10 August 1975; *Bundeszentrale fur politische Bildung*, 'Frauen in der RAF', Gisela Diewald-Kerkmann, 20 August 2007.

On the JRA's failures in Japan: 'Japanese Arrest Guerrilla Suspect', GDN, 21 July 1977; see CIA, International Issues Monthly Review, 23 February 1978, pp. 43–7.

For the JRA's hijacking, which coincided with a coup attempt in Bangladesh, see 'Hijackers Demand $6M Ransom', 29 September 1977 and 'Japan Wants Ransom and Hijackers Back', 5 October 1977, both in the GDN; also Farrell, pp. 185–9.

22. THE LAST AKTION

My account of the conversations at Mogadishu between hijackers and German representatives is based on two reports in *Der Spiegel* – 'Protokoll der "Landshut"-Entführung', 29 September 2008, and 'Hier spricht Captain Märtyrer Mahmud', 27 November 1977 – as well as Koch and Hermann's *Assault at Mogadishu*, pp. 138–48. On the biographies of the female hijackers, see Barry Davies, *Shadow of the Dove*, pp. 71–3, who interviewed Andrawes. The best source by far however is the sixty-page judgement in the trial of Andrawes in Germany in 1996, which draws on the testimony of multiple witnesses and of the accused to describe in great detail her route into violent extremism. There were several key events – Andrawes' wish to train in Jerusalem as a nun was thwarted by the Israeli victory in the war of 1967, the massacre of Palestinians in Beirut in 1975 at Tel al-Za'atar shocked her deeply – but one very important factor must have been the support and encouragement of her mother.

For Akache, see Schröm, pp. 156–7; Koch and Hermann, pp. 53–63; and *Hansard* of 17 November 1977 which tells us that Merlyn Rees, the Home Secretary, admitted to the British parliament that the suspected killer left through Heathrow airport shortly after the murders using a Kuwaiti passport. 'Soon after the murders had been committed, the police and the immigration service at Heathrow were alerted, but the descriptions of the suspect ... were insufficiently detailed to enable Akache to be identified and apprehended,' Rees explained.

To describe the first days of the hijacking (as far as Aden) I relied on the German judicial ruling on Andrawes, pp. 19–36; Koch and Hermann; Davies, pp. 15–16; Peters, *Tödlicher*, pp. 443–9. Also, 'Fünf Tage als Geisel: Wie zwei Überlebende die Qualen an Bord der "Landshut" erlebten', *Stern*, 7 April 2019, and 'Fünf Tage Todesangst', *Spiegel*, 11 October 2017; *Focus*, 'Die letzten Minuten des "Landshut" Kapitäns', 25 August 2007; 'Secret Tricks that Beat the Hijackers', the *Observer*, 23 October 1977; 'Macht keinen Quatsch', *Die Welt*, 16 October 1977; and Aust, pp. 381–4, 390.

For events at Mogadishu, see the Andrawes ruling, pp. 38–55; Koch and Hermann, pp. 130–52; 'Protokoll der "Landshut"-Entführung'; Peters, *1977*, p. 256; Volker, pp. 151–77; and a US cable, PLO Wadi Haddad Faction Activity, 26 April 1976. The excellent website of the 'Landshut77' project – landshut77.de – has long interviews with key actors including passengers, cabin staff, co-pilot Jürgen Vietor, the then West German minister of justice, and members of the GSG9 assault team.

Carter had already signalled the aim of winning over Somalia as a local ally in April 1977. Hours after the raid, Barre's officials put out a statement boasting of a successful operation by 'Somali security forces in conjunction with some German technical experts'. A month later, Barre revoked a friendship treaty with the USSR, expelled Soviet military experts and broke off diplomatic relations with Cuba. See 'L'attitude coopérative du président somalien devrait faciliter le rapprochement amorcé entre Mogadiscio et l'Occident', *Le Monde*, 20 October 1977.

For reaction in Germany and the Stammheim suicides, the contemporary media reporting is voluminous. Some useful examples include 'Deutsche können stark und menschlich sein', in *Der Spiegel* of 23 October 1977, 'Le Dénouement De L'affaire Du Boeing Et Ses Répercussions' in *Le Monde* of 20 October 1977, 'Bloody Drama Far From Over' in the *Observer* on 23 October 1977, and 'Schmidt Seeks To Clear Up Baader Suicide Doubts', GDN, 19 October 1977. See also the interview with Schmidt in *Todspiel*, documentary, 1997; Peters, *Tödlicher*, p. 520; Peters, *1977*, p. 271; Aust, pp. 397–9, 413–14; and a US DoS cable from Stuttgart, headlined Reaction To Death Of Baader And Associates, 21 October 1977.

On reporting of Haddad, see 'A Loose Alliance of Terrorists Does Seem to Exist', NYT, 23 October 1977, and for how the destination of the *Landshut* was Aden all along, Charbel, p. 122, and the Andrawes ruling, p. 36, which describes the disappointment of the hijackers to find such a hostile reception in Yemen. The ruling also suggests that Haddad had told Zohair and the others to draw out the hijacking for seven days before heading to Aden.

As with Meinhof, the final days and weeks of Baader and Ensslin have been exhaustively investigated and discussed. A question is whether either regretted the course they had followed. No one can be sure, of course, but in a meeting in prison with clerics shortly before she died, Ensslin recalled the great cause of her youth – the Vietnam war – and her belief that only violence could free the oppressed. Ensslin said she now feared ties between the US and West Germany would combine with the manufactured 'dependency' of the masses to bring about a terrible nuclear war. 'This must be prevented by any means, force if necessary,' she told her visitors. Shortly before his suicide, Baader told an official that the RAF had always avoided targeting 'innocent civilians' but had been driven to desperate measures by the German state. He appeared 'at the end of his tether', the official reported, 'pale, agitated [but] polite'. See Stern and Herrmann, pp. 280–81.

23. CARLOS REDUX

The two most useful sources for Ramírez's stay in Algeria are Oliver Schröm's *Im Schatten des Schakals* and Magdalena Kopp's *Terrorjahre*. This is also true for the story of Kopp's gradual and almost inadvertent slide into violent extremism. Schröm interviewed Kopp at length and worked hard to verify what she told him. For Weinrich, see Wolff in Adrian Hänni, pp. 281–305. Kopp added further details about both former lovers in a series of interviews shortly before she died. One appeared in the *Financial Times* as a lunch engagement – 'First Person: Magdalena Kopp', 20 October 2007.

I viewed Associated Press (AP) archive footage of Haddad's funeral on YouTube and in Bonnet's documentary; there are also photographs with Alamy, the stock image agency; see too US cable from Baghdad, Iraq Mourns Wadie Haddad, 2 April 1978.

For good background on Yuri Andropov and the KGB, see Andrew and Mitrokhin, *Vol.* 2, pp. 10–14. I have a copy of Haddad's KGB 'appointment' letter. Other useful documents are available online. On Soviet attitudes to the PLO see Andrew and Mitrokhin, pp. 144–5 as well as files in FCO 8/3462 1980 at Kew. On the superpower conflict more generally, I enjoyed Sergey Radchenko's *To Run the World*, the masterful Odd Arne Westad's *The Cold War*, John Lewis Gaddis' more conventional work of the same name and Paul Chamberlin's aforementioned *Killing Fields*. Lorenz Lüthi's *Cold Wars: Asia, the Middle East, Europe* is vast in scope. All contain passages covering Moscow's dealings with groups like the PFLP in the Middle East and elsewhere, as well as broader material on the geopolitics of the era.

On the shipments of weapons to the PFLP and Haddad's meetings in Beirut and Moscow with the KGB see memos in FCO file 93/1561, entitled PLO, from December 1978; Andrews, Mitrokhin, *Vol.* 2, pp. 251–3, and 'The KGB's Abduction Program and the PFLP', Isabella Ginor and Gideon Remez, in Hänni et al., *Terrorism in the Cold War, Vol. 1*. Charbel, pp. 105–07, has a very useful and detailed account of the quite difficult encounters between Haddad and senior Soviet officials, including the KGB, in Moscow. See also USSR Committee of State Security (KGB) memo, 16 May 1975, No. 1218-A/ov and that of 23 April 1974, No. 1071-A/ov, Andropov to Brezhnev about a meeting between the KGB station chief in Lebanon and Haddad in Beirut. The quote comes from Ekberg's unpublished English-language MS; see also Sayigh, p. 304, and Roland Dannreuther, *The Soviet Union and the PLO*, p. 45.

An astute US diplomat in Moscow told Washington in 1976 that the Soviet political leadership were 'caught between their dislike of terrorism and their unwillingness to take concrete steps against it which their friends among Arab and other third world states and the "national liberation movement" oppose.' 'The Soviets have always been uneasy about the use of terrorism as a political instrument, but they have qualified this distaste to accommodate its use in extremis, and this leads to problems of defining the permissible,' they added. See US cable, Moscow to DoS, Soviet Attitudes on Terrorism and FRG UNGA initiative, 24 August 1976.

That the Stasi was very much subservient to Moscow is clear from the 'Protocol Guiding Cooperation Between The Stasi And The KGB', 1978, available in translation online from the Wilson Center. Details of the service's instructions to authorities in Aden can be found in Charbel, p. 123.

My account of Kopp's first days in Baghdad is based on *Terrorjahre*, pp. 118–19, 125, but also a report of her interrogations by German prosecutors between 24 April 1995 and 18 July 1996, which I was given. There is now a wealth of sources on Ramírez's first trip to Prague. See Daniela Richterova, *Watching the Jackals*, pp. 244–6; Pavel Žáček in Hänni et al., *Terrorism, Vol.* 2, pp. 108–10; US DoS cable, PLO Wadi Haddad Faction Activity, 26 April 1978; the German judgement in the trial of Andrawes, which describes Ramírez's visit to the convalescing hijacker; and Davies, who describes their warm relations. The details of the money and the final flight from Baghdad are from Schröm, p. 186; Kopp, p. 126.

On who killed Haddad and how, see Charbel, pp. 22–7; Klein, *Striking Back*, pp. 207–08; and Bergman, *Rise Up and Kill First*, p. 212. Descriptions, or at least categorisation, of Israeli 'terrorist acts' can be found on the first page of the Rand Corporation's 'International Terrorism: A Chronology, 1968–1974', published in March 1975, and the US National Daily Intelligence Cable, 28 August 1978, p. 25. Some say toothpaste rather than chocolates were the vehicle for the toxin, but the sources for the latter are more reliable. George Habash and others close to Haddad were sceptical of poisoning as a cause of death: Habache, p. 106.

On the (false) claim of Iraqi involvement, see 'Haddad "Was Poisoned by Iraqis"', GDN, 25 August 1978; Amos, p. 375; Middle East Intelligence Survey, 1–15 April 1978. In Tel Aviv in 2023 and 2024, I spoke to Mossad officials who had taken a keen contemporary interest in Haddad's death and possibly been among those responsible for it.

24. 'THEY ARE ALL MAD'

Much of this chapter deals with the extremely complicated history of the Lebanese civil war, which I have done my best to render intelligible. For excellent accounts of the first round of the conflict see Chamberlin and Rogan. On Arafat, Gowers and Walker is good, as well as Aburish's biography. On the Palestinian armed factions: Sayigh. If you like 1970s Middle Eastern graphic design then *Off the Wall: Political Posters of the Lebanese Civil War*, by Zeina Maasri and Fawaaz Traboulsi, is highly recommended. In fact, it is recommended even if you don't. For anecdotes and espionage Arafat, try Aburish's entertaining *Beirut Spy: The St George Hotel Bar*.

The first round of fighting in the 1970s fatally weakened Lebanon's leftists and reinforced sectarian motivations for fighting at the expense of broadly secular ideologies. This is important. The PFLP along with many other PLO factions, and of course Lebanese leftists, framed the conflict in class terms as a battle between bourgeois Maronites and proletariat Muslims. As ever, things were not so simple. The Phalange, for example, recruited heavily among poorer Christian Maronites, especially farmers and lower middle-class urban families. Neither were part of the traditional powerful feudal elite. The Gemayels themselves were, but not one of the most prestigious families. The Maronites made up around 900,000 of Lebanon's 1.5 million Christians in 1973. See Sandra Mackay, *A Mirror of the Arab World*, pp. 108–09.

In Ramallah and elsewhere in the West Bank in 2023 and 2024, I was also able to talk to several former veterans of Fatah, the Black September Organisation and the PFLP who knew Ali Hassan Salameh personally, some very well. The best single published account by a country mile of the last years of Salameh's life is Kai Bird's *The Good Spy*. For this chapter's opening section, see pp. 177, 181–3. Peter Taylor's *States of Terror* is useful too. Bar-Zohar and Eitan Haber have some details, see pp. 202–03, 210, but no references. Some sources say Salameh's wedding to Rizk was grandiose, in the Lebanese style, but I found no reference to it in contemporary Lebanese media that I was able to consult, which suggests modesty rather than ostentation was the order of the day.

Kamal Jumblatt is another extraordinary character. A feudal leader, he admired Gandhi and travelled to India for spiritual retreats but also had significant street popularity, even among some Christians. See 'Un Grand Féodal Réformiste', *Le Monde*, 18 March 1977 and 'Kamal Jumblatt, the Uncrowned Druze Prince of the Left', *Middle Eastern Studies*, No. 2, 1988, pp. 178–205. Though Jumblatt was more motivated by his admiration for French republicanism and New Left thinking about 'humane socialism' than any sectarian impulses, his project would have inevitably meant the end of Maronite dominance, given the demography of the country, and so was bound to be fiercely opposed.

A further addition to Jumblatt's Lebanese National Movement (LNM) was a faction of Muslim mutineers from the Lebanese national army, which effectively disintegrated. The LNM also included the right-wing Syrian Socialist Nationalist Party, the Lebanese Communist Party and Marxist breakaway factions. All these had significant numbers of Christians, mainly Greek Orthodox, among their members. Then there were the Nasserist groups, of which the largest was the Independent Nasserite Movement, with its powerful militia, the Murabitoun (the Sentinels). Fatah was initially reluctant to get involved: see Abu Iyad, p. 179; Gowers and Walker, pp. 154–8.

For Salameh as a warlord, see Bird, pp. 177–8, Abu Iyad, p. 190; Al-Jazeera World, 2018, interview with Karim Pakradouni; Sayigh, pp. 370, 393, 403; Aburish, *Beirut Spy*, p. 224; Paul O'Neill, *Life*, April 1979; Bar-Zohar and Haber, pp. 208–09. On the trip to the US, see Taylor, p. 44, Bird, and my own interviews with former CIA officials, 2021 and 2022. On US views of Salameh, see US DoS cable from Beirut, Lebanese Situation,18 September 1976; Bird, pp. 172, 178–9; Taylor, pp. 44–5; Gowers and Walker, pp. 166–8; Charbel, p. 313; and O'Neill in *Life*. Salameh was described by a visiting senator as a 'leading pro-peace moderate' in US DoS cable, Summary Yasser Arafat's Main Points from Conversations with Landrum Bolling, 17 September 1977. On Ames' visit, see Bird, pp. 181–7; Taylor, pp. 44–5. Bassam Abu Sharif, in Jericho in 2024, spoke about his interactions with Salameh and Ames.

At a town hall meeting in Massachusetts in March 1977, President Carter referred to the need for 'a homeland for Palestinian refugees who have suffered for many, many years', an unprecedented expression of support for the Palestinian nationalist cause by a US president. Two weeks later, according to Bird, Salameh arranged for Ames to meet Arafat. The American found the PLO chairman as 'funny looking as his pictures' but 'a very bright and sincere man'. This was not a characterisation that many in Tel Aviv or even Washington would have recognised and Ames admitted that knowledge of this utterly unauthorised encounter would send his superiors 'into outer space'.

For Salameh in Austria, see Hänni et al., *Terrorism, Vol.* 2, 'Pact With The (Un) Wanted? The Wischnewski Protocol', Matthias Dahlke, pp. 175–93. On Kreisky and the PLO, see Thomas Riegler, 'Ein Österreichischer Weg: Die Reaktion Auf Den Internationalen Terrorismus Der 1970er und 80er Jahre', *Journal for Intelligence Propaganda and Security Studies*, Vol. 6, pp. 139–57; Yazid Sayigh, p. 415. On the PLO and West Germany, see *Spiegel*, 'Germany's Secret Contacts to Palestinian Terrorists', 28 August 2012.

That the conference was taking place in Vienna was a testament to the diligence with which Austria's moderate socialist chancellor Bruno Kreisky had pursued his 'internationalist' strategy over previous years. This sought to keep Austria safe from terrorism by seeking compromise and dialogue with Arab powers as well as more controversial actors, while trying to find elegant solutions to what Kreisky, a socialist and a non-practising Jew, saw as a complex problem. When in 1973 a transit station for Russian Jews on their way to Israel was attacked, Kreisky agreed to close it down, an apparent concession to violence that prompted anger in Israel and the US. In fact, the passage of immigrants through Austria did not cease and a new centre was quietly set up elsewhere. During the OPEC attack in 1975, Kreisky again sought to avoid confrontation and used his contacts with the Algerian government to defuse the crisis. Later, he helped the PLO with its often clumsy efforts to establish a dialogue with Washington, and even Israel. On the other hand, Kreisky also made sure Austria had its own specialised counter-terrorist unit, known as the Cobras.

Wild shooting by poorly-trained police may have caused many casualties during the Fatah attack in March 1978 in Israel. The operation had two aims, its organisers said later. 'We couldn't let Carter, Begin and Sadat get away with a so-called peace that would deprive the Palestinian people of their future,' said Abu Iyad. 'We had to show Israel that it was futile to exclude us from a settlement and remind the Arabs that it was dangerous to sacrifice us to their selfish interests.' See Abu Iyad, p. 216.

For the killing of Salameh, I used Bergman, *Rise*, pp. 119–223; 'The Top Mossad Spy Who Befriended His Terrorist Target – Then Had Him Killed', the *Times of Israel*, 24 December 2019; 'PLO Operative, Slain by Israelis, had Been Allegedly Helping US', David Ignatius in the *Wall Street Journal* on 10 February 1983; O'Neill in *Life*; Bar-Zohar, p. 204; Dean Brelis, *Time*, 'Death of a Terrorist', 5 February 1979; Taylor, pp. 46–7; Bird, pp. 207–09; Al-Jazeera's interviews with Murid al-Dajani, Nidal Salameh, Pakradouni; CIA, 'International Terrorism in 1979', January 1980, p. 4; my interviews with Mossad and former Fatah, PLO intelligence officials, Tel Aviv, Ramallah, 2023 and 2024, as well as a 2021 interview with a former CIA officer who reviewed Salameh case files.

One warning of an imminent threat to his life came to Salameh from an unexpected source. Bashir Gemayel, who had excellent contacts with the Mossad, told Salameh in early January 1979 to move out of his apartment as soon as possible to live in one of the refugee camps. Another came from a Fatah security official, who wrote a long letter, which Salameh never read.

25. THE RED AND THE BLACK

The amount you could – and probably should – read on the Iranian revolution is vast. The works cited below were all useful, but particularly good are Andrew Scott Cooper's mildly revisionist *The Fall of Heaven*, James Buchan's beautifully written *Days of God*, Baqr Moin's authoritative biography of Khomeini, Ray Takeyh's concise *The Last Shah* and the relevant chapters of Kim Ghattas' *Black Wave*. Christian Caryl's *Strange Rebels* nicely puts the revolution in a broader global context. For a new general history, try the epic *Iran: A Modern History*, by Abbas Amanat.

I read through much specialist literature on left-wing extremism and its counterparts. Some is cited below. Seyed Ali Alavi's *Iran and Palestine* is a thorough and fascinating overview. On the practice of Iranian Shiism, I cannot recommend highly enough Roy Mottahedeh's brilliant *The Mantle of the Prophet*.

You can watch the return of Khomeini to Iran in 1979 on YouTube. I also used much excellent reporting by Associated Press and others. There are many accounts, from many perspectives. Most end up in the same place: the Behesht-e Zahra cemetery. Ryszard Kapuściński, *Shah of Shahs*, conjures the moment with typical clarity. See p. 148 for this passage.

Some sources say Khomeini was born in 1904. For this account of Khomeini's early decades, I used Nikki Keddie's *Modern Iran*, pp. 190–92, Moin, Amanat, Cooper, Takeyh, and I read Jalal al-e Ahmad's *Westoxification* or, in my edition, *Occidentosis*, too.

On the unrest of 1963 see Dilip Hiro, *Iran under the Ayatollahs*, p. 46; Mottahedeh; and Ervand Abrahamian's *Khomeinism: Essays on the Islamic Republic*. On the deaths in the protests, Moin says 380 (p. 92), Cooper says thirty-two (p. 116), Amanat says 125 (p. 739).

For Khomeini in exile see: Abrahamian, *Khomeinism*, p. 50 and Moin, pp. 147–8.

On Shia practice and the marja'iyya, see Mottahedeh, pp. 187–94 and Cooper, pp. 52–3, with p. 253 for the large donation reference.

For Khomeini's new ideas, see Mojtaba Mahdavi in *The Oxford Handbook of Islam and Politics*, ed. John Esposito and Emad el-Din Shahin, pp. 180–200; Abrahamian, *Khomeinism*, pp. 23–32; Keddie, pp. 191–3; Mottahedeh, pp. 243–4, 255–6, 330 and lots elsewhere too. Traditionally, *velayat* or guardianship meant protection of those who had no other defenders – orphaned children, the mentally ill or destitute widows, for example.

Khomeini spoke little about how any leader would exercise power. He appeared to envisage a leader with a personal, unmediated understanding of God's truth which would allow him to make the right decisions. This meant there was little need for consultative bodies. Some speculated that he was influenced by the mysticism that had interested him in his youth. Others that he was an instinctive autocrat.

A reference to *enqelab* appears in Khomeini's book of 1971 but was probably inserted by the students who compiled the work. Shariati had translated Frantz Fanon's phrase 'The Wretched of the Earth' as Mostazafin-e Zamin in the early 1960s in Paris.

For economic problems, see Misagh Parsa, *Social Origins of the Iranian Revolution*, 1989, p. 64; Keddie, pp. 168–9; Kepel, *Jihad*, pp. 106–09; Axworthy, p. 98; Mottahedeh, p. 356; Takeyh, p. 205.

On the shah and *Ettela'at*, see Cooper, pp. 290–91, Buchan, pp. 147–50 and Keddie, pp. 225–6. The edition of *Ettela'at* of 7 January 1978 can be found online. For the protests that followed its publication: Cooper, pp. 289–93; Mottahedeh, pp. 371–3; Kapuściński, p. 113; Hiro, p. 71.

In his final months, the shah would frequently admit to being incapable of understanding how he had lost his throne. One important factor was a profound ignorance about the values and views of his subjects. Few in his entourage, with the possible exception of the empress Farah, made efforts to tell him unpalatable truths, and when he travelled in Iran the shah was greeted by respectful, sometimes adulatory, crowds which gave an entirely false impression of the state of his nation. Nor was his understanding of foreign affairs particularly profound. Though able to impress some interlocutors, particularly in Washington, his knowledge of geopolitics, economics or the world of finance was superficial. On most foreign trips, he saw very little of his destinations. He sometimes travelled to see his friend Anwar Sadat in Egypt, who was in the middle of conducting his highly controversial strategy of turning to the West and seeking peace with Israel. Most years, the shah spent weeks, even months, in St Moritz, skiing with his family and reading specialised aviation periodicals or arms brochures.

26. IN THE NAME OF THE OPPRESSED

For fascinating details of Abadan see 'The Rise and Demise of an Oil Metropolis', *MERIP*, summer 2018. For a very useful description of Iranian cinemas at this time, see passages in *The Shadow Commander: Soleimani, the US, and Iran's Global Ambitions* by Arash Azizi. On wonderful Iranian new wave films, 'Iranian Cinema's "Quiet Revolution" 1960–1978', by Ali Mirsepassi and Mehdi Faraji, in *Middle East Critique*, 2017.

For my account of the fire and the short, unhappy life of Hossein Takbalizadeh, I relied on Buchan, pp. 156–63 and a lengthy and well-sourced investigation by the Rahman Boroumand Center (www.iranrights.org/).

For reactions to the fire, see Cooper, pp. 376–81; a US cable from Tehran, Abadan Theater Disaster Roundup, sent on 22 August 1978; 'Terrorists Kill 377 by Burning Theater in Iran', WP, 21 August 1978; Takeyh, pp. 218–19.

The figure of eighty-eight casualties on Black Friday is from Cooper, p. 403. Hiro says 1,600 people, p. 77.

On Khomeini leaving Iraq: see Takeyh, pp. 224–5; Cooper, pp. 387–8; 'Iraq Backs Silencing of Shah's Critic', GDN, 27 September 1978 and Pierre Razoux, *The Iran-Iraq War*, pp. 93–4. Khomeini's closest aides warned supporters in Paris that he was on his way only when they changed planes in Geneva on their way from Baghdad. It is unlikely they told French authorities any sooner.

The account of Mohsen Sazegara's life, ideas and movements is based on multiple interviews with him between 2022 and 2025.

For the LMI overseas, see Matthew Shannon, 'American foreign relations, the Iranian student movement, and the global sixties', *The Sixties*, 4:1, 2011; Houchang Chehabi's comprehensive *The Liberation Movement of Iran*; and Ghattas, pp. 19, 27–9.

Along with Debray, Fanon and Marighella, many Iranian dissidents in the US also read with great excitement a book published in 1977 by the literary professor who had helped with Arafat's speech at the UN and was emerging as one of the most articulate and forceful advocates of the Palestinian cause. This was Edward Said, and the book was *Orientalism*.

For this section on Shariati, see Takeyh, p. 201; Christoper de Bellaigue, *The Islamic Enlightenment*, pp. 342–4; 'Ali Shariati: Ideologue of the Iranian Revolution', Ervand Abrahamian, *MERIP*, January–February 1982; Mottahedeh, pp. 16, 255–6, 330; Axworthy, pp. 66–7; Keddie, pp. 198–213; *An Islamic Utopian: A Political Biography of Ali Shariati* by Ali Rahnema; Kepel, p. 113; and Shahbrough Akhavi in *The Oxford University Handbook of Islam and Politics*, pp. 169–80. Much of Shariati's writing and lectures is easy to find online, in the original and translation.

For Khomeini in France, I have relied on much press reporting at the time, my interviews with Sazegara, and Moin.

On the tapes and their impact see Takeyh, p. 215; Cooper, p. 241; Ghattas, p. 22; Rasmus Christian Elling, 'In a forest of humans', in Mirsepassi, ed., *Global 79*, p. 173;

Mottahedeh, pp. 353–4; Axworthy, p. 80; Milani, pp. 217–18; CIA National Foreign Assessment Center, 'Khomeinism: the impact of theology on Iranian politics', March 1983. Among the first instances of use of the technology was in 1964, when the speech that led to Khomeini's arrest and expulsion had been recorded and circulated on cassettes. See Amanat, p. 738.

For the upheavals of late 1978, I used much contemporary media reporting but also Amanat, p. 885; 'Troops kill five students in Iran riot', United Press International (UPI), 4 November 1978; CIA National Foreign Assessment Centre, 'Opposition Demonstrations In Iran', 21 December 1978; Axworthy, p. 122; Kapuściński, p. 123. In early November, Sattareh Farmanian, a sociologist, described 'shuttered, empty, burned-out stores, broken pavements, flashing police lights, overturned cars and trucks' in Tehran and 'the smells of burning buildings and rubber tyres, billowing smoke and tear gas'. Quoted in Caryl, p. 142.

On the news of the shah's flight reaching Khomeini: Moin, p. 153. On Khomeini's return, Amanat is good, and so are lots of others.

That Khomeini was described as 'Imam' by supporters was another radical break with tradition. In Arabic, the term 'imam' describes a leader or prayer leader. In Iran, the title was reserved for the twelve infallible leaders of the early Shia, and members of the senior clergy had never previously accepted this title.

27. 'WE ARE DEALING WITH WILD ANIMALS'

The Fedayeen-e Khalq's leading role in the opposition and the revolution in Iran in the 1970s has been much neglected. My account relies on much reading of specialist literature, but above all long interviews with Farrokh Negahdar, online and in London between 2022 and 2025.

On the foundation of the FeK, their ideas and their strategy, try Ali Mirsepassi, 'Seeing the World from a Humble Corner', in *The Global* 79, pp. 59–103; Maziar Behrooz, *Rebels with a Cause*; Rahnema's *Call to Arms*, especially pp. 61–75; 'Armed Struggle and the Iranian Revolution', Shahrzad Azad, *MERIP*, June 1980, pp. 30–31; 'The Guerrilla Movement in Iran, 1963–1977', by Ervand Abrahamian, *MERIP Reports*, No. 86; and Keddie, pp. 210–20.

On the Iranian left and the PLO, Abrahamian, *MERIP*; Chehabi, *Distant Relations*, pp. 183–5; Rahnema, *Call to Arms*, p. 118; Alavi, p. 10; Abu Sharif, *Arafat*, p. 62; Habache, p. 287; author interviews, Ramallah, 2023; Verso blogpost, 'Abandoned Legacy: The Left of Iran and Palestinians', Omid Montazeri, 12 June 2024; Ghattas, pp. 14–15.

For Siahkal see many of the above sources but also Hamid Ashraf's review of the operation, 'An Analysis of One Year of Urban and Mountain Guerrilla Warfare: How did the Siahkal Insurrection Begin?', which is at Marxists.org.

For FeK successes and then failures in the 1970s see Behroz, pp. 68–9. Axworthy is good on the Goethe nights in Tehran, pp. 100–01. On the clashes in Tehran of February 1979 and the flight of Bakhtiar see Buchan, p. 238 and Hiro, p. 94. For the revolutionary trials: Buchan, p. 246; Axworthy, p. 148; Hiro, pp. 107, 126; and much useful contemporary reporting, for example, 'Iran Calls Executions Just the Beginning', WP, 16 February 1979. For the LMI et al. in Lebanon, see Alemzadeh, in *Global 1979*, p. 185.

Sazegara was helpful here too. On the history of the Pasdaran, see *Vanguard of the Imam* by Afshon Ostovar and Azizi.

The mistakes and misjudgements made by the Iranian left in 1979 may seem hard for us to understand in hindsight. Helpful here are Abrahamian's *Khomeinism*, and 'The Tragedy of the Iranian Left', by Ali Mirsepassi, in Stephanie Cronin, *Reformers and Revolutionaries in Modern Iran*. Shokrallah Paknejad, a prominent Iranian socialist, optimistically told a reporter in August 1979 that Iranians were living on the turn of the tide. 'People will turn away from the mullahs if they become a ruling class. This process has already begun. The people are less supportive of religion than they initially were.' He was executed in Evin prison during December 1981. See 'We Are Living Between Two Tides', *MERIP*, April 1982.

Moin is good on increasing regime repression, pp. 269–72. Many could see what was happening. The *Guardian*'s correspondent described armed regime supporters riding 'in great armadas through the streets on their motor bikes, traditional Shi'ite black flags and banners held aloft, and sometimes preceded by a mullah in a bullet-proof Mercedes'.

On the French intellectuals, Michel Foucault's somewhat delusional 'A quoi rêvent les Iraniens?', originally published in *Le Nouvel Observateur*, 16 October 1978 is widely available online. Both Sartre and Foucault refrained from criticising the revolutionary regime in Tehran through much of 1979. So did the USSR. Simone de Beauvoir rapidly revised her early enthusiasm when she saw the rapid regression of women's rights following the fall of the shah.

On Khomeini's own increasing extremism, see Moin, pp. 164–5, and the indefatigable Oriana Fallaci's NYT interview published on 7 October 1979. 'Our revolution is only six months old. What do you expect of a child . . . born in a field filled with locusts, after 2,500 years of bad harvests and 50 years of poisonous harvests? That past cannot be wiped out in a few months, not even in a few years,' Khomeini told her.

On the embassy takeover: see Mark Bowden's *Guests of the Ayatollah*, Buchan, Axworthy and Amanat for useful accounts; also 'Prisoner and Captor Look Back at the Iran-US Cold War', GDN, 14 August 2014, and 'We Planned A Three-Day Takeover of U.S. Embassy', *Kayhan*, 4 November 2002. The CIA research paper, 'Iran: the seizure of the embassy in retrospect', of November 1981, is interesting as is the mass of memos from bewildered British officials, now held in Iranian embassy PREM-19-76_1 and 2 in FCO archives. The adjective 'Muslim' had been added to the supposed Organisation of Students to distinguish them from the Fedayeen, while the 'Imam Line' distinguished them from the MKO. The reference to a 'line' was a direct borrowing from the radical leftist milieu.

Takeyh, p. 254, points out that the immediate trigger for the takeover was the shah, and reports of an unscheduled meeting between Mehdi Bazargan, the moderate, pragmatic Islamist picked as prime minister in February, and Zbigniew Brzezinski, Carter's national security adviser, at a summit in Algiers.

28. WHO DARES WINS

The opening scenes and the first hours of the takeover at Prince's Gate are based on multiple sources, but two 'instant books' by teams of reporters from the *Sunday Times* and the *Observer* were particularly helpful. See also: 'Threat to Blow Up Besieged Iran Embassy',

GDN, 1 May 1980; Cabinet papers Prem 19/1137, 'Terrorist Incident at the Iranian Embassy London', 30 April 1980; Official History, Home Office, QPE/8011/5/21, p. 9; FCO 8/3660, p. 96; Cramer and Harris, *Hostage*, pp. 22–3. The correspondence between the embassy and the Met can be found in FCO 8/3661, pp. 50–51.

For contemporary background on Khuzestan, try *Sunday Times* Insight's *Siege!*, p. 28; CIA, 'Khuzestan: Iran's Achilles Tendon', 4 December 1979; CIA, 'Iran: Economic Significance of Dissident Areas', 1 January 1980; FCO files 93/913. My interviews with former Ahwazi activists in London in 2023 were very useful. For the DRFLA's Libyan connection see US cable from Tripoli, Libya Sponsors Conference, 8 May 1978.

For Rashidi, my interviews with Ahwazi activists were essential here too. Also see 'The Siege Leader is Dead . . . But His Taped Voice Still Lives On', the *Observer*, 25 May 1980; Cramer and Harris, *Hostage*, pp. 1–8, 51; Amanat, *Iran*, pp. 1004–05.

On Nejad and the others, Insight's *Siege!*, pp. 6–8, the *Observer*'s *Siege*, pp. 38–42; 'Embassy Siege Gunman Tells How he Was Recruited' GDN, 22 January 1981; Memo on Iranian Embassy Siege, 28 July 1980, FCO 400/2, p. 198; FCO 8/3661, p. 40; 'Embassy Siege Factors the Police Could Not Overcome', Stewart Tendler, *The Times*, 23 January 1981; *Hostage*, Cramer and Harris. My conversations with friends of Nejad in December 2022 helped. The weapons were almost certainly procured by the Abu Nidal Organisation and sent to London, probably in the Iraqi diplomatic bag. The same group may also have had a role in training the hostage-takers, but there was no shortage of individuals, groups and government agencies in Baghdad who could have provided instruction in the minimal skills needed. See 'Network of Iraqi Spies Set Up in UK', the *Observer*, 16 March 2003.

On the Iranian diplomats and others inside the embassy, see both the *Sunday Times*' and the *Observer*'s books. For officials' views, see FCO 8/3661, p. 221 and the Memo on Iranian Embassy Siege, 28 July 1980, FCO 400/2 198. Also 'A Hostage's Tale', Mustapha Karkouti, GDN, 15 October 2008; Hiro, p. 113; and Cramer and Harris, pp. 1–10, 109.

On the attackers' failure to prepare and the conversations with Tehran, see the UK Home Office Official History, pp. 11, 24; Insight, pp. 33–4; FCO 8/3660, p. 105; Cabinet papers file 19/1137; FCO cable from Abu Dhabi to London, 30 April 1980; FCO 8/3660 NBP 400/2 has a useful cable from Tehran, 12 May 1980. There is a good account of Eagle Claw in Andrew Bacevich, *America's Wars in the Greater Middle East*.

Rashidi tried to contact the Ministry of Foreign Affairs in Tehran late on the first night of the hostage-taking, but only at the insistence of Afrouz, the chargé d'affaires. Sadegh Ghotbzadeh was one of the young modernising Islamists from the Liberation Movement of Iran who had helped Khomeini in France. In Neauphle-le-Château, he had distinguished himself both by a gift for succinct translation and assiduous efforts to seduce female Western journalists. After the revolution, he retained his taste for sharp suits and a pipe but managed to survive the mass resignation of the Bazargan government in late 1980. Ghotbzadeh's political instincts did eventually fail, however, and he was executed as an alleged traitor in Tehran's Evin prison in 1982, aged forty-six.

On Thatcher's decisions, see the cable FCO 400/2, 9 May 1980, The Arab Ambassadors and the Embassy Siege. Sandbrook, *Who Dares Wins*, xvi–xvii; Rory Carroll's excellent *Killing Thatcher* is helpful on her attitudes to terrorism. Of particular interest to police was a bank robbery in Sweden in 1973 during which hostages had become very supportive of their captors. This was dubbed 'Stockholm syndrome'.

On growing tensions and the shooting of Lavasani see Insight, p. 48; the Home Office History, p. 49; FCO 8/3661, p. 197; FCO 8/3660, pp. 34, 41–9, 67–8; and Cramer, p. 130.

There are lots of accounts of the raid. Those that veer towards military porn are to be avoided. Operation Nimrod by Russell Phillips is concise and clear. Two deaths of the attackers caused mild controversy but the SAS were cleared of any wrongdoing by police and a coroner.

On reaction see John le Carré, the *Observer*, 1 June 1980; Cabinet Office papers, LF 398; FCO papers, FCO 8/3660 NBP 400/2, including a cable from Bonn on 7 May 1980. Richard Nixon sent a congratulatory message, lauding 'an inspiring example to free people throughout the world'. A West German newspaper praised the British for showing how terrorism could be tackled 'in a liberal but at the same time determined manner', an implicit condemnation of its own government's policies over the previous decade. The Iraqi news agency reported a victory over the 'racist Persian regime'. Officially Moscow made no comment, though TASS strongly criticised the hostage-taking as a violation of international conventions on the sanctity of diplomatic representations and insinuated a possible US role in the takeover. The agency referred to 'Iranians from Khuzestan' as the attackers, underlining its support for Tehran's claims to the territory over those of Iraq. See 'Moscow On Iran', CIA briefing, 7 May 1980.

On the DRMLA being very much part of the nationalist, secular anti-colonial international, and not suicide attackers, see: CIA, 'Memorandum, Palestinian presence in Iran', May 1980; Cabinet papers 19/1137, 'Terrorist Incident at the Iranian Embassy London', 30 April 1980; 'Iraqis Told Us British Would Never Attack – Siege Gunman', GDN, 14 January 1981; Home Office report, p. 55; Cramer and Harris, p. 70; and *Hansard* of 1 May 1980. This point was made strongly to me by Ahwazi activists in London, 2023 over an excellent lunch in a small home in south London. It is also underlined by press reporting, such as '£6,000 Spree of Embassy Terrorists', 11 May 1980, *News of the World*. When Thatcher was briefed on the first day of the attack she was told of speculation that the DRMLA was 'aligned with the PFLP'. This was closer to reality than many thought.

The review of the Islamic world and other relevant documents can be found in FCO 8/3405, file 226/2-B; FCO 8/3485, 1980 Jan 01 – 1980 Dec 31, 'Islam in the Persian Gulf'. The CIA reports mentioned included CIA: 'Iran and the US presidential election', memo 18 August 1980, 'Iran: Implications of the Shah's Death for the Hostages', March 1980, and CIA: 'Iran: Fragmentation in the Future', October 1980, which did little to buck the trend of poor forecasting.

29. 'THE MOST BEAUTIFUL WORK'

Khomeini's speech about exporting the revolution was reported in Khomeini: 'We Shall Confront the World with Our Ideology', *MERIP*, June 1980.

Useful sources for the consolidation of the clerical regime include Hiro, p. 132, Amanat, p. 962, and Said Amir Arjomand's *Turban for the Crown*, pp. 167–9.

On Abol Bani-Sadr, see Buchan, p. 268, Axworthy pp. 431–2 and Moin, p. 179. Bani-Sadr's autobiography, published in English as *My Turn to Speak: Iran, the*

Revolution and Secret Deals With the US, 1991, is, like its author and subject, extraordinary, exasperating and occasionally impressive. For the shredded documents see Razoux, p. 170. The CIA had assigned Bani-Sadr a code name, which was a very stupid thing to do.

On the Mojahedin-e-Khalq, I relied primarily on *The Iranian Mojahedin*, by Ervand Abrahamian. The name was important. A *fedayi* was a fighter prepared to sacrifice himself, if necessary, in a cause. In the context of the late 1960s, this cause was 'liberation' – of a country or an ethnic community. It was rarely a religious one. In contrast, a *mojahid* was engaged in the holy jihad, the struggle, and that meant war for the faith. On the MKO going to Lebanon for training, Alemzadeh in *Global 1979*, pp. 190–92, is very good. The reference to Ali Hassan Salameh is from Alavi, p. 12.

For Shariati, the MeK appeared a clandestine means of actually implementing his ideas, while for the MeK, Shariati offered a way of reaching and recruiting young Iranians. In his lectures in Tehran, Shariati laid out the fundamental principles of the MeK's beliefs: that the enemies of freedom and fulfilment were capitalism, imperialism, Zionism, multinational corporations and other familiar foes, that the true message of both Shia Muslim and Iranian traditions was a revolutionary one, that radical transformation would be led by intellectuals, not the hidebound, reactionary clerics.

Some among the MeK went further. For them, the Koran and other key Islamic texts were 'living inspirations for revolutionary action'; the 'ummah' no longer signified 'a religious community' but 'a dynamic society in constant motion toward a classless society', while 'martyrs' were now 'revolutionary heroes'. A jihad was a 'liberation struggle'; and a mojahid a 'freedom fighter'. See Ervand Abrahamian and Olivier Roy's 'Mujāhidīn' in John Esposito, ed., *The Oxford Encyclopedia of the Modern Islamic World*, 1995. Keddie is also good on ideology, pp. 210–21.

Interestingly, members of the MeK were more likely to be from rural origins and clerical families, students of sciences rather than arts, and men, than recruits to the Fedayeen-e Khalq.

On the final struggle, see Axworthy, pp. 512–18; Abrahamian, pp. 211–18; and Eric Rouleau's reporting from Tehran in *Le Monde* in June and July 1981.

By end of October, well over 2,000 MeK members had been killed. By the end of the 1981, perhaps 3,000. The identities of more than 3,400 individuals executed between June 1981 and March 1982 had been verified by 2022, perhaps less than a quarter of the total. See Nasiri and Faghfouri Azar, 'Investigating the 1981 Massacre in Iran', *Journal of Genocide Research*, 2022.

For the flight of Bani-Sadr and Rajavi see 'The Great Escape', *Time*, 10 August 1981, and British Pathé News, 'France: Deposed Iranian President Calls For A New Revolution In Iran To Establish Freedom', broadcast on 23 August 1981. *Le Monde* covered this extensively too.

Sazegara spoke to me about his frightening experiences in 1981 and 1982. He also describes them in more detail in Joshua Muravchik's *The Next Founders: Voices of Democracy in the Middle East*. For the passages here on the Fedayeen-e Khalq, I spoke to Negahdar and read Maziar Behrooz, pp. 113–15. On Khamanei, Hiro's *Ayatollahs*, pp. 195–7 is good. The text of the Iranian Constitution can be readily found online, with different English versions depending on the political leaning of the translator.

On Iran's efforts to export the revolution, Esposito's *The Iranian Revolution* and David Menashri's *The Iranian Revolution and the Muslim World* offer good overviews, especially their respective introductions.

For Arafat and Iran, compare and contrast the following reports from the WP in 1979: 'PLO Chief, in Iran, Hails Shah's Fall', on 19 February and 'PLO Now Dubious About Iranian Revolt It Once Hailed', on 15 December. Also see Abu Sharif, *Dream*, p. 62; Alavi, pp. 47–64; and the accounts in Azizi, as well as Trita Parsi's *Treacherous Alliance*, pp. 84–5. On Kuwait, see Laurence Louër, *Transnational Shia Politics: Religious and Political Networks in the Gulf*.

Ghattas has a good account of unrest in Saudi Arabia, pp. 72–3, and the shoe quote comes from Trofimov, *Mecca*, p. 201. See 'The Cold War and the Communist Party of Saudi Arabia, 1975–1991', Toby Matthiesen, *Journal of Cold War Studies*, 2020, on how some leftists from the Eastern Province, in particular younger Shia Muslims, joined the protests. Some were detained and tortured, and two died.

30. THE BLACK FLAG

The takeover of the Great Mosque of Mecca – in Arabic, al-Masjid al-Haram, also called the Holy Mosque – in November and December 1979 in Saudi Arabia received little attention in the West until the middle of the 2000s. One reason was the lack of good, readable, authoritative books for general readers on the topic – and on the kingdom more broadly. The excellent Holden and Johns, *The House of Saud*, published in 1981, was not widely available, and fine histories like Madawi al-Rasheed's did not look in detail at the episode. This was remedied over the following decade with the publication of Robert Lacey's *Inside the Kingdom*, Yaroslav Trofimov's *The Siege of Mecca* and the more scholarly *The Meccan Rebellion* by Thomas Hegghammer and Stéphane Lacroix. All five, particularly the latter two, informed my account, along with some useful documentaries, archive footage, newspaper reporting from the time, an *Arab News* multimedia production of 20 November 2019, declassified diplomatic cables and internal memos, as well as many conversations in Saudi Arabia in 2008 and 2011.

For the executions, see Lacey, p. 36 and '130 Were Killed as Saudis Recaptured Mosque', WP, 5 December 1979. For Juhayman's childhood and youth see Trofimov, p. 18; Hegghammer and Lacroix, pp. 12–13; Holden and Johns, pp. 514–17. On changes in the kingdom, see reporting in *Time*, such as 'The Life and Times of the Cautious King of Araby', 19 November 1973, and 'A Desert King Faces the Modern World', 6 January 1975. Also good is: 'Le Gâteau Et Les Miettes', Eric Rouleau, *Le Monde*, 25 January 1977, and Ghattas, pp. 52–3. In 1975 Saudi Arabia's foreign assets were estimated by monetary experts at somewhere between $60 billion and $70 billion and climbing at the rate of $1 billion per month. See al-Rasheed, pp. 121–3, 138.

Juhayman's reasons for leaving the Guard and moving to Medina are explored by Stéphane Lacroix, *Awakening*, p. 90. For his encounter with the brothers, see Hegghammer and Lacroix, pp. 8–12; Holden and Johns, p. 518; Hegghammer; and the useful BBC Arabic service documentary *Mecca 1979, 40 Years On*. One of the more extreme beliefs of the brothers was that sandals could be worn during prayers and that their headquarters could be lit by a single lightbulb to allow further study of the Koran after dark during Ramadan.

Details of the shanty towns come from 'Le Coran et le Cimetière', Eric Rouleau, *Le Monde*, 26 January 1977. Villagers and former followers revealed useful details of the desert encampments where Juhayman lived for two years, and of whom he recruited, in *The Siege of Mecca*, Dirk van den Berg, K2 productions, 2019. In all, 300 former JSM and Ikhwan may have been detained between 1977 and November 1979. See US cable Jeddah to DoS, King Khalid's Comments In A Meeting With Secretary Miller, 24 November 1979.

On the epistles and the Mahdi see Hegghammer and Lacroix, pp. 17–18, 51; Lacroix, *Awakening*, p. 99; Kennedy, p. 343; Holden and Johns, p. 521; Trofimov, pp. 45–52. See too Filiu, *The Apocalypse in Islam*, especially pp. 97–102, on the broader theological traditions.

On the hajj and the new influx: Hegghammer, *Azzam*, p. 95; and Salah Oumoudden and Khaled al-Zahrani, 'Tourisification', *Via Tourism Review*, 20(20), 2021. The management and security of the pilgrimage had been one of the single most important duties of the caliph, when this office of supreme temporal ruler of the world's Muslims existed before its abrogation by Kemal Atatürk in 1924.

For the quotes on the kingdom without revolution, see Rouleau, 26 January 1977, and *Time*, 'The Desert Superstate', 22 May 1978. On Bin Baz and his complaints, see Lacroix, *Awakening*, pp. 24, 94–5; al-Rasheed, p. 144; Trofimov, pp. 41–2; US cables from Jeddah, Saudi Ulema Ban Table Soccer: Paper Criticizes Decision, 3 January 1979 and Public Morality In Riyadh, 6 June 1979.

For the takeover, see Trofimov, pp. 1–6, 68–71; Holden and Johns, pp. 512–16. 'The Mahdi and his men will seek shelter [here] because they are persecuted everywhere,' al-Qahtani told the bewildered pilgrims.

For the siege and the aftermath, Trofimov, p. 246; Radwan Radwan, 'How the 1979 Siege of Makkah Unfolded', *Arab News*, 20 November 2019; US DoS cable, Occupation Of Grand Mosque, 28 November 1979; 'Saudi Arabians Behead 63 for Attack on Mosque', WP, 10 January 1980; original newsreel released by Saudi government, viewable on YouTube; FCO 8/3419 'The Mecca Rebellion', FCO Research Note, August 1981.

Official figures claimed that of the 260 attackers, 117 were dead – ninety died where they fought and twenty-seven later in hospital. Thirty-eight persons were found not guilty and released. The remainder, including twenty-three women and teenagers, were given various prison and 're-education centre' terms following closed trials in a religious court.

On the internationalism, Trofimov, p. 229; US cable Kuwait to DoS, Booklet Attributed To Perpetrators Of Grand Mosque Incident, 29 November 1979; Lacroix, *Awakening*, p. 100; Trofimov, pp. 229–40; Holden and Johns, p. 520; 'Takeover of Grand Mosque Said to Be Political Act; Fundamentalists Joined Group', NYT, 17 December 1979; FCO 46/2227, FCO 8/3419, telegrams Jeddah to London. British officials stressed that the proportion of those involved in 'the Mecca incident' who were not Saudis was striking, although there was 'no evidence of external organisation'. FCO 46/2227; see also FCO 8/3419, telegrams Jeddah to London. Juhayman and his associates were less parochial than they appeared. One of the thinkers who had inspired the group was an Albanian-born scholar who spent most of his career in Syria, and though they were largely ignorant of what had happened in Iran, the rebels were well aware of the violent end of Shukri Mustafa's campaign to transform Egypt.

On Saudi efforts to shift blame outside the kingdom and comparison to a cult, see Trofimov, pp. 230–32; Holden and Johns, pp. 514, 521; 'Takeover of Grand Mosque Said to Be Political Act', NYT, 17 December 1979. Saudi claims of Soviet involvement were supported by US intelligence reports, US officials said to journalists.

31. A NEW INTERNATIONAL

In November 2001, I walked through the streets of Peshawar's University Town with an Islamist who had known 'Mr Osama' in the 1980s. He told me how bin Laden had spoken with fervent admiration of Juhayman. For bin Laden's visit to the damaged mosque, see Coll, *Bin Ladens*, pp. 227–8; for the days after the siege, see *Arab News*, *40 Years On*, 20 November 2019; and news footage online. Also Trofimov, p. 225.

For bin Laden's childhood and youth, I drew on my own 2003 book on al-Qaeda, pp. 45–6, including some previously unpublished interviews in Pakistan conducted between 1998 and 2001; Lawrence Wright's *The Looming Tower*, pp. 73–5; Bergen's *The bin Laden I Know*, pp. 7–9, 13; Coll, pp. 143–7; Jonathan Randal's *Osama*, p. 60; Najwa and Omar bin Laden, *Growing up bin Laden*, pp. 31–3; 'My son, bin Laden', GDN, 3 August 2018; Wright, pp. 76–7.

For the expansion of education in Saudi Arabia see Lacroix, *Awakening*, pp. 41–6, and for al-Thagr see Coll, pp. 144–7. A new nationwide policy adopted in 1970 defined the purpose of education as 'inculcating in [the student] a conception of the universe, the individual, and life [that] emanates from a total Islamic vision'. The numbers of Muslim Brothers were so great that in 1973 the organisation's most senior leaders chose Mecca for the first meeting for twenty years of the movement's advisory council.

For bin Laden's marriage (and car crashes), see Randal, p. 60; Coll, pp. 150–51, 199; bin Laden and bin Laden, pp. 51, 92. For the trips overseas: 'Bin Laden's Disdain for West Grew in Shakespeare's Birthplace, Journal Shows', GDN, 1 November 2017; 'Bin Laden's Oxford Days', BBC, 12 October 2001; Coll, p. 153.

Azzam's epiphany when he heard the fedayeen is reported in Hegghammer's authoritative *The Caravan*, p. 53. Accounts of Azzam's fedayeen days and the tensions between the Islamist and Marxists groups can be found in Sayigh, *Armed Struggle*, p. 244; Hegghammer, pp. 49–57, 59–61, 136; and Abdallah Anas and Tam Hussein, *To the Mountains*, pp. 23–4. Hegghammer is predictably good on Azzam in Cairo, Amman and the US, see pp. 71–80, 100–22.

For the World Muslim League and broader effort to export Saudi Arabia's preferred version of Islamic practice, see Kepel, *Jihad*, pp. 69–75; al-Rasheed, p. 139; 'What the 1967 War Meant for Saudi Religious Exports', William McCants, Brookings Institution, 30 May 2017; Hegghammer, pp. 109–11, 136–41. On Azzam's books and Qutb's influence see Hegghammer, pp. 133–4 and Calvert, p. 261. On donations to the Jihad and the bin Ladens, see Coll, pp. 250–53.

Though much of what Azzam was saying in his books was specific to the Middle East, the Arab world and the broader Islamic world, some themes echoed those prevalent elsewhere too: a new sense of transnational identities and activism, a paranoiac sense that shadowy cabals with hidden agendas were responsible for much that happened in the world, a rejection of both capitalism and Marxism, and an innovative vision of what faith or religious practice could and should mean to communities but, above all, to individuals. This placed personal satisfaction above obedience to a hierarchy and so was, like so much else, very 1970s.

32. DEATH ON THE NILE

For Sadat's daily routine, see pp. 171–2 of *Autumn of Fury*, the memoirs of his controversial and influential media adviser, Mohammed Heikal, one of the best-known journalists in the Middle East at the time. Dina Rezk has much on the views of Western diplomats of Egypt's ruler. See also the many profiles of Sadat in the Western media, such as 'Actor with a Will of Iron', in *Time* on 2 January 1978. Few were very critical.

The *Guardian*'s reporting on the economic crisis in Egypt in the later 1970s and early 80s was excellent, and so useful. See too Saad Eddin Ibrahim, pp. 105–07 and Heikal, pp. 185–90.

The shah was a friend of Sadat, and the gesture he made in offering the dying former monarch a final resting place was a courageous one that cost him politically. See 'Sadat Pushes State Funeral for Shah', WP, 29 July 1980 and AP, 'Deposed Shah Buried as World Leaders Stay Home', 30 July 1980. William Shawcross gives a useful and readable account in his *The Shah's Last Ride*, published in 1989. For other high-profile visitors see Heikal, pp. 174–5. On the visit of Diana and Charles, which I actually remember, see 'A Sea 'Scape for the Royals', GDN, 14 August 1981. Ibrahim reports *Dallas* on the TV on p. 38.

The concerns about Sadat's security are described by Rezk, who quotes Roy Atherton, American ambassador to Cairo, who recalled that 'Egyptian intelligence and security people were in despair because Sadat really did not take kindly to be told that he had to be on his guard from the security point of view.' The same point was made to me by a CIA official stationed in Egypt at the time, whom I interviewed in 2022.

On the tactics of the al-Gama'a al-Islamiyah, see Kepel's *Pharaoh*, pp. 142–3, 151 and Gerges, *Making of the Arab World*, pp. 332–3; for the military academy attack see 'Egyptians Say Fanatic Sect Attacked Military College', NYT, 22 April 1974 and Ibrahim's important research, originally published in the *International Journal of Middle East Studies* in December 1980 on pp. 423–53.

For the impact of the Iranian revolution on Egypt see FCO surveys of Egypt and the Islamic world in 8/3405 file 226/2-B; Ibrahim, 2002, pp. 22, 28; Abdullah al-Arian, *Answering the Call*, p. 180; Gerges, p. 34; Esposito, p. 5; Kepel, *Pharaoh*, p. 213; Walid Abdel Nasser, *The Islamic Movement in Egypt*, pp. 66–75; Juan Cole and Nikki Keddie, *Shi'ism and Social Protest*, pp. 247–75; Heikal, p. 267. The bestselling book was written by a twenty-nine-year-old Palestinian medical student called Fathi Shiqaqi, who was expelled back to Gaza where he would found the group Palestinian Islamic Jihad a year or so later. See 'Intifada's Gentle Man of War', the *Independent*, 15 December 1992.

On al-Zawahiri's childhood, youth and marriage, see Wright, pp. 37, 44; al-Zayat, pp. 16–18. For his first trip to Pakistan and return to Egypt, see al-Zawahiri's own book, *Knights Under the Banner of the Prophet*, published in December 2001, and Wright, pp. 44–6. I also drew on my own numerous interviews with local journalists, warlords, Islamists and others in Peshawar, conducted in 2001, 2002 and 2007. See too, al-Zayat, pp. 18, 27, 52.

The arrests of September 1981 were well covered in the Western media – see for example 'Fears Behind the Angry Face of a Pharaoh', Patrick Seale, the *Observer*, 13 September 1981. On the stories of the assassins of Sadat, and so Farraj too, the best account is in Heikal, pp. 242–52 and 265–70, but see also Kepel, *Pharaoh*, pp. 192–205; Roxanne Euben and Muhammad Qasim Zaman, *Princeton Readings in Islamist Thought*, pp. 321–43; Devin Springer, James Regens and David Edger, *Islamic Radicalism and Global Jihad*, pp. 39–42; and Ghattas, pp. 102–03.

For details of the parade and the aftermath of the assassination, see 'Assassinated At Army Parade As Men Amid Ranks Fire Into Stands', NYT, 7 October 1981 and 'Anwar Sadat Assassinated', UPI, 6 October 1981.

On the trials, '24 Plead Not Guilty In Cairo Trial; One Blurts Out He Killed Sadat', NYT, 1 December 1981; 'Doors Closed to Murder Trial in Egypt's "National Interest"', *Christian Science Monitor*, 3 December 1981; Robin Wright's *Sacred Rage*, p. 182; Wright, pp. 51–5; and al-Zayat, pp. 15, 22, 31–3. It is difficult to watch the Associated Press footage of al-Zawahiri shouting himself hoarse and not flinch before the sheer fury displayed. It can be found on YouTube. Try searching 'CUTS 15 12 82 MUSLIM EXTREMISTS TRIAL'.

On reaction in Beirut, Tehran and elsewhere, see Fisk's *Pity the Nation*, p. 143; 'Sadat's Arab Antagonists Salute His Killers', WP, 7 October 1981; and 'Moscow Shows No Sorrow Over Sadat', UPI, 7 October 1981. For Ramírez's reaction, see Schröm, *Schatten*, pp. 225–48.

Possibly the best source of all on Egypt at the time is *The Day the Leader Was Killed*, a short novel by Naguib Mahfouz published in 1983. The book describes the life of a middle-class family in Cairo and brilliantly captures the visceral shock of Sadat's killing.

33. CARLOS IN THE EAST

Sadly, the suggestion in Olivier Assayes' otherwise excellent film *Carlos* that Ramírez had a contract from the KGB to kill Sadat is difficult to substantiate. According to Andrews and Mitrokhin, *Vol.* 2, p. 167 the KGB had learned in December 1977 of a secret meeting in Damascus between leaders of Syrian intelligence and the PFLP at which a plan to kill both Sadat and Ashraf Marwan, his son-in-law and a Mossad spy, had been discussed. But I have come across no evidence that the service was in any way involved in the project or pursued it, even if Sadat's turn towards the US and away from the USSR offered a motive.

The scene in the Hill of Roses villa when Ramírez learned of the death of Sadat is related in Kopp, pp. 224–5; Schröm, p. 225; and Follain, p. 133.

For Ramírez's installation in Budapest, including gastronomy, see Follain, p. 123 and Laszlo Liszkaï's *Rideau*, pp. 83–4, 164.

On the beginning of Kopp's relationship with Ramírez, accounts differ, as I point out in the main text. Follain, p. 113, quotes Kopp in a *Stern* interview in 1997 calling Ramírez 'a real seducer'. But on p. 128 of her autobiography, Kopp says she tried to get Ramírez to leave 'but he just stayed, put his gun on the nightstand by my bed and made love to me, a sexual act devoid of any emotion, almost a rape. He had not achieved his goal of winning me over.' To the *Financial Times*, she said: 'I thought I was safe, but he raped me. I didn't dare struggle – his gun lay next to us.' See also 'Leben mit Top Terrorist Carlos – Mein Geliebter, der Killer', *Der Spiegel*, 11 Mar 2007 and Schröm, p. 188. As previously mentioned, Ramírez says he was 'seduced'.

Reports of Weinrich's passivity are credible. He discharged tasks carefully and competently but shied away from confrontation. Security officials in one eastern European government described Weinrich with contempt as a 'soft boiled egg', a brittle shell and nothing firm inside; Follain, p. 173.

On Ramírez in Czechoslovakia, see Pavel Žáček, 'Carlos the Jackal in Prague', in Hänni, ed., *Terrorism, Vol. 1*, pp. 107–22. Daniela Richterova's *Watching the Jackals*, and her 'The Anxious Host: Czechoslovakia and Carlos the Jackal 1978–1986', in *The International History Review*, Vol. 40, No. 1, 2018, pp. 108–32 are both very good too. I also used Liszkaï's *Rideau*, p. 21 and FENVAC transcripts of statements made by prosecutors in Ramírez's trial in Paris in November 2011 in which documents from behind the Iron Curtain played a key role. Also helpful was Mitrokhin, *Vol. 2*, pp. 245–6. For the Libyans, see Schröm, pp. 203–4, and Follain, pp. 176–7. The 'other group' was almost certainly Abu Nidal's faction which was based in Poland.

For details of the practical problems of tracking Ramírez, local security services' fears of reprisals and the spectacularly exaggerated estimates of the OIR's capabilities, see Liszkaï, *Rideau*, p. 99 as well as Richterova, pp. 249–50 and Follain, p. 133. For the media treatment of 'Carlos', see 'Secret Bedfellows? The KGB, Carlos the Jackal and Cold War Psychological Warfare', in *Studies in Conflict and Terrorism*, 2018 by Adrian Hänni, which has plenty of examples, such as the supposed nuclear threat. Also: Ovid Demaris, 'Carlos: The Most Dangerous Man in the World', *New York*, 7 November 1977, pp. 35–40; 'US Border Agents Send Data on Suspected Libyan Hitsquads', WP, 12 December 1981; a US cable from Cairo, Report Concerning Presence Of Carlos In Malta, 15 January 1979; and the CIA's Foreign Broadcast Information Service's 'West Europe Report' on 23 September 1981.

For Ramírez in Hungary, see Liszkaï, *Rideau*, p. 41, Schröm, p. 198 and Follain, pp. 124–5. Also, 'Television Shows Internationally Sought Terrorist with Hungarian Agents', AP, 7 July 1990; and Hänni, *Terrorism in the Cold War, Vol. 2*, 'Hungarian State Security and International Terrorism', Balasz Orban-Schwarzkopf. In the GDR and with the Stasi: see Kopp, *Terrorjahre*, p. 127; Stasi memorandum XV/3031/78; Follain, p. 120; Liszkaï, p. 90; 'Wie die Stasi Top-Terrorist "Carlos" protegierte', *Spiegel*, 30 October 2010; Schröm, pp. 203–20; Roland Jacquard, *Le Dossier Secret*, p. 197; and Herf.

In 1977, Moscow had circulated a file on the 'international terrorist Ilich Ramírez' to its Warsaw Pact allies, which would not have told them much they did not already know. A year or so later, the KGB had responded with some indignation to a request from the Stasi for clarification of the exact status of Ramírez following a memo sent to the East Germans by local security officials in Aden which reported that the Venezuelan had claimed to be a 'KGB agent'. See Herf and Stasi memorandum XV/3031/78. The Soviet archives are still inaccessible so we can only speculate, but it seems the KGB often simply ignored requests from its eastern European allies for guidance on what to do with unwelcome guests like Ramírez. See Mitrokhin, *Vol.* 2, p. 256; Richterova, p. 257. It was not all one-way however. A defecting senior Stasi officer said in 1990 that, by the early 1980s, 'many of the KGB's results were obtained from [us]. We no longer were subordinate partners but equals.' See interview by Lally Weymouth, in the WP on 14 October 1990.

For the CIA analysis, see its National Intelligence Estimate 'Soviet Support for International Terrorism and Revolutionary Violence' of May 1981. For a comprehensive account of the row the estimate caused, and much else, read Hänni, *Bedfellows*.

The words of Benzion Netanyahu et al. can be read in *International Terrorism: Challenge and Response*, Proceedings of the Jerusalem Conference, ed. Binyamin Netanyahu. A useful discussion of later conspiracy theories around this meeting, and a subsequent similar event in 1984, can be found in Anshel Pfeffer's rigorous and readable biography of Netanyahu, *Bibi*, pp. 200–01.

On the RFI attack see Schröm, p. 208; Follain, pp. 130–31; FENVAC transcript of testimony of judge Jean-Louis Bruguière, November 2011; report of interrogation of Magdalena Kopp by German prosecutors, 24 April 1995 to 18 July 1996; Hänni's biography of Bréguet, pp. 158–64; Liszkaï, *Le Monde Selon Carlos*, pp. 160–61; 'Minutes of Meeting between Czechoslovak and Hungarian Interior Ministry Officials on the Carlos Terrorist Group and Radio Free Europe Bomb Attack', 25 April 1981, Wilson Center; RFE Special Feature, *The 1981 Bombing of RFE/RL*, 9 February 1996.

And for its aftermath: Schröm, pp. 219–20; Hänni, *Bréguet*, pp. 166–8; Kopp interrogation report; 'Terrorist Organization "Revolutionary Organization November 17" and "Carlos the Jackal"', Spyros Repousis, *Journal of Money Laundering Control*, No. 23–4, March 2021; CIA, 'Leftwing Terrorism in Greece: a status report', June 1983.

On the plot to kill Sadat: Yallop, pp. 236–7; Liszkaï, p. 90. There is passing reference to the plot – 'They intend to carry out attacks against Sadat – in this case Libya is interested' – in the minutes of the meeting between Czechoslovak and Hungarian officials mentioned above. This may be based on what the Czechoslovaks had learned from a source codenamed Vezir, presumably an Iraqi communist, who reported a request from Ramírez to help with an effort to assassinate Sadat, described as an initiative of Libyan intelligence. See Hänni, *Terrorism in the Cold War, Vol. 1*, p. 112. Further corroboration of a Libyan link can be found, somewhat unexpectedly, in Susan M. Sandover, *Libya: A Love Lived, a Life Betrayed: 9/36*, Matador, 2016, p. 3.

On the plan to bomb a palace, see Richterova, p. 28. For the trips to Damascus and the *al-Watan* commission, see FENVAC, testimony of Jean-François Riou, Paris, November 2011; Follain, pp. 132–3; and the report by the German police of their interrogation of Kopp, who said that the Syrians were 'stingy' with money.

34. CARLOS IN THE WEST

The opening scene of this chapter is based on Kopp, pp. 143–5; 'Leben mit Top Terrorist Carlos', *Der Spiegel*, 11 March 2007; Schröm, pp. 189, 227–9; FENVAC, testimony of Yves Noël and Jean Dufour, November 2011.

The details of Bréguet's life before his involvement in the Paris attack are from Hänni's biography.

On Ramírez, the Syrians and the attack on *al-Watan*, see Hänni, pp. 166–70 and Liszkaï, *Le Monde Selon Carlos*, p. 150. The *al-Watan* interview can be found in *Le Figaro* of 15 December 1979, headlined 'Les aveux sans remords de Carlos'. According to testimony of Michel Guérin, ex-deputy director of the DST, in November 2011 in Paris, Ali al-Issawi had opened a file for an eventual attack on *al-Watan al-Arabi* immediately after the publication of the interview. Much else in the transcripts of the trial's hearings was helpful, as was the German report of the interrogation of Kopp cited previously.

On the arrest of Kopp and Bréguet, I used Kopp, *Terrorjahre*, p. 146; Follain, p. 139; Bonnet, loc 2817; contemporary reporting by *Le Monde* and *Libération* and the always helpful FENVAC transcripts, particularly the testimony of Inspector Yves Noël.

On the first wave of attacks against French targets, see Burdan; UPI, 'Assassins Posing as Flower Deliverymen Shot and Killed a Diplomat', 16 April 1982; Violet, *Carlos*, p. 210; 'L'ambassadeur de France évoque "un acte terroriste dans le style des actions de Carlos"', *Le Monde*, 19 April 1982. At the time, French intelligence were working on the assumption, based on outdated intelligence received from Bonn, that Kopp was still the lover of Weinrich. This misapprehension was not corrected for many years.

Vergès had become internationally known almost three decades earlier when he defended Djamila Bouhired, then facing execution for her alleged role in a Front de Libération Nationale bombing of a café in Algiers that killed eleven people. Vergès led a campaign to commute the capital sentence and married Bouhired, known throughout the Middle East as the 'Algerian Joan of Arc', when she was freed in 1965. He then defended a series of Palestinians accused of terrorism in western Europe, including several involved in the high-profile attacks launched by the PFLP at the end of the 1960s. Among his contacts was Mohammed Boudia. Vergès had then disappeared for several years, resurfacing in Paris and refusing, in a typically suave but determined fashion, to explain his absence.

For more on Vergès, watch the documentary *L'Avocat de la terreur*, 2007, by Barbet Schroeder. For the *défense de rupture*, try, if you must, *De La Stratégie Judiciaire*, which Vergès published with Editions de Minuit in Paris in 1968. Ramírez's threats, as communicated by his lawyer, were repeated widely in the French media.

On terrorism in France, and attitudes to it, see *Le Monde*, 'Les Etranges protections de Bruno Bréguet', 5 March 1982 and 'Le Dédale Terroriste', 7 March 1983; as well as a CIA 'Terrorism Review', March 1984, pp. 9–10. There also may have been a deal with the Abu Nidal Organisation.

When Mohammed Odeh was arrested in Paris and then freed by a French judge in 1977 on a legal technicality despite a pending West German extradition request, there was outrage in Washington as well as much sanctimonious sermonising elsewhere. See FCO 93/116 file 'The Abu Daoud affair', and Abu Daoud's book. There was domestic pressure on France too, particularly after a bloody attack in 1980 on a synagogue in Paris, the first such violence against the French Jewish community since the Second World War.

For attacks in Lebanon and the 'private war', see FENVAC transcripts, especially, of the concluding comments of presiding judge and the previously mentioned testimony of Bruguière.

On the attitudes of the Stasi and other eastern European services, I relied heavily on the FENVAC transcripts of the November 2011 trial, which included much relevant testimony; Hänni, ed., *Terrorism, Vols. 1* and 2, Follain and Richterova.

I learned that Ramírez bought himself a Cartier from Bonnet, loc 2587. The RFE's report into the 1981 bombing showed that he did this just as he had written to Weinrich describing the OIR's finances thus: 'Ali takes $15,000, there are only $15,000 left . . . , and I have just over $9,000 left.'

For the attempts of Mohnhaupt to reform the RAF, see Peters, *Tödlicher Irrtum*, pp. 531–3 and *1977: RAF gegen Bundesrepublik*, p. 559 as well as Smith and Moncourt, *Dancing with Imperialism*, p. 117. There is also the useful interview with Peter-Jürgen Boock in *Die Zeit*. On the Red Brigades' misogyny, see 'Warum dominierten Frauen die Rote Armee Fraktion?', *Die Welt*, 28 September 2010.

On 22 February 1980, the *Guardian* reported the new atmosphere in Germany with the headline 'The terror that ended more with a whimper than a bang'. The Red Army Faction statement of 15 September 1981 is available online. See 'German Terrorists Strike, but Propaganda Largely Fails', in the *Christian Science Monitor* two days later, for reaction. Feelings still ran high. In 1981, some 50,000 peaceful demonstrators protested the presence of Alexander Haig in Berlin, and a thousand militants burned cars, looted shops and stoned police.

On the defectors, see Peters, *Tödlicher*, pp. 477–9, 541–4; Assaf Moghadam, 'Failure and Disengagement in the Red Army Faction', *Studies in Conflict & Terrorism*, 2012; Taylor, *States of Terror*, pp. 78–86; Sigrid Sternebeck, *Der Spiegel*, 'Dann sind bald alle tot', 12 August 1990.

In a rare moment of weakness, Mohnhaupt had allowed herself to be convinced that Boock was suffering from intestinal cancer and so had exempted him from the RAF's strict ban on drug-taking. Worse, she had ordered the group's members to help procure 'medication'. This led directly to the killing by police of a junior RAF member and the arrest of several others as they tried to procure drugs for her former lover in Amsterdam and Hamburg.

On the Stasi and the RAF, see the collection of reports about Meinhof put online by the Stasi Mediathek. The German Central Archive's file entitled Anarcho-terroristische Kräfte: Die Rote Armee Fraktion und die Stasi is full of useful material. See also Thomas Riegler, '"Es muß ein gegenseitiges Geben und Nehmen sein": Warschauer-Pakt-Staaten und Terrorismusbekämpfung am Beispiel der DDR', in *Terrorismusbekämpfung in Westeuropa: Demokratie und Sicherheit in den 1970er und 1980er Jahren*, ed. Johannes Hürter; and Peters, *Tödlicher*, pp. 553, 561. On Mohnhaupt in Yemen, see 'Die Stasi deckte die westdeutsche RAF-Terroristin Brigitte Mohnhaupt in ihrem damaligen Versteck bei Palästinensern im Jemen', *Spiegel*, 6 January 2013. See also US cable from Berlin, GDR Media Treatment Of Terrorist Activities Against The FRG, 20 October 1977.

The move of some of the RAF defectors to the GDR was widely covered in the German press in the 1990s. The accounts in Smith and Moncourt, *Dancing with Imperialism*, pp. 473–7, and 'Das zweite Leben', *Die Welt*, 19 August 2016, are both useful.

On the attack on the nuclear power station see: FENVAC transcript of the testimony of Berthe de Marcellus in November 2011 and Follain, p. 137. Anne Hansen, a Canadian activist, told me in 2021 she had tried to join the RAF in Paris in the 1970s but had been told to go home to launch the struggle there. Arrested in Canada in 1983, she was convicted of bombing a factory and served seven years in prison. By then, she and her fellow activists were more motivated by the rights of indigenous communities, the fight against violent pornography and for the environment than global revolution, Hansen said.

Police in London identified two of the surviving three members of the assassination team as members of Abu Nidal's group and the third as an Iraqi intelligence colonel. See FCO 93/3511, 'Palestinian Terrorism Outside Israel' and FCO QPE/82/1/75/2, 'Shooting of Israeli Ambassador'.

Some readers may be wondering why Saddam Hussein might have commissioned Abu Nidal to kill Argov. The answer, the more reliable sources strongly suggest, is this: Saddam knew that Israel's political and military leaders wanted to intervene forcefully in Lebanon but lacked an immediate casus belli. So he sought to provide one. Saddam was painfully aware that Iraq's war with Iran was going badly, Tehran had rejected offers of a ceasefire, and a costly, prolonged conflict looked unavoidable. If Israel invaded Lebanon, he reasoned, he could call for a ceasefire with Iran so all 'Muslim forces' could concentrate their efforts against this new threat. Such an offer would be difficult for the regime in Tehran to refuse if it wanted to maintain its self-appointed role as the standard-bearer of resistance to the 'Zionist entity'. Even if this gambit failed, Saddam reckoned, Israel would become embroiled in a new conflict, Syria would receive a bloody nose and the PLO, which Saddam detested, would be seriously weakened. There was no ceasefire between Iran and Iraq but on everything else, he was absolutely right.

35. YASSER ARAFAT'S LAST STAND

My descriptions of Beirut in the spring of 1982 are based on Lina Mikdadi's *Surviving the Siege of Beirut*; Robert Fisk's *Pity the Nation*; Jonathan Randal's *Tragedy of Lebanon*; Tony Clifton and Catherine Leroy's *God Cried* and John le Carré's *The Pigeon Tunnel*, pp. 94–106, 118–24, plus a few novels, lots of more general reading and much archive footage online.

On the leftists still in Lebanon in 1982, details of the stories of German and Swiss extremists came from Thomas Skelton-Robinson and Adrian Hänni; 'The Red Army faction: encounters with phantoms', Goethe-Institut Lebanon, 2024, by Martin Klingus; US cable from Beirut, Reported Activities Of Terrorist Groups In The Middle East, 3 February 1978; Melkonian, *My Brother's Road*, p. 82, for neo-Nazis; 'Des terroristes entraînés au Liban', *Le Monde*, 27 August 1982; 'Germans Link P.L.O. To Domestic Terror', NYT, 27 May 1981; Charbel, p. 392.

For the US contacts with the PLO: see Ignatius, WP, 4 December 1988; Gowers and Walker, pp. 191–2 for the motorcade and the informal outreach.

The question of Sharon's war aims has been much discussed; see Schiff and Ya'ari, pp. 32–43 and Black and Morris, p. 372. Also David Landau's biography, of course. David Hirst describes decades of efforts by Israel to secure influence over Lebanon in the early chapters of his *Beware of Small States*. To Oriana Fallaci in late August 1982, Sharon swore blind that he had never intended or desired to enter Beirut. See: 'Israeli Defense Minister Ariel Sharon says he "fully obtained"' etc., 30 August 1982, UPI Archives.

The statistics are from Ariel Sharon, 'Gains From The War In Lebanon', NYT, 29 August 1982.

There are multiple accounts of this debate but Shlaim, pp. 41–15 and Landau, p. 182 are typically solid.

Different numbers for Israeli and PLO strengths are given. These are from Black and Morris, p. 371. Thomas Friedman in the NYT, on 11 July 1982, said 25,000, for example. Schiff and Ya'ari, pp. 109–50 are good on Syrian resistance. In late 2024 I stood on a spur above the Israeli town of Kiryat Shmona and looked across the hills to Beaufort Castle. Even the most non-military observer can see its strategic and tactical significance.

On the placement of military equipment among civilian infrastructure, see 'P.L.O.-Dominated West Beirut: Armed Camp In Crowded Capital', NYT, 25 June 1982 and also the reference to the PLO putting anti-aircraft guns on the roof of a hospital made by Fallaci, no great friend of the Israelis, in her August 1982 interview with Sharon, reprinted in *Interviews with History and Conversations with Power*, 2016. Abu Sharif, who had helped plan the PLO's defence of Beirut, described the city's buildings as the defenders' 'best barricades', which was not just a metaphor. Beneath Shatila camp were supposedly tunnels with stocks of ammunition, mortars and missiles, as reported here: 'Army Find Booty in Beirut Underground', GDN, 8 October 1982. Khalidi, in *Under Siege*, p. 282, vehemently rejects the charge that weapons were 'cold-bloodedly sited near civilians for protection', arguing that PLO commanders knew Israel had no compunction about striking civilian areas, and that anyway most PLO, Syrian and LNM forces and weapons were necessarily placed in the front lines.

For the Israeli attacks on Beirut and efforts to kill Arafat see Black and Morris, p. 380; Gowers and Walker, p. 215; Bergman, pp. 253–9.

On casualties, see Sayigh, p. 540; Rogan, *The Arabs*, p. 523 for casualties from UN figures; Walkers and Gower, p. 217 for Lebanese official figures; 'War Casualties Put at 48,000 in Lebanon', WP, 2 September 1982; O'Ballance, p. 116. Also, 'The Siege of Beirut – and the Reluctant Israeli Colonel', *Christian Science Monitor*, 29 July 1982.

For media coverage of the siege, see Gregory Orfalea, 'Sifting the Ashes', *Arab Studies Quarterly*, Vol. 11, No. 2/3, 1989; 'Arafat Leads The P.L.O. Into Toughest Salvage Operation', NYT, 11 July 1982; and Clifton and Leroy, pp. 28–30, as well as, obviously, much contemporary reporting.

What few reports from the city showed, though many observers in the city were struck by this most of all, was how life across the 'green line' in predominantly Christian east Beirut had continued uninterrupted through much of the siege. Food was plentiful, restaurants remained open, families headed to the beaches. Journalists who drove up from Israel ate well and visited Roman ruins. So too did Israeli officers. At night, residents stood on the roofs of villas in the foothills of the Chouf mountains and watched the explosions over west Beirut. Some celebrated; Clifton and Leroy, p. 31; author interviews with Israeli veterans, June 2024.

See Bird, pp. 278–9 for the Little Drummer Girl's encounter with Arafat, and Mikdadi, p. 57 for the joke.

Reagan was called by King Fahd of Saudi Arabia 'begging [him] to do something'. For his phone conversation with Begin, see Max Boot, *Reagan*, p. 546; Landau, pp. 195–6; 'Reagan Diaries Reveal President's Private Musings', Reuters, 9 August 2007; Avner,

Prime Ministers, pp. 603–16; and Landau, pp. 194–6. Begin, aware of growing misgivings in Washington, had written to Reagan, comparing Arafat in Beirut to Adolf Hitler in his Berlin bunker at the end of the Second World War.

My account of the departure of Arafat is based on Clifton and Leroy, pp. 133–4; Nassib and Tisdall, pp. 115, 122–7; 'Weeks Of Siege', Thomas Friedman, NYT, 20 August 1982; Landau, p. 197; Mikdadi, pp. 132–3; Walker and Gower, p. 217; 'Arafat's Defiant Fighters Pull Out', Shyam Bhatia, the *Observer*, 22 August 1982.

For Arafat's final escapes, see Bergman, p. 261, and my own interviews of former security officials in Israel, 2023.

For the flight of the various militants, see *Tried by Fire*, p. 203; Farrell, p. 198; author interviews, Israel 2023; 'Après La Chute Du Sanctuaire', *Le Monde*, 12 October 1982; and Irving on Leila Khaled, p. 84. If Shigenobu and the JRA did set out on a ship for Yemen they may well have jumped ship somewhere, because the next editions of their small newsletter, *Solidarity!*, were mailed from Vienna, Milan and Libya. See Farrell, p. 198.

The NYT editorial was referred to above. Sharon also told Fallaci that she was wrong to suggest that the massive damage done to Israel's international image rendered any victory Pyrrhic, insisting that 'the sympathy for Israel has not decreased and, though we care to have it, when it comes to our security, we can do without it.' The interview – which took ten hours at Sharon's Negev ranch – is available here: 'Sharon: "I Wanted Them Out of Beirut; I Got What I Wanted"', WP, 29 August 1982.

For the 'Mission Accomplished', see 'US Marines Withdraw From Lebanon', *Boston Globe*, 11 September 1982.

On Sabra and Shatila, I read a lot, and found the following most useful: 'Preventable Massacre', Seth Anziska, NYT, 16 September 2012; Chamberlin, *Killing Fields*, p. 502; Schiff, pp. 246–86; Fisk, pp. 358–87; and Khalidi's *Under Siege*, pp. 16–18. The report of Israel's own official investigation led by the president of the supreme court Yitzhak Kahan has obvious limitations but is also worth consulting.

On Reagan's reaction, see Patrick Tyler, *A World of Trouble*, pp. 281–2. For the father's letter: Shindler, p. 151.

For Arafat in Tunisia, see 'Arafat: Bourguiba Accueillera Samedi À Bizerte Un Millier De Combattants Palestiniens', *Le Monde*, 27 August 1982; O'Ballance, p. 139; 'Arafat Arrives In Greece', WP, 1 September 1982; Friedman, pp. 153–5; and le Carré, *The Pigeon Tunnel*, p. 106. Obviously, le Carré's *The Little Drummer Girl*, published in 1983, is essential reading – and typically evocative and entertaining too.

36. THE BLOODIEST YEAR

The demolition of the Iraqi Embassy in Beirut in December 1981 opened the way for a new era of terrorism. A massive bomb in a truck flattened the building, killing sixty-one, including, by design, the driver. Despite the similarity in tactics, the attack was ignored by the Israelis investigating the Tyre blast just eleven months later. Their cover-up and/or failures are still controversial today, as I learned in 2023 and 2024 from Israeli former military intelligence officers who served in Lebanon at the time or soon afterwards. Burton and Katz, *Beirut Rules*, contains a useful account of the attack. Biographical details of the teenager who drove the car were only released by Hezbollah some years later.

Beirut's brief moment of relative calm is well described by Fisk in *Pity the Nation*, pp. 464–5 and Friedman in *Beirut to Jerusalem*, p. 198. For Ames and for the embassy bombing, see Bird, pp. 295–305; Tyler, pp. 286–7; and Fisk, p. 479. There was a lot of contemporary media reporting of the growing violence, 'Islamic Jihad' and the embassy attack too of course, but I have omitted individual references.

On the Lebanese Shia, the literature is extensive. Ferdinand Smit, *The Battle For South Lebanon* is comprehensive. References here are from 'Lebanon and Its Inheritors', Fouad Ajami, *Foreign Affairs*, Spring 1985, and 'The Roots of the Shi'i Movement', Salim Nassr, *MERIP*, June 1985. The best single work on the fascinating, important al-Sadr is Ajami's *The Vanished Imam*, especially pp. 85–122, 168–171. Ghattas in *Black Wave* is useful, see pp. 18–19. Alemzadeh in *Global 1979*, pp. 178–210, is good on Iranian radicals' activism in Lebanon in the 1970s.

On Mughniyeh's youth, see Bilal Saab's 'Israel, Hizb Allah' and 'The Shadow of Imad Mughniyeh' in *CTC Sentinel*, June 2011; also Bird, pp. 328–9; Robert Baer's *See No Evil*, pp. 148–9; Hala Jabar's *Hezbollah*, p. 115; and Ronen Bergman, *The Secret War with Iran*, pp. 68–70.

On his recruitment to Fatah, see Charbel, pp. 225–323; the documentary *Anis Nakkache – Révolutionnaire ou Terroriste?*; Bilal Saab in the *CTC Sentinel*; Nicholas Blanford, *Warriors of God*, pp. 27–9, 46, 73; 'Mughniyeh Was Key Hezbollah Commander, Insider Says', AP, 27 February 2008; Baer, p. 155. I picked up useful information during interviews with Fatah and PFLP veterans in Ramallah in 2023. For Mughniyeh during the 1982 invasion, see Saab, *CTC Sentinel*; '"Ghosts of Beirut" Gets Hezbollah's Most Wanted All Wrong', Hussain Abdul-Hussain, *Asia Times*, 26 August 2023; Ibrahim al-Amin writing in *al-Akhbar* on 17 February 2011; and Bird, p. 278.

On the many Fatah fighters, Communists and others who turned to Islamism in Lebanon at this moment, see 'Brothers in Arms: How Palestinian Maoists Turned Jihadists', in *Die Welt des Islams*, 51, 2011, and 'From Maoism to Jihadism: Some Fatah Militants' Trajectory from the mid 1970's to the mid 1980's', *Jihadism and Terrorism*, Vol. 1, 2013, both by Manfred Sing. Also: 'The Disenchantment of the Left: Two Memories of the Palestinian Struggle', *Forum Transregionale Studien*, 5 June 2018, and Nicolas Dot-Pouillard, 'De Pékin à Téhéran, en regardant vers Jerusalem, La singulière conversion à l'Islamisme des "Maos du Fatah"', *Cahier de l'Institut Religioscope*, 2008, p. 39. See too: Baer, pp. 155–6; Schiff, pp. 144–55; and Aurélie Daher's useful *Hezbollah*, pp. 39, 50–51. Anis Nakkache, who is not entirely reliable, boasted to Charbel of recruiting eighty former Fatah fighters for Hezbollah.

On Islamist attacks in late 1982 and early 1983, see Fisk, p. 456; Daher's *Hezbollah*, pp. 49, 52–4. The CIA's Near East review, 'Lebanon: Radical Shias and the Beirut Bombings', 29 April 1983, was also useful.

For the arrival and activities of the Iranians in the Beqa'a, see Fisk, p. 469; Dominique Avon and Anaïs-Trissa Khatchadourian, *Hezbollah*, pp. 25–6; Ostovar, pp. 95–6, 113–15.

On the decisions of Khomeini and Assad see Hirst, pp. 188–9; Smit, pp. 169–70; and

Daher, pp. 52–4. For Mughniyeh's activity with the Iranians, Jaber, pp. 48–9; the CIA's 'Embassy bombing and the investigation', *Studies in Intelligence*, Summer 1983; Fisk, p. 479; Baer, pp. 172–3. On Israeli covert operations, Bergman, *Rise*, pp. 242–3.

On the Marines at the airport, the barracks bombing and its aftermath: *Peterson v. Islamic Republic of Iran*, 264 F. Sup. 2d 46 (D.D.C. 2003); Benis M. Frank, *U.S. Marines in Lebanon, 1982–1984*, p. 108 and Friedman, p. 204. See too, Matthew Levitt, 'The Origins of Hezbollah', *Atlantic Monthly*, October 2013; 'Report of the Department of Defense Commission on Beirut International Airport Terrorist Act', 20 December 1983. There are also helpful accounts in Bird, Patrick Sloyan's *When Reagan Sent in the Marines*, and Fisk, as well as useful material in the legal files for *Estate of Farhat v. The Islamic Republic of Iran*, 19-cv-03631-RCL (D.D.C. 2004), on evidence of Iran's responsibility.

For US reaction, 'Bush Says Act Of Terrorism Won't Change U.S. Policies', NYT, 27 October 1983; CIA, 'Prospects for Increased Terrorism Against the US in the Wake of the Latest Bombing in Beirut', 29 September 1984; Fisk, p. 519; Rand Corporation, 'Trends in International Terrorism in 1982 and 1983', August 1984; Lawrence Freedman, *A Choice of Enemies*, pp. 138–9; Bacevich, p. 71; 'U.S. Knew Iran Ordered, Funded Beirut Bombings, Intercepts Show', *Miami Herald*, 7 December 1986; US National Intelligence Council Memo, 28 October 1983, NIC-7758; *Peterson v. Iran*; Sloyan, pp. 146, 155; and Bird, p. 325. Also, 'Israeli Warplanes Bomb 2 Camps of Moslem Radicals', WP, 17 November 1983; Razoux, pp. 275–6; and Freedman, pp. 143–4.

On Kuwait bombings, see the CIA's summary: 'Bombings in Kuwait', 13 December 1983, and Robin Wright, *Sacred Rage*, pp. 113–32. On the *New Jersey*, see Fisk, p. 527; Bacevich, p. 70; 'U.S. Navy Uses Heaviest Guns To Blast Syrians', WP, 15 December 1983; 'Why West Beirut Went Over to the Shi'ites', GDN, 13 February 1984; 'Bob Hope on the Road to Lebanon', UPI, 10 December 1983; Frank, p. 127; and finally 'New Chapter for Lebanon', NYT, 27 February 1984. Images and footage of Hope and Brooke Shields on the *New Jersey* are available online.

37. THE REVOLUTIONISTS

The opening pages of this chapter refer to the DoD 'Report on the Terrorist Bombings of US Marines in Beirut, Dec 19 and 23 1983', and Rand's 1982–83 review, published in August 1984. The Rand database is available online. The hijack quote comes from Alex Hobson, '"A Lot of People Watching": Understanding the Theater of Terrorism', *Diplomatic History*, September 2023.

On Reagan's directive, see NSA Briefing Book No. 55, 21 September 2001; Tim Naftali, *Blind Spot*, pp. 138–42, and Brian Jenkins, *Combatting Terrorism Becomes a War*, Rand, 1984, p. 1.

For the spillover quotes etc., see the CIA's Terrorism Reviews of May 1984 and July 1985. The Islamo-fascist reference comes from an Italian newspaper commenting, interestingly, on a copy of Abdallah Azzam's *al-Jihad* magazine found there.

US agencies highlighted the threat from radical Islam: see CIA Intelligence Directorate, 'Islam and Politics: a Compendium', April 1984. A former Mossad official told me about the British attitude in Tel Aviv in 2024.

For the various failures and successes of Ramírez and his OIR, see Jacquard's *Le*

Dossier Secret, pp. 249–64 and testimony in the November 2011 trial in Paris of Ramírez, especially its ninth day.

For the final break with Ramírez and his OIR of Prague, Budapest and other regimes, see Richterova, Liszkaï, Schröm, Follain and the two volumes of Hänni, ed., *Terrorism in the Cold War*. For Weinrich's exchange with Abu Iyad, see Liszkaï, p. 186.

On the Barbie plot and more general relations with the Stasi at this time, see Follain, pp. 156–7; Violet, p. 240; and the *Le Monde* report of 9 January 1984 headlined 'Carlos "l'insaisissable"'. The West German agent was a Syrian migrant and smuggler based in East Berlin who was close to the OIR if not actually a member. Codenamed 'Cairo', he was eventually tracked and unmasked by the Stasi, but not before he had revealed a great deal of useful information to his handlers.

Though personally unbothered by the prospect of freeing Barbie, a Nazi mass-murderer, Ramírez was aware that others might view this particular 'revolutionary action' differently. 'Don't mention the [Barbie] scheme to the Socialist camp,' he warned Weinrich in one of the many letters the two men exchanged. The Stasi were very concerned too when the OIR posted their claim of responsibility for bombings in France from East Berlin – something that was immediately and widely reported in the West. It is worth noting that though Yuri Andropov, the KGB former director general who was now the leader of the USSR, was a confirmed hawk and Cold War tensions were higher than at any time since the Cuban Missile Crisis twenty-two years earlier, Moscow still strongly disapproved of the 'adventurism' of individuals like Ramírez.

Weinrich's further money problems are from Schröm, p. 266. For his and Ramírez's movements between 1983 and 1984 see 'Objectif France' in *Le Monde* of 14 October 1982, Jordan Baev's article 'Bulgarian State Security and International Terrorism', and Jordan Akrap's 'Yugoslavia, Carlos and International Terrorism during the Cold War', both in Hänni's *Terrorism, Vol. 1*.

For Kopp's final days in France and West Germany, see Kopp, pp. 156–7; Schröm, p. 271; and *Le Monde*, 'Magdalena Kopp est expulsée en RFA', 6 May 1985.

On Mohnhaupt's trial, 'Two Red Army Faction Terrorists Accused', UPI, 1 February 1984 and 'Wir oder sie', *Der Spiegel*, 29 January 1984. On the depots, see 'Waffen, Ausweise, Geld – und spektakuläre Festnahmen', *Tagesspiegel*, 19 January 2021. The concentric circles quote is from Varon, p. 302. For a general account of the RAF at this time, see Butz Peters, pp. 602–03 and 'Hier spricht die RAF', 3 February 1984, *Der Speigel*. On the IRA, Carroll, p. 249. 'Erklärung zu 77', Mohnhaupt's statement of 4 December 1984, is available online. For the verdicts, 'Toughest Ever Jail Terms for Terrorists', GDN, 12 January 1985. Some analysts described a new and frightening 'Euroterrorism', warning once again that 'predictions of the imminent demise' of groups like the RAF had been 'premature'. See, for example, 'Attacks in Europe Seem Coordinated', *Washington Times*, 11 March 1985. This was alarmist. The RAF's campaign was effectively over.

Khomeini's speeches are here: 'Khomeini on Anniversary', WP, 31 January 1984 and 'Iran: Five Years of Fanaticism', NYT, 12 February 1984. The jokey British official is from: 'How Britain Helped Iran's Islamic Regime Destroy The Left-Wing Opposition', Declassified UK, 21 January 2020.

For the section on Iran and martyrdom, I used Efraim Karsh, *The Iran Iraq War*, p. 42 and the following reports in the GDN: 'Red Dye Flows at Tehran Cemetery',

24 November 1983; 'Where the Martyrs Come in Hordes', 16 March 1984; and 'Death Holds no Fear for Iranian Mourners at the Spring of Blood', 27 October 1984. Also see Amanat, p. 1013, and Rahnema, *The Political History of Modern Iran*, pp. 438–9. Teenagers leaving for the front, often without the permission of their parents, were encouraged to write last testaments which then appeared in newspapers and propaganda publications of the Islamic Republic.

On the fate of the Communists, see 'More on Espionage Confession from Leaders of the Tudeh Party', IRNA, 1 May 1983, and Behrooz, pp. 113–15, 120–30. See also 'Iran Country Report', Amnesty International, 30 November 1983. Some of the names of the Communists came from a defector who had gone to MI6, which had briefed the CIA, which passed a list to the regime. See 'Tight Little Network', NYT, 5 May 1991. The accounts of Sazegara and Negahdar are based on my interviews with both.

For the 'Arab Afghans', see Hamid and Farrall, *The Arabs at War in Afghanistan*, pp. 92, 98–9; Hegghammer, *The Caravan*, p. 248; my own *Al-Qaeda*, pp. 72–7 and *The 9/11 Wars*; Abdallah Anas and Tam Hussein, pp. 150–52. Almost all aid from the US and other overseas powers was distributed by Pakistan's main military intelligence service, known as the ISI, which divided it among Afghan mujahideen factions according to its own strategic and ideological priorities. A small amount may thus have reached the Afghan Arabs indirectly, but in negligible quantities. Bin Laden and his comrades in arms made no appreciable difference to the course of the war in Afghanistan and were deeply disliked and distrusted by many Afghans.

On Azzam in Pakistan, see Hegghammer, pp. 252–3, 295–302. On Azzam and bin Laden during this time, see Bergen, *The bin Laden I Knew*, pp. 26–9, 39, 60; my own *Al-Qaeda*, pp. 56–9; Hegghammer, pp. 205–12.

On bin Laden's trip to Jaji, see Hamid and Farrall, who suggest a slightly different date, pp. 187–97, and Wright, pp. 100–01. You can find some pictures of Jaji in the early 1980s and rare descriptions of the fighting there online.

Epilogue

On Bréguet's death, see Hänni's biography, pp. 211–26. On Shigenobu, see 'Japanese Red Army Founder Shigenobu Freed from Prison', AFP, 28 May 2022. Yasser Arafat first explicitly renounced violence and recognised Israel in 1988, but was not taken seriously either by Israel or the US. On his death, see: 'Yasser Arafat Died of Natural Causes, French Investigators Say', GDN, 3 December 2013.

Select bibliography

Most of the works cited below were of direct assistance in the writing of this book. A handful have been included simply because they were very useful to my broader understanding, or because I enjoyed them sufficiently to find it impossible to leave them out. I have included a selection of newspapers and journals that were the most helpful, as well as some of the documentaries I viewed.

Ahmed Abdalla, *The Student Movement and National Politics in Egypt 1923–1973*, Al-Saqi Books, 1985

Ervand Abrahamian, *The Iranian Mojahedin*, Yale UP, 1989

Khomeinism: Essays on the Islamic Republic, California UP, 1993

Iran Between Two Revolutions, Princeton UP, 1982

A History of Modern Iran, Cambridge UP, 2018

'The Guerrilla Movement in Iran, 1963–1977', *MERIP Reports*, No. 86, 1980

Abu Daoud and Gilles du Gonchay, *Palestine: de Jérusalem à Munich*, Carrière, 1999

Abu Iyad (Salah Khalaf) with Eric Rouleau, *My Home My Land: A Narrative of the Palestinian Struggle*, Times Books, 1981

Bassam Abu Sharif, *Wadi' Haddad: Tha'ir am Irhabi*, Al-ruaa, unknown date, c. 2013

Arafat and the Dream of Palestine: An Insider's Account, Saint Martin's Press, 2009

Bassam Abu Sharif, Uzi Mahnaimi, *Tried by Fire: The Searing True Story of Two Men at the Heart of the Struggle Between the Arabs and the Jews*, Sphere, 1996

Saïd K. Aburish, *Arafat: From Defender to Dictator*, Bloomsbury, 1999

Saddam Hussein: The Politics of Revenge, Bloomsbury, 2001

Beirut Spy: The St George Hotel Bar, Unicorn, 2022

Jalal al-I Ahmad, *Occidentosis*, translated by R. Campbell, introduction by Hamid Algar, Mizan Press, 1984

Fouad Ajami, *The Vanished Imam: Musa al Sadr and the Shia of Lebanon*, Cornell UP, 1986

Seyed Alavi, *Iran and Palestine*, Routledge, 2019

Richard Aldrich, Rory Cormac, *The Black Door: Spies, Secret Intelligence and British Prime Ministers*, HarperCollins, 2016

Maryam Alemzadeh, 'Revolutionaries for Life', in *Global 1979: Geographies and Histories of the Iranian Revolution*, eds. Ali Mirsepassi, Arang Keshavarzian, CUP, 2021

Abbas Amanat, *Iran: A Modern History*, Yale UP, 2017

John Amos, *The Palestinian Resistance Movement*, Pergamon Press, 1980

Christopher Andrew, Vassily Mitrokhin, *The Mitrokhin Archive: The KGB in Europe and the West*, Basic Books, 2000

The World Was Going Our Way: The KGB and the Battle for the Third World, Penguin, 2006

Abdallah Anas and Tam Hussein, *To the Mountains*, Hurst, 2019

Abdullah al-Arian, *Answering the Call: Popular Islamic Activism In Sadat's Egypt*, OUP, 2014

Said Amir Arjomand, *The Turban for the Crown*, OUP, 1988

Alex Aßmann, *Gudrun Ensslin: Die Geschichte Einer Radikalisierung*, Brill Schoningh, 2018

Abdel Bari Atwan, *A Country of Words: A Palestinian Journey from the Refugee Camp to the Front Page*, Saqi, 2007

Stefan Aust, *The Baader Meinhof Complex*, Bodley Head, 2008

Yehuda Avner, *The Prime Ministers*, Toby, 2012

Dominique Avon, Anaïs-Trissa Khatchadourian, *Hezbollah: A History of the 'Party of God'*, Harvard UP, 2012

Michael Axworthy, *Revolutionary Iran: A History of the Islamic Republic*, Allen Lane, 2019

Arash Azizi, *The Shadow Commander: Soleimani, the US, and Iran's Global Ambitions*, Oneworld, 2020

Andrew Bacevich, *America's War for the Greater Middle East*, Random House, 2016

Tricia Bacon, *Why Terrorist Groups Form International Alliances*, Pennsylvania UP, 2018

Robert Baer, *See No Evil*, Arrow Books, 2002

Abol Bani-Sadr, *Le Complot des Ayatollahs*, La Découverte, 1989

Mordechai Bar-On, *Moshe Dayan, Israel's Controversial Hero*, Yale UP, 2012

Michael Bar-Zohar, Eitan Haber, *Massacre in Munich*, The Lyons Press, 2005

Karin Bauer, *Everybody Talks About the Weather . . . We Don't: The Writings of Ulrike Meinhof*, Seven Stories, 2008

Bommi Baumann, *Terror or Love?: Personal Account of a West German Urban Guerrilla*, Calder, 1980

Gillian Becker, *Hitler's Children*, Author House, 2014

Andy Beckett, *When the Lights Went Out: Britain in the Seventies*, Faber & Faber, 2010

Maziar Behrooz, *Rebels with a Cause: The Failure of the Left in Iran*, I.B. Tauris, 2000

Menachim Begin, *The Revolt*, Kindle edition, 2014
Peter Bergen, *The bin Laden I Know*, Free Press, 2006
Ronen Bergman, *Rise and Kill First*, John Murray, 2018
The Secret War with Iran, Oneworld, 2008
Paul Berman, *Power and the Idealists: Or, the Passion of Joschka Fischer and its Aftermath*, Norton, 2007
Muki Betser, *Secret Soldier*, Simon & Schuster, 1996
Kai Bird, *The Good Spy: The Life and Death of Robert Ames*, Broadway Books, 2014
Divided City, Simon & Schuster, 2010
Ian Black, *Enemies and Neighbours: Arabs and Jews in Palestine and Israel, 1917–2017*, Penguin, 2017
Ian Black, Benny Morris, *Israel's Secret Wars*, Grove Press, 1991
Nicholas Blanford, *Warriors of God*, Random House, 2011
Sophie Bonnet, *Salutations Révolutionnaires*, Grasset, 2018
Max Boot, *Reagan*, Liveright, 2024
Thomas Borstelmann, *The 1970s: A New Global History From Civil Rights to Economic Inequality*, Princeton UP, 2012
Marcel Bouguereau, *The German Guerilla: Terror, Reaction and Resistance: conversations with H.J. Klein*, Christie Books, 2013
Mark Bowden, *Guests of the Ayatollah*, Grove Press, 2018
Noel Brehony, *Yemen Divided: The Story of a Failed State in South Arabia*, I.B. Tauris, 2011
James Buchan, *Days of God*, Simon & Schuster, 2013
Daniel Burdan, *DST – Neuf ans à la division antiterroriste*, Robert Laffont, 1990
Jason Burke, *Al-Qaeda*, Penguin, 2003
The 9/11 Wars, Penguin, 2011
Elinor Burkett, *Golda*, HarperCollins, 2009
Michael Burleigh, *Blood and Rage*, Harper Press, 2008
Bryan Burrough, *Days of Rage*, Penguin, 2015
Fred Burton, Samuel M. Katz, *Beirut Rules: The Murder of a CIA Station Chief and Hezbollah's War Against America and the West*, Penguin, 2018
Jonathan Calvert, *Sayyid Qutb and the Origins of Radical Islam*, Hurst, 2010
Ian Carol, *From Jerusalem to the Lion of Judah and Beyond: Israel's Foreign Policy in East Africa*, Bloomington 1977
Rory Carroll, *Killing Thatcher*, Mudlark, 2023
Christian Caryl, *Strange Rebels*, Basic Books, 2013
Gerard Chaliand, *The Palestinian Resistance*, Penguin, 1972
Paul Thomas Chamberlin, *The Global Offensive*, OUP, 2012
The Cold War's Killing Fields, Harper, 2018
Ghassan Charbel, *Asrâr al-sundûq al-aswad* (*The Secrets of the Black Box*), Riyad El-Rayyes Books, 2008 (original in Arabic)
Houchang Chehabi, *Distant Relations: Iran and Lebanon in the Last 500 Years*, I.B. Tauris, 2006

Iranian Politics and Religious Modernism: The Liberation Movement of Iran under the Shah and Khomeini, Cornell UP, 1990
Duane Clarridge, *A Spy For All Seasons*, Scribner, 2009
Tony Clifton, Catherine Leroy, *God Cried: The Battle of Beirut*, Quartet Books, 1983
Helen Cobban, *The Palestinian Liberation Organisation: People, Power and Politics*, CUP, 1984
Juan R. I. Cole, Nikki R. Keddie, eds., *Shi'ism and Social Protest*, Yale UP, 1986
Steve Coll, *Ghost Wars*, Penguin, 2005
The Bin Ladens, Penguin, 2008
John Cooley, *Green March, Black September*, Cass, 1973
Andrew Scott Cooper, *The Fall of Heaven*, Picador, 2018
Con Coughlin, *Khomeini's Ghost*, HarperCollins, 2010
Chris Cramer, Sim Harris, *Hostage*, John Clare, 1982
Stephanie Cronin, *Reformers and Revolutionaries in Modern Iran: New Perspectives on the Iranian Left*, Routledge, 2004
Michael Curtis, ed., *The Middle East: A Reader*, Routledge, 1982
Aurélie Daher, *Hezbollah: Mobilisation and Power*, Hurst, 2019
Roland Dannreuther, *The Soviet Union and the PLO*, Macmillan Press, 1998
Saul David, *Operation Thunderbolt*, Hodder, 2016
Barry Davies, *Shadow of the Dove*, Bloomsbury, 1996
Christopher de Bellaigue, *The Islamic Enlightenment*, Vintage, 2018
Régis Debray, *Révolution dans la révolution? Lutte armée et lutte politique en amérique latine*, François Maspero, 1967
Christopher Dobson, *Black September: Its Short, Violent History*, Macmillan, 1974
Jutta Ditfurth, *Ulrike Meinhof: Die Biographie*, Ullstein Taschenbuch vlg, 2009
Simon Dunstan, *Israel's Lightning Strike: The Raid on Entebbe 1976*, Osprey, 2009
Gunnar Ekberg, *De ska ju ändå dö: Tio år i svensk underrättelsetjänst* (They're Going to Die Anyway, Ten Years in the Swedish Intelligence Service), Fischer & Co., 2010
Amos Elon, *The Israelis: Founders and Sons*, Holt, Rinehart & Winston, 1971
John Esposito, *The Iranian Revolution: Its Global Impact*, Florida UP, 1990
John Esposito and Emad el-Din Shahin, *The Oxford Handbook of Islam and Politics*, OUP, 2013
Roxanne L. Euben, Muhammad Qasim Zaman, eds., *Princeton Readings in Islamist Thought: Texts and Contexts From al-Banna to Bin Laden*, Princeton UP, 2010
Roger Faligot, *Tricontinentale: Quand Che Guevara, Ben Barka, Cabral, Castro et Hô Chi Minh préparaient la révolution mondiale*, La Découverte, 2013
Oriana Fallaci, *Interview with History*, Houghton Mifflin, 1977
Interviews with History and Conversations with Power, Rizzoli, 2011
Mamoun Fandy, *Saudi Arabia and the Politics of Dissent*, Palgrave, 1999
Frantz Fanon, *The Wretched of the Earth*, Penguin, 2001

William Farrell, *Blood and Rage: The Story of the Japanese Red Army*, Lexington, 1990

Niall Ferguson, et al., *The Shock of the Global: the 1970s in Perspective*, Harvard UP, 2010

Jean-Pierre Filiu, *Gaza: A History*, Hurst, 2014

Apocalypse in Islam, California UP, 2011

Michael Fischback, *Black Power and Palestine: Transnational Countries of Color*, Stanford UP, 2018

Robert Fisk, *Pity the Nation*, OUP, 2001

John Follain, *Jackal*, Orion, 1999

Benis M. Frank, *US Marines in Lebanon, 1982–1984*, US Marine Corps, 1987

Lawrence Freedman, *A Choice of Enemies*, Weidenfeld & Nicolson, 2008

Thomas Friedman, *Beirut to Jerusalem*, HarperCollins, 1998

David Frum, *How We Got Here: The 1970s*, Basic Books, 2000

John Lewis Gaddis, *The Cold War*, Penguin, 2007

James Gelvin, *The Israel-Palestine Conflict: One Hundred Years of War*, CUP, 2014

Fawaz Gerges, *Making the Arab World: Nasser, Qutb and the Clash that Shaped the Middle East*, Princeton UP, 2018

Hanin Ghaddar, *Hezbollahland: Mapping Dahiya and Lebanon's Shia Community*, The Washington Institute for Near East Policy, 2023

Kim Ghattas, *Black Wave*, Wildfire, 2021

Giorgio, *Memoirs of an Italian Terrorist*, Carroll & Graf, 2003

Michel Goldberg, *Namesake*, Yale UP, 1982

Andrew Gowers, Tony Walker, *Behind the Myth: Yasser Arafat and the Palestinian Revolution*, Corgi, 1992

Ernesto Che Guevara, *Guerrilla Warfare*, Penguin, 2021

Laure Guirguis, *The Arab Lefts: Histories and Legacies, 1950s–1970s*, Edinburgh UP, 2020

Aviva Guttmann, *Operation Wrath of God*, CUP, 2025

Georges Habache, *Les Révolutionnaires ne meurent jamais*, Fayard, 2008

Simon Hall, *Ten Days in Harlem: Fidel Castro and the Making of the 1960s*, Faber & Faber, 2020

Fred Halliday, *Revolution and Foreign Policy: the Case of South Yemen 1967–1987*, CUP, 1990

Mustafa Hamid, Leah Farrall, *The Arabs at War in Afghanistan*, Hurst, 2015

Jussi Hanhimäki, Bernhard Blumenau, eds., *An International History of Terrorism*, Routledge, 2013

Adrian Hänni, ed., with Thomas Riegler, Przemyslaw Gasztold, *Terrorism in the Cold War, Vol. 1*, Bloomsbury, 2020

Terrorism in the Cold War, Vol. 2, Bloomsbury, 2020

Adrian Hänni, *Terrorist und CIA-Agent: Die unglaubliche Geschichte des Schweizers Bruno Bréguet*, NZZ Libro, 2023

Karrin Hanshew, *Terror and Democracy in West Germany*, CUP, 2012

Thomas Hegghammer, *The Caravan: Abdallah Azzam and the Rise of Global Jihad*, CUP, 2020

Jihad in Saudi Arabia, CUP, 2010

Thomas Hegghammer, Stéphane Lacroix, *The Meccan Rebellion*, Amal Press, 2011

Mohammed Heikal, *Autumn of Fury*, Random House, 1983

Jeffrey Herf, *Undeclared Wars with Israel: East Germany and the West German Radical Left, 1967–1989*, CUP, 2016

Dilip Hiro, *Cold War on the Islamic World*, Hurst, 2020

Iran Under the Ayatollahs, Routledge, 1987

David Hirst, *The Gun and the Olive Branch*, Faber & Faber, 2003

Beware Small States: Lebanon the battleground of the Middle East, Faber & Faber, 2011

Bruce Hoffman, *Inside Terrorism*, Columbia UP, 2006

David Holden, Richard Johns, *The House of Saud*, Pan Macmillan, 1981

Shafiq al-Hout, *My Life in the PLO: The Inside Story of the Palestine Struggle*, Pluto, 2011

Albert Hourani, *A History of the Arab Peoples*, Faber & Faber, 1995

Johannes Hürter (ed.), *Terrorismusbekampfung in Westeuropa: Demokratie Und Sicherheit in Den 1970er Und 1980er*, De Gruyter Oldenbourg, 2014

Sarah Irving, *Leila Khaled: Icon of Palestinian Liberation (Revolutionary Lives)*, Pluto Press, 2012

Mahmud Issam, avec Huguette Cuchet-Cheruzel, *Je suis un fedayeen*, Stock, 1976

Saad Eddin Ibrahim, *Egypt, Islam, and Democracy: Critical Essays*, AUCP, 2002

Hala Jabar, *Hezbollah: Born With a Vengeance*, Columbia UP, 1997

Faleh A. Jaber, *The Shi'ite Movement in Iraq*, Saqi, 2003

Roland Jacquard, Dominique Nasplezes, *Carlos: Le Dossier Secret*, Jean Picollec, 1997

Tony Judt, *Postwar: A History of Europe Since 1945*, Vintage, 2010

Amy Kaplan, *Our American Israel: The Story of an Entangled Alliance*, Harvard UP, 2018

Ryszard Kapuściński, *The Shah of Shahs*, Quartet, 1985

Katherina Karcher, *Sisters in Arms: Militant Feminisms in the Federal Republic of Germany Since 1968*, Berghahn Books, 2017

Efraim Karsh, *The Iran Iraq War, 1980–1988*, Osprey, 2002

Nikki Keddie, *Modern Iran: Roots and Results of the Iranian Revolution*, Yale UP, 2003

Jeffrey Kenney, *Kharijites and the Politics of Extremism in Egypt*, OUP, 2006

Gilles Kepel, *Jihad: The Trail of Political Islam*, Bloomsbury, 2000

Muslim Extremism in Egypt: The Prophet and Pharaoh, California UP, 2003

Ian Kershaw, *Roller-Coaster: Europe 1950–2017*, Allen Lane, 2018

Arang Keshavarzian, Ali Mirsepassi, eds., *Global 1979: Geographies and Histories of the Iranian Revolution*, CUP, 2021

Moti Kfir, Ram Oren, *Sylvia Rafael: The Life and Death of a Mossad Spy*, Kentucky UP, 2010

Leila Khaled, George Hajjar, *My People Shall Live: The Autobiography of a Revolutionary*, Hodder & Stoughton, 1973

Rashid Khalidi, *The 100 Years War on Palestine*, Profile Books, 2020

The Iron Cage, Oneworld, 2009

Under Siege – PLO Decision Making During the Siege of Beirut, Columbia UP, 1985

Khomeini, *Islam and Revolution*, Taylor & Francis, 2013

Henry Kissinger, *The White House Years*, Simon & Schuster, 2011

Aaron Klein, *Striking Back*, Random House, 2007

Hans-Joachim Klein, *La Mort Mercenaire: Témoignage d'un ancien terroriste ouest-allemand*, Seuil, 1980

Peter Øvig Knudsen, *Blekingegadebanden 1: Den danske celle*, Gyldendal, 2007

Peter Koch, Kai Hermann, *Assault at Mogadishu*, Corgi, 1977

Gerd Koenen, *Vesper, Ensslin, Baader: Urszenen des deutschen Terrorismus*, Kiepenheuer & Witsch, 2003

Brendan I. Koerner, *The Skies Belong to Us: Love and Terror in the Golden Age of Hijacking*, Crown, 2013

Magdalena Kopp, *Die Terrorjahre: Mein Leben an der Seite von Carlos*, DVA, 2007

David A. Korn, *Assassination in Khartoum*, Indiana UP, 1993

Wolfgang Kraushaar, *Die Bombe im Judische Gemeindehaus*, HIS Verlag, 2005

Wolfgang Kraushaar, ed., *Die RAF und der linke Terrorismus*, HIS Verlag, 2007

Mario Krebs, *Ulrike Meinhof: Ein Leben im Widerspruch*, Reinbeck, 1988

Gabriel Kuhn, *Turning Money into Rebellion: The Unlikely Story of Denmark's Revolutionary Bank Robbers*, PM Press UK, 2014

Mark Kurlanksy, *1968: The Year That Rocked the World*, Ballantine, 2004

Robert Lacey, *Inside the Kingdom*, Arrow, 2009

Stéphane Lacroix, *Awakening Islam: The Politics of Religious Dissent in Contemporary Saudi Arabia*, Harvard UP, 2011

Shaul P. Ladany, *King of the Road: From Bergen-Belsen to the Olympic Games: The Autobiography of an Israeli Scientist and a World-record-holding Race Walker*, Gefen, 2008

Carmen bin Laden, *The Veiled Kingdom*, Virago, 2019

Najwa and Omar bin Laden, with Jean Sasson, *Growing up bin Laden*, Oneworld, 2009

David Landau, *Arik: The Life of Ariel Sharon*, Knopf, 2014

David Clay Large, *Munich 1972*, Rowman & Littlefield, 2012

Karl Laske, *Le Banquier Noir: François Genoud*, L'Epreuve des faits, 1996

John le Carré, *The Pigeon Tunnel: Stories From My Life*, Viking, 2013

Mark Leopold, *Idi Amin: The Story of Africa's Icon of Evil*, Yale UP, 2020

Matt Levitt, *Hezbollah: The Global Footprint of Lebanon's Party of God*, Hurst, 2013

Laszlo Liszkaï, *Le Monde Selon Carlos*, Eric Bonnier, 2017
Carlos à l'abri du rideau de fer, Seuil, 1990
Laurence Louër, *Transnational Shia Politics: Religious and Political Networks in the Gulf*, Hurst, 2008
Julia Lovell, *Maoism: A Global History*, Bodley Head, 2019
Lorenz Lüthi, *Cold Wars: Asia, the Middle East, Europe*, Woodrow Wilson Center Press, 2015
Zeina Maasri, Fawwaz Traboulsi, *Off the Wall: Political Posters of the Lebanese Civil War*, I.B. Tauris, 2008
Eileen MacDonald, *Shoot the Women First*, Arrow, 1992
Sandra Mackey, *A Mirror of the Arab World*, Norton, 2008
Shiraz Maher, *Salafi-Jihadism: The History of an Idea*, Hurst, 2016
Leena Malkki, *How Terrorist Campaigns End: The Campaigns of the Rode Jeugd in the Netherlands and the Symbionese Liberation Army in the United States*, Helsinki UP, 2010
Nur Masalha, *Palestine: A Four Thousand Year History*, Zed, 2020
Golda Meir, *My Life*, Weidenfeld & Nicolson, 1975
Markar Melkonian, *My Brother's Road: An American's Fateful Journey to Armenia*, Bloomsbury, 2008
Yossi Melman, *The Master Terrorist: The True Story Behind Abu Nidal*, Adama Books, 1986
David Menashri, ed., *The Iranian Revolution and the Muslim World*, Routledge, 2019
Giulio Meotti, *A New Shoah: The Untold Story of Israel's Victims of Terrorism*, Encounter, 2010
Lina Mikdadi, *Surviving the Siege of Beirut*, Onyx Press, 1983
Abbas Milani, *A Tale of Two Cities: A Persian Memoir*, Mage, 1996
Baqer Moin, *Khomeini: Life of the Ayatollah*, I.B. Tauris, 1999
Elaine Mokhtefi, *Algeria: A Third World Capital*, Verso, 2020
Benny Morris, *The War of 1948*, Yale UP, 2009
Jan Morris, *Destinations: Essays from Rolling Stone*, OUP, 1980
Roy Mottahedeh, *The Mantle of the Prophet*, Oneworld, 2000
Claude Moufflet, *Otages à Kampala*, Presses de la Cité, 1976
Joshua Muravchik, *The Next Founders: Voices of Democracy in the Middle East*, Encounter Books, 2009
Tim Naftali, *Blind Spot: The Secret History of American Counter-Terrorism*, Basic Books, 2005
Walid Abdel Nasser, *The Islamic Movement in Egypt*, KPI, 1994
Selim Nassib with Caroline Tisdall, *Beirut: Frontline Story*, Pluto Press, 1983
Elliot Neaman, *Free Radicals: Agitators, Hippies, Urban Guerrillas, and Germany's Youth Revolt of the 1960s and 1970s*, Telos, 2016
Binyamin Netanyahu, ed., *International Terrorism: Challenge and Response*, Proceedings of the Jerusalem Conference, Transaction Publishers, 1981
Ido Netanyahu, *Yoni's Last Battle 1976*, Gefen, 2013

Jens Nordqvist, *Baader Meinhof: Terrorismens årtionde*, Historisla Media, 2021
Edgar O'Ballance, *Civil War in Lebanon, 1975–92*, Palgrave, 1993
Observer, *The Siege*, Macmillan, 1980
Yehuda Offer, *Operation Thunder*, Penguin, 1976
Michael Oren, *Power, Faith, and Fantasy: America in the Middle East*, Norton 2008
June 1967 and the Making of the Modern Middle East, Penguin, 2002
Afshon Ostovar, *Vanguard of the Imam: Religion, Politics, and Iran's Revolutionary Guards*, OUP USA, 2016
Amos Oz, *Under This Blazing Light*, CUP, 1990
Ilan Pappé, *The Ethnic Cleansing of Palestine*, Oneworld, 2006
Alison Pargeter, *The Muslim Brotherhood: From Opposition to Power*, Saqi Books, 2013
Misagh Parsa, *Social Origins of the Iranian Revolution*, Rutgers, 1989
Trita Parsi, *Treacherous Alliance: The Secret Dealings of Israel, Iran, and the United States*, Yale UP, 2007
Pierre Pean, *L'Extrémiste: François Genoud, de Hitler à Carlos*, Fayard, 1996
Shimon Peres, *No Room for Small Dreams: Courage, Imagination, and the Making of Modern Israel*, Weidenfeld, 2017
Butz Peters, *1977: RAF gegen Bundesrepublik*, Apple Books/Droemer, 2016
Tödlicher Irrtum Die Geschichte der RAF, Argon, 2004
Anshel Pfeffer, *Bibi: The Turbulent Life and Times of Benjamin Netanyahu*, Hurst, 2018
Russell Phillips, *Operation Nimrod: The Iranian Embassy Siege*, Shilka, 2016
Alois Prinz, *Liber wutend als traurig sein: Die Lebensgeschichte der Ulrike Meinhof*, Weinheim, 2003
Yevgeny Primakov, *Russia and the Arabs*, Basic Books, 2009
Syed Qutb, *Milestones*, American Trust Publications, 1990
David Raab, *Terror in Black September: The First Eyewitness Account of the Infamous 1970 Hijackings*, St Martin's Press, 2007
Sergey Radchenko, *To Run the World: The Kremlin's Cold War Bid for Global Power*, CUP, 2024
Ali Rahnema, *Call to Arms: Iran's Marxist Revolutionaries: Formation and Evolution of the Fada'is, 1964–1976*, Oneworld, 2021
The Political History of Modern Iran, I.B. Tauris, 2023
An Islamic Utopian: A Political Biography of Ali Shariati, I.B. Tauris, 2014
Jonathan Randal, *Osama: The Making of a Terrorist*, I.B. Tauris, 2005
The Tragedy of Lebanon: Christian Warlords, Israeli Adventurers, and American Bunglers, Just World Books, 2012
Madawi al-Rasheed, *A History of Saudi Arabia*, CUP, 2010
Pierre Razoux, *The Iran-Iraq War*, Belknap Harvard, 2015
Simon Reeve, *One Day in September: The Full Story of the 1972 Munich Olympic Massacre and the Israeli Operation 'Wrath of God'*, Faber & Faber, 2005
Thomas Reigler, *Im Fadenkreuz: Oesterreich und der Nahostterrorismus 1973 bis 1985*, V&R, 2010

'When modern terrorism began: The OPEC hostage taking of 1975', *Handbook of OPEC and the Global Energy Order*, Routledge, 2020
Mathieu Rey, *Histoire de la Syrie XIX-XXIe siècle*, Fayard, 2018
Dina Rezk, *The Arab World and Western Intelligence: Analysing the Middle East, 1956–1981*, Edinburgh UP, 2017
Dave Rich, *The Left's Jewish Problem*, Biteback, 2018
Daniela Richterova, *Watching the Jackals*, GUP, 2025
Thomas Riegler, *Österreichs geheime Dienste: Vom Dritten Mann bis zur BVT-Affäre*, Klever, 2019
Jeffrey Robinson, *Yamani: The Inside Story*, HarperCollins, 1988
Eugene Rogan, *The Arabs*, Penguin, 2009
Eric Rouleau, *Truth and Lies in the Middle East*, AUC Press, 2019
Barry Rubin, *Revolution Until Victory? The Politics and History of the PLO*, Harvard UP, 1994
Barry Rubin, Judith Colp Rubin, *Yasir Arafat*, OUP, 2004
Eric Salerno, *Mossad Base Italia. Le azioni, gli intrighi, le verità nascoste*, il Saggiatore, 2010
Mark Sanagan, *Lightning Through the Clouds*, Texas UP, 2020
Dominic Sandbrook, *Who Dares Wins: Britain 1979–82*, Allen Lane, 2019
Chris Sands and Fazelminallah Qazizi, *Night Letters: Gulbuddin Hekmatyar and the Afghan Islamists who Changed the World*, Hurst, 2019
Daniel J. Sargent, *A Superpower Transformed: The Remaking of American Foreign Relations in the 1970s*, OUP, 2014
Yezid Sayigh, *Armed Struggle and the Search for a State*, OUP, 1997
Kay Schiller, Chris Young, *The 1972 Munich Olympics and the Making of Modern Germany*, CUP, 2018
Margrit Schiller, *Remembering the Armed Struggle: My Time with the Red Army Faction*, PM Press UK, 2021
Ze'ev Schiff and Ehud Ya'ari, *Israel's Lebanon War*, Simon & Schuster, 1985
Oliver Schröm, *Im Schatten des Schakals* [In the Shadow of the Jackal]: *Carlos und die Wegbereiter des Internationalen Terrorismus*, Verlag, 2002
Patrick Seale, *Abu Nidal: A Gun for Hire*, Random House, 1992
Tom Segev, *1967: Israel, the War and the Year that Transformed the Middle East*, Abacus, 2007
William Shawcross, *The Shah's Last Ride: The Story of the Exile, Misadventures and Death of the Emperor*, Chatto & Windus, 1989
Colin Shindler, *A History of Modern Israel*, CUP, 2013
Avi Shlaim, *The Iron Wall*, Penguin, 2014
Lion of Jordan, Penguin, 2017
Thomas Skelton-Robinson, *The Popular Front for the Liberation of Palestine and Left-Wing Terrorism in West Germany, 1969–1980*. English translation provided by author. Published as 'Im Netz verheddert: Die Beziehungen des bundesdeutschen Linksterrorismus zur Volksfront für die Befreiung Palästina

(1969–1980)', in Wolfgang Kraushaar, ed., *Die RAF und der linke Terrorismus*, Vol. 2, Hamburger Edition, 2006, pp. 828–904

Patrick Sloyan, *When Reagan Sent in the Marines*, Dunne, 2020

Ferdinand Smit, *The Battle for South Lebanon: The Radicalisation of Lebanon's Shi'ites 1982–1985*, Bulaaq, 2000

Colin Smith, *Carlos the Jackal*, Sphere, 1976

J. Smith, André Moncourt, *Daring to Struggle, Failing to Win: The Red Army Faction's 1977 Campaign of Desperation*, PM Press, 2008

The Red Army Faction, A Documentary History, Vol. 1: Projectiles for the People, PM Press, 2009

The Red Army Faction, A Documentary History, Vol. 2: Dancing with Imperialism, PM Press, 2013

Peter Snow and David Philips, *Leila's Hijack War*, Pan, 1970

Devin Springer, James Regens, David Edger, *Islamic Radicalism and Global Jihad*, Georgetown UP, 2009

Klaus Stern and Jörg Herrmann, *Andreas Baader: Das Leben eines Staatsfeinde*, Deutscher Taschenbuch Verlag, 2007

William Stevenson, *90 Minutes at Entebbe: The Full Inside Story*, Corgi, 1976

Sunday Times Insight team, *Siege!*, Times newspapers, 1980

Chelsea Szendi Schieder, *Coed Revolution: The Female Student in the Japanese New Left, 1957–1972*, Duke UP, 2021

Ray Takeyh, *The Last Shah*, Yale UP, 2021

Peter Taylor, *States of Terror: Democracy and Political Violence*, BBC Books, 1993

Petra Terhoeven, *Die Rote Armee Fraktion: Eine Geschichte terroristischer gewalt*, Beck, 2017

Nydia Tobón, *Carlos: terrorista o guerrillero*, Grijalbo, 1978

Jeffrey Toobin, *American Heiress: The Wild Saga of the Kidnapping, Crimes and Trial of Patty Hearst*, Doubleday, 2016

Yaroslav Trofimov, *The Siege of Mecca: The Forgotten Uprising in Islam's Holiest Shrine*, Penguin, 2008

Alwyn Turner, *Crisis? What Crisis? Britain in the 1970s*, Quarto, 2013

Patrick Tyler, *A World of Trouble: The White House and the Middle East – from the Cold War to the War on Terror*, Farrar, Straus & Giroux, 2009

Fortress Israel: The Inside Story of the Military Elite Who Run the Country, Granta, 2012

Jeremy Varon, *Bringing the War Home: The Weather Underground, the Red Army Faction, and Revolutionary Violence in the Sixties and Seventies*, California UP, 2004

Federico Vélez, *Latin American Revolutionaries and the Arab World: From the Suez Canal to the Arab Spring*, Routledge, 2016

Richard Vinen, *1968: Radical Protest and its Enemies*, HarperCollins, 2019

Bernard Violet, *Carlos: Les réseaux secrets du terrorisme international*, Seuil, 1996

Bernard Volker, *L'Affaire Schleyer*, Menges, 1977

Mary Anne Weaver, *A Portrait of Egypt*, Farrar, Straus & Giroux, 1999

Tim Weiner, *Legacy of Ashes: The History of the CIA*, Penguin, 2012

Yfaat Weiss, *A Confiscated Memory: Wadi Salib and Haifa's Lost Heritage*, Columbia UP, 2011

Odd Arne Westad, *The Cold War: A World History*, Penguin, 2017

Robert Wolff, 'Between Personal Guilt and Practical Internationalism: The Transnational Entanglements of the Revolutionary Cells'. English translation provided to author of 'Zwischen persönlicher Schuld und praktischem Internationalismus: Die transnationalen Verflechtungen der Revolutionären Zellen', in Adrian Hänni, ed., *Über Grenzen hinweg, Transnationale politische Gewalt im 20. Jahrhundert*, Campus, 2019

Lawrence Wright, *The Looming Tower*, Allen Lane, 2006

Robin Wright, *Sacred Rage: The Wrath of Militant Islam*, Simon & Schuster, 1985

David Yallop, *To the Ends of the Earth: The Hunt for the Jackal*, Little, Brown, 1993

Salim Yaqub, *Imperfect Strangers: Americans, Arabs and US – Middle East Relations in the 1970s*, Cornell UP, 2015

Montasser al-Zayat, *The Road to al-Qaeda*, Pluto, 2004

Film/TV/radio podcasts cited

Children of the Revolution, Mike Sullivan, 2010

Israel's Hunt for the Red Prince, Ali Hassan Salameh, Al Jazeera World, 2018

One Day in September, Kevin MacDonald, 1999

Munich: Mossad's Revenge, Tom Whitter, Channel Four, 2006

Anis Nakkache – Révolutionnaire ou Terroriste?, Timon Koulmasis, Arte, 2000

Face à Carlos le Chacal, Sophie Bonnet, TV5 Monde, 2018

Starbuck Holger Meins, Gerd Conradt, 2001

Stockholm 75, David Aronowitsch, 2003

Todespiel, 1997, Heinrich Breloer, 1997

The Siege of Mecca, Dirk van den Berg, 2018

Hijacked, PBS American Experience, 27 February 2006

Baader-Meinhof: In Love with Terror, Ben Lewis, 2002

Covert, 10: 'Entebbe: Hostage Rescue, Part 2', Audioboom, 24 July 2018

Nasrallah: une figure à la croisée des crises, Radio France Culture, 4 October 2024

Leila Khaled: Hijacker, Lena Makboul, 2006

De Terrorist Hans-Joachim Klein, Alexander Oey, 2005

Eugene Casey – Terrorist Carlos The Jackal, FBI Retired Case File Review, ep. 95, 2017

Selected news publications

Guardian
Liverpool Echo
Birmingham Post
Evening Standard
The Times
Irish Independent
Time
Newsweek
New York Times
Wall Street Journal
Village Voice
Washington Post
Los Angeles Times
Boston Globe
The New Yorker
The Atlantic
The Sentinel, Chicago
Libération
Le Monde
Le Figaro
L'Express
Le Nouvel Observateur
Der Spiegel
Jungle World
Neue Zürcher Zeitung
Frankfurter Allgemeine Zeitung
Die Tageszeitung
Stern
Die Zeit
Süddeutsche Zeitung
Die Welt
Trouw (NL)
Corriere della Sera
La Stampa
La Repubblica
Haaretz
Jerusalem Post
Jerusalem Times
Times of Israel
Yedioth Ahronoth
Ynet
+972 Magazine
Tel Quel (Morocco)
Ettela'at
Kayhan
Al-Ahram
Arab News
Al-Hadaf
United Press International
Jewish Telegraphic Agency
Reuters
Associated Press
Press Association
Agence France Presse
British Pathé News
The Mainichi Shimbun

Specialised periodicals

American Historical Review
Arab Studies Quarterly
British Journal of Middle Eastern Studies
Combating Terrorism Center – Sentinel
Comparative Studies of South Asia, Africa and the Middle East
Diplomatic History
Economic Development and Cultural Change
Foreign Affairs
International Journal of Middle East Studies
International Journal for Arab Studies

Japanese Studies
Journal of Cold War Studies
Journal of Contemporary Central and Eastern Europe
Journal of Genocide Research
Journal for Intelligence Propaganda and Security Studies
Journal of Money Laundering Control
Middle East Journal, Middle East Institute
Middle East Research and Information Project (MERIP)
Middle East Review of International Affairs
Prispevki za Novejšo Zgodovino
Review of African Political Economy
Studies in Conflict and Terrorism
Studies in Intelligence
The Sixties: A Journal of History, Politics and Culture
Welt des Islams

Official archives

National Archives, UK: Records of Cabinet Office, FCO, Home Office
Central Intelligence Agency, US, Freedom of Information Act Electronic Reading Room
Office of the Historian, Foreign Service Institute, United States Department of State
Ronald Reagan Presidential Library and Museum
Jimmy Carter Presidential Library and Museum
Federal Bureau of Investigation, The Vault, archives
The British Newspaper Collection, the British Library
The National Library Newspaper Collection, Israel
Mediathek des Stasi-Unterlagen-Archivs, Berlin, Germany
Romanian National Central Historical Archives (ANIC)
FENVAC, Fédération Nationale des Victimes d'Attentats et d'Accidents Collectifs, Paris
Arabian Gulf Digital Archives, UAE

Acknowledgements

I have many people to thank for their support, advice and encouragement, and what follows is a very abbreviated list. My apologies to anyone I have left out.

Enzo Mangini in Rome did wonderful work in Italian archives; Reem Makboul helped at the very beginning; Gina Bates diligently combed records at Kew and translated Persian. I was lucky to be able to tap the collective knowledge of Philip Oltermann, Michael Safi, Dina Rezk, John Davison, Thomas Hegghammer, Alia Brahimi, Seyed Ali Alavi, Alexander Buehler, Peter Neumann and Colin Shindler who all generously found time to read draft chapters.

A special thanks is due to Adrian Hänni for sharing his deep knowledge on so many occasions, carefully reading many pages, hosting me in Munich and guiding me round the Olympic Park. One day we will resolve the mystery of the exploding chianti, I hope. Thomas Skelton-Robinson repeatedly gave invaluable advice based on his detailed understanding of both German and Arab extremism during the 1960s and 70s. I am grateful to Leena Malkki, Alex Hobson and Thomas Riegler for passing on wisdom and useful documents. Saul David provided unpublished interviews conducted for his own fine book on Entebbe. Yoram Schweitzer offered introductions and advice. Many other experts, analysts and authors gave of their time and knowledge. And obviously I am in the debt of all the former diplomats, officials, spies and investigators who spoke to me – and the revolutionists who did so too.

Marshall Yurow very generously made available to me the unpublished manuscript of his forthcoming and painstakingly researched book, entitled *Volcano's Edge: Patrick Arguello Ryan, the Tragic Internationalist* as well as material from Arguello's notes and interviews with family. He also provided vital information on the origins of Sandinista links to Palestinian armed factions obtained by personal interviews with Nicaraguans involved at the time.

I owe a great deal to Joe Parkinson for his encouragement and advice during the hard early stages. Alex Perry offered much-appreciated criticism too. Corrections to the cover came from Anshel Pfeffer. Faisal Qureshi shared documents and enthusiasm; Yossi Melman his expertise and experience. Sophie Bonnet and Laszlo Liszkaï were generous and helpful in Paris. Sufian Taher was a patient and professional companion in the occupied West Bank. Steve Farrell, more than two decades after watching my back in Najaf and guiding me through the chaos of Arafat's funeral, somehow found time to read much of the manuscript closely, offering careful, perceptive and knowledgeable suggestions with his usual good humour and sense. Thanks too to friends in Amman, Cairo, Damascus, Jerusalem, Ramallah, Haifa, Tel Aviv, Baghdad, Beirut and Berlin for helping out. You know who you are.

I sent my first story from the Middle East in 1998 and for almost three decades now editors at the *Guardian* and, until very recently, the *Observer* too have allowed me to report from the region and some eighty countries elsewhere. This is an immense privilege, for which I am profoundly grateful. Without 'the desk' in London, and our brilliant administrators, all of us correspondents would be lost, often quite literally. So a big thank you to Devika Bhat, Georgia Bisbas, Jana Harris, Oliver Holmes, Nick Hopkins, Simon Jeffrey, Alex Olorenshaw, Paul Owen, Karen Plews, Paul Webster, Jamie Wilson and Kath Viner.

If a foreign correspondent is lost without an editor, an author is equally adrift without an agent. Sarah Chalfant understood exactly what I wanted to write, quite possibly before I did, and then found me what I needed. She then protected, encouraged and advised throughout the long process of getting the book written and published. My thanks to her and to Rebecca Nagel and Sam Sheldon and everyone else at The Wiley Agency.

This is my second book with The Bodley Head. Will Hammond was once again the best of editors, showing infinite patience despite the many delays and diversions. His continued belief in *The Revolutionists* was essential throughout the long writing process, but especially as the marathon entered its final miles. Stuart Williams, publishing director, was tremendously supportive since I first mentioned the idea of the book in his office more than ten years ago and kindly oversaw its final months. Matt Broughton designed the wonderful cover, Jessie Spivey brilliantly managed the marketing, Duncan Heath did a very fine job as copy-editor, John Garrett read the proofs with care, Bill Donohoe drew the wonderful maps and Ben Murphy compiled the very long index. I am very grateful too to Laura Reeves and Graeme Hall for all their hard work and professionalism during the production process.

In the US, my thanks are due to Emily Cunningham at Knopf who took on the book with enthusiasm, insight and understanding, Andrew Miller for his initial interest and early encouragement, Elka Roderick and Emily Murphy for publicity and marketing, and Tiara Sharma for her hard work on pictures and much else.

Finally, I have to thank many friends outside the worlds of journalism or writing for their support, patience and continued interest in *The Revolutionists*. I need to mention Mike Newman in particular, the best listener on the planet and so, among much else, the best companion for long walks in the Hertfordshire countryside any author could wish for. I have to thank too all the members of my family who have had to deal with the stresses and strains of this project in various homes in various countries for many years. This book is dedicated to my mother, who would have been happy and proud to see it finally published.

To Clara and Victor, I have several things to say. This will come as no surprise. Ours is not a home where anyone is short of words, after all. Firstly, I will now fulfil the promises made for 'when the book is finished' (except for buying the videogaming set-up, sorry, that was never going to happen). Secondly, never forget that long books are wonderful things. Thirdly, do not under any circumstances even begin to think about writing one.

List of illustrations

Every effort has been made to contact all copyright holders. The publisher will be pleased to amend in future editions any errors or omissions brought to their attention.

Index

ABOUT THE AUTHOR

Jason Burke, the International Security correspondent for the *Guardian*, has been a foreign correspondent for almost thirty years, reporting from the Middle East, South Asia, Europe and Africa.

He is one of our foremost writers on terrorism and the author of four critically acclaimed books: *The New Threat from Islamic Militancy*, shortlisted for the Orwell Prize; *The 9/11 Wars*, 'the best overview of the 9/11 decade in print' (*The Economist*); the groundbreaking *Al-Qaeda: The True Story of Radical Islam*; and *On the Road to Kandahar: Travels through Conflict in the Islamic World*.

He lives near London.